The Methodist Church in Michigan:
The Nineteenth Century

The Methodist Church in Michigan:
The Nineteenth Century

by

Margaret Burnham Macmillan

Professor of History
Western Michigan University

The Michigan Area Methodist Historical Society
and
William B. Eerdmans Publishing Company
Grand Rapids, Michigan

PREFACE

By Bishop Marshall Russell Reed, D.D., LL.D.

A few years ago when our General Board of Evangelism held an assembly in Washington, D.C., I was assigned to preach in our First Methodist Church in Arlington, Virginia. Arriving a little while before the hour of worship I was privileged to relax a few minutes in the minister's study. I took from a shelf what appeared to be a new book on Virginia Methodism. It was a history of the Methodist Church in Virginia by one of our greatest church historians, the late William Warren Sweet.

I read several pages and evidenced so much enthusiasm over it that my genial minister host, who was a member of the publication committee, autographed the book and gave it to me. It is a great story well told. As I read it on the way home, there was revived within me the hope that we might sometime have a worthy history of Michigan Methodism. There have been some small histories written and some interpretations of historic events in which our church was involved but no comprehensive Methodist history of the state.

There has been much interest in seeing a commendable history of Michigan Methodism come into being. Members of the Conference Historical Societies have been active in this direction and other interested Methodists have had a concern about it. They long faced a real difficulty in securing a financial underwriting for the project and most important of all, securing a competent historian to produce the history. In 1961 came the encouraging word that the two Annual Conferences in Michigan had voted to advance the necessary funds to publish this history.

Soon after came the good news that Dr. Margaret Burnham Macmillan, competent historian of the faculty of Western Michigan University, had agreed to write the history. Dr. Macmillan is the daughter of the late Dr. Smith Burnham, a member of the Western Michigan faculty for many years, an author of many works in American history, and a leading Methodist layman. The research and accumulation of materials as well as the actual writing of this two-volume history is a colossal un-

v

dertaking and we rejoice in having a historian so competent and so well acquainted with the church to undertake it.

The pioneers who brought Methodism to this particular state have long since left us, but some people have fond memories of these stalwarts. My own great-grandfather was one of the five charter members of the first Methodist society organized in Adrian in 1830. I have vivid memories of the Rev. Dr. Seth Reed, who died in 1924 at the age of 101, and who often told about the hardships of the early Michigan frontier.

With eagerness we look forward to the publication of the first volume of Dr. Macmillan's history of Michigan Methodism, covering the nineteenth century.

THIS BOOK SPONSORED BY
The Michigan Area Methodist Historical Society

TABLE OF CONTENTS

List of Illustrations

xii

List of Maps

List of Appendices

PROLOGUE

TWO STRANGERS VISIT DETROIT

In 1804, Detroit was only a modest cluster of about one hundred log cabins. A few narrow streets were surrounded by a twelve-foot high stockade. On opposite sides of the fortified area, two gates gave access to the town. Every night at sunset all Indians were required to leave the place and the gates were locked. Away from the river on higher ground stood a rundown fort named Lernoult for a former British commander there. The so-called "ribbon farms" lay in narrow strips north and south of the town on both the American and Canadian banks of the Detroit River. Most of them had stone wind mills with cloth sails. Within a mile of the river on the west was a dense, primeval forest penetrated by narrow Indian trails. Detroit had only a precarious hold on the edge of the river at the beginning of the nineteenth century.

By the census of 1800, the population of the Detroit area numbered 3,106. The place had just been in American hands since 1796 so only a few Americans lived there yet. The majority of the people were French, peasant farmers; but Indians, English or Scotch fur traders and merchants plus a couple of Catholic priests also lived in Detroit. Although five Protestant denominations had already held services there, the general tone of everyday social life was French and Catholic. Father Levadoux, who came to Detroit in 1796, wrote of the place:

> The town of Detroit is not very much . . . . but the shores of the river are inhabited for 12 leagues on both sides, making this parish extremely difficult to care for . . . . the people here are better instructed and much more religious than in the Illinois country. I cannot but praise their piety and good manners.[1]

[1] Edward J. Hickey, *Ste. Anne's Parish: One Hundred Years of Detroit History*. Richard D. Miles, *The Stars and Stripes Come to Detroit*, pp. 17-20. Both are booklets done for Detroit's 250th anniversary.

Cadillac had been accompanied by two Catholic priests when he founded Detroit in 1701. Just one hundred years later, Bishop Denaut of Quebec visited Detroit and confirmed 563 Catholics, ranging in age from twelve to eighty. In 1804, Ste. Anne's Parish was occupying their sixth church building.

The early predominance of Catholics in Detroit was a severe trial to the few Protestant ministers who came there then. The Rev. Elijah H. Pilcher, a Methodist minister appointed to Michigan for the first time in 1830, declared:

> The whole population became imbued with the French spirit and frivolity; and, of course, they were but little inclined to true piety . . . . no necessity was felt for any considerable mental culture . . . . the people gave themselves up to music and dancing, which tended to weaken the mind, vitiate the moral sensibilities, and to disincline them to religion. The mere ceremonies of Romanism did not lay any restraint on the people in these respects.[2]

It has sometimes been claimed that a Methodist minister was the first Protestant to preach in Michigan but this is not true. Moravian, Episcopalian, Baptist, Quaker, and Congregational services had all been held there before those of Methodism were.

The Moravians were prisoners here during the latter part of the Revolutionary War. They also established a mission on the Clinton River two miles southwest of Mount Clemens in the years from 1782 to 1786.

Chaplains from both sides in the Revolutionary War period also officiated briefly at Detroit. The Queen's Rangers and their British chaplain were of course Episcopalian. In 1796, an American chaplain, the Rev. David Jones, was there briefly. He was a minister of the Baptist Church.

Six members of the Society of Friends were in Detroit in 1793. They came in the hope that they might mediate for peace between the Indians, British, and Americans. While in the area, these Friends held their form of religious service at least seven times. But their hope of bringing peace to the frontier failed to materialize as wished. Not until General Anthony Wayne defeated the Indians at Fallen Timbers and then made the treaty of Greenville with the various tribes in 1795 did the frontier begin to calm down. Most of all, the withdrawal of

---

[2] E. H. Pilcher, *History of Protestantism in Michigan,* p. 11. Hereafter cited as *Hist. Prot. Mich.* Pilcher is often the only source for early Methodism in Michigan. He served over forty years here, knew all but one of the seven members of the first Methodist Society formed in this State, often talked with them about the early days, was widely acquainted with the early Methodist ministers, and travelled himself all over Michigan in its most primitive and pioneer conditions.

the British in 1796 from the fur trading posts within the original boundaries of the United States settled the northwest.[3]

A Congregational missionary, the Rev. David Bacon, was the only Protestant minister who made a sustained religious effort over a period of years in Michigan before the War of 1812. He came to Michigan first in 1800, sent by a Congregational church in Connecticut. He returned east, was married and then lived in Detroit from 1801 to 1804. His son, Leonard Bacon, was born in Detroit in 1802. The son became a minister of a wider reputation than his father. The Bacons wanted to work among the northern Indian tribes but were never able to do so. Whether a lack of money or the difficulty of the Indian languages hindered their plans is unknown today. But Mr. Bacon did gain the reputation locally of being unable to hold a congregation by his preaching. The children were the only people who came to his services more than once or twice. This Congregational missionary is known to have talked with the second Methodist minister to preach in Detroit. This was the Rev. Nathan Bangs. To him, Mr. Bacon admitted his complete discouragement and growing desire to return to New England. He thought there was an entire lack of any Protestant religious interest in Detroit. He is said to have told Mr. Bangs, "If you can do the people any good, I shall be glad of it, for I cannot."[4]

The First Methodist Minister Visits Detroit

In the spring of the year 1804, the arrival of a tall, vigorous man in Detroit could not have gone unnoticed especially because he soon announced that he was a Methodist minister and would preach the next Sunday at the old wooden Council House near the river. His name was Daniel Freeman and he was the first to preach the faith of John Wesley and Francis Asbury in Michigan. Little more than his name was known to Methodist historians for many years. But Canadian records reveal a few facts about him.

The Rev. Daniel Freeman was born in New Jersey in 1769. He was then thirty-five years of age when he came to Detroit to preach. Therefore he could scarcely have been "venerable looking" as one

---

[3] For the story of the Moravians, see W. F. Dunbar, *Michigan, A History of the Wolverine State,* pp. 146-147. Information on early Protestant visits to Michigan furnished by the Rev. Ronald Brunger, President Detroit Conference Historical Society. For the Quakers, see *Mich. Pioneer & Hist. Coll.,* XVII, 565f.

[4] E. H. Pilcher, *Hist. Prot. Mich.,* pp. 12, 20. Farmer, Silas, *History of Detroit and Michigan,* pp. 550-552. W. R. Prescott, *The Fathers Still Speak,* pp. 35-36. The Rev. Leonard Bacon was widely known as a preacher and hymn writer. He was the author of the hymn "O God Beneath Thy Guiding Hand" found in the Methodist Hymnal in use today as No. 493. Pilcher corresponded with Bangs many years later about their early Detroit experiences. Both men were agreed that the times in 1804 were not yet ready for Protestantism in Michigan.

author described him. Another said he had "a tall commanding personal appearance." If he was like most Methodist preachers then, he had a strong, enduring voice and always preached loud and long with specific emphasis on sin and personal salvation.

After undergoing a profound conversion personally, Mr. Freeman began to preach at the age of nineteen. He was fond of telling in his sermons how "years afterward he went back to the place where he had agonized with God for salvation and there he found a living well —an enduring fountain of bliss." Mr. Freeman was received on trial in the Philadelphia Conference, served two appointments there and may have been ordained just before coming to Upper Canada.

He was married to Phoebe Swazze, at a date now unknown, had a grant of land in Charlotteville in 1798, moved to Canada and founded the first Methodist society in the Long Point district. He was always hospitable to travelling Methodist preachers and held a good many services himself. He and his wife had a family of nine children. Perhaps they were the reasons why he located, or left the travelling ministry, in 1811 and went into the milling and cloth-dressing business. Mr. Freeman died in 1837.

This was a time when Bishop Asbury gave the Presiding Elders considerable freedom to arrange the various circuits as they thought best. Many preachers, after travelling on one circuit for three months, were shifted to another, Mr. Freeman may have been a local preacher, licensed by a Quarterly Conference, who came to Detroit entirely on his own initiative. Or he might have been a travelling elder appointed by the New York Annual Conference to a large circuit in Upper Canada.

Those were the days when the Canadian Methodists were still a part of the American Methodist Episcopal General Conference. For some years, the New York Annual Conference made a good many appointments to work in Canada. Perhaps Mr. Freeman was not actually ordered by anyone to come to Detroit. He may have been preaching his way along the Canadian shore almost from house to house. Either his intense religious zeal or just plain, human curiosity led him to cross the river to Detroit.

Whether he was sent or came of his own accord, Freeman's journey to Detroit showed considerable courage and energy. The land on both sides of the river was heavily forested, quite swampy, and infested with many insects. And the river had to be crossed in a small, open boat.

Presumably the Rev. Daniel Freeman stayed in Detroit only a few days, certainly not over a week. How could he have had any lasting influence in so short a time? The Rev. Elijah Pilcher knew several Methodists who had seen and heard Mr. Freeman. Over a quarter of a century later, they remembered that the first Methodist minister to officiate in Michigan "preached the gospel in a very plain and earnest manner, accompanied by the unction and power of the Holy Spirit."

One woman, Mrs. Maria C. McCarty, "received such convictions for sin as never left her till she was converted some years afterwards." She had been raised a Catholic but became a member of the first Methodist Society organized in Michigan in 1810. Her husband in addition to her sister and brother-in-law, Mr. and Mrs. Robert Abbott, were also members of that first Michigan Methodist Society. The seed of Methodism was surely planted in Detroit in 1804.

Although the Rev. Daniel Freeman never returned to Michigan, some of his relatives were later active members of the Methodist Episcopal Church there. A cousin, also named Daniel Freeman, was a Class leader, Sunday School Superintendent, and local preacher in Flint for many years. The cousin's son, Joseph S. Freeman, was also an active Methodist layman both in Flint and Houghton. A girl cousin of the original Daniel Freeman was the mother of the Rev. Joseph S. Sutton, a minister in the Detroit Conference for over fifty years.[5]

The Second Methodist Minister Visits Detroit

The Rev. Nathan Bangs had a long and distinguished career in the Methodist Episcopal Church. He was for many years a religious newspaper editor, an historian of Methodism, and one of the founders of the national Missionary Society. But when he came to Detroit he was only a young preacher just recently ordained a "travelling elder."

In July, 1804, the New York Annual Conference appointed Mr. Bangs to the "River Le French Circuit" in the western part of Upper Canada or Ontario. The geography of that region was not widely known then; the river named was really the Thames. In any case, the village of Detroit was an obscure appendage at the western end of the Thames Circuit.

It was the original intention of the Rev. Mr. Bangs to make Detroit a regular appointment on his plan for travelling the Circuit. But the hardships attendant upon just getting there plus the cool reception he received led him to make only three trips to the place in all. These occurred in the time between August and November, 1804.

Travelling to Detroit then involved many days of horseback travel

[5] John Carroll, *Case and His Cotemporaries; or the Canadian Itinerants Memorial: Constituting a Biographical History of Methodism in Canada from Its Introduction into the Province till the Death of the Rev. William Case in 1855.* I, 220, 243, 247. This book was five volumes in all. It is hereafter referred to as *Case & His Cotemp.* Helpful letters about Daniel Freeman were sent the author by the late Dr. William C. S. Pellowe and the Rev. Ronald Brunger. Dr. Pellowe had received information on Freeman from a Canadian lady who obtained it from E. A. Owen, *Pioneer History of the Long Point Settlement* and the Ontario Historical Society magazine for 1900. Mr. Brunger found the information on Freeman's later cousins in Michigan from a number of *The Michigan Christian Advocate* in 1909, See also E. H. Pilcher, *Hist. Prot. Mich.*, pp. 11-12, 16-17, 47.

through unsettled, heavy forests whether one went by Ohio or Upper Canada. The path could be found only by following the marked trees. Houses were few and far between and one might meet a band of Indians. After Mr. Bangs came through Canada to Lake St. Clair, he followed the shoreline to Sandwich. There he got a small boat and was rowed across the river to Detroit.

On his first two trips to Detroit, the Rev. Nathan Bangs preached on a weekday evening in the old Council House. The third and last time, he preached on Sunday in the same place. He himself once described his procedure in starting a new appointment. It was always the same. He stood up in front of the people, told them his name and age, described his education and conversion, and finished with the details of his call to the ministry and his motives in coming there. Then he said, "I am a Methodist preacher and my manner of worship is to stand up and sing, to kneel in prayer, and then stand up and preach while the people sit in their seats. If you don't see fit to join me choose your own method."

In those days, the hymn singing was of course entirely without musical accompaniment and was done by a process usually called "lining it out." The preacher read one or two lines and the congregation sang them. Then the procedure was repeated. None of the early Methodist hymn books had any printed music in them. The words were the important thing then.

After the singing, prayer, and preaching were all finished and just before he gave the benediction, Mr. Bangs always said to his audience, "All who wish to hear any more such preaching, stand up." The first time he preached in Detroit, everyone present stood up so the minister promised at once to come and preach again in just two weeks.

After his first service in Detroit, Mr. Bangs had noted that "the lighthearted people flocked to hear me." On his second trip there, he found the meeting place "was pretty well filled with hearers." But, alas, on his third visit even though it came on a Sunday, "only a few children came out to hear him."

During his sermon on the second trip he made to Detroit, a terrible storm with much thunder and lightning passed over the town. But Mr. Bangs kept on preaching with consistent steadiness. Afterwards, he learned that he had been in great danger particularly when he took up the candle in order to see to read the closing hymn. Two young men had put gunpowder in the candles, expecting they would explode during the sermon. Nothing happened during the service but the tricksters sat literally trembling in fear all through the storm because they thought "God was about to strike them dead for what they had done."

This incident together with that conversation he had with the Rev. David Bacon and the poor response to his preaching must have completely discouraged Mr. Bangs. He did not return to Detroit. Many years later, after correspondence with Mr. Bangs, the Rev. Elijah Pilcher wrote that the second Methodist minister to come to Detroit left there "wiping off the dust from his feet as a testimony against them." The people were left, as Pilcher said, "to pursue their follies unrestrained."[6]

It must be remembered that early Methodism was far more strict and puritanical than it is today. Also the unpleasant events of the Reformation were not forgotten. Hence most Protestant ministers were somewhat anti-Catholic then. In addition, those first Methodist ministers to come to Detroit could probably not understand one word of French. What they could see of the life there in early Detroit seemed incurably light-minded and frivolous to those frontier preachers. To them the place and its people did not seem to be worth the effort it took just to get there. No more Protestant services were held in Detroit until the year 1810.

To understand how and why Methodism was established in Michigan, after this extremely slow beginning, requires some examination of the situation and previous history of the United States, Michigan, and the Methodist Episcopal Church, as they were then. All three were very different from what they are today.

[6] Pilcher, E. H., *Hist. Prot. Mich.*, pp. 12-13. Carroll, John, *Case & His Co-temp.*, I, 27-31, 150. For Canadian information see Barclay, W. C., *Early American Methodism*, 1769-1844, I, 175-190. Ling, Louis, *A Century of Service, the History of Central Methodist Church in Detroit*, pp. 23-25.

PART I

THE UNITED STATES, MICHIGAN AND METHODISM

1804 — 1820

The histories of the United States and Methodism developed together. National events have frequently influenced denominational happenings. The Methodist Episcopal Church was the first religious organization formally to pledge its support to the new government under the constitution made in 1787. One month after George Washington took his oath of office as our first President, he received by appointment Bishops Asbury and Coke with ministers John Dickins and Thomas Morrell. First, Bishop Asbury read an address of congratulation containing a pledge of allegiance. In reply, Washington thanked them for their support, promised to be "a faithful and impartial patron of genuine religion" and then implored "the divine benediction on yourselves and your religious community."[1]

The United States

Even the flag of the United States was different in 1804. It had fifteen stars and the same number of stripes. Seventeen States made up the Federal union. Those already added to the original thirteen were Vermont, Kentucky, Tennessee, and Ohio.

The territory of the United States lay between the Rocky Mountains and the Atlantic Ocean, excluding Florida. How much was included west of the Mississippi River was not clear as the Louisiana Purchase of 1803 had not yet had its boundaries surveyed and precisely defined.

By the census of 1800, the population of the United States numbered

---

[1] William W. Sweet, *Methodism in American History*, pp. 120-121. Hereafter cited as *Meth. Am. Hist.*

1

5,308,483, of whom one-fifth were negro slaves. Two-thirds of the population lived within fifty miles of the tidewater area. A strip of uninhabited mountains, one hundred miles wide, lay between the eastern and western settlements. The entire population west of the Appalachian Mountains was not quite one-half million. A little less than one million able-bodied males were to be found in the whole United States. Only six percent of the people lived in cities or towns, all the rest being rural.[2]

Most of the land in the United States was untamed and unclaimed. Our mineral resources were largely unknown and undisturbed. The rural ways of life and work prevalent everywhere had changed very little from what they had been ever since the first settlement of North America.

The hostile western Indian tribes had been broken in half by the white settlements along the Ohio River but the halves were still very dangerous to newcomers. The Spanish in Florida helped keep the Indians on the warpath in the south and the British in the north. In defiance of the terms of the peace treaty of 1783, the British had remained in the fur trading posts at the Canadian border. Only after the making of Jay's treaty with Great Britain in 1794 and General Wayne's defeat of the Indians at Fallen Timbers reinforced by the treaty of Greenville in 1795 did the British evacuate Detroit and Mackinac.

Michigan

Modest American forces finally occupied Detroit on July 11, and Mackinac on September 1, 1796. Later the same year Wayne County was created to furnish an American local government. It included all Michigan for a time.

The year before Freeman and Bangs visited Detroit, 1803, all of Michigan had been made part of Indiana Territory. This should not be confused with the State of Indiana. It was really the remainder of the Northwest Territory after the State of Ohio had been created. Residents of Michigan were not very happy to be part of Indiana because the capitol was located at Vincennes, distant and inconvenient for Detroiters.[3]

Petitions were circulated asking that Wayne County be made a separate territory. Also the Indiana Governor, William Henry Harrison, visited Detroit in May, 1804. Not much more is known of his visit than that of the Rev. Daniel Freeman the same spring. Michigan became a separate territory with the capital at Detroit on June 30, 1805. But before that date fire had destroyed all the village.

On January 18, 1802, Detroit was incorporated as a town with a

---

[2] Statistics and comparisons based on the appendices in *The Federal Union* and *The American Nation* by John D. Hicks.

[3] W. F. Dunbar, *Michigan*, pp. 182-183.

five-member board of trustees and an annual meeting of all voters. The first action of the trustees was the adoption of a code of fire rules. Regular chimney sweeping in addition to household provision of ladders and buckets were required. In 1796, General Wayne had written of Detroit, "The town is a crowded mass of wooden or frame buildings and therefore subject to a general conflagration either by accident or from design."

On June 11, 1805, a fire broke out in the stable of John Harvey, the town baker. He had been smoking his pipe while harnessing his horse. The loose hay, sparks from the pipe and a high wind were a bad combination. The fire spread from his stable to his home and, with unbelievable rapidity, the entire town went up in flames. Every building in Detroit was destroyed with the exception of a warehouse near the river. Food was desperately short too. Father Gabriel Richard, priest of Ste. Anne's, organized groups to obtain supplies from the river farms.

A few days after the fire, the first presidentially appointed officers of the new Territory of Michigan arrived in Detroit or what was left of it. It must have seemed to them that little was left to govern. President Jefferson had appointed General William Hull as governor, Stanley Griswold as secretary, and Augustus Woodward as a judge. Michigan was entitled to three of the last under the Northwest Ordinance. The fire and the arrival of these three men seem almost like blessings in disguise today.

The new officers had foresight enough to see the unique opportunity before them. Permission was obtained from Washington, D.C., to plan a new city with wider streets and a more orderly arrangement of the public buildings and dwellings. Judge Woodward borrowed a plan of Washington from Pierre L'Enfant and adapted it to the needs of Detroit. A grant of 10,000 acres of government land was also secured and then distributed among the adult citizens. The terms of the grant required any surplus to be sold and the money therefrom used to build a courthouse and a jail.[4]

Unfortunately for Michigan, western migration was still following the Ohio and the Mississippi Rivers. The Indians were still quite hostile in the north. Interest had been aroused in the recent Louisiana Purchase. Ohio had just become a State but that did not mean it had continuous settlement extending to the Michigan boundary. Between the last villages in Ohio and Detroit lay a hundred-mile wide strip of land known as the Black Swamp. Four or five days of hard travel on horseback were needed to cross it. The water was not safe to drink and the swarms of flies and mosquitoes were terrible. In one stretch, no houses existed

[4] G. B. Catlin, *The Story of Detroit*, pp. 115-124. Detroit Public Library, *Detroit in Its World Setting*, pp. 46-51.

for forty miles. Difficult as travel through Canada was, that through Ohio was worse.

After 1806, the trade restrictions that President Jefferson labored to apply against Canada and Great Britain increased the hostility between Ontario farmers and American travellers to Detroit in the very area through which most people then went to Michigan. Worst of all for its future, Michigan was reputed to have such poor land that it was not worth farming anyhow. Neither American settlers nor Methodist ministers were interested in this area yet.

The Methodist Episcopal Church

In the years between 1783 and 1804, the Methodist Episcopal Church was the first to break its ties with Europe and nationalize its organization in the United States. Indeed it was independently established here before a separate Methodist Episcopal Church existed in England. Young American preachers were determined not to follow the Anglican ways which they thought unsuited to the American conditions.

As an ordained clergyman of the Anglican faith, John Wesley insisted that English Methodists might form Classes or Societies but must look to the State Church for the sacraments. But Wesley also knew that Methodists in America had not received communion nor had their children baptized in many years.

In September, 1784, John Wesley himself ordained Thomas Coke, Richard Whatcoat, and Thomas Vasey to the rank of Elder. He had already appointed them, at the last Annual Conference, to work in America. Coke was intended to be the Superintendent of all work in America and Francis Asbury his assistant. But Coke did not remain here long so the assistant became the first Bishop.

Francis Asbury was the only English Methodist missionary who stayed in the United States throughout the Revolutionary War. Even he found it necessary to live quietly in a small village in Delaware. Because of John Wesley's open opposition to the rebellion, many Americans believed all Methodists were Tories.

Soon after they arrived in the United States, the three English Elders met with Francis Asbury and John Dickins. The latter was then preaching at John Street Church in New York City. Together these five men drafted a call to all Methodist preachers to meet with them in Baltimore on December 24, 1784.

Of the eighty-three Methodist preachers then in active service, about sixty came to that Christmas Conference at Lovely Lane Chapel in Baltimore. There they organized the Methodist Episcopal Church in America in ten days. Afterwards Asbury wrote, "We spent the whole week in conference, debating freely, and determining all things by a majority vote. . . . We were in great haste and did much business in a little time."

Asbury refused ordination as Superintendent on Wesley's appointment alone. Only when unanimously elected by the Conference did he accept the position. Then he was ordained Deacon, Elder, and Superintendent on three successive days. By 1800, in spite of John Wesley's open opposition, Asbury had substituted the title of Bishop for that of Superintendent.

The Christmas Conference also drafted and adopted many rules for a great variety of things such as the order of services, the hymns to be sung, conduct required of ministers and members, the steps by which young men might become Elders, and the forms for local organizations. To answer all questions of faith, John Wesley's Twenty-five Articles of Religion were accepted. All the topics mentioned here and many more were printed for the first time in a *Methodist Discipline* in 1785.

Before that Conference of 1784 adjourned, several young men were ordained as "travelling elders." Such a one was authorized to give the sacraments, preach, and expound the Bible. One of those present at the Christmas Conference, the Rev. William Watters, noted in his diary, "We became, instead of a religious society, a separate church. This gave great satisfaction through all our societies."[5]

Among the Methodist doctrines, based on Wesley's Articles of Religion, were universal redemption, free will, free grace, and justification by faith. In other words, any man might be saved by his own act of belief in Jesus Christ. Once converted, anyone might grow into "Christian Perfection" or complete holiness. Methodists were generally quite opposed to the doctrine of predestination preached by Presbyterians on the frontier.

The *Discipline* stated that anyone might be admitted to a Methodist Society or Class who had "a desire to flee from the wrath to come and to be saved from their sins." In those days, it was easier to be admitted than it was to *stay* a Methodist. Six months of probation was required for full membership. A rigidly high standard of conduct was set and maintained too. Card playing, dancing, drinking intoxicating liquors, theater attendance, travel on the Sabbath, elaborate dress and fancy jewelry were all forbidden. Indulgence in any of them could get one expelled from the Methodist Episcopal Church.

The organizations of the early American Methodist Episcopal Church, as defined by the Christmas Conference in 1784, were those established in Michigan when this region finally was settled. Many of them have been greatly modified or else have disappeared from the Methodist Church of the 20th century.

[5] Account of the Christmas Conference and all quotations concerning it drawn from W. W. Sweet, *Meth. Am. Hist.*, pp. 110, 112-113. Also W. C. Barclay, *Early American Methodism*, I, 96-99.

John Wesley's basic unit was the SOCIETY defined always in the *Discipline* as:

> A company of men having the form and seeking the power of godliness, united in order to pray together, to receive the word of exhortation, and to watch over one another in love, that they may help each other to work out their salvation.

Societies were divided into Classes and Bands. A CLASS, usually about one dozen in number, was the fundamental unit on the frontier. It was made up of "believers" living in the same area. Each Class had a lay leader, whose duty it was to visit each member weekly. Class leaders comforted, advised, or warned as they felt necessary. They also collected money or useful articles given for the ministers, the local church, and the poor. In pioneer days, firewood, potatoes, or mittens were often the only items the members had to give.

Classes all had individual tickets of membership good for three months. These were lettered or numbered in such fashion that expired tickets could be instantly detected. No one was supposed to attend meetings more than two or three times without a ticket for that particular Class.

Old Class Ticket. In early Methodism, a Class Ticket signifying that the holder was a Methodist in good standing, was required for entrance into the Quarterly Meeting.

Harriet Carpenter Member.

METHODIST EPISCOPAL CHURCH,
FOUNDED A. D. 1784.

2 QUARTERLY TICKET, *April 5* 18 *56*

C. H. Oward Minister.

Let every one that nameth the name of Christ depart from iniquity.—2 Tim. ii, 19.

Quick as the apple of an eye,
O God, my conscience make!
Awake my soul when sin is nigh,
And keep it still awake.

Class leaders were very strict about many things. Those who came late after the doors were closed were not admitted. This was practiced so generally that even a minister arriving late would not usually enter a Class meeting. Such small, private gatherings were times of free, emotional religious testimony. Most leaders never hesitated to speak plainly of improper conduct that had come to their knowledge or even to expel a member if they thought it was necessary.

A BAND was a still smaller group, all of the same sex, in order to encourage more frank and free expression. Every Class or Band leader was responsible religiously to the appointed minister and financially to the stewards of the Society.[6]

A CIRCUIT was composed of many Societies and Classes. Three or four week Circuits were very common in 1804. This meant for the minister incessant travel to reach anywhere from twenty to twenty-eight places of previously announced preaching appointments. These were located in schoolhouses or private homes. Rare was the Circuit that possessed a separate church building.

Most of the Circuit riding ministers were eager to cover as much ground as possible. They often preached from twenty-five to twenty-eight times on a trip around a Circuit. But one sermon could be used over and over again until perfected. The only day most Circuit riders did not preach was Monday.

Large Circuits often had a senior and a junior preacher, who travelled in opposite directions in order to reach the standing appointments more often. Most Circuits had also local preachers and exhorters licensed annually by any Quarterly Conference. These men assisted at revivals and camp meetings or locally after the sermon. The Term CIRCUIT RIDER was applied to all grades of ministers from the travelling Elder, Deacon, and young man just "admitted on trial" to the exhorter and local preacher. The latter might be fully ordained to give the sacraments or only locally licensed to preach.

To aid the bishops the office of PRESIDING ELDER was created in 1792. The Bishops then travelled anywhere in the country as needed but the Presiding Elders were assigned to a definite district from the first. They knew all the preachers and their Circuits very well and so were able to help any Bishop in making the annual appointments. Collectively in an Annual Conference, they were known as the Cabinet. It was the Presiding Elder's immediate duty to hold all Quarterly Conferences. And they really were held four times a year in that early day.

According to the *Discipline,* the QUARTERLY CONFERENCE was "the basic body of control uniting the pastoral charge to connectional Methodism." Every pastor, stationed in one church only, and every Conference appointed Circuit rider was required to organize one. It included all Class leaders, trustees, stewards, local preachers, exhorters, and active unappointed or retired Elders. No matter what his occupation might be, every ordained minister was a member of some Quarterly Conference.

On the frontier, a Quarterly Conference was much anticipated and people came long distances to attend. It lasted from Friday night to Monday morning usually. Church business was transacted, sermons were

---

[6] Information on organizations based on the *Discipline* and on the discussion of the "Wesleyan Heritage" by W. C. Barclay in *Early American Methodism,* I, xv-xli.

preached, and communion was administered by the Presiding Elder. On many Circuits, he was the only one authorized to give it. Many of the appointed ministers were not yet fully ordained. Consequently, communion was offered less often, was regarded as a sacred privilege, and was open only to the members in good standing in their Classes and Circuits. Last of all, the Presiding Elder would "open the door of the church" and receive new members on probation.

Class leadership and Quarterly Conference were the sources of new ministers for the Methodist Episcopal Church in those days. A young, vigorous Class leader would be urged to take out a local license and try his skill at preaching. If all went well, then he would be recommended by the Quarterly Conference for admission on trial by the next Annual Conference session. There he would receive an appointment and also begin the Conference course of study. His next four years would be strenuous ones. If he passed the annual examinations in the prescribed studies, he might be ordained a Deacon in two years and, at the end of four years, become an Elder. It was generally felt then that the young minister ought not to marry within that fouryear period of education and trial.

All his active years of service would find any minister associated with the Quarterly Conference of his current appointment. Even after he superannuated or retired, he would be a member of one in the town and church where he lived. Through his Quarterly Conference, he might still find opportunities for preaching in his old age.

After 1796, the districts were united into ANNUAL CONFERENCES. Before that year all Methodist Circuits in the whole of North America formed one group which met in Baltimore in 1792. Three sectional Annual Conferences were supposed to be held each year after 1784. This did not work out satisfactorily as too many of the early Circuit riders were too poor and too far away to attend. Therefore, the General Conference of 1796 created the first six Annual Conferences with definite boundaries These were New England, which included Canada, Philadelphia, which included New York, Baltimore, Virginia, South Carolina, and the Western. The latter included all Methodist work west of the Appalachian Mountains.

Both State and sectional Annual Conferences had been held earlier but in haphazard fashion at the wish of the Bishops. With the geographical division more precise, more businesslike patterns of procedure began to develop. For nearly a century to come, the Annual Conferences were strictly ministerial in their composition. Included were the Bishops, the Presiding and the travelling Elders, the Deacons, and the ministers on trial. Only after many years of struggle were the laymen admitted to an equal vote in the Annual Conferences.

The Annual Conference was really the professional organization of Methodist ministers. It gave much time to reviewing the "characters" of the ministers. Standards were very high beginning with absolute obedience to the Bishops at all times. Matters of dress, manners, and marriage might come up. Total abstinence from all liquor was required and, after the 1870's from the use of tobacco. In the mid-19th century, membership in such a secret society as the Masons could cause questions in Conference too.

If serious charges were brought against any minister, the Annual Conference would arrange for a trial with a panel of from nine to fifteen ministers serving as the jury. A private or a public reprimand by the presiding Bishop might be voted or, more rarely, expulsion from the Annual Conference might be the result. Such matters were not hushed up and dealt with in private as they probably would be today.

Two high points in the last day or two of the Annual Conference session were the ordinations and the announcement of the appointments for the coming year. The Bishop, assisted usually by the Presiding Elders, ordained the Deacons first and then the travelling Elders. Often a minister's wife would kneel at the altar with him during the ordination.

Reading out the appointments was not then the rather cut and dried performance it tends to be today. Many ministers quite literally did not know where they were going until they heard the appointments read. Sometimes the shock was keen. The Annual Conference was then and still is the high point of any Methodist minister's year.

Even in the first decade of the 19th century, Methodism was beginning to develop a stationed ministry. The General Conference of 1804 ruled that any minister, appointed by a Bishop to a charge, could not remain in the same station or circuit more than two years.

The capstone of the whole Methodist system was then and still is the GENERAL CONFERENCE. It supervised the entire Church giving particular attention to "all matters distinctively connectional." In 1804, its time of meeting was already quadrennial in the month of May. It was not yet representative in composition. In actual practice, only the ministers living nearby attended.

Therefore the General Conference of 1808 adopted a constitution for the American Methodist Episcopal Church. This established a representative General Conference for the United States and Canada. The ratio was one delegate to every five members of each Annual Conference. A quorum was two-thirds of all elected delegates. This new body was never to alter the Articles of Religion, the episcopacy, and the Society rules unless all the Annual Conferences so recommended and the next General Conference approved the changes.

Certain financial arrangements previously adopted were then carried over under the new constitution. The General Conference of 1792 set the annual salaries of all travelling elders at $64 plus their expenses of travel. Wives were also to receive $64 "if they be in want of it." The General Conference of 1800 raised these salaries to $80 per minister plus "$16 each for children under seven and $24 each for those between seven and fourteen." In 1816, the ministerial salaries were raised to $100.

With such modest compensation, it is not surprising that the General Conference of 1796 created the Chartered Fund for which gifts of money were solicited. Nor that the Fund was to be used only for the needs of "distressed travelling preachers, their families, worn-out preachers, and the widows and orphans of preachers."

Interest in promoting good reading habits was shown quite early. The Methodist Book Concern was established in 1789. The General Conference of 1800 declared that it was the duty of every Presiding Elder and Circuit preacher to see that his District or Circuit was kept "fully supplied with books."

Methodist preachers came to Canada from the United States and also from England. Quite early, English Wesleyan Methodists differed in their ways from American Methodist Episcopalians. In 1800, the New York Annual Conference was created and Canada was transferred to its care from that of New England. Six itinerant American ministers received Canadian appointments from the just-started New York Annual Conference. In 1810, the work was again divided with Lower Canada left in the New York Annual Conference and Upper Canada transferred to the newly created Genesee Annual Conference. Detroit was an obscure part of the Thames Circuit in Upper Canada under the New York Annual Conference from 1804 through 1810.

The Western Annual Conference existed from 1796 to 1812. It grew very fast from fourteen appointments in 1800 to one hundred in 1812. Then it was divided into the Ohio and the Tennessee Annual Conferences. Methodist preaching had been held in Ohio by 1800 and in Indiana by 1801. The District of Ohio was created in 1803 with five Circuits and eight preachers. The new District grew so fast that, by 1811, it had nineteen Circuits and hence was divided into two Districts: Miami and Muskingum. That same Western Conference made Indiana a District in 1808 and Illinois one in 1811.[7] Geographical expansion was slowly bringing the Methodist Episcopal Church nearer Michigan.

But Territorial and State boundaries did not mean very much to the members of those early Annual Conferences. Circuit riders went anywhere that they heard or thought that their services might be needed. Before 1840, wandering Circuit riders from the New York, Genesee, Ohio, and Indiana Annual Conferences had all preached in Michigan. The connectional Methodist Episcopal Church was extending its network of societies and classes to the frontier in Michigan.

---

[7] Wm. W. Sweet, editor, *The Rise of Methodism in the West, passim.* This book contains the Journals of the Western Annual Conference sessions from 1800 to 1812. They are not so very detailed.

CHAPTER I

A BEGINNING AND A WAR

1809 — 1815

In May, 1809, the New York Annual Conference appointed the Rev. William Case to the Detroit Circuit in Upper Canada District. This was the only time that this Annual Conference made such an appointment. The Rev. John Carroll, who knew most of the early travelling elders on the Canadian-Michigan frontier, wrote of this first appointment to Michigan:

> Detroit . . . was . . . like the old Oswegotchie Circuit, which was named from a place in the State of New York but which lay wholly in Canada. . . . It was the intention of the bishop appointing, to make Detroit the bona fide head of the Circuit, which was to comprise both sides of the river, but . . . less was done there than on the Canada side where the principal part of the Circuit lay and where most of the success was realized.

The Rev. William Case was a handsome, energetic, young Irishman. Born in 1780, he joined the Methodist Episcopal Church in 1803, was received on trial in the New York Annual Conference in 1805, served as the junior preacher on three different circuits, and was ordained an elder in 1808. He was then given charge alone of the Ancaster Circuit in Upper Canada. He did not attend the Annual Conference session in 1809. But on June 20 Case received the news of his appointment to that remote Detroit Circuit.

Such an assignment meant preparation and soul searching to any Methodist circuit rider. Most travelling preachers were very concerned to procure a large, strong horse and a good saddle with capacious saddlebags. They journeyed round their circuits entirely on horseback, carrying their worldly possessions along with them.

These might include an extra suit of clothes, stockings, and perhaps an extra shirt. Books were always carried too. Included would be a

11

William Case (1780-1855) was the Father of Michigan Methodism. Appointed to the Detroit Circuit in 1809-10, he laid the foundations of the Church in Detroit and southwestern Ontario. Repeatedly appointed presiding elder, he was later famous as the father of Methodist Indian Missions in Canada. His converts began the Methodist mission work at the Soo.

Bible, *Discipline,* hymn book, and one or two theological works such as Fletcher's *Appeal* or Dexter's *Call.* Most ministers also had a bundle of cheap, religious tracts for distribution among their congregations.

The usual attire of a Methodist Circuit rider then was a dark, straight coat with long tails and a standing collar. He wore either knee breeches or pantaloons and a long, heavy waistcoat. The trousers were frequently patched on the knees. His hair was turned straight back and allowed to grow long, extending to his shoulders.

The early Circuit riders aimed to follow the settlers just as soon as possible after they came into new country. Generally, the pioneers built their cabins near springs in the river valleys. A travelling preacher might know the name of a former Methodist family but much more often the people he met were all strangers. In any case, he always stopped at every cabin, inquired for Methodists, and announced he had come to preach. Either he delivered a sermon then and there or announced a time for services several days hence. This gave the family time to notify the neighbors.

The specified time was usually noon or "first candlelight." A people generally without clocks would then know when to come. For many years all frontier Methodist preaching took place in school houses or private homes. In the latter case, the minister stood in the doorway to pray and preach with the women and children inside the house and the men clustered around outside. Dogs, chickens, and a pig or two might also be under the house.

The Rev. William Case followed the typical Circuit rider procedure on his journey from Ancaster to Detroit. He found so many cabins in which to preach and the roads were so bad, or even non-existent, that it took him until the last of September to work his way through western Upper Canada to Detroit. Mr. Case had a fine singing and whistling voice and, on long journeys, he sang or whistled his way along. Thus, "his own spirits were revived, his horse seemed livelier, all the birds began to sing and he went on his way rejoicing."

He must have felt the need of any encouragement possible because he approached his new work with many doubts. These he confided to his diary in specific detail thus:

> My appointment to the Detroit Country gives me trials and my mind is continually wading in deep waters . . . I feel a heavy burden almost continually on my mind, the cause of which I conceive to be this. 1 — Fears what my success may be. 2 — Being a stranger in a land where there is not a single person I ever saw before that I know of. 3 — The people are rude, unchristian, uncultivated and expect therefore that my trials will be great. 4 — And to meet all these difficulties, I fear I have neither wisdom, gifts, nor grace to conduct such an important mission, but in secret prayer to God "my only resource in trouble," I find some assurance of God's blessings. I have covenanted with Him to devote all I have and am to His service for the salvation of souls.[1]

Here was a missionary approaching a new field of work without money or a missionary society to back him in his efforts. In a letter to Bishop Asbury, Mr. Case told how he began in Detroit. He said in part:

> As I could not understand that there were any serious persons in the town and as I knew of none more worthy than the rulers ought to be I immediately went to the governor and having introduced myself to him as a minister of the Gospel, I requested the privilege of the Council House to hold meetings in. He appeared very friendly and used me as a Christian minister, and ordered the Council House to be prepared for meeting, where I preached to crowded and listening congregations during the time I stayed in that country.

Those large congregations may have come in part because of Mr. Case's manner of holding a service. The Rev. John Carroll said of him:

> He was wont . . . when he finished his sermon which was always persuasive to break out in one of his melodious strains by which he first spellbound and then melted his auditors. Next, he would pass

---

[1] Quoted from a typescript of Case's Journal for this time to be found in the Burton Collection of Detroit Public Library. Also quoted by Louis Ling in his booklet, *A Century of Service,* which is a history of Central Church in Detroit. Further information about Case in Pilcher's *Hist. Prot. Mich.,* pp. 16, 20-22, 31-35. J. Carroll, *Case & His Cotemp.,* I, 170, 187-188. Elmer Houser, "A Historical Survey of Detroit Methodism," *Michigan Christian Advocate,* for May 31, 1928, LV, #22, p. 3. W. R. Prescott, *The Fathers Still Speak,* pp. 32-33.

around the room, shaking hands and speaking a word to each, perhaps throwing his arms around the necks of the young men and entreating them with tears to give their hearts to God.

After being in Detroit some months, Mr. Case had arrived at a low opinion of the people there somewhat like that of the other early Protestant ministers in Michigan. He said that they were "wicked and dissipated" as many of them openly got drunk, played cards, danced, and paid no attention to Sunday observance. The great majority had never learned to read and consequently knew nothing whatsoever of the Bible. Perhaps the fact that Mr. Case had trouble in finding a place to live in Detroit may have influenced his opinions of the town. His troubles were only partly due to his being a Protestant in a Catholic village but also to his very modest salary of $100 a year, if he could collect it.

Soon after arriving in Detroit, Mr. Case met Robert Abbott. He was at that time the auditor-general of the Territory of Michigan as well as a merchant and furtrader. This man was to become the first Michigan born lay member of the Methodist Episcopal Church. He helped build the first Methodist Church in Detroit and for a great many years befriended a succession of Circuit riders.

Beginning a custom by which many a Methodist minister was helped, Mr. Abbott immediately invited the Rev. William Case to stay with him at his farmhouse about a mile from the town. But Mrs. Abbott was very hostile to Protestant preachers, having had Roman Catholic parents who told her that Methodist ministers tried to break up families.

Many years later, Mrs. Abbott admitted to the Rev. Elijah Pilcher that she once locked Mr. Case out of her house on a very cold day. When the minister then came home with her husband, she was as ugly to both men as she dared to be. She even listened at the keyhole when her husband and the minister were busy in "private conversation." How amazed she was to discover that they were praying together.

Full conversion was not experienced by Mr. Abbott until later. After the Rev. William Case had gone east to attend the New York Annual Conference session, Abbott and his family went to a camp meeting on the Thames River in Canada. It seems quite likely that the Rev. Daniel Freeman was the preacher there. He officiated on the Ancaster Circuit in 1810-1811 and located in that part of Canada after 1811. Perhaps the first Methodist minister to preach in Michigan was responsible for the conversion of the first lay member of the Methodist Episcopal Church there. Mr. Abbott underwent a serious and emotional religious experience in his tent at midnight. Afterwards he was wont to say that "the true light shone into his heart." Mr. Freeman may have been the immediate agent of Abbott's conversion but the way thereto had clearly been prepared by the Rev. William Case. Things were in readiness for another minister to organize Classes and a Society.

Reporting to Bishop Asbury at the end of his year here, Mr. Case said that another minister was much needed in Detroit to give more attention to the American part of the Thames Circuit. The work on the Canadian side of the Detroit River was well organized in a two weeks Circuit with twelve appointments in a travelling distance of 240 miles. Any minister appointed to Detroit might be able to help his Canadian colleague a little. Case himself had received his salary of $80 plus expenses of $30 and had actually been able to leave $10 on the circuit for the next minister to come there. He said that "some few were brought under awakening and three or four had found peace in believing, and expect to join in society when a minister shall again be sent among them."

The Rev. William Case never again was appointed to Michigan but enjoyed a long career as a Presiding Elder and missionary to the Indians in Canada. Hs assisted in the first camp meeting held in Michigan on the River Rouge in June, 1822. As an old man of 73, he attended the Michigan Annual Conference session of 1853 in Detroit. There he preached on Sunday and "reviewed the past with great interest and much pleasure." He is almost forgotten today but he cleared the way for those who organized the Methodist Episcopal Church in Michigan.

The First Society is formed in Michigan

The Genesee and the Western Annual Conferences each made an appointment to the Detroit Circuit in the summer, 1810. This never happened again and is probably due to the rapid settlement of the frontier and the constant effort of the Methodist Episcopal Church to push its ministers out where the pioneers were.

The new Genesee Annual Conference appointed Ninian Holmes to Detroit under Henry Ryan as the Presiding Elder of Upper Canada District. When Mr. Holmes finally reached Detroit in the fall of 1810, he must have been surprised to find another Methodist minister at work there. The Western Annual Conference had appointed William Mitchell to Detroit under the Ohio District; which in 1811 was split into Miami and Muskingum.

The difficulties of travel then and of crossing the Detroit River together with the two-week Circuit already established in Canada soon led Holmes and Mitchell to a division of their labors. The Genesee man worked in Canada and the Western man tended to the American side of the Detroit River. His preaching places may have been Detroit, Frenchtown later Monroe, and a little inland on the River Rouge. Except for the Council House in Detroit, all services certainly were held in farm houses which were simple log cabins.

The Rev. William Mitchell of the Western Annual Conference organized the first Methodist Episcopal Society in Michigan sometime in the fall of 1810. No records of this Society have survived but the chances are that this forward step was taken on a weeknight in a private home, possibly that of Robert Abbott. Just seven people constituted the first organization: three men and four women. Sometime early in 1811, Mr. Mitchell also organized a Methodist Episcopal Society in Frenchtown, later Monroe, on the River Raisin. Pilcher said that it soon had about twenty-three members.

Then in the spring of 1811, Mr. Mitchell succeeded in holding one of the special occasions of frontier Methodism. The first Quarterly Conference ever held in Michigan took place at the house of William Weaver on the River Rouge. Pilcher stated that Weaver was a Catholic. But perhaps his wife or some close relative was a Methodist. If it was like other Quarterly Conferences, two or three sermons were preached, love feast was held, baptism was given and, most important of all, communion was administered. This was a sacrament that only Elders could give and was the reason that Mitchell had been ordained an Elder a year ahead of the time it was usually granted by any Annual Conference. No Presiding Elders were present at this first Quarterly Conference. Mr. Mitchell presumably left Detroit fairly early in the summer because he was present at the last session of the Western Annual Conference held in Cincinnati. That was a very long trip to make on horseback all the way.

Consideration of the accomplishments of the Rev. William Mitchell during his short stay in Michigan give the impression that he must have been a minister of energy and industry. And Pilcher, having talked with people who knew him personally, said that Mr. Mitchell "was regarded here as a very good man and a fine preacher." But the records of the Western Annual Conference sessions leave a feeling of doubt about his career.

In 1807, William Mitchell was admitted on trial from the Licking Circuit by the Western Annual Conference although a few years previously he had been rejected by the Philadelphia Annual Conference. "After mature consideration," it was thought proper to give him a chance. In 1809, Mr. Mitchell was elected a Deacon and a full member of the Annual Conference. He served on the Little Kanawha Circuit the year before and after his election as a Deacon. In 1810, he was elected an Elder "in consequence of a Mission" says the record of the Conference session. As already noted, in going so far as Detroit was then, such a mission ought to have at least one minister entitled to give communion.

Mr. Case had apparently no particular trouble in raising his modest salary in 1809-1810 but Mr. Mitchell collected only $30 during his appointment to Detroit. In 1811, he was present at the Cincinnati meeting of the Western Annual Conference and was appointed to Tuscarawas.

In 1812, Mitchell "was expelled from the connection" and, as Pilcher said, "Here he is lost to our view."[2]

The members of that Society formed by Mr. Mitchell, the first seven Methodists in Michigan, were Mr. and Mrs. Robert Abbott, Mr. and Mrs. William McCarty, Mr. and Mrs. William Stacy, and Mrs. Sarah McComb. Their family relationships and high degree of neighborliness had some relation to their church activities. The Rev. Elijah Pilcher, early historian of Michigan Methodism, knew personally five of the original seven. He often consulted them about the early events of Methodism in Michigan. He is the source of much of what is known today about these early Methodists.

Mrs. Betsey Abbott and Mrs. Maria McCarty were born the Audrain sisters of a Catholic family in Detroit. Mrs. Abbott was at first openly hostile to the Methodist preachers, as shown in her treatment of the Rev. William Case. Mrs. McCarty had been emotionally affected by the preaching of the Rev. Daniel Freeman in 1804. After Mr. Abbott was so profoundly converted in Canada in June, 1810, it is probable that he and his sister-in-law influenced their respective spouses to attend and then join in the Methodist work of the Rev. William Mitchell.

When William McCarty had "a Christian experience," the first Class leader in Michigan Methodism had been found. He came of Irish ancestry and "possessed a warm and lively temperament, ready utterance and very respectable talents." In 1822, he was licensed as an exhorter and continued in such work until his death in 1844. He moved to a farm in Branch County near Coldwater in 1831. He was the sheriff of that County for several years. In Methodism, he continued active helping to form the second Society in the County and also serving as the Sunday School Superintendent. Pilcher said of Class Leader McCarty:

> He died very happy . . . aged fifty-five years, having been a member of the Methodist Episcopal Church for thirty-four years. It had been a very common remark with him that he expected "to go straight from Coldwater to heaven." While on his death-bed he said to his children, *"Live Religion."* To a Christian brother who called to see him a few days before his departure he said: "If I could get loose from this old body, how quick I would be there — in Heaven."

The early Class records, carefully kept and sewed together by McCarty for many years, have all disappeared. Pilcher said:

> When he died, the minister who preached his funeral sermon called on the widow and obtained these books, with the pledge that he would

---

[2] E. H. Pilcher, *Hist. Prot. Mich.*, pp. 16, 22, 32, 39. W. W. Sweet, *Meth. Am. Hist.*, pp. 166-169. John Carroll, *Case & His Cotemp.*, I, 193-199. W. W. Sweet, *Rise of Methodism in the West*, Journals of the Western Conference, *passim.*

return them — a pledge that he failed to redeem. As this minister shortly after left the place and the ministry, and died, it has been impossible to reclaim them.[3]

The former Audrain sisters long outlived their husbands. Mrs. Abbott "became decidedly attached to the Church she had so violently opposed." She was a Methodist Episcopal Church member for forty-eight years. In old age, she liked to reminisce of that first small class and the early ministers in Detroit. Her husband died in 1853. She lived in Coldwater with a daughter much of the time but died in Detroit in 1858 while visiting another daughter.

The second Audrain sister, Mrs. Maria McCarty, outlived the other six members of that first Class. In her last days, she maintained an ardently Unionist stand in correspondence with a sister in the south. Her children and grandchildren fought in the Civil War. She died in 1863. Pilcher wrote of Mrs. McCarty, "She was the first to rise when opportunity was given for those who wished to join in the first class of Methodists of the State of Michigan, and is the last to fall in death and go to her reward in heaven, of that class."

The third couple in the first Michigan Methodist Society were Mr. and Mrs. Stacy. He was the first to die of the original seven. Short, quiet, steady, and devout were the adjectives used by his contemporaries to characterize him. He was living on a farm on the River Rouge about seven miles out of Detroit when he died in 1827. It is likely that his farm was near the first log church built by the Methodists in 1818.

Mrs. Betsey Stacy outlived her husband for many years. She was remembered for her great power as an exhorter, being "large of stature, commanding and noble in her appearance, and of an ardent temperament." She married a second time, lived in Detroit, and was a member of the Congress Street Church at the time of her death in 1853.

The seventh member of that first Society was Sarah McComb, about whom Pilcher knew the least of any of that original group. He even spelled her name Macomb. Recently certain facts about her came to light.[4] She was born in 1772. Her first husband was Godfrey Corbus by whom she had four sons. They also lived on a farm in the River Rouge area near that first church building. Her first husband died in 1805 and, a few years later, Mrs. Corbus married John McComb not long before she joined that Methodist Society in 1810. After her second husband died, she moved with a son and his family to Branch County

---

[3] E. H. Pilcher, *Hist. Prot. Mich.*, pp. 40-54, 57. Quotations above are from pp. 45 and 57.

[4] The late Dr. William C. S. Pellowe discovered a fourth generation descendant of Mrs. McComb. She is Mrs. Margery Adams of Flint. She gave the *Advocate* and Dr. Pellowe the facts about her ancestor. See *Mich. Christian Advocate* for Dec. 6, 1962. LXXXIX, #44, p. 10.

near Coldwater in 1830. There she died in 1838. Numerous descendants of Sarah McComb are scattered all over the United States.

This family also has a long record of patriotic service to the United States. Mrs. McComb's second husband, John, fought in the War of 1812 and a grandson, Samuel Corbus, in the Mexican War. Still another descendant fought in the Civil War and later was a Circuit rider in Kansas. The present generation descendant, Mrs. Margery Adams, was a nurse ensign in the Navy in World War II.

One other woman was a very early member in 1810-1811 but not quite a charter member of the original Detroit Society. She was Mrs. Amy Witherell, wife of one of the Territorial judges named James Witherell. She had been converted to Methodism in Vermont long before she came to Michigan. Appalled by the primitive conditions of living and frightened of the ever present Indians, she took her three younger children east for the winter. With the outbreak of war, the rest of her family joined her in Troy, New York. They all returned to Detroit in 1817. She and her children were to be prominent Detroit citizens and loyal Methodists for many years to come.[5]

The New Society at Detroit Struggles to Survive

The Genesee Annual Conference in 1811 sent Ninian Holmes back to the Detroit Circuit with a junior preacher, Silas Hopkins, to assist him. The Presiding Elder of Upper Canada District was still Henry Ryan. Apparently Holmes was expected to give more attention this year to the American side of his appointment but his junior preacher

[5] E. H. Pilcher, *Hist. Prot. Mich.*, pp. 51-54.

Detroit had been settled for over a century. In 1812 it was still a small frontier town menaced by the British and the Indians. As late as 1830 the population was only 2, 222.

was entirely inexperienced. The Western and its successor, the Ohio Annual Conference made no appointments to Michigan until 1820.

Perhaps it was felt that the rewards of ministerial labor in Michigan were so meagre that preachers should not be wasted there. Or enough ministers were simply not available. But the earliest statistics indicate 134 members for the entire circuit of which around one hundred were possibly Canadians. To travel so far for about thirty members of the Society in Michigan may have been too time-consuming or expensive. Methodist ministers were all expected to be moving around to many places and not to be giving their efforts to one group. Here one of the inherent weaknesses of frontier Methodism is visible. The ministers did not stay long enough to do lasting work in an area. They barely got acquainted and then were moved elsewhere. Between 1809-1812 and 1815-1824, Detroit had ten different ministers assigned to it by the Methodist Episcopal Church.

Holmes, Hopkins, and Ryan all came to Detroit during the Conference year 1811-1812. The second Quarterly Conference in Michigan was held in late autumn at the house of Robert Abbott in Detroit. This was the first time that a Presiding Elder, the Rev. Henry Ryan, officiated at baptism and communion here assisted by the Circuit ministers. Let us look at these Circuit riders in turn.

Presiding Elder Henry Ryan was a frontier character. About six feet tall, of a stalwart frame, dark in complexion, and quick in movement, he was well suited to the rough and tumble life of that time and place. For seven years, he was Presiding Elder of the Upper Canada District when Detroit Circuit was one of its appointments. Many were the stories told of him. Bishop Hedding, writing years later, said of Mr. Ryan:

> A very pious man of great zeal in his work as a minister. A man who labored as if the judgment thunders were to follow each sermon. He was sometimes overbearing in the administration of discipline . . . but he was very brotherly and kind to me — often speaking to me in a manner calculated to urge me on to diligence in the great work. When we met in the place of intersection in the circuit, he would salute me with his favorite exhortation, "Drive on, Brother, drive on! Drive the Devil out of the country. Drive him into the lake and drown him!"

The Rev. John Carroll remembered what fine singers both Henry Ryan and William Case were as young ministers and then as Presiding Elders. Ryan had the stronger voice but Case's was the sweeter. No one could forget their entrance together upon a new field of labor. Carroll said:

> They would ride into town, put their horses at an inn, lock arms and go singing down a street some stirring ode, beginning with "Come let us march to Zion's hill." By the time they had reached the market place they usually collected a large assembly. . . . They suffered . . . a

little annoyance from some of the baser sort, who sometimes tried to trip them off the butcher's block which constituted their rostrum; set fire to their hair and then blew out their candles if it were in the night session. . . . Such opposition the preachers regarded as trivial and held on.

Presiding Elder Ryan travelled a large district in Upper Canada with ten difficult Circuits. He was supposed to visit all of them which involved him in about 4,000 miles of horseback riding per year. He owned a modest farm and was paid $80 each year for himself and $60 for his wife, plus some provisions for his family. No wonder that the Rev. John Carroll declared, "In such disinterested zeal we surely see an humble follower of Jesus Christ."[6]

The senior preacher on the Detroit Circuit in 1811-1812 was the Rev. Ninian Holmes. In 1807 he was admitted on trial to the New York Annual Conference. In 1809 he came into full connection and was ordained Deacon and Elder all at once. As he was about to be appointed to a frontier area in the Upper Canada District, he had to be prepared to give the sacraments there. Holmes was said to have been "a compact and sprightly, fervent and orderly preacher." He was tidy in both person and dress and was widely noted for his well polished boots and the particular care he always gave his horse. He liked to be well mounted but so did most Circuit riders then. When aroused by his subject or the circumstances, Holmes was a powerful preacher.

The Rev. Silas Hopkins, junior preacher on the Detroit Circuit in 1811-1812, was a native of Canada. He was considered to be pious, young, single, and "of slender ministerial ability." He began his ministerial career with this appointment to the Detroit Circuit but was never received into full connection as either Deacon or Elder. He served later as a local preacher.

Both Holmes and Hopkins seem to have been distracted from their ministerial careers by the War of 1812. The Rev. Ninian Holmes was said by Pilcher to have been in Detroit on the very day that General Hull surrendered the city to the British. The Rev. Mr. Holmes baptized a child of William McCarty's on that date. Quite possibly he may have remained in Detroit during most of the War of 1812.

The declaration of war with Great Britain in June, 1812, cut like a knife across all organized religious effort as it did so many other activities. The Genesee Annual Conference had been appointed to meet on July 23, 1812, at Niagara, Upper Canada, but the American Bishops and preachers did not think it wise to go into Canada and such Canadian Methodist ministers as were British subjects did not dare come over into the United States. Therefore the Genesee Annual Conference fell

---

[6] J. Carroll, *Case & His Cotemp.*, I, 23-26, 225-227. E. H. Pilcher, *Hist. Prot. Mich.*, pp. 36-39. L. Ling, *A Century of Service*, pp. 25-26.

apart into two halves for the duration of the war. This was a forecast of the official separation that came later.

The American members of the Genesee Annual Conference met at Lyons, New York, and made appointments on paper for the whole of the Conference. The Rev. George Washington Densmore was assigned to the Detroit Circuit but he never got there. It is likely that Governor Hull had surrendered Detroit to the British, on August 16, before Densmore was even appointed to come there. Undoubtedly the British would have refused him admission to the occupied city.

Canada was left entirely to her own Methodist ministerial resources for three years. Presiding Elder Ryan assumed command and held three Annual Conferences chiefly to appoint the preachers to their fields of labor. It must have been this emergency situation that caused some of the ministers to call Mr. Ryan "high-handed and tyrannical." Eventually the Rev. Mr. Ryan grew embittered also and left the Methodist ministry and the Church too in 1827.[7]

As the Canadian ministers were turned away from the United States by the War of 1812 so some American ministerial careers were deflected from Canada. The Rev. Nathan Bangs was appointed to the Presiding Eldership of Lower Canada in 1812 but "being unable to cross the line with safety," spent the rest of his working days in the United States.

Michigan was peculiarly hard hit by the War of 1812. The Indians seemed to be everywhere so that fighting went on within and on its borders. The British occupation of Detroit lasted from August 16, 1812, to September 29, 1813.

That tiny Methodist Society in Monroe simply disintegrated and why the Detroit Society did not do likewise is a mystery. By some miracle, the original seven members there held together, although without an ordained minister for three years. William McCarty must have been a powerful class leader.

Methodist ministers, throughout the Northwest Territory, were conscious of the decrease in church membership and the decline in moral standards noticeable everywhere. A famous Ohio Circuit rider, the Rev. Jacob Young, recalled that he was conducting a quarterly meeting at Ashtabula when news of the British invasion came. Preaching on Sunday morning, he noticed that people in his congregation were leaving a few at a time. As soon as he decently could, Mr. Young closed the services and went to the door where he met four men. One was in army uniform, one was beating a drum, another was playing the fife, and the fourth held aloft the American flag. Mr. Young said in part:

> I asked them what all that meant? They told me that Hull had
> surrendered Detroit to the British and that nine hundred British and

---

[7] E. H. Pilcher, *Hist. Prot. Mich.*, pp. 23-24. J. Carroll, *Case & His Cotemp.*, I, 239, 264, 269, 286.

Indians were on their way down the Lake toward that country; that
they had no time to lose; they must try to raise force enough to hold
them in check. . . . Next day I crossed the Pennsylvania line and stopped
at a little village . . . and told the doleful news. . . . Some were frightened and some were very angry, one man swore most profanely, loud
and long. I tried to . . . reprove him but . . . he said it was right to
swear and . . . if Hull had sworn more he would not have lost Detroit.
Everywhere people were alarmed — many were preparing to leave their
homes and go to Pittsburgh. I tried to dissuade them . . . the Indians
would not get this far . . . One woman was very angry — she had just
persuaded her husband to leave. She knew better — we would all be
destroyed.[8]

The Rev. James B. Finley, another wellknown Ohio pioneer preacher,
was of the opinion that "This year the war spirit unfortunately entered
into many professors of religion and as soon as they caught it they
began to lose their religion."[9]

[8] Jacob Young, *Autobiography of a Pioneer*, pp. 286-288.
[9] W. W. Sweet, *Meth. Am. Hist.*, pp. 173-174.

CHAPTER II

FIVE YEARS OF SLOW GROWTH

1815 — 1820

Conditions in Michigan After the War

Even before the treaty of Ghent was signed, eastern people were pouring into the Northwest Territory. As a foreign traveller said in 1817, "All America seems to be breaking up and moving westward." Hard times in eastern seaports, caused by the Non-Intercourse and Embargo Acts, the desire for good farm land obtainable cheaply, and the belief that the Indians were no longer as dangerous were the major causes of this flood of immigration. Among its results were two new States: Indiana in 1816 and Illinois in 1818.

Not one in fifty of these immigrants had his heart and mind set on moving to Michigan. The maps of that day had the words "Interminable Swamp" spread in big letters across the peninsula of Michigan. Morse's *Traveller's Guide* said that Michigan consisted of "sand hills crowned with a few stunted trees and a scanty vegetation but generally bare and thrown by the wind into a thousand fantastic shapes."

Before the Northwest Territory was politically organized at all, James Monroe had visited parts of it and then reported to President Jefferson that it was "miserably poor, especially that near the Lakes Michigan and Erie. . . . The district, therefore, within which these fall will never contain a sufficient number of inhabitants to entitle them to membership in the confederacy."[1]

---

[1] George Fuller, *Econ. & Soc. Begin. of Mich.*, I, 51. John Caruso, *The Great Lakes Frontier*, pp. 350-352.

Indian titles to the land had not been extinguished by treaties in Michigan. Furthermore Congress had passed in 1812 an act setting aside two million acres of land in Michigan for army volunteers. Governor Lewis Cass of Michigan kept pressing Edward Tiffin, Surveyor General of the United States, to have this tract of land platted and thrown open to settlers in the hope this action would bring more Americans to Michigan. The resulting Tiffin Report increased Michigan's sad reputation. The government surveyors arrived in the late fall and started work between the Maumee and Raisin Rivers. They endured constant rain, sleet, and mud. Then they reported to Tiffin that this was the poorest land that they had ever seen and not even worth the cost of surveying.

Surveyor General Tiffin passed this estimate on to Josiah Meigs, Superintendent of the General Land Office. He in turn told President Madison that not one acre in a thousand was worth farming. The result was the transfer of the military bounty lands to Illinois and Missouri. This action infuriated Governor Cass. After much correspondence, he managed to get the surveys resumed in September, 1816. But Michigan was a long time in recovering from the effects of the Tiffin Report.

The United States Surveyor General was a Methodist. And at least one of those men who worked on the map of Michigan was a Methodist. He was Colonel Joseph Wampler, who came here from Tuscarawas County, Ohio. He had been appointed deputy surveyor general and his first contract here was to do eighteen townships in eastern Michigan. He agreed to do this on October 18, 1816, and began the work the following February. In 1821, he had a contract to survey land in Oakland County. He was "commonly understood among the early settlers to be a Methodist preacher." This probably means that he had been licensed back in Ohio by some Quarterly Conference as an exhorter or local preacher. Wampler's Lake in the Irish Hills was named for him. Judson Collins Methodist Youth Camp is located there today.[2]

Many of those, whose military, political, or professional positions brought them to Detroit soon after the end of the war, were impressed with the destitution and demoralization of its people. Governor Cass declared, "This country is totally exhausted of all its resources, and except as a frontier is scarcely worth possessing. . . . Through fear or policy, the British suffered the Indians to pillage the poor miserable inhabitants at pleasure." Territorial Secretary William Woodbridge said, "Many of the inhabitants had nothing to plant, nothing to eat, and no money to buy with."

By united efforts, Cass, Woodbridge and Woodward got $1500 from the War Department for relief. Later permission was obtained for the

[2] Mrs. Reginald Angus of Brooklyn, Michigan, called the facts about Colonel Wampler to my attention. See *Proceedings of the Land Board of Detroit*, for 1915, M. A. Burton, editor. C. Burton, compiler, p. 214.

most desperate poor to draw supplies from the government stores until another crop could be raised. Hundreds of thieving, starving Indians added to the grimness of the situation. Judge Witherell wrote to his wife, "Should peace continue, it will be many years before people will feel their scalps quite as safe as in Vermont."

This was really Detroit's first economic revolution. The importance of the town as a fur trading center was diminishing due to the decline of the European fur trade during the Napoleonic Wars and to the gradual disappearance of the wild life in an area being cleared for farming.

Conditions were not improved by the haphazard, agricultural methods of the French peasant farmers. They discarded the wool from their sheep and hauled the manure out on the winter ice of the Detroit River.

Transportation either by water or land was hazardous, slow and uncomfortable. Harbors had never been cleared of the sand bars, no lighthouses existed, and local storms were both sudden and violent. Money was scarce and a local system of using due bills prevailed.

Mail delivery once a week from the east was theoretically supposed to be in operation. But most citizens of Detroit allowed a minimum of two months in which to write to an eastern coast town and then receive a reply. No regular local newspaper yet existed.

Worst of all, the Territory of Michigan was not yet entitled to a delegate in Congress and the nearest member of the Federal House of Representatives lived at least two hundred miles away. A merchant and future mayor of Detroit said, "Everything seemed to be entirely unhinged."[3]

Much testimony to the decline of Christian standards of conduct can be found. Writing to the Rev. Mr. Backus in the spring of 1815, Solomon Sibley said, "the war has produced a great relaxation of morals in this place." As late as 1826, the Rev. William Simmons wrote, "This has for so long a time been a military post that that spirit seems to have been more assiduously cultivated than the spirit of the Gospel." The Rev. E. H. Pilcher said that the failure to appoint a Methodist minister to the Detroit Circuit for three years was a subject of deep concern to the Genesee Annual Conference.

The young minister who was appointed to Detroit also had a low opinion of his place of assignment. The Rev. Joseph Hickox felt that only "the grace of God" would enable any missionary to persist in such a town. He said in part:

> Detroit was a sink of iniquity. The original inhabitants were Canadian French, characterized by all the loose morals of secluded Catholicism. Besides, it had been under martial law for three years, alternately

[3] Quotations and summary of conditions in Detroit drawn from F. R. Dain, *Every House a Frontier, Detroit's Economic Progress, 1815-1825.* Chapter I on Detroit in 1815, *passim.* The future mayor was John R. Williams.

under the British and American dominancy. The pandemonium created by rum-drinking British soldiers, Indians and French may be more easily imagined than described. It was awful. Though the morals of our troops were of a higher grade than the others, yet war in its mildest form is an enemy to righteousness and temperance. The only Americans in the city were a few traders, whose antipathy to religion was proverbial.[4]

Hickox and Montieth: A Methodist and a Presbyterian Arrive in Detroit

Meeting in June 1815, at Lyons, New York, the Genesee Annual Conference appointed Joseph Hickox to the Detroit Circuit under the Upper Canada District. As was the practice then in making such assignments, Hickox was ordained an Elder one year in advance of the usual term. Thus he would be able to give the sacraments in his isolated location.

Joseph Hickox was born in 1788 near Hartford, Connecticut of Congregationalist parents. When he was fifteen, his mother and he were both converted to Methodism by the first preacher of that denomination whom they had ever encountered. Young Hickox came up through the usual training for a Methodist minister then. He was in turn a Class leader, an exhorter, and a local preacher. Licensed by the Rev. William Case, it was understood that he would soon enter the itinerant ministry. He was admitted on trial to the Genesee Conference in July, 1812. After three years, each on a different eastern circuit, he was chosen to reestablish the Methodist Church in Detroit.

The new travelling Elder had the usual tedious and difficult trip to his Circuit. The forests, swamps, and savages were all against him. He thought that the Indians were shooting at him instead of game on one occasion, was taken for a spy at another time, and preached wherever he could find people who would listen.[5]

The Rev. Joseph Hickox was twenty-seven in 1815, unmarried, "possessed an earnest piety and zeal," and was not afraid of anybody from a British officer and an Indian chief to a Catholic priest or a Presbyterian minister. Most of these he encountered during his work on Detroit Circuit.

Mr. Hickox found seven people in Detroit who wished to continue the Methodist membership they had held before the war. Presumably these were the original seven of the Society established in 1810. The men who had helped William Case in 1810 were equally useful in 1815 and began work in much the same way his predecessor had. Robert Abbott

---

[4] E. H. Pilcher, *Hist. Prot. Mich.*, p. 58.

[5] E. H. Pilcher, *Hist. Prot. Mich.*, pp. 58-59, 63, 71-75. The surname of this preacher is not always spelled the same. Pilcher, who knew him, wrote it Hickox but the *General Minutes* spell it Hickcox. W. R. Prescott, *The Fathers Still Speak*, pp. 33-34.

introduced the minister to Governor Cass, who promised the use of the Council House for his preaching services. The Governor also declared that he and his family would be "constant attendants." The Rev. Joseph Hickox said the Council House was always filled at services he conducted, the audience was quiet and attentive, and the higher army officers at the fort were usually in courteous attendance.

Pilcher testified that Hickox was "a very smooth, easy and eloquent speaker — never at a loss for thoughts or words in which to express them, and always attracted large congregations."

The town was crowded with Indians and soldiers because the Generals Harrison, Brown, and Cass were in process of negotiating a general treaty of peace with all the frontier Indians. But Mr. Hickox had a very large Circuit which required much time spent in Canada which which could not be traversed quickly. The very best he was able to do was a trip to Detroit once in three weeks. He himself admitted that "my stay in Detroit was necessarily so short that I could not follow up . . . by pastoral visitation any impression that might have been made by the labor of the pulpit."

The Rev. E. H. Pilcher knew Mr. Hickox and also had often travelled exactly the same Circuit beginning just fifteen years later. Therefore he was sure of the facts when he wrote:

> The rides and labors of the missionary to fulfill the duties connected with Detroit Circuit . . . were very fatiguing and excessive. . . . The preaching places in Michigan, for the two years in which Mr. Hickox travelled the Circuit were Detroit City, River Rouge, and Frenchtown, now Monroe. . . . On the Canada side of the river it was to include Malden, Sandwich, the new settlement down the lake about sixty miles below Detroit, and the River Thames . . . . Three times every three weeks he had to pass through a wilderness of fifty-seven miles without human habitation and to swim his horse five times each trip. In the winter, when the clumsy ferry boats were stopped, he had to leave his horse on the Canada side and to walk up and down the river seeking the strongest ice.[6]

Of the three preaching places in Michigan, Monroe surely received less attention than the other two. It was forty miles away and was reached through "a lonely wilderness" over a poor excuse for a road. The War of 1812 had wrought great havoc in the area and, under its stress, the small Society that had been organized in 1811 had disintegrated. Even Hickox, a very zealous missionary, admitted that he only got to Monroe "occasionally."

The other preaching places in Michigan, Detroit at the Council House and among the members living on the River Rouge, received about equal attention. Mr. Hickox strictly maintained his once in three

6 E. H. Pilcher, *Hist. Prot. Mich.*, pp. 63, 75, 62.

weeks preaching schedule: in Detroit and then in private homes on the
River Rouge. He had a choice of houses in which to preach there. The
Rev. E. H. Pilcher said:

> There were several of the Corbuses, Thomases and Hanchetts residing
> on the River Rouge, from three to eight miles out of the city, who soon
> became members so that the Society increased with considerable rapidity;
> nevertheless it was subject to considerable fluctuations.[7]

The recurrent question of which Methodist Church in the State of
Michigan was *first* specifically stated in terms of descendants, that is
Central of Detroit or Dearborn, can *never* be settled. These two
churches were *twins*. Pilcher and Hickox both wrote of *a* Society (in
the singular) in Michigan. Its parent was the Methodist Episcopal
Church. William Mitchell started and Joseph Hickox restarted the work
in and around the area of Detroit. The way of that time was the large
Circuit and any travelling Elder regarded *all* of his preaching appointments as equally important. The average Circuit rider was if anything
more concerned about finding new places in which to preach than he
was about those previously established.

Dependable statistics for this early Methodist work in Michigan
cannot be found. The early Class books disappeared. And the record,
in the Genesee Annual Conference *Minutes* for the first year that Mr.
Hickox was here, includes all the members on both sides of the Detroit
River. He began with seven in the Detroit *Society*, reported 140 members on the entire *Circuit* at the end of his first year of work, and then
said thirty members in Detroit, Michigan, at the end of his second year
there. This 1817 record is the first indication of definite numbers of
Methodists *in Michigan* beyond the original seven. Methodist travelling
Elders were supposed to receive $100 per year then. How much Mr.
Hickox actually got is unknown.

In the early summer of 1816, Mr. Hickox departed to the Annual
Conference which was held that year at Paris, New York. He rode
about one thousand miles on horseback to and from the meeting.
Sometime in 1816 Mr. Hickox married a wife whom he found on the
Thames part of his circuit in Canada. With an eye to the future, he
had already selected and made legal entry for a piece of land on the
River Rouge about sixteen miles outside of Detroit. But he did not
get a chance to live there until 1820.[8]

From the Methodist viewpoint, the most important thing that happened, while Hickox was gone to the Genesee Annual Conference, was
the arrival in June, 1816, at Detroit of the Rev. John Monteith. He
was a Presbyterian minister, a native of Gettysburg, Pennsylvania, a
graduate of Princeton College, and sponsored by the American Board

[7] *Ibid.,* p. 57.
[8] E. H. Pilcher, *Hist. Prot. Mich.,* p. 76.

of Commissioners for Foreign Missions of the Presbyterian Church. He got along better with the Catholic Father Gabriel Richard than he did with the Methodist itinerants.[9]

Bishop McKendree, at the Genesee Annual Conference, reappointed Joseph Hickox to the Detroit Circuit for a second year, remarking as he did so, "no other man could be found who would endure so much hard service."[10]

The Rev. Henry Ryan was still the Presiding Elder of Upper Canada District. Early in the Conference year, he came to visit Detroit and preached to a large crowd in the Council House. If he held any Quarterly Conferences on that trip, no record of such meetings has survived. It seems likely that he would have felt it his duty to hold at least one.

Unfortunately, what had been a pleasant first acquaintance of ministers Hickox and Monteith was now terminated over whether the Presbyterian minister should have the exclusive use of the Council House on all Sundays. Mr. Hickox was evidently striving to maintain the same extensive plan of Circuit labor which he had carried on the previous year, or even to increase it.

The disagreement began, in the presence of Presiding Elder Ryan, when Hickox asked Monteith to announce his regular appointment for evening worship "a week from the next Sabbath." Monteith replied that he planned to preach then and asked the Methodist minister to change to any weekday evening. Presiding Elder Ryan even urged Hickox to comply in order "to make all things smooth." But the Circuit rider was stubborn and refused. All this talk was held in public.

The consequence was an unusually crowded Council House on the next journey Hickox made around his Circuit. Mr. Monteith had first possession of the pulpit by dint of getting there first. Neither would yield at all to the other so the congregation heard two sermons that evening. After preaching second, Mr. Hickox announced that he was there by specific permission of the Governor and would withdraw his appointment only when "the same authority that admitted me here . . . excludes me from the place." In a more subdued way, Monteith still urged a weekday time on the Methodist minister on the grounds that only the Circuit rider could preach "extempore . . . and get a congregation at any time at three hours' notice."[11]

The Rev. Joseph Mitchell, a venerable local preacher of Methodism, spent the winter of 1816-1817 in Detroit. Because crossing the River in winter was so difficult, Mitchell and Hickox divided the Circuit between them. The latter worked entirely in Canada and the former preached in Michigan. The Rev. Joseph Mitchell had the reputation

[9] Woodford & Hyma, *Gabriel Richard, Frontier Ambassador*, pp. 92-95. E. H. Pilcher, *Hist. Prot. Mich.*, p. 64.

[10] *Ibid.*, p. 76.

[11] E. H. Pilcher, *Hist. Prot. Mich.*, pp. 64-68.

of being a plain and very powerful preacher. Pilcher was told by Hickox of one occasion when "Father Mitchell" preached in the Council House:

> The Governor, and all the civil and military officers and men of note were present. The preacher's theme was the necessity of the new birth . . . with finger pointing with significant force, and eyes fixed upon the persons addressed, he cried out, "You, Governor! you, lawyers! you, judges! you, doctors! you must be converted and born again, or God will damn you as soon as the beggar on the dung hill." Deep silence prevailed and a lasting impression was made . . . . The next morning Governor Cass sent him a complimentary note, containing *five dollars,* saying it was the best sermon he ever heard.

Once early in the winter the Rev. Mr. Monteith called on Father Mitchell and tried to get him to agree not to preach any doctrines. But the old minister soon convinced him of the depth of his personal belief in Methodism and the equal depth of his hatred of Calvinism.

Pilcher considered it most unfortunate that Hickox did not stay in Detroit and build a strong Methodist Church on the foundation that the Rev. Joseph Mitchell had helped him lay. But that would have been contrary to all the rules and everyday practices of the Methodist Episcopal Church of 1817.

All that is known of the rest of Joseph Mitchell's life is that he left Detroit in the spring. The Rev. Joseph Hickox served on three different Circuits in New York and Canada in the three succeeding years. Then his wife's health grew so bad that the minister was compelled to locate. It was feared that she was in "a consumptive decline." That was a very common affliction then. The minister gave up being a travelling Elder at the Genesee Conference Session of 1820, moved his wife and family to that farm on the River Rouge, and lived there until 1836. But he continued to function as a local preacher, making himself useful at camp meetings, Quarterly Conferences, funerals, and in visitation of the sick. His later years were spent in Illinois and Wisconsin. Pilcher corresponded with Hickox about early Methodism in Michigan and was allowed the use of the latter's early diaries. Hickox died in 1867.

Presbyterian ministers were usually better educated than Methodist Circuit riders, preached a sterner theology, and mostly were called to guide an organized group of people already members of that denomination. They were not apt to go looking for people who needed the Christian faith. Their Calvinism was repulsive to the Arminianism of the Methodists. Methodism spread on the frontier faster than Presbyterianism did. Monteith and Hickox would have been apt to disagree over something else if they had not collided over use of the Council House.

Then too the Rev. John Monteith was continuously on duty in Detroit from 1816 to 1822. In that same period, eight Methodist ministers, not counting Presiding Elders or local preachers, came and went in Detroit presumably preaching every two to three weeks. Mr. Monteith was also backed by an organized, national, missionary society and, soon after his arrival in Michigan, was asked in a public meeting to stay for a year at a salary of $800.

At the close of his first year there, Monteith organized the First Evangelistic Society of Detroit. This was to be a cooperative enterprise of all Protestants in the city with Monteith as pastor. How many Methodists were active in the group is unknown.

In 1820, the name of the new group was changed to the First Protestant Society. It then built a modest church on a lot on the east side of Woodward near Larned Street. Mr. Pilcher said that the Methodists "contributed their full proportion toward the erection of the house." Whether they decided of their own accord to drop out of the common group of Protestants, in order to erect a city Methodist church, or were forced out by the Presbyterians, gaining a majority of the membership, is not clear today. Pilcher hinted that they were voted out of their place of worship. Whatever the cause, in 1825, the First Protestant Society became the First Presbyterian Church.[12]

Rapid Changes in Detroit and Michigan

The five years after the end of the war were a period of continuous change in Michigan. In government, Governor Cass began to establish the boundaries of the present county system of Michigan. Wayne County was reduced to almost its size today. Because of grumbling about the "arbitrary government" of the governor and judges, Detroit was re-incorporated with a locally elected board of trustees. It was known from then on as the City of Detroit. Another accomplishment of the Governor's was publication of a Michigan Code of Territorial Law. As the Superintendent of Indian Affairs, Governor Cass also gave almost continuous attention to the extinction of Indian rights to the land in Michigan. What probably caused the most talk was the Governor's importation of the first carriage seen in Detroit. Considering the general condition of the roads then, where it could be driven is a mystery.

The economic changes were equally rapid. A new market was built on Woodward Avenue. A Bank of Michigan was authorized but did not open for business until 1819. In July 1818, the first auction of public lands was held at the Council House. The same month a "Mechanics Society" was organized. And an institution called "the public whipping post" was installed near the market. It was in use until 1831.

President James Monroe paid a five day visit to the city in August 1817 but of more importance to the future of Detroit was another ar-

---

[12] E. H. Pilcher, *Hist. Prot. Mich.*, pp. 68, 92. W. F. Dunbar, *The Mich. Record In Higher Education*, p. 30.

rival in August, 1818. This was Walk-in-the-Water, the first steamboat on Lake Erie, which had come in forty-four hours and ten minutes actual running time from Buffalo. On this trip and for years afterward, the steamers made way stops at Dunkirk, Erie, Cleveland, and Sandusky. Before long a flood of settlers and visitors came to see for themselves the conditions in Michigan. A more modest but doubtless welcome change was the establishment of a regular ferry service between Detroit and Windsor, carried on at first by canoe and later by rowboat.

The cultural development was remarkable for so pioneer a town. The Catholepistemiad, forerunner of the University of Michigan, was established by Mr. Monteith and Father Richard. In 1818, a non-denominational Sunday School Association was organized to teach reading in addition to religion. In 1817, the Detroit Gazette was started as well as a subscription library and a musical society. In January 1818, a lyceum for "literary, scientific, patriotic, and benevolent" purposes was founded.

Citizens were starting to settle in the much maligned interior of Michigan. The first inhabitants of what would be Wyandotte and Birmingham appeared in 1817, of Dearborn and Pontiac in 1818, and of Royal Oak in 1819. A post road was set up in 1820 from Detroit to Pontiac and Mount Clemens. In the autumn of 1818, about a dozen citizens, led by Governor Cass, explored Oakland County on foot for twelve days and returned with glowing accounts of its beauty and fertile soil. In 1820, came the Governor's trip with Schoolcraft to the Upper Peninsula.[13]

Slow Growth and the Building of the First Church

The next session of the Genesee Annual Conference was held at Elizabethtown, Canada, in June, 1817. Bishop George there appointed the Rev. Gideon Laning to go on "a mission to Detroit." Only the part of Detroit Circuit in Michigan was included. It did not include Canada as an appointment to "Thames Circuit" in Canada was also made. Mr. Laning presumably would be expected to give more attention to each preaching appointment in Michigan Territory. This man was then twenty-five years old and very active "though married." He was born of Methodist parents in New Jersey, converted in western New York, became an exhorter and then a local preacher before he was twenty years of age. In 1812 he was admitted on trial to the Genesee Annual Conference and put in five years on five different Circuits before he came to Michigan.

His eloquent sermons and polite manners had considerable effect on his various congregations. Pilcher said, "Mr. Laning preached in William McCarty's private dwelling on the Rouge on Sabbath morning

---

[13] All chronological summaries based on the Detroit Public Library's *Detroit in Its World Setting, a 250-Year Chronology, 1701-1951.* pp. 59-64.

and in the Council House in Detroit at night." Laning himself remembered, "It was affecting in Detroit City, on a bright moonlight evening, to have the Council House yard and adjacent street filled with attentive hearers. O that my health had been such that I could have continued on the mission."

On weekdays, Mr. Laning tried to extend the work. He had a "large congregation" at Monroe, was well received at Maumee Rapids in Ohio, and found a new preaching place "at a settlement about fifty miles in a northwesterly direction from Detroit." He did not give its name. Perhaps it was so new that a name had not been chosen. He said of this last place, "I never saw any people more hungry for the preached word . . . they had never been visited by a preacher before. The whole community would turn out on a weekday and drink in every word. One man told me he had left his harvestfield and walked eight miles to hear me."

One of the commonest hazards in Michigan pioneer life caught up with Mr. Laning. He fell very ill with an attack of malaria. Finally Mr. Laning found it necessary to go south for his health if he was ever to work again. After five years on appointments in Pennsylvania, Maryland, and Virginia he returned to active duty in the Genesee Annual Conference in 1823. In all, he was a Methodist minister nearly forty years.

The Rev. Gideon Laning revisited Michigan in 1857. He was very impressed by the changes that time had wrought. Instead of less than thirty Methodists in one society, he found 25,000 in two Annual Conferences and numerous churches. He said in part:

> Where I had to follow an Indian trail to get to the settlement, and ford rivers, or have the horse swim by the side of a canoe while holding him by the bridle, or if no one was present to paddle it, to lie down and be drawn to the opposite shore, there were railroads now, and every facility for travel. Cities and villages had sprung up as if by magic, where there was only a dense forest forty years before."[14]

Due to his illness not much more than half of his appointed year in Detroit could have been served by Mr. Laning. Presiding Elder Ryan found a local preacher named Thomas Harmon in Canada, who assisted in Detroit both before and after Laning left and went South. Harmon was said to be "a rough, bold, fearless kind of man.'" It was wellknown that he had fought on the Canadian side in the War of 1812. Pilcher thought that the Michigan people did not like Harmon as well as they had Laning. But the Circuit report at the end of the year

---

[14] E. H. Pilcher, *Hist. Prot. Mich.,* pp. 69, 79-81, 86. G. B. Catlin, *The Story of Detroit,* p. 220. Another variation in the spelling of a surname is found here. Pilcher spelled the name Laning but the *General Minutes* spelled it Lanning.

was forty members, a gain of ten. Also the first Methodist church in Michigan was built in the spring of 1818 under Mr. Harmon's supervision.

The Rev. Thomas Harmon, Robert Abbott, and William McCarty had the most to do with planning, locating, and building the first Methodist Episcopal Church in Michigan. Pilcher said that "Abbott took a very active part in raising subscriptions for building the church and he acted as collector and treasurer." Harmon was the Circuit preacher and McCarty the Class leader for the group who resided on or near the River Rouge. Possibly Gideon Laning, before his illness, had some part in the planning and the collection of money. Certainly Joseph Hickox and William Stacy also helped. Each of them owned a farm in the vicinity of the location chosen.

Such building projects usually began with the circulation of subscription papers, which invited both members and non-members to pledge money, materials or labor. Money being very scarce, many people would promise to help in getting out the logs and dressing them. Nobody preserved the original subscription list. The common frontier practice was to hold a church-raising day on which all available male labor rolled up the sides and then laid the rafters of the roof. Women members were busy cooking a hearty meal for the workers.

Many years later Silas Farmer located in the *Detroit Weekly Gazette* of April 3, 1818, a notice sent in by Robert Abbott of the erection of the first *Protestant* Church in Michigan by a Society of Methodists organized at the River Rouge in 1810 and now having a church building in the same area. He said it was erected *on* the 31st of March which sounds like a log structure raised in one big day's work. He signed the notice "one of the trustees of the River Rouge Methodist Episcopal Church." Abbott was not correct on his "first Protestant" claim as the Moravians had a modest chapel in Michigan in 1782.[15]

This first church building was located between five and six miles out of Detroit on the north side of the road not far from the River Rouge. The exact site cannot be given. A committee of the Dearborn Historical Commission looked into this matter while assisting in preparation of a marker to be placed by the Detroit Annual Conference in 1954. They concluded that the marker would have to say "Near this spot" the first church stood.

The whole area is within the Ford River Rouge plant today and the marker was placed at Butler Road near Greenfield Road. The site was within what later became Dearborn Township. The uncertainty was because Thomas Sargent and wife Margarette gave one acre of land for the church building from within their own Private Claim #52,

---

[15] E. H. Pilcher, *Hist. Prot. Mich.*, pp. 87-88. Also items in a miscellaneous file on the Dearborn Church in Burton Historical Collection, Detroit Public Library. Among these items is a dedication program for the marker on site of earliest church.

Lot #2. Their plot of ground was 7.52 acres of land on the River Rouge. The deed for the church acre was dated November 21, 1817, but was not recorded until April 24, 1821. May Thomas Sargent and his wife have been Methodists?

Early Methodists were prone to locate their churches in rather remote areas or at least not in the midst of the business section. They felt that their members would be too ·disturbed by the distractions of worldly affairs. As they were often called "shouting Methodists" in those days, might there also have been some concern about not disturbing the neighbors?

While it once was thought that the Methodists were more suited to rural than urban areas, it was a deliberate choice at first. The home locations of the important members also had an influence on the selection of sites. For a few years just then, Robert Abbott, William McCarty, and William Stacy all were living on farms in the River Rouge area.

Robert Abbott's notice in the *Gazette* about the Society and church on the River Rouge does not mean that it had become an independent unit with a minister stationed there. Pilcher said, "They had come to

The first Methodist Church in Michigan, a log building about 24 x 30 feet, built March 31, 1818, on the River Rouge six miles west of Detroit.

Interior view of the first Methodist Church in Michigan, which was used ten years.

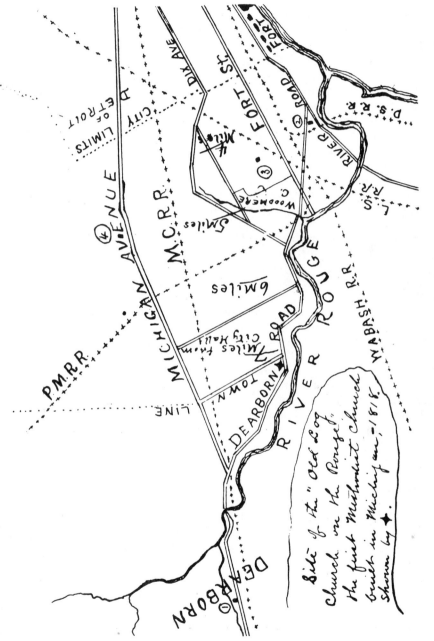

LOCATION OF THE FIRST METHODIST AND ALSO THE FIRST PROTESTANT CHURCH FOR WHITE
PEOPLE BUILT IN MICHIGAN

have more members there than in the city of Detroit and had built a church there. The society or church, as originally organized had a majority of its members in the city and they held their meetings in both places."

Just at the time the first church was built, some of the city Methodists were involved in that First Evangelistic Society. The historian of the Detroit First Presbyterian Church said that Mr. Monteith was careful to set up a church "partaking somewhat of the features and doctrines of a Presbyterian Church yet not sufficiently so to repel those of other religious persuasions of a Protestant kind from cordially uniting with them." Among the trustees of the First Evangelistic Society, chosen in 1818 but not known publicly until 1821, were James Abbott, Thomas Palmer, and B. F. H. Witherell. These men may have been Methodists earlier and certainly were later. As Methodist services did not occur in Detroit every Sunday for some years yet, regular church attendants might hear the Methodist Circuit rider in the Council House one Sunday and the Presbyterian minister in his modest church the next.[16]

Although that first Methodist church built in Michigan, located on the River Rouge, was built, used, abandoned, and burned before the day of photographs, John Baughman, the last minister to preach there, described it to Mr. Pilcher in detail. Also the latter had seen it often after it was no longer used for church services.

The outside of the log church was about 24 by 30 feet. The logs composing it had been hewn which meant that by use of a chalked line and the broad axe the sides had been roughly squared and smoothed. The ends of the logs were notched together and squared with some use of clay or moss in the cracks between the logs. Four windows had been cut in the log frame, one in each end and one on each side of the door in the front of the building. Baughman thought the length of the building and the entrance door fronted south toward the road and the river but Pilcher remembered it as having the narrower width and only a window toward the road.

The interiors of all Methodist churches were extremely plain then. An altar, a crucifix, stained glass, decorated walls, comfortable pews, or kneeling cushions were anathema to most Methodists. They suggested Episcopalianism or Catholicism too clearly. It was thought to be too worldly to use any musical instrument whatsoever, from the violin to the organ, to accompany the hymn singing. The words rather than the music were the important part of this activity. Even a steeple with a single bell was often considered too worldly and too expensive.

The interior walls in that first church on River Rouge were the plain hewn logs. The ceiling, about twelve feet from the floor, had round, peeled logs for joists with rough boards laid loosely over them. The

---

[16] *Mich. Pioneer Coll.*, I, 417-429. E. H. Pilcher, *Hist. Prot. Mich.*, p. 88..

floor was of plain, rough boards nailed down to sleepers. It was not the custom to raise the floor very far from the ground or to dig a cellar. Churches raised on blocks, as some of them were, offered too tempting a resting place to chickens and pigs, who were apt to disturb the services by their crowing or grunting.

The pulpit was directly opposite the door quite close to the one wall with no window and approached by a few steps on one side. No effort at pulpit adornment or symbol was made. Only the plainest of flat boards were used. Perhaps there was a low railing just in front of the pulpit at which members might kneel during the communion service. The whole thing was large, clumsy, and ugly. Years later, the editor of the *Northwestern Christian Advocate* was wont to refer to such an old-fashioned pulpit as "the odious preach-pen."

The congregation sat on rows of backless benches with one wide central aisle. These benches were made of thick planks with auger holes bored therein and round sticks inserted for legs. Such seating must have been acutely uncomfortable for a long service. Men and women usually sat separately on opposite sides of that center aisle.

The members of the congregation were plainly dressed in homespun, deerskin, or calico garments. In summer the men were mostly barefooted and the women put on shoes just before getting to the door. Probably they also wore sunbonnets. In the winter, most of the congregation must have lingered by the large stove which stood in the center aisle with a long pipe smoke stack running back out of the roof.

Such inside arrangements were common in most Michigan churches through the days of the Civil War. As sawmills spread over the country, church people either sheathed their log buildings in sawed boards or built a simple frame church. A "plain and decent" church was the goal for many years everywhere.[17]

That log building on the River Rouge was used as a Methodist church for ten years. If it may be assumed that all travelling Elders, appointed to Detroit Circuit between 1818 and 1828, officiated in the log church as part of their work then fifteen ministers and four Presiding Elders preached there. The Rev. Joseph Hickox must be added for he continued in the local ministry after he had settled on his farm near the church.

The Methodist services that the Rev. Nathan Bangs described in 1804 had changed very little by 1818. The hymn-singing, with which the service opened, was vigorous, sincere, and probably horribly unmelodious. Methodist theology was well reiterated in these hymns. Everyone knelt for prayer and the petitions were fervent, personal, and lengthy.

[17] Description of first church in Michigan given by Pilcher, *Hist. Prot. Mich.*, pp. 83-85. See also Paul N. Garber, *The Methodist Meeting House*, chapters I and II on the church and its sanctuary and the church on the frontier.

Pioneer Methodist sermons were ardent, repetitious, and always extempore. A fully written sermon or even the use of notes was considered a sign of weakness in a minister. He expected emotional interruptions even what would be called today hysterical responses from his audience. Common ejaculations were "Amen," "Praise the Lord," "Hallelujah,'" or "The Lord Help." The preacher paid no attention to crying babies, crowing roosters, grunting pigs, or noisy rowdies.

The Rev. W. B. Williams, a Congregational minister, described Methodist preaching in Charlotte, Michigan, in the 1840's. What he said was just as true of the early pulpit performance as of later. He wrote in part:

> Whenever we could capture a minister of any denomination we gladly set him to preaching. Wesleyan sermons and prayers sounded strangely enough to those familiar only with the staid and proper worship of the Unitarian Churches of New England. Men would bawl at the top of their voices until they were hoarse, as if the Lord were deaf or they lived so far away from Him that they could only with difficulty make Him hear. Preachers would speak until they frothed at the mouth and were almost exhausted.[18]

Methodist pioneer preachers were widely known for their penetrating voices but the prize must go to the one who, on his way home from Detroit late at night, encountered a large bear right in the middle of the road. He leaned over his horse and "gave a scream such as only a full fledged Methodist preacher could furnish voice to give and the bear ambled away."[19]

Although no records exist to confirm these events, quite a number of Quarterly Conferences must have occurred in the log church on the River Rouge. Four Presiding Elders, James B. Finley, John Strange, William Simmons, and Zarah Coston, made at least one visit apiece to the Detroit Circuit during the time that the first church was in use. If they followed the customary procedures then, they preached several times, held business sessions, and closely examined the moral and financial health of all members, Class leaders, and local preachers.

Sunday services included love feast, baptism, communion, and reception of new members. A love feast might partake of bread and water and go on to prayer and intimate relation of diverse religious experiences. Only members of the Society attended this. Baptism was necessary to join the church and might take the form of sprinkling or immersion. The latter was quite common then hence such ceremonies on the banks of the River Rouge must have taken place now and then. Communion was the high point of the day and took place only occasion-

---

[18] *Mich. Pioneer Coll.,* XXII, 526-531.

[19] From reminiscences of the Rev. Riley C. Crawford about his father-in-law. *Mich. Pioneer Coll,* XVII, 232.

ally. Many of the regular Circuit preachers were not fully ordained yet. Hence only the Presiding Elder could administer the bread and wine. Joining the Methodist Episcopal Church always meant a preliminary probation of six months before full membership.

By the time the Rev. E. H. Pilcher came into the area to preach, the first log church had been abandoned for religious services but was still standing. Pilcher said of it:

> We used to pass it often and have gone into it to look at it with feelings of reverence, as its having been a place where much good had been done; for one who used to worship in it once said to us, "There was much of divine power in their meetings, and prayer and praise there ascended to Heaven. Peace and joy filled their hearts, while they walked in fellowship and love."[20]

Their last two years of connection with the Genesee Annual Conference were not particularly helpful to Michigan Methodists. The Rev. Gideon Laning reported forty members here in 1818. The general statistics show thirty members reported in 1819 and sixty-two in 1820.

The Rev. Alpheus Davis succeeded Mr. Laning on the Detroit Circuit in 1818. He was in poor health when he came to Michigan and quite early in the year was transferred to the Ancaster Circuit, near Hamilton, in Upper Canada. Mr. Davis was a popular and useful preacher so he was able to increase the total membership on that Canadian Circuit by 303 in one year. His delicate look was mentioned by various ministers then. His looks did not belie his health for Mr. Davis died of pulmonary consumption in October, 1820.

Apparently an exchange of pulpits took place between Ancaster and Detroit for the Rev. Samuel Belton of the Canadian Circuit finished out the year in Michigan. This double shift was arranged by the Rev. Henry Ryan, who was still the Presiding Elder of Upper Canada District. Thus the decline from 40 to 30 members on the Detroit Circuit in 1819 was largely the fault of Mr. Belton. He was of Irish birth and in appearance was "above the middle size, well developed, prepossessing, and of a dignified carriage." It was also said that Belton was plump and "filled his respectable clerical clothes." He was a "commanding and eloquent" preacher when "at liberty." If the statistics are to be trusted, he was not too effective with the pioneer people of Detroit.[21]

---

[20] Pilcher, *Hist. Prot. Mich.*, p. 84. For the love feast, and other early ceremonies of Methodism see W. C. Barclay, *Early American Methodism*, I, XXXV.

[21] Very little official evidence can be given for this Davis-Belton exchange. Pilcher in his *Hist. Prot. Mich.* does not mention Belton and assumes Davis remained all year. It must have been a double transfer arranged by Presiding Elder Ryan. John Carroll in his *Case & His Cotemp.*, II, 142, 151-152 gives more details on Davis and Belton than any other early writer. Carroll also says that Belton was sent from Detroit to York, later Toronto. In 1822, Belton may also have supplied the pulpit of that First Protestant Society in Detroit just after Monteith left there.

In July 1819, the Genesee Annual Conference appointed the Rev. Truman Dixon to the Detroit Circuit. This was the last time that Conference sent a minister to Michigan as this Territory was transferred to the Ohio Annual Conference in 1820. Pilcher knew very little about Mr. Dixon because he located or left the ministry in 1825. But Pilcher concluded because Mr. Dixon more than doubled the number of members in the local Society here that "he was a man of good abilities as a preacher and attended faithfully to his work here."

John Carroll must have known Truman Dixon for he said that he was of Irish stock but grew up in the United States. He had scarcely any early educational advantages but his naturally vigorous mind and eloquent utterances made him a popular preacher. He was also evidently a man of great vigor for he made every effort to extend the circuit and enlarge the membership. He appears to have been the one who organized the Society at Mount Clemens in January 1820, and he very likely preached at Pontiac, Birmingham, and along the St. Clair River. Sometime in the winter he also preached the first sermon in St. Clair County to the three families then living on Harsen's Island. This is the largest island in Lake St. Clair and is nearer Canada than the United States. Presumably Mr. Dixon reached there by crossing the ice on foot.

Judging from the evidence of their daily lives and activities, nearly all those early Methodist preachers in Michigan would have agreed with the Rev. Joseph Hickox when, at the end of his first year in Michigan, he wrote:

> When the chaotic condition of the country and the multitudes who are perishing for the lack of knowledge are considered, the privilege of preaching the world-wide gospel and a free salvation is so great that the labor and dangers of doing so sink into insignificance, and the remembrance of that work is full of sweetness to me.[22]

[22] Quoted by Pilcher in a paper on the "Life and Times of Rev. Joseph Hickox" which he read before the Detroit Pioneer Society in 1873. *Mich. Pioneer Coll.*, I, 472-481. For Pilcher's comment on Dixon in his *Hist. Prot. Mich.*, p. 83. J. Carroll, *Case & His Cotemp.*, II, 219. Rev. Ronald Brunger brought more information on Dixon to my attention.

PART II

THE UNITED STATES, MICHIGAN AND METHODISM

1820 – 1840

The United States

The United States of 1820 was beginning to resemble the American nation of today. Congress had changed the flag law in 1818 to the basic plan still in use. The original States were symbolized by thirteen red and white stripes. These would remain the same but the stars were to increase in accord with the number of States. To the sixteen States of 1800 had been added Ohio, Louisiana, Indiana, Mississippi, Illinois, Alabama, and Maine by 1820. The United States of 892,135 square miles in 1800 now had an area of 1,792,223 square miles due to the Louisiana Purchase and the acquisition of Florida. Our total population stood at 9,638,453, lacking just under a million of having doubled since 1800. Still employed in agriculture were 83% of the working population.

The population growth in the two new States, southern neighbors of Michigan, was interesting. Ohio's 45,365 people in 1800 had become 581,434 in 1820. Indiana's 5,641 had risen to 147,178. But in contrast, Michigan Territory had 3,106 in 1800 and had grown only to 8,896 in 1820. Of the latter number, 1,442 had settled in Detroit. Michigan's geographical location and lack of transportation still handicapped her growth.

The American people were far more nationalistic than in 1800. The War of 1812 had given us a new national song, the Star Spangled Banner, and a new national hero, Andrew Jackson. American economic independence was being asserted too. Textile mills were well established

in New England. The tariff law of 1816, intended to be genuinely protective, received the votes of Congressmen from all sections of the
country. A Second National Bank was also chartered in 1816.

Only a few far-seeing men realized that negro slavery and its ac-
companying sectionalism were already dividing the United States. The
Missouri Compromise of 1820 was passed only after a bitter struggle in
Congress. By the middle of the 1830's, the question of slavery was di-
viding even the ministers and members of the Michigan Methodist
Episcopal Church.

Michigan

Lewis Cass was still Governor and eager to do all he could for the
people of Michigan Territory. He hoped to draw more American settlers here by clearing all the Indian claims from the land and achieving
a more democratic, territorial government. Michigan was still run by a
governor, a secretary, and three judges. In 1818, Congress gave the
Territory an elected delegate who could speak but not vote in the lower
house of Congress. That enormous Wayne County of 1800 had been cut
in size by the creation of three new counties. These were Monroe,
Macomb, and Oakland. Wherever enough settlers appeared, townships
were also platted often only one to a county. These were then later
reduced to the usual sixmile square size.

It was a slow process to make treaties of purchase with the Indians, get the surveyors out to make maps of tiers of townships for sale,
and finally open a land office nearby. In 1807, Governor Hull had begun with the purchase of a large section of southeastern Michigan.
Governor Cass continued with a small portion of land on the southern
boundary in 1818 and a much larger area by the treaty of Saginaw in
1819. Almost half of the Lower Peninsula was cleared of Indian claims
by 1820.

A Land Office was opened in Detroit in 1818 but it could sell only
fully surveyed areas with titles clear of Indian rights. The Land Law
required a first effort to sell 320 acre lots at public auction to the
highest bidder. Then the same size plots might be sold at $2 an acre
with a down payment of $160. This was too high a price and too large
an acreage for most settlers. Therefore, in 1820, Congress amended the
Land Law to allow the purchase of eighty acres for $1.25 per acre. A
man could now get a family-size farm for $100.[1]

The decreases in the size and price of the public lands on sale in
Detroit had an immediate effect. "The number of land sales at Detroit
in May, 1823, were seven times greater than in the same month of previous years." Congress soon authorized a second Land Office at Mon-

---

[1] F. C. Bald, *Mich. in Four Centuries*, pp. 146, 154.

roe. The two offices together sold more than four times as much land in 1824 as one office had in 1822.[2]

Another helpful thing was the continued negotiations with the Indians by Governor Cass. Five million acres of land were turned over to the United States by the treaty of Chicago in 1821. The Indians had given up all land south of the Grand River and also granted a right of way for roads from Detroit and Fort Wayne to Chicago. When the surveyors for these roads found fertile land in southwestern Michigan, settlers soon appeared there.

The steamboat service from Buffalo had been a great benefit but the transportation barrier was really broken by the completion of the Erie Canal in 1825. In May of that year, the *Detroit Gazette* estimated that the steamboat brought over three hundred passengers weekly to Detroit and still more came by sailing vessels. Winter no longer stopped the newcomers. They often found travel easier then than in the spring when bottomless mud prevailed everywhere.

American settlers came to Michigan in ever-increasing numbers during the 1820's and 1830's. Detroit was frequently unable to provide overnight lodging in public hotels for this flood of people. Many Detroit residents took in immigrants for a few days. The custom was to provide the necessary implements of pioneer farming in Detroit if at all possible. Often the father of the family made trips of investigation to several areas before settling on the particular portion he would buy.

Western and southern interior settlement of Michigan came more rapidly than that to the east and north. The plan for a road to Chicago, the new Land Office in Monroe, the establishment of Washtenaw County plus the laying out of the villages of Ypsilanti and Ann Arbor therein contributed to drawing the settlers west and south. Exploration of the River Raisin revealed rich lands on its upper banks and brought the settlement of Tecumseh in Lenawee County. Although St. Clair and Mount Clemens were plotted in 1818 and made county seats, they did not at first attract settlers in large numbers. The lands around Mount Clemens had been bought by speculators. The prices they set were too high for the average settler when such quantities of cheap, public land were readily available. St. Clair County was a little to one side of the main stream of settlement. It was also heavily forested and said to be swampy and disease-ridden.

The rapid population increase brought the second stage of territorial government to Michigan. By an act of Congress in 1823, a Legislative Council of nine members was created. Father Gabriel Richard was elected the Territorial Delegate in the U.S. Congress. This is said to be the only time that a Catholic priest represented a Territory in the

[2] Comments based on F. R. Dain, *Every House a Frontier, Detroit's Economic Progress, 1815-1825*, chapter III on "The Settlement of the Hinterland," *passim*.

Congress. The cornerstone of a Territorial Capitol was laid in Detroit that same year but the building itself was not completed for many years. In 1824, a Detroit City Charter was adopted. Henceforth, the people were to be governed by a mayor, Common Council, and a City Clerk.

Michigan was at last being spoken of more favorably in the eastern press. The *New York Spectator* of March 4, 1823, declared that Michigan added to its natural advantages of soil, climate, and interior streams those of cheap transportation and abundant low-priced public land. Other papers were impressed with the high quality of the movers to Michigan. In that same spring of 1823, the *Buffalo Journal* said:

> For a few days past our wharves and taverns have been literally thronged with people emigrating to this new country (Michigan), nearly all of whom appear to belong to the most valuable class of settlers — practical farmers, of moderate capital and good habits.[3]

The Methodist Episcopal Church

The American Methodist Episcopal Church in 1800 had 64,894 members organized in seven Annual Conferences. By 1820, twelve Annual Conferences had 273,858 members. The rapid growth in the membership came in two periods separated by the War of 1812. Methodism actually decreased in 1814 over three thousand members and its increase in 1815 was only thirty-six. Beginning in 1817, the Methodist Episcopal Church grew very rapidly for about twenty years. The Circuit rider under district Presiding Elders and the Bishops at large carried on the work through the Class meeting, Society, Quarterly Conference, and Annual Conference. The power of the Bishops increased because a movement to make the Presiding Elders elective rather than appointive failed. The first effort at lay representation in all the Annual Conferences also was rejected.

The General Conference remained, as established in 1808, a quadrennial assembly of elected travelling Elders plus all the Bishops. The General Conference of 1820 took several actions that had some significance for Michigan Methodism. It adopted a standard hymn book, prepared by the Book Concern, provided a western book agent in Cincinnati, and approved a general missionary society to operate throughout the Methodist Episcopal Church and to send its missionaries anywhere in the world. Auxiliaries were to be formed in every Annual Conference, Church, or Society that was interested. The local organizations were to raise money both for their own work and that of the national missionary society.[4]

---

[3] F. R. Dain, *Every House a Frontier*, pp. 83-84.
[4] W. W. Sweet, *Meth. Am. Hist.*, pp. 169, 177-178, 191-193. W. C. Barclay, *Early American Methodism*, I, 205-210.

The National Methodist Missionary Society had already been established and in action for a year. Interest was keenest in work among the Indians and the negro slaves. United States government money was then available for work among the Indians *if* the missionaries would try to teach them agriculture and try to bring them to a settled life. Attempts of this nature would be made repeatedly in Michigan.

All the Michigan appointments were shifted by that 1820 General Conference from the Genesee to the Ohio Annual Conference. In the long run, this benefitted the local Methodists. The connection with an entirely American Annual Conference rather than with one having Canadian and English members, eliminated a certain amount of friction.

Interdenominational agencies now began to be organized to work together for great religious and social reforms. The American Bible Society, the American Education Society, and the American Colonization Society were all started in 1816.

The last named society was formed for the purpose of freeing the slaves by returning them to Africa. Out of this effort came the new country of Liberia with which American Methodist Episcopal missionaries were particularly concerned. The first Methodist foreign missionaries were sent there but with sadly small results due in part to the deadly climate for the white man.

Other religious reform societies of similar nature were the American Sunday School Union formed in 1824, the American Tract Society in 1825 and the American Home Missionary Society in 1826. Methodists generally were not very cooperative with these new groups in the earlier part of the 19th century. They preferred to work through their own denominational organizations and their own Bishops and ministers.[5]

[5] W. S. Hudson, *American Protestantism*, pp. 82-89.

The history and achievements of Michigan Methodism in its years under the direction of the Ohio Annual Conference, and in the southwestern part under the Indiana Annual Conference, must now be examined. Perhaps the decades between 1820 and 1840 are the most important years in this State's development of Methodism for it was then that a separate Michigan Annual Conference, conterminous with the State boundaries, was born.

CHAPTER III

DETROIT METHODISTS ATTEMPT TO BUILD A CHURCH

1820 – 1825

In such a time of upheaval and change for Michigan as the third and fourth decades of the nineteenth century, the organized branches of religion were inevitably affected too. Methodist church work in Michigan, for the years from 1820 to 1825, lacked general continuity and unbroken individual work. The scanty evidence gives an impression of disjointed indeed almost haphazard efforts with little result. In those five years, twelve Methodist ministers labored in Michigan if the Presiding Elders and the local or retired preachers are included. Michigan was successively a member of the Lebanon, Miami, and Sandusky Districts under the Ohio Annual Conference. Worse still, in 1820, the Presiding Elder was James B. Finley, in 1821, it was John Strange, then Finley again, next Strange reheld the position and in 1824, Finley did so for the third time.

The chief reason for the lack of continuity lay in the higher administrative pressure for ministerial attendance at every Annual Conference. A famous Indian missionary, the Rev. John H. Pitezel, pointed out that for many years Conference attendance necessarily mear: two or three months of absence from a minister's charge. He thought that the Catholics always took advantage of such long absences, especially in the Indian mission field in the Upper Peninsula.

Between 1820 and 1825, the Ohio Annual Conference met successively at Chillicothe, Lebanon, Marietta, Urbana, and Zanesville. None of these places meant less than two hundred miles of horseback travel for a Michigan appointed Elder and some of them were more than three hundred miles away.

The hardships of such travel are almost beyond belief today. A journey to the settled parts of Ohio always involved crossing the "Black Swamp." The water there was unsafe to drink, the mosquitoes, flies, and hornets incessantly annoying, and the safe stopping places were few and far between. In one area, no houses at all could be found for at least forty miles.

Some ministers regarded appointments to Michigan as a form of punishment. To some extent it may have been. Appointments commonly covered an entire county or more. Most of the early Circuits in Michigan were set up on a four weeks plan. That meant incessant travel and preaching at least once a day on all weekdays except Mondays and on Sundays at least two or three times.[1] The Methodist mode of operation then and the primitive frontier conditions prevented continuity of effort by the ministers. Therefore, even thus early, the efforts of the laymen and women were important in the Methodist Episcopal Church.

A feeling of need for a local church of their own was forming among the Detroit *city* Methodists. On May 10, 1820, a meeting was held to consider where they could get some land and how they might raise enough money to build a church. Samuel Davenport presided and B. F. H. Witherell served as secretary. The latter's mother, Amy Witherell, and his sister, Mary A. W. Palmer, were lifelong active Methodists but he himself, although a member, did not work as much in the Methodist Episcopal Church in his later years. Like his father, James Witherell, he was a judge in Detroit. That meeting decided to petition the governor and judges for a lot for the church location. They also decided to circulate subscription papers for pledges of money and materials with which to build. The committee chosen to handle both these duties was composed of Robert Abbott, Samuel Davenport, and William W. Pettit.[2]

Nothing whatsoever was done by this committee for nearly two years. Pilcher said that this delay was due to the fact that "they had not as yet been entirely shut out from other places." Remembering

[1] R. A. Brunger, "Preachers go to Annual Conference" in *Mich. Ch. Ad.*, for May 24, 1962, LXXXIX, #21, 4-5, 18-19. J. H. Pitezel, *Lights and Shades of Missionary Life*, pp. 78-79. Also Pitezel's "Historical Recollections" being a paper read before the Historical Society of the Michigan Annual Conference in 1872. E. H. Pilcher, *Hist. Prot. Mich., passim.*

[2] From a clipping in the Palmer Scrapbooks, Burton Collection, VI, 105. E. H. Pilcher, *Hist. Prot. Mich.*, pp. 95, 97.

that he came to Detroit in 1830 and knew all those early Methodists, Pilcher's comments are helpful. He wrote:

> Some time during the year 1821 the Society became more fully in-
> stalled in the City of Detroit . . . . Previous to this time, although the
> preaching was constant in the city — that is, once in three or four weeks
> — the Society met sometimes in Detroit, and sometimes on the River
> Rouge in the log meeting-house. As yet, no vigorous effort had been
> made to build a Methodist church in the city. Our people had been
> content to occupy, occasionally, the house which had been built by
> Protestants in common, under the name of "The First Protestant Church
> or Society."[3]

The efforts of an experienced travelling Elder were clearly needed in Detroit. The Rev. John P. Kent was sent there in August 1820, under Presiding Elder James B. Finley of Lebanon District, Ohio Annual Conference. Admitted on trial in 1815, Mr. Kent became an Elder in 1819. He was young, unmarried, a hard worker, and "an able preacher."

All that year Mr. Kent devoted his best efforts to the Detroit Circuit, trying to set up a plan of the work and preaching "where he could find an open door." He undoubtedly preached at the Council House in the city and possibly at the First Protestant Meeting House, certainly at the log church on the River Rouge and, Pilcher said, "extended his Circuit as far south as the Maumee Rapids."

The result was that Mr. Kent's health was so impaired that he had to retire from the work for a time, becoming a superannuate at the Ohio Annual Conference in September 1821. He reported twenty members for Detroit Circuit whereas Mr. Dixon had reported sixty-six the year before. Whether Dixon included Canadian members is unknown. But from this time on, all local membership reports here included only those members residing in Michigan.[4]

Methodists in Michigan had an important visitor in the spring of 1821. The Rev. James B. Finley, Presiding Elder of Lebanon District, made a tour of the Detroit Circuit. Considering the extent of his District and the hardships of travel then, the wonder is that he got here at all. Lebanon District included territory from the Ohio River through the southeastern Michigan settlements. Admitted to the Western Conference in 1809, Finley became a Presiding Elder in 1819. Bold and fearless, free and easy in manner, educated in the Bible and the classics by his father, a frontier preacher in Kentucky, Finley was, as Pilcher said, prepared for any emergency.[5]

---

[3] *Ibid.*, pp. 91-92.

[4] W. W. Sweet, *Circuit Rider Days along the Ohio,* Journals of the Ohio Annual Conferences, 1812-1826, pp. 196, 202.

[5] Pilcher, *Hist. Prot. Mich.*, pp. 180-185. J. B. Finley, *Autobiography or Pioneer Life in the West, passim.*

Just getting to Detroit would have stopped a less resolute man than Finley. He was unable to travel by the Indian trail because the "summer freshet" was so high. Then he hired two Indians to take him by canoe to the river mouth where he hoped to catch a steamer to Detroit. Night fell and forced them to stop. Finley never forgot the ensuing night. In his *Autobiography*, he said in part:

> We concluded to tarry . . . with an old Frenchman . . . who occupied a miserable shanty on the bank and lived principally on muskrats. The place was dreadfully infested with fleas and mosquitoes. My comrades joined in partaking of our host's hospitalities but I was not sufficiently hunger-bitten to eat muskrats. To protect myself from the foes which swarmed around me I sat all night on a box.

The wind was so high next day that the waves filled their canoe with water and upset it. Finley got thoroughly soaked and had to walk four miles to Portland carrying his saddle bags. He was more disturbed by the fact that his books did not dry out very well than by his physical exhaustion. The next morning he got on board the steamer and finally arrived at Detroit next day.

He stayed with Jerry Dean in Detroit. He was a layman who befriended a long succession of Methodist Episcopal ministers newly come to Michigan. Dean was a saddler by trade and had moved to Detroit in 1820 just after he married. He had first joined the Methodist Episcopal Church in Ohio and had known Mr. Finley there.

Instead of having the help of the Circuit preacher, the Rev. John Kent, Finley found only a letter from him explaining that he was ill at Maumee Rapids and would be unable to help in church visitation. But Mr. Kent had not just been idle for he enclosed in his letter a plan of full appointments for Mr. Finley for the ensuing week. Another staunch layman, Robert Abbott, provided a horse for Presiding Elder Finley's use on the Detroit Circuit.

The Rev. James Finley preached in Detroit on successive Sundays at the Council House in the presence of the Governor and his wife. In between those Sunday appointments, Finley put in four hard days on the road. The first day he preached twice and swam the River Rouge three times. Finley said, "I then went to two or three places out north and preached as far as Pontiac." Could he have meant Royal Oak, Mount Clemens, or Birmingham?

The Presiding Elder himself was very pleased with the response to his efforts in Michigan Territory. He wrote that his "preaching was of great interest and profit to myself and many others. My soul was much united to the dear people; for they seemed to be as sheep without a shepherd."

If Michigan had been able to retain the services of the Rev. James B. Finley, Methodism might have been established both widely and strongly even at this early time. Certainly the Detroit Methodists tried to get him appointed there. Mr. Finley himself wrote:

> A petition was sent . . . to the bishops for me to be stationed at Detroit. This petition was signed by Governor Cass . . . and the principal citizens . . . they pledged themselves to pay all expenses, and support me besides building a church. It was confidently believed by them that their prayer would be heard; but Bishop McKendree thought the Indian mission of more consequence than Detroit . . . . Bishop Roberts was in favor of sending me to Detroit and the matter continued in suspense until late in the Conference. My own judgment and feelings led me to Detroit, because I believed that at that time all the English inhabitants of the place would have joined the Church. But the senior bishop prevailed and I was sent among the Indians.[6]

En route to Ohio, Finley rented an Indian pony and thus avoided some of the hardships he had encountered coming to Michigan. He corresponded with Governor Cass and came to Michigan again but strictly on the subject of extension of the Indian missions.

At that time, belief was strong that all the Indians might be Christianized and thereby somewhat civilized. The founding of the Methodist Missionary Society in 1819 coincided with the passage by Congress of a law to establish schools among the different tribes. Reading the Episcopal Address to the General Conference of 1820, Bishop McKendree had said "the voice of God . . . was calling the Church to meet the need for the spread of the Gospel among the Indians."[7] No one appears to have had any idea of how swiftly the white man would settle the country and drive most of the Indians beyond the Mississippi River.

---

[6] J. B. Finley, *Autobiography*, pp. 356-357.
[7] W. C. Barclay, *Early American Methodism, 1769-1844*, II, 112.

James B. Finley (1781-1856) was a prominent Methodist leader in Ohio, who made his mark on Michigan. He was the first Presiding Elder from Ohio to visit Michigan in the spring of 1821. He served the Wyandot Indian Mission at Upper Sandusky, 1821-27, and organized the first Indian class in Michigan on the Huron in December 1823.

Elias Pattee (1784-1860), was a colorful, zealous, early pioneer preacher in Ontario and Michigan, who served the Detroit Circuit in 1823-25, the St. Clair Circuit in 1828-29, the Huron Mission 1835-36. He had a large family of children, and often had to locate to provide for his family.

The next appointment to Detroit, the Rev. Platt B. Morey, was inadequate and even tragic. He was a young, local preacher of uncertain health, just admitted on trial, and elected a Deacon in September 1821. He started out around the Detroit Circuit in October but never completed even one single visit to each of the preaching appointments. Taken very sick, he was cared for at the home of Mrs. Sally Noble. She was one of the first members of the Mount Clemens Church. Mr. Morey died in December 1821. The Rev. Joseph Hickox preached Morey's funeral sermon. He was the first Methodist minister to be buried in Michigan soil.[8]

The new Presiding Elder of Lebanon District, the Rev. John Strange, persuaded the Rev. John Kent to fill the rest of the year on the vacant Detroit Circuit. That period was from January to September, 1822. At the Ohio Annual Conference, Mr. Kent reported 130 members for Detroit Circuit when he had been able only to find twenty the previous year.

Several causes contributed to this substantial increase. New settlers were coming to Michigan in ever-increasing numbers. Presiding Elder Strange made one visit to Detroit that year where he preached "with great power." Perhaps Mr. Kent recovered his health or was a very effective preacher. Probably the most important cause of increased membership was the holding of the first Methodist camp meeting in Michigan in June 1822.[9]

Mr. Kent and Presiding Elder William Case organized and then preached at that first Methodist camp meeting in Michigan. It was held on the farm of William Stacy, one of the seven in that first society. As Joseph Hickox had located on a farm near that same river, the Rouge, probably he also assisted. William McCarty was still the class leader in that area and had just been licensed as an exhorter by Kent in April 1822. He too must have shared in the work of that occasion as he had a lifelong reputation for effectiveness at such revivals.

The first Michigan camp meeting came rather late in the history of that institution. Hundreds of such meetings had already been established in Ohio, Indiana, and Illinois. The origin of the camp meeting of the frontier type lies in Kentucky. That had been a combined effort by Presbyterians, Baptists, and Methodists. But by 1822, other Protestant denominations had mostly dropped out and it was regarded as a peculiarly Methodist device.

The camp meeting was never an *official* institution of Methodism. This means it was not described minutely in the Discipline with the time and form prescribed. It was only a custom that the Presiding

[8] Pilcher, *Hist. Prot. Mich.*, pp. 90-91. W. W. Sweet, *Circuit Rider Days along the Ohio*, p. 214.

[9] Pilcher thought that eleven of the reported 130 members were at Monroe where Kent had revived a society. *Hist. Prot. Mich.*, p. 210.

Elders and Circuit riders found helpful. No exact time was ever established at which all of them must be held. The time tendency was toward late summer or early fall. Thus a circuit camp meeting might take the place of the fourth quarterly conference just before the ministers all journeyed to the annual conferences. It has been claimed that the circuit rider and the camp meeting together tamed the wild west.[10]

Pilcher said of that first Michigan camp meeting, "It was a very good and profitable time. The whole country turned out to see the novel spectacle of a meeting in the woods. . . . The Church was much benefitted by it." A French Catholic woman was among the converts in spite of the loud objections of a relative who was present. Presumably all the ministers there preached loud and long and, knowing Mr. Case's reputation for a fine singing voice, we may guess that he led the singing of hymns and what were called "spiritual songs."

Scarcely any details of the early Michigan camp meetings have survived. But a "Detroit settler" described one to Alexis de Tocqueville in 1831. Upon being asked if religion had ever reached that "half-peopled country," the Detroit man replied:

> Almost every summer . . . . some Methodist preachers come to make a tour of the new settlements. The noise of their arrival spreads with unbelievable rapidity from cabin to cabin it's the great news of the day. At the date set, the immigrant, his wife, and children set out by scarcely cleared forest trails toward the indicated meeting place. They come from fifty miles around. It's not in a church that the faithful gather but in the open air under the forest foliage. A pulpit of badly squared logs, great trees felled for seats, such are the ornaments of this rustic temple. The pioneers and their families camp in the surrounding woods . . . . During three days and three nights, the crowd gives itself over to almost uninterrupted religious exercises. You must see with what ardor these men surrender themselves to prayer, with what attention they listen to the solemn voice of the preacher. It's in the wilderness that people show themselves almost starved for religion.[11]

Being converted at a camp meeting was not the same as becoming a full member in good standing of the Methodist Episcopal Church. That required six months of probation during which one demonstrated by his conduct and attendance at class meetings that his conversion was genuine. Bishop Kennedy estimated recently that about one quarter of the converts at a camp meeting became full members of the Methodist Episcopal Church. If that be true then the Rev. John Kent may have had as many as between three and four hundred converts at that

---

[10] C. A. Johnson, *The Frontier Camp-Meeting, passim.* W. W. Sweet, *Meth. Am. Hist.*, pp. 155-160. Pilcher, *Hist. Prot. Mich.*, p. 91.

[11] Quoted from G. W. Pierson's *Tocqueville and Beaumont in America* by C. A. Johnson in *The Frontier Camp Meeting*, pp. 231-232.

first Michigan camp meeting. This estimate is based on the report of 130 members on Detroit Circuit to the Ohio Annual Conference of 1822.

Both more frequent preaching and increased lay activity were now to be observed in Detroit City. That committee, appointed back in 1820, to seek a lot and build a church had finally done something. On March 21, 1822, members of the society resident in Detroit obtained incorporation with a view to being legally able to hold property. They drew up articles of association which stated their religious purposes, gave them the right to own land, money, and goods, and created a board of nine trustees to run the business affairs of the church. This document was then approved by two of the judges, the attorney general of Michigan Territory and finally Governor Cass. Then eighteen Methodists signed it.[12]

Today the most interesting thing about this early Methodist document is the list of signers. Several had been active in the River Rouge log church, still in active use in 1822. Of course, Robert Abbott heads the list. He is thought to have moved back to the city from his farm about this time. Joseph Hickox signed next. This was probably because he had been their own minister previously. Joseph Corbus and Joseph Hanchett were also River Rouge church members. Jerry Dean was just beginning long years of service to Detroit Methodism. Three others — Israel Noble, Nathaniel Champ, and Philip Warren — were mentioned in 1829 by a Presiding Elder as "Methodists of the good old Stamp." William Hickox may have been a brother of Joseph and James Abbott was a brother of Robert.[13]

The Detroit Methodists proceeded to circulate papers for subscriptions and applied to the city authorities for a lot. The Methodists were allowed to select their own site and so chose a lot at Gratiot and Farrar Streets. This was outside of the city on "the Common." It was believed then that churches ought to be located on the edge of town or in open country. Whether such a custom was in quest of quiet or an avoidance of the more worldly parts of town, where saloon or theater might be, is not quite clear. Pilcher thought the location chosen an enormous mistake.

The members in Detroit must have realized their error for later they tried to get another location but were refused it on the ground that they had already made their choice. To obtain another lot, it would have had to be paid for in full immediately. As trouble was being experienced

---

[12] This document is given in full with signers by Pilcher in *Hist. Prot. Mich.*, pp. 95-97. He calls it "Constitution of the Methodist Episcopal Church of the City of Detroit."

[13] Pilcher, *Hist. Prot. Mich.*, p. 96, 191. The rest of the signers, given in the same order as Pilcher did, were James Kapple, James Reed, John Ramsey, Joseph Donald, H. W. Johns, Edwin Goodwin, Robert Lewis, and John Farmer.

in raising the money to build the church, perforce the first Detroit church was built on the first location after all.

Alfred Brunson and Samuel Baker Are Appointed to Detroit

The Ohio Annual Conference of 1822 decided to *double* the effort in Michigan and so appointed two ministers to the Detroit Circuit. The Rev. Alfred Brunson was first named and the Rev. Samuel Baker second on the list for Michigan. In double assignments, the first one listed was the Senior Preacher and the second, often inexperienced, was Junior Preacher. The older man was expected to give some advice and supervision to the younger minister.

Alfred Brunson had been in Michigan as an Ohio soldier during the War of 1812. He fought at the battle of the Thames and spent the winter in Detroit. He returned, nine years later, as a travelling elder of the Methodist Episcopal Church. Brunson observed in his reminiscences, "On my first trip here I came to drive out the British and the Indians and now I am back to drive out the Devil."

Much less is known of Samuel Baker because he died young and Brunson lived to a ripe, old age and also wrote his memoirs. Mr. Baker was a southerner from Baltimore, Maryland, and unmarried when he came here while his fellow minister Brunson had a wife and five children.[14]

After a rough passage via sailing ship from Ohio, Brunson and all his family reached Detroit. A cold reception awaited them. Although he had written ahead to rent a house for his family, nothing whatsoever had been done. He had to leave his family with the wife of the class leader while the two men rented a house and moved in their possessions from the dock.

Having paid the rent out of his own pocket, Brunson was quite overcome to learn that his family had been given no food all day long. He himself had eaten with the class leader. When he got home about sundown, he found everything in confusion, the children crying, and his wife determined to do no settling whatever until she had fed their children. Many years later he wrote:

> I thought if this was a specimen of the treatment I was to receive I must fare hard indeed and my heart sunk within me . . . It was so unexpected that . . . I had no more spirit in me. My wife saw this in my sunken countenance and, tho she felt bad and hungry enough to weep, she thought that it would not do for both of us to be down at the same time; so she rallied and cheered me up, "Never mind, we'll soon get something to eat and get along somehow and things may be more favorable hereafter." . . . We had carried some provisions with us and had

[14] A. Brunson, *A Western Pioneer*, 2 volumes, *passim*. W. W. Sweet, *Circuit Rider Days along the Ohio*, p. 214. Pilcher, *Hist. Prot. Mich.*, pp. 92-93, 134-136.

> procured some wood and soon had a fire and supper and then being
> weary, worshipped God, spread our beds on the floor and lay down to
> rest.[15]

Inevitably the incident became known and profuse apologies were made
not only by the couple immediately concerned but by several other
Methodists.

Brunson and Baker reported 161 members on their circuit at the
Ohio Annual Conference of 1823. This increase of thirty is somewhat
surprising when the difficulties of their daily work are considered.
Two ministers were trying to reach all the white settlements in the
Territory except Sault Ste. Marie. Only twelve preaching appointments
constituted the entire circuit but conditions of travel were so bad that
four weeks were needed to cover them all. Most of the appointments
were filled every two weeks with the exception of Detroit. With two
ministers travelling the Circuit in opposite directions it was possible to
provide preaching every Sunday in the city by one or the other of the appointed ministers. This was called a "half Station."

According to Brunson, the circuit was as follows: from Detroit to
Pontiac, then by the upper Huron or Clinton River to Mount Clemens,
and so to Lake St. Clair and back to the city by the Detroit River.
Next they went up the River Rouge seven miles to the log church and
the "upper settlements." Thence the route was reversed to the river
road leading to Monroe, from there by an Indian trail nine miles up the
River Raisin and back to the lake road by which they went to Maumee
at the foot of the Rapids in Ohio. All that was left to do then was to
ride fifty-eight miles to Detroit and start all over again. Just the description of the route is tiring.[16]

Not the least of Brunson's tribulations was his poor health in addition to that of his family. Four of his five children had both measles
and whooping cough that winter. He himself suffered from inflamma-
tions of both lungs and liver. His doctors wanted him to stop preaching
but he felt compelled to preach "or what little pay I got would be
stopped." He actually preached with a huge blister on his breast which
broke while he was in the pulpit. But his financial plight was clearly
his worst anxiety.

The financial reports of any early 19th century Methodist Annual
Conference read very strangely today. The column headings in the
statistics were Quarterage, Table Expense, and House Rent. The last
is plain enough in a time and place where no parsonages had been
built. By Quarterage is meant a sum of money which each member
promised to pay by the date of the quarterly conference. Church

[15] A. Brunson, *A Western Pioneer*, II, 261-265.
[16] A. Brunson, *A Western Pioneer*, II, 267. Pilcher also traced the route of the
circuit. *Hist. Prot. Mich.*, p. 135.

stewards circulated subscription papers on which these pledges were written in accord with one's ability to pay. The individual amount was often very small or in terms of wood or mittens or anything else of which the pioneer had rather more than he did of money.

Table Expense was for providing the minister and his family with food. It usually was paid in farm products and by holding a donation party. These occurred about twice a year and large amounts of potatoes, pork, apples, flour, sugar, etc. were then unloaded in the parsonage kitchen and cellar.

Each of the three main divisions of income was reported in two columns labeled Claims and Receipts. This meant what the preacher was promised and what he actually received. The difference between the two was sometimes disastrously large. General Harrison once remarked to the Rev. James B. Finley, speaking of Methodist travelling preachers, "Their condition is just the same as though they had taken the vow of poverty. The great mass of them live poor, die poor, and leave their families to the charities of the church."[17]

Brunson's desperate financial plight in Detroit was all too common then. To begin with, he had to pay house rent himself as soon as he landed there. A subscription paper circulated for his benefit had pledges totalling $200 but actually only $100 was paid him. When Brunson went on the southern part of the circuit and left Baker to preach two Sundays in succession in the city, "some of the outsiders who had subscribed refused to pay alleging that they had subscribed for me but I had gone they knew not where and left him to fill my place." Evidently some Detroiters did not like Baker's preaching.

Eventually they divided the circuit so that Baker went to Monroe and Maumee while Brunson was on the River Rouge and in Detroit City. They agreed to divide the collections "as if we both went all around." Each minister said it was the other's idea. The junior preacher felt that the senior preacher wanted "the cream of the circuit." Both of them were financially distressed. Baker complained to Presiding Elder Finley that he had to buy all his horse feed, had not received any travel expenses, and had no idea how much Brunson had received.[18] The senior preacher finally found a "hired girl" to help his wife run a boarding house. Even so he was compelled to leave for the annual conference session $100 in debt. This he paid during the next year "out of my own funds." The mystery is how he ever got any funds of his own.

Brunson must have had some part in raising funds for that planned church building in Detroit. He did tell Presiding Elder Finley in a letter on February 20, 1823, that $1,000 had been subscribed toward the

[17] R. A. Brunger, "Methods of Church Finance: Old and New" in *Mich. Ch. Ad.*, for October 18, 1956, LXXXIII, #42, 6-7.

[18] From MSS letters of Brunson and Baker in Methodist Historical Collections at Ohio Wesleyan University, Delaware, Ohio. Copied by Rev. R. A. Brunger.

building of a meeting house and it was hoped that work on it could start in the spring. On May 27, he reported to Finley that construction was under way, that they expected to get the brick building erected during the summer, and to hold meetings in it by the next fall. But before that time came, Brunson had departed to the annual conference and appointment to an Ohio charge.

Other matters concerned this early Detroit pastor more than building a church. He was pleased to report that city membership had more than doubled going from 21 to 46. This may have been due in part to the holding of the second camp meeting in Michigan, announced for May 23, 1823. Brunson was so ill that he did not attend but four Canadian preachers came and presumably conducted the services. They were Case, Slayter, Parker, and Pattee. Case had often officiated in Detroit and Pattee would be appointed there the next year.

Relations with his ministerial colleagues were a special problem in one way or another to Brunson during his stay in Detroit. Any circuit rider then worked in close association with the fellow preacher on the same appointment. They might not be together very much on such large circuits but it was important that they should agree on the division of their circuit travel. Also the "moral character" of any travelling or local elder in the region would be reviewed by the senior preacher upon a complaint being made.

From their correspondence with Presiding Elder Finley, it is evident that personal antagonism between the two men, Brunson and Baker, was reinforced by sectional differences. Early in the conference year, Brunson wrote that Baker was "pious, holy, zealous" but could not preach. And Baker thought that, purely from a financial point of view, Brunson was trying to monopolize the best parts of the circuit. Toward the end of the year, Brunson began to think that it may have been wrong to complain of Baker. Really his "southern dialect" was his chief handicap.

Whatever their mutual attitudes had been during the year, the ministers were glad to unite their forces for the difficult trip to the Ohio Annual Conference. In the course of his recurrent visits to Monroe, Baker had acquired a wife, Miss Sarah Harvey. This couple with Brunson and a couple of friends travelled on horseback about two hundred miles via the Black Swamp to Urbana, Ohio. Water was not safe to drink, houses few and far between, and the insects peculiarly vicious.

To Brunson's surprise, Baker's friends in the Ohio Conference encouraged him to make a formal complaint of the way he had been treated by his circuit colleague. This led to the appointment of a special committee of investigation before whom Baker was forced to acknowledge as Brunson reported:

> His leaving Detroit was on his own proposition and not mine . . . .
> He had expressed entire satisfaction with me at the time; but on coming

to Conference and conversing with some of his old friends, he had, at their instance, complained; but in reality he did not blame me at the time and did not know that . . . he could or should have done any way different from what I did. Upon this, the committee, who were all of southern stripe, advised him to drop the matter to which he agreed and they reported the matter settled.[19]

Moral and social standards of conduct were always extremely high and strictly enforced for all Methodist ministers. Not only must their characters be examined and passed by each annual conference but a church trial might occur on charges ranging from slander and contumacy to drunkenness and sexual offenses. Such charges then had more open review and embittered public trial than they would today. Little consideration was given to the feelings of the accused minister's family or to the impression outsiders would receive of the Methodist clergy.

It was Brunson's unhappy duty to deal with charges brought against his immediate Detroit predecessor, John Kent. This seems to have been what would be called a breach of promise today. In a letter of April 27, 1823, Brunson explained to Presiding Elder Finley that Kent had promised to marry Caroline Starks, then denied he had, and "kept improper company with her." Both the Disciplinary and legal aspects of the case troubled Brunson. Kent was not then attached to the district of which Detroit was a part. Therefore he would have to appear before a special committee appointed by the Ohio Annual Conference to deal with the charges. Because Samuel Baker was absolutely the only disinterested minister then available, Brunson had set him to taking the evidence of the girl and her parents. Kent had evaded all efforts toward a friendly settlement and "acts very queerly for an innocent man."

Finally on June 11, Brunson reported to Finley that the entire matter was dropped "for the sake of peace." He felt Kent took advantage of the situation. Brunson was sick again, Baker was away preaching on the circuit, and Kent seized the opportunity to obtain a signed release from both the girl and her parents. The senior preacher still felt that "a breach was there" but Kent had left town and many other matters demanded Brunson's attention.

In his letters to Finley, Brunson earnestly recommended the Rev. Elias Pattee for appointment in Michigan Territory. He was a local elder, once a member of Genesee Annual Conference, who had located on account of poor health and a big family. Now he was moving to Michigan and was eager to assume the work of a travelling elder here. Brunson had examined Pattee's "parchments," legal documents of ordination, had heard him preach acceptably, and knew he had a year's supply of food on hand from his crops. A final asset of this minister's was that "he is enured to the climate and will not in all probability be affected

---

[19] A. Brunson, *A Western Pioneer*, I, 278-279.

by those complaints common to our Ohio boys." It is not surprising that Pattee was Brunson's successor at Detroit.

Brunson, in his relations with the clergy of other denominations in Michigan, combined a general uneasy suspicion with individual, warm-hearted cooperation. Both he and Baker cited instances where the Presbyterians were striving to get well established in a preaching place ahead of the Methodists. Brunson had reference to Mackinaw and Baker to the Monroe and Maumee area.

Twice during his year in Detroit, Brunson worked closely with a young Presbyterian minister not yet fully ordained and so not able to give the sacraments. Upon this minister's request, once a quarter Brunson administered communion to both church groups. When so requested, he also baptized Presbyterian as well as Methodist children. Brunson said, "In the mission field we met as brethren, laborers with God in one common cause . . . the Christian courtesies as of brethren in one common harvest field seemed to prevail. I saw . . . the missionary spirit is the millennial spirit."[20]

Both Methodist and Presbyterian ministers were shocked by the wideopen Sunday markets in French Catholic Detroit. After each had preached a denunciatory sermon, together they got the Detroit City Council to order that markets might be held on Saturday nights but must be closed on Sundays. How effective this was is not known.

One day in the spring of 1823, Sergeant Ryan of the U.S. Army, just arrived from the post at Sault Ste. Marie, called on Brunson to tell him how four soldiers had set up a class at that place "destitute of all other means of grace." They had originally been converted at Sacket's Harbor, located at the east end of Lake Ontario in New York. Transferred to northern Michigan, they had missed the regular religious services. Their class had a dozen members, held regular meetings, and had won several converts. Brunson wrote all this to Finley and declared, "It done my very soul good to hear him tell of the good meetings they had had in that distant land. It fired me and my wife both with a missionary spirit and was it not for the size of my family I would volunteer for some of these outposts."

Brunson was most anxious for Finley to come and talk with Governor Cass about missionary work among the Michigan Indians. He had learned that a sum of Federal money, $2,000 a year, was available to those who would teach the Indians to cultivate the land. Presiding Elder Finley was also the Superintendent of the Wyandot Mission at Upper Sandusky in northern Ohio. He made the desired trip to Detroit in December after Brunson had gone to an appointment in Ohio.

In just one year in Detroit, Alfred Brunson saw the enormous opportunities that would soon open before the Methodist Episcopal Church

---

[20] A. Brunson, *A Western Pioneer*, I, 268-275.

in Michigan. On May 27, 1823, he wrote to Finley that more than three hundred people had already come to the Territory that spring and thousands more would certainly arrive before fall. He very much feared that the "New England missionaries . . . will flock here like pigeons." If at all possible, the Methodists ought to try to get in "ahead of their pious peculations." Brunson was of the opinion that "There is at present more Methodists in the Territory than all other denominations except Catholics and we get once in a while one of them converted."

This valiant, pioneer preacher specifically recommended making Michigan Territory a District containing one station in Detroit and two circuits. Perhaps the minister stationed in Detroit could also serve as the presiding elder. This would aid the local preachers very much and allow holding quarterly conferences and camp meetings without having to ask for the assistance of Canadian preachers.

It is odd that Brunson himself did not want to stay in Michigan when he saw so clearly the opportunities here. But he had a large family, heavy debts, and was convinced that two prominent presiding elders were testing his capacity for obedience in sending him to Detroit. So at the Ohio Annual Conference in 1823, Brunson went "privately" to Bishop Roberts and stated his desperate financial plight. In consequence, he received appointment to a more settled Ohio circuit presumably of more wealth.

In the course of going to Ohio, returning to Detroit to get his family and moving them back to Ohio, Brunson travelled over nine hundred miles. About two-thirds of it was on horseback and the rest by lake steamer. Figures give no idea of his hardships enroute. The horseback travel was via the Black Swamp, the lake trip through a violent storm in which all his family were very seasick, and the landing in Ohio was by a small boat through rough waves in which they barely escaped drowning.[21]

Three New Ministers Labor in Michigan

That new church building, which Brunson had seen under way before he left for the annual conference, was a long way from being completed. Subscription money ran out before the brick walls were finished. The mechanics of Detroit agreed to work together on a Sunday in the fall to roof the building before winter began. They surprised the Detroit Methodist Society with this contribution. Such was the strict attitude toward Sabbath observance in those days that most of the Methodists would have preferred to have their building go unroofed rather than see the Sabbath thus violated.

The place was left unplastered and seated with rough, wooden benches. It could only be used for meetings in the summertime. Its

21 A. Brunson, *A Western Pioneer*, I, 276-280.

The first Methodist Church in Detroit, a brick church, was
built in 1823-26, on the common, in an out of the way location. It had rough board seats and a gallery on three
sides. A plank walk to it was built in 1829. This Church
was used until 1833.

remote location in the small Detroit of that time was an added dissatisfaction. Consequently after one decade of partial use, the "old brick
church on the Common" was sold to a Universalist group and a new
frame building was erected in a central location on Woodward Avenue.[22]

The Ohio Annual Conference of 1823 appointed Elias Pattee and
Billings Plympton to Detroit Circuit. Pattee was the only one of the
early ministers appointed to Michigan who served two consecutive years
here. This probably was due to the fact that he had a large family to
support and was able to do some farming in Michigan.

The Rev. Elias Pattee was thrice married and had seven children.
Periodically he was overcome by financial and also physical exhaustion.
His formal education was limited but his natural ardor for the Methodist
Church was great and he gave all that he had in zeal and lung power to

---

[22] Pilcher, *Hist. Prot. Mich.*, pp. 98-100.

his preaching. Pilcher thought that Pattee was "a man of moderate talents and limited education but of great zeal." John Carroll described him as a large, commanding figure, wearing knee breeches, handknit stockings, and fine shoe buckles. This garb set off his "portly symmetrical body." He had a very loud voice, much emotional zeal, and was then thought to be a fine preacher. One early frontiersman declared, "That big Petty come and with his big fist did kill the Devil." Pattee's health compelled him to locate, or retire, from preaching in 1838.[23]

The junior preacher during Pattee's first year in Detroit was Billings Plympton. Little is known of him beyond the facts that he was young and in his second year of work in the ministry. Pilcher declared that he was "a noble-spirited and zealous Christian." He served only that one year in Michigan.

Isaac Hunter succeeded Plympton as junior colleague with Pattee. He also was here only the one year. Unfortunately he came in an irritable frame of mind as the result of an embittered quarrel with another minister in his previous appointment. An antipathy quickly developed between Hunter and some of the people to whom he preached. This was shown in a mean way one night by cutting off his horse's mane and tail. Hunter's very visible anger, upon discovering what had happened to his horse, was said, by Pilcher, to have pleased the practical jokers responsible for the trick.

Where the three Methodist ministers appointed to Michigan in the years 1823-1825 preached or how they divided up the circuit is uncertain. Pilcher noted that they confined their efforts to Michigan and did not go to Maumee Rapids, Ohio. They gave more attention to the country part of Detroit Circuit than they did to the city. Michigan was drawing more settlers and these ministers were eager to reach the newcomers in order to form classes and societies among them. Probably all three of them preached in the log church on the River Rouge, in the old Council House in Detroit, and at the home of Joseph Hickox some miles west of the first log meeting house.

To Mr. Pattee goes the credit of being the first Christian minister to extend the Church into Washtenaw County. A tiny settlement, first called Woodruff's Grove and later Ypsilanti, had been made in 1823. The terrain was most difficult. Swamps, heavy forests, neither roads nor bridges all made travel hazardous. Ypsilanti was reached by following the blazed trees and the return was in the same way. The nearest Methodist preaching appointment was on the River Rouge at least twenty miles distant. When Mr. Pattee came and preached in Ypsilanti, in

[32] For comments on Pattee and the two junior preachers, Plympton and Hunter see Pilcher, *Hist. Prot. Mich.*, pp. 93-94, 101-102, 147-148. J. Carroll. *Case & His Cotemp.*, I, 147, 246. W. W. Sweet, *Circuit Rider Days along the Ohio*, pp. 240, 258.

May 1825, and organized a society there a few weeks later, he was showing true pioneer zeal.

Also Mr. Pattee did all he could to help that struggling little society in Detroit complete and pay for its church building. Each year of his appointment to Detroit, the trustees of the church corporation authorized him to travel outside of the territory in order to collect funds for paying their debts and completing the building. He is thought to have gone to Ohio the first year and may have gone to New York City on a similar mission in 1825. The first year he reported the collection of $291.82 over and above his travelling expenses. The second year was better and he gathered in $625.25, of which the trustees allowed him $175 for his services. Pilcher stated that Mr. Pattee spent $2.50 more than he collected but that is not true. The official church records disproved that story entirely. It is one of the few incidents which Pilcher either misunderstood or did not investigate sufficiently.[24]

The membership reports to the Ohio Annual Conference indicate that Pattee also had some success in gaining new members. Brunson had reported 161 members in 1823 but Pattee and Plympton had 242 members in 1824. Curiously the statistics for 1825 give exactly the same number of members — 242 — as in the previous year. Was this a mistake in arithmetic or did the work not grow at all? Pilcher rather implied that Isaac Hunter was not as useful a junior preacher as Plympton had been. More attention by more ministers was the crying need of the Methodist Episcopal Church in Michigan.[25]

Michigan Territory received only the most scanty attention from the presiding elders in the years from 1823 through 1825. In 1823 Detroit Circuit was changed from the Lebanon District to the Miami District. John Strange was the presiding elder but did not visit Detroit. In 1824, Detroit Circuit was shifted again from Miami District to a new one, Sandusky, with James B. Finley again the presiding elder. But he held two positions simultaneously being both a presiding elder and superintendent of the Upper Sandusky Indian Mission. The first place in Finley's interests was occupied by the Indian work.

Through Alfred Brunson, Finley had learned of the chance of getting U.S. Government money for the Indian work, had then been in touch with Governor Cass, and finally had made a trip from Ohio through southeastern Michigan into Canada. He was not presiding elder when he came to Michigan in December 1823 and January 1824. He wanted to establish branches of the Wyandot Mission in northern Ohio certainly and in Michigan if possible.

Finley and a few chiefs, who were Christian converts, stopped at

---

[24] Silas Farmer, *History of Detroit & Mich.*, p. 564. Pilcher, *Hist. Prot. Mich.*, pp. 99-100.

[25] Pilcher, *Hist. Prot. Mich.*, pp. 147-148, 249-251.

an Indian camp on the Huron River near Flat Rock. These were people from the Wyandot and Shawnee tribes. A white man, called Brother Honiss, had lived among them for years. Finley preached both Sunday evening and Monday morning, receiving such a response that he was able to set up a class of twelve members. He was proud that this was the first Indian class formed in the entire Michigan Territory. Later it was called Huron Mission.[26]

On this same trip, Finley preached in Detroit, at Robert Abbott's house on the River Rouge, at Pontiac, and at three "new settlements." He even exhorted from house to house in Detroit.

The plans Finley had hoped to make for the Indian work fell through for the time being. Governor Cass received him cordially and arranged a conference for him with Major Baker, who was in command of the garrison at Detroit and had recently returned from work on fortifications in the Saginaw region. This officer discouraged Finley from proceeding with Indian religious work at that time. Most of the Indians were widely scattered hunting in the woods and only one chief was in the Saginaw region. He was Kish-a-kauk-o, who was violently opposed to missions and also to "religion of every kind." Even his own tribe had tried to depose him which had made him more wicked than ever. In view of the fact that most of these Lower Peninsula Indians would be moved west across the Mississippi River within the next quarter of a century, a good deal of what these early Michigan Methodists tried to do for them was wasted effort.

Other Protestant denominations were now beginning to work quite strongly in Michigan. The First Episcopal Church in Detroit was organized in 1824. After meeting for years in the Council House, the Methodists had been compelled to give up its use while the Legislative Council was meeting there. Then the Episcopal Society had been just a mite quicker and had obtained the use of the building upon the adjournment of the Council. The time at which they were to use it was the same as that the Methodists wanted.

Robert Abbott and Jerry Dean applied in person to Governor Cass for the use of the Council House at the time for which the Episcopalians had the reservation. They hoped the Governor would evict the other group. Cass refused to dispossess one "respectable society" in order to let another one meet there. He offered instead the use of a large room in the Academy Building and future occupation of a fine room in the Court House then under construction. Also the Methodists might use the Council House at any time that the Episcopalians were not there. None of this pleased the Methodists at all. By habit their wishes were

[26] W. C. Barclay, *Early American Methodism*, II, 123-124. J. B. Finley, *History of the Wyandot Mission*, pp. 229-230, 232-234.

set on the Council House on Sundays in the mornings and evenings. And their own remote brick building was not usable in the winter.[27]

In the next decade many changes would come both to Michigan and to Methodism here. A formal separation from the Canadian Methodists came in 1824 with the organization of all the Canadian circuits into a separate Conference. This did not quite satisfy the Canadian Methodists so in 1828 this Conference became the Methodist Episcopal Church in Canada, independent in all ways of the United States.

The Ohio Annual Conference, in October, 1825, created the Detroit District. Its membership began with the presiding elder of the new District, who would also serve as the stationed minister in the city of Detroit. Also included was Detroit Circuit, with two ministers appointed to it, and finally two assignments in Ohio: Fort Defiance and Wyandotte Mission. All those ministers appointed to the new Detroit District would of course continue to belong to the Ohio Annual Conference. This was an extremely modest beginning but it had great potential for future development.[28]

[27] Letter of Cass to the Methodists, October 8, 1824. *Mich. Pioneer Coll.,* XXXVI, 488-490. Territorial Records.

[28] W. W. Sweet, *Meth. Am. Hist.,* pp. 131, 169. Also *Circuit Rider Days along the Ohio,* Journals of the Ohio Annual Conferences, 1812-1826. p. 273.

CHAPTER IV

A FOURFOLD INCREASE IN SEVEN YEARS

1825 — 1832

The new Detroit District was under the supervision of the Ohio Annual Conference for the ensuing eleven years. All the Methodist ministers who worked in Michigan then came from the State of Ohio. Their family origins were apt to be found in the south usually in the States of Virginia or Maryland.

But the great majority of the settlers here in the next few years came from New York State and their ancestors were New Englanders. Thus the ways of ministers and people were strange to each other. Methodists were prone to mention in testimonial meetings how they had been converted "down in old York State" and how they wished for the ministers and sermons they once had known. Efforts were made to get some of the New York Methodist preachers to come here but met with little success.[1]

As already noted, the office of Presiding Elder was combined with that of the stationed preacher in the city of Detroit. This dual assignment to one man was quite common on the midwestern frontier. Although the appointments to Fort Defiance and the Wyandot Mission were officially part of the Detroit District, the Presiding Elder was not expected to visit them. This may have been because experienced men were working at both places. It may also have been due to the extreme hardships of travel in that particular area. Detroit Circuit seems to have meant anywhere in Michigan outside of the city of Detroit.

[1] Pilcher, *Hist. Prot. Mich.*, p. 108. The writer remembers that her grandfather, a Detroit Conference minister, always spoke of York State in affectionate terms and, even as an old man, went back there to visit frequently.

The modest personnel which started the Detroit District consisted of six ministers for four appointments. The one with the dual job, and therefore the most work, was the Rev. William Simmons. He was young, vigorous, and full of zeal for the cause. He preached regularly in "the old Academy." How much supervision he gave to the new District is hard to determine. Pilcher said that Simmons made a trip west in the spring of 1826 during which he preached at Ypsilanti and Ann Arbor. He must have held some Quarterly Conferences and given communion during this trip. It is known that he also performed the marriage service for two daughters of a Deacon Maynard at this same time. By correspondence he had some contact with business men on the St. Clair River, who made a financial offer to get a Methodist preacher sent there. But Mr. Simmons went back to Ohio in the fall of 1826 where he was transferred out of Michigan to an appointment in that State.

Three of the six ministers were still inside Ohio and were not the concern of the Presiding Elder at Detroit. Elias Pattee was at Fort Defiance and James B. Finley at the Wyandot Mission with J. C. Brook to assist him. The first two were men of long experience. Therefore they ran their appointments with little outside aid or interference.

The remaining two were assigned to Detroit Circuit. They were John Baughman and Solomon Manier. The latter, like Simmons, remained only the one Conference year in Michigan. The records do not even agree on how this minister spelled his name. Pilcher spelled it Manier in his *History of Protestantism in Michigan* but a family descendant here in Michigan spells it Minear. And the Ohio Annual Conference *Minutes* spell it both Minnear and Manear. He was admitted on trial in 1822 in Marietta, Ohio, and served on the Muskingum, Brunswick, and Wayne Circuits before coming to Michigan. There he had received salaries each year of less than $100. He must have been young, of vigorous health, and full of Methodist religious zeal.

One of his descendants has declared that Solomon Minear was born in Virginia in June 1796 and married in Ohio in 1828. The family tradition is that Minear preached once a month, in his year on the Detroit Circuit, to "the Indians and the Astor trading post." He served in the Ohio Annual Conference for seventeen years and then moved to Illinois. He is believed to have been trained in medicine as well as theology. Hence he practiced as both preacher and physician for forty years in the State of Illinois.[2]

---

[2] Pilcher, *Hist. Prot. Mich.*, pp. 108-109. *Mich. Pioneer Coll.*, XVII, 229, 682. Letter to the author from the great-great-grandson of Solomon Minear, Charles W. Baughman of Middleville, Mich. The latter says that Minear died and was buried in Paris, Illinois. Also letter to the author from R. A. Brunger on Sept. 2, 1962, about Solomon Minear. Undoubtedly Minear preached in Michigan very early in the history of the Methodist Church in this State but he could not have been either the first Protestant or the first Methodist minister to do so.

John A. Baughman, First Lifetime Michigan Methodist Minister

The first travelling elder to give the major part of his life to serving the Methodist Episcopal Church in Michigan was the Rev. John A. Baughman. Born in Maryland in 1802, he was admitted to the Annual Conference on trial at the age of twenty. He came to the Detroit Circuit for the Conference year 1825-1826 and the succeeding year was on the Monroe Circuit. Such work required a young and very vigorous man because the distances were great, real roads non-existent, swamps and creeks too plentiful, and settlements so new that it took search to find them. Mr. Baughman was either the first to preach or else the first to leave a regular Methodist appointment in ever so many places in Michigan.

In November 1825, he preached in the house of Colonel Allen in Ann Arbor and then in July 1827 he organized a society of five members there. The Allen and Rumsey families had just taken up the land from the U.S. Government in 1824. Baughman was the second Methodist minister to preach in Ypsilanti as Elias Pattee had preceded him there. A Presbyterian minister had preached once in Tecumseh but Baughman made the first regular preaching appointment there in 1826. He was also the first Methodist to set up a similar appointment in Pontiac. To appreciate how near the edge of the frontier this minister was working, it must be understood that neither Adrian nor Jackson had yet been founded.

While on the Monroe Circuit in the Conference year 1826-1827 Mr. Baughman met and married Mrs. Sarah Harvey Baker. She was a Methodist convert in 1821, had married the Rev. Samuel Baker early in 1823 and then, only a few weeks later, gone with him to the Ohio Annual Conference at Urbana. Right after the Conference ended, Mr. Baker was taken suddenly and violently ill and died in a few days. His wife was forced to return to Monroe alone on horseback. She triumphantly survived the experience of being lost in the woods of the Black Swamp. She then soon married the next Methodist minister to preach in Monroe and shared the itinerant life with Mr. Baughman for the rest of his career. He died in Detroit in 1868 and she outlived him by five years.

Baughman's Conference memoir in 1868 described him as "a man of extraordinary physical strength, with a loud voice, a cheerful temper and untiring industry." Pilcher, who knew him well, wrote that he was "young, handsome, sleek, polished and educated . . . refined in character and manners."

The last minister to preach in that log church on the River Rouge, before it was abandoned in 1828, was Mr. Baughman. He provided Pilcher with a detailed description of the place. It is presumed that

Baughman officiated there during the year, 1827, when he was on the Monroe Circuit.

In addition to all his work in the Methodist Episcopal Church, Mr. Baughman also served as an agent of the American Bible Society for four years and agent of the Conference Tract Society for one year. He was Presiding Elder of the Detroit District for two years. He was also an elected member of the General Conference of 1844, that being the one which finally split over slavery. The Rev. John Baughman was a member of the Ohio, Michigan, and Detroit Annual Conferences, serving in all twelve years in Ohio and thirty-two in Michigan. His last sermon was preached "with unusual fervor and the power of the Holy Spirit" in the Jefferson Avenue Church in Detroit just two weeks before his death.

A letter written by Joshua Dick to his brother from Batavia County, Ohio, early in 1833, gives an idea of John Baughman as a preacher. He wrote in part:

> I went to meeting on New Year's Day and heard Jno. Baughman preach. Never before was displayed in my hearing such a flow of divine eloquence. It was from these words. Knowing the time . . . he proceeded first to show what time was. Then to show the value of time from a consideration of the vast work that should be done in it. He then proceeded to show the shortness of time; . . . . From observation . . . ten years of our lives passes before we are capable of being engaged in the service of our Creator . . . which leaves us only three score years to prepare for a never ending eternity and it has also been concluded that the last ten years when the body is generally wornout or feeble . . . we are then incapable of being engaged in actual service . . . hours in each day must be spent in refreshing this body with food and sleep which leaves but a very short time for us to prepare for another world. He traced the subject through various windings with great success. I never saw a congregation so generally affected. Everyone appeared to feel the force of divine truth. I never was in my life better entertained than I was that day.[3]

✳   ✳   ✳   ✳   ✳

The Michigan contingent of the Ohio Annual Conference — Simmons, Baughman, and Manier — undoubtedly travelled together to the session of 1826 at Hillsboro. It was still the custom for those compelled to cross the Black Swamp to set out on horseback together to face the dangerous terrain. Those three must have gone with a sense of achievement

---

[3] This letter is in the historical collections of Ohio Wesleyan College, Delaware, Ohio. A photostat is in the Detroit Conference Historical Collection, Adrian College Library. The writer's name is not quite certain. It was either Dick or Dial. Baughman's Conference memoir is found in the Detroit Conference *Minutes* for 1868, pp. 184-185. His wife's memoir is to be found in Pilcher's *Hist. Prot. Mich.*, pp. 148-150. Pilcher has a great deal to say about Mr. Baughman too, especially on pp. 83-84, 228, 250-252, 320.

for their one year of effort. They had increased the total membership of the Michigan Methodist Episcopal Church over one hundred in all.

Also Presiding Elder Simmons carried a letter from some business men, in the St. Clair River area, promising to pay $50 toward the support of a Methodist minister if one could be sent there. They felt that the Presbyterian efforts in their area had been disappointing and therefore they wished to have a Methodist missionary attempt to raise the moral tone there.[4]

In 1826 for the first time, Detroit City was reported separately to any Annual Conference. The local church there had added only ten members. This was due in part to the isolated location of the partially finished brick church. On winter days of meeting in the old Academy they were annoyed by a singing school conducted upstairs by another church.[5]

Michigan received only one more minister in 1826 and that double duty for the man at Detroit was continued. The Rev. Zarah H. Coston was put in charge of the city station and also made Presiding Elder of Detroit District. One man was sent to each of the other Appointments. A geographical expansion of the work was started. John Janes was appointed to the Detroit Circuit, while Monroe had John Baughman and St. Clair James Donahoo. In addition to that local pledge of $50, the latter also received $50 from the Missionary Society. This was because he was going to establish the work in a new region. Mr. Donahoo was later said to have done much more good there than so modest a sum entitled the local people to expect.[6]

The above four places of appointment did not at all indicate the only towns where these Methodist ministers officiated. They all travelled to every place they could reach on foot or on horseback. If a settlement did not invite one of them to hold services there then he would ask if he might preach there and, if rejected, he would stay and preach anyway. He thought such sinners were the very people who most needed him. By such means the pioneer Methodist Church grew and prospered.[7]

---

[4] So stated by Simmons to Pilcher, *Hist. Prot. Mich.*, p. 226.

[5] Early Michigan Methodist statistics are not reliable, nor complete. A special Conference committee, set up to "gather statistics on the progress of Methodism in Michigan" and report in 1855 said that Detroit Circuit had 150 members in 1825 and Detroit Dist. in 1826 had 270. This they divided into City 70 and Circuit 200. Mich. Conf. *Minutes* for 1855, pp. 39-44. Pilcher had seen once an old classbook that said Detroit City had 60 members in 1825. But in his *Hist. Prot. Mich.*, published in 1877, Pilcher stated that Detroit City had 70 and Detroit Circuit 290 members in 1826, a net increase of 138. *Ibid.*, p. 109. The varying figures of that time cannot be reconciled.

[6] Pilcher, *Hist. Prot. Mich.*, pp. 110, 226-227. W. W. Sweet, *Circuit Rider Days along the Ohio*, p. 273.

[7] M. D. Osband, "History of the Pioneer Church of Nankin," *Mich. Pioneer Coll.*, XXVII, 150-160.

Such a frontier preacher usually wore in the pulpit a long single breasted coat with a straight collar and buttoned up tight to his white lawn tie. If his pants became thin on the knees, he would have them cut off and turned around so that any patch would come at the back of the leg and only the seam would show in front. One minister noted that he saw his Presiding Elder in the pulpit in such mended trousers.

The members of the congregation were clad in the plainest of home-spun garb. Many of the men were barefoot in the summers. Methodists then were extremely strict about over-worldly dress. A gold watch chain, rings, fancy trimming on a dress, ruffles, even flowers would get one excluded from Class meeting. Every Circuit minister considered it his duty to read Wesley's sermon on dress once a year to every congregation. He or a local elder were always on guard at the door to exclude from a Class meeting or a love feast any whose garb was not plain or even visiting Methodists not members of that particular Class.

The Michigan Circuit rider preached about twenty-eight times in going around a fourweeks route. The same sermon did duty in many places and eventually became a highly polished piece of work. Major attention was given to reaching all appointments on time not to close book work in a pastor's study. M. D. Osband, who knew many pioneer preachers, once wrote, "The position of a circuit preacher was no sinecure. Their energies were sometimes taxed to their utmost powers of endurance but it was not brain work. They were in no danger of falling from cerebral exhaustion. Some of them must have had muscles strong as iron."

Of the four Ohio Conference ministers sent to Michigan in 1826, only Baughman served here most of his life. The others transferred out of Detroit District and Ohio Annual Conference within five years. Zarah Coston served in Detroit and as the Presiding Elder for three years. Pilcher declared that Coston was "a faithful, good man, and an excellent preacher . . . but the disadvantages were more than a match for him." An Ohio man never forgot how he had heard Coston preach in front of the jail for the benefit of a man under sentence of death.[8] After leaving Detroit in 1829, Coston served for many years in the Pittsburgh Annual Conference.

The Rev. John Janes served two years on the Detroit Circuit. He must have been young and energetic for he had a very extended route to follow. He also preached in Ann Arbor the second half of his second year here. There he acquired a wife, Miss Hannah Brown. She and her sister, having seen a newspaper notice of a camp meeting signed by Coston, had written to him asking for regular ministerial visits to Ann Arbor. The Brown sisters were among the first members of the Ann

---

[8] In 1825 at Newark, Ohio. "Recollections of Newark, Ohio." *Ohio Arch. & Hist. Publications*, XX, 220.

Arbor Methodist Society. Mr. and Mrs. Janes were long active in the Ohio Annual Conference.

The Rev. James Donahoo faced the most difficult Circuit of all. St. Clair geographically was long and narrow. Religiously, it was reputed to be full of people who spent their Sundays "in horse-racing, drinking, gambling and other demoralizing practices." Donahoo had been a member of the Ohio Annual Conference since 1821. He was said to be "of respectable talents and good social habits, sprinkled a little with oddity and Irish wit." He reported thirty members of the new St. Clair Circuit to the Ohio Annual Conference of 1827.

Like Alfred Brunson earlier, Donahoo learned of an opening for a Methodist mission at Sault Ste. Marie. He had met a local preacher, the Rev. J. H. Smith, who had just returned from a trip up north "and brought this news of an opportunity." Neither trained men nor money were available in sufficient supply then. The Ohio Annual Conference made no appointments either to St. Clair or the Soo in 1827. It seems today as if those opportunities were not followed up quite as they ought to have been.[9]

An examination of the Ohio Annual Conference statistics for 1827 shows that Detroit City Station had just maintained its own, being reported at seventy members, exactly the same as the previous year. The increase had come on the rural frontier. Pilcher recorded it as 123. Five ministers reported in 1828 that Detroit City had lost five members and the outstate church had gained sixty-two. The entire territorial membership in 1829 increased only seventy-five of whom thirteen were in the city church. The increase in 1830 was 205, that in 1831 was reported as 358, and in 1832 it was 495. Pilcher considered that, in the 1820's, the Methodist Episcopal Church in Michigan "was not any more than keeping pace with the population."[10]

The First Michigan Methodist Sunday School

Figures on adult work alone do not reveal all the effort being put forth by the Methodists. The time had come when the needs of the children were to be considered and the laymen were to assume an increasing part in church activities. A union Sabbath School had been organized in Detroit since about 1820. Now the Methodists began to feel the need for one of their own, which the Church alone could control.

The two 19th century pillars of the Methodist Episcopal Church in Detroit, Jerry Dean and John Owen, started the first Methodist Sunday School. Dean was its first Superintendent. That remote building location was again a serious handicap to the Methodists. Teachers were

[9] Letter from Donahoo about the Soo is found in Maurice F. Cole, *Voices from the Wilderness*, p. 80. Pilcher, *Hist. Prot. Mich.*, pp. 110, 219-220, 228-229.
[10] Pilcher, *Hist. Prot. Mich.*, pp. 114-116.

very scarce and the union Sunday School had more prestige. After three years of hard struggle, Dean persuaded his friend, John Owen, to give up his work in the union Sunday School and take the superintendency of the Methodist one. At once, Owen overcame the distance handicap by renting one room, formerly a lawyer's office, right in downtown Detroit, on Woodward Avenue near Congress Street.

Sometime in 1827 the Methodist Episcopal Sunday School began to meet in that room that Owen had rented. It was held there until the local church erected a new building nearby in 1834. No Conference statistics on Sunday Schools were kept then. And all the local records have long ago disappeared together with the early class meeting books. The fact that the Sunday School was held in one room would indicate that the numbers were few with perhaps only three or four teachers.[11]

Changing Michigan

Secular events were profoundly changing Michigan and would soon affect the churches therein. The United States troops were removed in 1826, the old fort and land surrounding it given to Detroit and destuction of the stockade and earthworks undertaken. The dirt removed was deposited along the river in an effort to improve the harbor. In 1827 stage coaches began to make regular runs to Toledo and Congress authorized construction of three roads in Michigan. These were to go from Detroit to Port Huron, Saginaw, and Chicago. Roadmaking then usually meant clearing away the stumps and trees, laying logs in marshy spots, and providing drainage where necessary. The exact routes of these roads were of extreme importance for they determined the lines of Michigan settlement, the location of new towns, and eventually the establishment of Christian churches, including the Methodist.[12]

Methodist Ministers and Appointments
1827 – 1828

The Ohio Annual Conference appointments to Michigan in 1827 were a recession in the number of charges but a slight gain in the number of the ministers sent to the State. Coston was returned for his second year in that dual position as Detroit City minister and Presiding Elder. This was the last year such an arrangement was made. No one was sent to St. Clair. The Detroit Circuit appeared for the last time but with two ministers: John Janes and William Runnels. Monroe also was given two men, both of them new to Michigan, being George Walker and James Armstrong.

---

[11] Pilcher, *Hist. Prot. Mich.*, pp. 128-129, 142-143. Pilcher tried to find the exact date of origin of the Sunday School but failed.

[12] Detroit Public Library, *Detroit in its World Setting*, pp. 70-72.

These men were young, came to Michigan for only a year or two, and eventually transferred to other Annual Conferences. Things were in a state of flux then, not only in the settling of Michigan but also in the boundaries and exact areas of the various Annual Conferences. Pilcher testified that the ministers here in 1827-1828 were "all men of fine preaching abilities."

In 1828 the Annual Conference in Ohio shifted the ministers again, bringing both advance and retreat to Michigan. Zarah Coston's duties in Detroit had been cut in half and so he served only as the Presiding Elder in his third and last year there. The District was growing and required more close supervision. Most of the appointed ministers were young and not yet authorized to administer communion. One of the high points of every Quarterly Conference was the service of the Lord's Supper by the Presiding Elder. Those were also the days of strict obedience to the *Discipline*. Pilcher said that, in his experience, the young preachers not only needed their superior to give communion but also required his advice because they were "unaccustomed to the administration of discipline."

Only one more minister had been sent here but geographical differentiation had been continued. A new man, Arza Brown, came to Detroit City, George Walker was returned alone to Monroe and experienced Elias Pattee was sent to St. Clair. The new stations were named Oakland with William Snow there and Huron with Benjamin Cooper. It appears that Pattee and Brown were the only ministers authorized to administer communion besides the Presiding Elder.

The early Conference *Minutes* give no information on where the preaching appointments were on those huge frontier circuits. Fortunately Pilcher took the trouble to describe the routes and geography of these charges in his *History of Protestantism in Michigan*. With the exception of two log churches, all the preaching appointments he listed were in oneroom schoolhouses or private homes. When preaching in a home, the minister usually stood in the door with the women sitting on the beds, the children on the floor, and the men standing clustered outside around the door. No wonder the early preachers cultivated a loud attention calling voice.

St. Clair and Monroe were the most remote and difficult of all the circuits in 1828. The first lay along the river from Algonac to Port Huron. The people were few and worldly, and were isolated from the other circuits. One Society organized by a Canadian existed in Algonac. The Monroe Circuit preacher was expected to cover southern Wayne County, Monroe and Lenawee Counties, and then go to the Maumee Rapids in Ohio. The only villages were Monroe, Flat Rock, and Tecumseh. Much of the route lay through mud and more mud in swamps and marshes.

Oakland and Huron, the new Circuits, must have furnished a minister labor for every day in the week. They lay directly in the path of advancing settlement so the preacher undoubtedly made new appointments every time he traversed the Circuit. One complete round alone took him three or four weeks and then he started all over again. The Oakland charge included northern Wayne County in addition to all of Oakland and Macomb counties. Among the settlements were Troy, Bloomfield, Farmington, Pontiac, Mount Clemens, Romeo, and Utica. This Oakland Circuit had the second log church built by the Methodists in Michigan. It was three miles northeast of Pontiac and was widely known as the "Donation Chapel."

The Huron Circuit covered western Wayne County and all of Washtenaw County. Its route lay along the Rouge and Huron Rivers. The settlements with preaching appointments included Nankin, Plymouth, Ypsilanti, Dixboro, and Ann Arbor. This Circuit was changing faster than any of the others as the settlers pushed on, even ahead of the roads, into the woods in eager search for the best lands.

The year 1828 was a time of advance for Michigan Methodism in many areas and recession in one. That first log church on the Rouge was abandoned as a place of worship. It stood vacant for some years and then was burned apparently because it had become an eyesore. The location was not particularly convenient, the population was moving west, and dissension had arisen among the members. Some were also pioneering in other States.

Pilcher said that a few members were jealous of Robert Abbott. One man tried to get Abbott out of the Society by claiming he had run off with their funds. When Abbott returned from a trip to Canada, he brought a charge of slander against this member and secured his expulsion from the Society. But a bit later Abbott moved back to Detroit City and became active in the church there. Another original member, William Stacy, had died. The Corbus family also had moved away. Internecine quarrels and membership shrinkage were too much for that old log church to endure.

Although their meeting house was abandoned, this does not mean that the Methodists left the neighborhood. Pilcher himself came to Michigan in 1830, often went into the abandoned building, and knew the area well. He stated that "we preached in a private house a little above it," Might this have been the home of the Rev. Joseph Hickox? Presumably the Society functioned still but it was only one of a large number of places where the minister appointed to Huron Circuit preached during his monthly round.

The name Dearborn appeared first in 1833 as a township and later was incorporated as Dearbornville Village in 1838. In that latter year, the Methodists built a small frame church there. None of the early class or Society records have survived to tell more about that first log meeting house. It is believed that the small Society became part of an appointment known as Huron Mission in the Conference *Minutes.* All meetings must have been held in private homes from 1828 to 1838.[13]

Beginnings in Southwestern Michigan

Methodism was now about to leap over one hundred miles of wilderness to begin work in the southwest corner of Michigan Territory. Settlers reached there via Ohio and Indiana not from Detroit. The boundary lines were neither fully settled nor actually surveyed yet so some people may not have realized that they were leaving the recently created States of the southern half of the Northwest Territory.

But early realization of their complete lack of religious services must have been strong. A county had been organized and a representative to the Territorial Legislative Council elected and sent to Detroit. There he would certainly have soon met the Rev. Arza Brown. In addition to being the stationed Methodist minister in Detroit City, he served as chaplain at the Legislative Council session of 1829. He gave close attention to his duties there. Indeed, his Presiding Elder, Zarah Coston, felt his chaplaincy was so important that he advised Mr. Brown not to try to attend the Ohio Annual Conference in 1829.

It is likely that it would be through the help of Chaplain Brown that the territorial delegate from southwestern Michigan was able to bring the religious needs of his part of the Territory to the attention of Mr. Coston. Upon learning of the local desire to be supplied with religious services, Presiding Elder Coston responded himself. In the summer of 1829, he went as far west as Niles and spent three weeks in that area, preaching probably every day. Pilcher said that Coston several times preached in the home of a member of the Society of Friends. He located a few people who had been members of the Methodist Episcopal Church elsewhere but was not able to find anyone whom he considered suitable for a Class leader. How much more one would like to know about this journey! Certainly Coston got there on horseback for the roads could scarcely have been more than plans on paper yet.

Presiding Elder Coston must have done his duty by these new settlers at the next Conference session too. That fall the St. Joseph Mission was created and Erastus Felton was sent there. This new appointment included all the southwest Michigan settlements. Felton was able to organize several small Societies, including one at Niles started in 1830. However, the chief settlement then was at White Pigeon.

---

[13] Pilcher, *Hist. Prot. Mich.*, pp. 83-85, Moore"s *History of Dearborn Area, 1709-1940.*, p. 371. Also pamphlet, First Methodist Church *Directory* for 1948, p. 21 for "Milestones in the History of the First Methodist Church." Found in Detroit Conference Historical Society Collection in Adrian College Library.

Where no Methodist work at all had been, Mr. Felton reported seventy-six members at the Ohio Annual Conference in 1830.[14]

Methodist Ministers and Appointments
1829 – 1832

The Ohio Annual Conference of 1829 made several changes in the Michigan appointments. A new Presiding Elder, Curtis Goddard, was sent to Detroit. He was to stay for three years. The Rev. Arza Brown was left a second year in the Detroit City station. He must have been useful to the new Presiding Elder. Oakland Circuit retained William Snow for a second year. The rest of the charges had new men appointed as follows: Huron Circuit went to Leonard B. Gurley, Monroe Circuit to Jacob Hill, St. Clair to Samuel Latta, and the new St. Joseph Mission, as already noted, to Erastus Felton. These men were young without much ministerial experience or any knowledge of Michigan.

At first sight, the 1830 appointments by this same Conference appear about the same as the year previous because the same Presiding Elder was retained and the number of places receiving ministers was the same – seven – but the total number of ministers here in 1829 was seven and in 1830 it was ten.

Three more ministers was a substantial increase in terms of the working force then. Their assignments reveal where the need was greatest because the population was increasing the fastest. They were assigned as the second, or junior, preachers on the Oakland, Ann Arbor, and St. Joseph Circuits. The name Huron Circuit was dropped and Ann Arbor substituted. The men on that particular circuit were riding an additional eighty miles to preach at Jackson and Grass Lake. Much of the route was only an Indian trail. All the circuits outside Detroit were being enlarged on every round the preacher made.

Presiding Elder Goddard dealt with a constantly changing personnel on his Detroit District during the years from 1829 to 1832. If the man was one he had known in a previous year then he was found in a different charge. Arza Brown was moved from Detroit City to Oakland Circuit. Leonard Gurley, on the Huron Circuit in 1829, was sent to the vast St. Joseph Mission. There he labored with Erastus Felton who was there both the previous and succeeding years.

Young men of little experience and with southern backgrounds were still being sent to Michigan. Their tendency was to work here a year or two and then transfer to another Conference. James W. Finley, serving the Monroe Circuit from 1830 to 1832, transferred out of the Ohio Annual Conference in 1832. William Sprague, junior preacher in 1830 with Arza Brown on Oakland Circuit, located in 1839. Leonard

[14] Pilcher, *Hist. Prot. Mich.*, pp. 113-114, 264.

Gurley, coming in 1829, transferred elsewhere in 1831. The same was true of his co-worker Erastus Felton. Laboring on the difficult St. Clair Circuit in 1830 and the equally tough St. Joseph Mission in 1831, Benjamin Cooper transferred out of the Ohio Annual Conference in 1832. Some of these changes were due to the action of the General Conference of 1832, which put southwestern Michigan under the supervision of the Indiana Conference.

Only on the newly named Ann Arbor Circuit were there appointments of more lasting value to Michigan Methodism. Henry Colclazer, just twenty-one, was the senior preacher and Elijah H. Pilcher, only twenty years of age, was junior preacher. Colclazer was to serve the Michigan Methodist Episcopal Church until 1846 and Pilcher until 1877. Both were to minister to many churches, act as Presiding Elders and, as elderly men, serve in other Conferences.[15]

Elijah Holmes Pilcher

Perhaps the most versatile of all the Methodist ministers in the history of Michigan was the Rev. Elijah H. Pilcher. He held every position open to a minister in any State then, except the bishopric, founded at least thirteen Methodist churches in Michigan, helped to start Albion College and Bay View, and wrote the only detailed history of early Methodism in Michigan. Somewhere he also found the time and inclination to become a lawyer and a physician. Where he found the energy and enthusiasm for all his work is a mystery to modern Methodists.[16]

Born on June 2, 1810, near Athens, Ohio, Elijah Pilcher went two years to Ohio University, left for financial reasons, and taught school for one year. All the rest of his career, and he lived until April 1887, was spent in the service of Methodism.

A camp meeting was the scene of Elijah Pilcher's conversion at the age of ten. When he was nineteen, he received a local license to preach and the same year was admitted to the Ohio Annual Conference. He was sent to the Nicholas Circuit in what is now West Virginia for his first year of ministerial labor. His next appointment, in 1830, was as junior preacher on the Ann Arbor Circuit. It was the first year in Michigan for so-named a circuit and its minister too. The ensuing term was the only time in fifty years that Pilcher held a subordinate position.

---

[15] Pilcher, *Hist. Prot. Mich.*, pp. 115-116. Also Pilcher gives an alphabetical and chronological list of "Itinerant preachers in Michigan from 1809 to 1877." This includes a separate list of ministers appointed to the city of Detroit. See pp. 446-457.

[16] Pilcher, *Hist. Prot., Mich., passim.* Scattered all through his book are references to Pilcher's career in Michigan. A biography of him was written by his youngest son, James Elijah Pilcher, *Life and Labors of Elijah H. Pilcher.* See also R. A. Brunger, "Elijah H. Pilcher, Methodist Preacher Extraordinary," in the *Michigan Ch. Ad.*, for Feb. 20, 1964, XCI, #8, 4-5, 18-19.

Elijah H. Pilcher (1810-87) was a pioneer preacher in Michigan; a presiding elder for many terms; a lawyer and a doctor; one of the founders of Albion College, The Michigan Christian Advocate, and Bay View; the author of "Protestantism in Michigan."

Among the churches he served for several years each were Adrian, Ann Arbor, Jackson, Battle Creek, Kalamazoo, and Detroit Woodward. He was a Presiding Elder for twenty-one years. He was elected a delegate to the General Conference five times.

All his life Pilcher was a student. He first became convinced that a knowledge of law would help him in counselling the members of his various churches. Later when he became a Presiding Elder, such knowledge was even more important to him. He studied with a lawyer

An early circuit rider coming into a settler's clearing.

in Marshall and was admitted to the bar in 1846. As many a circuit rider did then, much of his study was on horseback en route to his next appointment. Then he took up the study of medicine and intermittently worked at it until he attained his medical degree in 1859. At first he had been guided by a physician in Jackson, later he combined the ministry of the Ann Arbor Church with regular attendance at the University Medical School for two years. Somehow he slipped in the achievement of an M.A. degree in 1848, and an S.T.D. in 1865.

The most extensive in time and effort of all Pilcher's labors was his *History of Protestantism in Michigan.* For many years, he collected documents, made inquiries by letter, and interviewed early members of the Michigan Methodist Episcopal Church. He was personally acquainted with five of that first class of seven people in Detroit in 1810. The greater part of his book was probably written before the Civil War but he was unable to obtain means of publishing his work until 1878. Our knowledge of the Michigan Methodist Episcopal Church in its early days would be very scanty without his aid.

Thanks also in part to the zeal with which Pilcher kept a diary himself and then obtained access to those of his colleagues, the work demanded of pioneer circuit riders and the conditions under which they lived can now be understood more clearly. Elijah Pilcher knew all too well out of his own vast experience what the early hardships were.

The name of Ann Arbor was omitted from the Ohio Annual Conference appointments in 1831 and that circuit was divided with the region east of that town under Ypsilanti and all west of it under Tecumseh. The regular route ran from Ann Arbor to Marshall, then south to Cold-

Grand Rapids in 1830. From such tiny and humble beginnings, began the cities of our state.

water, east to Clinton, next to Tecumseh and Adrian. The final stops were at Manchester and Saline en route back to Ann Arbor to start all over again. It amounted to nearly four hundred miles of travel and at least twenty-seven preaching appointments.

The east and west roads had been established but there were no connecting north and south roads. The first time that Mr. Pilcher tried to go from Marshall to Coldwater, he was forced to give up and backtrack through Marshall and Jackson to Ann Arbor and so reach the rest of his circuit from the east.

His troubles on October 10, 1831, remained vivid in his mind. He wrote of them in part:

> Having hired a man to go with me to find the way to Coldwater, we set out. Left my clothes and books at Marshall and filled my saddle-bags with oats for the horses and bread and raw pork for ourselves. We supplied ourselves with an ax, a gun, a pocket compass and a map, and so started to find our way to Coldwater. We wallowed through marshes and creeks as we came to them; we marked the trees on the south side, so that we could follow the same way back . . . . Thus we continued until night overtook us. Wet and tired, we kindled a fire, made a hut of brush, roasted our meat, and ate supper and went to bed after family prayer. My great-coat made my bed, my saddle and saddle-bags my pillow. Slept some. The wolves howled most hideously most of the night.

The next day they could not advance at all in the right direction so finally Pilcher gave up and reversed his way on the circuit route. After reaching Coldwater from the east, he started north again, finally found his own previous blazes on the trees and so got to Marshall.

There he found his junior preacher, the Rev. Ezekiel S. Gavit, waiting for him. But the very next day, Pilcher started back to Coldwater. He was accompanied about halfway by Gavit. Pilcher remembered well that:

> We labored hard and made the way plain and parted after prayer here in the wild woods. Thus I have spent four days carrying an axe and blazing the trees to make a way to get around our circuit. My right shoulder is so sore and lame that I can scarcely lift my hand to my head. But I am resolved to persevere.[17]

Among the restrictions on a young circuit rider was the attitude toward marriage of his church and also of many a father with attractive daughters. Most Conference travelling elders disapproved of the young preacher who married while still on trial in Conference, learning to preach, studying the required books, and constantly en route to his next appointment. Parents were apt to take a dim view of a minister's poverty, threadbare clothes, and inability to provide a decent home for

[17] Both this and the previous quotation from Pilcher, *Hist. Prot. Mich.*, pp. 123-125.

William Barrus and wife, Mary Ann, were two of the five charter members of the Adrian Methodist society in the summer of 1830. They were typical of the pioneers of southern Michigan, and were the great-grandparents of Bishop Marshall Reed.

their daughter. In 1832, Elnathan Gavit was appointed to the Monroe Circuit where he noted several intelligent, attractive and refined young ladies. He even recommended one of them to his successor, William Sprague. Gavit was quite pleased when his matchmaking was successful. Many years later, Gavit declared, "I dared not as much as squint at any of them, much less to make any propositions."[18]

Parsonages and church buildings were practically non-existent in Michigan Territory. Many another newly married circuit rider must have had an experience similar to that of the Rev. Arza Brown. After two years in Detroit City, he married in Farmington, Ohio, and took his new wife to the Ohio Annual Conference where they learned of his appointment to Oakland Circuit in Michigan. His salary for the year would be $180. Years later Mr. Brown reminisced a bit for Pilcher's history:

> Taking leave of beloved parents and friends, we left in our carriage for our distant field of labor. A toilsome journey it was, through mud and storm. After ten days we reached our Circuit. The territory embraced within its limits was new . . . no parsonage . . . . I succeeded in obtaining a room in a house in Auburn. This house was weather-boarded but not ceiled. A partition of rough boards divided the rooms. It was a cold house in a cold climate; and in this small cold room we spent the cold winter of 1830-31. But we were, in this manner of living, sharing the privations incident to this new country with our dear friends . . . . Now and then I borrowed a team and . . . would go to the forest, chop, load, and draw home my own firewood . . . . Early in the spring, I was so fortunate as to obtain a larger and more comfortable room in Bloomfield . . . Here our daughter Mary was born, and we resided until the close of the year.[19]

Both ministers, Brown and Pilcher, thought that the religious work on their Circuits was greatly helped about 1830 by the arrival and settlement in southeastern Michigan of several local preachers. These men were generally devoted to the work, efficient and deeply pious personally. Among them were Marcus Swift, who came to Nankin, Laban Smith and John Young, who settled in Bloomfield, Allen Tibbitts of Plymouth, Abel Warren of Washington, and Joseph Bangs of Tecumseh. The latter was a brother of Nathan Bangs, who had preached in Detroit in 1809. Mr. Brown also noted that these ministers had devoted and helpful wives. He said that generally such couples "continued steadfast in the faith, daily witnessing a good profession." The Temperance movement and the abolition societies were also objects of special attention on the part of these local preachers and their wives.

Three camp meetings were held during the summer of 1831 in

---

[18] Elnathan Gavit wrote his autobiography many years later under the title *Crumbs from my Saddlebags or Reminiscences of Pioneer Life,* pp. 181-182.
[19] Pilcher, *Hist. Prot. Mich.,* pp. 192-194.

southeastern Michigan. Two of them were on Mr. Brown's Circuit. In one of the two camp meetings on Oakland Circuit, Arza Brown had the help of Elijah Pilcher. The latter was highly skilled in dealing with the young rowdies who often tried to disturb the meetings. He would wear a farmer's everyday coat instead of the usual ministerial frockcoat and so work his way into the midst of any group on the edge of the congregation who looked like trouble-makers. Pilcher always strove for good order and genuine conversions before the meetings ended. Mr. Brown believed that "the power of God was gloriously displayed in the awakening and conversion of very many precious souls."

All Methodist preachers then were paid in various and curious ways for their services. In travelling to Conference or around their Circuits, they generally were able to stay and to eat in the homes of fellow Methodists without charge. But now and then, such homes were few and far between, so occasionaly the ministers were forced to put up at hotels and pay for their lodging and meals. The Rev. Elnathan Gavit told of one tavern host's scheme of credit for travelling preachers. A long sermon rated 25¢ credit, a short one 50¢, a long family service got only 12½¢ but a short family prayer and reading one Bible chapter was rewarded with 25¢. Donation parties of food and hand-knitted mittens and scarfs were more common in a minister's life than cash or the above scheme of credit.

The widespread custom of lodging the minister with one of his church members got him into some curious situations. He was lucky if he had a clean, quiet bedroom alone. Frequently he had to sleep with another preacher or even with some of his host's children. The bedding was often dirty or insect infested.

Quarterly Conferences created special problems of lodging and meals. People often would come as much as fifty miles, arrive either Friday night or Saturday morning, and expect to stay until Monday morning. Usually men slept in the hay mow in the barn and women in blankets on the cabin floor. Families gave the best they had to the Presiding Elder.

Once a family prepared their only four poster bed and even hung up sheets around it to give a bit of privacy. All this was for the Rev. Henry Colclazer, then the Presiding Elder of Ann Arbor District. He was completely bald and always wore a full black wig but none of the people there knew it. As was his usual custom, Colclazer hung his wig on the bedpost when he retired. When the host, a Mr. Boutwell, went to call the minister the next morning, his eye fell on the wig, and he yelled out that the Indians had been there and sca|ped the minister. The latter was awakened by the noise and clapped on his wig immediately but by then Boutwell was screaming, "Murder, Murder!" Everyone was awakened and Boutwell was with some difficulty brought to realize what he had done. Then he was so chagrined that he fled to the barn and stayed there all day missing most of the meetings.[20]

The Year 1832

This was the year of change and excitement for Michigan and its Methodist Episcopal Church. A net increase in total membership of over 400 occurred and the first Quarterly Conferences were held in Jackson and Calhoun counties. The towns were Jackson and Marshall. Near Northville, one camp meeting was held in contrast to three the year before.

The Black Hawk War greatly excited people in the spring of 1832 as it was widely feared that the Michigan Indians would go to fighting too. The militia were called out but did not leave Michigan Territory.

Later that same year, Michigan was dreadfully frightened by an outbreak of cholera. This dread disease was brought to Detroit by soldiers on a transport going up the Lakes. Many people died of it in Detroit, Ann Arbor, and Marshall. Some villages kept armed guards on their roads leading east and stopped anyone coming from the direction of Detroit. Were the circuit riders stopped from going their rounds? The Ohio Annual Conference came just at the height of the epidemic so perhaps they were all absent from Michigan Territory then.

Denominational changes added to the sense of a break in 1832. The new Presiding Elder was James Gilruth. He was to stay here for four years. Also the General Conference of 1832 placed southwestern Michigan under the Indiana Conference until 1840. This was done for greater convenience of travel in reaching the people there. But it delayed a little the coincidence of the State and a Methodist Episcopal Conference of Michigan. Pioneering continued farther north but rapid changes were impending for southern Michigan and Methodism in the ensuing eight years.

[20] Lorenzo Davis, "Recollections of early ministers of Washtenaw County." *Mich. Pioneer Coll.*, IX, 160-161.

CHAPTER V

THREE YEARS AND THREE LEADERS: GILRUTH, ROBE, AND CLARK

1832 – 1835

Michigan and its Methodist Episcopal Church joined the main stream of American development in the mid-1830's. Michigan Territory became a State in January 1837. Its population of 31,640 in 1830 had grown to 212,267 by 1840. Detroit had increased from 2,222 to 9,192. While the city was having a little over a fourfold growth, the State had nearly a sevenfold increase. This may be one reason that the City Methodist Church did not grow as fast as many of the village churches, such as Tecumseh and Ann Arbor.

That Detroit District of the Ohio Annual Conference with sixteen ministers and 1678 members in 1832 had by 1840 become a Michigan Methodist Episcopal Annual Conference with six Districts employing seventy-five ministers for 11,523 members. The almost sevenfold increase in the membership of the Church closely followed the rate of Michigan population growth. Unfortunately the number of Methodist ministers serving there increased only between four and fivefold. Every year the Conference *Minutes* of this period have a few appointments marked "to be supplied." Presiding Elders hoped to fill such vacancies with local preachers or Class leaders.

1832 was the year that Andrew Jackson was re-elected to the presidency over Henry Clay. National issues were concerned with the protective tariff and the re-charter of the Bank of the United States. The nullification crisis in South Carolina was of some interest to a few Michigan Methodists. The Presiding Elder of Detroit District, James Gilruth, carefully followed the question in the newspapers and noted developments in his diary. But the incident was too remote for the ordinary citizen to be much concerned about it.

The wild speculation in western lands, the Specie Circular, the deposit of surplus U.S. Funds in favored State banks and the hard times after the Panic of 1837 all had a direct effect on Michigan. Methodists were just as short of ready cash as every one else. This delayed building the first Methodist churches and parsonages.

National Methodist missionary funds were a great help here for years. Presiding Elder Gilruth was always detained an extra day at the Ohio Annual Conferences to get "drafts and money for the Mission purposes in Detroit District." Part of his salary came from this source. Five appointments in his District were missions and southwestern Michigan was part of a missionary District in the Indiana Annual Conference. The New York Annual Conference also in 1832 sent John Clark as missionary to the Indians at the Soo and Green Bay.

During the years from 1832 through 1835, Methodist ministers were sent to Michigan by three Annual Conferences: Ohio, Indiana, and New York. Yet Presiding Elder Gilruth was a unifying influence throughout his District. The years from 1835 through 1840 saw the birth of a Michigan Annual Conference, its partial supervision by the Ohio and Indiana Annual Conferences and its eventual independence. Statehood and the rapid growth in church membership led the General Conference of 1840 to the decision that in the future the Michigan Annual Conference should include only the State of Michigan.

James Gilruth

Membership statistics or lists of appointments with the names of ministers holding them in successive years give little idea of the human hardships and problems involved in establishing Methodism in a newly settled area. James Gilruth was the first Methodist minister to serve four years as a Presiding Elder in Michigan. He also kept a detailed daily diary during his years here.[1] Would that more Methodist ministers had done likewise!

James Gilruth was born in 1793, grew up in the backwoods of Ohio,

---

[1] W. W. Sweet printed one year, 1834-1835, of Gilruth's diary in his *Religion on the American Frontier*, Volume IV. The descendants of James Gilruth had the record of the rest of his Michigan years photostated for the use of the author. They are invaluable for this time in the history of Michigan Methodism and the author is grateful for their use. Page references to Gilruth's diaries do not help in location of a particular item. When Gilruth finished one small notebook, he began on another numbering it in continuity with the last previous page. None of them coincide with the year by the calendar. Only the full date of the entry is of any help in finding it again. Article on Gilruth by R. A. Brunger in *Mich. Ch. Ad.* May 9, 1963, XC, #19, 4-5, 19.

and was converted in 1819. The same year he was received on trial in the Ohio Annual Conference. On September 25, 1832, he wrote in his diary, "I said when Thou didst set my soul at liberty 'Yes Lord I will preach even if Thou would send me to hell to preach to devils only have mercy on my soul. I cannot draw back.'"

He was large physically being over six feet in height and weighing two hundred pounds. Once a small preacher, with whom Gilruth was assigned to sleep at the Ohio Annual Conference, was so afraid of being "overlaid" that Gilruth slept on the floor. He noted his extreme disgust with the other minister's "unmanly hang." The new Presiding Elder had the booming ministerial voice, a naturally serious expression, and a strong desire to improve himself by his own study and reading.

He read everything in the way of a book that came his way, from Rollins' *Ancient History* and Plutarch's *Lives* to the poetry of Homer and Burns. He borrowed the apocryphal books of the Bible and bought a booklet containing the Presbyterian confession of faith. He even read a life of Mary Queen of Scots. The *New York Christian Advocate* and the newspapers were always part of his weekly reading. He delighted in "agreeable conversation" with fellow ministers but feared that in friendly argument he might be "too much adicted to positiveness."

Most of his four years in Michigan, he and his family lived in a house in Ann Arbor of which the rent was 75¢ a week. His family consisted of his wife and several daughters. One of them was born in Ann Arbor. He was capable of turning his hand to almost any domestic task. He built a wagon with a cover, kept up a garden, repaired his own and his family's shoes, and gave much time to the care of his horses.

He was a skilled, self-trained physician, prescibing for himself, his wife, his children, and suffering Methodists too. Sometimes he pulled teeth but he was usually paid a small sum for doing that. Treating his own vexatious cough, which had kept him from preaching, he tried turpentine and raisins but felt that he was more relieved by a heavy sweat and sleeping with his feet toward the fire. When his wife was very ill, he bled her and she said she felt some relief. He disapproved of alcoholic remedies but once when he had a bad fall from his horse he was persuaded to take one spoonful of whisky. He then thought it relieved his pain.

Mr. Gilruth had been in Michigan as a soldier in 1814 at Fort Gratiot. Perhaps that was why he was dismayed by the news of his appointment there. On September 24, 1832, he was taken aside by James B. Finley and informed that he would be appointed to the Detroit District. He "felt much opposed." But by the next day he was partially reconciled. He wrote in his diary, "I find then nothing will do but I must be a District man. I regard not the labours for myself but my poor wife and children how will they come out — less at home than on a circuit, O God if it is thus, be it so."

The Rev. Jacob Young, an older minister experienced as a Presiding Elder, took Gilruth to supper that same day. They talked at length about the duties of a Presiding Elder. Gilruth made a careful record of the advice that Young gave him. Among the various items were these:

> Correct your rashness in speech in the pulpit and elsewhere. What faults you find with our discipline keep it to yourself except to some old and well tried preachers. Thinking men will find some faults. Form some simple by-laws to govern the q t. Conference and get them adopted. Read or keep the discipline you will get its spirit.

The preparations Gilruth made for his first journey as Presiding Elder to Michigan were typical of those he made seven times thereafter either from or to Ohio. He always took particular pains with his wagon, renewing worn wheels or putting on a new cover. Food was prepared for meals on the road and inquiries were made about hospitable Methodists along the way.

He was disturbed when it was necessary to stop for the night at some tavern and pay a high price for poor accomodations. It was also against his principles to travel at all on Sundays. He usually preached then in some small town either in the school house or a large barn.

The roads were so bad that he fully expected to have his wagon broken to pieces. On his first trip to Michigan, he got stuck in a mud-hole, had to hire a man to pull the wagon out with his oxen, and as a result made only seven miles that whole day. When he finally got to Ann Arbor and had unpacked his wagon, he noted that it had been "one of the most fatiguing journies I have encountered since I began to move my family from place to place." These Ohio trips averaged in time anywhere from ten days to three weeks.

On his first trip to Michigan, a chance encounter was helpful to the new Presiding Elder. On October 29, 1832, he "fell in with Brother Curtis Godard," his immediate predecessor for three years on the Detroit District. Gilruth felt their meeting was "an agreeable thing and we talked of that country till late."

The very day he arrived in Monroe, Michigan, Mr. Gilruth preached at night. Two days later he left his family in Lodi Plains and rode to Ann Arbor. He found lodging with Dr. Packard and preached again that night. A Methodist "brother" helped him get his wagon and family to Ann Arbor, find a house, and then unload his goods.

The new Presiding Elder immediately began "making preparations to set out on my District." This entry appeared often in his diaries for the next four years. It implied a great deal of work not primarily for himself but rather for his family and horses. Wood was hauled and cut into useable lengths. Sugar and flour in one hundred pound bags must be obtained. A smaller bag of maple sugar was usually included. Hay and oats were perennially needed in large amounts. Horses ran away, went lame, or needed shoeing. Repairs to family footwear might also be necessary. After building a stable and doing other heavy work, Gilruth wrote on December 5, 1832, "Thus have I slaved — not to be burdensome to others; nor waste that designed for better purposes — I am fatigued but of a peaceful mind."

Procedure in exact accord with the terms of the *Discipline* was the prime goal of every Presiding Elder. Many of the Preachers on his District were young, inexperienced, and unfamiliar with the application of Methodist rules to human problems. Every Quarterly Conference must include all Class leaders, trustees, stewards, exhorters, and local preachers. In so new a region, the Presiding Elder might be the only minister there fully ordained and widely experienced.

Sometimes in one weekend, the Presiding Elder preached three or four times, held a business meeting, administered communion, and dealt with appeals from suspended or expelled members. In the intervals of formal meetings, much conversation with the stationed ministers ended in advice, warning, or even the engagement of some local preacher to help the inexperienced man with the sermons. The Presiding Elder often slept in the same bed with the local man who would then talk confidentially with his superior.

Most Presiding Elders quickly laid out a route for covering their territory. This was much needed in Detroit District as it was large and sparsely settled. For three years and three times each year, Gilruth started northeast from Ann Arbor into Oakland and Macomb Counties to hold Quarterly Conferences on Farmington, Mount Clemens, and St. Clair Circuits. Saginaw Mission was so remote that he did not always get there. He then turned south to Detroit and went on to Monroe. On up the River Raisin to Tecumseh and Clinton was his route. If someone did not delay him, he had a day or two at home in Ann Arbor then. Next came the seventy-mile trip to Calhoun Mission. En route he would stop at Dexter, Jackson, Grass Lake, and end at Marshall. An average of two and one half months elapsed between his visits to the various appointments.

Travel via his diary with James Gilruth during the last two months of 1832 is revealing. A school house in the woods on the Farmington Circuit was the scheduled place of his first Quarterly Conference and the time set was Saturday at 1 P.M. "Not a soul was there" but at seven minutes past the time announced, three people came in so Gilruth at once began the service. He usually preached long sermons of one to two hours in length so by the time his sermon was over, he had about twenty in his audience. The planned routine included an evening service and exhortation, communion first thing on Sunday morning, an experimental meeting for an hour, more sermons and exhortations, and finally the taking of a "public collection." Full members generally paid their pledges to the Class leaders. A congregational public collection was not the regular practice then.

The first two Sunday morning events were intended for church members. Often a younger preacher was stationed at the door to allow only Class members with current quarterly tickets to enter for communion. If a woman was dressed in bright colors or wore jewelry, the minister might exclude her. The experimental meeting is believed to have been an hour of personal testimony and prayer by the members. Gilruth was aided on Saturday night and Sunday by Marcus Swift, the Circuit preacher, and by Laban Smith, a local minister. As was usual, the Sunday sermons drew the largest crowds. Being nearby, Gilruth rode home to Ann Arbor on Monday.

The next day he rode to Detroit where he stayed the first night with Jerry Dean and the second with Israel Noble. Gilruth went to Detroit to attend a meeting of the trustees of the local church. He also talked with the Rev. Henry Colclazer, then the stationed minister of the Detroit church, picked up a letter from Bishop Emory, and toured the city. He thought the place had improved enormously, especially in its wharves, in the eighteen years since he had last seen it.

Making two stops to preach on the way, Gilruth rode next to Mount Clemens. On the second night en route, he stayed with Truman Fox of Auburn and soon discovered that Mrs. Fox was not a Methodist. He decided, "She was some tinctured with Calvinism — if God knows one will be damned — he must be damned. I found it useless to reason and consequently directed her to read the Word, obey and believe. She seemed thoughtful but I doubt a deep impression was made."

His second Quarterly Conference, held at Mount Clemens, was much like the first one on the Farmington Circuit, except for the addition of the baptismal service. Two men were immersed and two women were poured. No agreement on the mode of baptism existed then. Gilruth read all the preliminary ritual but, disliking to get the only clothes he had with him wet, a minister named Warren performed the actual baptism. Marcus Swift, Laban Smith, and Bradford Frazee all assisted in the services by prayer, preaching, or exhortation. Gilruth noted they had "a comfortable season."

On the succeeding Monday, the Presiding Elder had a long talk with the Mount Clemens preachers, Leonard Hill and Richard Cheney. He also conferred with Bradford Frazee and paid him his first installment as the Saginaw missionary. Everyone agreed that it was impossible to get through to St. Clair so his planned route could not be followed.

Arriving home, Gilruth preached a man's funeral in a German

settlement near Ann Arbor on November 29, 1832. He observed that "the congregation were mostly Germans and I suppose one half could not understand one word I said. At the grave they sung a hymn in German and I prayed."

In the week he remained at home, he preached to the Ann Arbor Society, completed building a stable, hauled in quantities of horse feed, and mended his shoes. On December 7 he started to Detroit, stopping over 'night with the Rev. Joseph Hickox at his farm on the River Rouge. Jerry Dean was again his host in the city. Gilruth was somewhat displeased with the Detroit Quarterly Conference. The attendance was poor, the members did not follow the *Discipline*, and only one was converted. The Presiding Elder also preached to the colored people of Detroit "in a most plain and familiar manner." He hoped that it had some influence on them.

En route to Monroe the next day, Gilruth fell in with Elijah Pilcher, one of that Circuit's preachers. The two men attended a temperance meeting and then went to the Indian school on the Huron River at Flat Rock. Twenty were present and Gilruth preached on baptism. A day later, the two ministers went on to Monroe by an Indian trail which was swampy and ran through unsettled country. At Monroe Quarterly Conference, Pilcher and E. C. Gavit preached and Gilruth served communion.

The route to Tecumseh and Clinton was the worst ever. Besides Gilruth was "vexed with indefinite directions given me to find a place by the people of this territory." At Clinton for the first time the audience was large. Therefore Gilruth preached at the school house and two other ministers at the hotel. Seven members were received on trial by the Society. On Monday the Presiding Elder rode twenty-two miles to Ann Arbor and spent the evening in again mending his boots.

The seventy-five miles to Calhoun Mission was Gilruth's longest trip anywhere on his District. Both going and returning he stopped at Jackson. Quarterly Conference was held at Marshall where Andrew Dixon was the appointed minister. He was young and inexperienced so the Presiding Elder felt it necessary to "explain and correct" Dixon's sermon. The first round of Quarterly Conferences was completed by meetings at Dexter and Ypsilanti early in January 1833. Attendance was poor at both places. The time of year may have been the cause.

On his second journey around Detroit District, Gilruth went to several places unvisited on his first round. He began at Pontiac where he was much tried by the slow business meeting. Then he accompanied Bradford Frazee to Grumlaw on the Saginaw Mission Circuit. This was the first Quarterly Conference ever held there. Not enough church members were present to allow the celebration of communion and love feast. Gilruth thought it was "a poor dull two day meeting." Frazee decided it was impossible to get through to Saginaw so both of them

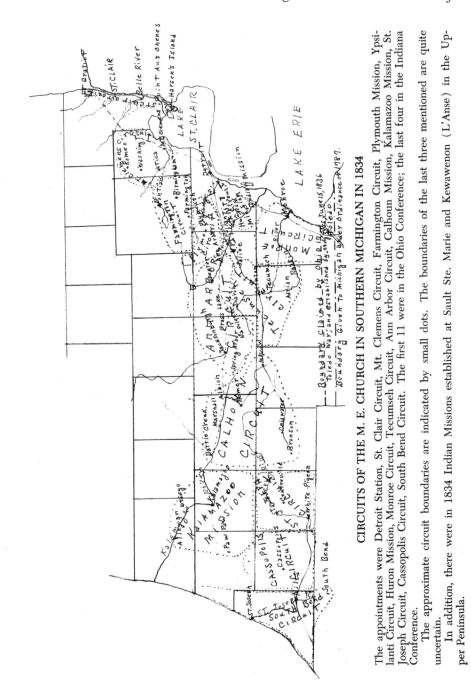

CIRCUITS OF THE M. E. CHURCH IN SOUTHERN MICHIGAN IN 1834

The appointments were Detroit Station, St. Clair Circuit, Mt. Clemens Circuit, Farmington Circuit, Plymouth Mission, Ypsilanti Circuit, Huron Mission, Monroe Circuit, Tecumseh Circuit, Ann Arbor Circuit, Calhoun Mission, Kalamazoo Mission, St. Joseph Circuit, Cassopolis Circuit, South Bend Circuit. The first 11 were in the Ohio Conference; the last four in the Indiana Conference.

The approximate circuit boundaries are indicated by small dots. The boundaries of the last three mentioned are quite uncertain.

In addition, there were in 1834 Indian Missions established at Sault Ste. Marie and Kewawenon (L'Anse) in the Upper Peninsula.

returned to Pontiac. En route Gilruth preached on prayer at a house near the road. He also had an argumentative encounter with some Baptists about "close communion."

After holding the second Quarterly Conference at Mount Clemens, Gilruth started to St. Clair. He hired a guide, borrowed a sleigh and travelled via the frozen Clinton River and Lake St. Clair. They proceeded at five miles an hour. When the horse began breaking through the ice crust, the journey was finished on horseback. The Circuit missionary, Ezekiel S. Gavit, acted as pleased to see his Presiding Elder as if he had met his father. They spent the entire evening going over the affairs of the mission. Gavit was in poor health so Gilruth did all the preaching at Quarterly Conference with a little aid from a Canadian minister named Dean, from the Thames Circuit. At Quarterly Conferences on the border, a Canadian minister was frequently present. With another guide to help him avoid the marshes, the Presiding Elder went on to Detroit.

In addition to holding the second Quarterly Conference there, Gilruth organized a Detroit District Bible, Tract, and Sunday School Society. He conferred one evening with B. F. H. Witherell about "the best plan of building a Meeting House in the Station." During the weekend, February 15-18, 1833, Gilruth preached three times and Colclazer and Elias Pattee each once. The Presiding Elder noted that "Pattee's feelings was some hurt with Brother Colclazer about his not having sufficient liberty to exhort but on talking it over all was healed."

The routine went on. Quarterly Conferences were held at Ypsilanti, Monroe, and Tecumseh. The latter place agreed to hold a camp meeting at Gilruth's next visit. Everything went well at Tecumseh. On March 10, 1833, Gilruth preached "with life and power on following peace and holiness." Nine people were baptized and fifteen joined the Society. The Presiding Elder officiated at all the services including the immersion of five people. About the latter service, he noted, This was indeed cold bathing but both they and I felt well. Two or three of them came out of the water shouting — I spent the P.M. reading and drying my clothes not having any change with me and others not being large enough." The night crowd filled the house to overflowing but Gilruth went to bed and left the Circuit preacher, James Davidson, to conduct the services. Next morning he was pleased to learn that six more had joined the Society.

Things rarely went so smoothly as at Tecumseh. En route to Calhoun Mission, he could not hold a meeting at Jackson due to the prevalence of smallpox there. The Calhoun Mission Quarterly Conference was held at the home of a local preacher named Tibbetts. Only twelve people took communion and the entire congregation did not exceed fifty. Joseph Corbus accompanied Gilruth around this Circuit. The Presiding Elder was disturbed to learn that people in the area generally thought that Andrew Dixon was incompetent as a preacher. After he got back to Ann Arbor, Gilruth wrote to Dixon that he must get a certain local preacher to fill the appointment at Marshall. The Presiding Elder believed Dixon lacked "that solidity of judgment that is requisite to make a Methodist preacher." In the Swartsburgh Society, Gilruth cancelled an exhorter"s license because he had married a couple without any authority to do so.

His travels about Michigan did not give Gilruth a very high opinion of it. On March 17, 1833, he wrote, "Never was I in a country so cheerless in the winter as Michigan, scarcely a bird of any description to be seen and but few animals all is nearly an unanimated land. . . . Spring comes just about a month later than it does in southern Ohio." After holding the Farmington Quarterly Conference in a barn, Gilruth complained that "the place was cold and so was the meeting."

Early spring was the most difficult of all the seasons for travel in Michigan. This was due to the bottomless mud everywhere. On April 23, 1833, Gilruth started to St. Clair by a trail that followed the section line laid out by the first surveyors. Brush, logs, and swamps combined to make it the worst road he had yet seen.

At noon he fed his horse some oats he had carried in a handkerchief and then ate a paper wrapped sweet cake himself. He rattled the paper which frightened his horse so that it bolted and threw him off. He fell on his stomach on a projecting snag and dislocated one finger. His fellow traveller, the postman, finally persuaded him to take a little whisky. The horse was wild and hard to handle for an hour. That night Gilruth noted, "This day's experience has taught me that in racking pain it is a poor time to exercise prayer or praise. Felt much humbled and resigned to the Divine will."

The Presiding Elder preached to twenty people in St. Clair and again talked with E. S. Gavit "on the concerns of the church." Then en route to Detroit, Gilruth had another unpleasant experience with his horse. The road was so bad that he had gotten off to lead his horse when it suddenly sank into the mud up to its belly. In its frantic struggle to get out, the horse threw off the saddlebags and filled one end with muddy water. This accident dirtied all his clothes which he could not get washed until he arrived in Detroit two days later.

None of these happenings kept him from holding the Detroit Quarterly Conference on time nor from preaching with powerful effect on his audience. "One woman was so filled with joy as to constrain her to praise the Lord with a loud voice but for fear of giving offence she ran out of the house." He also had time to talk at length with Mr. Colclazer about "Human Nature"; to call on Robert Abbott, to read the *Christian Advocate*, and to write out a number of Sunday School and Tract Societies forms for constitutions.

When he left Ann Arbor again on May 17, 1833, his wife and child went along to a two day meeting among the Indians at Flat Rock where he was assisted by an Indian exhorter. So small a number of children attended the mission school that he was doubtful its expense was justified. En route they saw huge flocks of pigeons going north and, on the road to Monroe, he drove to the Lake Erie shore and they watched the "tumultuous waves" for some time.

Monroe Quarterly Conference was well attended and very successful. Gilruth, Pilcher, E. C. Gavitt, and William Sullivan all preached during the weekend. They held two prayer meetings and gave communion. The Episcopalians offered the use of their new church building which Gilruth accepted for communion and preaching. They also used the court house. To complete the occasion, the Monroe Circuit stewards paid him his full quarterage allowance. Unfortunately on the way home, his wife was thrown out of the wagon and hit her head. Both were exhausted when they reached home and his wife also had a sore throat. As she had not improved two days later, Gilruth bled her after which she seemed to feel better.

During the summer of 1833, Gilruth held eight Quarterly Conferences of which four were combined with camp meetings. The first one was at Clinton. The Ann Arbor and Saginaw ministers assisted with the services. One man was licensed to preach and another one refused. Of the latter, the Presiding Elder noted in his diary:

> Another was recommended who had been a local preacher in England but who had never read our discipline this appeared to me a case, however good the man, improper to give license to preach until he has first examined our doctrine and discipline the conference being of the same opinion he was not licensed to preach but his license to exhort was renewed.

The camp meeting services had to be held in the tents because the rain was continuous. At night the tent for the preachers leaked and they all got well soaked. Yet the people voted to finish the meetings and everyone stayed through the next Tuesday. Gilruth had contracted a bad cold and cough and the rainy weather did not help his condition.

The next Quarterly Conference was scheduled for Cocoosh Prairie on Calhoun Mission. Gilruth preached several times and even called from house to house both going and returning. He spent one night each with Joseph Corbus, Allen Tibbets and William McCarty, all oldtime Methodists. A minister named Crane, just arrived from the Troy Annual Conference and wishing to travel Calhoun Mission, preached at the Quarterly Conference there. Gilruth was of the opinion that Mr. Crane preached "a plain discourse the greatest merit of which consisted in the correctness of the language." Andrew Dixon also preached much better than the Presiding Elder had expected him to do. But attendance was quite poor and communion was given to three ministers and three church members. Gilruth declared, "A corncrib would hold all the members of this mission." The Presiding Elder was a little low in spirit due to a trying experience with a runaway horse. It had taken five men several hours to find and return the minister's only means of travel.

In the summer of 1833, camp meetings were also held at Ypsilanti, Farmington, and Mount Clemens. The first was conducted during another rainy time, at the second Gilruth lost his voice entirely after speaking on Universalism for two hours. He said he left that subject unfinished. For the first time in Gilruth's Michigan experiences, outside disturbances occurred for two nights in succession in the grove at Farmington. But Gilruth concluded the whole thing did not amount to much more than "some howling around." The camp meeting at Mount Clemens was poorly attended and the work went slowly. Yet at that particular camp meeting and Quarterly Conference, two men were recommended for membership on trial in the Ohio Annual Conference. One of them, Duncan McGregor, was the first man converted to Methodism *in Michigan* who became a travelling minister. Unfortunately his health was poor and he was forced to locate and so leave the church work after only two years of service.

On July 10, 1833, accompanied by his wife and two daughters, Gilruth set out for the St. Clair Mission Quarterly Conference. This was rather different than the awful journey which he had taken there in April. They all went in his wagon to Detroit, stayed all night with Jerry Dean, and then took the steamer to St. Clair. It was an easy and delightful voyage. The work of the Quarterly Conference was divided up between Gilruth, E. S. Gavit, the Circuit preacher, and Mr. Dean, that Canadian minister. Gilruth found time to take his wife over into Canada "so she might have it to say she had been out of the United States."

The family and the minister returned to Detroit by the same steamer and there he held his last Quarterly Conference of the year. The audiences were small, dull, and unresponsive in spite of the best preaching efforts of three ministers: Janes, Gilruth, and Billings. But the thermometer stood at 98° in the shade. Gilruth felt that "the heat tended much to depress and flag the exercise of the mind." On Saturday evening, he and a number of other men went bathing in the Detroit River.

On July 29, 1833, Gilruth and his family left Ann Arbor to attend the Ohio Annual Conference which was to meet in Cincinnati. It was a long, dusty trip during which almost everything went wrong. His double axletree for his team broke, his wife developed a sick headache, and one of his horses had the bots. He sat up most of the night with the horse. They heard cholera was raging in Columbus and avoided the town. Leaving his family with a brother-in-law, Gilruth went on

<hr>

2 Pilcher, *Hist. Prot. Mich.*, pp. 127, 451.

with one horse. He soon met Bishop Roberts and the Rev. Jacob Young so they travelled together "visiting all the way."

Once the Annual Conference began, Gilruth was busy every minute. He copied the Conference Minutes, defended the ministers of the Detroit District, and worked on the next year's appointments. This last was a new experience and he wrote in his diary, "At night I met the bishop and P. Elders in their stationing Council. This was a strange scene to me I had no idea of the pulling and hauling in the stationing business before."

Michigan Territory had increased the membership of the Methodist Episcopal Church by 873 members during the year 1832-1833. Of these about one quarter were due to the efforts of the four ministers sent by the Indiana Annual Conference to that missionary district of southwestern Michigan. All the rest were the product of the labors of Gilruth and the ministers of the Detroit District.[3]

James T. Robe and the Work in Southwestern Michigan

The First Presiding Elder sent from Indiana was James Armstrong. He had the reputation of being "a man of great power in the pulpit." He served two years as Presiding Elder. His labors were probably beyond his strength for he died in 1834. Three ministers served the Michigan portion of Armstrong's District in 1832 and two in 1833. The Circuits were St. Joseph and Kalamazoo Missions. Only one of the Indiana appointees to Michigan, James T. Robe, labored at any length in the churches of this State.

Born in New Jersey in 1807, James Robe came to Indiana in 1830 and joined its Methodist Annual Conference in 1831. He labored that first year on Wayne Circuit. When he learned that his appointment for 1832 was to the Kalamazoo Mission, he began to wonder whether he really was called to the ministry. This Mission included all land north of the St. Joseph River and west of Climax to Lake Michigan. Robe felt that he was being sent to induce him to resign. An older minister told him to go because "the Lord is opening a door in that faroff country for you to be honored and His name magnified."

Robe's first Class had nine members and was on Toland Prairie. The emphasis then was not on the few small villages but rather on the rich prairies south and west of them. Eventually James Robe established twenty-six Classes, to each of whom he preached once in four weeks.

---

[3] All figures of membership in this chapter are based on statistics of growth compiled by Pilcher for the Conference in 1855 in preparation for the division of the State into two Conferences. See Michigan Annual Conference *Minutes* for 1855, p. 41.

James T. Robe (1807-88) was the great pioneer preacher in
southwestern Michigan in the decade of the 1830'3. He died
in Kalamazoo.

Pilcher stated that Robe was the first minister of any denomination to
preach in Kalamazoo. This he did in the log cabin of Titus Bronson,
founder of Kalamazoo. The first Society in Kalamazoo was formed in
the fall of 1833 by Robe's successor, Richard Meek. Presiding Elder
Armstrong and Robe together held the first camp meeting in the southwestern part of Michigan in August, 1833, on Big Prairie Ronde. As in
eastern Michigan, preaching took place in homes, barns, and school
houses.

When Robe was returned here in 1834, the Circuit had been divided
and he preached in fourteen places once in two weeks. Surviving early
records are scanty and occasionally conflicting but the first Methodist

Classes were either established or strengthened by James Robe in Allegan, Climax, Comstock, Galesburg, Kalamazoo, and Schoolcraft.[4]

During the time that southwestern Michigan was part of the Indiana Annual Conference, the individual appointments increased very slowly. In 1832-1833, St. Joseph and Kalamazoo Missions were listed. But in 1834, the District was called Laporte and Cassopolis was added to the charges. Richard Meek was sent there. In 1835, District and the appointments remained the same but all the ministers were new, stayed in Michigan only a few years, and then located or transferred elsewhere. After being listed in 1834 and 1835, Cassopolis was dropped as an appointment for several years. Instead the three appointments from 1836 to 1838, were Niles, Kalamazoo, and St. Joseph. Richard Hargrave was the Presiding Elder from 1834 through 1837. His major efforts were undoubtedly made in Indiana.

John Clark and Indian Work in Upper Michigan

In the same year — 1832 — that Gilruth began work for the Ohio Annual Conference in southeastern Michigan and Robe for the Indiana Annual Conference in southwestern Michigan, John Clark was sent by the New York Annual Conference to labor among the Indians at Sault Ste. Marie, Michigan, and Green Bay, Wisconsin. All three of those pioneer ministers received some help from the national Methodist Missionary Society. But the work in the Upper Peninsula was almost entirely among the Indians whereas that in the Lower Peninsula soon found the needs of the ever-increasing white population so great that Indian missions got only incidental attention. Possibly Indian work in the Upper Peninsula was enlarged by the belief of that first Methodist missionary that Indian converts should at once be trained to minister to their own tribes.

John Clark, of Pilgrim ancestry, was admitted to the New York Annual Conference in 1820, served as a Presiding Elder from 1828 to 1831, and was stationed in New York City the year before he came to do missionary work among the Indians of Michigan and Wisconsin. After four years there, he served three years on the Texas frontier, and then two more terms as a Presiding Elder. Finally as pastor of Clark Street Church in Chicago, he was one of those who influenced Mrs. Eliza Garrett to give the money that founded Garrett Biblical Institute.

Missionary Clark found that the way had been prepared for him in Michigan by a famous Indian preacher named John Sunday or Shah-

---

[4] Pilcher, *Hist. Prot. Mich.*, pp. 255-256, 260-261. MSS histories of the Methodist churches at Galesburg, Schoolcraft, and Kalamazoo are found in the Michigan Annual Conference historical collection at the Albion College Library. See also S. N. Griffith, "Sketch of early Methodist History in Southwest part of Michigan," *Mich. Pioneer Coll.*, II, 158-171.

wundais. His early life had been ignorant, immoral, and drunken. Then in Canada he came under the influence of the Rev. William Case and experienced a complete religious conversion. He developed a gift for preaching to his own people although many whites were influenced too. His familiarity with the Indian languages and religion enabled him to reach large numbers of his own race. Henry Schoolcraft once said that Sunday "produced a great sensation . . . and overthrew the loose fabric of their theology and mythology with a strong hand." Sunday had been preaching at the Soo and winning a few converts for about two years before Clark came.

In June 1833, Clark, together with his wife, their two small children, two women assistants, and a lay general helper, arrived at the Soo and went to work at once. The aid of the Indian chiefs was sought in setting up a mission and a school. A day school, a Sunday School, an Indian Methodist Class, and regular prayer meetings were established. All meetings were in the house where the family and all the workers lived. Four Indians were employed, one as an interpreter and the rest as exhorters. During the winter, two more Classes were started, one of which was among the white soldiers of Fort Brady.

The list of Clark's weekly activities is almost unbelievable. On Sundays he preached at 10:30 A.M. to the town citizens, at 12:30 P.M. to the Indians at the office of the Indian Agent, at 3 to the garrison, and in the evening he held a prayer meeting at the fort. Tuesday evenings he taught a Bible class for the army officers and their families, Wednesday evenings he preached to citizens and Indians in the town, Thursdays he taught the private soldiers in a Bible class, and Friday evenings he held prayer meetings in the fort. On Saturdays he did the many chores that went with all pioneer living then.

Extensions of the Indian work were undertaken. One effort succeeded and the others failed. About two hundred and fifty miles from the Soo was an Indian settlement at Kewawenon on Keweenaw Bay off Lake Superior. John Holliday, Indian Agent there, was disturbed by "the degraded, drunken and quarrelsome" condition of the Indians. He asked Sunday to come and start a mission like the one at the Soo. The adults at first were very hostile. A school was started with only two little girls. Interest spread and soon one of the medicine men was converted. A few months later Clark made Kewawenon a branch of the Soo mission and reported a Class of thirty-one members there.

In August 1834, this energetic missionary tried to start a mission on Grand Traverse Bay among five Chippewa villages. He sent three local Indian preachers to start Sunday services and also set up a school. After a mildly successful beginning, the Indians were alienated by certain fur traders connected with a Catholic mission thirty miles away. A similar effort on Saginaw Bay off Lake Huron also failed. On Clark's request, William Case sent three young missionaries there but a cholera scare stopped all public meetings so that the men were forced to return to Canada.

By the end of 1834, two stations had been set up at the Soo. At the fort was a Class of twelve adults and a Sunday School. Two miles down the river was Missionville, the Indian station, with thirteen houses, a school, and a mission building. A Class, a day school, and a Sunday School flourished. Each place also had a temperance society.

Keeping adequate help was a real problem. The women assistants soon went back east. Daniel Chandler, just admitted to the Troy Annual Conference volunteered and Clark sent him to Kewawenon to labor with two Indian assistants.

In June 1835, Clark gave a week to helping Chandler. He went to Kewawenon on purpose to aid. He held services every day, conferred with all the chiefs, gave baptism and communion on the Sunday, and finally officiated at a love feast and preaching services. The Indians were persuaded to give a plot of ground on which to build a mission and a school.

Chandler was reappointed for another year with three Indian assistants. They were also instructed to find out if a mission could be established on the Ontonagon River. During the winter, Clark was pleased to learn from one of Chandler's letters that the mission was flourishing. The Watch Night meeting just held was "crowned with displays of grace."

In 1836, Clark was transferred to the Illinois Annual Conference to head the Chicago District and Chandler became a member of the new Michigan Annual Conference with appointment to the Soo and Kewawenon. Easterners had begun these remote Indian missions but Michigan soon furnished her own ministerial leadership there.[5]

Continued Effort and Increased Growth
1833 – 1835

But after all, the major, continuous penetration of Michigan by Methodism came through the southeastern part of the Territory. Therefore the preachers sent there by the Ohio Annual Conference were of most importance. In 1833, the Presiding Elder, the number of appointments and ministers sent thereto were the same as in 1832. Of the sixteen ministers under Gilruth's supervision, four were new to the District.

One change was made in the circuits. Saginaw Mission was dropped

[5] Details of early Methodism in the Upper Peninsula given in a booklet by William C. S. Pellowe, R. A. Brunger, and John Marvin, *History of Methodism in the Upper Peninsula of Michigan,* published by the Detroit Conference Historical Society. W. C. Barclay, *Early American Methodism,* II, 153-159. (Chapter on Indian Missions east of Mississippi River) B. M. Hall, *Life of Rev. John Clark, passim.*

and one called Huron Mission was created. The terrain of the first was so difficult and the number of whites resident there so small that equal effort would show better results elsewhere. The new mission lay along the Huron River. It included an Indian mission at Flat Rock and the region of the old first log church. This was only a temporary arrangement for Huron Mission was placed in Ohio's Maumee District in 1834, in Detroit District in 1835, combined with the charge at Ypsilanti in 1836, then placed with Dearbornville in 1837, and disappeared entirely and finally from the list of appointments in 1838.

The year 1833-1834, was a year of great personal tribulation to James Gilruth. He never got back to Michigan until mid-November due. to the serious illness of his wife, their children, and himself. They all endured high fevers and much digestive disturbance. The winter weather must have been more severe that year because Gilruth frequently noted in his diary that he broke his journeys in order to "call to warm."

His horses were still a trial. At Dexter in January 1834, he was leading his horse to drink when it pranced, kicked him in the leg, knocked him down, and dragged him several feet. Gilruth noted, "I was some hurt." In May 1834, his horse fell suddenly and pitched him over his head into the mud. The Presiding Elder was bruised and dirtied all over. Later the same day the horse mired down clear to his belly, rolled and got up, mired down again, and, in struggling to escape, nearly killed itself on a buried snag. By nighttime Gilruth was tired and sore as well as firmly resolved never to travel by that road again.

His personal tribulations did not keep the Presiding Elder from holding his regular round of Quarterly Conferences at much the same times and places as he had during the previous year. In general, he first travelled northeast, next south, and then west on his District. Repetition of geographical locations gives scarcely any idea of his increasing influence that year of 1833-34.

The influx of population and the work of experienced clergy combined to produce visibly greater effect. Many of the Quarterly Conferences were more largely attended and their participants too were more enthusiastic than ever before. At Monroe in late December, Gilruth was assisted in the preaching by the Circuit preachers: Pilcher and Sprague. The Presiding Elder preached in the morning on "the fruits of the spirit" and in the evening on "putting on the whole armour." Both times he felt that he enjoyed "life and liberty." He especially noted the evening response thus:

> There was a general move and before I was done the people were nearly all on their feet — the cries of penitents and the rejoicing of believers were incessant and strong — the exercise was changed to a prayer meeting. It was a time of great noise so that all most all the town came to see . . . . This has been a good day to my soul — Our meeting

throughout was solemn and impressive but some part, what will be called extravagant perhaps was so but souls were converted and many others roused to seek salvation.

Gilruth counted fifteen who joined as probationers and the Conference *Minutes* for 1834 show an increase of twenty at Monroe.

Quarterly Conference at Lyons Meeting House on Ypsilanti Circuit also drew a crowd. The numbers were so great that the group was divided with Gilruth preaching to half and a local preacher to the rest. When Gilruth met the Ypsilanti Circuit minister, Marcus Swift, in Northville in July 1834, he discussed with him the problems of how and when his Circuit should be divided. Ypsilanti Circuit reported 486 members in 1833 and 645 in 1834. The number was the same in 1835 but this was due to the creation of Plymouth Circuit in 1834. The latter counted 411 members in 1835 after just one year of existence.

Huron Mission also drew large congregations. As a mission having an Indian school at Flat Rock, it received financial aid from the Federal government and also from the national Methodist Missionary Society. It was located in the part of Michigan Territory most accessible to settlers. And its appointed preacher, William H. Brockway, was young, energetic, and zealous. He was twenty years of age and had just .been admitted on trial by the Ohio Annual Conference. He was to become superintendent of all the Indian missions in the Upper Peninsula for ten years. Later he was a trustee and agent of Albion College and also a chaplain in the Civil war. He never superannuated, or retired, but gave fifty-eight years to the active Methodist ministry.[6]
In February 1834, the Huron Mission Quarterly Conference drew so large a crowd that the school house would not hold them all so the meeting was moved to a private house and divided between two rooms with Gilruth standing in the doorway between to preach. Elias Pattee helped with communion and he and Brockway both preached during the weekend.

In May 1834, an even larger Quarterly Conference was held on this same mission. Response to Gilruth's sermon was most vocal, indeed at times his voice was submerged "by the rejoicing of the saints and the crys of penitents." Prayer services were held in several different homes after the main meeting had ended. These were actively participated in by the Indians. They sang hymns and prayed in their own language. Even the Presiding Elder was impressed by the size of the audience. He estimated at least three hundred people were present. This might be thought small in some cities but said Gilruth, "For a place so new as this . . . it was great and is said to be the largest collection of white people ever seen in Huron Township."

[6] Pilcher, *Hist. Prot. Mich.*, pp. 284-285.

By no means all his efforts met such response. In March 1834, Quarterly Conference could not be held on Calhoun Mission because none of its official members were present, except for the Presiding Elder and the Circuit preacher, Thomas Wiley. Several times on St. Clair Mission, Gilruth preached to only "a few souls." After holding Quarterly Conference in Washington Township, Macomb County, he confided to his diary, "My confidence . . . in man is not increased by my acquaintance with professors."

At heart, James Gilruth was a genuine pioneer Circuit rider. He was vexed by demands for a preacher stationed at only one church and even more tried by the introduction of pew rents. By this custom, the best seats in the church went to the members with the most money. In June 1834, he made a note that the Ann Arbor church people "want to have a stationed preacher and not to be connected with a Circuit."

His Detroit visits were not always happy ones. By 1834, the Detroit congregation had built a white frame church at Woodward and Congress streets. Their Presiding Elder had little to do with either the building or its financing. But he was most displeased by their adoption of pew rents as a mode of paying for the new building. In mid-July 1834, he wrote in his diary:

> Found myself under strong temptations to feel unpleasant. I fear the spirit of distinguishing pride is all about this house — it is pewed and the best pews rented, the poor Methodist must sit on the back seats — the poor coloured man I see not where — I am vexed — and were it not that official duty bound me my voice would never be heard within its walls, until the seats were free — What! must I beg a seat in my father's house from one of satan's servants who holds a seat.

The administrative anxieties inherent in his position were increased for Gilruth by the necessity of dealing with several appeals from the results of trials before Quarterly Conferences. The first one took place in January 1834 on Tecumseh Circuit. The Circuit preacher, Bradford Frazee, had expelled a member and the man appealed the minister's action to the Quarterly Conference but it only confirmed his expulsion. These early church trial records never are very enlightening about the exact nature of the charges.

Even the Presiding Elder himself wished later that he had kept fuller notes of the exact proceedings. This may have been because he himself was involved in one trial. A Class steward on the Mount Clemens Circuit accused Gilruth of "acting from Masonic principles so much so as to exert an unrighteous influence in the quarterly conferences." Nothing came of this except a formal reproof of the man by his own Quarterly Conference. This was the heyday of the Anti-Masonic Party in the United States.

The relations between the Presiding Elder and the ministers of his District were as friendly as possible. He was anxious about a few of the new men. Duncan McGregor he thought was a weakling. On January 8, 1834, he happened to meet McGregor on the Tecumseh Circuit and had a long, plain talk with him about his work and conduct. Gilruth noted this meeting in his diary and concluded the entry, "Poor hypoconderic creature." McGregor located and left the ministry in 1835. But not all were weaklings . After preaching at Donation Chapel on the Farmington Circuit, Gilruth met another new minister named John Kinnear. Of him the Presiding Elder said, "This is an agreeable young man and will make a useful preacher." Kinnear only served in Michigan until 1839 when he transferred to another Annual Conference.

Always on the watch for budding preachers, Gilruth asked a young man, just licensed for the first time by the Warren Quarterly Conference, to preach that evening. Unfortunately "he took his text conmmenced and became confounded." Gilruth immediately went into the pulpit, took the same text, and then labored hard with it. Afterwards the Circuit preacher, Leonard Hill, exhorted for quite a time. The results of all this, if any, were not recorded.

Toward the end of the Conference year, Gilruth was distressed to discover that dissatisfaction with Bradford Frazee existed in several places on Tecumseh Circuit. After most careful consideration, the Presiding Elder decided that Frazee was "an excellent preacher and a good disciplinarian but in the manner of exercising Discipline he is blamed with harshness." This minister was transferred to the Kentucky Annual Conference at the end of the year. Perhaps Gilruth helped bring about the change.

June was often the month when young ministers got married, just before they went to the Annual Conference session. On June 2, 1834, Gilruth married the Monroe junior preacher, William Sprague, to Jemiah Hall. On June 22, 1834, he married the junior minister, on Mount Clemens Circuit, William Sullivan, to Harriet Bennet. Gilruth had very positive ideas on the propriety required for a Methodist wedding. He said the Sullivan-Bennet marriage was "done in a sober and christian like manner free from all pomp and parade."

On February 24, 1835, Gilruth married Henry Colclazer and Aseneth True at Ann Arbor. After recording this wedding in his diary, Gilruth commented:

> Their deportment on the occasion was calm and dignified — after the ceremony was over a supper in hand was served round — a certain Mrs.
> - - - requested me to be seated by the bride to which I pled an excuse —
> That I wished not to conform to the vain ceremonies of this world.

The Ohio Annual Conference session was set for August 20, 1834, in Circleville. Late in July Gilruth arranged to travel with Samuel

Bibbins, who was going to be ordained. They made a double yoke so that both their horses might be harnessed to Gilruth's wagon. His family remained in Ann Arbor that year. After a leisurely journey, which included some preaching, a call on Gilruth's married daughter, and bathing in the Maumee River, the two men arrived in Circleville the day Conference began.

The session lasted nine days. Gilruth considered it was one of "the longest and most laborious Conferences" he had ever attended. This may have been due to the fact that Bishop Soule was taken very sick midway and the Presiding Elders had to finish making up the appointments. New Circuits were being laid out. Three young men previously on trial were dropped. Various new committees were created. One of them was to find out whether all meeting houses and parsonages were built and occupied in accord with the *Discipline.*

The Presiding Bishop was deeply concerned over "the extensive increase of Methodism and the necessity of keeping up the spirit of religion." Taking all the required collections was just as important as preaching or meeting a Class said the Bishop. He concluded, "I pray you in the name of God not to let the institutions of Methodism go down in your hands."

During Conference, Gilruth made a private call on Bishop Soule. He was immediately asked to help prepare the parchments of ordination for the eight new elders just elected. Those appealed cases in his Quarterly Conferences must have been on Gilruth's mind. He took advantage of the opportunity to ask about certain legal technicalities that had bothered him. Later he wrote in his diary, "Musing on the various conversasions (*sic*) I had with the Bishop and David Young on the powers and nature of our government O how monarkal (*sic*) their views."

As the Conference closed, Gilruth learned that cholera had broken out in the towns on Lake Erie. This news alarmed him and he hurried home as fast as possible. Near Monroe he encountered a minister named Brockway who informed him that "cholera and other sickness were raging at Ann Arbor." The Presiding Elder hurried on ahead on the other ministers and found his family all in good health. But he himself took to his bed with a high fever the very next day after a morning spent in visiting and praying with the sick. His immediate remedy was twenty grains of calomel. Although too sick to travel, Gilruth still was able to copy the journal of the recent Ohio Annual Conference session amounting to twenty-six pages in his diary.

Instead of the sixteen ministers in 1833 on Detroit District, Gilruth had thirteen placed in nine appointments in 1834. Huron Mission and Monroe were under Maumee District. A new Circuit called Plymouth Mission was created. Neither Tecumseh nor Mount Clemens received a second minister as they had in 1833.

Only three new ministers came to Michigan that year and none of them stayed very long. Hiram Geering transferred in 1837 and F. A. Seaborn was expelled that same year. Lorenzo Davis served ten years and then located. One sign of a shortage of ministerial help was the phrase "to be supplied" on the Conference list of charges and their appointments. The words appeared twice on the Detroit District list for 1834-1835. As already noted, finding local preachers to fill such vacancies was the duty of the Presiding Elder.

Gilruth's Part in Starting a Methodist Seminary

Presiding Elder Gilruth's third year on Detroit District, had increased responsibilities connected with starting a Methodist seminary of learning. The problem had been on his mind for some time. On March 27, 1833, he noted in his diary, "Spent the evening with Dr. Packard and Brother Thompson till 10 talking of measures and means in relation to establishing a Methodist seminary in Michigan." By resolution the Ohio Annual Conference of 1833 had made the matter his direct responsibility. The matter had been twice discussed during the week of the session. Finally the Presiding Elder and all preachers on any station or circuit in Michigan were appointed to find out if it was practical to set up a seminary in that territory. Specific authorization was given to receive offers of land from "the inhabitants of any place who may desire to have said seminary located among them."

This resolution brought Gilruth a good deal of extra work. On February 25, 1834, he "spent the morning in Conversasion (*sic*) respecting our contemplated college." This talk was with Marcus Swift. On March 20, 1834, Gilruth spent the evening at Dr. Packard's home in talking again about a seminary. A day or two later, Bradford Frazee rode with Gilruth to Spring Arbor to "view the place as a location for a seminary." He visited with a Mr. Smith, one of those who had offered land for the school. Next day Gilruth inspected the suggested site with great care. He thought it "moderately pleasant."

After holding the Calhoun Mission Quarterly Conference, he returned and had dinner with several other men. After which "during a steady shower of rain," they all visited the lands offered for a seminary. This trip was on March 31 and on April 5, 1834, he went to Sandstone or Berrien Village to see a Mr. Mather who had offered a quarter section of land for the college.

On June 9, 1834, he again had a long talk with Dr. Packard about the seminary plans. On June 18, 1834, still another site on the north bend of the River Raisin was examined. Gilruth did not think this plot was central enough in location for a school intended for the use of the entire Territory.

On August 29, 1834, the committee reported to the Ohio Annual Conference that it favored the site at Spring Arbor. The same committee was continued with more work assigned it. Trustees must be nominated, a territorial charter obtained like those for the Methodist seminaries in the other States, and last but not least subscriptions must be taken in order to build and endow the school.

On September 23, 1834, Gilruth sent notices to all the ministers on his District to meet at Ypsilanti on October 24, for the purpose of making plans for getting the charter. On October 17, he spent all day going from one lawyer's office to another. He was seeking a college charter from which he might make a tentative draft of one for the Spring Arbor seminary. He lamented in his diary, "I was by no means as successful as I could wish. I have my fears I shall have too much of this business on my hands."

Preparation helped though when that meeting on October 24 took place, Gilruth, Colclazer, and Crain were appointed to draft a bill and petition to the legislature. This having all been done in advance, such papers were presented immediately for consideration. The plan was for a self-perpetuating board of twenty-one trustees for the institution. Gilruth noted that the plan was amended "to secure that ⅔ of the trustees be members of the Methodist Episcopal Church and then adopted — of this I have my doubts — But it is the policy of Methodist preachers to have full control or not have anything to do with such matter."[7]

On December 20, 1834, Colclazer brought a draft of the proposed seminary charter to Gilruth for his approval. Not until March 19-20, 1835, was the charter passed by the Territorial Legislature at Detroit. Gilruth was present both days and lobbied directly for the charter. First he saw the chairman and his committee members, who immediately reported the bill back to the House exactly as he wished it. Gilruth noted that he himself spent the entire day of March 19 either in the Council room or visiting the individual members of the body. In Committee of the Whole, the House seemed to hesitate a little. So Gilruth suggested one small change which immediately procured the passage of the entire bill with no trouble. The Preamble of the charter began with the words "Whereas the Ohio Annual Conference." Gilruth simply asked that the word *Ohio* be struck out of the charter. He explained the result in his diary:

> This took as I expected . . . . The high feeling . . . against Ohio for her asserting her authority over a gore of land the right to which is in dispute between that State and this Territory hindered us . . . military preparations are making on both sides . . . O the madness and folly of

[7] This portion of the diary on the seminary is printed in part of the year 1834-35 selected by W. W. Sweet for inclusion in his *Religion on the American Frontier,* IV, 391-392, 395.

wicked men!! These movements will not settle the matter supposing the parties should shed the blood of thousands.

The seminary had its charter but nothing more. The matter dragged on for several years with no visible results. In efforts made in May and again in June, 1835, Gilruth could not even get a quorum of the trustees to come together at Spring Arbor. In 1852, Elijah Pilcher, one of those concerned in the enterprise, explained the delay without naming those immediately involved. He said in part:

> Various efforts were made to secure the erection of buildings and the establishment of the school without success . . . . The original projectors became much discouraged, . . . on account of the difficulties thrown in the way by some of the professed friends of the object.[8]

Closing Gilruth's Third Year on Detroit District

Between the tasks connected with starting a seminary in Michigan, Presiding Elder Gilruth strictly kept up his daily duties required by the *Discipline.* He preached often, held the Quarterly Conferences regularly and, on three occasions, met with a Class and made the closest investigation of its usual practices. In each Class so examined, he dropped one or two members, in which he felt "justified from the State of things." One Sunday in Detroit, he fasted all day and preached three times. Afterwards he was fearful that he might have spoken with "too much point and plainness to sit well on carnal professors."

His first mention in his diary of a visit to Dearbornville was on January 10, 1835. He went there to hold Quarterly Conference and was aided in so doing by ministers named Church, Sayre, and Warren. The business meeting, love feast, and also preaching were held in the school house. The communion he noted was taken by "a respectable number of communicants."

Even his night's lodging might involve more work. On January 11, 1835, such a case arose. "But I being solicitated to put up with a Mr. Putnam (inn-keeper hard by) whose wife found peace at this quarterly meeting I consented and spent the evening till past 11 Discoursing and exhorting them on the things of God." Homely errands sometimes led to religious arguments. Going to get his new boots in Ann Arbor, he got into argument on "disinterested benevolence." The idea was that of any man's eternal damnation would save the world then he ought to be willing so to suffer. Gilruth called this idea "a mean delusion — a piece of Romish supperioragation (*sic*)."

A special anxiety in the early part of 1835 was the city church in Detroit. Gilruth wanted the members to give up their annual pew

[8] Quoted by Willis F. Dunbar in his *The Michigan Record in Higher Education,* p. 40.

rentals. He felt that they must strive not to obey the ideas of worldly and carnal men. On February 15, he spent the evening with B. F. H. Witherell, urging him to have all seats in the new Detroit Church "made free by Deed and that the Deed be made according to the form of Methodist Discipline."

On March 18, Gilruth stayed all night with Robert Abbott at his home "a little below the city." They talked all evening about the Detroit Church and the Presiding Elder was very angry when he learned that use of the bass viol had been introduced in the Sunday services. He declared that he would stop the use of any musical instruments "or brake (*sic*) down in attempting it."

Sixty years later, Thomas W. Palmer said of this early church:

> It was a bare, cheerless building inside, heated by stoves and pipes running the whole length of the auditorium. Here the music was by a volunteer choir, with no musical instrument for many years, when Mr. John Owen . . . accompanied the choir on his flute. It is doubtful whether anyone less influential than Mr. Owen could have effected the innovation. Afterwards, a bass viol, or . . . a cello, was added and thenceforward musical progress was made.[9]

Yet so conservative a Presiding Elder religiously was also a strong anti-slavery man. He attended lectures by abolitionists, read their pamphlets, and got into warm arguments on the subject. He thought African colonization of the slaves was utterly impractical and that the abolitionists would never be able to destroy slavery by political means. Their organizations for that purpose were all within States where slavery was already illegal. Marcus Swift and Luther Whitney were both abolitionists and young Methodist ministers under Gilruth's supervision. Many years later, they declared that they would have lost their employment entirely if Gilruth had not sympathized with their views and protected them just as far as he possibly could.

As his third year on Detroit District drew to a close, Gilruth often noted in his diary, after either camp meetings or Quarterly Conferences, "a general move in the congregation" or "a considerable number joined society." A joint camp meeting was held by the Ann Arbor, Tecumseh, and Ypsilanti Circuits. Many people attended on Sunday, no rowdyism occurred, and between forty and fifty were converted. Gilruth held that "This meeting will tell in eternity."

On July 14, 1835, the Presiding Elder went by appointment to preach and baptize at a place on the north branch of the Clinton River. He was quite surprised at the large number present "considering the newness of the settlement." He baptized three men and two women by immersion. Afterward he observed, "It was a solemn and impressive time."

[9] *Mich. Pioneer Coll.*, XXXI, 497-498.

The Ohio Annual Conference met in Springfield on August 19, 1835. Gilruth was much worried at that Conference by illness among the ministers and his relatives. His family were staying with a relative who had children suffering from the measles. He and his wife had been so very careful to keep their children away from contact with that disease in Michigan. The Rev. William Brockway had the "colera morbus" and was so sick that Gilruth brought the Doctor to see him. The Rev. Elijah Pilcher, with whom Gilruth was rooming, had a very high fever. Gilruth noted his many anxieties in his diary and concluded, "O God be gracious and suffer not thy servant to be hindered in his ministerial duty by this providence."

Michigan Methodism showed a net increase of 1256 members for the Conference year 1834-1835. Such growth demanded administrative adjustments and more ministers than were available. Bishops Andrews and Soule were both present at Conference. Gilruth noted his complete agreement with the statement by Bishop Andrews that "once an Annual Conference was a season of joy, a jubilee but now they are a toil and burden."

The ties of Michigan Methodism with the Ohio Annual Conference were now gradually to be broken. Gilruth's last year here was quite different from the other three. His District was smaller and he was giving much time and effort to the establishment of a model Christian Community. His diary had a prevailing tone of sad farewell quite unlike the entries of the previous years in Michigan. The years from 1832 through 1835 had brought many changes in the Methodist Episcopal Church in Michigan Territory but the next five years would produce even more.

CHAPTER VI

A MICHIGAN METHODIST ANNUAL
CONFERENCE

1835 – 1840

Although the Ohio boundary quarrel delayed admission of Michigan as a State until January 1837, the real work on a constitution and the settlement of boundaries came in 1836. So in the Methodist Episcopal Church, plans for the creation of new Annual Conferences and their Districts were made by the existing Annual Conferences in their autumn meetings the previous year. Then the quadrennial General Conference, meeting in May of the next year, considered the proposed changes via memorials to them and finally approved, rejected, or modified the plans. Any new Conference was organized the next fall.

Preliminary Steps Toward a Michigan Conference

The first official action to create a Michigan Annual Conference was taken by the Ohio Annual Conference at its session of 1835. On August 25, a committee of eleven, one from each District nominated by its Presiding Elder, was chosen "to take into consideration the division of Conference." William Sprague and Elijah Crane were the members with previous Michigan experience.

On August 27, this committee recommended the formation of a Michigan Annual Conference to include besides Michigan the Maumee District in Ohio. The rest of Ohio was to be divided into two Annual Conferences at the National Road. If these three were created then the next Annual Conference sessions should be held in Chillicothe, Mansfield, and Ann Arbor. If only two were made then the meetings should be in the two Ohio towns previously mentioned.

Because all these changes required General Conference approval and communication was very slow, the committee also recommended that the next Annual Conferences should if at all possible be delayed until October 1, 1836. The same day the committee report was adopted, eleven delegates to the General Conference were elected.

The Ohio Annual Conference session of 1835 also created a second District in Michigan. It was to be called Ann Arbor and included the town of Ann Arbor, Tecumseh and Calhoun Mission, all previously part of Detroit District. Monroe was added from the Maumee District to which it had belonged in 1834. The entirely new appointments were Saline, Coldwater Mission, and Grand River Mission. Henry Colclazer was made Presiding Elder of the new District. He supervised eleven ministers, six of whom had served in Michigan before and five were entirely new.

Gilruth's reduced Detroit District retained Detroit City, St. Clair, Mount Clemens, Farmington, Ypsilanti, and Plymouth. The last was no longer a mission. Of three remaining missions, only Lapeer was new as Huron Mission was a transfer from Maumee District and Saginaw Mission was last attempted in 1832. Twelve ministers were assigned to the District and only Lapeer Mission was left to be supplied. Only board and travelling expenses were available as pay for the year's work there. No wonder Gilruth was unable to find anyone to supply there. Only four of the Detroit District ministers were new to the region. The Presiding Elder would no longer have to take that long and lonely trek west to Calhoun Mission but he still faced much hard travel to the north and east in going to Saginaw, St. Clair, or Lapeer.

Gilruth's Last Year on Detroit District

Although Ann Arbor was no longer part of his District Gilruth maintained his home there for the one year that remained to him to serve on the Detroit District. Perhaps he still felt needed there. At its first Quarterly Conference, the new Presiding Elder was not present so Gilruth took charge, preached, and handled the business session.

On going to Huron Mission, he found that the appointed minister, a man named Buckles, had not come nor could anything be learned about him. Elias Pattee had come to the rescue and had announced the meeting. So Gilruth put him in charge until the stationed minister should appear. He gave Pattee $5 of the mission money to keep the work going. Pilcher noted that Mr. Buckles came in 1835 and located in 1836 so he was very little help to Michigan Methodism.

Signs of growth were evident as Gilruth proceeded around his District. Often both a school house and a private home were used and an overflow stood outside. In such circumstances, he stood in the doorway or near a window and preached very loud. He did this at Northville, Ann Arbor, Plymouth, and Pontiac. He was pleased at the last place by the "very large and attentive congregation," the public collection of $18, and the very friendly way in which he was entertained. He concluded "that this quarterly meeting has advanced Methodism in this place at least 50%."

Progress in building was also evident. At Mount Clemens he found two men hauling timber to build a Methodist church and he allowed them to use his horse to get out the heavier pieces. At Plymouth he inspected "a new parsonage that Brother Crain is giting (*sic*) erected, the first I believe in the territory." In July 1836, he appointed a board of trustees to build a church in a village called Piety Hill.

His usual tribulations still bothered the Presiding Elder. He suffered from pains in his back and hips. Whenever he baptized people by immersion, he uneasily wondered how it would affect his back. He had one bad experience with the muddy roads in June 1836. It had been unusually rainy, the water was high everywhere, and most of the bridges were floating. At one spot near Plymouth, Gilruth was forced to take off his clothes, wade over with his saddlebags, and then lead his horse across. At the next bridge, he tried with a long stick to determine how deep the water was. The stick broke, he pitched in head first, and, as he wrote later, "I was now in a sad pickle."

The reactions of the congregations were sometimes trying too. Preaching to a large and responsive gathering at Ten Mile Creek, he was most annoyed by a young man "who busied himself cracking hazel nuts during the sermon. He however was glad to make an apology before the congregation to escape being handled by the law for disturbing the audience during service." At a prayer meeting in Ann Arbor, "some of the brethren became too noisy for edification." At a very large gathering on Plymouth Circuit, when Gilruth was preaching in the doorway, he was much annoyed by the dogs running in and out so finally "Being vexed with one I gave him a violent kick which sent him heels over head out of doors at the movements of whom I had like to have lost my gravity."

Now and then he got involved in religious arguments. He talked several times with "a vain self-conceited universalist." When he spent the night with Elder Twist, a Baptist minister, they discussed "Election and reprobation (he being a strong Calvinist Baptist) but all in a temperate Christian spirit." In June 1836, Gilruth fell in with a Roman Catholic travelling the same road. They had an argument about purgatory. The Catholic said the Protestants had expunged it out of their Bible. Finding the man "ignorant and set," Gilruth finally told him to get a Catholic Bible, read the New Testament, and see if he could find purgatory anywhere in it. One evening in April 1836, several preachers had dinner at a house where the wife was a Methodist but the husband a Presbyterian. He was most determined that "no Methodist preachers should put up at his house. We readily took our horses and retreated."

On April 3, 1836, Gilruth had a long theological argument with two Methodist preachers: William Herr and Lorenzo Davis of Detroit and Farmington respectively. They discussed Watson's *Theological Institutes* and went on to other similar books. The Presiding Elder said:

> I gave my views of how we were to understand the Bible in all matters of faith and practice vis. as it reads and that all Commentaries I had ever seen rather tended to corrupt than clear the mind unless it were when the commentator corrected the translation or gave the history of some custom refered to but not described in the Bible . . . . I finally grew rather warm and expressed my mind farther then I had intended to have done when I commenced.

The frequent illness and early death so common on the frontier occasionally brought a most touching need of Gilruth's services. In March 1836, he baptized a child "ill unto death" and added to his record only the remark "it was a time of feeling." Abel Warren, a local preacher, had a 19-year old daughter in the last stages of consumption. Gilruth said, "She has lately found the Lord and seems to enjoy much peace." At her father's request, the Presiding Elder administered communion to her, all the family, and a few close friends, among them the Luther D. Whitneys of Mount Clemens Circuit. Gilruth felt "it was a refreshing season to all."

A few incidents reveal the attitude to Methodism of those who were not Methodists. On December 1, 1835, Gilruth stopped at an inn near Plymouth only to be annoyed by a loudly swearing traveller and his large and noisy family. Finally the Presiding Elder emphatically told the man to stop. Later he noted:

> The whole family sobered when they found I was a Methodist preacher and one that was not backward to defend the cause of Christ. Never did a charm produce a more sudden effect. All was sober and we conversed freely on religion and other topics. The innkeeper charged me nothing.

After the Quarterly Conference at Romeo on April 16, 1836, held in the Presbyterian Meeting House, one man who had just attended his first love feast told Gilruth that it would be his last "till he was conscious of more fitness."

En route to Quarterly Conference at St. Clair on April 20, 1836, a woman ran out and hailed Gilruth from a new cabin "three miles below Bell River." Finding that she was an "old Methodist" recently settled there, he stayed to dinner and had a long talk with her. When he pointed out that it was a very sparsely settled area and that they could have "no privaleges (*sic*) of schools and meetings here she confidently affirmed that they would have them that the Lord would provide."

The years 1835 and 1836 were years of wild land speculation throughout the middle west. A few Methodist ministers expressed their dislike of the very high prices, the excessive interest rate on loans, and the repeated land sales that really were a form of gambling. In May 1836, Gilruth talked with an Ohio minister who had $6,000 out at 10% interest. He also noted another conversation with a Methodist "Brother" in which they both deplored the spirit of speculation abroad in the United States then.

In 1835, the Rev. James Robe had also noticed the same desire for quick wealth through land sales in southwestern Michigan. Robe wrote to the *Christian Advocate*:

> There is here a mighty contest going on between religion, the world and infidelity. The last named enemy will no doubt fade away before the light of the glorious gospel of Christ. But the contest between the world and Christianity is very doubtful as yet. How often have I thought of the words of the Apostle, while I have been viewing with pain the spirit of speculation that inundates our country and professors of religion have embarked in it very considerably also — "Love not the world nor the things that are in the world."[1]

For several years Gilruth had been deeply interested in establishing a Christian community in which all work and also earnings would be shared in common. For some time he had carried with him a draft constitution for such an ideal group and had discussed it with men who seemed genuinely interested. Now he determined to go ahead with the project. Perhaps his disgust with the speculation he saw around him combined with the end of his four-year term on the District to bring him to the point of action. In June 1836, he met with two Ohio preachers to plan their transition from appointed Methodist travelling Elders to members of a community holding all property in common. He was confident that what they were about to do would find favor "in the eyes of the Lord."[2]

With so great a change in his life impending, Gilruth felt very sad about leaving Ann Arbor and the Detroit District. On July 31, 1836, at the close of his last Quarterly Conference in Detroit, he wrote in his diary:

> Here I have now wound up the regular business of the District over which I have presided for these 4 years past and it is no small satis-

---

[1] Quoted by S. N. Griffiith in his "Sketch of Methodism in southwestern Michigan" in *Michigan Pioneer Coll.*, II, 166.

[2] The ideal community lasted just about one year. The necessary farm work was too heavy a burden on the ministers. Gilruth also found out that one of the other minister members had heavy debts which he had never mentioned. Gilruth returned to the ministry at first in Ohio and later in Iowa.

faction to know that I have not left a case of difficulty unsettled . . . .
When I came to sign the minutes and make out the licenses and sign
them I felt a kind of feeling steal over my soul for a moment . . . like
that felt when we take the parting hand of friends to meet them no
more.

One reform he greatly desired had just been achieved in the Detroit
City Church. All the meetings had been far more crowded than usual.
Gilruth thought that was due to "the seats being now free (done last
week) things look rather more Methodistic."

En route to Ann Arbor, Gilruth did one last errand. He stopped
at the home of the Rev. Elijah Crane on the Plymouth Circuit to leave
a subscription paper for the signature of those who might promise aid
to Spring Arbor Seminary. Then he noted in his diary, "I have now
closed up all my travelling on the District."

Back on June 16, 1836, Gilruth had read some of the Journal of the
General Conference. Before he and his family left Ann Arbor perma-
nently, they must have known of the official creation of the Michigan
Annual Conference.

Among the many committees of the General Conference of 1836
was one on Conference Boundaries. This committee was made up of
one member from each Annual Conference. Its report was adopted by
the General Conference on May 20. The 11th resolution therein formally declared "Michigan Conference shall embrace all that part of the
state of Ohio not included in the Pittsburg, Erie, Ohio and Indiana
Conferences, and all the territory of Michigan except so much as is
included in the Laporte District, Indiana Conference."[3] This arrangement was the common pattern then. Erie and Pittsburg Conferences
included eastern Ohio, the Ohio Conference included part of West
Virginia, and the Indiana Conference took in bits of both Ohio and
Michigan.

More important for the Methodist Episcopal Church at large was
the strong, anti-abolitionist attitude displayed by the General Conference
of 1836. It censured two New England delegates for attending an
abolitionist meeting in Cincinnati. The pastoral address to the Church
at large urged every minister "to refrain from the agitating subject of
abolitionism and from patronizing any of the abolition publications."[4]

The First Session of the Michigan Annual Conference: Organization,
Personnel, Appointments

From September 7 to 15, the Michigan Annual Conference held its
first session at Mansfield, Ohio. Bishop Joshua Soule presided and H. O.

---

[3] General Conference Journals, I, 458, 470 (covers years 1796-1836).
[4] W. W. Sweet, *Meth. Am. Hist.*, pp. 237-238.

Sheldon was Secretary. The citizens of Mansfield opened their homes very generously to the ministers and their wives. All parts of the session were held in the Congregational Meeting House. As every Methodist Annual Conference still is, that first session was opened with hymn singing, scripture reading, prayer, and the roll call. Forty-seven ministers answered to their names and two more came the second day. Local preachers and those on trial were allowed to be spectators. Bishop Soule was anxious for a correct start. The *Minutes* note that "The President addressed Conference in its commencing its business on the importance of beginning on the oldfashioned Methodist plan that we can never mend Wesley . . . exhorting Conference to abide by the book of Discipline."

Parliamentary rules were adopted and standing committees appointed. Among the latter were one on missions, another for examination of ministerial candidates, a third on books, and a fourth on "proposals for establishment of a college under the patronage of this Conference." With the division of Conferences, Ohio subscribers to a Michigan seminary would not be available. Neither should Michigan Methodists be asked to contribute to Augusta College in Kentucky.[5]

The Michigan Annual Conference conducted its examination of the characters of the ministers exactly as John Wesley did. Among the first to be passed were William Brockway and Luther Whitney. But Abraham Buckles was discontinued. Perhaps, due to his failure to appear promptly at his appointment, Gilruth made an unfavorable report on him. Elias Pattee was superannuated, or retired, over his own protest. Twenty-two men were admitted on trial, the same number left on trial, three located or left the ministry, and then finally sixteen deacons and seven travelling elders were ordained.

In a meeting at 7 a.m., the Michigan Annual Conference Missionary Society was established. Special attention was given to Indian missions. Twelve Indian and nine "colored" members were reported. A Conference course of study for ministers was accepted. A refund of $5 was voted to a preacher who had received a counterfeit bill. After some argument about the powers of a Presiding Elder, it was voted that he can "remove a preacher from the charge of a Circuit in the interim of Conference if the good of the work requires it."

The Michigan Annual Conference was established with five Districts: three in Ohio, namely Wooster, Maumee, and Norwalk, then two in Michigan, namely Detroit and Ann Arbor. A total of nineteen appointments in Michigan was divided into ten in Detroit District under Presiding Elder William Herr and nine in Ann Arbor District under Presiding Elder Henry Colclazer. Southwestern Michigan was left part

---

[5] From a photostat of first session *Minutes* of Michigan Annual Conference, 1836, found in Detroit Conference historical collection, Adrian College Library.

of Laporte District in the Indiana Annual Conference. The custom of sending two men to large Circuits as senior and junior preachers still prevailed. Four places in the Detroit District and two in Ann Arbor District were missions. A bit of the money from the national missionary society might be expected there. From having been only a preaching appointment, Romeo was made a station. Ypsilanti and Huron Mission were combined in one charge. New missions were Livingston and Bean Creek.

The Michigan part of Laporte District retained Richard Hargrave as Presiding Elder for his third year and also the same number of appointments, being three. But Cassopolis had been dropped and Niles appeared for the first time. In 1835, three ministers had served these places but in 1836 each appointment received two. Three of the six men had worked in this area before.

The Indian missions in the Upper Peninsula soon would be made a missionary area with its own superintendent sent by the Michigan Annual Conference. Meantime a certain amount of shifting occurred. D. M. Chandler superintended the Soo and also Kewawenon for a year or two, then in 1837 both were added to Detroit District and thence shifted to Ann Arbor District in 1838. It is unlikely that the Presiding Elders of these two Districts gave much attention to such remote missions. Not until William Brockway was sent there as superintendent, to remain for ten years, did the Upper Peninsula begin in 1839 to receive more adequate attention.

The new Presiding Elder of Detroit District, William Herr, had been superintendent the previous year of Livingston, Huron, Saginaw, and Lapeer missions. Gilruth had some acquaintance with Herr, hearing him pray at Dearbornville Quarterly Conference and preach at Pontiac. Twice the two ministers stayed at the same house at night and enjoyed extended conversation. Gilruth noted that he found Herr "a companionable man." Herr remained in Michigan as Presiding Elder only two years and then was transferred out of the Michigan Annual Conference.[6]

Of fourteen men appointed to Detroit District in 1836, eight had been there previously and six were new. Five of the six men were gone from Michigan within a decade. Only three of the men appointed to Detroit District by the first session of the Michigan Annual Conference made their careers in the State. They were William H. Brockway, Larmon Chatfield, and David Burns.

The Rev. Edward Thomson was stationed in the Detroit City Church only from September 1836 to the same time in 1838. But he had a long and varied career elsewhere in Methodism. He was Presi-

---

[6] Herr's appointment to the superintendency of the four missions is not in the official *Minutes* of Ohio Conference. But Gilruth stated in his diary in August 1835 that Herr was so assigned.

Bishop Edward Thomson (1810-70) attended the University of Pennsylvania and served as a doctor. He joined the Ohio Annual Conference in 1832. He served the Detroit station from 1836 to 1838 and had charge of the Norwalk Seminary, 1838 to 1843. He served as editor of the Ladies' Repository; Pres. of Ohio Weslyan University; Editor of the Christian Advocate. He was elected bishop in 1864; the first elected bishop to have served in Michigan.

dent of Norwalk Seminary and later of Ohio Wesleyan. He edited the *Ladies Repository* for two years and the *Christian Advocate* four years. In 1864 he was elected a Bishop and continued in that office until his death in 1870. Pilcher, who knew him, said "he was small in stature but large in intellect," of deep piety, and decided convictions.

Mrs. Anna B. Jameson visited Detroit in the summer of 1837. Of Irish birth, she had come from Toronto by stagecoach and planned to go on to Chicago. On Sunday, she visited all the church services in Detroit "merely as a spectator." After the Roman Catholic mass, she continued to the "Methodist Chapel." There she said:

> I found a small congregation of the lower classes. A very ill-looking man . . . was holding forth in a most whining and lugubrious tone; the poor people around joined in sobs and ejaculations, which soon became howling, raving and crying. In the midst of this woeful assembly I observed a little boy who was grinning furtively, kicking his heels and sliding bits of apple from his pocket into his mouth. Not being able to endure this long with proper seriousness, I left the place.

Mrs. Jameson never mentioned the preacher's name. Was it Edward Thomson or might it have been a local preacher occupying the pulpit while the stationed minister was at a camp meeting or Quarterly Conference elsewhere?[7]

---

[7] Anna B. Jameson, "Winter Studies and Summer Rambles," in *Michigan History Magazine*, VIII, 74-75.
For Pilcher's opinion of Thomson, see his *Hist. Prot. Mich.*, pp. 189-190.

On the Ann Arbor District, Henry Colclazer was Presiding Elder for the second year. He came to Michigan in 1830 and after three years in the Detroit City Church served two years in the Ann Arbor one. He was a very able man, who aided Methodism and education in Michigan for many years. He helped to establish a Methodist college and later was the first librarian of the University of Michigan. In 1836, Colclazer supervised thirteen men on the Ann Arbor District. Nine had worked there previously and four were new. Seven out of the thirteen died, located, transferred to another State, or were expelled within ten years. Besides Colclazer, those whose life work was done in Michigan were James F. Davidson, John Pitezel, and Elijah Crane.

A Few Statistics of Growth

Judging from the figures that Elijah Pilcher collected in 1855, part of the preparation for division into two Conferences in Michigan, most of the preachers in the first year of the Michigan Annual Conference's existence applied themselves to their duties with the Circuit rider's usual zeal. The total increase in members was 439 in the Conference year 1835-1836 but it was 1,033 in 1836-1837. OutState increase was greater than that in and around Detroit. The Ann Arbor District added 510 as compared to Detroit District's 380. St. Clair lost twenty-one members and Mount Clemens dropped from 401 to 123. But Lapeer rose from 186 to 215.

In the Ann Arbor District, Coldwater increased from 259 to 387 members and Saline from 428 to 590. The town of Ann Arbor lost members, going down from 137 to 120 and Monroe dropped from 200 to 180. Changes in the area of particular Circuits or shifts and increases in settlement population may explain the differences in these early statistics.

The growth of the Grand River Mission was different from most of the other Circuits. It was established in 1835 with Osband Monette as the assigned minister. His Circuit ran from the mouth of the Looking Glass River at Portland all the way along the Grand River to Grand Haven. Less than 500 people lived in the village of Grand Rapids then. Monette labored hard and reported twenty-seven members in 1836 where none had been previously. But assignments were still usually only for one year on such frontier circuits. Therefore, Monette was succeeded by Frederick A. Seaborn in 1836.

This preacher had entered the Methodist ministry in 1834 so he must have had two years of experience when assigned to Grand River Mission. But evidently the Conference examination of his character could not have been very thorough. He left the Circuit early in the year "in disgrace." The *Minutes* of the second session of the Michigan Annual Conference reveal that F. A. Seaborn "confessed to adultery, sent his

credentials back and was then expelled." For several months, no religious services of any kind were held by the Methodists on any part
of the Grand River Mission Circuit. Nor were any statistics for that
year reported.

Mrs. Mehitable Stone, then living in Ann Arbor and about to move
to Grand Rapids, knew of this deplorable religious situation there.
She went to her brother-in-law, Henry Colclazer, and asked him to send
a good, strong minister to Grand Rapids. She promised, if such a
one was appointed, to be responsible for his board and care. Assigned
to the Grand River Mission by the Michigan Annual Conference in
1837, the Rev. Orin Mitchell made his headquarters at her house. It
was there in her home that the first Methodist Episcopal Society of
Grand Rapids was organized. Mrs. Stone was one of the five original
members of that group. Mr. Mitchell reported sixty-eight members
there in 1838 and by 1840 there were 151 in the Society.[8]

Fifty years later in looking back on the beginnings of Michigan
Methodism, the then editor of the *Michigan Christian Advocate* thought
that independence was not really attained by Michigan Methodists until
the second session of the Michigan Annual Conference, which met in
Detroit in 1837. He thought that the Ohio Annual Conference was still
dominant in 1836 and Michigan was just an appendage to the larger
organization. Today it looks as if independence only came in 1840
when the State and the Annual Conference at last coincided in their
respective boundaries.[9]

The Second Session of the Michigan Annual Conference:
Personnel, Appointments, Problems

By September 6, 1837 when the Michigan Annual Conference met *in*
Michigan at Detroit, the former Territory was a State and the Methodist
Episcopal Church was holding its second session within the region its
name denoted. Pilcher attended this session and afterwards wrote of it:

> The Conference was well entertained for all denominations opened
> their houses for the purpose, and Methodism received much advantage
> from it. Other denominations were forced, however reluctantly, to culti-
> vate a higher respect for them . . . . They were very favorably im-

[8] For F. A. Seaborn incident see photostat of the Second session Minutes for
1837 of the Michigan Annual Conference to be found in the Detroit Conference
historical collection at the Adrian College library. The story of Mrs. Stone is
found in her obituary headed "A Mother in Israel" in the *Northwestern Christian
Advocate* for Feb. 24, 1864. Vol. XII, 59.

[9] Comment by the editor of *Mich. Ch. Ad.* was in connection with a reprint
of the earliest Conference Minutes believed to have been done in 1887. From a
clipping by some Detroit Conference minister pasted in a scrapbook at a later time.
Adrian College Library in Conference collection.

pressed with the ability and dignity of the body. Though the Conference was composed very largely of young men, they were young men of ability and great promise.[10]

Bishop Robert R. Roberts presided and the Rev. Edward Thomson was secretary. Most of the business meetings were held in the Presbyterian Church on Woodward near Congress Street. Among the Conference committees were one to supply the pulpits and superintend the congregations during the session, another to get a Book Depository established within Michigan, a third to investigate the lack of progress in the Spring Arbor Seminary plans, and a fourth was concerned with Finance.

The last one listed was probably the most important. A uniform system of collecting and recording the offerings of the various congregations was much needed. Such difficulties would not be experienced in providing for aged preachers, their widows and children if only all ministers were vigorous in action on money matters. It was finally resolved that any minister who neglected to take up a Conference decreed collection would be censured and forfeit any claim on the Annual Conference funds. The future seminary was a real problem as no money at all had been collected for it. A committee was appointed to confer

[10] Pilcher, *Hist. Prot. Mich.*, p. 177.

Bishop Robert Richford Roberts (1778-1843) was ordained in 1802 by Bishops Asbury and Coke. He was elected bishop in 1816, the sixth bishop to be elected. He lived on the frontier in southeastern Indiana and served the west. He presided at the first session of the Michigan Annual Conference to be held in Michigan, at Detroit in 1837; he also presided over the Conference at White Pigeon in 1841.

with the Spring Arbor trustees and "ascertain if it is best to prosecute the same and to receive proposals from any other places."

Some attention was given to Sabbath observance. A Presbyterian minister, Mr. Isham, and two laymen asked the Conference to join with the other evangelical denominations to the State in a convention for improving Sunday observance. Joint action of that kind was not cordially entered on by most Methodists then. Neither did the Conference show any desire to work with the agent of the American Sunday School Union. As to violation of the Sabbath, the Conference resolved to discourage it by "precept and example." It was urged that everyone attending a Quarterly Conference remain there until Monday morning.

Ministerial matters took up much time. One man discontinued due to ill health, another was expelled, thirteen were admitted on trial and thirteen deacons were elected. On account of the continuing shortage of ministers, the Presiding Elders were authorized to use any man recommended by any Quarterly Conference even though not admitted on trial to Annual Conference.[11]

The Michigan Annual Conference added another District, named Flint River, to make three in the State. The Flint River District was flung across the state from Lapeer to Grand Rapids, and as far south as Dexter. The Detroit District gave up three appointments to the new District and added the Upper Peninsula also Dearbornville combined with Huron Mission. This was the first listing of Dearborn in the Conference Minutes although it had been a preaching appointment for many years. The Presiding Elder was still William Herr. He had eleven men in nine appointments to supervise. Only three new ministers came to Detroit District and all were gone a year later.

The Ann Arbor District kept its Presiding Elder, Henry Colclazer, for his third year there. The new appointments were Dundee Mission and Adrian. Calhoun Mission disappeared but is thought to be much the same as Marshall was. This District had fifteen men in nine appointments. Of the fifteen only four were new to Michigan and all of them stayed at least seven years.

Under the Indiana Conference in southwestern Michigan the same three appointments were filled by five men, of whom four were new to this State.

The new Flint River District was a makeshift patchwork. It lasted only one year. Three places on it were from Detroit District: Saginaw, Livingston, and Lapeer. One — Grand River — came from Ann Arbor District. Brand new were Flint River Mission, Dexter, Shiawassee, and Clinton Mission. This last meant the county not the village. These

---

11 Facts about second session drawn from photostat of *Minutes* for 1837 in Detroit Conference historical collection, Adrian College library. All these early Minutes are very brief, have occasional mistakes, particularly in figures, and now and then omit items mentioned in other early material about Michigan Methodism.

eight appointments were filled by eight men under supervision of a new Presiding Elder, Samuel Shaw, who stayed in Michigan only one year. Four of the ministers sent to this new District were new in Michigan and three of them transferred elsewhere within ten years. It was tough, pioneer work so perhaps they had some excuse. As always, the Methodist Episcopal Church was attempting to bring in the Church just behind the first settlers.

In the Conference year 1837-1838, total Methodist membership in Michigan increased 1,689 compared with one of 1,033 the previous year. Again there was greater growth outState than in Detroit. Ann Arbor District added 578 members and the new Flint River District 1,277 more. But Detroit District lost eighty-six members. This was due in part to transfers from Detroit to Flint River District. Still Detroit City Church added only four members and Ypsilanti fell from 464 to 190. But Romeo grew from 352 to 545 and isolated St. Clair from 109 to 199 members. In Ann Arbor District the changes are hard to explain. Why should Coldwater fall from 387 to 92? Or Monroe decline from 180 to 112? But the station church at Ann Arbor added sixty-one new members and Spring Arbor grew from 168 to 476. And in the southwestern region, Kalamazoo added 127 new members.

Winter Revivals

The years from 1836 to 1840 were a time of great effort and widespread success in the revivals carried on during the winter months in many Methodist societies. Success in enlarging their membership through such a revival often coincided with the first efforts to build a church. "Protracted Meetings" began in mid-January and might continue as much as eight weeks. Services were held every night in the week except Saturday. The usual order began with hymn singing, then came a prayer, next a long sermon, and finally exhortation by a different preacher. People were invited to come forward and kneel at the "mourner's bench" where ministers or older members would talk and pray with them.

The whole service was far more emotional than many Methodists could accept comfortably nowadays. The entire congregation took an audible part in singing and in the utterance of what might be called holy ejaculations. Cries of Amen, Praise the Lord, Hallelujah, or The Lord Help were frequent. A whole village might become interested in the efforts to convert a hardened sinner. Human beings were expected to be weak and backslide often in those days. So another revival would be needed before long. Such religious meetings were common in most Michigan towns throughout the 19th century.

Pilcher, in his *History of Protestantism in Michigan* mentioned a great many such revivals. He said very successful ones were held in

Ann Arbor, Tecumseh, and Monroe in the winter of 1837-1838. The
Rev. R. R. Richards held nightly meetings at a school house on the
Tecumseh Circuit. Attendance was good, great interest was shown,
and many were converted. Peter Davidson was repeatedly urged to
attend and as often refused. Pilcher said:

> He became so angry at Mr. Richards for holding the meetings that
> he threatened to flog him; but before he got ready to do this, the Spirit
> of God got such a deep hold on him that he felt this was his last chance
> for salvation. He had been a very wicked man. He submitted and was
> very powerfully converted and became a very zealous Christian. It
> seemed as if he could not do too much for Mr. Richards.

The Ann Arbor Church had the most extensive and productive revival
of any that took place in 1837-1838. Pilcher was the local pastor then
and years later he still felt the importance of that time. A joint effort
was made with the Presbyterians and continued for months. Pilcher
kept up the meetings in his own church after the Presbyterians stopped.
Thus he was able "to carry with him a large proportion of the converts."
This one revival gave the Methodist Episcopal Church 118 new members. Whether these all joined the church in Ann Arbor is not clear.
Neither is it made plain whether that number all survived the required
six months of probationary membership.

Pilcher himself thought that the benefit of this particular revival
lay "in the persons converted." He meant the three Collins brothers
— Walter, Isaac, and Judson — all converted at that time. The oldest,
Walter, was really reclaimed and became a missionary among the Indians in Texas. Isaac was long a minister in the Kansas Annual Conference. The youngest, Judson, was fourteen when he too was converted and joined the Ann Arbor Church. In 1847, he became the first
Methodist Episcopal missionary in China.

The Third Session of the Michigan Annual Conference
Ministerial Selection and Training

The last time that the Michigan Annual Conference met outside of the
State was in September 1838, at Tiffin, Ohio. Bishop Waugh presided
and Edward Thomson was again serving as secretary. Sixty-three ministers were listed as present. Much the same committees, as in the first
and second sessions, were appointed. In spite of efforts to stop such
discussion, the abolition of slavery was again a cause of dispute. Then
a resolution was adopted that declared debate about slavery was "preju-
dicial to the interests of the Church." It was said to be the duty of
every member of the Conference to refrain from forming abolition
societies or even attending their meetings. Any preacher who neglected
circulation of official Methodist periodicals to give preference to any
abolition paper, violated his own duty to the Methodist Episcopal

First Train entering Dearborn, in January 1838.

Church. This last was ordered printed in every Methodist paper that circulated in Michigan.

A pleasanter tone is found in another resolution saying:

> It would greatly conduce to the domestic comforts of Methodist preachers if those who have the privilege of occupying the parsonages would occasionally make permanent improvements in the parsonages by setting out useful fruit trees and shrubbery . . . the ministers are urged so to do if it will not be attended with expense or with injury to their ministerial labors.

Much concern was shown about the qualifications and training of new preachers. Quarterly Conferences were urged to be more careful in granting local licenses to preach. Evidence of a minimum knowledge of English and arithmetic must be obtained, preferably by an examination with the Presiding Elder present. The Bishop was asked to draft a better course of reading to be required of those admitted to the Annual Conference on trial. A four year course with annual examinations over the subjects specified for each year was needed. The Church had very few theological seminaries then. Frontier Conferences usually frowned on such theoretical training. They felt that young preachers should study and learn by practice, as much from the examples offered by older ministers as from books.

That Conference of 1838 admitted twenty-eight men on trial, continued twenty-six on trial, ordained eighteen deacons and finally seven travelling elders.

The morals of the ministers concerned Conference too. A resolution, eventually laid on the table, condemned "horse jockeying" or trading them for profit. Such transactions were much too common. No minister could so indulge without the ruin of his ministerial character.

A minister's wife was a touchy subject too. Arthur Elliott was publicly reproved because:

> He had connected himself in matrimony with a lady not possessed of religious character and for his unchristian deportment in neglecting the society of his brethren and associating with those who know not God and in his foolishness of appearance and in neglecting his work on his circuit.[12]

Charges and Their Appointments in 1838-1839

The Michigan Annual Conference still had three Districts but one had been changed in name and area, from Flint River to Marshall. Two out of the State Districts still included some Michigan appointments. To the three previous Michigan appointments in the Laporte District of Indiana had been added Allegan and Berrien Mission. This District had a new Presiding Elder, Aaron Wood, who remained only one year.

Four Michigan appointments had been moved to Ohio's Maumee District. These were Monroe, Palmyra, Dearbornville, and Dundee Mission. John Janes was the Presiding Elder. This same arrangement was continued in 1839.

The Detroit District had a new Presiding Elder, George Smith, who supervised twelve men in eleven appointments. Five of these were new to Michigan and all of them were gone from the work here inside of ten years. New stations and the transfer of old ones had narrowed the Detroit District and stretched it out north and east to Lake Huron. Ypsilanti and Plymouth were put in the Ann Arbor District. A three way division of Flint River District gave Detroit District three more charges. These were Flint River Mission, Lapeer, and Saginaw Mission. The Upper Peninsula work was placed under Ann Arbor District. New stations in Detroit District were Pontiac, Oakland, and Port Huron Mission. The St. Clair Circuit became the Palmer Circuit; St. Clair was called Palmer for a time. This Circuit was being cut down and the emphasis centered around Port Huron.

The Ann Arbor District retained Colclazer as its Presiding Elder for his fourth year. It had thirteen men filling ten appointments. Five of those men were new to Michigan and transferred inside of two or three years. Colclazer must have reworked his plan for District travel

---

[12] From photostat of *Minutes* of third session, Mich. An. Conf., in Detroit An. Conf. historical collection, Adrian College library.

because six of the previous year's ten appointments were no longer part of his District. The removals were Monroe, Dundee, Bean Creek Mission, Coldwater, Marshall, and Spring Arbor. Instead he was newly responsible for seven charges: Ypsilanti, Plymouth, Northville, Livingston, Dexter, and two Upper Peninsula missions.

There is no evidence that Colclazer ever saw the work at the Soo and Kewawenon but perhaps he felt that the man appointed there was quite capable of looking after them. William Brockway had taught an Indian school at Flat Rock when he first came to Michigan in 1833. Colclazer had known Brockway in his days there.

The new Marshall District was much like Flint River District to which it succeeded. Both covered much unsettled terrain with few roads and many swamps. The Flint River District had sprawled across south central Michigan from Lapeer, Flint, and Saginaw to the counties of Livingston, Clinton, and Shiawassee. A dip south took in Dexter and one northwest the Grand River Mission. Now the Head of the District was at Marshall with stations southeast at Coldwater, Jonesville, and Spring Arbor. Then the Clinton, Ingham, and Shiawassee Circuits lay north of Spring Arbor. Finally Lyons and Grand Rapids were due west of Clinton County and its mission. This was a region with more roads and seems a bit more manageable area for a Presiding Elder to travel than was Flint River District. Only three of the previous charges were kept in Marshall District. They were Clinton, Shiawassee, and Grand Rapids. Three were transferred from the Ann Arbor District and three were entirely new. These last were Lyons, Jonesville, and Ingham Mission.

The ministers who were to work on this new District had Elijah Pilcher as their Presiding Elder. George Smith, just appointed to Detroit District was the only one who matched Pilcher's term of service. Each man served six terms in five Districts of Michigan, giving twenty-two years apiece to the Presiding Eldership. Today's District Superintendents are usually older ministers with long terms of service. Pilcher was twenty-eight in 1838 while Colclazer and Smith were each twenty-nine. Only a vigorous, young man could cope with the kind and length of travel required of any Presiding Elder then.

Just as he had done on his first charge in Michigan, Presiding Elder Pilcher widened the trails and drew settlers after him as he went his rounds. Between Marshall and Grand Rapids or Lyons, no settlements existed. Pilcher was the trail blazer between the Territorial Road and Grand Rapids. The religious result was the establishment of the Eaton Circuit in 1840.

Working with Pilcher on the Marshall District were thirteen ministers, of whom four were new to Michigan. By 1844, one of the four had been expelled, one transferred, and two had located. Detroit had only one appointment of two ministers to the same Circuit, Ann Arbor had three and the Marshall District had four. Perhaps it was felt that the new area needed more effort.

A comparison of the statistical reports of 1838 and 1839 shows a small loss in membership in both Detroit and Ann Arbor Districts, the first was down twelve and the second sixteen. Marshall District, for which no exact basis of comparison with the previous divisions exists, had 2,322 members in 1839. Five of the appointments on this new District, which had reported earlier, showed a combined increase of 739. Grand Rapids, made from the former Grand River Mission, declined from sixty-eight to fifty-five but probably this was due to a cut in the size of the Circuit. Detroit City remained a static church but Romeo, with two ministers on the Circuit, rose from 545 to 764 members. Mount Clemens gained eighty-three. Ann Arbor and Ypsilanti each lost about fifty members but Adrian gained ten and Plymouth ninety-six.

More Revivals

Winter revivals and summer camp meetings continued much as they had earlier. Pilcher noted four outstanding revivals in 1838-1839. James Davidson led "a very gracious revival" by which 319 members were added to the Coldwater Methodist Church. James Shaw and R. R. Richards held a series of meetings at Romeo. Interest and opposition were both aroused so the net result was 219 more Church members, the greatest gain on the entire Detroit District that year. One husband was so opposed to his wife's conversion at Romeo that he publicly threatened to horsewhip the preacher. But Mr. Richards calmly presented "the claims of the Gospel" to him and brought both husband and wife into the membership of the Methodist Church. In the first two months of 1839, the work at Jackson was strengthened by a revival at Concord, Jackson County, which brought many young people into church membership. This work at Concord and also at Jackson was on a Circuit that came out of Spring Arbor. The fourth strong revival, mentioned by Pilcher, was at Albion in April 1839. From it the Methodist Church there "derived great strength."[13]

Continued Efforts to Start a Seminary

Albion village was platted in 1837 by the Albion Land Company of which Jesse Crowell was the principal agent. It was in the center of Michigan east and west while an important road running through it

---

[13] Pilcher, *Hist. Prot. Mich.*, pp. 217, 274-276, 369, 398.

had been surveyed from Monroe to Marshall. The school planned at Spring Arbor had never gone into operation because it had little money and only 173 acres of land in a location not so desirable as had at first been thought. The trend of settlement was west along the state roads; Spring Arbor was not on one of these.

At the Michigan Annual Conference in 1837 a committee of three ministers — Thomson, Billings, and Wells — had been appointed to investigate the Seminary situation and if possible get it started. These men were also authorized to confer with the trustees about the possibility of relocation of the project.

In 1838, the committee recommended that a new group of six — three ministers and three business men — be appointed "to confirm the present location . . . or to locate the seminary at some other place." If necessary, the six were also to get the charter changed by the Legislature. The Albion Land Company, through Jesse Crowell, gave sixty acres of land for a college site and accompanied their land offer with a large subscription. The committee, the trustees, and the Michigan Annual Conference each in turn accepted the offer.

On April 12, 1839, the Michigan Legislature changed the charter. The school was to be called the Wesleyan Seminary at Albion. The number of trustees was reduced from twenty-one to thirteen. Election of the Principal was taken from the trustees and given to the Michigan Annual Conference. All lands or moneys previously owned were transferred to the new organization.

Another committee of the 1839 session of the Michigan Annual Conference conferred with the Albion Seminary trustees. Having received their report, the Conference then decided that the trustees should employ the Rev. Loring Grant to solicit funds for the seminary buildings. He was a retired preacher from the Genesee Annual Conference, who had recently moved to Albion. The seminary was not able to open for classes until 1843.[14]

Other Aspects of Methodist Growth

The scanty records reveal other beginnings. At Flint, a Sunday School had been organized in 1838 which had a superintendent, four teachers, ten "scholars," and 150 volumes in its library. Flint built a parsonage in 1839 and was planning to start a church. Romeo built a small, frame church in 1839. As soon as the basement was done, services were held there. A board of trustees was also organized to hold title to the new building. The Ypsilanti Church in 1839 started an organi-

---

[14] Pilcher, *Hist. Prot. Mich.,* pp. 383-386. Robert Gildart, *Albion College, 1835-1960,* pp. 22-35.

zation that was still in existence in 1950. It was a women's society "to sew for the poor and needy."[15]

The Fourth Session of the Michigan Annual Conference

The 1839 Conference session was held in the new Ann Arbor church in September. It was finished, dedicated, and Conference was held there all in the same week. The first church was south of the river at Fifth and Ann Streets. The dedication services were scheduled for the afternoon of the first day of Conference. The local choir had made special preparation for this service and expected to be accompanied by a flute and a bass viol. Bishop Joshua Soule was the president of the Conference that year. Presiding Elder Colclazer decided that the Bishop must be warned of the choir plans. Pilcher states that the warning took place on the street as the men were approaching the church. The bishop immediately turned away saying, "Go on, brethren, and dedicate your church. I will have nothing to do with it." The dedicatory sermon was preached by Jonathan Chaplin, the Detroit City minister. Elijah Crane was then the stationed minister in Ann Arbor. Presumably he and Presiding Elder Colclazer dedicated the new building.[16]

In some ways the Annual Conference of 1839 was like its predecessors. Committees were chosen and examination of the characters of the preachers proceeded as usual. Discussion of slavery was still being repressed if possible. By a vote of 75 to 1, the Conference refused to concur in an effort by the New England Conference to tighten the general rule on slavery to prohibit all such trade in human beings. A special committee was appointed to inquire "whether the laws of Michigan are sufficient to secure church property where the trustees are appointed according to Discipline." Plans were laid to set up a Michigan Conference Preachers Aid Society.

Impending changes in conferences and districts were clearly visible. Early in the week, a committee of one from each District was created "to enquire into the expediency of dividing this Conference." It was to confer with the Ohio Annual Conference, recommend new boundaries, and select the places for the next Conference sessions. If changes were made, Marshall and Norwalk were chosen but if nothing was done then the one meeting should be at Norwalk, Ohio. Six men were chosen to examine the candidates next year and so listed that the first three were from Ohio and the last three were Michigan ministers. A quick

---

[15] Lawrence & Potter, History of Court Street Church in Flint; G. Brabb, Centennial History of Romeo M. E. Church, L. Skinner, History of Ypsilanti Church. All these individual church histories are in bound alphabetical files by name of town where church is located in the Detroit Conference historical collection, Adrian College Library. Pilcher, *Hist. Prot. Mich.,* p. 184.

[16] Pilcher, *Hist. Prot. Mich.,* pp. 233-234.

division might then be made if necessary. Five delegates to General Conference were elected. Two were from Michigan, they being Pilcher and Colclazer.

The Indiana Conference and Michigan

The wording of two resolutions, adopted by the Indiana Annual Conference five years apart, indicates some anxiety on its part to be rid of the responsibility for southwestern Michigan some time before the shift was made. Toward the end of the Indiana Conference session of 1834, their delegates to the General Conference were instructed "to *consent* that the northern boundaries of this State shall be the bounds of this Conference." But at the Conference session of 1839, their delegates to the General Conference again impending "were hereby instructed to *use their influence* to make the line dividing the State of Indiana and Michigan the northern boundary of this Conference."[17]

Preparatory to the expected change, that southwestern corner of Michigan was removed from the Laporte District and named the Michigan District of the Indiana Annual Conference, with John Ercanbrack as the Presiding Elder over nine preachers filling eight appointments. Four new charges were also created in 1839: White Pigeon, Edwardsburg, Centreville, and Paw Paw Mission. The changes in 1839 were greater than those in 1840.

After word had been received that the General Conference of 1840 had made the desired change in boundaries, then that same Michigan District of the Indiana Annual Conference became the Kalamazoo District of the Michigan Annual Conference. The same Presiding Elder then was given eleven preachers in nine appointments. Only one new charge was added, that being Prairie Ronde.

Eight ministers on this new Kalamazoo District were the same in 1839 and 1840. Four new men came to the Michigan District in 1839 and three to Kalamazoo District in 1840. Only two of the new men were of outstanding value to Michigan Methodism. James V. Watson became the first editor of the *Northwestern Christian Advocate* in 1852 but he died in 1856, mourned as a great loss. The other was Ransom Richards who was to give many years of service in Michigan.

After the General Conference decisions in 1840, the chairman of the Michigan Annual Conference Board of Stewards put in a claim of $41.80 to the Indiana Annual Conference "for the benefit of those preachers who were struck off together with the Michigan District." The Indiana treasurer was at once authorized to pay the claim. It seems a very modest amount for eleven ministerial pensions.

[17] From MSS record of Indiana Annual Conferences from 1832-1848. Indiana Methodist Archives, Library, De Pauw University. This record has unnumbered pages and hence must be used by dates only. Italics in quotation those of the author.

New Districts, New Charges, 1839-1840

Comparatively considered, Detroit District underwent less upheaval than the southwest and southeast parts of Michigan. George Smith was retained as Presiding Elder in 1839 and 1840. He supervised ten appointments with fifteen ministers in 1839 and in 1840 nine appointments with thirteen preachers. Farmington had been transferred to the Ann Arbor District. Seven ministers worked in this District both years. Six came new to Michigan in 1839 and three in 1840.

Neither were the Ann Arbor District arrangements too different. Presiding Elder Alvan Billings continued in office. Ten appointments in 1839 were nine in 1840 by the subtraction of Adrian and Tecumseh and the addition of Farmington. Fifteen ministers worked under Mr. Billings in 1839 and thirteen in 1840. Eleven of them had served in Michigan previously. The new men included Daniel Jacokes and Larman Chatfield, both of whom gave the rest of their lives to serving Michigan Methodism.

Elijah Pilcher entered upon his third year as Presiding Elder of Marshall District but with several changes in its charges. Spring Arbor was dropped, Jonesville transferred to a new District, and three new Circuits were established. These were Albion, Mapleton, and Eaton Mission. Sixteen ministers in 1839 were fifteen on his District in 1840. Seven places had two preachers in 1839. These were cut to five such in 1840. Pilcher asked in 1839 that two ministers be sent to the Grand Rapids Mission in addition to the same at Lyons. This was also done in 1840. Of fifteen preachers under Pilcher's supervision in 1840, ten had served in Michigan before then. Only David Thomas of the five new men worked in Michigan until he died in 1870. All the rest left within the decade.

The southeast corner of Michigan was changed to a new District just about as southwest Michigan had been. The new District was named Monroe and composed of four appointments from the Maumee District in Ohio, plus three taken away from the Ann Arbor and Marshall Districts. A new Presiding Elder, Elijah Crane, previously a preacher in Ann Arbor and Marshall, was assigned to the new Monroe District. An area receiving the efforts of seven men in four appointments in 1839 had eleven serving seven charges in 1840. Ten of the ministers had worked in Michigan before 1840.

In 1838 William H. Brockway was appointed to the Sault Ste. Marie and Kewaweenon Indian Missions in the Upper Peninsula. In 1839 he reported 65 Indian members and 78 cents raised for Conference Collections! The 1839 appointments were "Indian Mission — W. H. Brockway; Sault Ste. Marie — W. H. Brockway, George King." In 1840 these appointments reported 33 and 43 members. A Mission District was formed in 1840 with Brockway as its superintendent. Five ministers worked with him at the Soo, Kewawenon, and Mackinac. Two of these were Indians, John Kahbeeje (the name is variously spelled) and Peter Marksman.

The General Conference of 1840 decided that the boundaries of Michigan Annual Conference would hereafter coincide with those of the State. Independent of political barriers but not yet rid of geographical handicaps, Michigan Methodism had at last become what its title suggested: The Michigan Annual Conference. It had seventy-five ministers organized in six Districts of which the smallest had three appointments, one had seven, another had ten, and three had nine each. A gain of 2,228 members over the previous year made a total of 11,523 lay members of the Michigan Methodist Episcopal Church in 1840.

The Fifth Session of the Michigan Annual Conference

Meeting at Marshall in the fall of 1840, the Michigan Annual Conference did not display quite the united and enthusiastic spirit that might have been expected of their new geographical situation. The abolitionists, ministerial character, and even where to hold the next session were all subjects of controversy among the ministers.

Until the open split in 1844 between northern and southern Methodists, local and national church officials tried to repress any discussion of slavery. The Michigan Annual Conference attempted to comply with the desire of the bishops that such questions be avoided if at all possible. For some years, known abolitionists did not get the better appointments. The 1839 session of the Michigan Annual Conference refused to ordain Marcus Swift and Samuel Bibbins as travelling elders due to their strong abolitionist views. Both men were widely known and repected in the Farmington-Northville area. The feeling in favor of these men ran so strong that John Pitezel, appointed to Northville in 1839, finally gave church membership letters to some thirty people. He said he "preferred the few in unity to the many in a state of discord." No wonder Northville reported 216 members in 1839 and 130 in 1840.[18]

That 1840 session of Conference gave considerable time and attention in closed sessions to the characters of certain ministers. Some doubt was felt about John Baughman, who had been a zealous worker in Michigan since 1825. It was finally decided to pass him with "a private reproof for absenting himself from his Circuit."

A more serious case was that of John Sayre, accused of trying to seduce the wife of a local preacher on Tecumseh Circuit where he had been the junior preacher. He had been tried by the Quarterly Confer-

[18] From a typed copy of the History of the Northville Methodist Church by Paul Cargo, written for 125th anniversary of the church in 1959. Found in Michigan Historical Collections, Rackham Bldg., University of Michigan, Ann Arbor.

ence on a charge of immorality in October 1839. Detailed testimony had been taken, including that of the woman in question. The Ann Arbor District Presiding Elder and the Conference committee on Sayre considered him guilty. He was already suspended so the Annual Conference expelled him by a vote of 23 to 17. The next day, he returned his credentials as a minister to the Conference secretary.

A class of fourteen were admitted on trial but an elder of the "Free Communion Baptist Church" was not accepted. The Conference felt that they did not have reliable information about his qualifications. He was referred to the Quarterly Conference of the Circuit where he lived for a local preaching license if they considered it proper. Sixteen men remained on trial and twelve deacons plus five elders were ordained. This session even found it difficult to agree on their next place of meeting. A vote between several places was taken and White Pigeon chosen.[19]

Some pioneers felt the shortage of qualified ministers and the consequent lack of religious services very deeply. In the region where Hastings would develop, Alonzo Barnum wanted to do something about the lack of Sunday services. Later he wrote:

> I proposed to my neighbors to come together and I would read a sermon of Wesley's to them and we would spend an hour in worshipping the Lord, who made us. The people seemed very willing and on the Sabbath we met for the first time. I prayed to my heavenly Father that he would open some way that the gospel might be preached to us likewise. The good Lord heard my prayer and sent Brother Daubney to preach to us for the first time. He came forty miles.

Daubney was a local preacher, then living at Gull Prairie. Later the missionary from Eaton County, Isaac Bennett, also preached and then helped them form a Class of twelve members. Barnum was chosen the Class leader.

The Michigan Annual Conference in 1841 created Hastings Mission, a large Circuit, and appointed Daniel Bush to labor there. He travelled a largely unsettled area with not more than ten or twelve buildings. His parsonage was an upper room in a log cabin belonging to one of the Class members. Bush cut his own firewood and reached his room by a ladder. He remembered most vividly his first meeting with Alonzo Barnum when he wrote many years later:

> I introduced myself and when I told him a new mission had been formed and that I was the preacher in charge he raised his hands and eyes to Heaven, great tears rolled down his face and he exclaimed,

[19] *Minutes* of fifth session of Michigan Annual Conference in 1840 bound in Volume I of Mich. Conf. *Minutes*, Detroit Conf. Hist. Coll., Adrian College Library.

"Praise God, my prayers have been heard at last." We both knelt at the roots of the tree and held a prayer meeting. I soon had a regular preaching place in his house.[20]

[20] From History of the Hastings Methodist Episcopal Church by Daniel Striker, written in 1891 for the semi-centennial celebration. Published in *Mich. Pioneer Coll.*, XXII, 565-624. Quotations are from pp. 571, 574.

PART III

THE UNITED STATES, MICHIGAN, AND METHODISM

1840 – 1860

The area of the United States in 1840 – 1,792,223 square miles – was exactly the same as it had been in 1820. But hardly anything else in America remained unchanged. Three more States – Missouri, Arkansas, and Michigan – had entered the Federal union. The population had increased about 75% or from 9,638,453 to 17,069,453. Gainfully employed population in agriculture had declined from 83% in 1820 to 77.5% in 1840.

In the years from 1820 to 1840, the city of Detroit had increased in population just over fourfold but the State of Michigan had achieved a sevenfold growth. The rates of increase began to reverse between 1840 and 1860. Michigan had a population of 212,267 in 1840 which grew to 749,113 in 1860. This was between a three and fourfold increase. The city of Detroit grew fivefold in the same years. It had only 9,192 people in 1840 but reported 45,619 in 1860. This made it the nineteenth city in size in the United States. This fact may partially explain why Methodism enlarged its church work in Detroit at that time.

The first factories were flourishing in the east by 1840 and railroads were reaching Michigan. The Michigan Central Railroad began running trains as far as Jackson in 1841 and next to Kalamazoo in 1846. The land speculation of the mid-1830's had dwindled and many Michigan citizens were poverty stricken in the 1840's. President Jackson's restrictive bank policies did not have their full effect here until then.

All but three of the banks had closed by 1845 and money was very scarce in Michigan.

As to politics, the Whigs and Democrats still clung to the animosities that had divided them in Jackson's day. The Whigs had just elected William Henry Harrison President but he died after one month in office. Tyler was inclined toward Democratic policies. Michigan on the whole was a strongly Democratic State until about 1853.

This was a time when third parties flourished too. The Anti-Masonic Party had some following in Michigan but far more Methodists were attracted by the Liberty Party, an abolition group. Texas had gained independence but had not been admitted to the United States because of northern fear that it would strengthen the pro-slavery forces. Anti-slavery societies flourished in Michigan and Garrison's paper, *The Liberator*, was widely circulated here. During the 1840's the Liberty Party had an official newspaper, *The Signal of Liberty*, published in Ann Arbor. One of its editors had been a Methodist minister. Every year more people felt that slavery was an unadulterated evil that must be stamped out.

Nowhere was this change more evident than in the Methodist Episcopal Church. Schism that had been narrowly averted in 1840 came in 1844. Secessions from membership had already occurred in Michigan. Here the Wesleyans and the Methodist Protestants were to exert an influence far beyond that suggested by their small membership.

In the twenty years preceding the Civil War, Michigan Methodism exhibited all possible stages of development from the primitive Circuit, too vast for any one preacher to reach effectively, to the city appointment where one married minister officiated in one church with rented pews and had aspirations to build a really showy church. He lived in a parsonage too. All this was true of many of the churches in the four southern tiers of Michigan counties.

North of that area, the Circuit riders met all the old hardships of weather, sickness, and long journeys. They still preached to their congregations in school houses and private homes too. The most extreme hardships were those endured by those zealous men who attempted to christianize the Indians in both the Upper and Lower Peninsulas. Total growth in membership was not quite so great nor so consistent as in the 1830's. Indeed, the Methodist church membership in Michigan decreased in the years 1845, 1847, 1849, and 1852.

Yet signs of achievement can be found too. A Methodist seminary at Albion was actually opened. Work among the Indians put Methodist ministers on the ground where they would be the first Protestants to preach to the miners of Ontonagan and Eagle River. More Districts were created. In 1856, the State was divided into two Annual Conferences. Above all, the attitude to slavery changed profoundly. Neutrality or mild hostility to abolitionism became openly expressed hatred of the institution of slavery itself. The Michigan Annual Conference resolutions plainly reveal this changed attitude. The years of dissension and development between 1840 and 1850 must now be examined in detail.

The First Methodist Episcopal Church in Adrian, built in 1838-40. The Michigan Annual Conference met here in 1842 and 1849; The Detroit Annual Conference was organized here in 1856. This Church was superseded by the one on Broad St. in 1864. This first Church later became a Christian Church and was torn down in 1965.

Smith's Chapel near Edwardsburg in southwestern Michigan, was built in 1840, and is typical of the white frame churches built thenceforth through the 19th century in all parts of our state. Services were held regularly in this oldest Michigan Church to the fall of 1966.

Chapter VII

A DECADE OF DISSENSION AND DEVOTION

1840 - 1850

Starting a Methodist Ministerial Career

The recollections of ministers who lived and worked in the 1840's make the period more vivid than any statistics ever can. Fortunately, two men who began their work then have written their reminiscences and then had them published in the *Michigan Pioneer Collections*. Both Stephen C. Woodward and Riley C. Crawford were admitted on trial to the Michigan Annual Conference in 1841.

Woodward, or Woodard as some of the records spell his name, was converted in 1838 and soon felt he was called to preach. But he said, "All the natural elements of my being shrank from the response to such a call. I thought the Lord had undertaken a very difficult task in trying to make . . . a preacher out of such an ignorant diffident boy as I was."

He might never have preached if the Circuit preacher, Duncan Mac-Gregor, had not arranged a place and time for him and then insisted that Woodward must appear. He himself was positive that no one would come to hear him and that he could not talk over five minutes in all. To his utter astonishment, the house was full of people and, after he had announced his text, he was able to talk for one hour. This made him think that he must be "quite a preacher." The next time that MacGregor came around, a license to exhort was issued for Woodward. A few months later, it was exchanged for a license to preach and, in the summer of 1841, he was received on trial by the Michigan Annual Conference in its meeting at White Pigeon.

Woodward was evidently not present for he said that he "did not think he would get in" and so was quite surprised when, in a Detroit newspaper, he saw his name and assignment to Livingston Circuit in the Ann Arbor District. He was to be the junior preacher with Flavel Britain.

The preparations for such work were quickly made. Woodward wrote many years later:

> With a trembling heart, I packed my saddle, bade my friends fare-
> well and started out in the name of the Lord on the great mission of
> my life. I had in my saddlebags all my worldly effects, which consisted
> of a Bible, hymn book, discipline, . . . and a few clothes. As I went
> through Milford and Howell, I was glad I didn't have them on my cir-
> cuit . . . . I then found I did. I dreaded villages, for I thought that
> people in villages knew more than country people did. I have since
> learned I was mistaken.

The work went slowly his first year or two. The Societies had no
churches and were very small in numbers. Woodward's salary his first
year was $37. He mentioned a skeptic and non-church member who,
nevertheless, wanted Woodward to come and preach in a new community "to help get a good class of settlers."

In 1845, Woodward was ordained a Deacon. He could now marry
and baptize people. He was assigned to Mapleton Circuit, a quite new
appointment on Marshall District. He travelled there one hundred miles
on horseback, with less than one dollar in his pocket and entirely among
strangers. At the first house on his Circuit where he stopped, the woman
guessed at once who he was and expressed open disappointment. The
Presiding Elder had promised them "an old man" whom they had agreed
to pay $100. Those were the days when middle-aged to elderly men
of considerable experience were preferred. Woodward was to be the
senior preacher on the Circuit to serve in cooperation with Nathan
Mount, who was admitted to the Michigan Annual Conference in 1842.
Naturally Woodward was offended and so he told the woman:

> The Presiding Elder you said made you that promise knows me.
> I was converted, joined the church, licensed to preach and recom-
> mended to the Conference under his administration and he picked me
> out for this circuit. I did not covet the job of coming up here in the
> woods but I am here and if I live and the Lord favors me with health
> I shall probably stay during the year and the people will have to put up
> with it some way.

His first encounter with his colleague on the Circuit was also vivid
in Woodward's memory. He said:

> I saw a man coming towards me on a large horse with a pair of big
> saddlebags in his saddle. He was poorly clad and looked as though he
> might be a Methodist preacher. I said to myself that is Nathan Mount
> my colleague . . . I soon found he wanted me to go thirty miles with
> him to marry him.

Woodward was paid 25¢ by the bridegroom for the ceremony.

In 1845, Woodward organized a new Circuit around Grand Rapids.
He knew of two established preaching places in the entire area when
he went there. By the end of the Conference year, he had nine preaching places and 120 members to report.

Services were held in all kinds of homes and schools. Occasionally he was much tried by dogs and pigs. But it was his settled policy never to stop preaching. He always boarded round with the members for he received less than $500 in money for seven years of work. As he got hold of books, he studied them thoroughly and then sold them in order to buy more. His clothes were patched until they fell to pieces. When his pants grew thin at the knees, they were often cut off and turned around so that he could get more wear from them.

While serving on Lyons Circuit, Woodward married and set up housekeeping with his bride in Portland. They had no table, bed or chair but they slept on the floor and borrowed bedding and chairs. Woodward declared, looking back over his life, "I never left a charge owing a dollar to any man . . . . I am glad I have been a Methodist preacher."[1]

Riley C. Crawford was the other preacher, admitted to the Michigan Annual Conference in 1841, who wrote his reminiscences. He came the same way that Woodward did, by license of the Quarterly Conference, of the Pontiac Circuit. But he did not suffer quite as much from nervousness as Woodward had. Crawford had preached first in a school house at Bloomfield Center. He said:

> The house was crowded with my friends, who were bent on hearing my first sermon, and we had what we used to call "The Shout of the King" in the camp; but my father used to call it a Methodist powwow. Father was an Episcopalian and did not take any stock in a noisy kind of religion.

Crawford was appointed junior preacher on the Palmer Circuit. This included the region along the St. Clair River and inland some fifteen miles. His preparations for his first Circuit were much like those of Woodward. His father gave him a horse, his uncle loaned him a saddle and bridle, and a local Doctor furnished a pair of saddlebags large enough to hold all his possessions. He had eighteen preaching places, was told he would receive $100 in salary, and have to board around for his "Table Expenses." He fell short about $40 of his salary.

Even so, he got married at the end of his first year but his wife lived at her father's house most of the time. After a couple of years of hardship, Crawford was appointed to the Shiawassee Circuit and they rented the ballroom of an unfinished hotel. It had been lathed but not plastered. He partitioned the room so that half of it could be used for the pastor's study and occasional guest room. The other half had the family bed "and everything else too." Four years later, when he was appointed to Port Huron, he felt he had really arrived. He had a church all alone, a salary of $200, and a stay of two years.

---

[1] Quotations from S. C. Woodward, "Reminiscences of the early Itineracy," *Mich. Pioneer Coll.*, XIV, 553-560.

All his life, Crawford remembered that, when his sister died at sixteen, no religious service was held because "not even the Methodist itinerant had yet found his way to the new settlement." This experience made Crawford very responsive to calls to conduct a funeral and thereby he got into some odd situations. Once he was called to conduct the funeral of a very young child in a private house where the family were all strangers to him. He arrived exactly on time for the service. A small table was set out with a Bible and a hymnal on it. A large crowd had gathered and Crawford first led in the singing of a hymn. After a short prayer, he gave out another hymn and, while the singing continued, took up the Bible to locate his text. When he opened the book out dropped a number of playing cards perhaps as much as a third of a deck. The entire crowd saw them. While the minister was surprised and somewhat embarrassed, he knew that his feelings were nothing to the "keenest mortification" that he saw in the faces of the bereaved parents. He concluded, "I pitied them . . . . I never saw any of them again."[2]

Crawford, like Woodward, gave many years of service to the Michigan Methodist Episcopal Church. Crawford lived on until 1910. He was one of the first retired ministers to live and die in the Clark Home. When he died there he was the oldest Methodist minister in his Conference both in physical age and also in years of service to the Church.

Opening and Financing the Albion Wesleyan Seminary

Loring Grant, that agent employed by the trustees of the planned seminary, had been busy since 1839 raising money for the project. A curious scheme seemed to meet with success then. A subscription of $100 guaranteed free tuition for four years and lesser sums proportionally. Even a "perpetual subscription" was offered. This could be used by any member of a family at any future time. The money secured went to erect the first building and not a penny was left to pay the salaries of the teachers. Before Albion finally cleared herself of this scheme, she endured great financial distress.

On July 6, 1841, a large crowd came to Albion for the ceremonies connected with laying the cornerstone of that first building. The trustees officiated at laying and sealing the cornerstone after which an address was given by Henry W. Taylor of Marshall. The Marshall Brass Band played, what Pilcher called, "Soul Stirring music."

The school opened by stages. On October 27, 1842, a primary school, meeting in a temporary frame building, was opened. The Seminary itself was ready for students in November 1843. The Rev. Charles F. Stockwell was the Principal, aided by five teachers. Some of the first

[2] R. C. Crawford, "Fifty-two years of itinerant life in the Michigan Conference of the M. E. Church," *Michigan Pioneer Coll.*, XXII, 266-281. Also *Ibid.*, IV, 41-53. *Ibid.*, XXXVIII, 686-689.

classes met in the Methodist church. The student body numbered 117 that first winter and was 183 in the succeeding summer term. In 1845, six Indians were enrolled in a separate department. They lived in a long, low building back of the first large three-story building. The aim was to provide missionaries and interpreters for work among the Indians.

The by-laws of Wesleyan Seminary were reprinted in a later class annual. The entire day was regulated by bells: for rising, chapel prayers morning and evening, meals, and classes. Before going to bed at night, a pail of water must be brought to each room. No dirt could be thrown out the windows. Restrictions were numerous. No liquors, tobacco, firearms, nor gunpowder could be kept in the rooms. Students must not visit taverns or groceries. "The sexes are not to visit each other's rooms in any case whatever." Observance of Sunday was particularly strict. Church attendance was required both morning and afternoon and no noisy disturbance was allowed. No student could leave the campus or town without advance permission.

The earliest students remembered raids on a farmer's cornpatch or chicken coops. Entrance to a locked dormitory was then achieved by one student climbing up the lightning rod and quietly letting the others in. The Michigan Central ran on strap iron rails beside the campus and an early wreck there excited all the students. A man named Sabin was the steward. Long afterward, he was remembered for his punishment of disrespectful students. Those whom he thought deserved reproof got no pie with their Sunday dinners.

Pilcher was impressed by the first "exhibition" held in March 1844. He described the occasion thus:

> A grand affair. An exciting occasion. The decorations of the hall, the music, the speaking — everything seemed under the influence of enchantment. It might have been regarded as an indifferent affair in an old country and a long established institution, but it was indeed, a "high day" for this country, which had but so recently been the home of savage beasts and wild Indians.[3]

Revivals, Stationed Ministers, church building

The regular work of the year was earnestly kept up by the churches during the decade about as previously done. Camp meetings in summer and revivals in winter flourished. The curious sect of the Millerites, with their belief that the end of the world was coming in 1843, had some influence on all revivals in the years from 1841 through 1843. The first camp meeting ever held in the Grand River Valley took place in Ionia County in June 1841. Presiding Elder Pilcher and Larman Chatfield were in charge. The numbers in attendance were not so large but

---

[3] Pilcher, *Hist. Prot. Mich.*, pp. 385-387. W. F. Dunbar, *Mich. Record in Higher Education*, pp. 108-109. Robert Gildart, *Albion College*, Chapter III.

the general work in that area was helped by the conversion of "a goodly number of sinners." Adrian and Pontiac both had very successful revivals in 1842-1843. Pilcher said of the meetings in Adrian in the winter and spring of 1842 under the guidance of the Rev. James V. Watson:

> This was remarkable . . . because of the manifestations of Divine power among the people. Many were prostrated and would lie for a long time without the power to move, and when they came to be able to speak, uttered the most joyful expressions. It was not simply the most excitable persons that were affected in this way, but all classes irrespective of age or sex. Many were converted and added to the Church.[4]

The desire of church congregations to have their own minister full time was growing in the 1840's. The Circuit rider's short stay once in three or four weeks was no longer thought sufficient. Sometimes a church became "half a Station." Two ministers were assigned to the same Circuit but arranged their appointments so that they alternated Sundays in a growing church. This gave that congregation .preaching every Sunday.

Kalamazoo had been part of a four-weeks Circuit with Sunday services every two weeks in 1839, it was made a half station in 1840, then head of the District in 1841. This last meant the Presiding Elder resided there and gave some attention to the local church. In 1844, the Kalamazoo charge was made a station at the village. Marshall became a station in 1839, Pontiac in 1842, both Niles and Jackson in 1843, Albion in 1846, and Flint in 1847.

The Michigan Methodists in the 1840's began to build churches in earnest. In 1840 the Methodists already had churches in Detroit, Monroe, Algonac, Allegan, Ypsilanti, Perrinsville, and Ann Arbor. In 1840 Smith's Chapel near Edwardsburg was built; likewise churches in Marshall, Birmingham, and Albion. Adrian built a church in 1840; a parsonage in 1845. The year 1842 saw churches erected in Tecumseh, Dundee, Clinton, Romeo, Flint, South Lyons, Franklin, Ridgeway, Grand Rapids, and Kalamazoo. Algonac built its second church in 1843. Pontiac completed "a small but neat building" in 1843; Flint finished a parsonage the same year. Coldwater, Milford, and Davis built churches in 1844. Port Huron erected a modest church in 1844; and finding it too small, built again in 1856. Washington built a church in 1846; Kawkawlin in 1847. Flushing erected its first edifice in 1848. Jackson built a church between 1848 and 1850. Then it struggled a long time with the burden of debt thereon.

The Michigan Annual Conference Minutes in 1847 reveal that there were then 15 Meeting Houses (as they were yet called) in the Detroit

---

[4] Pilcher, *Hist. Prot., Mich.,* pp. 300-303. References to revivals, stations, building churches, etc. all based on Pilcher.

District, 13 in the Ann Arbor District, 14 in the Marshall District, 21 in the Monroe District, 19 in the Kalamazoo District, and 4 in the Grand Rapids District — a total of 86. The parsonages were much scarcer. The Detroit District had only 2, Ann Arbor 7, Marshall 2, Monroe 8, Kalamazoo 4, and Grand Rapids surprisingly had 6. The Indian Mission District had 4 parsonages, making a total of 33 for the state. We know little about the early parsonages. Most of the early churches were modest frame structures.

Expansion in Detroit

More adequate attention at last began to be given to the city of Detroit. A First Charge and a Second Charge there were given in the Conference list of appointments for the first time in 1844. J. V. Watson was sent to First Church and R. R. Richards to Second. These were both very able ministers who came into the work there via the Indiana Annual Conference and the Kalamazoo District. Pilcher said two appointments were made in 1843 to the one Methodist church in Detroit with a view to starting the Second Society before the next Conference session. William Phelps, well-known in business and a local preacher in First Church, was persuaded to help start the Second Society and become superintendent of its Sunday School. The new group grew very slowly because they lacked a building for their services. Sometimes they met in the old State Capitol and again in the United States District Court room. Mr. Richards persuaded the Society to buy a lot on the corner of Congress and Randolph Streets. Tradition says the price was $2,000 for the entire piece of land which would be reckoned worth more than that per square foot today. A plain brick church was built and dedicated in 1846.

Meanwhile the First Society in their frame building, built in 1834 on the corner of Woodward Avenue and Congress Street, found it too small and unassuming. Therefore they too built a new church of brick on the corner of Woodward Avenue and State Street. Ex-President Martin Van Buren, returning from a trip to Lake Superior, stopped in Detroit for several days in July 1842. On Sunday morning, he attended the services in the First Methodist Church and in the afternoon visited the Catholic and also the Episcopalian Churches. How one would like to know what the guest thought of the Methodists and they of him.

Some members of First Church thought it was now too far away from their homes so they planned a small church west of Woodward Avenue. General Cass gave them a lot on the northeast corner of Lafayette and Fourth Streets. First Church then gave them their old frame building. So Third Church began services there with sixteen members. The names of these new churches were soon changed to Congress Street Church and Lafayette Street Mission. The latter was covered with clapboards, its chairs sat on a bare floor, the two stoves had long pipes, and the lights were whale oil at first.[5]

Changing Districts and Declining Membership

In 1840, six Districts had been organized in the Michigan Annual Conference. These were Detroit, Ann Arbor, Monroe, Marshall, Kalamazoo, and an Indian mission District in the Upper Peninsula. This set-up remained the same in 1841 and 1842. Then another District called Shiawassee was added but kept for two years only. The name was changed to Grand River in 1845 but eight of its twelve appointments were just the same as before. The Michigan Annual Conference retained its seven Districts for seven years, from 1843 through 1849.

A decline in total membership began in 1845 and was even more noticeable in 1847. After some years of not more than one or two new appointments in any District, Detroit added five in 1849. And in 1850 an eighth District named Flint was created. Presumably the reasons in part for this static situation may be found in the churchwide dissension over slavery.

When Elijah Pilcher, with the help of A. M. Fitch, prepared statistics of their membership from the beginning to the Conference session of 1855, he noticed the decline in the State's membership. Then he compared the relative increases in total population and in Methodist Episcopal Church membership. In 1820, one in 444 of the population was a Methodist. In 1830 the ratio was one in 41, in 1840 it was one in 18 but in 1850 it had reversed to one in 23. In explanation of this change, Pilcher said, "the increase of population was very largely made up of foreigners, a large proportion of whom are altogether inaccessible to our ministry." Pilcher probably meant the Germans, whose numbers in Michigan increased by thousands every decade.

German Methodism begun in Michigan

Methodist work, conducted in the German language, among the new settlers of that nationality in Michigan was started outside the State. The center from which all the German work in the middle west spread was Cincinnati and its chief leader was William Nast. Michigan German Methodism was made a District eventually but it never was a separate State Annual Conference.

The German work in this State was usually connected with North Indiana or North Ohio Annual Conferences. The Rev. Peter Schmucker, a missionary at large to German-speaking people, visited some groups

[5] G. B. Catlin, *The Story of Detroit*, p. 397. M. M. Quaife, *This is Detroit*, p. 129. Alice Nash, *Golden Jubilee History of the Tabernacle M.E. Church*, pp. 11-15. Pilcher, *Hist. Prot. Mich.*, pp. 198-99.

in Detroit, Monroe, and Ann Arbor in 1846. Then he asked the Ohio Annual Conference session of that year to send German-speaking preachers here. John M. Hartman was appointed to Detroit and Johann H. Seddlemeyer to Ann Arbor

The First German Church in Detroit was organized by Hartman in September 1846. He also established Societies at Roseville, Redford, St. Clair, Newport, and Pontiac. He did not have the troubles that the Ann Arbor German preacher met. Seddlemeyer was opposed in every possible way by the Lutheran pastor there. Nevertheless a Society was organized in 1847 and a modest church erected in 1848. The work spread very slowly, seeming to flourish the best in small villages.

In 1854 we find the first record that a Michigan District had been created in the Cincinnati Annual Conference. From 1864 to 1933, all the German churches in Michigan were supervised by a Central German Annual Conference.

In 1933, all German Methodist churches in the United States were merged with the English-speaking Annual Conferences in which they were located. The need for foreign language churches was dying out. The new and more restrictive immigration laws prevented the oldtime flood of newcomers. The hostile attitude toward all things German during the first World War had some influence too. And last but not least, the old members, who came here from Germany were all dead and gone. Their descendants had little need of or sympathy for a German-speaking Methodist Episcopal Church.[6]

Schisms in the Methodist Episcopal Church

Far more serious for the future of the Methodist Episcopal Church in Michigan than any division due to language were those caused by slavery and authoritarian administration. The Methodist Protestant Church and the Wesleyan Connection appeared in Michigan about the same time and held roughly similar views. But the Methodist Protestant movement was centered in Baltimore and did not appear in Michigan until its second decade. Small groups of Wesleyans were meeting here before any national relationship existed. The Methodist Protestants were chiefly concerned about lay representation and control of the autocratic power of the bishops. They held anti-slavery views but not quite so strongly as the other group did. Yet both seceders were in the end organized about the same as any Congregational Church would be. They relied on an elected President and then joint committees of min-

[6] Paul Douglas, *The Story of German Methodism, Biography of an Immigrant Soul, passim.* Also articles written by members of the Detroit Conference Historical Society: in 1959 — M. J. Betz, "Brief History of German Methodism in Michigan." in 1962 — E. J. Weiss — "Development and Growth of Methodism among German Speaking People in Michigan."

isters and laymen chosen by public vote in an annual conference. Endless debate accompanied their actions and a Methodist Episcopalian found it hard to perceive how either group ever accomplished anything.[7]

1) *The Methodist Protestants*

The Methodist reforms, wanted in the 1820's, were election of the Presiding Elders by the Annual Conference members instead of appointment by the bishop, more consultation of the ministers themselves before appointments were made, and a general limitation of the episcopal power. When the General Conference of 1828 refused to consider the petitions of the reformers, the organization of a separate Methodist group began.

The next two years brought the organization of at least twelve Annual Conferences in an Association. In November 1830, the Methodist Protestant Church was organized by a general convention in Baltimore. The use of the word Protestant implied that the Methodist Episcopal Church had become too much like the hierarchal organization of the Catholic Church. In place of a "Bishop," the Methodist Protestant Conference had a "President." Appointments were to be made by a "stationing committee" composed of fellow ministers. Their first *Discipline* did not mention Michigan. The movement did not yet reach this far west.

In 1840-1841, President Ancel Bassett of the Ohio Methodist Protestant Annual Conference made an exploratory tour in northern Ohio and Michigan. He travelled 350 miles, presumably on horseback, and is known to have spent Sundays in Adrian, Jackson, and Franklin. In April 1842, he published an account of his trip and, in May 1842, brought the situation here before the Methodist Protestant General Conference in Baltimore. So "authority was given for organizing an annual conference in Michigan." Next the Ohio Methodist Protestant Annual Conference agreed "that if the State of Michigan could find three ordained ministers in the State they might form an annual Conference for themselves accordingly."

Seven Elders and one Deacon were found so the Michigan Methodist Protestant Annual Conference was organized at Franciscoville in Washtenaw County on July 14, 1842. The Rev. James Gay was elected President. The other Elders were Laban Smith, J. T. Pratt, O. Earles, C. Blake, J. Mulligan, and E. Hall plus Deacon B. F. Paris. They agreed their territory would be all the Lower Peninsula and the first northern tier of Indiana counties. Eight men were received on trial. Two reso-

---

[7] *The History of American Methodism*, I, Chapter XIII on "The Formation of the Methodist Protestant Church" by D. R. Chandler. Also II, Chapter XIV on "The Church Divides" by R. M. Cameron. Note especially pp. 22-47 on the Wesleyans and abolitionists.

lutions were adopted. One declared, "We use no alcoholic wine but that in all our services we get wine without spirit or use raisins to make the wine." The second agreed "We have no fellowship with Slavery or Slave holding in this Conference."

At Concord in September 1843, the only resolution adopted said "We renew all our former resolutions on the subject of Slavery and the Sacrament." By 1850, the Michigan Methodist Protestant Annual Conference felt so strongly about slavery that it refused to elect any delegates to their General Conference of that year. They felt that to do so would be compounding with the evil of slavery. The Methodist Protestants in Michigan before the Civil War constituted a small and struggling Church. Undoubtedly their hostility to slavery was strengthened by the Wesleyans.[8]

2) *The Wesleyan Methodists*

The Wesleyan separatist group grew out of the disgust of many Methodists with the pressure for conformity to the lukewarm opposition to slavery fostered by the General Conferences. When Marcus Swift was refused the Eldership in 1839, he withdrew from the Michigan Annual Conference but kept on with preaching and lecturing. Early in 1841, he withdrew entirely from the Methodist Episcopal Church. A number of other members and their families also left the Nankin Society at the same time. Swift soon established a small local society of strong, abolitionist views.

A number of societies of this sort were also organized in 1841 in New England, Pittsburgh, and Iowa. Luther Lee, Orange Scott, and Laroy Sunderland were among the leaders in this separation. In November 1842, the first number of the *True Wesleyan* was published. Several of these ministers announced therein their withdrawal from the Methodist Episcopal Church. Such a public statement brought them news of other groups taking a similar action. Steps for united action were now started.

A preliminary convention of nine ministers and forty-three laymen met at Andover, Massachusetts, to plan their future steps. This led to a second, and far more important, convention in May 1843. It is usually called, from the place of its meeting, the Utica Wesleyan Convention. Marcus Swift attended this organizational meeting. Much of the Methodist Episcopal *Discipline* was copied, especially in doctrine. But the

---

[8] Early records of the Methodist Protestant Church are most inadequate especially in the statistics. A scrapbook on the M.P.s is in the historical collection of Detroit Conference Hist. Soc. Adrian College Library. Note particularly articles therein by Harlan Feeman and Charles Bragg. Also Lyman E. Davis, *Democratic Methodism in America, passim.* H. E. Woolever, *Highroad of Methodism Heights of Separation and Union,* (He was Secretary of Joint Comm. on Methodist Union, 1939).

rule on slavery forbade buying or selling any human being or even claiming it was right to do so. The new group was also strongly opposed to liquor and all secret societies. They copied from the Methodist Protestants their lay delegates and elected President or chairman. People from nine different denominations had attended the meeting at Utica. This may be why the new group was named "The Wesleyan Connection in America."

The growth of the new Wesleyan Church was phenomenal. Here in Michigan in two years it had over a thousand members and seventeen preachers. Nationally it had six Annual Conferences by 1844 and fifteen thousand members. These members were apt to be young, ardently idealistic, and industrious for many reform causes.[9]

The enthusiasm for starting church related colleges was strong in the Wesleyans. By 1845, they had set up a school at Leoni a few miles east of Jackson. The Wesleyan Annual Conference appointed the trustees, who bought 270 acres or land, collected pledges for $4,000 and obtained one thousand volumes for a library. Between fifty and sixty students attended the school its first year. The State Legislature chartered the school in 1848 with appointment of the trustees in the hands of the Wesleyan Connection. The name of the school became Leoni Theological Institute.

Within a week afterwards, a charter was also granted to Leoni Seminary, which is thought to have been sponsored by the Methodist Protestants. Its trustees included ministers of that Church. It seems never to have built a separate plant but it did have about forty pupils for a short time. Both schools suffered great financial hardship for some years. In the early 1850's, the Wesleyans changed the name of their Institute to Michigan Union College. But this did not seem to help their difficulties. Such was the ancestry of Adrian College.[10]

Two Wesleyan Leaders:
Laura Haviland and Guy Beckley

Mrs. Laura Haviland began life as a Quaker whose activities in behalf of the slave were disliked by the Adrian Friends.

From childhood, she knew of Methodism through attendance upon their prayer meetings at an uncle's but her parents disapproved of the emotional zeal of the sect then. After her marriage she and all her family left the Quakers and became Methodists of the Episcopalian branch for a short time. When the Michigan Methodist Episcopal Church split over slavery, she at once joined the Wesleyan Methodists

[9] W. W. Sweet, *Meth. Am. Hist.*, p. 241.

[10] W. F. Dunbar, *The Michigan Record in Higher Education*, pp. 123-125. F. W. Stephenson, article on Adrian College, 1959, done for Detroit Conference Historical Society, in historical collection at Adrian College Library.

because "this branch of our Father's family was the nearest our own views."[11]

Laura Haviland must have been a woman of boundless energy for she ran a farm, started a school known as Raisin Institute, and received runaway slaves in her home. She never hesitated to go south in some slight disguise and aid frightened slaves to escape. She would then come home and tell her experiences at meetings often held in the Adrian Court House. Her neighbors were so concerned about her safety that they kept guns at hand and guarded her home at night. One southerner came to Adrian and tried to get a local lawyer to help put Mrs. Haviland in jail. That attorney told him, "You will find no jail in this State that will hold that woman." Once she herself took six slaves across to Canada and "to see them leap for joy was rich pay for all my care in their behalf . . . I left each with 50¢ and returned to my own sweet home." Her son once declared, "Mother is a stranger to fear tho she might be in great danger."

[11] L. Haviland, *A Woman's Life Work, passim.* Her reminiscences written when she was an old woman. By the help of Dr. William C. S. Pellowe, the author, in the summer of 1963, had a talk with Miss Edith Haviland, the grandniece of Laura Haviland. The family still have many of her possessions and speak vividly of her and her exploits.

The Statue of Laura Haviland before the City Hall in Adrian, said to be the only statue to a woman in the state. Laura Haviland ran the underground railroad station at Adrian; she was an aggressive abolitionist and instrumental in the freeing of many slaves.

An Under Ground Railroad Station at Union City, Michigan. At these homes fugitive slaves from the south were sheltered, and then taken to the next station enroute to freedom in Canada.

Guy Beckley too ran a station on the Underground Railroad. He was also a Methodist Episcopal minister, editor of a weekly abolitionist newspaper, the *Signal of Liberty*, and helped his brother in business in Ann Arbor. He was born in Vermont, ordained there and served the Methodist Episcopal Church in New England for ten years. He located upon moving to Michigan but was still authorized to preach, perform marriages, and officiate at funerals. His ministerial relationship was with the Ann Arbor First Church Quarterly Conference.

Before moving to Michigan, Beckley had been an agent of the American Antislavery Society. He so continued in Ann Arbor. It required much lecturing and writing about the evils of slavery. In 1840 he became chairman of the Executive Committee of the Michigan State Antislavery Society. Later he was its treasurer and Vice President. This work took him all over the southern part of Michigan. He lectured in many of the village Methodist Episcopal churches between Detroit and Niles. After his brother died in 1843, Beckley was forced to give more attention and time to their jointly owned store and less to lectures and sermons.

His greatest influence was exerted through a weekly antislavery paper which he edited with Theodore Foster. *The Signal of Liberty* was published weekly from April 28, 1841, to February 5, 1848.[12] Only

[12] Copies of the *Signal of Liberty* were read in the Michigan Historical Collections, Rackham Bldg., University of Michigan, Ann Arbor. The most useful years for the study of Methodism are between 1841 and 1844.

two publication dates were missed in contrast to the carelessness of most such reform papers then. Foster later testified that the paper could not have been kept going without Beckley's aid. As editor, he never was afraid to write exactly what he thought. Part of the time the paper was the organ of the Liberty Party in Michigan. Beckley also wrote exactly what he thought of the Methodist Episcopal Church. He broke off his connection with the paper in 1846 due to the pressure of his business interests. Taken suddenly ill, he died in December, 1847, at the age of 42 years.

In a time when Methodist denominational papers had not been started in either Detroit or Chicago, the *Signal of Liberty* played a useful role through the information that it furnished. It gave all the details of Methodist Episcopal and Wesleyan Annual Conferences, announced meetings of either a religious or social reform character, and printed and replied with great vigor to many letters from its readers.

Editors Beckley and Foster were often sharply critical of the autocracy of the bishops in the Methodist Episcopal Church. They stood for lay representation equal with that of the clergy and for election of the Presiding Elders. Above all, they attacked the church attitude on slavery. Time and again, the *Signal* declared the Methodist Episcopal Church is "a slave-holding and slave-defending church." An editorial published on December 12, 1842, stated, "From what we know of the Methodist Episcopal Church in this State, we have reason to believe that she would permit her members and ministers to buy and hold slaves if our laws did not forbid it."

Such comment stirred up the readers, particularly two Methodist Episcopal ministers named John Scotford and Bradford Frazee. Each engaged in extended correspondence with the paper and Editor Beckley. Just one letter often ran two or three columns of fine newspaper print. Each preacher angrily denied that abolition views were "a bar to advancement in the Church." Scotford said the true attitude of the Church was deliberately misinterpreted. It was vital to keep communication with the South open and free. He said in part, "We must not forget some of these ministers grew up in a land of slavery, are used to it and think the Scriptures justify it. Would it do any good to treat them harshly? Many southern States prohibited by law the freeing of any slaves. Scotford finally concluded that the Church had taken the wrong stand on slavery and really he only disagreed with Beckley on how deeply the Church had erred.

But on April 10, 1843, Scotford was angry again, wrote at length of how unfairly he had been treated and denied all over again that the Methodist Episcopal Church held to slavery *as a Church*. Scotford's closing remark was that now he knew just how the man who fought a skunk felt when he said, "A victory under such circumstances is far worse than a defeat."

Bradford Frazee was intent on attacking the picture of slavery that the editors presented to northern readers. He had served in southern churches for seven years and did not believe the atrocity stories printed in the *Signal of Liberty*. His letter brought a long editorial reply and letters from other readers too. Stories of branding, ear cropping, whipping, and torture were printed. Weld's *Slavery As It Is* was cited as authority. Frazee certainly did not so regard it. He kept writing to demand some specific cases and places by name and ended, "You are imposing on the public."

Unfortunately for Beckley, all that written argument got him into real trouble with his church. Frazee brought charges of "slander, falsehood, and inveighing against the *Discipline*" against Beckley in the Quarterly Conference of the Ann Arbor First Church. A preliminary committee of four ministers heard Mr. Frazee and then drafted the formal charges, which all concerned things that Beckley had written in the *Signal of Liberty*. No witnesses were heard. Frazee was allowed the help of Judge Dexter with the prosecution but Beckley had no lawyer and was closely restricted to what he had written in his newspaper.

The Presiding Elder, Henry Colclazer, had charge of the proceedings on July 20, 1843. Afterwards Beckley devoted nearly three pages of his paper to the details of his trial.

Beckley made a long statement of his opinions and then reviewed all his correspondence with both Frazee and Scotford. The editor then charged that he was the victim of an organized effort to get him expelled from the Methodist Episcopal Church. He had been so told by both ministers and laymen. Also he himself had noted that some of Frazee's letters were not in his own handwriting. Within the last few months, Beckley had been interviewed by five Methodist Episcopal Elders, to whom he spoke his opinions freely. All of them had urged him to publish what he said and he had done so in good faith. If these men had given half as much effort to ridding the Church of slavery as they had to ridding it of him, they might be believed when they said "they are as much opposed to slavery as anybody."

In his general defense, Beckley reviewed all the items on slavery in the *Discipline*, quoted all General Conference resolutions on slavery, and ended with those of various Annual Conferences. He concluded that, for sixty years, the Methodist Episcopal Church had been on the retrograde on slavery. Only the most sincere repentance and reform could remove its accumulated guilt. He had always advised Church members to try to change the situation from within. For the last three years, he had talked and written "with an unmixed desire to glorify God, save the Church and benefit the slave." If he was now expelled, Beckley prayed he might be able to say, "Father forgive them, they know not what they do."

Frazee made a comparatively brief reply in which he insisted that he was an anti-slavery man and said, in an insinuating way, that in all large bodies, like the Church, some were discontented because they were not promoted as fast as they felt they deserved.

The votes of the Quarterly Conference judges were almost unanimous in acquittal of Beckley. On the charge of slander, they were thirteen for to two against him. On falsehood, they were twelve for to one against him. On "inveighing against the Discipline of the Methodist Episcopal Church," they were ten for to two against him. Those voting against Beckley were the Rev. A. M. Fitch and Mr. Lewis Barr. President Colclazer then announced that the charges were not sustained and "the character of the accused was passed."

Beckley had said that he did not want to leave the Methodist Episcopal Church but, just ten days after his trial, he helped start the Ann Arbor Wesleyan Church. His name appeared on the "unstationed" list of the Wesleyan Connection in 1844 but in 1845-1846 he was Chairman of the Ann Arbor District of that denomination. He was also one of the first trustees of the Leoni Wesleyan Institute. In his Ann Arbor store, he sold the Wesleyan *Discipline* and *Hymnbook*.[13]

Beckley was very modern in his sensitivity to any racial discrimination. Early in the summer of 1843, he gave some attention to a "deplorable exhibition of negro hatred in Detroit." It was the custom to hold a joint July 4 picnic for the white Methodist, Baptist, and Presbyterian Sunday Schools. That year "a respectable delegation of colored men" came to ask if the children of two of their Sunday Schools, one Methodist and one Baptist, might join in the celebration. The joint committee on arrangements rejected them.

Beckley had heard that the two Presbyterians and one Baptist on the committee favored admitting the colored children but the four Methodists voted against them. The four were John Owen, Hiram Ryan, Henry Canniff, and William Phelps. The rumor was that Owen objected because the committee was not instructed on the question and well-to-do Methodist parents would surely object to the presence of children of "humble and degraded rank."

Such editorial comment brought an immediate reply from William Phelps of the committee. He denied that Owen ever said what Beckley claimed he did. No colored delegation came to the joint committee meeting. Phelps admitted one colored Baptist, ahead of the meeting, asked if a colored delegation could appear. They were refused on the grounds that time was too short, this was an entirely new subject, they would not dare to decide it without consultation with their respective Sunday School officers.

---

[13] John E. Kephart, "A Pioneer Michigan Abolitionist," *Michigan History*, March 1961. XLV, 34-42. This article gives more detail on Beckley's connections with the Liberty Party.

In the August 14 issue of the *Signal of Liberty,* Beckley observed that no one denied the basic truth that the colored Baptists applied and were refused. The argument that time was too short was nonsense. He concluded:

> If four adult men who were deemed of sufficient intelligence to instruct children in the church religion and direct the affairs of the Sunday Schools could not of themselves solve the weighty problem whether it were right to exclude little children from a Sabbath School celebration, on account of their color, we humbly think they would do well not to occupy so perilous a post in future.

The Eighth Session of the Michigan Annual Conference

The Annual Conference session of 1843 was held in Ann Arbor. Editor Beckley attended all the sessions and then devoted three columns in his paper to its doings. He said it had one hundred travelling preachers and 16,363 members. The official *Minutes* of that session give little more than information about the appointments. It makes no mention of the long discussion of slavery which Beckley reported. Perhaps this was because Biship Soule was presiding and he tried to stop all talk about abolition of slavery.

Resolutions on slavery, passed by the New York and Genesee Annual Conferences, had been laid before the Michigan Annual Conference. These were intended to refuse church membership to any slaveholder in States where the law allowed emancipation. It was clear that slaveholding members would still be allowed in southern States. These resolutions were rejected by a vote of 57 to 1. Beckley noted that many ministers did not vote at all on this matter. Then a motion was presented to exclude all members who made a business of buying and selling slaves. This one was adopted by a vote of 64 to 0.

Bishop Soule tried repeatedly to get the members of the Annual Conference to stop both discussion and adoption of new resolutions against slavery. He explained that action on this subject in northern churches had no effect at all on slavery and, in most cases, made the negro's situation worse. He declared, "We in Michigan could not comprehend the difficulties of those who live where slavery has existed for centuries."

What he saw and heard and reported at that Annual Conference must have reenforced Beckley's decision to leave the Methodist Episcopal Church. Together, Methodist Episcopal neutralism and the two secession movements decreased the number of Church members for some years. Probably the continuing hard times increased this decline.

But in another decade, the views of the Methodist Episcopal Church North had changed to open abolitionism. The schisms contributed to this policy change. In the most recent *History of American Methodism,* the author, Richard M. Cameron, says:

> It often happens that when a minority group takes a determined stand on a matter of principle or secedes from a larger body, the results of its action are felt quite as much in the inert body it has left as in its own new entity, separate ar ⅃ free though it be. The Methodist Episcopal Church began to move in an antislavery direction so swiftly and so soon after the Wesleyan Methodists made it clear they meant business that it can hardly have been mere coincidence.[14]

Michigan Methodist Missionaries

The most sacrificial work done by any of the members of the Michigan Annual Conference was that of the missionaries, one to China and ten or twelve among the Indians.

The first Methodist missionary work in China was begun by Judson Collins. Graduated from the University of Michigan in its first class in 1845, he taught in the Wesleyan Seminary at Albion. He was then received on trial in 1846 in the Michigan Annual Conference. On a temporary appointment to the Tompkins Circuit, he began preparations for work in China.

The Methodist Episcopal Church had no plans for such work then and only after persistent, repeated applications to the Missionary Secretary, Dr. Durbin, was Collins finally authorized to go. He had felt a call to work there ever since his first days in college. Indeed he declared he would work his way there as a common sailor if the Church would not send him.

Collins went to China in the spring of 1847 but labored there only three years and nine months. The climate and disease were too much for him and he was forced to return to Michigan to recuperate he hoped. But his health was completely wrecked and he died at his father's house in May 1852. He was only twenty-eight then.

Pilcher always looked on Collins as his "spiritual son" and rejoiced that Collins had been converted in a revival he himself had conducted while stationed at the Ann Arbor First Church. Later Pilcher's own son, Leander W. Pilcher, became a missionary to China.[15]

Valiant efforts were made to continue and expand the Indian Missions in Michigan. The same old obstacles, in the nature of the life the Indians lived and the evil done by the traders who sold the Indians whisky, were stronger than ever. To these must be added the steady increase of the white population intent on grabbing all the good land.

In the 1840's the discovery and development of the great copper and iron deposits in the Upper Peninsula changed entirely the work

[14] *Hist. Am. Meth.,* II, 44.
[15] Pilcher, *Hist. Prot. Mich.,* pp. 236-239.

Judson Collins (1823-52) was a member of the first class of the University of Michigan, an early teacher at Albion, one of the two first Methodist missionaries who went to China in 1847. He burned out his life for the gospel. His name is perpetuated in a church camp today on Wampler's Lake.

of the missionary to the Indians in that region. Next in the 1850's the railroads were built across the State in several directions, the plank roads had been built, and the lumbering industry using steam power mills developed in the Lower Peninsula. Such radical changes plus the efforts of the United States government to remove the Indians to reservations west of the Mississippi River brought an end of many Indian missions or the survival of one little church in an area where once there had been several preaching places.

The two parts of Michigan had each an outstanding missionary to the Indians who was both articulate and reminiscent about his labors. The Methodist minister most effective among the Indians of the Lower Peninsula was Manasseh Hickey and one among the three or four who labored successfully in the Upper Peninsula was John Pitezel. He wrote a book about his northern experiences and Hickey some shorter reminiscences.

Mannasseh Hickey joined the Michigan Annual Conference on trial in 1844, became a full member in 1846, and from then to his death in 1903, was active in the work of the Church. Early in his career, he was appointed to the Nottawa Mission south of Battle Creek. He picked up some of the Indian language but usually preached through an interpreter. A visitor, A. D. P. Van Buren, was much impressed with the way the Indians sang the hymns in their native tongue and the reverent silence they kept in their little chapel.

Scattered over a wide area, the Indians were hard to reach and influence regularly. Hickey persuaded a band of Indians to buy 160 acres of land together on the Grand River near Portland. Then he planned eleven log houses and a mission center to be arranged along the river like a street. His salary was only $150 a year for all his expenses. But he had a genius for getting people to give labor or materials.

First, he found a surveyor who laid the plot off into small equal lots. Next he held a log cutting and gathering bee. After getting the walls up together, he gathered donations from all the merchants he knew. He had nails, brick, planed lumber, shingles, and window frames given. He himself worked at the shingling and laying of floors until he wore through one knee of the only pair of trousers he had there. He tied his handkerchief over the hole and limped a little whenever he could remember so to do. He added, "Whether I limped or not during my sermon I cannot tell."

One merchant said he would give him some lumber if Hickey would preach to "a hard crowd of sinners." Notice was widely sent of the meeting which was held in a school house with the light provided by two pounds of candles. A big crowd came and the young minister, who had been preaching only three years, was frightened when he realized what a tough audience he had. His knees were literally shaking when he went into the pulpit. In 1881 Hickey still remembered:

> During the opening prayer He who called me from the plough on my father's farm and who eighteen hundred years ago said to his Disciples "Lo! I am with you always" came with his Divine power and took away the fear of man from our heart. We preached with much zeal and the audience were moved to tears.

Afterwards, in commenting to the merchant on how well behaved the crowd had been, he replied, "If a dog of them had lifted his tongue I would have threshed the floor with him."

In August 1850, Hickey went across country to an Indian camp meeting in Saginaw County. From eight hundred to a thousand Indians attended with perhaps two or three hundred pagans among their number. Hickey estimated that the Indians were from Canada and thirteen counties of Michigan. The Presiding Elder, George Bradley, and several other pioneer ministers came to help.

The ponies had bells tied around their necks and were then turned loose in the woods. Next huge fires were built in an effort by the smoke to keep off some of the mosquitoes. A special preachers tent was also erected.

Sixteen Indian chiefs were present along with several medicine men. One of the latter was converted to the anger of his wife. He had been

The Oscoda Indian Mission with its log parsonage. It is said that a log meet-inghouse was erected here in the 1840's, and a bell now in possession of the Conference Historical Society was purchased between 1845 and 1848, to call the congregation together. They never knew when the preacher was coming; the bell would announce him. Near the end of the century the Bay City dis-trict had Indian Missions at Saganing, Oscoda, Frost Lake, and Pinconning.

uncertain about religion for some time and finally, after a night of agony, won relief and declared, "The light is come in my soul." Pre-siding Elder Bradley baptized this Indian later in the day. When asked if he renounced "the Devil and all his works" this convert replied, "I will and the medicine dance too." Hickey noted that he saw this same Indian in 1872 and found he had held fast to his religion.

This was a time of great hostility on the part of the traders to the missionaries. They were afraid the ministers would destroy the whisky trade with its huge profits. Word was brought to the ministers during this camp meeting that a bunch of rowdies and irreligious were planning to break up the night meeting on Saturday and then get the Indians all drunk. The Presiding Elder very quietly talked this all over with the chiefs and the missionaries and all agreed to close up on Saturday afternoon. Then in small bands, they would scatter from eight to fifteen miles away and camp over Sunday. Those going the same way would hold together and the missionaries would scatter too so that each group might have preaching on Sunday. Hickey could never forget how:

Rev. George Brown from Kaw-Kaw-lin had a very large canoe with a cook stove, beds, chairs, trunks, and a feeble, sick wife and a little girl. It was very affecting to see him have to pack, move, build another tent, and hold service after all this work, just to avoid rowdies.

But the scheme worked. In two hours everyone had quietly left and the rowdies found only the tent poles and the smoking embers of the fires.

From this time on, they had less trouble with white opposition. Hickey remembered that on the next fourth of July, a huge celebration was held at the mission in Danby. He made a speech and then four hundred people ate dinner together. They put all their wagons together and everyone stood around them for the meal. It was carefully planned so that an Indian and a white man alternated all around the wagons.

Together with four other Methodist ministers, Hickey tried to extend the mission work to the "Clay Banks" about forty miles down the Lake Michigan shore from Grand Haven. It was a hard place to reach and the Indians repulsed them after much talk. Their chief declared he had no faith in anything the white man ever promised as he would never keep his word anyhow. Another band whom they visited were already Catholic and "we did not seek to unsettle them." A modern historian concluded that Hickey had some success with individual Indians but not in the mass as a tribe. The Indians were always restless and enough missionary aid was never provided.[16]

John H. Pitezel was admitted on trial by the Michigan Annual Conference in 1836. In August 1843, he was appointed to the Soo at the personal request of Superintendent William Brockway of the Indian Missions of the Upper Peninsula. Pitezel gave nine years of his life to this missionary work. During that last four, he was Superintendent of all the work there. He possessed an observant eye and a ready pen so years later he published a book based on his diaries of that time. Its very Victorian title was "Lights and Shadows of Missionary Life: containing Travels, Sketches, Incidents and missionary efforts, during nine years spent in the region of Lake Superior."[17]

Pitezel's friends told him he was being exiled. And just before he and his family took the steamer north, he preached at Detroit which led him to the thought that never again would he "stand before such an intelligent congregation of white people."

The journey north included a stop at Mackinac Island, where his eyes were opened to the conditions among the Indians where the trader

16 "Reminiscences of Rev. M. Hickey, clergyman of the M.E. Church," *Mich. Pioneer Coll.*, IV, 23-33, 544-556. Wm. R. Prescott, *The Fathers Still Speak*, p. 68.

17 All quotations from Pitezel are taken from his book. The author is grateful to Miss Kay Bush for arranging a loan of the copy of Pitezel's book owned by her father, Mr. Harry L. Bush of Paw Paw, Michigan. See also booklet on the "History of Methodism in the Upper Peninsula of Michigan," section on "Methodist Indian Missions" by R. A. Brunger, pp. 9-14.

and his whisky had access to them. Pitezel felt that such Indians "were debased below the level of the brute." The trader was an ever present obstacle to the success of any Christian missionary.

Another shock awaited them at their house at the Soo. The place had been entirely in the hands of the Indians for three months. It was filthy, the children had a skin disease, and everyone was vermin infested. The most strenuous efforts by everyone for the next week produced some improvement in both the house and the children. Considering how hard they all had worked, Pitezel wrote in his diary, "If as Mr. Wesley says, 'Cleanliness is next to godliness,' these acts of physical renovation were intimately connected with the spiritual interests of the mission." Seeing his wife's struggles to make the Indian children work, he felt that the labor needed to make them help "was about equivalent to doing it herself."

After he had seen other mission houses, he decided it was a mistake ever to send single men to this work. They did their own cooking after a fashion, were alone so much they began to feel expatriated, and towards the end of the Conference year, left the place early in order to visit their parents. Then the work would disintegrate or the Catholics would take advantage of the situation and win away the most promising converts.

The plight of the missionary's wife was especially trying. Such a "Christian lady" had an overabundance of troubles. The very sounds and smells were strange to her. The language was unknown and queer sounding. The long Sunday services through interpreters grew monotonous and she was usually the only white female in the church. Her domestic cares were very irksome. She came to the mission expecting to keep house in her wonted way. The Indians walked in without knocking, squatted and spat on her clean floor, complained they were hungry, and often ate everything she had in the house.

If her husband was long absent, she worried about him too. If she went along with him, she was exposed to long hours of travel in open boats or walking in deep mud. She would have to sleep in tents or even in the open. She was constantly exposed to the observation of destitution and degradation ending sometimes in famine and murder. If she had children, all too soon she saw them imitating their Indian playmates. Yet Pitezel also thought that his wife was the Protestant missionary's biggest asset. "She teaches civilization in the management of her domestic relations." He often noticed the difference in the progress made in "house-wifery by the Indian women at our stations and those at Catholic stations. The comparison favors the former in great part due to the example set by the female missionary."

All missions were "given to hospitality" said Pitezel. This was especially true on New Year's Eve. In preparation for the service on December 31, 1843, the Soo mission folk baked a whole barrel of flour into bread and cooked a barrel of bean soup. Large numbers of Indians came including some pagans, who were "ignorant of God but professed to be seeking religion. They were deplorably degraded."

After long observation at the Soo, Pitezel decided that the Indians there were no slower nor more ignorant than the whites. Soo village had enjoyed mission preaching for twenty years but its Society was very weak. It had only a few scattered members and made slight response to any preaching. The truly converted Indians were neat, quiet, reverent, and also attentive in church. And how they did sing the old hymns in their own language.

The utmost Christian faith and patience were required in organizing and teaching an Indian school. The children were far more amenable and picked up English faster if they were kept at the mission all the time. Attendance was apt to fluctuate a great deal because the children usually went along when their parents went hunting or maple sugar gathering. By nature and everyday life, Indian children were restless and unsettled. The average mission teacher was often embarrassed and even frightened by his recalcitrant charges.

Nowhere were Pitezel's standards higher nor more rigorously maintained than in his own work and life. When the Indians were living in their winter wigwams, he often prayed and then preached in them. The stench and smoke from the fire were almost suffocating. Once he noted, "I did not know but I would be forced to follow the example of some other missionaries and preach in a sitting posture; but felt as if I could not be reconciled to this apparently indolent way of preaching."

Far more serious was the problem of how he should keep the white man's social and intellectual standards which he had brought north with him. Temptation to slide down into the Indian ways was ever present. Pitezel saw this clearly. He said:

> The missionary appointed to labor among the Indians has it in his own power to shape . . . his own course. He can let himself down to the condition of the Indian, or by habits of diligent study and an adherence to the customs of civilized life raise the Indian to the sphere in which he moves . . . the latter course we chose. In the school and in the field, as well as in the kitchen, our aim was to teach the Indian to live like white people . . . . But to throw aside our books and spend the long winter evenings in chatting and smoking and laughing with the Indian . . . was to us anything but tolerable.

Pitezel certainly practiced what he believed. He had written, "Deprived to a great extent of civilized society the missionary can only atone for this loss by communing with his books." During the winter of 1843-1844, he read the scriptures every day. While he read the Old Testament in English, he was also very slowly reading the New Testament in Greek. He finished this last task on February 7, 1844, noting that he had never expected to do so. He was twenty-four when he learned the Greek alphabet and he had only slight instruction before he began to read the New Testament in its original language. He found it enormously difficult to master a dead language all by himself. He also reviewed his Latin that same winter.

He faithfully kept a list of the books he read. It included Dr. Olin's *Travels in Egypt and Arabia*, the first two volumes of Bancroft's *History of the United States*, Robinson's *Biblical Researches in Mount Sinai*, and Lanman's *History of Michigan*. This is quite a list when it is remembered how much physical labor his everyday life demanded.

The physical hardships endured during Pitezel's nine years of travel in the northland are almost unbelievable today. The missionaries in the Upper Peninsula rarely travelled on horseback. No roads existed yet. They went on foot, on snowshoes, and by boat or Indian canoe. They endured wild storms, high winds and waves on Lake Superior, muddy swamps, and ill marked routes.

Once while he was walking with another man on the edge of frozen Lake Superior, a driving rain began. The only thing they could do was keep going. The rain froze as it fell and soon Pitezel's pant legs froze stiff. His sole complaint, in his book, was that he found this "a little inconvenient in walking." The first experiences in extended use of snowshoes were always very bad. Pitezel's feet were not yet hardened to the effort needed so he blistered his feet badly and even lost some of his toenails. In his later journeys in the north, Pitezel made snowshoe journeys of one hundred miles and over with ease.

He did not try to attend the Annual Conference of 1844 but eventually Pitezel received word that he had been transferred to Kewawenon (near L'Anse today). That was the mission started by Clark and Sunday on Keweenaw Bay. It was 250 miles from the Soo, fall was coming on, and the Superintendent was away.

The missionary tried to rent a Mackinaw boat from the American Fur Company but they had none to spare. Finally on his own responsibility, he spent $20 in the purchase of a bark canoe with sails and oars in addition to paddles. Many of their possessions had to be left at the Soo. They loaded only clothing, bedding, and as much food as possible. Among the provisions were four barrels of flour, one of pork, a keg of butter and a similar one of lard, one hundred pounds of sugar, a box of soap and one of candles.

In all they were twelve days en route. They sailed and rowed and, if the waves were too high for safety, they made camp and waited. They also rested and held services in the woods on Sunday. The returning missionary, a man named Brown, his wife and three-months old baby left at once in the Pitezel's canoe. They were sixteen days in reaching the Soo and their food gave out before they arrived.

Pitezel went to work on the mission house at Kewawenon immediately. It was a hewed log structure, with a cedar bark roof. All the old mortar was picked out, new lime mortar used, a new roof laid, and finally the whole building was whitewashed inside and out. Pitezel labored himself so hard at these tasks that he was almost too exhausted to preach on Sunday. He mourned his inability to achieve even one day a week for study and hoped he would not forget how to use a pen. He concluded, "No person is fit to be a missionary who is not willing to labor with his hands."

The Kewawenon Mission was Pitezel's appointment for three years and he did not go south to Annual Conference until 1846. He had a modest success in Indian revivals and was pleased when a few of the supposedly Catholic Indians joined the Methodist Church on probation. He felt it was his duty if possible to stop the Catholic priest's "proselyting efforts." Yet when the Catholic Mission at L'Anse bought a new church bell in 1845, Pitezel was pleased to buy the old one. Until then, the Methodists had called to church services by use of a conch shell.

Summers brought long canoe trips with the Indians to La Pointe, Grand Island, and Sandy Lake. Some of these were other Protestant missions and others were payment points for the government grants to the Indians. In the latter trips, Pitezel went along in an attempt to keep the Indians from spending all their money on whisky. The boundary between Indian missions in Minnesota or Wisconsin and Michigan was not sharply drawn in that period. The mode of travel and the locations made it far easier for an Upper Michigan man to supervise several missions.[18]

Significant changes were beginning in Upper Michigan due to the discovery of vast amounts of copper and iron there. In 1845, by raising a surplus of potatoes and then making a four day boat trip to Eagle Harbor, Pitezel had been able to sell his potatoes for $45 in gold. This was an enormous help in preparing for the winter. In 1846, in reappointing Pitezel to Kewawenon, Bishop Janes added to his duties "a roving commission to explore the mining region and do what he could to establish religious worship among the miners." Today that seems more of a challenge than the Indian mission work. Joseph Holt was sent to Kewawenon to teach the school and preach on Sundays whenever Pitezel was away.

In obedience to his new position, Pitezel made a long trip on foot and by boat all over the Keweenaw Peninsula. He visited the Cliff Mine, just discovered and opened. Both mine owners and workers received him warmly. He "had the privilege of proclaiming the gospel eleven times — in some places where the cross of Christ had never

---

[18] W. C. Barclay, *Early American Methodism*, II, 159-160; III, 329-342. Summary and comment on Indian missions in III, 363-364. See also two articles by R. A. Brunger, "John H. Pitezel Pioneer Missionary on Lake Superior," in *Mich. Ch. Ad.*, for April 1 and 8, 1965. XCII, #13, 3-4, 18-19. And in #14, 7, 18-20.

before been preached." He took particular note of families with children and left preaching appointments for his next visit there. On his return trip, he preached twelve times and even delivered a temperance lecture. Afterwards thirty men signed the total abstinence pledge. He had the framework of a church under way before being called away.

Everywhere he went, Pitezel made an effort to collect statistics of population by questioning the mining agents and also the steamboat captains. He estimated the population on Keweenaw Peninsula numbered about five hundred and in the whole Lake Superior region were at least one thousand whites.

Pitezel's next appointment was to Eagle River on a "mining mission." It was already one of his regular preaching appointments but "no society was formed and no immediate prospect of one could be seen." The missionary and his wife were both dismayed by their prospects. They had no money, had a very hard trip merely to get to Eagle River and knew that the prospects for success were very dim when they did get there. Finally after much thought, Pitezel wrote in his diary:

> I was rebuked by that passage . . . "Behold the fowls of the air, for they sow not, neither do they reap, nor gather into barns and yet your Heavenly Father feedeth them." This is enough, will God feed his birds and not his children. The want of religious society in our prospective field was a serious drawback in our feelings. But we had always made it a matter of conscience to go, if possible, to an appointment and therefore resolved to venture our all on the goodness of the Appointing Power, and, at least, throw our length that way.

A friend loaned him $8, the mining company provided a small log cabin and a stove, and let him charge for provisions at their store. Their house was better than that of their neighbors. The religious meetings had to be held in a school house or a dining hall. And the kind of men who worked in mines were not so very friendly to religion. Many had been away from their families for years, quite a number were Catholics, and all of them were there solely to make money quickly. But some who felt no religious interest themselves were glad to have a church started because they thought it might bring a little moral restraint over the miners.

Neither Pitezel nor his wife had expected to be so much annoyed by the incessant noise. It was a situation unlike any either of them had ever encountered. Pitezel wrote of it:

> Mining must go on day and night. There is a constant annoying din. Bells ring for shift changes, men talk, cars rumble, minerals drop, and six ponderous steam stampers work all night. Machinery whines and the blasts of explosions are heard. And the mules in a nearby barn fight.

In spite of the obstacles, Pitezel got a Class of twelve organized. He learned that the miners were frank, warm-hearted, generous in charity, and wonderful hymn singers in a congregation. He made some efforts also in the Ontonagon region but had small success except at the Cliff Mine.

An expansion of his duties came in 1848 when the Michigan Annual Conference appointed him Superintendent of the entire Indian Mission District. This meant even more travel if such a thing was possible. The previous Superintendent, William H. Brockway, sent word for him to come immediately to the Soo so that the papers of the Mission District might be transferred and the work in general discussed. For family reasons, Pitezel felt he could not go. Eventually another missionary handled the actual transfer of the mission business papers.

Just four days after Brockway's letter reached him, Pitezel recorded an important event in his diary as follows, "This morning Mrs. Pitezel was delivered of an interesting little son. I think we have realized an answer to many prayers. She came out of this trial beyond our most sanguine hopes." Eventually the whole family took the steamer to the Soo and, after moving twice, settled down there.

Besides general supervision of all the Indian and mining missions, Pitezel was also expected to serve as the pastor at the Soo. His opinion of the white people in his congregation there was low. He thought "the moral soil at the village was cold and sterile — the people were too easily distracted." But he tried to do his duty by them in his preaching. On July 21, 1850, he preached a sermon on the death of President Zachary Taylor, calling it "The fashion of this world passeth away." Pitezel was Superintendent of the Indian Missions from 1848 through 1852. At that time the situation in the entire Upper Peninsula was changing almost week by week. He himself was conscious of the rapid development around him and occasionally preached to the white congregations on what God had wrought in their country since 1844.

Origins of Methodism in the New State Capitol

In 1847 the Michigan Legislature finally selected a site for the permanent capitol of the State. Detroit wanted to keep it but many citizens thought it ought to be more centrally located. So much local pride and argument were aroused that the Legislature chose a spot without even one log cabin on it. This was "the township of Lansing in the County of Ingham." So rapidly was a frame capitol building erected that the Legislature met there in 1848.[19]

Ingham Methodist Mission had been set up as part of the Marshall District in 1838. Preaching had occurred at the log cabins of the area and a small Society had been organized at Lower Town, as the only

---

[19] F. C. Bald, *Michigan in Four Centuries*, pp. 253-254.

settlement near Lansing was then known. As soon as the location of the new capitol was announced, the Rev. Orrin Whitmore, then minister on the Mapleton Circuit, made Lansing one of his regular preaching appointments. Thus says Pilcher, Methodism sent "the first minister of any denomination to establish services here."[20]

In the summer of 1847, William Comfort, of the Lyons Circuit, came to Lansing and set up a church, although one already existed in what was to become the northern part of the city of Lansing. At the Annual Conference of 1847, Francis Asbury Blades was appointed to Mapleton Circuit with the specific understanding that it included Lansing. The same year, Lansing became Head of a District when Presiding Elder James Shaw fixed his residence there. One year later, Lansing was made a Station with Ransom R. Richards giving his full time to the charge. This was vital if a strong church was to be established there. The State had plenty of Circuit appointments still with services only once in two or three weeks. In addition, all the ministers sent to Lansing in these early years were very able men. Lansing made its first appearance in the Annual Conference statistics in September 1849 when seventy members were reported.

Seth Reed

The most interesting and longest ministerial career in Michigan Methodism began when Seth Reed was admitted on trial to the Michigan Annual Conference in 1844.[21] Often called "the grand old man of Michigan Methodism," Seth Reed answered to his name on the Conference roll call seventy-nine times in successive years. Born in 1823, he died in 1924, some nine months past his one hundreth birthday. Ministers who remember him have told the author that his deep voice saying "Present" sounded to them like the past of Methodism incarnate. In his ninetieth year, the Detroit Annual Conference asked him to preach to them on his life. This he did for an hour and a half and then made a book from his sermon, calling it *The Story of My Life.*

After teaching school two years, Reed decided that it was his duty "to select the highest and best plan for his life work." Hence he began to preach with a Quarterly Conference license on the Grand Rapids Circuit. He was also recommended to the Michigan Annual Conference, which admitted him on trial in the fall of 1844. Many years later, Reed still remembered how he was impressed, at his very first Annual Conference with what "great and good men" the preachers were. He mentioned, as having impressed him particularly, Pilcher, Colclazer, and Baughman.

[20] Pilcher, *Hist. Prot. Mich.,* pp. 406-408.
[21] See article by R. A. Brunger on "Seth Reed Centenarian of Michigan Methodism." in *Mich. Ch. Ad.,* for June 16, 1966, XCIII, #24, 3-4, 16-17.

Seth Reed (1823-1924), Michigan's Centenarian, was a pioneer preacher in Michigan, a presiding elder four times, an outstanding preacher, founder and the first superintendent of the Chelsea Methodist Old People's Home, when in his eighties. He answered the Conference roll call for 79 years consecutively.

His first Conference appointment was to the Grand Rapids Circuit, which did not include the village itself. The charge was a four-weeks Circuit in four counties. Reed had all the hardships of horseback travel that any Circuit rider endured. Once he was knocked off his horse by a projecting limb of a tree. He was unable to catch the horse and it ran to the house where Reed usually made his next stop. The farmer caught the horse, put it in his barn, went in his house, and told his wife that the preacher was on his way there and she was "to get a chicken ready" for the next meal.

In 1845 Reed was sent to the Mapleton Circuit in cooperation with another minister. This charge covered three counties, was wilderness in spots, and bears were occasionally encountered on ministerial journeys around the Circuit. Money was very scarce then and a Circuit rider was paid in almost anything useful. Later Reed estimated, "My salary for the year, including hay, oats, socks, mittens and cash amounted to $59.56."

Seth Reed was among the ministers who assisted in 1848 at that large Indian camp meeting which Manasseh Hickey described. But Reed was the one who noted the names the Indians had for each minister. He himself was "Straight up through the Sky," Hickey was "The Thunderer" and Larmon Chatfield was "Projecting Heavens." Incidentally Reed, as a young man, was known locally as "Death on stilts." He suffered terribly from asthma and certainly no one expected him to live for a century.

Once while Reed was preaching at that Indian camp meeting, Hickey reacted in a way that Reed never forgot. A large audience of perhaps eight hundred was listening to Reed preaching from the text, "But they that wait upon the Lord shall renew their strength; they shall mount up with wings as eagles; they shall run and not be weary; and they shall walk and not faint." This was a congenial theme to the Indians and they were audibly responsive. Suddenly Hickey began to roar and made said Reed:

> A noise such as I never heard before or since. Hickey had his mouth wide open, his arms and legs extended shouting with all his might. The audience caught the spirit and let loose their voices in billows of praise the like of which I never expect to hear till I hear them on the other shore.

Repeated experience taught Reed which methods were best for dealing with unruly members of the audience. One group at a school house had often disturbed him so finally one night, after the benediction, he told the audience how one man at another appointment of his had disturbed them so greatly that Reed investigated and learned that the man was an *idiot*. Then Reed said quietly, "Some of the men in this community think these young people are *not* idiots. If the neighbors are mistaken, the future conduct of these young people will show it." Reed never had any more trouble there.

Also he would go up to a noisy group, with a paper and a pencil in his hand and start taking down their names or at least pretend to do so. This procedure usually brought the hurried departure of the entire group.

Once at a camp meeting, three young ladies were standing on their chairs to see the scene at the mourner's bench and were thus annoying those seated immediately behind them. Reed very quietly said, "If one of those three young ladies knew she had a hole in her stocking, she would sit down at once." Immediately all three went down and began a surreptitious examination of their ankles.

Seth Reed's name is associated with many Methodist developments in Michigan throughout the rest of the 19th and also the early 20th centuries. He will be mentioned often in this History.

Changing Records and Changing Times

Until 1848, the official *Minutes* of the Michigan Annual Conference were printed only in the fat volumes of the *General Minutes.* All Annual Conferences were reported therein. Finally a very modest pamphlet only fifteen pages in all was printed by order of the Michigan Annual Conference in 1848. These first *Minutes* had no cover, did have many typographical errors, used very dingy paper, and did not contain the Journal of the Day.

The statistics of membership and finance in 1848 reveal that some of the ministers could not add correctly. Names of ministers and towns were often misspelled. Apparently no proofreading at all was done. The first one was compiled by four ministers and printed at Adrian.

Occasionally the committee reports are revealing. The committee on Sabbath Sanctity, in 1849, declared that stage coaches, steamboats, and railroads should not run on Sundays. No good Methodist should even think of going anywhere on Sundays by any of the listed modes of transportation. Also "securing grain, making sugar, travel on worldly business, visiting friends or going to the Post Office is inconsistent with the Christian profession."

During that same decade of the 1840's, the United States had annexed Texas, Oregon, and the Mexican Cession. Over the last the Mexican War was fought. Gold was discovered in California in 1848. The quarrel over slavery grew more embittered each year. Some southern States were talking secession until the Compromise of 1850 temporarily hushed the controversy. Most of these events were too far away to disturb Michigan so very much. Possibly the gold discovery and certainly the slavery agitation did affect many Michigan citizens. The committee, appointed to supervise the printing of the *Minutes* of the Michigan Annual Conference in 1850, put in at the beginning an apology for the result of their efforts. They knew that many of the documents were incomplete and imperfect. Some of the ministers never appeared at Conference and others could attend only part of the time. Great haste was necessary in getting the material in shape to print. Then the committee concluded that the apology for all this, if one was needed, must certainly be found "in the health of our Country and of the Conference at the time."

Chapter VIII

A CHANGING CHURCH IN CHANGING TIMES

1850 — 1860

From the Compromise of 1850 to the outbreak of the Civil War was a period of uneasy contention in the United States and the Methodist Episcopal Church. Many northerners were dissatisfied with the terms of the Compromise. Due to the proximity of Canada and the active Underground Railroad here, Michigan citizens were very disturbed by the stricter Fugitive Slave law. They particularly disliked the provisions which allowed any law officer to call upon any bystander to help arrest a fugitive and any U.S. Commisioner to receive twice as large a fee when he decreed return of a runaway slave as when he did not. Along with several other northern States, Michigan adopted a Personal Liberty Law, nullifying the Fugitive Slave law within its boundaries.

No evidence that Methodist Episcopalians were active in the Underground Railroad could be found. If any of them were involved, the work was most secret and no record of it was kept. Local tradition says that the Homer Methodist Episcopal Church was one of the stations but proof seems to be lacking. But the Wesleyans then and now had the reputation of being the most active workers for the Underground Railroad. Erastus Hussey, station master in Battle Creek, said that Guy Beckley led such work in Scio and Ann Arbor while Laura Haviland ran the station in Adrian. Beckley died in 1847 so Mrs. Haviland had a longer period for her humanitarian efforts. It was widely known that she would help any fugitive slave and put him on his way to Canada. Her plans for protection of her work were carefully laid out and everyone knew his part. She described the details in her book, A Woman's Life Work. She said in part:

A runaway slave could never be returned from this community . . .
let any slaveholders disturb an escaped slave at any time of day or night
and the sound of a tin horn would be heard with a dozen more answer-
ing it in different directions, and men enough would gather around the
trembling fugitive for his rescue. For women can blow horns and men
can run . . . . Hon. Ross Wilkins, U.S. judge residing in Detroit, can
legally require any fugitive so claimed to be brought before him and not
allow anything to be done until the decision is reached. And there are
many active workers to assist escaping slaves in that city, who would
rush to their aid and in ten minutes see them safe in Canada. If the
claimant had a score of witnesses and a half bushel of papers it would
mean nothing for we claim a higher law than that.[1]

Church papers, anti-slavery publications, and local newspapers all
described incidents of a harrowing nature in connection with efforts to
capture and return slaves to their masters. Northern hostility to slavery
was reinforced by the publication of *Uncle Tom's Cabin* in 1852. Methodists, such as were already abolitionists particularly, would probably
have read it from week to week as the various chapters were published.

Political and religious news also reached Michigan much faster in
the 1850's because the State was so rapidly increasing her connections
with the rest of the United States. In 1852, the Michigan Central Railroad reached Chicago. In that same year, the *Northwestern Christian
Advocate* was started in Chicago. It soon had hundreds of subscribers
in Michigan. In 1854, the first rail connections with New York City
were achieved when the Canadian Great Western Railway was completed to Windsor. A ferry then took passengers and freight to Detroit.
In 1855, the first ship locks at the Soo were finished and opened to
traffic. In 1856, the railway connection of Detroit with Toledo was completed. In these same years, Wells, Fargo and Company, an express and
stage coach line west, was organized. All these changes made it easier
and much quicker for political and religious news to reach Michigan.

Political Developments

Political confusion was very great in the 1850's. The long established
parties, Whigs and Democrats, were splitting over the problem of slavery
in the newly acquired West. The Liberty Party had been largely absorbed in the Free-Soil Party. It got enough votes in 1848 to keep Cass
from becoming President. Even the Know-Nothings, or Native Americans, whose chief tenet was hostility to foreigners and minorities, got
a good many votes.

Senator Douglas began the year 1854 by introducing a bill to or-

[1] L. Haviland, *A Woman's Life Work,* pp. 93-94. Erastus Hussey wrote his
reminiscences about the Underground Railroad in 1885. Found in a Slavery scrapbook, Burton Hist. Coll., Detroit Public Library.

ganize the remainder of the Louisiana Purchase into two territories, Kansas and Nebraska, on squatter sovereignty. When doubt of the meaning of this was expressed, he added a sentence that specifically repealed the Missouri Compromise. Thus the whole of a vast area would be thrown open to slavery, the question being left to the inhabitants of the region to settle. This made Kansas a field of guerilla war and contributed to the birth of the Republican Party. The first State organization and convention of the new party was held in an oak grove on the edge of Jackson, Michigan, on July 6, 1854.

Such a huge crowd as this Jackson gathering drew must have contained many Methodists. One of the speakers and one in the audience are known to have been Methodist ministers. The Rev. Riley C. Crawford, minister of the First Methodist Church in Jackson, made a speech but exactly what he said is not known. It may be presumed that he was strongly anti-slavery and opposed to the Kansas-Nebraska Act. The Rev. Isaac Bennett, long a pioneer Circuit rider, was present at the Convention and joined the Republican Party the day it was organized in Michigan. He noted in his pocket diary on July 6, 1854, "Today attended a political meeting at Jackson to consolidate political parties against incroachments (*sic*) of slavery; meeting harmonious; candidates for State offices nominated."[2]

National and State Methodist Opinions of Slavery

The histories of the American Methodist Episcopal Church sometimes call the years from 1844 to 1861 "the paper war." Feeling was so strong that the peaceful plan of separation proposed in 1844 could not be carried out. Dividing the assets and properties of the Methodist Book Concern was a special cause of discord. Border Conferences were hauled both ways by those, who were eager to pull them over to their side of the quarrel. Bitterness was so strong that the General Conference of 1848 refused to receive a fraternal delegate from southern Methodism. It was agreed to extend to him "all personal courtesies." Naturally the southern delegate, Dr. Lovick Pierce, declined such an offer.[3]

In 1854, the 19th session of the Michigan Annual Conference expressed its opinion of recent events in no uncertain terms. Its resolutions on the Compromise of 1850 and also the Kansas-Nebraska Act said in part:

[2] For Crawford's presence and speech at the Republican meeting see Charlotte Lockwood, *Church on Main St., A History of First Methodist Church, Jackson, Mich.*, p. 21. For Bennett's attendance see his Memoir in Michigan Annual Conference *Minutes* for 1892, pp. 80-83.

[3] W. W. Sweet, *Meth. Am. Hist.*, pp. 256-257. *The History of American Methodism*, II, 144-145. (Chapter 16 by A. E. Jones).

> We share fully in the general indignation . . . created by the repeal of the Missouri Compromise, by which it is made possible that one of the fairest portions of the National Domain once consecrated . . . to freedom forever, may become the theatre of such a system of oppression . . . as could not be introduced into any other civilized country upon the face of the earth. We view with the deepest abhorrence the operations of the Fugitive Slave Law, and will use all proper means whatever to contribute to the formation of such a Public Opinion as will peremptorily and absolutely demand its repeal by the National Congress.[4]

No mention of slavery was made in the Annual Conference resolutions from 1850 through 1852. But from then until the Civil War, annual resolutions in much the same wording were adopted. Perhaps a bit longer than the later ones but typical of most of them was the statement made in 1854. It said:

> American slavery is an invasion of the rights of God: it is an infraction of the eternal law of Jehovah; it wages war with the administration of Divine Justice and Goodness; it is opposed to the spirit and teachings of the Bible; it is distracting and dividing, if not destroying, the Churches of Christ in this land; it is subversive of all the true interests of the Nation, and in its present alarmingly aggressive movements is threatening the very existence of our Federal Union and Republican Government.

By 1855, the Michigan Annual Conference was urging all Christian men "to vote right upon this subject as well as to pray right." Presumably they meant the new Republican Party. In 1858, Seth Reed was appointed to secure by correspondence common action in the General Conference of 1860 to change the rule on slavery in the *Discipline*. The strong statement desired by the Michigan ministers failed to be adopted in 1860. It got only a simple majority and needed a two-thirds vote. What was adopted did condemn slavery as a very great evil but then it only "affectionately admonished all our preachers and people . . . to seek its extirpation by all lawful and Christian means."[5] Very few Methodists had any idea that the end of slavery would be achieved by a great Civil War.

Resolutions are cold things and the emotions of one parsonage family can be seen in the memoir of Mrs. Catherine M. Bartlett in The Detroit Annual Conference *Minutes* for 1907. In 1859, she and her husband, the Rev. A. R. Bartlett, were serving a small church in Lexington on the shores of Lake Huron. The couple were known to hold strong anti-slavery views. Her memoir writer said of her in part:

[4] *Minutes* of the 19th session of the Mich. An. Conf. in 1854 pp. 33-34.
[5] W. W. Sweet, *Meth. Am. Hist.*, p. 263.
The History of American Methodism, II, 209-215.

On every church or political issue she not only had a decided opinion but felt in it an almost personal interest. The victims of oppression whether of intemperance or slavery, church or state, had her deepest sympathy and her eldest daughter's first memory is of tears while the church bells were tolling at the time of John Brown's execution.

Unchanging but Growing Michigan Methodism

Many of the incidents involving slavery had no effect at all on Michigan. The border States were not its concern. Again a remote geographical location had an effect. Inspection of the local church records gives the impression that Methodism carried on in Michigan in the 1850's much as it had in its earlier years here. Circuit riders still travelled vast distances but a bit farther north than before. Presiding Elders and their quarterly visits were still important and the ministers were just as much concerned with camp meetings and protracted winter revivals. The national events may have had some connection with the slow growth of the Church in membership during the first part of the Fifties. Michigan Methodism gained 726 members in 1850, 670 in 1851 and then decreased 300 in 1852. After that it did better for in 1855 the increase was 2,508. This contributed to the decision to divide the State into two Annual Conferences in 1856.

The familiar pioneering pattern of advancing Methodism was still visible. After several years of Class meetings, a Methodist Episcopal Church was organized in Dowagiac in 1850. It began in the hotel ballroom and met there or in the school house for several years. The Circuit of which it was a part included Decatur, Cassopolis, and Lawton. In 1855, the Dowagiac Church bought the land, on which its building still stands, and began to erect its own house of worship. This was dedicated by Bishop Ames in 1859. Tecumseh became a station in 1851 as did Sturgis. In 1856, White Pigeon was also made a station.

Efforts to extend the Church into the Grand Traverse Area were made by David R. Latham. He had intended to preach in Kansas but felt that the need was greater here. In June 1857, he began to preach at Old Mission, started a Class of nine members and then a Sunday School of two teachers and eight pupils. His congregation was a mixed one composed of Indians, sailors from the revenue cutter Michigan, and white pioneer farmers. William H. Brockway came in the summer, being Superintendent of the Lower Peninsula Indian District, but a regular Quarterly Conference could not be held as neither officers nor members existed yet. Brockway took Latham's church letter to Isabelle Indian Mission and it recommended him to the Michigan Annual Conference. Not being there for examination that year, Latham was not admitted on trial to the Annual Conference until 1858.

However, the Michigan Annual Conference of 1857 created two Circuits, composed of Old Mission and Elk Rapids on one hand and

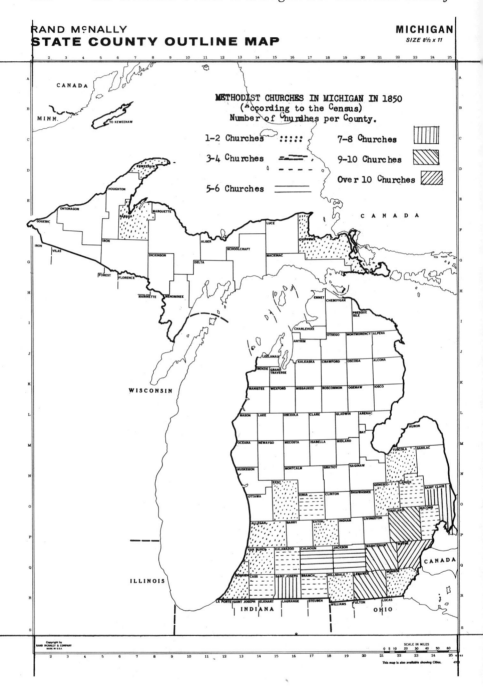

Northport and Traverse City on the other. Latham's first Quarterly Conference was held at Old Mission with an attendance of three, consisting of the Class leader, Mr. Pratt, Circuit Rider Latham, and Presiding Elder Penfield. They divided the work between them. Latham made the nominations, Pratt voted on them, and Penfield declared the results.

Latham's regular routine of work included teaching school at Old Mission during the week, preaching there on Sunday mornings, walking to Traverse City, preaching there on Sunday evenings, and then walking back to Old Mission again. Once in the winter, he got lost on the ice of the bay in a heavy fog. His Circuit was called Whitewater in 1858 and included Elk Rapids. The terrain was even more difficult and all his travel was on foot via the beach. No wonder he left the next year to be an Indian School Agent farther west.[6]

Equally pioneer conditions but more rapid growth was found in the Upper Peninsula. John Pitezel continued to be the Presiding Elder there until 1852. It is a sign of the change coming over that region that he was ordered to attend the Wisconsin Annual Conference in 1852 for the purpose of arranging the transfer there of Indian Missions at Sandy Lake and Fond du Lac, Minnesota. These had been under the care of the Michigan Annual Conference only a couple of years.

More attention was needed by the work among the miners, especially the Cornish Methodists who came in increasing numbers to the Upper Peninsula. Many of them had been local preachers and Class leaders in England. They were to furnish both the ministers and the congregations in large numbers for the next fifty years.

The organization of churches proceeded rapidly. The Marquette one was organized in the fall of 1851 by William Benson in the upper hall of a house afterwards a hotel. Presiding Elder Pitezel held their first Quarterly Conference in June 1852. By 1856, the Marquette Society had built a modest frame church and also a parsonage. In 1854, Grace Church at Houghton was started by Lewis W. Earle. This is often called the "Mother Church of the Copper Country." Many of the other Methodist churches of the Upper Peninsula were its offshoots. Among the places which had Methodist preaching in the Fifties but did not organize a church until later were Ontonagan, Calumet, and Hancock.[7]

Another sign of growth was the establishment of a *second* Methodist church in some southern Michigan towns. Adrian set up a second church

[6] M. L. Leach, "History of the Grand Traverse Region," *Mich. Pioneer Coll.* XXXII, 72-93. Also histories of the individual churches mentioned, to be found in the Conference coll. at Albion and Adrian College libraries.

[7] MSS History of First M.E. Church in Marquette by P. Ross Parish, written in 1883. Found in Mich. Conf. hist. coll., Albion College Library. Histories of the other Upper Peninsula churches are found in the Detroit Conf. hist. coll. in Adrian College Library.

Greensky Indian Church. In the 1840's the Chippewa Indian Missionary, Peter Greensky, established a mission on a hill north of Lake Charlevoix, where Indian chiefs once held their councils. The Indians built this Church in the 1850's. It is a fine example of the pioneer log style construction, with hand-hewn timbers and notched corners. Windows, doors, and much of the lumber were brought by canoe from Traverse City to Pine Lake (Lake Charlevoix) and then carried two miles to this site. Methodist services for the Indians have been held here regularly ever since.

in 1851 but had some trouble in keeping it alive due to internal dissension over renting the pews and also the use of music. In the same year, a second charge was established in Ann Arbor. Grand Rapids had an effective revival in 1853, led by Andrew J. Eldred. Over three hundred were converted of whom fifty-seven eventually became full members of the church. Thus Grand Rapids was made large enough for it to consider starting another Society. Under the guidance of the Rev. Resin Sapp, a forceful preacher long useful in Michigan Methodism, a second Methodist Church was organized in 1855. Fifty-seven members of First Church transferred to start the new Society. This was about one-fifth of the entire membership of First Church. It took this new group thirty years to achieve a church building.

In Detroit, a New York City missionary named Carter was brought in to start a *French* Methodist Episcopal Society. It had long been needed. The new group met at first in the Congress Street Church at 3 P.M. on Sundays. On Christmas Day, 1851, a special service in both French and English, was held and the members of First and Third churches were invited to attend. Eventually the French Society managed to build a modest church on Rivard Street but it was not too successful. Pilcher said that the French Church was discontinued after about fifteen years. He was of the opinion, "Good had been done — some had been converted and added to the Church, who were steadfast in the faith — but the success did not seem to warrant the continuance of the Mission."[8]

In actual construction of church buildings, this was not so busy a decade as those just before and after. The meeting houses were still built of wood in a very plain manner. And usually one was achieved by the dedicated efforts of one or two men. In the Hastings Church, the minister in 1859-1860, named Jeremy Boynton, was unusually skilled in getting the members to work together. The historian of the Church said:

> Soon after his arrival he said, "We must build a church. Few, if any, had faith that it could be done, but steps were taken . . . headed by the pastor. The first thing was a call for volunteers to chop, score and hew, to be lead by the stalwart pastor. During the evening the men were usually seen and it was ascertained who could go the next day and on the following morning as soon as it was light . . . with ax on the shoulder, dinner pail in the hand, with chalk line and charred sticks for the chalk, the company were marching for the forest to cut logs and get out timber for the new church . . . . All were volunteers, the stone needed and the hauling were donated too, all painting was done by the pastor and one other man.

The ladies did their part by preparing a lavish dinner at the time of laying the cornerstone. This brought in $75 which was considered a very large sum then. So eager were they to use the church that when the frame was up and enclosed, a temporary floor and seats of boards laid on wood blocks were installed. Quarterly Conference was then held there even though there were no doors nor windows. The finished building was dedicated by Presiding Elder Holdstock in September, 1860, with the sermon given by the President of Albion, Thomas Sinex.[9]

After years of being part of a large Circuit called Bean Creek Mission, the Morenci Methodists got tired of meeting in homes and school houses. In 1851, the north side of the village was platted for the first time, a lot was given to the Methodists, a subscription list was circulated at once, and a modest frame building dedicated in 1852. The contract included "an elegant steeple." Josiah Osgood, a layman, was determined

---

[8] Pilcher, *Hist. Prot. Mich.*, pp. 199-200. Also a series of clippings from the Detroit Free Press of 1851-1852 filed under Detroit, Churches, in the Burton Collection, Detroit Public Library.

[9] From a history of the Hastings Church, *Mich. Pioneer Coll.*, XXII, 595.

The Second German M. E. Church in Detroit was organized in 1857, and built its brick edifice on the east side of Sixteenth Street (then Lasalle Ave.) between Michigan Avenue and Dalzelle Street. The Church cost $1500. Detroit had the First German Church organized in 1847, and much later the Thirty-second Street German Church was built in 1882.

Lafayette Street M. E. Mission, 1849. Later the Tabernacle Church, this was the third M. E. Church organized in Detroit.

that Morenci should have a good bell. He went to Troy, New York, visited the foundry and picked out several bells. From a mile away, he then selected the one with the best tone. The bell was shipped to Toledo and, thence with ox teams, delivered to Morenci. So great was the excitement on the day it was hung, that Osgood locked the building or else the young men would have rung it all night. The bell was still in use, on a different church, when Morenci celebrated its centenary in 1936.[10]

[10] Centennial history of Morenci M. E. Church by Arthur Ackland. In Burton Coll., Detroit Public Library

A few other Societies built a church or remodeled in the Fifties. The first church at Allegan burned in 1853 and a new one was built on the same location. It was much like the old one. That meant frame construction, shingle roof, a square tower on an oblong room, and outside steps to a wide front door opening into a small vestibule. The pulpit was opposite the doorway but the choir and modest organ were at the back. Some churches, arranged in that way, followed the custom of turning their backs on the preacher and facing the choir when they stood to sing a hymn.

In 1859, the Ypsilanti Church enlarged its seating capacities by cutting the building in two, moving one end of it back sixteen feet and filling the resultant space with pews. Originally the first church at Northville had a high pulpit, square box pews, and two front doors. The pastor in 1854, William Taylor, had a central aisle, more modern pews, a platform, and uptodate pulpit furniture installed. This meant a smaller pulpit, a sofa, and two chairs, the latter undoubtedly covered with haircloth.[11]

Individual church histories occasionally reveal differing local customs. The Society at Palo did not have its own building until 1870. Before that, it met in a school house, or over a store or in the Masonic Hall. When evening meetings were to be held, it was the custom for the various families to bring their household lamps. In time another custom developed. "It was not uncommon for the young men to vie with each other for the privilege of carrying home the lamps that they might light the way for the young ladies."[12]

Pew rents were quite generally used in the stationed churches at that time. After a successful revival in 1857, the Dixboro Church erected a building in 1858 but with quite a large debt on it. The male members of the Society met to decide whether to rent the pews or not. After long debate, it was so decided by a close vote. Therefore, another resolution was added that all the pews should be free at Quarterly Conferences and protracted revivals. The Church at Quincy regularly rented its pews at $20 each per annum, in order to pay its pastor's salary. One member remembered that her father always took two pews for his family and two for his friends and guests.[13]

Much emphasis was given by the Michigan Annual Conference in

11 Booklet on "One Hundred Years of Allegan Methodism," *Mich. Conf. Hist. Coll.*, Albion College Library. Lulu Skinner, History of the Ypsilanti Church, Paul Cargo, History of the Northville Church. The latter two found in Detroit *Conf. Hist. Coll.*, Adrian College Library.

12 Clippings from Ionia County newspapers for 1934, *Mich. Conf. Hist. Coll.*, Albion College Library.

13 R. A. Brunger, History of the Dixboro Church, *Detroit Conf. Hist. Coll.*, Adrian College Library. Cora Clizbe, article on the Quincy Church in *Quincy Herald*, August 3, 1936. *Mich. Conf. Hist. Coll.*, Albion College Library.

the Fifties to increasing the number of parsonages. Every year one of the standing committees was on parsonages. In general, parsonages were found in a ratio of from one-half to two-thirds of the number of church buildings. A committee reported to the Michigan Annual Conference in 1855 that twelve parsonages had been built during the past year. That committee gave the reason for pushing such construction when it said, "It is a serious embarrassment to a preacher when entering upon a field of labor to find no house provided for the accommodation of his family." Congregations were also urged annually to provide the "heavy furniture" for their parsonages.[14]

A Changing Ministry With Seminary Education

The character of the itinerant ministry of Methodism was changing rather more than the congregations were then. More ministers married early in their careers, even during the period when they were on trial, more churches had stationed pastors, and the custom of equal poverty for all Elders was being destroyed by the salary votes of Quarterly Conferences. A station church demanded more variety in its preaching, a better educated man in its pulpit, and more social activity on the part of minister and family. Hence the Official board would offer more salary to obtain an outstanding pulpit orator. People soon grew dissatisfied with the results of horseback study of a few books by a Circuit rider. They began to demand the product of a professional theological seminary.[15]

Ministerial education had been the cause of argument in the Methodist Episcopal Church for about ten years already when, in 1855, Garrett Biblical Institute was incorporated and proceeded to build near Northwestern University. Not being in Michigan, the Annual Conferences of this State participated in its work only through two annually appointed Visitors or advisers from both Annual Conferences, soon to be created here.

But argument about the correct way to educate a minister continued. The age of a minister and the way he had entered his Annual Conference colored the opinion he held about religious education. In 1860, the Michigan Annual Conference committee on education said in part:

---

[14] *Minutes* of 20th session of Mich. Annual Conference, p. 13. Figures about churches and parsonages built do not always agree in committee reports with those given in statistics of all the Societies. Statistical tables each year reported on members, church property, Sunday Schools, and amounts raised for various causes. The summary at the end frequently contains mistakes in its totals or additions. Minutes were not yet done with much care.

[15] W. C. Barclay, *Methodist Episcopal Church,* 1845-1939. Vol. III. Chapter II on "A Changing Church in a Changed Society." The first topic discussed is "A Changing Itineracy" pp. 40-44.

>Our free Schools are bringing the blessings of education within the reach of all . . . it is indispensable that the standard of ministerial qualifications be correspondingly elevated and extended to make us suitable religious instructors of an intelligent and cultivated people. The times are greatly changed, and the literary advantages enjoyed by our fathers in the ministry are not sufficient for the present generation.

All young men thinking of entering the ministry were strongly urged to attend Garrett Biblical Institute.

In 1858, the Detroit Annual Conference declared that it was no longer possible to educate a young man as a junior preacher on a four-weeks Circuit under the guidance of an experienced, older man. The Circuits had been reduced in size or made stations for one man. A young, untrained man was a real burden. He lacked the ability to compete with able ministers of other denominations. Hence the work suffered.

The greatest need was for money to loan to promising men for support while they studied. In 1859, a plan for a Ministerial Education Society was laid before the Detroit Annual Conference. This contemplated only a modest loan of $100 per annum. Raising the funds with which to start this organization was its most difficult aspect. Like other worthwhile projects, it was much delayed by the urgent demands of the Civil War era.[16]

More About Seth Reed

In the decade from 1850 to 1860, Seth Reed served six churches in Michigan. In 1850, he was appointed to Pontiac where he held a fine revival and received the largest public donation party of his life. He had expected to be returned there but instead was sent to Ypsilanti for two years. Again he held a successful revival and thereby added sixty members to his church. While he was stationed there, the Normal College opened, the first such institution in Michigan. Reed gave the dedicatory prayer on October 5, 1852, and the State Superintendent of Public Instruction, John Pierce, made the main speech. Reed liked to remember that he also gave the prayer at the golden anniversary of the Normal College in 1902.

Monroe was Reed's next charge and, although not a happy experience, he stayed there the regular two years. The town was suffering from hard times, mainly due to the steamboats not stopping there any more. Then in 1854, Monroe had an epidemic of cholera, which

---

[16] *History of American Methodism,* II, 193-196. A section on theological education is found in Chapter XVI, The Years of Disagreement by Arthur E. Jones, Jr. For education reports and resolutions see the *Minutes* as follows: Michigan Annual Conference for 1860, p. 24. Detroit Annual Conference for 1858, pp. 26-27. Same for 1859, pp. 26-29.

caused widespread panic. Reed sadly noted that the Church lost sixty-four members by death or removal between 1853 and 1855.

The Monroe Church interior was arranged with a high pulpit between two front doors. Right below the pulpit was a large stove with ill-fitting pipes running around the room. His very first Sunday there, the fumes made Reed very sick. Upon recovering from his illness, he was most surprised to find that the congregation had been busy. The stove had been removed, a furnace installed, the pulpit moved to the rear, all the pews reversed, and some shaky galleries torn out.

The First Church in Ann Arbor was the scene of Reed's next labors. He was there two years also but did not feel entirely happy although a fine revival occurred. Also the church was enlarged and a parsonage built. Reed was a little too conscious of those University professors in his congregation. Years later he admitted that he was embarrassed in Ann Arbor by his lack of formal education.

Port Huron was his assignment in the years from 1857 to 1859. Again he remembered a fine revival. And a parsonage was built, which was opened with a banquet in the new dining room. During the time that the parsonage family was eating, a few members moved all their household goods in and even set up their bedsteads "for a surprise." At this point in his biographical sermon, given in 1913, before the Detroit Annual Conference, Reed stopped, took out his watch, and then told how his Port Huron Bible Class held a surprise party for them. They gave his wife a purse and him that very identical watch. He had carried it faithfully ever since – a period of at least fifty-four years.

From 1859 to 1861, Reed was stationed at Woodward Avenue Church in Detroit. This was one of the two ancestors of today's Central Church in Detroit. His salary was $1,000. According to Reed, that was "the most then paid in Michigan."

A comparison of the statistics on ministerial salaries as shown in the Detroit Annual Conference *Minutes* for 1860 is revealing. Reed and D. C. Jacokes at Lafayette Street Church, also in Detroit, each got $1,000. Yet the Detroit District's Presiding Elder, James F. Davidson, was supposed to have $700 and actually received $676. Trenton, Wayne, and Northville each promised to pay $500 per annum. Farmington paid $400 and Lee Chapel only $390. That same year the salaries in the Ann Arbor District ran from $200 to $750. On the Port Huron District, the range of pay was from $200 to $700. The days were almost over when a single man got $100 and a married man $200 in Michigan.

In 1861, the sixth session of the Detroit Annual Conference met in Reed's church in Detroit. The Civil War had begun and two of the four Methodist ministers in the City had gone as chaplains. Therefore, Reed of Woodward and John Levington of Walnut Street, a small mission, with a little aid from Presiding Elder Hickey, ran the day-to-day arrangements of the Conference session. The Rev. Thomas Eddy, editor of the *Northwestern Christian Advocate* in Chicago, was present to report the session for his paper. He observed that "Brother Reed especially, as Conference met in his Church, was pressed with duties but his cool patient systemizing enabled him to get through them all." The two-year restriction on the length of a minister's service in one church was still in effect. Mr. Eddy was sure that Reed would have a third year at the Woodward Avenue Church "if the wishes of the people had succeeded."[17]

Changes in Methodist Sunday Schools

Gone were the days in many churches when the entire Methodist Sunday School could meet in one room. On June 8, 1851, a procession of seven hundred Sunday School students marched to the Woodward Avenue Methodist Episcopal Church for dinner and a program. On November 23, 1854, the Detroit Methodist Sunday School Union was organized. It was composed of all the city's Sunday School officers and teachers belonging to that denomination. The aims were to improve the teaching and to increase the membership. Quarterly meetings were held in turn at the different Methodist churches and the Union also tried to establish more Sunday Schools wherever it was thought they were needed. This led in time to the organization of the Fort Street and Simpson Methodist Episcopal Churches. On August 2, 1855, the Sunday School Union and all the Methodist Episcopal Churches in Detroit joined in an excursion and picnic on the steamer May Queen to Wyandotte. Fourteen hundred people went along on this occasion.[18]

General Educational Attitudes

Every year during the 1850's, the Michigan Annual Conference adopted several resolutions on Education. These were concerned with the State system of education and also their own collegiate institutions. In view of the attitudes in 1966, it is interesting to note that the Methodist ministers were firmly sure that daily Bible reading and prayer, on a non-denominational basis, should be sustained in every public school. The ministers were repeatedly urged by Conference committees on Education to visit and take an interest in their local common schools. High approval was registered of the founding of the State Normal College in 1852 and also of the Michigan Agricultural College in 1857. Genuine interest was also taken in Northwestern and Garrett. But the deepest concern was felt for the seminary at Albion.

[17] Seth Reed, *Story of My Life, passim. North. Ch. Ad.,* IX, 324. Also *Minutes* of Detroit Annual Conf., for 1861, pp. 6, 19-21.
[18] Silas Farmer, *History of Detroit and Michigan,* p. 579.

Origins of Albion College

Financially the situation of the Wesleyan Seminary at Albion remained desperate. If one may judge by the questions repeatedly raised by the Michigan Annual Conference to be asked in writing of the trustees of the Seminary, the ministers were ignorant and very uneasy about that institution. Those old subscription notes, good indefinitely for tuition at Albion, were the chief subject of dispute. Were all or any of them worthless? This question received varying answers.

The whole situation was made more difficult by a bad fire in the newly erected North Building, in the fall of 1853. It had only been in use about a year. Most of the girl students lost all their personal belongings while the Seminary lost three classrooms and a laboratory. Most of the chemical equipment was carried out and stacked up against the campus fence. The male students were all ousted from their rooms and told to find rooms in town. Many students simply went home.

The site of the fire was cleared that summer and in 1854 North Hall was rebuilt. Somewhat modified, this building still stands on the Albion College Campus. It was never again used as a dormitory. The clubs and boarding houses of Albion date from the time just after the fire.

Three changes in the presidency of the Seminary came within

Albion College (then the Wesleyan Seminary at Albion) in the late 1850's. The Central Building was completed in January 1844; the North Hall (at the left) was built in 1854; South Hall began in 1856 was not finally completed until 1870.

this same decade. Clark T. Hinman, President from 1846 to 1853, left to become the first President of Northwestern. He died suddenly in 1854. Ira Mayhew, who succeeded Hinman, served only fifteen months as President. Then he left to become Michigan Superintendent of Public Instruction. Mayhew was then succeeded by Thomas H. Sinex, who served for ten years and was the first President of Albion College. It looks as if the Seminary had not yet attained a standing which made trained men willing to give a lifetime to its service.

Three changes were made by the Michigan Legislature during this period, all designed by the trustees to strengthen the school if possible. The first law, passed on February 18, 1850, added the title "Albion Female Collegiate Institute" to that of "Wesleyan Seminary." It obviously provided a college education for women but not for men. Full college authority probably could not have been obtained then. The degree of "Mistress of Arts and Sciences" was conferred on 116 women between the years 1851 and 1863.

After the creation of two Annual Conferences in the State in 1856, the Legislature passed another Act about Albion in 1857. The title was again changed, becoming "Wesleyan Seminary and Female College at Albion." Provision was also made for future equal division of elected trustees between the Michigan and Detroit Annual Conferences. At that time the trustees were thirteen in number with the President of the Seminary as the thirteenth.

The final and most important change by the Legislature was taken on February 25, 1861. That awkward long title was dropped and the Seminary became "Albion College" as it has been ever since. Conditions had changed from the time when the Seminary was started. The public schools were good enough and numerous enough in 1861 to decrease the need for a preparatory seminary. The trustees hoped that the title change might help the desperate financial situation of the school. Men and women were to be admitted on exactly the same basis. Both the Church and the Legislature opposed *denominational colleges* when the Seminary was started in 1835.[19]

Origins of Adrian College

That Wesleyan educational institution at Leoni, known in the early Fifties as Michigan Union College, also underwent changes. It had much the same financial problems as Albion. But the trustees in Leoni felt that their situation might be improved by moving the school to a more accessible town. The Rev. Asa Mahan, well known as President of Oberlin College, had come to Jackson as minister of the Congrega-

---

[19] Pilcher, *Hist. Prot. Mich.*, pp. 386-389. W. F. Dunbar, *Mich. Record in Higher Education*, pp. 109-111. R. Gildart, *Albion College*, pp. 25, 56-59, 64-78. This last has much financial detail.

tional Church in 1855. Jackson was near Leoni so that Mahan often visited there and lectured at the college's literary societies. Then in 1857, Mahan moved to Adrian to become pastor of the Plymouth Congregational Church. When he learned of the desperate financial situation of Michigan Union College, he decided to try to bring it to Adrian.

What he did, all within six weeks, seems almost impossible. Mahan aroused the interest of the leading citizens of Adrian, got twenty acres of land donated as a site for the college, and raised $30,000 for buildings. Naturally the trustees accepted such an offer. Then Mahan and his local committee hired an architect and had two new brick buildings ready to occupy in the fall of 1859. In the spring of that year, the school had been incorporated as Adrian College and Mahan elected its President. The charter provided that six of the twelve trustees must be drawn from the Wesleyans.

The actual moving of the school from Leoni to Adrian was done by ox team at night. Apparently the faculty and the students feared that the citizens of Leoni would try to prevent their departure. Naturally there was some local opposition to losing the college. Mahan also served as Professor of Intellectual and Moral Science at Adrian College. He thought that he was free to speak his mind on any controversial topic. His attitude plus the Civil War eventually brought more trouble for Adrian College. But it enjoyed a good start at Adrian, having 235 students in 1862.[20]

[20] William C. S. Pellowe, "Asa Mahan — Sage of Adrian," *Mich. Ch. Ad.*, for June 11, 1964, XCI, #24, pp. 4-5, 18-19. W. F. Dunbar, *Mich. Record in Higher Education*, pp. 124-126.

In 1859, a struggling Weslyan Methodist school at Leoni, known as Michigan Union College, was moved to Adrian to become Adrian College. Dr. Asa Mahan, pastor of the Congregational Church, got 20 acres of land donated as a college site and raised $30,000 for buildings. He became the first president. Two brick buildings were ready for occupancy in the fall of 1859. In 1866 Adrian College became a Methodist Protestant institution.

Methodism and the University of Michigan

Colleges then quite generally emphasized their classical courses. In so new a State as Michigan, the clergy were often the only men available with the education needed to teach in a college. Four faculty homes were among the first buildings on the Ann Arbor campus of the University of Michigan. Custom led to each home being set aside for a Professor who belonged to one of the four chief Protestant denominations in the State. These were Methodist, Baptist, Presbyterian, and Episcopal.

Among the Methodist faculty in the early days were: Henry Colclazer, first librarian of the University and also the Presiding Elder of Ann Arbor District; Daniel D. Whedon who was Professor of Logic, Rhetoric, and Philosophy; and Erastus O. Haven who came from the New York Annual Conference to be the Professor of Latin. He stayed from 1853 to 1856 when he left to be the editor of *Zion's Herald* in Boston. Later he would be President of the University very briefly. Pilcher said that at the time of Haven's coming, "It was understood that the Regents of the University of Michigan were desirous of obtaining a Methodist Professor."

Naturally the Methodist Episcopal Church in Michigan approved of this early policy just as it also liked the early rule requiring the students to attend one of the village churches on Sundays and also the daily chapel exercises. The Michigan Annual Conference in 1853 said in one of several resolutions devoted to education:

> We rejoice to see the prosperity of the University of Michigan and approve of the action of its Regents . . . recognizing the need of christian influence in the Institution, by the election of Professors connected with various denominations of christians in the State.

In those early years, no permanent executive head of the University had been chosen. The professors from the four chief denominations each served in turn as President for one year. The wrangling between professors themselves and professors and Regents was almost incessant then. Some people felt that the Methodists wanted to hold too many of the professorships. The abolitionists played some part in all the quarrels too. The Regents were mostly Democrats and had an established policy against abolitionism.

All these jealousies and conflicting opinions resulted in a serious situation when the Regents adopted a resolution to dismiss Professors Whedon, Agnew, and Williams. The immediate cause was several abolition lectures and sermons Whedon had given around the State. Eventually Whedon and Agnew left but Williams kept his position. Mr. Haven had a somewhat similar treatment but was strong enough in the State so that the Regents dropped the matter entirely.

A new State constitution, a new Board of Regents, and a permanent President, Henry P. Tappan, changed the whole situation at Ann Arbor. The new leader was a very able man with independent ideas and a forceful, formal bearing. Some people thought he was condescending toward Michigan in general. He dropped the policy of having professors from each of four denomnations and was not so strict about church and chapel attendance. He wanted to make the University a place with a national reputation for its outstanding scholars. He certainly put the whole organization on a firmer footing but he alarmed many of the more devout Methodists in the State. About this time a student died after a riotous party at which he had been forced to drink too much. This was again a shock to total abstinence Methodists, of whom there were many in those days.

It is not surprising that both the Detroit and the Michigan Annual Conferences adopted long, strong resolutions about the University of Michigan at their sessions in 1857. One of the Professors, Alexander Winchell, is believed to have instigated these resolutions. He was an enemy of President Tappan both in religion and education. On the other hand, the editor of the *Michigan Argus*, Elihu B. Pont, did not approve of the resolutions at all and eventually withdrew from the Ann Arbor Church over the matter. The Michigan Annual Conference was a bit plainer spoken perhaps in its resolution. Here is part of it:

> With respect to the Michigan State University, while we believe that in its facilities for thorough mental cultivation it is second to no kindred institution of the land, we are compelled to fear that it is so defective in those moral and religious restraints . . . which ought always to be thrown around students of literary institutions, that it cannot be patronized by our citizens without imminent peril to the moral and religious character of those youths who may be sent there for instruction, and until there is a decided improvement in this respect, we must say to the christian public within the bounds of our Conference, *beware*.

The idea of Methodist work with college students, as expressed in the Wesley Foundations at State institutions of learning, was about half a century in the future then.[21]

The Temperance Movement

Two aspects of social reform received about equal attention from the Michigan Annual Conference in the Fifties. Abolition of slavery was one and the fight against liquor was the other. The fight for abo-

---

[21] W. F. Dunbar, *Mich. Record in Higher Education*, pp. 69-81. Pilcher, *Hist. Prot. Mich.*, pp. 239-242. Mary E. Lumy, "A History of the First Methodist Episcopal Church, Ann Arbor, Mich." typewritten copy from which items were copied for this History by R. A. Brunger. Burke Hinsdale, *History of the University of Michigan*, pp. 35, 159-160. Mich. Annual Conf. *Minutes* for 1853, p. 20; same for 1857, pp. 21-22. *Minutes* of Detroit Annual Conf., for 1857, p. 26.

lition of slavery was rather more emotional and received rather more attention in Michigan than Temperance did at first. The faith in a State law of prohibition was strong then. Maine adopted such a law in 1851 and soon twelve other States had followed her example. Michigan attempted such a law with little success. The first Prohibition Act passed the Legislature in 1853 and was accepted by a majority of the voters that year. But the Michigan Supreme Court declared the law unconstitutional. Huge petitions were circulated favoring another such law. Methodist ministers were active workers for signatures to these petitions. In 1855 another prohibition law was passed and remained on the State statute books until 1875 when it too was repealed and forgotten.[22]

The subject of Temperance is not mentioned in the *Minutes* of the Michigan Annual Conference until 1853. Beginning then some Temperance resolutions were adopted each year through 1860. These showed considerable faith in a *law*. First, a law like that of Maine's was urged. When one was finally adopted, it was admired and faith in its constitionality was expressed. Toward the end of the decade, disappointment over the failure to enforce the law was voiced.

More specific recommendations were also made. The Michigan Annual Conference in 1856 charged every minister to preach at least once a year on Temperance. Public lectures on the same subject were also urged. The Detroit Annual Conference of 1856 resolved that "all those ministers who treat this subject with neglect are recreant to those great trusts committed to them."

By 1860, it was evident that something more than good will was needed for Temperance. The Michigan and Detroit Annual Conferences that year approved the plans of the Michigan State Temperance Alliance and commended its agent, J. B. Merwin, to the churches. The Detroit Annual Conference said specifically that such an organization was needed not only for more efficiency and permanence but "also secures the friends of the cause in all parts of the State from the imposition of irresponsible lecturers." Again the ministers were reminded to preach "once or more" on Temperance during the coming year. Finally it said, "We urge upon all our people the importance of total abstinence from *all* that will intoxicate. . . . We will urge the impropriety of our members renting buildings for the sale of intoxicating liquors."

One agency outside the Methodist Episcopal Church was popular with some ministers in their drives for Temperance. This was the Independent Order of Good Templars. It was secret with a ritual

[22] For general background of Temperance in Mich., F. C. Bald, *Mich. in Four Centuries*, p. 268. W. C. Barclay, *Methodist Episcopal Church*, III, 54-56. For Mich. or Detroit Conference attitudes on Temperance see any of the *Minutes* for the years mentioned. A committee on Temperance functioned each year.

and a promise of total abstinence in its vows. Evidently it was meant to appeal to young people. A few Michigan ministers were active officers in the I.O.G.T., as it was often called. But many Methodists were very opposed to secret societies of any kind then. This kept down ministerial aid to an organization that was quite flourishing for a time.[23]

Immediately following the Temperance resolutions passed by the Detroit Annual Conference in 1860, were some on the use of Tobacco. This subject was there treated for the first time by the Conference committee. It declared that the ministers must "wholly abstain from the ordinary use of tobacco in all its forms." Such use was an evil which they must preach against and in no way encourage. Any young man thinking of becoming a minister in the Detroit Annual Conference ought "wholly to discard this base practice before they seek admittance to this body."

Administrative Changes

Reorganization of the Districts and placement under them of the charges went on annually at that time. During the decade of the Fifties, the eight Districts of 1850 doubled and the State was split into two Annual Conferences. A great many changes of appointments were made from one District to another. Jackson, was in the Ann Arbor District in 1851, shifted to the Marshall District for the years 1852 through 1855, and then made a part of the Lansing District in 1856.

Michigan Methodism's eight Districts in 1850 were Detroit, Ann Arbor, Monroe, Kalamazoo, Grand River, Flint, Marshall, and an Indian Mission District in the Upper Peninsula. The Districts were unchanged in 1851. A new District named Coldwater was set up in 1852. It drew five appointments from Marshall District, three from Kalamazoo, and three from Monroe. Only one charge, Addison, was a new appointment. Also the Indian Mission District was called Lake Superior Mission District but the seven appointments remained the same.

In 1853 another new District was created. That was Romeo, taken off the Detroit District for the most part. The name changes were two. Monroe District was now called Adrian District with much the same appointments but presumably the Presiding Elder changed his place of residence. The Grand River District was renamed Grand Rapids. In 1854, the Districts remained the same being ten in number.

In 1855, a new Indian Mission District in the Lower Peninsula was created. The experienced William H. Brockway was made its Pre-

---

[23] See the unpublished correspondence of E. E. Caster and W. H. Hicks found in the Detroit Conf, Hist. Coll., Adrian College Library. These men were young Methodist ministers in the 1850's. The I.O.G.T. was often mentioned by them. Mr. Caster believed in it, was a member and officer in it, and also the Masons. Mr. Hicks had his doubts about both secret organizations.

siding Elder. Only four appointments were listed but there must have been more preaching places. It is likely that this general change was made in preparation for the establishment of two Michigan Annual Conferences.

Two Conferences in Michigan

The Michigan Annual Conference session of 1854 began the preliminary preparation for a division of the State into two Conferences. Such a change would be proposed to the General Conference in 1856. Questions of expediency and location of the boundaries were certain to arise. Therefore, the Michigan Annual Conference appointed a special committee of five ministers "to secure enlightened and harmonious action." These men were Elijah H. Pilcher, James F. Davidson, William H. Brockway, John H. Pitezel, and George Smith. These ministers had long travelled the Circuits of Michigan and also served as Presiding Elders. Pilcher and Smith were so functioning in 1854.

That special committee made a written report in 1855. It said the territory now occupied was so large that, in order to attend the Annual Conference sessions, many ministers were forced to undertake very long and expensive journeys. The area would certainly make two Annual Conferences "of respectable size." The Michigan Principal Meridian was suggested as the line of division. It had already been surveyed and ran through the middle of the State east of Lansing and Jackson.

All of the Upper Peninsula would be attached to the eastern division and all the Indian missions in the Lower Peninsula would be placed in the western part. Mutual support of Albion College was to be pledged by both Annual Conferences. Superannuated preachers or their widows would be divided between the two new Conferences in ratio to their numbers of active preachers. If division occurred as planned, the Michigan Annual Conference would meet at Coldwater and the Detroit Annual Conference at Adrian.[24]

The Michigan Annual Conference of 1840 had 4,958 lay members and seventy-seven ministers. In 1855, it had 21,378 members and 189 ministers. That special committee certainly managed an even division of the State's Methodists. It has been shown that:

> Of the 189 preachers, 98 went into the new Detroit Conference and 91 remained in the new Michigan Conference. Of the 174 pastoral charges, 98 were assigned to the Detroit Conference and 76 to the Michigan. Of the lay membership, 10,623 remained with the Michigan Conference, while 10,755 came into the Detroit Conference.[25]

[24] *Minutes* of Mich. Annual Conf. for 1854, p. 36; *Minutes* of same for 1855, pp. 9, 12-13.
[25] William C. S. Pellowe, *Beginnings of Methodism in Mich.*, p. 10.

THE ANNUAL CONFERENCES OF EPISCOPAL METHODISM
THAT HAVE SERVED MICHIGAN

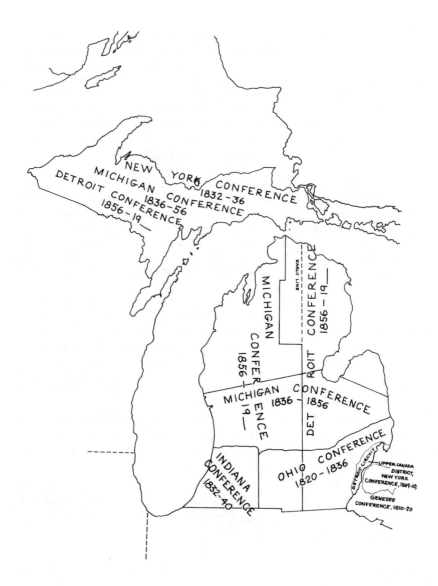

A member of that special division committee in 1855, John Pitezel, wrote many years later:

> Michigan Conference sent out a noble swarm from the parent hive constituting the Detroit Conference. This swarm — now forty — has grown in number, strength and influence to be the peer of her not to be despised venerable mother.[26]

The Detroit Annual Conference Districts, as established in 1856, were seven, of which six were old and one a new creation. The latter was named Owosso and was made by transfers from other Districts. Seven came from Flint and three from Ann Arbor. The previous Districts, which were maintained were Detroit, Ann Arbor, Adrian, Romeo, Flint, and Lake Superior.

Six Districts were the portion of the Michigan Annual Conference. Five had been previously organized: Marshall, Coldwater, Kalamazoo, Grand Rapids, and an Indian Mission District. Lansing was the new District with four of its appointments drawn from Grand Rapids. This new District presumably had several new appointments too. That is hard to determine because what looks like a new charge in the Conference records may have been a preaching place on another Circuit previously.

More Administrative Changes

Each Annual Conference in Michigan had added a District in 1856. Only Detroit did so in 1857, with the new Port Huron District containing twelve appointments of which ten were transferred from Romeo District. In the Michigan Annual Conference, the Indian Mission District was renamed Isabella Indian Mission and had one less appointment than the year previously.

In 1858, it was the Michigan Annual Conference which added a new District. This was the Grand Traverse District with six appointments. Four were transferred from Grand Rapids District. This District probably was created to save the Presiding Elder many miles of travel. Manistee and Pentwater appear as separate appointments for the first time.

In 1859, no changes were made in the Districts by either Annual Conference. Rather growth is revealed by the general increase in the number of appointments per District. Marshall District increased from sixteen to twenty charges. A more average change was two more per District.

In 1860, change rather than increase occurred. The Indian Mission District covering the Lower Peninsula was given up and the missions

---

[26] *Michigan Christian Advocate,* a clipping from MCA pasted in a Palmer Scrapbook, XIV, 124, Burton Coll., Detroit Public Library.

were divided between Lansing and Grand Traverse Districts. A noted Indian preacher and interpreter, Peter Marksman, was transferred to the Detroit Annual Conference. Then he was appointed to Iroquois Point and Sugar Island in the Lake Superior District.[27]

The Michigan Annual Conference also created the Niles District with twelve appointments, all of them being transferred from the Kalamazoo District which had twenty the year before. Next, three charges were taken from Grand Rapids District to Kalamazoo. In the Detroit Annual Conference, a new District, of only three charges was organized and called Superior City District. This was in northern Wisconsin, and only continued two years. The eight Districts in the entire State of Michigan in 1850 had grown to sixteen Districts in 1860.

Other changes than geographical can be detected in the successive lists of appointments. Almost every single District increased in the number of its appointments opposite which was not a name only the phrase "to be supplied." Was the supply of local preachers and exhorters decreasing or were these villages left without a Conference appointed minister tough places in which to work?

The list of the special assignments at the end of the tables of regular appointments was growing throughout the decade. Sometimes, as many as four preachers were assigned to Albion College as teachers or as President. A minister who was a professor in the Agricultural College, another at the University of Michigan, and one at Garrett were noted. T. C. Gardiner was the Agent of the American Bible Society, R. C. Crawford was the chaplain at the Michigan State Prison, and James Summerville held a similar position at the "Juvenile House of Reform."

A different source of Methodist preachers for Michigan was found in English Methodism beginning with one such minister coming here in 1856. In the early 20th century, such men were to come to Michigan in increasing numbers. John Wesley was a descendant of an uncle of the original John Wesley in England. The immigrant John Wesley came to the United States in 1856 with his wife, their six small children, and his wife's mother. They were enroute six weeks as they travelled via sailing ship. Almost every imaginable hardship befell them, such as terrible storms, various falls and injuries, and, as the voyage had lasted much longer than expected, their food supply was exhausted before land was sighted.

Upon landing in New York City, Wesley went at once to the Methodist Book Concern office. He had been a Class leader and also a local preacher in England. So he inquired "after some conferance (*sic*) where I might get employed as a minister." After showing his cre-

---

[27] See article by R. A. Brunger, "Peter Marksman — Chippewa Indian Missionary" in *Michigan Ch. Ad.*, for March 3 and 10, 1966. XCIII, #9, 3-4, 20-21; #10, 10-11, 18-19. Marksman was outstanding among the Indian Methodist preachers. He worked with Pitezel, Brockway and many other early Methodists for many years.

LOCAL PREACHER'S LICENSE.

TO ALL WHOM IT MAY CONCERN.

This Certifies that *Thomas Stanfield*, having been examined by us concerning his gifts, grace, and usefulness, we judge that he is a suitable person to be licensed as a LOCAL PREACHER in the METHODIST EPISCOPAL CHURCH, and we accordingly authorize him to preach the Gospel, subject to the requirements of the Discipline of said Church.

Signed, by order of the Quarterly Conference of *Fowlerville Cr.*, in the *Owosso* District, this *Ninth* day of *June*, 18 66.

_____ Orlando Parker _____ Presiding Elder.

The Local Preacher's License of Thomas Stanifer, Conway Township, Livingston County. Stanifer was a farmer, and representative of local preachers whose service meant so much to the influence and progress of nineteenth century Methodism. They preached and conducted funeral services in the absence of the circuit preacher.

dentials, he was told that the Detroit Annual Conference was in session at Adrian and "short of men to work."

He and all his family came by train to Toledo, being three days and nights on the way. After various vicissitudes, including taking the wrong train and being rendered practically penniless by having to pay has way back, finally they arrived in Adrian. The Conference was over but Presiding Elder Pilcher interviewed him, examined his papers, and assigned him to the second charge at Adrian.

John Wesley served in all twenty-one appointments in the Detroit Annual Conference. He retired in 1889. Then he preached occasionally until his death in 1900. His sermons were said to have been "scriptural, clear, practical, and convincing."[28]

[28] Wesley's Diary, mostly of the trip over and his early days in America is given in full, with annotations by Lewis Beeson, in *Michigan History*, March 1964. XLVIII, #1, 47-65.

Michigan Methodism Just Before 1861

The Michigan Annual Conference session in 1854 appointed a committee of ten ministers "on the State of the Church." The chairman was Andrew M. Fitch. The members were mostly experienced ministers but not Presiding Elders in any number. They drew up a long and rather pessimistic report.

First, they cited many figures which showed great growth in Districts, Circuits, stations, ministers, and members. Then they attacked these statistics as being unread by many members anyhow and also not giving a true picture of the real state of Methodism in Michigan. Two aspects of the Church were of concern.

The financial condition of the salaries of the travelling Elders alarmed them. An average of over $6,000 annually was the deficiency in meeting the claims of the ministers on their various charges. That old time method of claiming quarterage, table expenses, and house rent was still in effect. The committee felt that something was radically wrong either with the system or its application in practice.

In spiritual affairs, they had made very careful inquiry and ascertained that about one-half of the members did not attend the Classes regularly. The ticket system, formerly used for the love feasts, "has come to an end with us." Prayer meetings were not too well attended but members were still faithful in attendance on "the public preaching of the Word." Greater faithfulness on the part of stewards and Class leaders was needed and, above all, firm enforcement of the *Discipline* by the pastor. Also more pastoral visitation was needed in every church in the State.

Perhaps a few random incidents in conclusion of this chapter may reveal more than any statistics could. A spectacular comet had caused widespread alarm in 1857. The Rev. Resin Sapp chose to preach on the comet in the church at Galesburg. The interest of the congregation was intense. Twenty years later, the editor of the Michigan Christian Advocate remembered and wrote of it:

> Many feared the world would dissolve and this would be the end of the earth . . . before Mr. Sapp concluded all fear had vanished. His accurate mathematical calculations, his convincing array of astronomical facts, his plain presentation of the Providence of God . . . and his concluding exhortation to the people to put their trust in God were all perfectly well adapted to the end accomplished.[29]

In February 1861, the assistant missionary secretary of the national society, together with the Rev. Thomas H. Jacokes, paid a visit to the Isabella Indian Mission. Two other prominent local ministers, Francis

---

[29] Piece about Resin Sapp from editorial page of *Mich. Ch. Ad.* for March 3, 1877.

B. Bangs and Israel Cogshall, were also in attendance. The journey there was by sleigh one hundred and twenty miles from Albion. The missionary in charge was Eramus D. Young. He and his wife had actually learned to speak the Chippewa language as a courtesy to the Indians. Some one of the four ministers later wrote of their visits to the editor of the *Northwestern Christian Advocate* as follows:

> The mission was in a prosperous state. A new church edifice was dedicated on the Sabbath of the visit — a neat frame, of good size, lighted with lamps, painted, carpeted, etc. and furnished with a handsome Bible presented by Rev. T. C. Gardiner. The house was out of debt but a good quarterly collection was taken. At the communion some two hundred red men and women surrounded the Lord's Table . . . . Brother Young, the missionary, was laboring successfully and both himself and wife are spoken of as admirably fitted for mission life. They teach good doctrine and furnish the example of a model Christian home.[30]

On the other hand, a letter six months later the same year from Brighton, Michigan, reported to the same church paper that a protracted revival at which the local pastor had been helped by the Rev. Elijah Pilcher, had not been very successful. Both men had labored hard but few were "powerfully convicted." The writer lamented that it was almost impossible "these troublesome times to persuade men to believe to the saving of the soul."

Someone else in Michigan wrote another letter of complaint to the same editor in October 1861. The editor thought it both too long and too doleful to print in its entirety. In part it said:

> Not long after a person is converted to the religion of Jesus Christ before the minister or someone in the church is ready to assail him to know whether he is right on politicks. If he is not an abolitionist he is persecuted and quickly finds . . . that he has no place in the church. O man, what a state of things is this in the church of Christ.

The Rev. Myron A. Dougherty was stationed at the Grand Rapids East Church for the years 1859-1860. Later he wrote:

> I was stationed in Grand Rapids the year before the Civil War broke out. All the people were in fearful excitement . . . . Nearly all my congregation . . . were loyal Union men and red-hot Lincoln men. I was the same. Nearly every sermon was preparatory of the great struggle just before the country . . . . My sermons were a strong mixture of gospel and politics . . . .In the midst of all this excitement, God gave us a glorious revival and a large number were converted.[31]

[30] See *North. Ch. Ad.,* for Feb. 13, 1861, IX, 51.
[31] Quoted by Joseph Ware in 75th anniversary *History of First M.E. Church of Grand Rapids,* pp. 11-13.

PART IV

THE UNITED STATES, MICHIGAN, AND METHODISM

1860 – 1880

The continental, continuous area of the United States had been completed by 1860. Texas, Oregon, the Mexican Cession, and the Gadsden Purchase had all been annexed between 1845 and 1853. The area of the United States had risen from 1,792,223 square miles to 3,026,789. In the next twenty years, only Alaska was added and it was not of much importance for years. But five new States had joined the Union and the eleven Confederate States had been returned to the United States by force. The new States were Kansas, West Virginia, Nevada, Nebraska, and Colorado.

The 31,443,321 people in the United States in 1860 had increased to 50,155,783, by 1880. Also that 1860 census included four million slaves who were counted as free people in 1880. Michigan's 1860 population of 749,113 had slightly more than doubled by 1880 to 1,636,937. Detroit, the 19th city in population in the United States in 1860 had become the 17th in 1880. Its 1860 population of 45,619 had become 116,340.

Statistics give no idea of the tragic era involved in that twenty years. A civil war, military reconstruction of the south, and hard times after the Panic of 1873, influenced every aspect of life in the United States. After eleven States seceded, it took four years of hard fighting to restore the Union and end slavery. The death of Lincoln, the mistakes made by both Johnson and Congress added to the bitterness of the period.

Scarcely had recovery begun than profound economic developments changed many things in everyday life. Extension of the railroads, development of iron and copper mining, industrial production of salt, and the rise of labor unions had great influence upon Michigan. The Panic of 1873 began in the eastern United States but the general over-expansion, extravagance, and corruption were nationwide. The greatest unemployment, bankruptcy, and crime came in the middle west between 1875 and 1878. No occupation nor profession in the United States was untouched by the general hard times.

The politics of the time were very one-sided. To be a Democrat in Michigan was nearly the same as being a traitor. This State was very Republican throughout this period. Johnson, Grant, and Hayes were the Presidents after the Civil War. Nobody could classify them as great political leaders.

The Methodist Episcopal Church made a real patriotic contribution during the Civil War. No Methodist should forget Lincoln's reply to a delegation from the General Conference of 1864, which made a formal call and pledge of support at the White House. While he felt that the United States Government had been well sustained by all the churches yet "the Methodist Church sends more soldiers to the field, more nurses to the hospitals, and more prayers to Heaven than any."[1] Religion and patriotism were almost synonymous in many Methodist congregations. The American flag was displayed near the pulpit and sometimes flew over the steeple. Many a minister was torn between his duty to his church and that to his country.

The years just after the Civil War were unhappy for the Methodist Episcopal Church at large. Relations with southern Methodists were very strained. Northern Methodism tried to extend its control to churches in the south neglected or even abandoned during the war. This certainly increased the animosity of southern Methodism. And the northern

[1] W. W. Sweet, *Meth. Am. Hist.*, p. 299.

Bishop Metthew Simpson (1811-84) was famous for being a personal friend of President Abraham Lincoln, who gave the funeral address in Springfield. He was a peerless orator. Baptized by Bishop Asbury; he was ordained by Bishop Roberts. He presided over the Michigan Conference sessions in 1860, 1863, 1866, and 1874; and over the Detroit Annual Conferences of 1863, 1871, and 1874.

church efforts to help and educate the former slaves were also resented by southern whites. Minor splits in Michigan Methodism, due to abolitionism were partially healed soon after the war but nothing of the sort happened in the south. To aggravate the situation more, lay representation was ever before the Church in the latter 19th century.

Michigan was less disturbed by the Civil War than such states as Illinois or Ohio. Their proximity to slaveholding or seceded States gave them an immediate fear of invasion. The only time Michigan had such fears was at the time of the Trent Affair. The arrest of Mason and Slidell from a British steamer en route to England, led many Detroiters to fear that a war with England might develop. That might mean bombardment of the city from Windsor, Canada. Methodists living on farms in remote areas went on with their usual routine work and church attendance.

Geographical location with transportation facilities had a connection with personal realization of the Civil War. After Lincoln's first call for troops, proximity of a town to a railroad rather than priority in offering determined which militia companies were first accepted. The towns between Detroit and Niles on the Michigan Central Railroad had many volunteers in the fighting from 1861 to the end of the war.

A company or a regiment was frequently raised within a certain county. Relatives and friends made up a small group that enlisted and fought together. This improved morale at first but after a major battle, the casualty lists were a shock to a town.[2]

Not one Methodist Church in Michigan had over 500 members then and most of them numbered from 100 to 300. Every Methodist soldier absent at war was missed by the people of his church. The smaller churches in the south central part of Michigan lost more members than those in the far north or around Detroit.

Pioneering in the northern counties of the Lower Peninsula went on continuously during the Civil War. A large acreage of what was thought to be good land was available from the State and Federal governments. The new Homestead law made it even easier for a poor man to obtain a farm. In the issue of July 3, 1861, the *Northwestern Christian Advocate* noted that a large migration into the northern parts of Sanilac and Huron counties had gone on during the spring and summer. Over 2,000 acres of land had been disposed of to actual settlers in just one week.

The wartime activities of the Michigan Methodist Episcopal Church deserve closer attention and remembrance. Even the church functions of the home-staying Methodists were greatly affected by the Civil War.

2 F. B. Woodford, *Father Abraham"s Children, Michigan Episodes in the Civil War*, p. v. (Foreword by W. A. Harbison).

CHAPTER IX

THE CIVIL WAR YEARS

1861 – 1865

Michigan Methodist Reaction to the Outbreak of Civil War

News of the attack upon Fort Sumter produced much the same excitement and patriotism among Michigan Methodists as it did in the other northern States. The Rev. M. A. Dougherty, pastor of the First Methodist Church of Grand Rapids, wrote afterwards:

> I remember the evening of the day we got the news that Fort Sumter had been fired on. The opera house was filled to overflowing by the most excited and wildest crowd I ever saw, and yet the occasion was one also of great solemnity. Enthusiasm was mingled with the terrible thoughts of the bloody carnage and horrors of war. Yet our church services were well attended and directed largely to the care and encouragement of the soldiers, stationed there or passing through the city on their way to the front.[1]

In Jackson First Church a meeting of the trustees had been scheduled for the evening of April 15, 1861, but at the time set, only a few were there. And they quickly adjourned to two days later. Like everyone else in town, the trustees wanted to attend the hastily called public mass meeting in Jackson Hall.[2]

A few Detroit churches were still hostile to abolitionism and cautious about open political discussion. Seth Reed said several members of his Woodward Avenue Church had been conservative, sympathetic with the south, and hostile to the national government's defense of the Union. The *Detroit Free Press* was then a Democratic paper opposed

---

[1] J. B. Ware, 17th Anniversary *History of 1st Methodist Church of Grand Rapids*, p. 13.
[2] C. Lockwood, *Church on Main St.*, p. 22.

212

to the anti-slavery movement. On the day after the attack on Fort Sumter began, an editorial in the *Free Press* said in part:

> The President has called for a volunteer force to go south and put down the rebellion; we hope . . . there will be a fire in the rear, and that such men as Hogarth and Ketchell and Reed will be placed where they will receive the first fire.[3]

The men named were then the ministers respectively of the leading Presbyterian, Congregational, and Methodist Detroit churches.

The Rev. John M. Arnold, who succeeded Seth Reed as minister of the Woodward Avenue Methodist Church, declared that every major battle or new call for troops "was commemorated by a sermon." The leading members of his congregation warned him that "it would not do to discuss national matters in that pulpit." This made Arnold more determined "to push the claims of patriotism in the sacred desk."[4]

But sour comment on the war was an exception. The majority of the ministers and members of the Michigan Methodist Episcopal Church were ardently patriotic. When the Michigan Annual Conference met at Battle Creek in October, 1861, it was said that the patriotism of its members was "all in a blaze." When one of them asked for a location in order to enter the army "either to pray or fight," Bishop E. R. Ames put his request before the Conference with the remark "the brother evidently thinks that blue pills and blood-letting is the best medicine for this rebellious disease." Today it seems a queer remark but the Conference in 1861 was both amused and pleased thereby said the *Northwestern Advocate* editor.

In September, 1863, the Detroit Annual Conference in session at Romeo was opened by "a brother who prayed heartily and sincerely for national success in crushing the rebellion. An "Amen" came forth whose force caused the windows to dance as though Colonel Loomis had planted a battery in the street."[5]

More formal comment on the official attitude of the Michigan Methodist Episcopal Church toward the Civil War may be found in the committee reports and resolutions adopted during the Annual Conference sessions. The standing committee on slavery, common in the 1850's, was dropped and one on "the State of the Country" took its place. Its annual reports usually advocated "a high toned christian patriotism," declared that God had made this one country via its geography, and slavery had been the only "prime disturbing element." Each committee in turn asked for the "firm and cheerful support of the government of their fathers."

[3] Seth Reed, *Story of My Life*, p. 66.
[4] M. A. Boughton, ed., *Autobiography of J. M. Arnold*, p. 26.
[5] Clipping from the *Detroit Advertiser*, Burton Collection, Detroit Public Library.

It was reiterated that slavery was the real cause of the war and fighting must go on until rebellion was crushed and slavery utterly abolished. Naturally then both the Annual Conferences approved the steps taken by army officers to free runaway slaves and enlist them in the Union army. Their approval of Lincoln was stronger after he issued the Emancipation Proclamation. Toward the end of the war in 1864, the approach of victory was thus hailed:

> We recognize the hand of God in the late splendid victories which have crowned our military movements; and we humbly trust that triumph will follow triumph, till the glory of the Republic will stand acknowledged in all the earth.[6]

What Was the Duty of a Methodist Minister in Wartime?

How much a "high toned christian patriotism" demanded of Methodist ministers and laymen was not always clear. In the excitement due to Lincoln's first and second calls for troops, pastors and members often volunteered together. Frequently a minister raised a local company promising to go as one of its officers and not necessarily the chaplain either. Volunteers composed the regiments in the first two years of the war and only 4,281 men were ever raised by draft in Michigan. This was due in part to the practice of crediting the State with its volunteers against draft quotas. Also hiring and paying a substitute was allowed. Ministers were subject to the draft as much as any layman.[7]

Annual Conferences, bishops, fellow preachers, and religious paper editors agreed that the field of military action was not a place for ordained ministers. When Andrew J. Eldred, Presiding Elder of Niles District, was elected chaplain of the 12th Michigan Volunteers, the Ministerial Association of his District declared they "saw a call of Providence for his appointment to the chaplaincy" and urged the bishop to so act. But they also said, "We can't give any countenance to the course of brethren who drop the sword of the spirit for Cesar's (sic) sword and bestow more sympathy for the weapons of a carnal warfare than for the panoply of God."[8] Not over a dozen Michigan Methodist ministers left their charges and served as soldiers.

Wayland had two of its pastors leave to enlist in the army and then die there. The Rev. Newland Cleveland, appointed at Wayland from 1859 to 1861, was offered a lieutenancy in the 12th Michigan Infantry. He resigned to accept, fought at the battle of Pittsburg Landing, and

---

[6] Similar resolutions can be found any year from 1861 thru 1865. Quotations are from Detroit Conference *Minutes* for 1861, pp. 35-36, and from Michigan Conference *Minutes* for 1864, p. 36.

[7] F. B. Woodford, *Father Abraham's Children*, pp. 251-252.

[8] Jan. 1, 1862 in *North Ch. Ad.*, X, 6.

soon afterward died of typhoid fever. His Conference memoir said he died "in response to what he believed to be his duty."

The Rev. Washington I. Blowers served the Wayland Circuit from 1862 to 1864. During the Michigan Annual Conference session of 1864, he had advance notice that he would be drafted. So he volunteered at once and received a bounty for doing so. The Rev. F. D. Hemenway said he so acted because he was "so averse to serving as a conscript." The *Northwestern Christian Advocate* editor said he did it "to secure the bounty for his family." Blowers went with the army to Nashville, Tennessee, where he died of erysipelas after an illness of sixteen days. F. D. Hemenway said, in his memoir of Blowers, "This is a sad, mysterious, glorious record by a young man of high promise. Who can say it was wasted?"

The death of the Rev. Henry Carlton also caused doubts. He had served six appointments successfully in the Detroit Annual Conference but felt he must answer the presidential call for volunteers. He raised a company, became its Captain, joined the 22nd Michigan Infantry, and was ordered to Nashville, Tenn. En route, presumably standing on the car platform, a low bridge knocked him under the train and he was instantly killed.

The Rev. Samuel Clements Jr., sent a notice of his fate to the *Northwestern Christian Advocate* for insertion in its "Soldiers Death Roll." Although Carlton was a minister "with talents above the medium," his death notice would not appear in the Detroit Annual Conference memoirs. He had located or left the ministry to serve in the army. Clements concluded:

> Whether he acted rightly in leaving the ministry and entering the army as a combatant may be a question with some. But if he erred, it was a mistake not a crime and he acted in accord with what he thought his duty.

In 1865, The Detroit Annual Conference was again saddened by the death of the Rev. Francis L. West. A preacher since 1859, he served just one Sunday on his new appointment to Davisville Circuit. He was suddenly drafted, sent to the 23rd Michigan Infantry in Tennessee where he served not quite three months. On guard duty, he was shot by guerrillas, robbed and left alone. When found, he was removed to hospital and died next morning.[9]

A few Michigan Methodist ministers survived serving in the army but returned home with impaired health. James A. Sprague was sta-

---

[9] All information about ministers who died based on their memoirs in the various Conference *Minutes*. Also on Soldiers Death Rolls in *North. Ch. Ad.*, as in order discussed above are in XIII, 99; XI, 235; XIII, 196.

tioned at Palo in 1861. He decided it was his duty to enlist, took his wife and three children to her father's house at Lyons, and went to war. He was captured and held in Libby Prison until the end of the war. He suffered from badly broken health the remainder of his life.[10]

Joseph B. Varnum was admitted to Detroit Annual Conference in 1861. He also felt it his duty to leave his charge at Laingsburg in 1863 and serve as a private in the 2nd Michigan Infantry. In March 1864, he was wounded in knee and hip so received a furlough. He was mustered out in 1865 and, although somewhat lame, returned to his ministerial duties.

Serving the Methodist Church at Hillsdale in 1861, the Rev. Thomas J. Hill raised 130 men for the army, was commissioned a Captain, and went to war. After six months of service, he was so ill that he was forced to resign. He never was in good health again although he occasionally rendered ministerial service.

Silas P. Warner was a fourth minister who went to war. His ministry began in 1851. He was stationed at Grass Lake in 1861. His memoir in 1908 said:

> At the earnest solicitation of a number of men in his church and in the community . . . he organized a company of soldiers and as their captain served with honor, receiving a severe wound upon the field.

He was unable to return to active service in the Annual Conference until 1869. But he was a zealous pastor until 1888 and he lived until 1908, being the oldest member of the Detroit Annual Conference at the time of his death.[11]

It was possible if drafted to hire for $300 a substitute to serve in the army. Only one minister who did so was found. He was David R. Latham of the First Methodist Episcopal Church in Grand Rapids. The substitute was a widower with a three-year-old daughter, whom the Lathams cared for in their home while her father was gone to the war.[12]

Michigan Methodist Civil War Chaplains

Available records show that twenty-four Michigan Methodist ministers served as army chaplains. Nine were from the Michigan Annual

[10] *History of Carson City Church*, Mich. Conf. Hist. Coll., Albion College Library.

[11] For Varnum Detroit Conf. *Minutes* for 1896, pp. 43-45. For Hill Centenary booklet of St. Louis Church, Mich. Conf. Hist. Coll., Albion College Library. For Warner Detroit Conf. *Minutes* for 1908, pp. 38-40.

[12] J. B. Ware, *History First M.E. Church of Grand Rapids*, pp. 11-13.

Conference and fifteen from the Detroit Annual Conference.[13] Of some, a great deal is known and of others nothing beyond the factual statement of such service usually found in their memoirs.[14]

Great variation in the length of time given to the chaplaincy also existed. Only one Michigan Annual Conference minister was a chaplain throughout the war. This man was Joseph Jones of Charlotte. He was Canadian born and served with a regiment containing many Methodists. A Captain was Silas P. Warner of the Detroit Annual Conference and among the privates were N. Garlick of the Michigan Annual Conference and a local preacher, "Brother Hutt." While in Virginia in 1865, Chaplain Jones gave some attention to restoring the northern Methodist Church in Petersburg. As soon as the city was fully occupied, he applied for the use of the best Methodist church building there, in order to preach a loyal and anti-slavery gospel.[15]

None of the chaplains from the Detroit Annual Conference served throughout the entire war. But William C. Way was chaplain of the 24th Michigan Infantry Regiment of the Iron Brigade from the mustering in on July 26, 1862, to its mustering out on June 30, 1865. He was the only Michigan Civil War chaplain of any denomination of whom this was true. He was also the war correspondent of the *Detroit Tribune* while in the field. The regimental history is full of references to Chap-

---

[13] Michigan Annual Conference chaplains:

William H. Brockway	Lewis Earl	Joseph Jones
Israel Cogshall	Andrew Eldred	Holmes Pattison
Benjamin Doughty	Francis Glass	Moss Smith

Detroit Annual Conference chaplains:

William Benson	Daniel Jacokes	James Smart
Jonathan Blanchard	William Mahan	George Taylor
David Curtis	Franklin May	D. Burnham Tracy
Lyman Dean	Benjamin Pritchard	William Way
Arthur Edwards	Addison Shaw	Elisha Wright

These lists may not be complete. Records were not meticulously kept then and some ministers were first in the army as fighting men and then later became chaplains. As they had located to go in the army, the chaplaincy is not in the church records. The lists were made up from Michigan and Detroit Conference *Minutes* for 1861 through 1865. Also Appendix A in W. W. Sweet, *The Methodist Episcopal Church & the Civil War.* Also lists by Dr. William C. S. Pellowe in *Mich. Ch. Ad.,* for Sept. 14, 1961. LXXXVIII, #32, 10-11, 21.

[14] For complete discussion of all our knowledge of the Michigan Methodist chaplains, see the author's booklet "The Methodist Episcopal Church in Michigan during the Civil War." In the Civil War Centennial Observance series by the committee on "The Impact of the Civil War on Religion in Michigan." pp. 35-55. Eleven chaplains are discussed in the centennial booklet of whom seven are considered in this history.

[15] For memoir of Jones see Michigan Conference *Minutes* for 1877, pp. 53-54. For letters from him, *North. Ch. Ad.,* X, 302; XIII, 124.

lain Way. The high point of his years of service was at Gettysburg. Writing of July 1, 1863, the regimental historian said:

> The Pennsylvania line had been reached and the forces of the enemy must be met very soon, though none suspected that he was within a few hours' march. Before resuming the daily journey it was deemed proper to assemble the regiment for prayer. During Chaplain Way's invocation, cartridges and hard tack were distributed among the men. Time was precious and not to be lost.

The regiment fought hard at Gettysburg, lost a good many men, and left many wounded in the hospitals. Therefore, Chaplain Way was detached on special hospital duty from July 4 to September 13, 1863. His wife, Eliza M. Way, was with him and also aided in the hospitals. He found time to write twice to the *Detroit Tribune* from Gettysburg. On July 7, 1863, he said:

> Gettysburg is one vast hospital . . . . I went upon the field with two of our regiment and buried several of our fallen comrades and there witnessed a savage vandalism. Our dead were robbed of everything, their bodies stripped of clothing and shoes.

On July 15, he stated to the Detroit newspaper:

> I have been constantly engaged in the comfort of our wounded and am astonished at their cheerfulness. Their "stumps" are doing nicely . . . . The town is filled with sadhearted relatives. It is saddening to stand near the Express office and see the coffined remains of hundreds being sent to their former homes. Many are dying and it is almost impossible to get a coffin.

The Rev. Mr. Way returned to the pastorate immediately after the war was over, accepting an appointment to Farmington in September, 1865. He died in 1896 after thirty-nine years in the ministry. Both the G. A. R. and the Masons had a part in conducting his funeral.[16]

Jonathan Blanchard served as a chaplain for about one year and nine months. Before the war, he had been the Presiding Elder of the Romeo and then the Adrian Districts. In the fall of 1862, he became chaplain of the 26th Michigan Infantry. He was soon noted for his kindness and piety. "He always kept up vocal devotions in his tent, morning and evening, as if he had his family about him." Apparently always of delicate health, he contracted the ever-prevalent camp diarrhea in the army and "wasted away in spite of all medical efforts." He died at Ann Arbor on March 22, 1864. Presiding Elder E. H. Pilcher, then living in Ann Arbor, wrote the memoir of Blanchard for the *Northwestern Christian Advocate*. He concluded it with the prayer, "May

---

[16] Way's memoir is in the Detroit Annual Conference *Minutes* for 1896, pp. 46-48. Many of his letters are quoted by O. B. Curtis in his *History of the 24th Michigan of the Iron Brigade*, as on pp. 71, 80, 118, 155, 185, 214, 270.

we be as ripe as he for the rest of Heaven." Blanchard was the only Methodist chaplain from Michigan who died during the war.[17]

One Michigan Annual Conference chaplain was captured by the Confederates. In 1863, a surprise raid by the Confederates into Kentucky ended in the capture of a number of Michigan and Wisconsin soldiers. Each State group captured included its chaplain. The Michigan one was Israel Cogshall and the Wisconsin man C. D. Pillsbury. Soon after recovering from their mutual surprise, they learned that chaplains and surgeons would not be held but exchanged at Vicksburg, Mississippi. Their captivity lasted fourteen days for it took a hard, cross-country journey to reach the place of exchange. They continually changed trains and waited in an enemy land. Finally they came north via river steamboat and then train. Chaplain Pillsbury wrote of their experiences in detail to the *Northwestern Christian Advocate*. He ended his long narrative thus:

> Mutual hardships, toils, privations and sufferings had made strong friends of two who first met as strangers in the army. Two chaplains can never forget their journey together as prisoners through the Southern Confederacy. To travel a prisoner, in company with a single friend, thousands of miles through the enemy's country, knowing neither whom to trust, nor what awaits, is to experience some of the stern realities of the soldiers' life.[18]

Two of Michigan's Presiding Elders, one from each Annual Conference in the State, served as chaplains. The one from the Michigan Annual Conference was Andrew J. Eldred, Presiding Elder of Niles District in 1860-1861. He was chaplain of the 12th Michigan Infantry from October 5, 1861, to September 10, 1863. A number of the men of the 12th Infantry were Methodists from Eldred's District. The chaplain drew Methodists to that regiment and their numbers in turn helped to hold him with that organization. Eldred was also an aide to General Prentiss, saw many battles, and was present at the siege of Vicksburg.

While there, his only daughter died suddenly in Michigan and, feeling he was needed at home, Eldred resigned and was honorably discharged to return home to his ministerial labors. All the regimental officers, from the Colonel to the surgeon, signed "an unsolicited tribute" to Eldred on his leaving. They said he would be greatly missed, regretted the cause of his going, rendered him their "fraternal regards" and wished him well in his future work. They appreciated his "ability,

[17] Memoir of Blanchard in *North. Ch. Ad.*, XII, 139. R. A. Brunger, *History of Tecumseh Church*, p. 55. Also William C. S. Pellowe, Study of Methodist chaplains, *Mich. Ch. Ad.*, LXXXVIII, #32, 10.

[18] For Cogshall's diary of same incident, *Indiana Mag. Hist.*, for 1946. XLII, 69-87. Pillsbury's letters in *North Ch. Ad.*, XI, 185, 198, 222, 230, 270, 278.

integrity, and patriotism" and were sure his voice would "be heard in support of the flag." Eldred went home to the church at Niles in 1863 and to the Albion charge in 1864-1865.[19]

The chaplain, who had been a Presiding Elder in the Detroit Annual Conference was James S. Smart of Flint District. He was intensely patriotic and drew young men to enlist when no one else could. He was "a strong man with an explosive voice and an earnest manner, bold and harsh in debate and abhorred compromise."

The Sunday before the regiment left Saginaw, Smart preached to the men and held a two-hour prayer meeting. He said he had 200 Christian men in the regiment and "a more respectful and attentive audience one could not wish to see and, if they fight as they pray, we need have no fears."

During his year of service, mostly in Kentucky and Tennessee, Smart wrote often to the *Northwestern Christian Advocate*. He was most unfavorably impressed with the country and the people. One was dirty and devastated and the other disloyal. Everything was fifty years behind the times and blighted by slavery. The sights he saw made him both angry and disgusted with the south.

Part of his service was in Bowling Green, Kentucky, in work with the sick and wounded soldiers in the hospitals there. He thought it strange that all the Protestant churches had been turned into hospitals and "the Romish Chapel" left untouched.

Smart conducted many military funerals, visited hospitals every day, and preached in the Court House on Sundays. In one of his letters to the *Northwestern*, Chaplain Smart declared:

> I find many of our soldiers really hungry for the word of life . . . . If the real presence of Jesus is manifest anywhere on earth, it certainly is at times among these very men. One man, in my own regiment, was at first very opposed to religion. Taken seriously sick, left in hospital alone, . . . he could think only of One who said, "Lo I am with you always," When I visited him, I found him humbled and of his own accord he asked for prayer. Now he is recovering and the New Testament is his constant companion. Still very weak, he can read only a little but he feasts on every verse. The Spirit illuminates the Word.

When Chaplain Smart came home from the war, his usefulness to his church had just begun. For two years, he was financial agent for Garrett Biblical Institute and then did the same work for Albion College for four years. Then he was Presiding Elder for the Flint District again.[20]

---

[19] *Ibid.*, XI, 324. Eldred mentioned in History of Carson City Church.

[20] For memoir of Smart see Detroit Conference *Minutes* for 1892, pp. 56-60. For his letters as a chaplain see *North. Ch. Ad.*, for the years 1862 and 1863, X, 340, 348; XI, 19, 316. Brief mention of Smart by William C. S. Pellowe in article on Methodist Chaplains in *Mich. Ch. Ad.*, LXXXVIII, #32, 11.

One other chaplain deserves mention for his varied activities in the war effort. George Taylor was born in England, had been a Methodist preacher since 1837, came to Michigan in 1847, and had served many churches in the Detroit Annual Conference. When the war began, he enlisted but Governor Blair at once appointed him recruiting agent for the State of Michigan. He became chaplain of the 8th Michigan Infantry in 1862. He was then fifty-two years of age and soon found field service too strenuous. In six months, his health was so bad that he was discharged in 1863.

At the next Annual Conference, he asked for a supernumerary relation. This meant being left as an extra minister without any specific church responsibility. He then became Chief State Agent for the U.S. Christian Commission. It was a national relief and religious organization for soldiers. It grew out of the Y.M.C.A. movement. Taylor travelled all over the State, making speeches for the cause and collecting thousands of dollars in addition to many supplies for the soldiers. He also persuaded many men and women to serve as agents in the fighting areas.

In 1865, under urging by John Owen and with his Conference's consent, he became financial agent of the Michigan Soldiers and Sailors Monument Association. After Grant became President, it was said that Taylor was his "Detroit pastor." Taylor was the pastor of Congress Street Methodist Episcopal Church in 1849-1850 when young Lieutenant Grant was stationed in Detroit. He probably attended that church occasionally. When Taylor visited Washington during Grant's presidency, the former parishioner insisted that Taylor stay at the White House. In spite of his poor health, Taylor lived to the age of 88 and served in the Methodist ministry for 69 years.[21]

Michigan Methodist Laymen as Soldiers: Numbers and Influence of Their Absence on Home Churches

The exact number of Michigan's Civil War soldiers who were Methodist laymen cannot possibly be determined. Ministers who located, or left the church, before going in the U. S. army themselves paid no attention to recording other men who had enlisted. Home-staying ministers were careless or else noted the general loss in membership without any special record of those who were soldiers. Annual Conferences in many States urged their members to keep military records but scarcely any did.

The editor of the *Northwestern Christian Advocate* considered that most ministers treated such military records in the wrong way. When members of their own congregations enlisted, certificates of membership

[21] For memoir of Taylor, see Detroit Conference *Minutes* for 1897, pp. 42-43. Also article by William C. S. Pellowe previously cited, pp. 11, 21.

should have been given each one of them. Instead they were either dismissed by letter or else dropped from a church's record of membership and the names marked "Gone to the army." The editor felt that no one should consider these soldiers lost to the Methodist Church or indeed to all religion. He concluded, "Absence in the service of our country should no more cause the forfeit of church membership than of civil rights."[22]

After extended inquiry, the *Northwestern's* editor thought that some States had as high as 10,000 Methodists in the U.S. Army. The exact number of Michigan's Civil War soldiers who were Methodists cannot be accurately determined. Michigan's total population in 1860 was 775,881 and in four years the State sent 90,048 men to war. Of that total number, 14,855 died and the terrible thing is that 10,136 died of disease and only 2,820 were killed in action while 1,387 died of their wounds.[23] Several thousands of the men who served were Methodists, possibly five or six thousand.

The inadequate records show that Michigan Methodism suffered a decline in membership. This was greater in 1862 and 1864 than in the other years of the Civil War. And the western half of the State, Michigan Annual Conference, lost more of its church members than the Detroit Annual Conference did.

In 1860, the Detroit Annual Conference had 14,552 members and in 1865, it counted 14,535. Michigan Annual Conference in 1860 had 13,828 members as contrasted with 12,748 in 1865. Comparison of the Districts of the two Conferences is also revealing. Between 1860 and 1865, adult membership increased between 200 and 300 in the Detroit and Adrian Districts. But the Ann Arbor and Owosso Districts each lost not quite one hundred members. Flint District lost 520 and Port Huron District 232 members. The remote Lake Superior District rose from 344 to 545 members.

In the Michigan Annual Conference, five Districts — Marshall, Coldwater, Kalamazoo, Lansing, and Grand Rapids — all declined at least 500 members each at some time during the Civil War. Grand Traverse District with only 74 members in 1860 had become Manistee District with 584 members in 1865. Niles District, created from Kalamazoo District in 1862, had 754 members at its beginning and 1739 in the year 1865.

The changes in the membership of some of the village churches is even more noticeable. In the city of Detroit, Woodward Avenue had 269 members and Congress Street 182. By 1865, the two had combined to form Central Church and it had 509 members. Birmingham had

[22] *Northwestern Christian Advocate*, X, 396.
[23] All military statistics from F. B. Woodford, *Father Abraham's Children*, pp. 3-5.

268 members in 1860 and 136 in 1865. Owosso had 46 in 1860 and 93 in 1865. Ypsilanti had 386 in 1860 and 264 in 1865. But Marquette rose from 55 in 1860 to 80 in 1865.

In the Michigan Annual Conference, Marshall fell off from 183 members in 1860 to 124 in 1865. Homer had 166 in 1860 but only 102 in 1865. But Albion reported 164 in 1860, and 230 in 1865. And Jackson had 121 in 1860, and 180 in 1865. Battle Creek rose from 182 in 1860, to 231 in 1865. Yet also on the line of the Michigan Central Railroad was Niles and the church there fell off from 185 in 1860 to 145 in 1865. Further north, Pentwater with only 19 in 1860 had 52 in 1865.[24]

Whether religion continued to mean anything to a pre-war member of the Methodist Episcopal Church, after he had enlisted, is difficult to decide. Many Civil War letters make no mention of religion, and the denomination of those that do is hard to determine. In general, Protestant church attendants, after they became soldiers, were critical of many chaplains, disliked the constant swearing and gambling, and had no opportunity for "Sabbath observance" for months at a time.

In spite of war interference, Private John D. Faxon of Duplain tried faithfully to keep up his religious life. On April 20, 1862, he wrote to his wife from Leesburg, Virginia:

> Sabbath is not regarded as a day set apart for rest or worship. A few of us are locked up in a room, trying to be quiet, four are sitting around the counting desk writing. I have spent the Sabbath reading, the best employment I could find . . . . Have not heard a sermon since I have been in the State. It would seem real good to hear the Word preached again.

When Faxon did get a chance to attend a local Methodist church, he found only a few there and had to listen to a poor sermon by a minister whose piety he questioned. Next day he found out it was the loyalty of the preacher he should have doubted for the man was "secesh" and was to be required to take the oath of loyalty. Later, on a visit to Washington, he found a Methodist Class meeting. Attracted by the sound of hymn singing, he went in, was warmly welcomed, took part in the service, and was "asked to close by prayer being the first time I have prayed in public since I left Frederick. I done the best I could."[25]

Henry W. Hicks was a Methodist Protestant minister at the time of the Civil War. Later he joined the Methodist Episcopal Church.

[24] Statistics are all taken from tables given in the various Annual Conference *Minutes* for 1860 and 1865. The figures for 1860 were used for comparisons, as being the last year untouched by Civil War influences.

[25] Three diaries and 115 letters of John Harvey Faxon and his wife and brother have been preserved. The Faxon Collection is in the Michigan Historical Collection, Rackman Bldg., University of Michigan, Ann Arbor.

Occasionally former members of his church in Capac wrote to him during the war. On November 18, 1864, from Murfreesboro, Tennessee, Captain P. B. Goodell wrote:

> Brother Hicks dont forget a poor pilgrim as you seat yourself by your fire to read a portion of God and to bow the knee around the family alter (sic) to thank God for his goodness to you and yours. I would like to attend a meeting once more in Michigan . . . . I could shout Halleuyah (sic) to hear once more of sinners being converted the boys that are professors are still hanging on but we are getting cold dont forget us I believe I could sing the good old way first rate if I could get into a good warm meeting.

On March 18, 1863, J. J. Huntley also wrote to Hicks from a Washington hospital where he was with a badly wounded hand. He said in part:

> I am sorry to say that there is men here that left home praying men but now they have forgot God and have commensed [sic] to curse and swear it makes my heart ache to hear them so I have talked to them . . . I asked them if they could not get along without it . . . . I want you to pray for me and for all soldiers for brother this is the worst place to live a christian life that ever need to be a man had to be on his lookout all of the time but God is able to help them that call on him aright. I do hope that this war will come to an end so that we can all enjoy the privalage [sic] of goin to meetings and that helps very much.[26]

Wartime Michigan Methodist Church Work

In spite of the shock and excitement of the great conflict, most Michigan Methodist churches kept up their usual yearly round of activities. The Detroit newspapers and the *Northwestern Christian Advocate* contained hundreds of notices of summer camp meetings, winter protracted revivals, watch night services on New Year's Eve, district Sunday School meetings, and district ministerial associations. Donation parties for ministers flourished. Pressed to find space for more war news, the *Northwestern* ran this item on March 12, 1862:

> It is impossible for us to give all the news of local surprises and donations. We may state in general terms that the membership of the Detroit Conference are exhibiting gratifying instances of liberality to their pastors this winter.

Methodists kept up church building throughout the war too. The Detroit Annual Conference *Minutes* show that their 125 churches valued at $234,600 in 1860 had increased to 135½ valued at $463,900 in 1865.

---

[26] All letters to and from Hicks are in Detroit Conf. Hist. Coll., Adrian College Library. Apparently Hicks kept all the letters he got.

The Michigan Annual Conference had 82 churches in 1860 valued at $167,500. These had grown to 100½ valued at $284,005 in 1865.

The editor of the *Northwestern,* Thomas Eddy, often visited Michigan to speak at new churches. He took part in the corner stone laying service at a new church in Niles in 1862 and was present in 1863 when Bishop Simpson dedicated the completed building. Adrian also built anew in those same years, changing from a modest brick church of $4,000 valuation to one also of brick but estimated to have cost $45,000. Editor Eddy described the Adrian building minutely in the *Northwestern,* telling of its fine Gothic style and seating capacity of 800. He thought that as architecture it was "the finest by far of our denomination in Michigan."

The Rev. Mr. Eddy also attended the dedication of a new church in Saginaw in 1864. Going there meant use of both railroad and stage coach. Returning he had plenty of trouble. Both stagecoach and railroad train broke down and he was forced to walk part of the way carrying his baggage. When he finally got to Pontiac, the Methodist minister there entertained him at dinner and they discussed the new church building there too. In the next issue of the *Northwestern,* Mr. Eddy wrote:

> Methodism is asserting its rightful position in Michigan. The old class of church edifices are being replaced by better ones; liberal things are being designed for the Lord, and the Peninsular State so rich in soil and other resources is determined that Christianity in earnest shall have its proper place and influence.[27]

Of all the Michigan Methodist activities during the Civil War, the most surprising is the increase in foreign mission offerings. Of all the changes that the war might cause, the one that alarmed the Methodist Church most was the danger to the foreign mission movement. On April 24, 1861, Mission Headquarters in New York City sent out a letter to be printed in all northern Methodist religious papers. It raised just one question. "Will the Church stand by her Missions in these times of peril?" For lack of financial support, all foreign missionaries might have to be brought home. The border Annual Conferences, such as Baltimore, Kentucky, and parts of Pennsylvania would not be able to make their usual contributions. The writer of the mission letter declared, "We must look to the interior churches and conferences for help. The people will respond nobly if the pastors do their duty."

Bishop Simpson gave up a planned trip to California to plead the mission cause in as many annual conferences as possible. Presiding Elders, ministers, adult members, and children rallied round to do their

[27] All references to the editorial visits to new churches in Michigan taken from the *North. Ch. Ad.,* trip to Niles X, 204; XI, 345. to Adrian XII, 380. to Saginaw XII, 76.

share for missions. In Michigan, almost equal concern was shown for missions and Sunday Schools. Work for the two was frequently combined by districts and churches.

Seth Reed drafted the plans for Detroit District in 1862. Special mission meetings were to be held. Every minister was charged to bring the subject before his congregation in his sermons. Special agents were to circulate all the year and collect all the mission money.

If asked whether the Church could meet such a demand, Reed firmly replied, "She can and will if all will ask the Lord what am I to do." Detroit District was peculiarly well equipped to meet this challenge. Last year, this District gave 31¢ per member for missions. Far more could be done because:

> No State in the Union has suffered less, financially, from the war operations than ours and in no part of ours less than in the Detroit region. A vast amount of money has been put in circulation here in a few months past. A common remark has been "business was seldom better." We must test for God our abilities and Christianity now. Taxation for the government in its need is accepted. Shall not the loyal subjects of Christ's kingdom willingly bear tax for it in its time of trial? . . .. In the Detroit District, we can and ought to do more for missions.[28]

At Milford in August 1862, the pastor had a missionary society organized in the Sunday School. Mission papers were circulated and a missionary sermon preached the first Sunday of each month. Four church ladies collected outside among the adults and also monthly in the Sunday School.

On the previous Sunday, Presiding Elder Pilcher had preached at 5 P.M. and the children had charge of the singing. Most of the families present had already made a mission pledge but to encourage the children $6.30 was contributed. "Silver change was thrown in the windows by persons who stood outside for relief from the oppressive heat." The two resolutions adopted declared that the children love the missionary cause and "if called by Jesus as missionaries to the heathen in foreign lands they will cheerfully comply."[29]

Life memberships in either the Conference or national Mission Society in New York were often taken for the minister and his wife. As the war went on, some were taken in the names of absent members serving in the United States Army. By 1863, the work was better organized and showed real results.

The Rev. Elisha E. Caster, stationed in Bay City, wrote to the Northwestern editor of his arrangements. First came a monthly missionary prayer meeting with a collection, next a Sunday School missionary society also with collectors, third a pastoral missionary sermon on the

---

[28] *North. Ch. Ad.,* X, 26.
[29] *North. Ch. Ad.,* X, 252.

first Sunday of each month, and then, on the afternoon of that first Sunday, all efforts were climaxed by a missionary concert. He described it thus:

> The little folks, assisted by the congregation, sing with great gusto, a few selections from "Golden Showers" intermingled with laconic speeches by ministers and laymen. A public report of the doings of the society in the last month is made by which all are stimulated . . . at the end four little boys, who seem to feel very proud of the honor, walk down the aisles with box in hand to receive the freewill offering. It is difficult to get rid of these little fellows until something is dropped into their boxes. Then "We are marching on" is sung and the meeting is dismissed . . . . We get from $3 to $5 each time . . . our lowest figure is 50¢ per member . . . Bay City expects to stand first and claim the banner for raising more money in proportion to the membership than any other appointment on the Flint District.[30]

This letter brought a vigorous response from Methodist ministers elsewhere in Michigan. Midland City was waiting to contribute $100, East Saginaw $100, and Saginaw City $63. The Saginaw minister added, "Unless Brother Caster makes a vigorous onslaught on the coffers of his people, he will be seen far in the rear at Conference." Ann Arbor had raised its offering from $35 the last year to $380 this year and Ypsilanti from $85 to $400. The Rev. T. C. Gardner declared on March 11, 1863, "The cause of God as connected with our beloved Methodism is moving steadily forward in Michigan . . . every department of our church interests is receiving earnest attention . . . the contributions are way above any anticipation."[31]

Meetings of State or District Methodist Sunday School Unions were held many times during the war. It a returned chaplain could be obtained to address them, the war would be brought home more clearly to lay Methodists. A Sunday School Institute of the Detroit District was addressed by the Rev. William Mahan, a chaplain with the 8th Michigan Infantry. His talk was reported to the *Northwestern* by the Rev. S. Clements:

> Another source of interest to the meeting was the presence of Rev. William Mahan . . . who was at home on a furlough. He had recently left . . . the war scenes at Port Royal and Beaufort, North Carolina, and the relations he gave of the horror of those scenes, of the wretched condition of the country, ruined by rebellion, of the degraded condition of more than ten thousand contrabands now within the lines of the division produced a deep sensation in the minds of the audience.

At Albion where Resin Sapp was pastor, the annual Michigan Conference Sunday School Union program was held in October, 1862. Mr.

---

[30] *North. Ch. Ad.,* XI, 142. The Rev. Elisha E. Caster was the maternal grandfather of the author of this book.
[31] *North. Ch. Ad.,* XI, 73, 220.

Sapp described what they did in the Albion Sunday School. Every week the children memorized and recited a few Bible verses. One child was selected to read a story the next Sunday and all wanted to hear it. All summer the children were urged to bring bouquets to Sunday School. Each week a flower boy or girl was chosen to arrange the bouquets on a table in the front of the church. The pastor had observed that this custom had improved the flower gardens of Albion. He also had noticed that his Sunday School was more religious than his church members. He said, "Their knees were not so stiff and could bend more easily in prayer."[32]

In 1860, the Detroit Annual Conference had 311 Sunday Schools with 15,167 scholars. In 1865, it had 321 Sunday Schools with 18,701 members. It gave to missions in 1860 some $3,514.45 and in 1865 it had made an almost triple increase to $10,180.39.

The Michigan Annual Conference had 308 Sunday Schools with 14,062 scholars in 1860 and in 1865 had 351 Sunday Schools with 17,032 pupils. Its mission offerings increased 350% from $2,122.88 in 1860 to $7,376.64 in 1865.[33]

Considering the difficulties inherent in a time of Civil War, the Michigan Methodist Episcopal Church was doing well to increase its giving to missions, to continue building churches and parsonages, and to enlarge its Sunday Schools. The other side of the situation was found in the decline in adult membership, in the troubles of its denominational colleges, and in the failure to increase the salaries paid to the ministers in proportion to the general increase in the cost of living in war time.

Michigan Methodist Colleges in War Time

Both Albion and Adrian Colleges were affected by the Civil War, the first rather more than the second. Naturally male students of college age were more likely to be drafted or to volunteer than to continue their education. In spite of its changes in name and charter, Albion College had continued to be in financial distress. The trustees had made the mistake of using money meant for an endowment fund for current expenses. The grounds and buildings needed much attention and the teachers were miserably paid. The College Agent of the Sixties, the Rev. M. A. Daugherty, wrote of Albion:

[32]. *North. Ch. Ad.*, X, 339.

[33] All statistics taken from the Conference *Minutes*. Those for the Detroit Annual Conference for 1860, p. 29; for 1865, p. 53. For the Michigan Annual Conference for 1860, p. 21; for 1865, p. 32. Care must be taken not to depend on these statistics too closely for some ministers were very careless in their arithmetic and others went off to war and never reported their statistics for a particular year at all. Probably all totals should be a bit larger in numbers.

The institution was without means, and what was far worse, was left without many friends, and with an army of open enemies or indifferent constituents. The college and its managers were covered with odium. Every prominent minister and layman in both conferences had scholarships, anathema for the trustees, and hostility or coldness for the institution itself.[34]

As might have been anticipated, the entire college teaching staff of nine people resigned at the end of the school year in 1864. Somehow, someway, seven more faculty were employed and college opened as usual in the fall. Its monetary problems were not solved until after the Civil War.

Adrian College was not at first as hard hit by the war as Albion. It continued to grow until 1864 when internal quarrels within the ranks of the Wesleyans and financial trouble too brought a demand for the resignation of President Asa Mahan. The trustees wished to see the College become the joint property of the Wesleyans and Methodist Protestants. A change of that kind could not be made until after the Civil War ended.

The coincidence of changes in the Presidency of the college in three Michigan institutions during the Civil War seems rather unusual. In each case in varying degree, the situation arose out of disagreements between the trustees, the alumni, and the head of the college.

The Adrian trustees finally forced out Asa Mahan. The Rev. John McEldowney, then a professor in the college, served as President from 1864 to 1867. Then he decided to return to the Methodist Episcopal Church. And Mahan again became the President of Adrian College.

At Albion College, the Rev. Thomas Sinex resigned as the President in 1864 and returned to the ministry. He had served the College ten years. He came to Albion from college work in Indiana and left to move to California where eventually he became President of the College of the Pacific.

The Board of Regents of the University of Michigan had been engaged in a long quarrel with their President, Henry Tappan. In 1863, they removed Tappan from the presidency. By telegram, they offered the position to the Rev. Erastus O. Haven. He was then the editor of *Zion's Herald* in Boston but had previously been a professor at the University. Knowing not a thing about the situation to which he fell heir, Haven became the next President of the University.

The reason that Michigan Methodists were interested in the Rev. Mr. Haven was that he was an ordained Methodist minister and well known all over the State for his sermons and lectures. The Methodists

[34] R. Gildart, *Albion College, 1835-1960*, pp. 78-79. Also see W. F. Dunbar, editor, *Michigan Institutions of Higher Education in the Civil War*. A publication of the Michigan Civil War Centennial Observance Commission.

were also pleased that Dr. Benjamin F. Cocker was the Head of the Department of Philosophy in the University. He too was an ordained Methodist minister.

President Haven served for six years in the executive office. He largely succeeded in healing the wounds left by the dissension with Tappan. Perhaps his most important action was to induce the State Legislature to begin regular financial support of the University.[35]

Wartime Work of Michigan Methodist Ministers

In the closing days of the Civil War, home staying ministers were quite concerned about the increasing cost of living and the inadequate salaries they received. More than one editorial in the *Northwestern* was devoted to discussion of ministerial salaries. They were far too low before the Civil War and that had doubled the cost of living. Yet few charges had made any substantial increase in their minister's salary. Peace would bring increased demand for ministers everywhere. And "a narrow policy may well result in a narrow supply — low wages will get you cheap men." Editor Eddy cautioned that "our ministers should not be mercenary and worldly but no more should laymen be mean and covetous."

Two Michigan Presiding Elders made appeals for increased pay for their ministers through the *Northwestern*. On July 27, 1864, the Rev. Henry Penfield urged the Niles District to increase ministerial support by 1/6 or more. He ended his letter, "Do not disappoint me." On August 3, 1864, the Rev. William E. Bigelow appealed to all estimating committees and Quarterly Conferences to increase salaries in proportion to the rise in the cost of living. All members ought to raise their pledges. He concluded, "Shall the most vital interests of the church suffer for want of pecuniary support when the country is literally flooded with money?"

Reports of the stewards, given in the annual conference *Minutes,* show some increase in ministerial pay but not a general doubling. Larger towns increased salaries from ½ to ⅔ but villages and circuits added a few dollars or nothing.[36]

In 1860, the Detroit Annual Conference had 132 travelling elders which had grown to 141 in 1865. The Michigan Annual Conference had 122 such preachers in 1860 and 127 in 1865. Over and against the total of twenty-four army chaplains and about twelve military officers, around

---

[35] W. F. Dunbar, *The Michigan Record in Higher Education,* pp. 76-81, 110, 124-126. R. Gildart, *Albion College,* pp. 64-65, 78-79. E. H. Pilcher, *Hist. Prot. Mich,.* pp. 239-243.

[36] *North. Ch. Ad.,* XII, 228, 239, 241, 324. Also all the Civil War *Minutes* of the Michigan and Detroit Annual Conferences, *passim.*

one hundred ministers in each of the two annual conferences in Michigan remained in their assigned appointments throughout the Civil War.

To what extent the regular work of the stationed Michigan Methodist minister was still much what it had been in peace time or was profoundly changed by the Civil War is difficult to determine. The answer is in part dependent on the minister's geographical location and personal character. Sermons might be preached at the same times as in previous years and pastoral calls on the parishioners be made as before but sooner or later some hint of the war crept into the most religious activities.

The editor of the *Northwestern* declared in the issue of April 20, 1864, that the impending General Conference ought to be as short as possible. The delegates ought not to be away from their own home churches for any length of time. Mr. Eddy then stated his reasons for that opinion, saying:

> They are needed in their pulpits to be among the earliest to speak for the country — the country may need all healthy influences before the last of May. The ministers are also needed in homes of bereavement. Will there be many more before the first of June???[37]

A good many Methodist Episcopal churches must have had soldiers' funerals held in their edifices during the Civil War. But specific mention of such occasions is rare. All Battle Creek Methodist soldiers, who were buried there, had their funerals from the First Methodist Episcopal Church. The historian of that Church mentioned five officers given such services before burial in a Battle Creek cemetery.[38]

In August 1864, the Soldiers Death Roll of the *Northwestern* listed the death of George Bradley of Isabella County, Michigan. He was thirty-eight years of age, belonged to the 8th Michigan Infantry, was wounded at North Anna, Virginia, and died in a Baltimore hospital. His funeral was held by the local Methodist minister at his home and was followed by the service of baptism for his infant daughter, "at his dying request."[39]

On February 7, 1862, Mrs. Mary Faxon wrote to her husband, Private John Faxon, from Moscow Village where she was visiting "Brother Copelius" and his wife. After telling of the two sermons and a wedding which she had attended, she continued:

> On Monday Brother Copelius preached a funeral discourse, from "'Let me die the death of the righteous." It was a soldier who hurt himself drawing a cannon uphill and came home to die, a noble looking

[37] *North. Ch. Ad.*, XII, 132.
[38] C. D. Pittee, *History First M.E. Church of Battle Creek*, p. 2. Written in 1907. A typed copy in Mich. Hist. Coll., Rackham Bldg., University of Michigan, Ann Arbor.
[39] *North. Ch. Ad.*, XI, 267.

youth, dressed in full uniform, corporal I saw by his sleeves, after the congregation were all seated, the bearers came in two by two bringing the flag — the stars and stripes — and spread it over the coffin, and marched around on the other side and out, it looked solemn, I could not but think of my own husband all the time, they said he was glad to die.

John Faxon survived the Civil War and was licensed as an exhorter by the Ovid Circuit Quarterly Conference on August 5, 1865. His brother, William Faxon, was one of the first lay delegates elected to the Michigan Annual Conference in 1871.[40]

Elisha E. Caster and Francis A. Blades

Comparison of the work during the Civil War of two Michigan Methodist Episcopal ministers shows the great variations possible then. One was younger and held somewhat smaller appointments during the years 1861 through 1865. Elisha Ezra Caster was admitted to the Detroit Annual Conference in 1857 and served churches at Owosso, Bay City, and Marquette in the war years. The other was Francis Asbury Blades, admitted to the Detroit Annual Conference in 1844 and appointed to the First Churches at Ann Arbor and Adrian during the war. He became a Presiding Elder in 1865 but Mr. Caster did not attain that rank until twenty years later.

Judging from his pocket diaries and letters to Henry W. Hicks, then a Methodist Protestant minister, Elisha E. Caster was scarcely touched by the war in his work or personal life. His diaries always record his sermon topics and brief estimates of his success with them. In the winter months, he was very busy with protracted revivals. In good weather, he did much calling on the members or even going from house to house along a block of some street. Once he even talked to men whom he called "the inmates of two taverns." After he was sent to Marquette, he devoted some energy to keeping the church and parsonage warm. He also procured a bell for the church steeple.

Caster did attend a few Civil War soldier funerals in Bay City, observed a national day of fasting and prayer, and preached occasionally on some topic associated with the war. Upon receiving news of the death of Lincoln, he preached about it and gave a lecture thereon in another church than his own.

A few comments in his letters to his friend, Henry Hicks, were revealing of his attitudes. From Owosso on May 17, 1861,

> The soldiers are here on parade preparing to kill systematically and according to law, O when shall war and strife cease! Shall the nation's walls ever be called Salvation and her gates praise. Shall the time ever

[40] John H. Faxon Papers, Michigan Hist. Coll., Rackham Bldg., The University of Michigan. Also Michigan Annual Conference *Minutes* for 1871, *passim*.

arrive, foretold by Isaiah, when "Violence shall no more be heard in our land wasting nor destruction within her borders." I believe the prophets.

In December 1862, he complained to Hicks that the Conference *Minutes* were late in delivery that year. It must be due to the Secretary being a Democrat and having had the *Minutes* printed at the *Detroit Free Press* plant. Both Hicks and Caster had voted for Lincoln in 1860 and were also to do so in 1864.

From 1863 through 1865, Elisha Caster served on the Marquette charge. In those days, the steamer trip there took five days and scarcely any vessels ran during the months from November to mid-April. The town lived in isolation in the winter. Nevertheless, Mr. Caster was pleased with his appointment there. The church building was "a perfect model, carpeted and highly grained throughout."

Perhaps one reason he thought it a good charge was the salary. The previous year at Bay City he had received $400. Now he was paid $1,000 his first year at Marquette and $1,400 the second. The donation parties were "all cash" too. This salary may have been in part the result of the Civil War as the great demand for iron and copper had caused a modest boom in the Upper Peninsula.

Only a very few of Caster's letters and diary entries relate to the Civil War. He did note that his patriotism was severely tried by some of the northern generals. In 1865, important events were noted in his diary as follows: on April 14, "News of the capture of Gen. Lee and his army reached us this afternoon, and created the wildest enthusiasm. Church bells rung and cannon fired until 12 o'clock at night. Bonfires, etc." on April 17, "This evening news of the President's death." on April 18, "The whole village draped in mourning for the President." on April 25, he gave an address in the evening at the Episcopal Church on the death of President Lincoln. When he heard that Jefferson Davis had been captured while disguised in his wife's clothes, Mr. Caster wrote a letter to Mr. Hicks on June 5, 1865, in which he said, "I presume you are feeling very comfortably over the fact of the return of peace especially since there has been signal success on the side of right and Madame Jefferson has been taken petticoats and all!" Then he condemned the Democrats in no uncertain terms as all copperheads. He thought that party "came near ruining this noble country."[41]

The other minister in this comparison, Francis A. Blades, was much more prominent in the war effort. He was serving at Ann Arbor First

---

[41] All quotations from Elisha E. Caster's pocket diaries are from his records kept in pencil for the years from 1863 through 1865. These are in the possession of his granddaughter, the author. It is not known what became of his earlier diaries. The letters to Hicks are in a collection of 280 all written to Henry Hicks in the years from 1856 to 1912. This collection is in the Detroit Annual Conference historical collection, Adrian College Library.

Church when the war began. Mr. Blades declined a colonel's commission, offered him early in the Civil War, but he did do much recruiting far various regiments. Governor Blair often sought his advice and so did Senator Chandler.

Under special orders from the Governor, Blades visited the Army of the Potomac first to investigate the treatment of the Michigan soldiers in army camps and second to check on the loyalty of the troops to the Union. He reported that the only traitors were to be found in front of the army or well to its rear. While with the army, he was once directly fired on by the rebels who thought he was President Lincoln. Mr. Blades declared that he was willing to be shot at if he could be honored by being mistaken for Abraham Lincoln. In August 1862, Mr. Blades was one of four fraternal delegates to the Canadian General Conference. This was the first such appointed group ever sent by the American Methodist Episcopal Church to the Canadian Methodists.[42]

Home Efforts to Aid Northern Soldiers

The minds and hearts of the Methodist ministers and laymen were often turned toward their absent soldier members. Much money, clothing, and food was given to the soldier relief organizations. The emotions of that time appear in a letter from William H. Faxon to his soldier brother, Private John Faxon. He said that his brother was greatly missed at the Class meetings and the singing school. The local Quarterly Conference had just taken place at which the Presiding Elder "referred to our Brothers and Husbands in the field of battle beautifully." William Faxon admitted that he had cried at the Quarterly Meeting and now while he was writing this letter. E. Nethaway, a friend, also wrote John Faxon about the church activities at Elsie. He said in part:

> We had a good quarterly meeting but there was a feeling of sadness came over me at the thought that so many seats were here vacant which were wont to be filled by those we loved and my heart went up to God in prayer that those who were away might be the subjects of His peculiar care.[43]

Home-staying Methodists, ministers and members alike, applied themselves to good works for the benefit of all Union soldiers. The *Detroit Free Press* of May 16, 1861, gave notice to all the "Patriotic Ladies of Detroit" that flannel shirts were much needed for the Second Regiment. Cut materials ready to make up could be had by any church

---

[42] For Francis A. Blades see *Mich. Pioneer Coll.*, XXXV, 387-392. Also *North. Ch. Ad.*, X, 281.

[43] First letter to Faxon written Dec. 23, 1861, and second one Jan. 2, 1862. Both are in the John H. Faxon Collection of Civil War papers, Michigan Hist. Coll. of the University of Michigan.

group upon application to the Woodward Avenue Methodist Episcopal Church.[44]

Many Methodists worked for the soldiers in the State and national interdenominational agencies. Among them were the Sanitary and Christian Commissions, the American Bible Society, the Tract Society, the Michigan Soldiers Relief Association, and the Ladies Soldiers Aid Society. On November 19, 1861, William H. Faxon wrote to his brother John from Ovid that a donation party for the soldiers had just been held at the church. Over $12 in cash was taken in and then "today the old folks attend and bring in everything needful for their comfort that can be thought of it will be forwarded at once to the Sanitary Commission."

Used to working together for their church, Methodist women soon joined the women of other Protestant denominations in the soldiers aid societies to collect and send food, clothing, Bibles, and tracts to the fighting men. Usually they met weekly to plan and sew. Public notices may refer to a Methodist Church Ladies Aid Society or a more general Soldiers Aid Society. In Hillsdale, Mrs. S. W. Cook, President of the Society (kind not named) got out a proclamation to the women of the northwest. It said in part:

> Falter not nor grow weary. Let every Aid Society buckle on the armor anew. Let every farmer whose cellars are filled with plenty, send to the Commission what he can spare. Let our young people have profitable good times for the sufferers. Let us all keep on working as the boys keep on suffering and fighting.[45]

Constant group activity for the soldiers during the Civil War had some influence upon the Methodist women's organizations after the war. The patriotic habit of working together was continued in peacetime church activities.

Among lay members of the Methodist Church who were agents or delegates of the various soldier relief societies were John Owen and Laura Haviland. Owen had long been a prominent Detroit Methodist and friend of good causes. He was the State Treasurer in 1861 and gave valuable aid in financing the war in Michigan. He was also a member of the national board of the United States Christian Commission. One of their field delegates mentioned early in 1865 that Owen had just made a helpful visit to the army in Virginia.

Presumably Owen was more interested in the soldiers. Laura Haviland was far more concerned about the negro freedmen. She made a number of relief trips to Missouri, Arkansas, and Tennessee. On such visits, she carried letters from the Adrian Postmaster and the local Con-

---

[44] From a clipping in the Burton Hist. Coll., Detroit Public Library.

[45] History of First Methodist Church of Hillsdale, a booklet without indication of date, author, or place of publication. In Michigan Conference Hist. Coll., Albion College Library.

gressman, stating who she was and what her purpose was in going there. She always travelled with several trunks laden with blankets, warm clothing, and almost anything that refugees might need that she could get donated. Apparently she was not afraid to go anywhere or among any class of people — black or white, Union or Confederate.[46]

Methodist Field Delegates of the United States Christian Commission

One other form of war service was open to the Methodist minister appointed to a charge. That was six weeks of work as a field delegate of the U.S. Christian Commission. Except for its limited time, the work was much like that of a chaplain. "Minute Men" were prepared to leave, on ten minutes notice, to aid the wounded on the battlefields. The aims of the Christian Commission were "to carry home comforts to the homeless, friendly counsel to the friendless, and gospel teaching to the army and navy."

The Christian Commission began in the efforts of the Y.M.C.A. to do something for its members in wartime. Organized at New York City in the fall of 1861, it went out of existence in 1866. Its ministerial and lay field delegates numbered 4,119. Of that total, 458 were Methodist ministers. Fifteen of them were from the State of Michigan. The Detroit Annual Conference furnished twelve and the Michigan Annual Conference three.[47]

The Y.M.C.A. was not yet strongly organized in Michigan. Field service was rewarded with "the consciousness of doing good." Only the unavoidable expenses on a very modest scale were paid. The overall records of such work were most inadequately kept. Neither the central organization nor the field delegates felt the need of detailed accounts of their work until it was all over. The only exception to this failure to keep a running historical account of the work can be found in the letters of midwestern ministerial field delegates to the *Northwestern Christian Advocate*. It had so many reports from field delegates in 1865 that it was unable to print more than half of them.

The United States Christian Commission was established in Michigan at Detroit on June 15, 1863. The Rev. George Taylor became its

[46] Laura Haviland, *A Woman's Life Work, passim.* the later chapters particularly deserve notice.

[47] W. W. Sweet, *The Methodist Episcopal Church & the Civil War,* Chapter IX. Official Report of Mich. Branch, U.S. Christian Comm., found in Adjutant General's *Annual Report,* Mich., for 1864, pp. 901-4. Lemuel Moss, *Annals of the U.S. Christian Commission.* He lists all field agents and Sweet gives all Methodist field agents. But both lists are probably incomplete. Elijah Pilcher makes no mention of his own service as a field agent in his *Hist. Prot. Mich.* Neither does his son, Leander Pilcher, in the biography he wrote of his father. An extended search for accounts of field service by Mich. Methodist ministers themselves yielded only those by Seth Reed and W. W. Johnson.

State Agent and may have done field service too. He travelled all over Michigan, preaching and lecturing for the Christian Commission. He was present at the Detroit and Michigan Annual Conference sessions in the years 1863, 1864, and 1865. He also attended as many district ministerial meetings as he could manage. Some ministers felt that Taylor signed up more ministers for future field service than the national organization was able to assign usefully.

The Michigan Annual Conference did not send any field delegates until 1865 when three were accepted. These ministers were James Hoyt, Welcome W. Johnson, and George D. Lee. The west half of the State was very busy trying to cope with the war losses of ministers and members plus the urgent need to expand into a growing northern area.

The Detroit Annual Conference sent four ministers to field work in 1863. Their names were James E. Parker, Elijah H. Pilcher, Seth Reed, and John Russell. Then it managed to give six in 1864, who were James R. Cordon, S. L. Ramsdell, William H. Shier, George Stowe, Joseph Sutton, and George Taylor. But probably due to the end of the war in April, 1865, only two ministers served that year. They were Ira Donelson and George W. Lowe. More men may have served in the field work from both Conferences but the facts are hard to establish. Most of the churches made no mention anywhere in their records of their minister's absence on such field duty.

The Rev. W. W. Johnson, then of the Galesburg Church, wrote to the Northwestern of his army experiences in Virginia in 1865. He had been at City Point where the Christian Commission was building chapels and holding preaching every night. Johnson considered the preaching, by a minister from Philadephia, was "too much starch and not enough slam-bang for soldiers."

When the news came that a large number of exchanged prisoners were expected on the next boat from Richmond, Johnson had gone at once to the dock. He found the crew laying dead men on the shore. They had died en route home from captivity. Going on board, Johnson found the cabin crowded with 400 men, "dirty, filthy, and with barely enough to cover them." He admitted, "I could not refrain from weeping." He shook hands with those near him and asked if they would like him to sing and pray. Receiving a very warm response, "I broke out in 'His name yields the richest perfume' — O how they seemed to rejoice that they could again hear the sound of prayer and praise. They wanted me to go on north with them." Johnson expected to preach to the Pennsylvania Heavy Artillery and then go on up the lines, as far toward Richmond as possible, preaching and praying when and where an opportunity was offered.[48]

48 Letters from Johnson printed in *North. Ch. Ad.*, XII, 402; XIII, 1, 79. Only his name and denomination are given in L. Moss, *Annals of U.S. Christian Commission*, appendix.

The Rev. Seth Reed, then of the Ypsilanti Church, was asked to do field duty for six weeks with the Army of the Cumberland in Tennessee and Alabama. His Official Board "said to go and they would take care of things at home." He went off to field duty in September, 1863, with $36 in his pocket, $11 being his own money and $25 given him by the local Commission Agent.

His first field experience was a visit to a large barn hospital full of sick and seriously wounded soldiers. The only light was given by a few candles and the air was filled with sighs and deep groans. Reed admitted, "I was not anticipating the shock which the scene produced upon me — for I had to retreat immediately and seek quiet before I could do anything for the suffering."

From then on Reed was much too busy to think of himself. In his pocket field record, he noted twenty-one times that he distributed books, papers, tracts, New Testaments, and housewives. The latter was a small sewing kit with buttons and also threaded needles. He often prayed

The Tent of a Christian Commission Worker in the Civil War. Michigan ministers such as Seth Reed, worked under such conditions as portrayed here.

with individuals and small groups, preached whenever possible, usually three times on Sundays, sent telegrams, and wrote letters for dying soldiers.

He saw many pathetic scenes and recorded a few of them. Michael Flyn said he was religious and tried hard to maintain a Christian attitude. His wife's letters were a great help and Reed noted, "I saw some of her letters much worn."

On October 18, 1863, en route to his quarters from Sunday services at which he had preached, Reed saw some soldiers busy washing and 'drying their clothes. He at once went over to them. Said one "This is our washing day." Reed said, "O boys I would not take Sunday for Washing Day." They looked at each other in astonishment finally one says to the other — *"this is* Sunday isn't it."

Like many of the chaplains, Reed was most unfavorably impressed with the south. The utter desolation, the heaps of ashes where homes once had been, and the bitterness of the southerners caught his attention repeatedly. He became convinced that hatred of the north was taught in the Sunday Schools and that all southern Methodists were "violent secessionists." He saw large numbers of escaped slaves and was very shocked when he saw that some of them had white skins, blue eyes, and auburn hair. He also noted that most of the churches in the south, regardless of the denomination, were in a rundown even dilapidated condition.

While Reed was stationed in Nashville, Tennessee, an unfinished hotel crowded with Confederate prisoners collapsed from the fourth floor down. Reed worked with those digging out the killed and wounded. He asked one victim who he was and was surprised by the reply, "Oh — I am a Methodist preacher and I wish this thing was ended." Reed gave the man a handkerchief to wipe his face with and said, "Well I am a Methodist preacher and I too wish this thing was ended."[49]

Michigan Methodist Reaction to Lincoln's Death

Equally with the rest of the northern States, Michigan was deeply shocked by the death of Abraham Lincoln. The churches generally draped their pulpits, window arches, and flags in mourning. Most ministers preached special sermons on his loss. The coincidence with Easter probably added to the solemn effect. The *Northwestern Christian Ad-*

---

[49] Seth Reed, *The Story of my Life*, pp. 71-75. Also Reed's pocket field record book, similar to that carried by all the field delegates of the U.S. Christian Commission. This is in the Michigan Historical Collection of the University of Michigan, Ann Arbor. In addition to Reed"s personal notes, it contains much printed information and instructions about how the delegates were to dress, travel and behave. They were always to be "Christian gentlemen."

vocate reported in detail sermons in Michigan at Ann Arbor, Adrian, Detroit, and Kalamazoo.[50]

Detroit Central Church had a special Sunday sermon by the Rev. John M. Arnold on "The Retributive Providence of God manifest in the war and particularly in its results upon the South." A few days later, a formal funeral service was held at which Arnold, Presiding Elder Clements, and former Chaplain Smart officiated. Arnold discussed Lincoln's character and declared that his name would be equal with that of Washington in the future. Clements invoked Divine guidance and said, as others did, that Lincoln had completed his earthly tasks and sterner hands were needed to wield the sword of justice. Smart remembered that most of the saviours of the world had met violent death. He thought it significant that Lincoln died on the same day that Jesus Christ did and also at the dawn of peace.

In Kalamazoo, Pastor Hemenway said, in the conclusion of his sermon, "Jesus reigns above rulers, rebels, and assassins. This is a new test of Republican institutions but above is the changeless, supreme kingdom."

The Rev. Francis A. Blades began his sermon in Adrian by reading the latest Washington dispatches to relieve congregational anxieties. He devoted much attention to the place of Lincoln's death, declaring that Christians generally would be shocked by his dying in a *theater.* His comment was:

> If it had been in his own house or in the discharge of his duty, would have been some relief . . . .But by the hand of an assassin actor. The theater of America is from this day immortal in infamy. This may be the lesson — that a man should never go where he is unwilling to die.

Blades also thought Lincoln was too easy on the south and hence "good may come of it . . . . Mr. Johnson's little finger will be heavier on the rebels than Lincoln's whole body."

In Ann Arbor, President Haven of the University "poured out the fullness of our sorrow-stricken hearts in prayer," and the pastor, B. F. Cocker preached. Among other things he said:

> Yesterday was the saddest, darkest day of all this terrible war has brought . . . . Twenty million people feel today that they have lost a *Father* . . . . But we must not linger in shock and feel that all is gone. The army victory is certain, the Emancipation Proclamation is not repealed, and the Lord God reigns . . . . May the new President be, as

---

[50] *The Northwestern Christian Advocate* gave most of its columns for three issues to Lincoln's death. the sermons thereon, and the funeral in Springfield. It printed very long summaries of sermons in eleven cities in its area. The material was all headed "The Bereavement. Northwestern Methodist Pulpits." Found in volume XIII, 129, 132-133, 142-145.

Lincoln was, noble and just, but also wise and firm to deal with men not to be trusted and, if the future security of the nation demands it, to hang or banish. God always raises up the right man at the right hour.

Methodist Preparations for Peace

The General Conference of 1864 changed the rule on slavery in the *Discipline* from an equivocal statement to an outright prohibition of slaveholding, slave buying, and slave selling.

Looking toward the changes that peace might bring, it also created a general church extension society, changed the time rule on ministerial appointments from a limit of two years to one of three, and laid plans for an enormous celebration in 1866 of the centennial of American Methodism. It also elected three new bishops, all of whom were church paper editors.[51]

The spirit of the members of the churches of Michigan Methodism, from the smaller rural ones to those in growing urban situations, promised fully as much for the future development of the denomination as did any decisions of the General Conference. It is revealed in such letters as the one that the Rev. A. J. Sprague, of the Elk Rapids Circuit wrote to the editor of the *Northwestern Christian Advocate* on August 2, 1865. He said in part:

> The war has made heavy drafts on our sparsely settled townships, yet even here the gospel has been sustained, souls converted and the Sabbath School has not lost its power . . . . It is well sustained by the wives of our soldiers. We of this new country truly realize that the path to freedom has been red with blood — the blood of our fathers, sons, and brothers, and as if this were not enough, the blood of Abraham Lincoln, who, under God, was the preserver of our nation. Yet we thank God for principle is triumphing and the tree of Liberty is taking deeper root in our American soil, its branches spreading far and wide welcoming the oppressed of every land, nation, kindred and tongue.[52]

Ahead were years of frustration and painful adjustment for the Methodist Episcopal Church. But it would grow in the process of change. New occasions would bring new vistas of duty and service to humanity.

[51] W. W. Sweet, *Meth. Am. Hist.*, pp. 298-302.
[52] *North. Ch. Ad.*, XIII, 245.

Chapter X

PEACE AND NEW PROBLEMS

1865 — 1872

The After Effects of Civil War on Methodism

Although the Civil War was over, its influence lingered in the Michigan Methodist Episcopal Church. That wartime standing committee on "The State of the Country" was maintained in Michigan by both Annual Conferences until 1867. After that a committee on the Freedmen was at work for over half a century. In 1868, the Michigan Annual Conference created a committee on "The State of the Church." Other standing committees for long periods were those concerned with Education and Temperance.

No doubt most Methodists agreed with the sentiments expressed in the 1865 report of the Detroit Annual Conference committee on "The State of the Country." Its members were John A. Baughman, William C. Way, Dean C. Wright, and George Taylor. Way and Taylor knew war by personal experience as chaplain and Christian Commission Agent. This committee's report began:

> Since the last annual meeting of our Conference, God has mercifully brought us from a state of terrible war and bloodshed to most glorious peace. And it certainly becomes us, as a body of Christian ministers, to most devoutly acknowledge the merciful kindness of our Heavenly Father in this wonderful deliverance wrought for us.

The greatest evil in the United States had been ended by the abolition of slavery. Now the new, colored citizens must be helped and elevated in every possible way. The right to vote must be given "as soon as they are capable of exercising it." Any minister had the right to teach his congregation the principles of "Christian morality in politics as well as in all other relations of life."

242

Even before the war ended, the northern Methodist Episcopal Church was pushing into conquered areas to take and use the southern Methodist churches. A few thought the split dating from 1844 would shortly be healed by the return of southern Methodist churches to the welcoming arms of the northern church. That Detroit Annual Conference committee on "The State of the Country" thoroughly approved all authorized efforts "to extend the influence of . . . an unsullied Methodism in all the southern States." This aggressive attitude was resented in the south and probably helped delay the unification of the whole Methodist Church.

A similar committee in the Michigan Annual Conference reported much the same ideas. Joseph Jones, a former chaplain, was chairman of the committee. It said that "next to Almighty God, our thanks are due . . . to the army and navy of our country." It recommended an amendment to the Michigan constitution in order to "forever exclude the word 'white' in relation to persons, from our Statute." Also the national Missionary Society must spend more money on the southern work.[1]

Feelings about the Civil War and the south were strong in Michigan for a long time. Hence people here were Republican in politics for a great many years. But the State escaped the vindictiveness found in some of the border and southern States. Again geographical location remote from the center of the conflict had much influence.

A Partial Wesleyan Reunion

Michigan Methodists had an added reason for looking at the future with hope. Slavery was the chief cause of the Wesleyan withdrawal from the Methodist Episcopal Church in 1841. The abolition of slavery opened the way for a modest reunion here. Seven Wesleyan ministers applied for readmission to the Detroit Annual Conference in 1867. The ministers wishing to return were Luther Lee, John McEldowney, Samuel and Elisha Bibbins, Ephraim VanNorman, Isaac Johnson, and Marsenus Wiltsey. They were admitted together as a group at Saginaw by Bishop Edmund S. Janes. Although they had been present as guests from the first day of the Conference session, their final admission did not come until the evening of the sixth day, September 9, 1867.

What an experience the occasion must have been! After religious services, the seven ministers presented themselves before Bishop Janes. He welcomed them and then "gave each of them the hand of fellowship in behalf of the Conference." Dr. Luther Lee had been chosen to speak

---

[1] For Detroit Annual Conference committee report on the State of the Country see *Minutes* for the 10th session in 1865, pp. 17-20. For the similar committee report of the Michigan Annual Conference see *Minutes* for the 30th session in 1865, p. 18.

to the Conference which he did "with much feeling." Finally the entire Conference sang the Doxology.

All seven of these Wesleyan ministers were received as elders and each was given a certificate of good standing. Samuel Bibbins was superannuated and so retired at once. The rest of them received appointments to various churches that same evening when the assignments were read. The places to which they were sent give an idea of their calibre as ministers. VanNorman was to go to Northville, Elisha Bibbins to Franciscoville and Waterloo, Wiltsey to Laphamville, Johnson to Mason, and Luther Lee to Court Street Church in Flint.

Perhaps the best known of the seven was John McEldowney. He had been a professor of Mathematics at Michigan Union College in Leoni. Later he had held a similar position at Adrian. From 1864 to 1866, he had served as President of Adrian College. He may have left there because of inner Wesleyan dissension and the effort to make Adrian College a project of the Methodist Protestants. The Detroit Methodist Episcopal Conference suitably appointed him a professor in Albion College with his church connection in the Manchester Quarterly Conference. McEldowney went to Albion to teach Mathematics but transferred to Greek and Latin in 1868. He was also the acting president for a brief period in 1870.

Luther Lee had been one of the most active abolitionists in Michigan. He lived to preach his semi-centennial sermon before the Detroit Annual Conference in 1879. In the course of that sermon, Lee remarked that he was mobbed five times by pro-slavery people but was never seriously hurt although once he did have a brand new suit ruined. At once, the Rev. John M. Arnold stood up and moved that the Detroit Annual Conference pay Dr. Lee for that suit. As a result, Lee recieved $50. Every year for a long time, Dr. Lee preached in Flint's Court Street Church on the Sunday nearest his birthday. He was very active in preaching and supply work almost to the day of his death in December, 1889, at the age of 89. McEldowney was also very active after his retirement in the newer churches of Detroit until his death in March, 1904, at the age of 80. These two men were the most valuable to the Methodist Episcopal Church of the seven Wesleyans who returned in 1867.[2]

The Non-Episcopal Methodists and Adrian College

The decision to leave the Wesleyans and return to the Methodist Episcopal Church, as those seven ministers did, may have also been in-

[2] *Autobiography of Luther Lee*, p. 310. Detroit Annual Conference *Minutes* for 1867, p. 90. Also memoirs of Lee and McEldowney in the same Conference *Minutes* for 1899 and 1904. Also for McEldowney see R. Gildart, *Albion College*, p. 95.

fluenced by internal dissensions over a variety of questions. At that time a great number of "smaller and, as we believe, more scripturally constituted Christian denominations of kindred sentiments and liberal principles" were trying to draw closer together "in building each other up." So wrote a Free Will Baptist minister to the Michigan "Methodists" in 1872.[3]

That minister might have had reference to the Wesleyans, the Methodist Protestants, the Independent Methodists, the Free Methodists, the Free Will Baptists, the Congregational and even the Presbyterian churches. The proceedings of the Methodist Protestant Conferences here in Michigan, even though kept most inadequately, look very congregational to one who reads them in the mid-20th century. The chairman of the sessions of Conference was called the President and practically everything he did had to be afterwards approved by the whole Conference session.

Almost everything that was done in Conference sessions demanded a committee first. Obviously the most important, because they assumed the tasks of the bishops in the Methodist Episcopal Church, were the Pastoral Relations, the Stationing of the ministers, and the Boundaries of Circuits and Missions Committees. One with an interesting title, although its exact duties are not too clear, was the Committee on Difficulties. These more important committees were elected by vote of the ministers and lay delegates rather than being selected by the President. The committee reports were not as extensively printed in the Minutes as those of the Methodist Episcopal Conferences were. Otherwise much of what these M.P. Conferences did was exactly like the procedures of the M.E. Conferences. The examinations of ministerial character, the survey of those wishing admission on trial, and the efforts to provide more money for the Preachers Aid Society were just as conscientiously carried out by either group.

Certainly also the hostility to liquor, to gambling, to violation of Sabbath observance, and to secret societies was very strong in all the branches of Methodism in the state of Michigan.

But the non-Episcopal forms of Methodism in Michigan were much smaller in numbers and in funds than the Methodist Episcopal Church was here. In the years 1865 to 1872, only three or four churches in either M.P. Conference in Michigan had over one hundred members apiece. Also the salaries of the ministers, even including the President of the Conference, were most inadequate and in at least half of the charges not anywhere near paid in full. Upon a couple of occasions, the Conference itself took up a collection for its President in an endeavor to see that he received the $700 salary he had been promised.

The Methodist Protestants in Michigan met some of their problems

---

3 *Minutes* of the 31st session of the "Methodist" Church for 1872, p. 22.

The Plymouth Methodist Protestant Church in Adrian was erected in 1857. At first it was by turns a Presbyterian or Congregational Church. Dr. Asa Mahan was pastor from 1858 until 1861 when he became president of Adrian College. The M. P. Methodist Society was organized April 14, 1867 and met at first at the College, then in the Opera House. It took over this building in 1879.

because of their location on the remote western edge of the area where their denomination was strongest. The eastern and southern Conferences had held together in spite of the Civil War but, beginning in 1858, the northern and western Conferences had drawn apart and taken a much stronger stand against slavery. With the negroes set free and the war won, many people hoped that the various Methodist minorities might draw together into a stronger church and a better support for Adrian College.

Individualism and independence were strong in Michigan Methodists whatever their branch was. The Wesleyans particularly did not want to rejoin any larger group and their Conference in the majority voted against it. In the end, the northern and southern wings of the Methodist Protestants were the only ones that reunited. The regrouping held to the name *Methodist* only for a decade and then, in 1877, returned to being called the Methodist Protestants until the unification of 1939.[4]

A good many individual resignations, transfers, and such evidently occurred in this Reconstruction Era. The seven who went back to the Methodist Episcopal Church have been noted. In the Michigan Annual Conference record for 1870 of the M.P.'s, listed under the heading "Left by Letter" are four names as follows: "J. T. Husted, gone to Congregationalists; Milo Smith, gone to Baptists; W. S. Buxton, gone to M.E. Church; C. B. Waldo. After the last name, an unknown hand has written in pencil "gone to the - - - bad -"[5]

Adrian College had been deeply disturbed by the Civil War and

[4] *History of American Methodism*, II, 397-399. Chapter XX is by D. R. Chandler on the Methodist Protestant Church from 1865 to 1900.

[5] *Minutes* of the 29th session of the Michigan Annual Conference of the Methodist Church (formerly Methodist Protestant) in 1870, p. 19.

all the talk of unification of the non-Episcopal Methodists. The College was in desperate financial condition and the trustees were hoping for much money from the Methodist Protestants. Since 1862, the project had been under discussion and finally in 1866, Adrian College was turned over to the "Methodists" by simply electing a majority of the trustees from the new Church group.

It was agreed that the new board of trustees was to pay all the outstanding debts and provide an endowment of $100,000. This sum had been intended to start a new college, possibly in Ohio, but Adrian got the money instead. Unfortunately the College lost two brick buildings by a bad fire just at that time. It is not strange that the board of trustees were unable to provide adequate financial aid nor that the student enrollment declined a good deal in the 1870's.[6]

Creation of the Methodist Freedmen's Aid Society

The deep concern widely felt in the North for the former slaves brought the Methodist Episcopal Church into a new field of missionary endeavor. At first, the care of the negroes was felt to be the business of the Federal Government and Methodist influence was used to get Congress to establish the Freedmen's Bureau. Some Michigan Methodists also helped the Northwestern Freedmen's Aid Society. Since this organization was interdenominational, the Methodist Episcopal Church began to feel that it must do its own work for the freedmen. This was joined with the effort to establish northern Methodist churches in the south. If the same amounts of money and effort had been given through the southern Methodist churches, the ill feeling between the two main branches of Methodism might not have been so bitter nor so long lasting. But in August, 1866, the Freedman's Aid Society of the Methodist Episcopal Church was created in Cincinnati. Most of the northern Annual Conferences approved it in 1867 and the General Conference did likewise in 1868.

Both the Annual Conferences in Michigan in their sessions of 1866 appointed committees on the Freedmen. Each was a committee of three with two members former army chaplains. The Michigan Annual Conference did not print its committee report but the Detroit did. It laid most emphasis on the desperate need of the freedmen for education by a permanent plan. This was especially urgent because the national Methodist Missionary Society "does not make appropriations for schools connected with domestic missions." Creation of a Conference Freed-

[6] Franklin W. Stephenson, Adrian College. An article written for the Detroit Conference Historical Society. In the Conference historical collection, Adrian College Library. W. F. Dunbar, *The Michigan Record in Higher Education*, pp. 125-126.

men's Aid Society was recommended and nominations for President, Secretary, and Treasurer were suggested. It may be presumed that the Michigan Annual Conference took similar action.

Beginning in 1867, the reports of the Conference Freedmen's Aid Society Treasurers were printed in the *Minutes* of both the Annual Conferences in Michigan. For at least ten years, the sums raised were very modest and many churches took no collection at all for the freedmen. In 1871, the Michigan Annual Conference committee on the freedmen stated that ¾ of all the churches had not reported any collection for the negro work. In the opinion of the committee, the ministers of such churches were "remiss in the proper discharge of duty."[7]

New Demands and Increased Financial Needs

A decided increase was taking place in the number and variety of causes for which the ministers were expected to collect. The Centenary celebration and its local projects coincided with the years in which the Freedmen's Aid Society was getting under way. The needs of Albion College were very evident. A Church Extension Society had been created by the General Conference of 1864. If it was to perform its appointed work, large sums of money must be put at its service. The foreign missionary cause asked for regular yearly collections. Such worthy organizations as the American Bible Society, the Temperance and Tract Societies all were eager for money and workers. Many parts of Michigan were still so newly settled that the first Methodist Meeting House there was still to be built. Small societies simply must have much outside help to do so. Every year Annual Conferences urged building decent parsonages provided with the necessary "heavy furniture." The Methodist Protestants felt so strongly about parsonages that the Conference allowed any minister to refuse a charge without a decent house for him and his family. Whatever the branch of Methodism in Michigan, many of its smaller churches were unable to fulfill all the urgent requests that their minister received in the course of a Conference year.

A sense of impending change and growth was felt by some ministers as soon as the Civil War ended. That committee on the "State of the Country" of the Detroit Annual Conference session of 1865 did not give all its attention to rejoicing that the war was over. It also declared:

> This new aspect of things imposes new duties, there can be no doubt; and that it calls upon us as a church and ministers to enter upon new

[7] Examples of the very modest contributions can be found in any of the Annual Conference *Minutes*. In 1867, the Michigan Annual Conference reported $175.41 from eleven places with the largest sum being $23.85 from Three Rivers. The same year, the Detroit Annual Conference raised $583.80 for the freedmen but Detroit Central Church gave $500 of that total sum and the rest of it came from twelve different towns.

and enlarged fields of usefulness, is not less true . . . . We are now called upon to take a calm view of the present, and a proper perspective survey of the future, as far as human sagacity may penetrate, and wisely adapt ourselves to the new exigencies that may arise.

A comparison of the standing committees of the earliest Michigan Annual Conferences with those of the 1860s gives an idea of the continuous tasks and the new duties. Early and late, the Annual Conferences of this State were concerned with Public Worship, Sunday Schools, Bibles and Tracts, missions, parsonages, and memoirs of recently deceased ministers. Other longstanding concerns were temperance, Sabbath observance, and education. The committees on slavery in both Conferences in the 1850s had been replaced by a Freedmen's Aid Society in each organization. Two new committees made their appearance in the records of both Detroit and Michigan Annual Conferences in 1865. These were for the Centenary Celebration and the Church Extension Society. The first was of the most immediate concern because of the time element involved.

The Centennial Celebration of 1866:
Goals and Results

The year 1866 was the centennial of the first Methodist meeting held in the United States. It was a modest gathering at the home of Philip Embury. He was a local preacher who had come from Ireland to New York City in 1760 with his family and other relatives. His cousin, Barbara Heck, grew very concerned about the lax life of this little group in the strange city. Under her urging, Embury preached to four people in his home and soon formed them into a Methodist Class. Its members were Barbara Heck and her husband, Embury and his wife, and a slave named Betty. From this modest beginning came John Street Church in New York City.

So vast a growth from so small a seed impressed all the Methodists. The Michigan Annual Conference's Centenary Committee said that it was most concerned to convey their profound debt of gratitude to God for raising the Methodist Episcopal Church in only one century "from nothing to the most numerous, wealthy and mighty body of Christians in the land."[8]

The connectional operations of the Methodist Episcopal Church are shown in plans for such a project as the Centennial celebration of 1866. The General Conference in 1864 had set October 1866 as the special time of centennial observance and appointed a general centennial committee of the Board of Bishops, twelve ministers, and twelve laymen.

[8] Michigan Annual Conference *Minutes* for 1865, p. 19. W. W. Sweet, *Meth. Am. Hist.*, pp. 53-55.

This committee met at Cleveland in February 1865 to plan execution of its twin goals :"the spiritual improvement of our members" and collection of a fund of Thanksgiving. This last was to be used for the Church institutions "best calculated to bless the world for the century to come." Ten worthy causes were chosen as objects of fund raising.[9]

The Annual Conferences chose the objects of fund raising in their areas. Those selected in the State of Michigan were Albion College, Garrett Biblical Institute, a building for the New York City national Mission House, the Irish Fund, and a general fund for the education of ministers and missionaries. All unspecified funds given were to go to this Education Fund and a Board of Education was created to administer it.

The Michigan Annual Conference declared that any unspecified gifts received in their half of the State were to be divided 85% to the Albion College Endowment Fund and 15% to Garrett. The Detroit Annual Conference gave 5% of its Centenary collections to the new Mission House and $5,000 for a building at Garrett to be named Wellington H. Collins Hall. Collins, brother of the China Missionary was the Presiding Elder of Detroit District who died suddenly in 1858 near the close of his four year term of office. Albion College claims were left for decision to the Conference Centenary Committee.[10]

Each Annual Conference in Michigan appointed a large committee composed equally of ministers and laymen to supervise all details of

[9] W. W. Sweet, *op. cit.*, pp. 317, 319. Detroit Annual Conference *Minutes* for 1865, pp. 21-23.
[10] Michigan Annual Conference *Minutes* for 1865, p. 19. Detroit Annual Conference *Minutes* for 1865, pp. 22-23.

David Preston was a prominent Methodist layman and philanthropist, who was active in the building of Detroit churches, and in raising an endowment fund for Albion College.

the Centenary. The Detroit Annual Conference committee had forty-four members and that of the Michigan twenty. Each Conference put seven of its Presiding Elders among the ministers appointed. Detroit included such experienced workers as E. H. Pilcher, J. A. Baughman, Manasseh Hickey, and James Smart. Albion College President G. B. Jocelyn and E. O. Haven, University of Michigan President, were also on the Detroit Committee. The Financial Agent of Albion College, W. H. Brockway, was on the Michigan Conference committee. The best known lay members were John Owen and David Preston of Detroit. The latter was the head of a private bank there.[11]

The goal of the Centenary committees was "a thorough and efficient canvass so that every member of our congregation may have the privilege of presenting his Centenary offering to God." As usual the connecting links were the Presiding Elders on the committees. They were urged to appoint a committee of ten to operate in every charge. District committees would eventually report to the Conference committee.

Considering the careful plans, practically every Methodist Episcopal Church in Michigan must have had a memorial sermon and a weekday historical address. But scarcely any of them noted such programs in their church records. Central Church in Detroit held a Centenary Jubilee on October 25, 1866, in their new chapel. After a "Union Love Feast" and several addresses, the memorial sermon was preached by E. O. Haven.[12]

In addition to the Centenary ceremonies, Michigan Methodism had its own anniversary to observe. 1866 marked the tenth year since the division of the State into two Annual Conferences. Ordinarily the Conference sessions were held in successive weeks so that one bishop might officiate at both. Now plans had been made for a reunion of the Conferences if their sessions might occur simultaneously. Therefore, the Michigan Annual Conference met at Hillsdale from September 6 to 11 with Bishop Simpson presiding and the Detroit Annual Conference met at Hudson from September 5 to 10 with Bishop Ames presiding. These towns are hardly more than ten miles apart. On Friday, September 7, 1866, the two Annual Conferences spent the day together at Hillsdale "in delightful and interesting reunion services." The Detroit Annual Conference returned to Hudson late in the day and resumed its regular business in the evening. Characters of men on trial and also

[11] See both Detroit and Michigan Annual Conference *Minutes* for the years from 1865 through 1868. Detroit Annual Conference did not print the names of their Centenary committee until 1866 but it may have functioned earlier. The Michigan Annual Conference committee names are given in the *Minutes* for 1865.

[12] Silas Farmer, *History of Detroit and Michigan,* p. 579.

Bishop Erastus O. Haven (1820-81) joined the New York Conference in 1848. He served as Professor in the University of Michigan 1853-56; as editor of Zion's Herald, and from 1863 to 1869 as President of the University of Michigan. The University doubled in size during this administration; his Sunday afternoon lectures were long remembered. He went on to become President of Northwestern, Sec. of the Board of Education; Chancellor of Syracuse U., and Bishop in 1880.

of those about to be admitted were painstakingly examined. Sufficient energy was also found to hear and accept two reports of standing committees. Adjournment with the doxology and benediction must have been welcome.[13]

In the year of the Bicentennial of American Methodism, it is difficult to estimate the religious and financial results of the Centennial observance. Was there the great spiritual awakening hoped for in the special meetings held in October, 1866? Generally the Centenary efforts covered three years from 1866 through 1868. Presumably the annual reports of adult membership ought to show a decided increase in 1867 and 1868. The general statistics of the Conferences in Michigan do not show any striking growth in membership as a result of the Centennial.

Rather the end of the Civil War and the return of former, soldier, church members was the more significant factor. A very large increase in membership in 1866, particularly in the Michigan Conference, was followed by five years of moderate increase ending in a decrease of just

[13] Detroit Annual Conference *Minutes* for 1866, pp. 14-15. The Michigan Annual Conference *Minutes* for 1866 did not print any of the Day Journal at all so nothing except the financial campaign can be observed.

over a thousand in total Methodist Episcopal Church membership in Michigan in 1872.[14]

The actual cash results of the Centennial campaign are hard to determine. This is due in part to the careless way in which Conference statistics were collected and printed then. An average of a dozen ministers in each Conference either were late with their reports or else did not make any. Even the arithmetic was not always correct. In the same year's *Minutes,* a sum of money for the Centenary or the Missionary Society might be one amount in the general statistics and an entirely different one in the committee reports. References to notes, pledges, or real estate in the hands of a committee leaves one in doubt as to how much *cash* was really there. Neither Conference thought it necessary to print the Centenary committee reports for each year of that special effort. The expenses of financial agents was another variable factor.

It appears that the Michigan Annual Conference raised more money for the Centenary goals than the Detroit Conference did.

Around $56,000 was collected by the Michigan Annual Conference. But that grand total included a lot of unpaid pledges and the expenses of the collection agents. The Detroit Annual Conference reported in 1866 the "subscription" of $26,192 from sixty-five leading charges in the region. No final report of the cash collections seems to have ever been made. The Michigan Annual Conference earmarked about 90% of its collections for the endowment fund of Albion College. The Detroit Annual Conference gave about ⅔ of its Centenary funds to Albion College but spread the rest of it around in small amounts to Garrett, to the New York Mission House, to the Irish Fund, to the Church Extension Society, and finally to the General Education Fund. The location of Albion College within the bounds of the Michigan Annual Conference may have given its ministers a more personal knowledge of its most serious financial plight.[15]

[14] Membership statistics for 1865-1872 in Michigan

Year	Detroit Conf	Michigan Conf.	Total Members	Yearly Change
1865	14,535	12,748	27,283	Decrease- 584
1866	15,358	17,260	32,618	Increase- 5,335
1867	16,856	17,620	34,476	Increase- 1,858
1868	17,910	17,836	35,746	Increase- 1,270
1869	18,174	20,484	38,658	Increase- 2,922
1870	19,501	21,627	41,128	Increase- 2,470
1871	20,353	22,376	42,729	Increase- 1,601
1872	20,147	21,549	41,696	Decrease- 1,033

[15] "On Centenary Cause" in Michigan Annual Conference *Minutes* for 1868, pp. 68-69. Centenary committee reports in the Detroit Annual Conference *Minutes* for 1866, pp. 46-47; for 1868, pp. 208-209.

The Financial Rescue of Albion College

At the close of the Civil War, Albion College was in a desperate condition. Much of its modest endowment was worthless. It consisted of promissory notes against some future, college scholarship. Many of these were held by Michigan Methodist ministers. The struggling college could not possibly honor all those potential requests for what amounted to free tuition because the ministers in their turn could not possibly supply the needed cash.

The Albion College faculty in this period numbered from seven to ten and most of them carried very heavy teaching loads. The third college building stood unfinished and unused for long periods. When the trustees got a little more money in hand, they would order a bit more work done on this building, South Hall. It took fourteen years of intermittent labor to finish it. The College and Preparatory Departments together never had more than about three hundred students in the years from 1865 through 1872. Much of the time the College had only forty to fifty students. The Rev. Myron A. Dougherty, then the College Financial Agent, declared:

> The institution was without means, and what was far worse, was left without many friends, and with an army of open enemies or indifferent constituents. The college and its managers were covered with odium . . . . The north and central buildings had grown dilapidated, the grounds unsightly, being uninclosed and dug into pits to get gravel to mend the ways of the village.[16]

The combined labors of a few devoted Methodist laymen and ministers saved Albion College. George B. Jocelyn was President of Albion from 1864 to 1869 and again from 1871 until his death in 1877. Under his leadership, Albion enjoyed a slow but steady growth in numbers and raised an endowment fund of around $200,000. The latter was the result of two major efforts, one during the Centenary from 1865 to 1869 and the other from 1871 to 1873.

Credit for the achievement of a respectable endowment fund belongs to two Detroit Conference laymen, David Preston and John Owen. The first labored mightily for Albion College all over Michigan for years. In 1871, he offered to raise $60,000 from Michigan Methodists within two years after the Albion College financial agents raised $50,000 from fifty people or less. Preston himself spoke in many churches, wrote hundreds of letters, and sent out thousands of printed fact sheets about the financial situation of the College. He also provided many pictures of the Albion College buildings to hang in Methodist Church vestibules.

The ministers who labored the hardest for Albion College in the years from 1865-1872 were its financial and endowment agents ap-

---

[16] Quoted by R. Gildart, *Albion College*, pp. 78-79.

pointed by the two Annual Conferences in Michigan. In that seven-year period the Rev. Myron A. Dougherty labored the longest, serving from 1867 to 1871. Other Michigan Annual Conference members who rendered similar service for a year or two included William H. Brockway, Thomas Lyon, and D. F. Barnes. These last two were also general Centenary agents. The Detroit Annual Conference ministers giving similar service were Seth Reed and Robert Bird. For several years, if any substantial amount of money was raised and laid aside for the endowment fund of Albion College, then it was necessary to borrow at a high rate of interest in order to meet the current expenses. Eventually by the mid-1870s, the endowment fund was large enough to warrant more attention to the improvement of the College's academic reputation.[17]

Today it seems as if the Methodist Episcopal Church both nationally and in Michigan had undertaken too much financial effort in too many different areas for the somewhat disturbed Reconstruction period and so soon after a great Civil War.

Church Extension in Michigan

Certainly a new national organization established by the General Conference of 1864, the Church Extension Society, had its troubles in winning wide financial acceptance by the Methodists of Michigan. The Society made an over-ambitious beginning and almost went down in bankruptcy in its first two years of existence. The needs were so great everywhere, the desire to satisfy them so keen, and the bank credit of the Society so meagre that when the first Secretary, S. Y. Monroe, was killed in a railroad accident the whole organization almost collapsed.[18]

Several factors created a need for a national Methodist Church Extension Society. The days when a circuit rider travelled a four-weeks circuit preaching almost every day were nearly over. Circuits were much smaller. A minister often was sent to a charge of three or four small villages but he attempted to preach in each one on Sundays. Rival denominations were much more active too. People no longer were satisfied with an overcrowded meeting in a school or small house. A new church building was an enormous help to a travelling minister. It was a visible focus of religious faith in that community. The Committee on Church Extension of the Detroit Annual Conference said in 1865:

> Foreign pecuniary aid in the erection of houses of worship for the use of feeble societies, has long been a felt want by those laboring in our frontier settlements. From want of such aid many opportunities to obtain suitable locations for building are lost, and the influences of such losses . . . have been and are severely felt.[19]

[17] R. Gildart, *Albion College,* pp. 78-84, 93-96, 113-116.
[18] W. C. Barclay, *History of Methodist Missions,* III, 134-136.
[19] Detroit Annual Conference *Minutes* for 1865, p. 23.

It was then widely believed that the northern Methodists must establish churches everywhere in the conquered south. The Michigan Annual Conference of 1865 gave $160.50 in a special offering to help pay for a northern Methodist church in Richmond. That same year the Detroit Annual Conference said that it thoroughly approved of efforts "to extend the influence of an unperverted Christianity, and an unsullied Methodism, in all Southern States." And the Conference's Church Extension committee referred to "vast fields throughout the entire South already white for the harvest."[20]

In 1862, the U.S. Congress adopted a Homestead Act, which enabled any American citizen to acquire his own farm. He must live on the land and improve it for five years. A flood of settlers were soon going west to the Great Plains area. This was largely a treeless frontier hence only small sod houses were built for homes.

The strong Methodist feeling that these new pioneers must be followed by circuit riders, just as had been done on earlier frontiers, influenced the creation of the Church Extension Society in 1864. In the heavily forested, eastern United States, a modest church might be built by the combined physical efforts of pastor and people. But on the last frontier, imported materials would have to be purchased at great expense. It was expected that much of the money raised by the new Church Extension Society would be spent on the Great Plains.

The earlier custom of allowing a financially burdened minister to travel in other Conferences for the purpose of raising money for his mortgaged home church was beginning to cause irritation. Wealthy Methodists were repeatedly solicited or sometimes a minister collected a sum equal only to his travelling expenses. A national organization ought to be more businesslike.

Few Methodist ministers in Michigan needed additional arguments about the vast need for organized efforts to collect funds for more church construction. Indeed, some of them felt all the church extension money that could be collected in this State was most urgently needed right here. The Detroit Annual Conference session of 1872 declared "a considerable portion of this Conference is Mission ground having slender means of contribution and urgently requiring aid."

In 1870, the committee on the State of the Church of the Michigan Annual Conference reviewed the entire situation of the western half of the State. It particularly criticized the carelessly kept statistics, the negligence about titles to church property, and many irregularities in the administration of the *Discipline*. Their deepest concern was reserved for twenty-one counties in the northwest part of Michigan. It was "as truly missionary ground" as any in Africa. Settlers there on homesteads

[20] Michigan Annual Conference *Minutes* for 1865, p. 8. Detroit Annual Conference *Minutes* for 1865, pp. 20, 23.

taken from the U.S. government, lived in mean shanties, had no comforts nor conveniences, and could barely support their families. The population was between 40,000 and 50,000. The Methodist faith must be taken to such people but how could a minister live while he labored there? The area needed at least $5,000 spent there annually by the Methodist Episcopal Church. The committee said "every dime raised for church extension within the bounds of this Conference should be expended on this field." If this should be done, collections for church extension would increase fourfold in a year's time.[21]

Both the Detroit and the Michigan Annual Conference sessions were addressed in 1865 by the Rev. S. Y. Monroe, corresponding secretary of the national Church Extension Society. Both Conferences then appointed standing committees on church extension, drafted constitutions for Conference Church Extension Societies, and elected the usual officers plus a Board of Managers. Recommendations of the national society were followed except that a lay member was added to the clerical members from each district on the Board of Managers. Of course, John Owen and David Preston were very active in this work. The latter was elected treasurer of the Detroit Annual Conference Society but a minister, Francis Glass of Coloma, was made treasurer of the Michigan Conference Society. The Conferences agreed that the collections for church extension would annually be taken in November.

The financial results of the new society's labors were very small at first. Not until 1872 did either Conference Society raise over $1,000 for church extension. In the years between 1865 and 1872, the Detroit Annual Conference usually raised about twice the sum that the Michigan Annual Conference did.[22]

The retention for use in local emergencies of money supposedly collected for general church extension work can be seen in some of the Conference statistics. The Detroit Annual Conference report on church extension collections in 1869 noted "There are receipts from Ann Arbor District, Rev. S. Clements, P.E., of moneys applied on local matters, not included above." The amount was $71.41 and the total church extension fund that year in that Conference was $755.11. A similar notation was made in 1870 for the same district and Presiding Elder. That time $444.05 had been applied to liquidation of the indebtedness of the Oakville Church. Yet in 1869, the Detroit Annual Conference had adopted certain resolutions which declared that $2,500 ought to be raised in the coming year for church extension and "no local circumstances can justify a neglect to take a collection for the purposes of this society." Then

[21] Michigan Annual Conference *Minutes* for 1870, pp. 73-76. See also Detroit Annual Conference *Minutes* for 1872, p. 95.

[22] The one exception was 1867 when the Michigan Conference collected $665.24 to the Detroit Conference's $226.36. Statistics from general recapitulation of finances in *Minutes* of year and Conference indicated.

it was pointed out that "collections taken for contiguous churches and passed over directly to them are not funds of this society, and cannot be reported and counted as such.[23]

For some years, Michigan Methodism probably received more money from the national Church Extension Society than was sent in from all individual church or either Conference collections. The Michigan Annual Conference in 1868 collected $557.41 and authorized the treasurer of the Church Extension Society to pay the money he had in hand "in the proportion of $300 to Pentwater and $600 to Decatur." The next year this Conference asked the national Society for $238 for Decatur and $122 for Pentwater. It had collected in all $508.11.

The Detroit Annual Conference in 1866 collected $475.90 but was apportioned $2,500 by the national Church Extension Society. This sum was divided by a Conference committee between eight churches in five Districts. Four churches each got $100 and two were each awarded $200. Then the Owosso Church received $500 and the one at East Saginaw $1,200.[24]

This last named church was in financial trouble all through this period. A small membership in a raw, new, lumbering town was quite unable to cope with its debts. In 1865, the scheme so often tried in earlier pioneer times was authorized for the East Saginaw minister. For the ensuing year, he was authorized "to solicit aid abroad to erect a church edifice in that . . . promising field." But rich laymen and strange ministers asked why aid was not sought at the national Church Extension Society. Or they said curtly that they gave only through regular channels. In 1871, the Detroit Annual Conference requested its Church Extension Society to retain all moneys it raised in the next year in order to pay the debt on the East Saginaw property. Either this was not done or else the sum raised was insufficient.

The Detroit Annual Conference session of 1872 was held in the East Saginaw Church. On its last day, regular business was suspended so that the large audience might be told of the debts still burdening that church. Subscriptions or pledges of $16,000 were immediately taken and a special committee was appointed to collect the actual cash from the promises.

Yet even so, the Rev. E. E. Caster, minister in charge of the East Saginaw Church in 1877, wrote on February 3 to the editor of the *Michigan Christian Advocate*, "One of the most effectual contrivances for paralyzing the energy of a church is a good round debt on the house of

[23] Detroit Annual Conference *Minutes* for 1869, pp. 258, 260; same for 1870, p. 380.
[24] Michigan Annual Conference *Minutes* for 1868, p. 13; for 1869, p. 11. Detroit Annual Conference *Minutes* for 1866, p. 41.

worship. Every society in this city has tried it thoroughly and it works like a charm."[25]

Muskegon and Marquette were among the other churches enduring like financial burdens. In 1859, the church at Muskegon had a theoretical value of $12,000, a membership of twenty, and a debt of around $2,000. The congregation could not possibly pay it "without foreign aid." The minister there was authorized "to go abroad to solicit funds." He must have been unable to collect any amount that mattered because, in 1865, the Michigan Annual Conference voted to assume the debt of the Muskegon Church and to apportion it among the ministers of the group by calling the roll. The Marquette Church was in similar straits in 1872. There a congregation of 151 had built a church of $25,000 value only to find it impossible to pay their debts without mortgaging all their holdings. Their predicament was due in part to "an unauthorized promise that $5,000 to $10,000 would be furnished by the Church Extension Society."[26]

By no means all the Societies had such extended financial troubles in building and paying for a church building. Substantial growth in the number of Methodist churches took place between 1865 and 1872 but was unevenly distributed over the State. The Detroit Annual Conference had 135½ churches in 1865 and 208½ in 1872 but the new buildings were mostly in the northeast. Owosso District added twenty-two churches, Flint District thirteen and one-half but the Ann Arbor and Adrian Districts each added two church buildings. The Michigan Annual Conference had 100½ churches in 1865 and 186 in 1872. The Coldwater District remained just the same but the Kalamazoo District added nineteen and a half new buildings. The Marshall and Lansing Districts each added eleven while a brand new District, in the Grand Traverse area had fourteen churches.[27]

Judging from the general mode of church architecture then and also the very modest values placed on the new buildings in Conference statistics, the usual Methodist patterns prevailed. Nine out of ten village churches were rectangular wooden boxes with modest spires and perhaps a small porch with slender columns at the main entrance. Such buildings were distinctly "preachers' churches" designed for one purpose only, that of providing maximum seating for the hearing of sermons. A few were beginning to build on an amphitheater plan "to make the

[25] *Mich. Ch. Ad.*, III, #5, p. 2. Detroit Annual Conference *Minutes* for 1865, p. 56; for 1871, p. 428; for 1872, p. 46.

[26] For the Muskegon church see Mich. An. Conf. *Minutes* for 1859, p. 30; for 1865, p. 7; and for the Marquette church see Detroit An. Conf. *Minutes* for 1872, pp. 33-34.

[27] One half a church might be held jointly with a society in a nearby town or in the same village with some other Protestant group. For comparative statistics see Detroit An. Conf. *Minutes* for 1865, pp. 53-54 and for 1872 p. 71. Also see Mich. An. Conf. *Minutes* for 1865 p. 32 and for 1872 p. 53.

preacher more visible and audible." Brick was being used more often too.[28]

Both Annual Conferences in the State grew concerned about the plan of building used, the Michigan one being more frequently explicit on the subject. Its Annual Conference session in 1868 adopted several resolutions about church architecture. These recommended the use of a plan and specifications obtained from a competent architect, an arrangement that suited "Methodistic peculiarities" and that all churches be built with chapels or basements "for the accommodation of love feasts, Sunday Schools, Prayer and Class Meetings." In 1870, the same Annual Conference advised the use of the Gothic style, galleries, and furnaces in basements rather than stoves in the main auditoriums. The Gothic architecture was supposed to help prevent echo.[29]

Building Central Church of Detroit

The finest Gothic Methodist Episcopal Church yet built in Michigan, Central of Detroit, was completed in 1867. At a time when the trend was toward church division, it was built by the unification of two churches. These were Congress Street and the older First or Woodward Avenue. Somehow the energy and money to start the project had been found during the Civil War. The desirability of relocating the Detroit Methodist churches had already been discussed but nothing had been done. In a growing city, the churches could be more advantageously located for the spread of Methodism and also the convenience of the members.

A catastrophe brought about the desired changes. On July 18, 1863, the Congress Street Church and parsonage were destroyed by fire. The Society decided to build in a new location and so bought five lots on the northeast corner of Woodward Avenue and Adams Street. The Woodward Avenue Church members were desirous of moving up town so they sent a committee to confer with the Congress Street Church people when they learned of their land purchase. The result was an agreement in February, 1864, for the two Societies to unite in building a stone edifice costing not less than $50,000 on the site owned by the Congress Street group. It was built in the name of the First Methodist Episcopal Church, as being "the older incorporation." But the Congress Street Society was allowed to decide on the name by which it would be known in future. So the title "Central Methodist Episcopal Church" was chosen. This first joint committee also agreed to contribute $2,500 to build a chapel for the eastern part of the city on Jefferson Avenue and in part to support its pastor for three years.

[28] Garber, Paul, *The Methodist Meeting House*, Chapter IV on Church extension Expanding.
[29] Michigan An. Conf. *Minutes* for 1868, p. 10; for 1870, pp. 78-79.

On March 14, 1864, a Building Committee was selected, composed of five men: John Owen, David Preston, L. L. Farnsworth, John Kendall, and Aaron Fisher. Preston bore the chief burden of financing the construction just as he did in so many other Michigan Methodist projects. Owen was the treasurer but Preston made the public pleas for money. His forceful, appealing speech on Dedication Day was long remembered in Detroit.

The property of the Woodward Avenue Church was sold for commercial use for $23,000 and the land of the Congress Street Society for $13,500. The committee decided that both a church and a chapel were needed. This required more land so two more lots on the Adams Street side were purchased. The chapel with seats for five hundred people was built first. It was dedicated September 21, 1865. Neither the new chapel nor the old church were big enough to seat the combined congregations so for two years two ministers were appointed to Central and they preached alternately morning and evening to the two congregations. On July 2, 1866, the congregation pledged $13,200 for the church building and on July 4 the cornerstone was laid. The building was completed and then dedicated by Bishop Simpson on November 17, 1867. The committee next decided that a parsonage ought to be built too so two more lots on Adams Street were bought on September 28, 1868. But the parsonage was not erected until 1883.

From the first services held there, the Central Methodist Episcopal Church was noted for the high quality of its preaching. The Rev. James

Central Methodist Church, Detroit, as it appeared nearly a century ago. Built in 1866-67 at a cost of $92,000, the Church was a union of the former Woodward Avenue and Congress Street M. E. Churches. Through the years it has remained a notable and beautiful church, a Detroit landmark.

M. Buckley served the Church from 1863 to 1866. Later he was the long time editor of the *Christian Advocate* in New York City. The Rev. Joseph H. McCarty was transferred from Providence, Rhode Island, to aid Buckley with the preaching from 1865 through 1867. The Rev. Lewis Ransom Fiske came to assist McCarty in 1866-1867 and then served alone at Central for a couple of years. He became the President of Albion College. From 1870 to 1873, William X. Ninde was the appointed minister at Central. Eventually he became a Bishop. During these years, the Central congregation paid their minister from $500 to $1,000 more than the salary of the Presiding Elder of the Detroit District.

The women of Central Church had an early record of help given to charity, missions, and Sunday Schools. The Woodward Avenue Church had a Ladies Missionary Society organized in 1844. This became the Missionary and Benevolent Society in 1855. After the merger of the two Societies was agreed upon, the ladies organized as the Church Furnishing Society. Then in 1867, they again changed to a Benevolent Society, whose aims were to provide care for the sick and poor in their Church.

The Sunday School work of Central was one of its strongest aspects. Back in 1855, the Woodward Avenue Church had one of the first young people's prayer meetings in Detroit. After the merger, the children of the two churches began to meet together in a public hall on September 25, 1864. Interest was repeatedly shown in starting mission Sunday Schools in the poorer sections of Detroit. Later these would lead to organization of another Society and finally building of a church. In

The First Methodist Episcopal Church of Kalamazoo, built in 1866-69 was a notable edifice for its time. With dimensions of 135 x 80 feet, and a steeple 170 feet high, it cost $50,000, a venture of faith for a church of the time with less than 500 members.

Bishop William X. Ninde (1832-1901) served two notable pastorates at Central Church, Detroit (1870-73; 1875-78); he taught at Garrett Biblical Institute and became its President. Elected Bishop in 1884, he presided over the Detroit and Michigan Annual Conferences in 1884, and the latter in 1887. He established his residence in Detroit and there he is buried.

January, 1868, the Central Church was active in helping to make the Sunday School Union of Detroit into the Sunday School and Missionary Union of the Methodist Episcopal Church of Detroit.

The united Sunday School of the new Central Church had a financial project of its own for the new building. It had a separate tower with bell, the whole being 175 feet high. The Church proper was seventy feet in height. The fine bell hung in the tower in 1867 bore on one side the inscription: "Presented to the trustees of the Central Methodist Episcopal Church Detroit by the teachers and children of the Sabbath School." On the opposite side of the bell was another inscription: "Bell, speak every year, every month, every week, every day, every hour, to all the children, to all within the sound of thy voice: 'Time is passing; walk in the ways of virtue, of truth and of life.' "[30]

The original Central Church was 123 by 58 feet of an elaborate Gothic pattern with fine stained glass windows. The main auditorium seated 1200 comfortably and by crowding could seat 1500. With all its interior furnishings, the main church cost $92,000, the chapel cost $27,834, and the nine lots purchased cost $15,900. Did anyone who worshipped in this elaborate Methodist Church ever think of that simple

[30] Inscription on bell in a clipping from the *Detroit Post* of 1867 in file on Detroit/Churches, Burton Collection, Detroit Public Library. Silas Farmer, *History of Detroit & Michigan*, pp. 566-579. E. H. Pilcher, *Hist. Prot. Mich.*, p. 199. *Northwestern Christian Advocate*, XII, #15, 113. XIII, 332, 310. Elmer Houser, "Historical Survey of Detroit Methodism, *Michigan Christian Advocate*, for June 14 and 21, 1928. Discussion is by decades so note that for 1860-1870, June 21, pp. 3, 16.

log cabin on the River Rouge, the only house of worship which the
Methodists possessed just fifty years previously.

The Detroit Annual Conference held its fourteenth session in the
new Central Church during the first week in September, 1869. The
ministers must have been eager to see such "a beautiful and commo-
dious house of worship" as their resolution of thanks for its use called
the new church. Bishop Levi Scott presided and Arthur Edwards was
Secretary. Among the visitors introduced were the Episcopal post chaplain at Detroit plus the Presbyterian, Baptist, and Congregational ministers of the First churches of those three denominations in the city.
Ministers from the Canadian Wesleyan Conference also attended. Among
the national church officials who came were Dr. Harris, Corresponding
Secretary of the Missionary Society, the agents of the Western and New
York Book Concerns. Best known of all the visitors was "Chaplain"
McCabe, Assistant Secretary of the Church Extension Society. He was
famous all over the north for his lecture on life in Libby Prison during
the Civil War.

*　*　*

When a first look is taken at the Michigan Methodist Episcopal
Church of 1869-1870, it seems as if all was flourishing. Closer examination of Conference Minutes, diaries, letters, and sermons of the time
leaves some doubt. Church building was proceeding well and church
membership was increasing. But it was not a time of deep spiritual
growth nor of enriched Christian brotherhood between the ministers
of the State's Conferences.

*　*　*

Legal and Financial Problems Increase

The first three years after the Civil War were generally quiet ones
for the two Annual Conferences in Michigan. Then legal problems and
petty bickering between individual ministers began to develop. The
Detroit Annual Conference session of 1868 adopted a resolution in-
structing its ministers "to look carefully to church property and the
titles for the same." And the same session authorized the trustees of the
First Church at Lapeer to sell their parsonage and apply the proceeds
on the church debt. In some way not made clear in the *Minutes*, the
sale authorized in 1868 involved the Lapeer Methodist Church in a
court case which dragged on for two years. It compelled the Detroit
Annual Conference session in 1869 to raise $150 for court costs and to
appoint the Presiding Elder of Romeo District and two other experienced
ministers to aid in prosecution of the case. Yet the times were such that
in 1872 the Detroit Annual Conference authorized seven churches to sell
their parsonages in order to pay their debts.

The Michigan Annual Conference did not get involved in the quest-tions relating to land ownership until 1871. The Conference then appointed a committee on Temporal Economy consisting of Daniel D. Gillett, Resin Sapp, and Israel Cogshall, all experienced men. They consulted "a leading jurist" before making their report. They were agreed that "the tenure of our church property . . . is loose, vague, and, in too many instances, wholly indefinite and void." But it was probably on a par with that of the other denominations in Michigan. The Committee offered, to the extent of five pages of fine print, many recommendations for reform. Model forms for organization of a board of trustees, for the elections of trustees, and for certifying the title of the trustees to the county clerk were all carefully printed in full. Such advice was felt necessary as always using the same name for the church concerned, giving the names of all trustees in full, and electing a secretary who carefully entered every action taken in a permanent record book. In 1872, this same Conference was still uneasy about the tenure of its church property so it authorized another committee to seek more legal counsel.

More Church Trials

Bickering between fellow ministers, between a Presiding Elder and a minister on his District, or a Quarterly Conference and its minister members, travelling or local, was on the increase then. Unfortunately, such quarrels often ended in a formal trial by a select committee of the Annual Conference. The strong sense of discretion of the secretary, who recorded such trials, usually has made it impossible to determine today the inner nature and true cause of a particular case.

The Michigan Annual Conference felt it necessary in 1870 to deplore "a growing practice in our church trials to conform to the spirit and practice of pettifogging." It prayerfully recommended that "our church trials be conducted more in harmony with the spirit of the gospel and the dignity of the Christian ministry." Such a standard was easier to utter than to practice.

The Detroit Annual Conference dealt with one ministerial church trial in 1867, two in 1869, three in 1870, and two in 1872. The Michigan Annual Conference handled one such case in 1870, two in 1871, and one in 1872. In most of these cases, the record is not at all clear as to the exact charge, except that it was "conduct unbecoming to a minister." One case concerned a member expelled from the Ypsilanti Church but due to inadequate evidence against him, the decision was reversed. A local preacher had his case returned to the Lafayette Street Church in Detroit for a new trial. The Rev. James S. Smart in 1870 brought an elaborate set of charges against his Presiding Elder, D. C. Jacokes. It involved the minute handling of the finances of the Adrian First Church. The special Conference Court decided that the charges were not sustained and the suit was dismissed. That same year, a charge of "un-christian Conduct" against Franklin W. May was sustained. The special Court ordered him "reprimanded in private by the Bishop." In 1871, the Michigan Annual Conference dismissed charges against John H. Richards as "founded in misrepresentation" and also reversed the expulsion of J. R. Skinner from the Lawrence Quarterly Conference.

Far and away the most troublesome and long continued of all the church trials of this period was that of John Levington and the Detroit Annual Conference. For a decade he harassed the sessions of that Conference. Levington had almost a phobia against Free Masonry. In 1870, he introduced resolutions attacking Masonry as "un-Christian, wicked, blasphemous and destructive" of Church and State. He declared "no adhering Mason can . . . be admitted to or continue in the Christian ministry." After a short debate, the Detroit Annual Conference quietly laid Levington's resolutions on the table and no doubt hoped they had thus heard the last of them.

But in 1872 Levington almost disrupted the necessary work of the Detroit Annual Conference. In 1871 he had been appointed to the Brighton Church on the Ann Arbor District with Samuel Clements as his Presiding Elder. By Conference time, each tried to charge the other with "lying, slander, and teaching grave error." The entire record of the Clements- Levington cases takes up twenty-eight pages of the forty-seven that constitute the Journal of that session — the seventeenth of the Detroit Annual Conference.

A fruitless effort was made to hush up the whole quarrel. The papers were handed to two special committees for examination with a view to deciding whether grounds for a trial existed. Each committee reported insufficient ground for a trial. Therefore, the characters of Clements and Levington were quietly passed.

But the very next day the matter was reconsidered. Such cases were ordinarily heard by a "select committee of fifteen" with a president and secretary. But the ministers voted to try the Clements and Levington cases "in the presence of the whole Conference." Parts of the first three days of the session and all the third and fourth afternoons were given to the trials.

In the Clements case, the only witness against the Presiding Elder was Levington himself. He repeated at great length much minutiae about how Clements acted in giving communion with the aid of Levington and also what he wrote and said about the witness in almost endless repetition. Levington was sure that Clements was deliberately persecuting him. On the fourth day of the session, the Conference voted to dismiss all the charges against Clements and to pass his character. The charges against him were "trivia."

The trial of Levington was put off until the next day. Then a paper signed by twenty-seven ministers was formally presented. Under their

signatures was a sentence "None of the above are Free Masons." The
paper contained a plan for dealing gently with an over-excited man.
It stated that Levington's mind had been devoted so long and intensely
to "a single class of topics" that his nervous system was affected, "his
ability as a pastor impaired" and he had in reality become a superannuated man. No good would be done by continuing with the trial. Yet
the ministers wanted to act toward Levington "with Christian charity
and fraternal regard." Therefore it was resolved that all charges against
him be dismissed, that his character be passed, and that he be superannuated "with his appropriate claims upon the funds of the Conference."
In more modern terms, Levington was compelled to retire but given
the usual ministerial pension. This action was formally passed by a
counted vote of 112 to fifteen.

Disastrous Fires

The Great Fire in Chicago, Illinois, took place on October 8-9,
1871. It was a serious handicap to the business and session of 1872 of
the Detroit Annual Conference. This was because all the Conference
journals, letters and committee reports were destroyed in that Chicago
fire. The Rev. Arthur Edwards was the Secretary of the Detroit Annual
Conference and also the editor of the *Northwestern Christian Advocate*.
Its office was in the Chicago Methodist Book Depository, which was
entirely destroyed along with all its contents. Also with the Conference
records, presumably the fine new Conference trunk for its papers, costing $65 and given by E. H. Pilcher in 1868, was burned completely.

Fire and the general lack of adequate insurance was a real affliction
of the Michigan Methodist Episcopal Church at that time. Algonac had
a bad fire in 1866 just after its insurance had expired. Due to the careless ways of lumbering then, the first great forest fire came in Michigan
in 1871. It began on the west coast in Holland where most of the town
was burned. A similar fire soon broke out in Manistee where it burned
half the town. Fanned by strong winds and in a time of long drought,
the fire destroyed almost everything in a wide band across Michigan
from Lake and Osceola Counties to Tuscola and Huron in the Thumb.

Many a small pioneer church or parsonage must have been destroyed.
The Rev. Marvin J. Scott, just admitted to full connection in the Detroit Annual Conference and then appointed to Sand Beach (Harbor
Beach) in the Port Huron District, lost literally everything that he
owned. On his first Sunday on his new Circuit, he went to meet his
appointments only to find on his return home "every earthly possession
swept away by forest fire from which he escaped death only by standing
in a lake for protection from the flames."[31]

[31] Memoir of Scott in Detroit Annual Conference *Minutes* for 1895, p. 45. F. C.
Bald, *Michigan in Four Centuries*, pp. 289-290.

Ministerial Social Attitudes:

1. Temperance

Methodist Episcopal ministers were still very strict in their social attitudes. This was clearly shown in the printed standing committee reports of each Annual Conference session. Every year from 1865 through 1872, both Conferences had committees on Temperance which usually made long reports. The Michigan Annual Conference did not print as many of these as the Detroit did but their Temperance committees were appointed and functioned. The high standard set in this area was explained by the Detroit committee in 1869 thus:

> Temperance . . . is the total abstinence from the use of, or traffic in, intoxicating drinks. A more comprehensive meaning includes the voluntary subordination of all human passions and appetites to the control of enlightened reason and conscience. Nothing short of the habitual observance of this rule is thorough temperance; rigid self denial is its radical idea, a christian grace of special value.[32]

Every committee report attacked in vigorous terms and at length the evils of strong drink, its cost in money, its terrible effects on the human body and soul plus the social and political corruption it always brought. Voluntary, total abstinence by the individual Methodist was urged with no exceptions allowed. Uses of wine and ale were but preliminary steps "which take hold on hell" and "lead down to the chamber of death." It was also held that politically the license system was "wicked in principle and . . . pernicious in practice." The only answer was complete prohibition of liquor by the State.

Year after year, Michigan ministers were urged to preach on Temperance, to arrange for its study in the Sunday Schools, and to supply the teachers therein with total abstinence pledge blanks. The juice of pure, unfermented grapes must be used in communion services. Temperance literature must be circulated. Use of a local temperance paper, called the *Peninsular Herald* and published in Romeo by a Methodist minister named Russell, was particularly recommended. Approval was given to a secret temperance society known as the I.O.G.T. or Independent Order of Good Templars. Nationally organized, its convention was held in Detroit in 1867. Some of the Michigan Methodist ministers and their wives were very active in the local chapters.[33]

---

[32] Detroit Annual Conference *Minutes* for 1869, p. 264.

[33] Quotations are from the Detroit Annual Conference *Minutes* for 1869, pp. 264-266, or from *Minutes* for 1867, p. 100. The I.O.G.T. is often mentioned in the diaries for 1866-1871 kept by the Rev. E. E. Caster and now in the author's hands. He and his wife both held office in the local chapters in the towns where he was stationed and he attended both their State and national conventions.

2. *The New Immigration and Roman Catholicism*

Closely related to their temperance views were the opinions of Methodist ministers on the recent European immigrants, Roman Catholicism, Sunday observance, and popular amusements. That Detroit Annual Conference of 1869 held in Central Church also declared in its Temperance committee report:

> By far the most alarming feature of intemperance now presented to the American people is the large yearly influx of foreigners, with their wine and beer drinking and sabbath desecrating social customs. Assembling as they do, in large numbers in public places, and on the sabbath day, attended by bands of music, their semi-military appearance attracts the attention of youth, which, together with the elaborate and often flattering notices of the secular press, all tend to the avowed purpose of engrafting these customs upon the civilization of this country.

Among the numerous visitors to that same Detroit Annual Conference session of 1869 was Dr. William Butler, representing the American and Foreign Christian Union. This was an organization formed to fight the errors of Catholicism. Dr. Butler both lectured and preached to the Conference on Romanism. Afterwards, the Conference appointed a special committee, of Joseph McCarty, Elijah Pilcher, and Benjamin Cocker to confer with Dr. Butler on the claims of his organization. Their report said in part:

> We recognize in the Roman Catholic Church an organization not only hostile to spiritual religion, but also to the spirit and institutions of our republican government. Her priests are nearly all foreigners, both by birth and education, and have taken the most solemn oath of allegiance to a civil prince no less than a spiritual ruler . . . . It is the open boast of Romish priests that this country will be won over to their faith.

The committee urged individual Methodists to labor for conversion of Roman Catholics to a true Protestant faith but it did not approve of official Conference support for Dr. Butler's society. "It should be left to the various Official Boards to decide in each case, whether collections shall be taken for this object or not."[34]

The late Dr. William C. S. Pellowe, then Curator of the Detroit Annual Conference historical collection in Adrian, pointed out to the author, in a letter on November 6, 1964, that the Conferences in Michigan never took an official stand against Romanism nor were there ever Methodist acts of violence or destruction of church property. But Dr. Pellowe also wrote, "The Methodist Church at one time was noted for its strong antagonism to Romanism. When a new Methodist minister came

[34] All quotations about Romanism and immigration still taken from the same 1869 Detroit Annual Conference *Minutes,* pp. 265, 278.

to a town there were two men who knew he would be their enemy . . . the tavern-keeper and the R. C. Priest."

In 1871, the South Haven Methodist Episcopal Church was destroyed by fire. It had not been entirely paid for but the congregation felt compelled to rebuild. In the Laymen's Electoral Conference of that year, Mr. Lannin, the lay delegate from South Haven, declared that the building had been destroyed "by those opposed to the suppression of the liquor traffic." The Church Extension Society let the South Haven congregation have $500 and a special appeal to the Michigan Annual Conference session was made jointly by the pastor at South Haven, Andrew R. Boggs, and its lay delegate. With the help of a special committee, pledges for $500, to be paid in ninety days, were obtained.[35]

3. Sabbath Observance and Popular Amusements

The Detroit Annual Conference usually had a committee on the "Sanctity of the Sabbath" throughout these years but the Michigan Annual Conference had one only in 1871 and 1872. The general tone of all the committee reports was much the same. The Sabbath was designed to be a religious day devoted to spiritual ends not to rest that was idleness. Rest from one's daily labor surely was needed but not a day of secular amusement. The growing laxity of Sabbath observance alarmed successive committees. In annual turn, they called on the ministers to preach more often on this subject and always to set a good example themselves and in their families.

Only in the year 1867 did the Detroit Annual Conference appoint committees on Divorce and on Popular Amusements. But the attitude taken then on each matter was sufficiently vigorous to leave a lasting influence. The committee on Divorce said that only for adultery was divorce ever acceptable. Even then "neither the guilty nor the innocent party should be allowed to marry while both survive."

The committee on Popular Amusements showed what seems a very extreme attitude today. It disapproved of all games of chance, all private theatricals, all dancing even in the family circle, all pantomines and tableaux in the churches, and even "billiard tables in the rooms of the Y.M.C.A. and Temperance Lodges." The committee thought all those amusements awakened the passions and developed into positive evils. Many of the church members saw no wrong in those things and even participated in them, sometimes inside the church building to raise money for benevolent causes. Thus "the line which publicly separates between the Church and the world has gradually become fainter and is in danger of being almost obliterated."[36]

---

[35] Michigan Annual Conference *Minutes* for 1871, pp. 13, 16, 81-82, 84.
[36] Detroit Annual Conference *Minutes* for 1867, pp. 96-99.

4. Use of Tobacco

Less unanimity existed about the smoking of tobacco. In 1871, the Detroit Annual Conference appointed a committee on "the use of Tobacco." It was forced to present a majority and a minority report. John M. Arnold and David B. Tracy, a former Civil War chaplain, wanted to make a short report saying that the effects of tobacco on the health were still uncertain, that its use was a matter of "private individual prerogative," and it was unwise to be dictatorial on the subject. The Conference over-ruled them and accepted the minority report of Solomon S. Littlefield. This stated that the use of tobacco was "an expensive, troublesome, and disgusting habit," that it hindered the usefulness of a Christian minister in many families and that members of the Detroit Annual Conference ought to "abstain from this self-indulgence." All this the Conference accepted with little trouble but the minority report also offered a resolution to question "those who propose to join the Conference at any time hereafter . . . so that it may be clearly known whether they use tobacco in any of its forms before the vote is taken upon their admission." An effort to defeat the last resolution failed. So the Detroit Annual Conference had a new requirement for all the young men wishing to become ministers.[37]

Administrative Developments

From 1865 through 1871, the Detroit Annual Conference retained eight Districts of the same names. These were Detroit, Ann Arbor, Adrian, Owosso, Flint, Romeo, Port Huron, and Lake Superior. Between 1871 and 1872, the Owosso District was dropped and Saginaw took its place. Twenty-one of the appointments on the Flint District were transferred to the new Saginaw District along with six of the former Owosso appointments. But the loss of so many charges by the Flint District was balanced by the transfer of nineteen places from the disappearing to the remaining District. These shifts must have entailed much replanning of their visits to Quarterly Conferences by the Presiding Elders of the new or rearranged Districts.

Rather than changes in the larger divisions like Districts, the major shifts were of appointments from one to another District or the combination of small villages into new circuits. Presumably much of it was done in an attempt to lighten the Presiding Elder's burden of travel. The Upper Peninsula changed or grew the least. The Flint and Port Huron Districts were never two years quite the same. The Flint District had

---

[37] Detroit Annual Conference *Minutes* for 1871, pp. 424, 446-447. Similar action was taken in the Michigan Annual Conference in 1872. *Minutes* for that year, p. 12. Candidates for admission to both Conferences in Michigan were henceforth warned that the use of tobacco would hinder their acceptance.

twenty-two appointments in 1866, thirty-two in 1867, twenty-one in 1868, twenty-seven in 1869, and thirty-one in 1870. The Port Huron District grew more slowly, having sixteen appointments in 1867, twenty in 1868, and twenty-five in both 1869 and 1870.

The Michigan Annual Conference made its shifts in District arrangement in 1866 and 1869. It had eight Districts in 1865, these being Albion, Coldwater, Kalamazoo, Niles, Grand Rapids, Ionia, Lansing, and Manistee. The last name was dropped in 1866 and two new Districts, named Pentwater and Grand Traverse, were created. The first had nine appointments and the second only eight. The defunct Manistee District had been equally divided with seven appointments going to each new District. These rearrangements were evidently designed to meet future growth. And it came. Each new District just about doubled in two years. The Pentwater District had fourteen appointments in 1868 and Grand Traverse had nineteen then. In 1869, a tenth District was created, named Big Rapids, and given five charges from Grand Rapids District, two from Ionia, and three brand new appointments. The Districts of which only the name is given had settled down and did not add over one to three appointments per year. As of 1872, the ministers of the two Conferences had not yet complained about the eighteen Presiding Elders needed to administer Methodism in the State of Michigan.

But the ministers did feel strongly about a change suggested by some of the church papers in 1871. This was to set a new rule that the bishops should serve only four years unless re-elected. The Detroit Annual Conference declared that such a change was quite uncalled for and no limit whatsoever on the term served by the bishops should be allowed. So strongly did they feel that a recorded vote was demanded which resulted in just one vote for a restricted term for all bishops and 147 votes against any limit at all on the bishop's time in office. The Rev. Joseph Sutton was the minister who favored a limited term for the bishops. He had been a member of the Conference since the year 1846. So he should have known the situation!

Other changes initiated in these years began most modestly but eventually would be of considerable importance. A State-wide effort by both Conferences together was suggested in three areas. These were camp meetings, conventions, and Sunday Schools. The State camp meeting place did not materialize for a few years yet but Albion offered the use of its District camp meeting ground to each Conference.

Mutual effort brought about a "Methodist State Convention" at Albion for three days in December, 1870. It seems likely that those present must have inspected the college buildings and discussed its problems. But their deepest concern was for the work in the northern part of the Lower Peninsula. Resolutions were adopted and sent to each Annual Conference in 1871 requesting that the national missionary board and the Church Extension Board each be asked "to make larger appropriations in the northern part of our State." The Rev. Arthur Edwards had a dual role here. As Secretary of the State Convention, he sent its resolutions to each Conference and then, as the   Secretary of the Detroit Annual Conference, he was ordered to forward these same resolutions to the two Boards mentioned.[38]

The greatest success was achieved in the State-wide organization of the Sunday Schools. Out of meetings of joint committees of ministers from the Detroit and Michigan Annual Conferences came a State Sunday School Union and a State Sunday School Normal Institute. The latter encouraged holding more District and local Sunday School Institutes. The universal object was improvement of the teaching in Sunday Schools. More sytematic methods and materials were being introduced at large in Methodism under the name "Berean Series." More charts, maps, pictures, and mottoes were coming into use too.

A new anniversary in the Methodist calendar — Children's Day on the second Sunday in June — was winning observance too. In 1872, the education committees of both Conferences in Michigan recommended its use annually. A special program and collection must be planned for all Sunday Schools. The money obtained on Children's Day must go to the new Student Loan Fund of the national Board of Education. It was intended to help deserving and needy young Methodists attain a higher education. The first loans were made to young men planning to become ministers.

Many good Methodists did not yet think that a college degree and then three years of seminary training were necessary. Even ministers were in disagreement on this subject. Both Conferences in Michigan still maintained their examinations by appointed committees on the studies for four years of work done on one's own initiative alone. An effort to raise the standards was under way. Year after year, the Conferences by formal resolution, exhorted those examining committees to be more strict and not admit those who stood "below the medium."[39]

First Steps in Lay Representation

Equal lay representation in the General and Annual Conferences of the Methodist Episcopal Church was a reform demanded at intervals throughout the 19th century. After the Methodist Protestants left the Church, a lull occurred during the peak of the slavery agitation. Modest steps toward the attainment of lay representation did not come in Michigan until after the Civil War. The Detroit Annual Conference accepted the change earlier and more readily than the Michigan Annual

[38] Detroit Annual Conference *Minutes* for 1871, pp. 415-416.
[39] Detroit Annual Conference *Minutes* for 1872, pp. 58-59. Michigan Annual Conference *Minutes* for 1872, p. 59.

Conference did. A lay member of the Michigan Methodist Church today finds it difficult to understand why opposition to the admission of lay delegates to the Annual Conferences was so strong.

The history of Methodist development had some influence. The founder, John Wesley, asserted in 1790, "As long as I live, the people shall have no share in choosing either stewards or leaders. . . . We are no republicans, and never intend to be." Coke and Asbury, who knew early American conditions, both declared lay delegates would destroy the Church and its itinerant plan for the preachers. A lay delegate would be incapable of considering the good of the whole and inevitably would advocate only local interests. Conditions in the Methodist Protestant Church in Michigan added to the suspicion of lay leadership here. The area lay on the western edge of the region of the greatest Methodist Protestant influence and hence was small and usually struggling hard just to keep going.

Bishop Simpson took up the battle for lay representation in the General Conferences of 1856, 1860, and 1864. All three either defeated his plan or ignored it. The Board of Bishops said in 1860 that lay delegation could be introduced in the General Conference with safety if the form was that of a "separate house." This mild approval led a few eastern Annual Conferences to place laymen on their District and Conference Boards of Stewards and occasionally on their education, Centenary, and Church Extension committees. This last step was taken up by the Detroit Annual Conference of 1865 but the Michigan Annual Conference did nothing about lay delegation until 1869.

The General Conference of 1868 agreed on a plan to start lay representation in a very modest way. It then asked all the Methodist Episcopalians, both clerical and lay, to vote on the plan. Legally speaking, the members of the various churches were only expressing an opinion on the principle of lay representation and it required a vote by the ministers in their various Annual Conferences to change the *Discipline*. The exact change was in the so-called "Second Restrictive Rule." This dealt with the representation of the ministers in the quadrennial General Conference. Two lay delegates from each Annual Conference were to be chosen every four years by a special Electoral Conference. As General Conferences met in the spring of every fourth year, the special lay meeting would have to be held at Conference time the previous year. The Electoral Conference might adopt a few resolutions on any subject of urgency as it met to choose the two lay delegates to attend the coming General Conference. But those two things were all the laymen had to do legally until 1900 when collateral lay annual conferences were finally established.[40]

[40] Summary of the development of lay representation based on the section on Lay Representation in Chapter XXVI, Structural and Administrative Changes, by Nolan B. Harmon, *History of American Methodism*, III, 51-56.

Much of the State of Michigan was still a pioneer land and its Methodist ministers were used to running their churches themselves and so were many of the members fully accustomed to having them do so. Perhaps some ministers feared loss of their authority over the Classes and Societies. Those were still the days when both ministers and members might be expelled from Church and Conference. A few of the ministers, in private letters, even declared that they would leave the Church if lay representation was established. Of course, they cooled down in time.

The increase in the cash funds handled by the ministers, the secular nature of debts, mortgages, fire insurance, contracts to build a church or parsonage, and all the other paraphernalia of business in a developing city church with a stationed minister, usually then staying three years in one charge, certainly increased the need for business men in church administration. This situation must have been much more evident in the Detroit Annual Conference in the years between 1865 and 1872 than it was in the west half of the State of Michigan.

The Detroit Annual Conference of 1865 appointed a committee on lay delegation for the first time. Because the General Conference of 1864 did not flatly reject lay representation but rather urged the ministers and members to give deliberate consideration to such a big change, the Detroit Conference committee said that the time had come "to avail ourselves still more fully of the experience and counsel of our Lay brethren." Such a change would bring better cooperation, development of the latent power among the members, and advice from "the best business talent of the Nation."

The committee recommended two steps to be taken at once as some of the eastern Conferences had done. Each Board of District Stewards should be requested to elect two laymen to attend the next session of the Detroit Annual Conference. These men should then be assigned to all the committees and the Board of Conference Stewards. Seven laymen attended the session of 1866 and were assigned to the committees on the State of the Country, Albion College, and the Centenary cause. Each year the request for lay delegates was formally voted. The peak of this preliminary period was reached in 1869 when all eight Districts sent two men each and then they were assigned to fourteen committees.

The committee on Lay Delegation of the Detroit Annual Conference of 1868 declared that "the question lately so absorbing and perplexing is now simple enough and upon the threshold of solution." A few months previously, the General Conference had adopted a plan for modifying its membership by admitting two lay delegates from each Annual Conference. These men must be twenty-five years of age and at least five years just previously members of the Methodist Episcopal Church. At that time, the ministerial delegates numbered one for every thirty members of an Annual Conference.

The new plan provided for an election in each Church, for or against lay delegation, in June, 1869. All full members over twenty-one could vote. If the vote was favorable and so reported by Presiding Elders to whatever bishop was in charge of the next Annual Conference session, then the ministers should vote on an amendment of the *Discipline*. It was worded to allow lay delegates to the General Conference to be chosen at an electoral conference of laymen to be held on the third day of any Annual Conference session immediately preceding the larger quadrennial session. A ¾ vote of all the ministers actually voting in each Annual Conference was needed for adoption. Lastly, the General Conference of 1872 would complete the process. If it accepted the change in the *Discipline* by a ⅔ vote then previously chosen lay delegates would be admitted to that session.

The Detroit Annual Conference committee made a very long report explaining the details of all steps and reminding the ministers that they themselves would not have to vote until next year. But it was the duty of Presiding Elders and ministers to warn the Quarterly Conferences to appoint tellers and explain to all adult members the importance and nature of their votes in June, 1869.[41]

The *Minutes* of the 1869 session of the Detroit Annual Conference reveal that 3,339 adult Methodists voted for lay delegates and 695 were against change. All eight Districts reported some opposition but only in Owosso and Romeo areas was the opposition over one hundred votes.[42]

The vote in the Detroit Annual Conference by the ministers must have been a solemn occasion. The time for the vote was set the day before by a motion introduced by several prominent ministers, including Arthur Edwards, Manasseh Hickey, Lewis R. Fiske, John M. Arnold, and Francis A. Blades. So on Saturday, September 4, "Promptly at ten o'clock Bishop Scott called up the special order, the vote on the change of restrictive rule submitted by the General Conference of 1868." Elijah H. Pilcher made the motion to concur. He must have been specially selected because of his strong sense of History and also his thirty-nine years of service in Michigan. This was a recorded vote by name with 133 for the change and twenty-five against. What seems odd today is that sixteen were absent and one changed his vote on Monday.[43]

Either the Michigan Annual Conference was rather opposed to lay delegation or its *Minutes* were most inadequately kept. Not until after the session of 1869 had begun was even a committee on lay delegation

---

[41] Detroit Annual Conference *Minutes* for 1868, pp. 173-176.

[42] Detroit Annual Conference *Miiutes* for 1869, p. 233. Owosso District cast 144 votes against lay delegation, Romeo 116, and Port Huron 93. The least opposition was in the Lake Superior District with only 27 votes against the change.

[43] Detroit Annual Conference *Minutes* for 1869, pp. 225, 229, 231-233.

appointed. It made a short report just before the vote on the restrictive rule was taken. Warning was given that this was only a vote on the Disciplinary rule itself and the General Conference plan was not endorsed. The only reference to the vote of the people in the churches in June, 1869, was this committee's statement that they regretted that the local vote was not larger. Yet it had given a "decisive majority" in favor of lay delegation. The committee wanted only a plan which would "not interfere with the divinely designated authority of the Christian ministry." It was every minister's duty to vote by his "conscientious convictions." The result was 94 votes for and 44 votes against lay delegation. No record of how individuals voted was kept.[44]

In 1870, both Annual Conferences in Michigan had at least one or, in most cases, two lay delegates present from all the Districts. Many of them were assigned to the standing committees. Resolutions were adopted, in both Conferences, reminding the Presiding Elders and Quarterly Conferences that it would be their duty to see that one lay delegate from each Charge was elected to attend the Electoral Conference slated to be held on the third day of the next Conference session. The Detroit Annual Conference also declared that a simpler and less objectionable plan must be devised. Hence they approved only the first lay electoral conference and the plan for lay delegates to the next General Conference.[45]

The year 1871 was significant in the development of lay representation. The Annual Conferences across the nation generally held their first Lay Electoral Conferences. But uniformity in the manner of meeting did not yet prevail. The Detroit and Michigan Annual Conferences treated their lay gatherings quite differently.

The Detroit Conference never really met in a joint session with the lay gathering. Bishop Simpson and a committee of five prominent ministers were appointed to visit the Electoral Conference and convey "Christian salutations." The next day one layman, W. M. McConnell of the Detroit District, read a short address from the Lay Electoral Conference to the Annual Conference. Much of it was only conventional politeness but strong opposition to a limited term for the bishops was expressed. The laymen felt that a term of quiet growth was needed by Methodism far more than agitation of "injudicious changes." The first lay delegates to General Conference chosen from the Detroit Electoral Conference were John Owen of Detroit and Henry Fish of Port Huron. The first had been active in every good work of Methodism and the second had worked mostly in the Sunday School Union.[46]

[44] Michigan Annual Conference *Minutes* for 1869, pp. 6, 7, 10, 64.
[45] Detroit Annual Conference *Minutes* for 1870, pp. 314-316, 353. Michigan Annual Conference *Minutes* for 1870, pp. 10, 73.
[46] Detroit Annual Conference *Minutes* for 1871, pp. 417, 420-423, 439-440.

The Michigan Annual Conference Session of 1871 met in Grand Rapids with Bishop Janes presiding. It received the entire Electoral Conference "amid great applause," listened to an address by J. W. Stone of Allegan, and then to the "earnest, eloquent and affectionate" response by the Bishop. The ministers were so impressed that they requested a copy of Stone's address to print in the *Minutes* and also provided for publication of the entire record of the Lay Electoral Conference. Unfortunately the Detroit Annual Conference did not do that. The address that Stone read had been drafted by a committee and approved by the Lay Conference. It opposed any changes whatsoever in the system of itinerancy or the general superintendence of the bishops. The first lay delegates elected to General Conference from the Michigan Annual Conference were Hampton Rich of Ionia and Charles R. Brown.[47]

The year 1872 brought for the first time participation in a General Conference of lay delegates from all Annual Conferences. But lay representation in Michigan declined until 1875 when an Electoral Conference was called again. Not one word about laymen can be found in the Michigan Annual Conference *Minutes* for 1872 except in connection with David Preston's work for the Albion College Endowment Fund. Although the Detroit Annual Conference had not met jointly with their Lay Electoral Conference, it did have a habit of lay assistance more firmly fixed. Eleven laymen from six Districts were registered in 1872 at Conference. The Ann Arbor and Lake Superior Districts were unrepresented.[48] Lay representation had taken a very small step into the Methodist Episcopal Church. It had a long journey before it yet.

Missions and the W.F.M.S.

The Methodist Episcopal Missionary Society warranted the most optimism about the Church during the years from 1865 through 1872. The impetus that missionary giving had gained during the Civil War was mostly maintained. The financial reports of the new societies, formed since 1865, usually showed collections in hundreds of dollars but rarely over $1,000 in all for either Annual Conference in Michigan. But the Mission Society, by patient collection of small sums, reached results annually in the thousands. Three or four times the amounts collected for freedmen or church extension was usually gained for missions. Long establishment and strong leadership nationally helped give the Mission Society its strength.

Fifty years of foreign effort by this Society was thought to be a real

---

[47] Michigan Annual Conference *Minutes* for 1871, pp. 7, 9-10, 15-16. For the proceedings of the Lay Electoral Conference see pp. 78-86. No home address was given for Charles R. Brown.

[48] Detroit Annual Conference *Minutes* for 1872, pp. 10-11.

achievement. Hence the General Conference of 1868 set up plans for a nationwide celebration of the missionary semicentennial on April 4, 1869. Both of the Annual Conferences in Michigan agreed in their sessions of 1868 to celebrate in their individual churches with a memorial missionary sermon and a special collection solely for the purpose of building a missionary house in New York City. These moneys were to be reported separately at the next Conference session. Either such special appeals were not effective or the people had little ready cash or the ministers did not bother to take the collections. The Detroit Annual Conference collected $30.97 for the Mission House and the Michigan Annual Conference $103.80. The adult and the Sunday School missionary societies together in the Detroit Annual Conference collected $9,369.46 in 1869. The same groups in the Michigan Annual Conference collected $8,959.15 that same year.

The missionary work of Methodism was about to receive an enormous advance through the creation of the Women's Foreign Missionary Society. It was born in Boston on March 30, 1869, the same week as the semicentennial of the Missionary Society. Three women, Mrs. Parker, Mrs. Butler and Mrs. Flanders, were founders of the Society at Tremont Street Church. The first two had recently returned from service in India with missionary husbands. Their goal was to reach the women of India and China with Christian teachers and Bible readers. Men missionaries were completely unable to reach the women in Moslem or Hindu households. The organization was designed to tell American women at large of the degraded conditions of life for women in the Orient and to gain their financial support by personal sacrifice of tiny sums like 2¢ a week or $1 a year.

When enough money had been collected, the W.F.M.S., as it was often called, intended to send out its own women missionaries and to publish a periodical to be called the *Heathen Woman's Friend.* The first number of the new paper appeared in May, 1869. The first women missionaries sent to India, Dr. Clara Swain and Isabella Thoburn, arrived there early in 1870.

The Methodist Episcopal Church was run strictly by *men* in those days. When word of what the women were doing spread, consternation was the usual reaction. The ministers were sure that the W.F.M.S. would hurt the regular collections for missions, that rivalry would ensue on the fields abroad, and that such public activity was not at all becoming to women. Only a short time was needed to show how wrong these ideas were.[49]

By Annual Conference time in 1870, the W.F.M.S. was organized in six coordinate branches across the United States. The Chicago branch

[49] For a detailed account of the founding of the W.F.M.S. see W. C. Barclay, *History of Methodist Missions*, III, 139-148.

included Michigan, Illinois, Indiana, and Wisconsin. Miss Sallie A. Rulison was the assistant corresponding secretary for the branch. Her concise reports were printed in their *Minutes* by both the Detroit and Michigan Annual Conferences in 1870. Nineteen auxiliary societies had been established in the Detroit Annual Conference with a total membership of 926. Four societies were in Detroit, two in Flint, and two in Saginaw. Membership in these local societies ranged from eleven to 219, this last being in Central Church, Detroit. That same year twenty-three societies were organized in the Michigan Annual Conference with 730 members. The author's grandmother, for whom she is named, helped to organize the auxiliary society in the Church at Climax. She became its first President and when she died in office in 1877, the resolutions adopted by the Climax W.F.M.S. were printed in the *Michigan Christian Advocate*.[50]

The Detroit Annual Conference expressed its approval of the new women's society briefly in 1870. It said the W.F.M.S. was a "legitimate, valuable and promising agency of the cause." The Michigan Annual Conference did not express an opinion until 1871. Then a committee reported that an organization of "women to labor in behalf of women through the agency of women" was most helpful and the Conference would give it "our hearty cooperation." Perhaps this was because the new society had raised within the west half of the State of Michigan the sum of $970.18 the past year. This had been done by collecting the mites of the women who saved it "by personal economy as the result of new missionary zeal."[51]

❄   ❄   ❄   ❄   ❄   ❄

What a lot of changes had come to the Methodist Episcopal Church in Michigan in the seven years since the Civil War ended. A Statewide Methodist Convention and a Sunday School Normal Institute drew together people from both sides of Michigan for mutual aid on common problems. The needs of those beyond their immediate community aroused greater sympathy too or the Freedmen's Aid Society, the Student Loan Fund, the Church Extension Society, and the Women's Foreign Missionary Society would never have been able to establish their branches and auxiliaries in the State of Michigan. Perhaps the most significant change of all was the meeting of those first Lay Electoral Conferences. Increased strength to deal with new tasks would even-

---

[50] The author's grandmother was Margaret Smith Burnham, known as Maggie in her own life. She is still remembered in the Climax Church and thus the author had the honor of speaking at the 25th anniversay of the W.S.C.S. there. For her death notice and the W.F.M.S. resolutions thereon see *Michigan Christian Advocate*, III, #15, 2. (April 14, 1877) Detroit Annual Conference *Minutes* for 1870, pp. 398--99. Michigan Annual Conference *Minutes* for 1870, p. 72.

[51] Detroit Annual Conference *Minutes* for 1870, p. 327. Michigan Annual Coference *Minutes* for 1871, p. 36.

tually be given the Michigan Methodist Episcopal Church by its laymen *and* laywomen.

But peace and unity within were needed to achieve the Methodist potential. The addresses to the Annual Conferences by those first lay delegates described the spirit that was needed. The Michigan Annual Conference laymen promised their "sympathy and cooperation," declared that they felt "more called upon to serve than direct," and prayed that their "united efforts" might advance Methodism throughout the world. The Detroit Annual Conference laymen expressed much the same loyalties but cautioned against excessive change in the fundamental institutions of Methodism. They declared that "the Church needs years of fruitful quiet far more than she needs further agitation. The springtime of planting has past, and we now pray for a peaceful summer in which to advance and secure the harvest."[52]

[52] Michigan Annual Conference *Minutes* for 1871, pp. 84-86. Detroit Annual Conference *Minutes* for 1871, pp. 422-423.

CHAPTER XI

THE CHALLENGE OF HARD TIMES

1872 – 1880

The "peaceful summer in which to advance and secure the harvest" which the Detroit Annual Conference laymen had hoped for in 1871 did not materialize. The history of the United States in the decade of the Seventies was the exact opposite of peaceful. Corruption in high political office, widespread strikes accompanied by violence and destruction, economic panic, and a presidential election in 1876 unlike any previous one were among the worrisome events of that time. An urban United States was in process of being born but few of the American leaders of that day, from Presidents to Methodist bishops and ministers, understood what such rapid changes portended.

Triggered by the spectacular failure of the investment firm of Jay Cooke in September, the so-called panic of 1873 lasted for over five years. It was one of the worst depressions in our history. In Michigan, general hard times were particularly noticeable in the years from 1875 to 1879.

Poor economic conditions were aggravated by the rising labor movement and the uncertain monetary policies of the Federal government. The Knights of Labor, an industrial union, were spreading rapidly from east to west. A secret terrorist group, the Molly Maguires, flourished among the coal miners. A cut in wages brought on an ugly railroad strike in 1877. This soon spread widely and frequently involved violence to persons and property. In 1880, the Detroit Council of Trades and Labor Unions was organized. Civil war financing by the issue of "Greenbacks," legal tender without redemption in specie, and the Coinage law of 1873, which ended the making of silver dollars, undoubtedly had their influence upon the depression. They also created endless argument. Every town had its fanatical Greenbackers and Free Silverites.

National and local government had rarely been more corrupt than in the 1870's. Grant may have been personally honest but, in his second term as President, one scandal after another was uncovered in city, State, and Federal governments. The Tweed Ring, revealed in New York in 1871-1872, was only the most notorious of many corrupt city gangs. Dishonesty on the Indian reservations and in tax collections forced out of office Grant's own personal secretary and a member of his Cabinet.

Inventions that would revolutionize the daily life of every American citizen were being made too. Thomas Edison was at the peak of his inventiveness then, creating the phonograph in 1877 and the incandescent electric bulb in 1879. Alexander Graham Bell invented the telephone in 1876 and the first telephone exchange in Detroit was opened in 1878 with 124 customers listed. A rotary printing press was developed in 1875. This printed both sides of a sheet of paper at once and then cut and folded it. The carpet sweeper was patented by Melville Bissell of Grand Rapids in 1876. Greatly improved then were harvesting combines, flour milling machinery, bicycles, and also cameras.[1]

The first factories were making their appearance in Detroit. The Michigan Stove Company began manufacture in 1872. The first car wheels made in the west were produced by George Russel at his Hamtramck Iron Works and his sons established the Russel Wheel and Foundry Company in 1876.

Transportation was changing too. The last stage coach lines in Michigan ceased operation from Detroit in 1873. The Michigan Central Railroad, running across the State to Chicago had been in use since 1852. Now the Detroit and Bay City Railroad was completed in 1873. Two railroads were building toward the northern tip of the Lower Peninsula. Methodist ministers, with any distance to travel, came to the Annual Conferences by railroad in the 1870's. Each year one minister was named Railroad Secretary to obtain half-fare tickets for his colleagues from the railroads running to the place of session. Always on the last day of Conference, a resolution of gratitude to the railroads for their kindness was unanimously adopted. This however did not prevent the committee on the Sanctity of the Sabbath from asking the railroads each year not to run their trains on Sundays. Particularly deplored were Sunday railroad excursions to camp meetings and other religious assemblies.

If the areas of social and educational reform or scientific advance are observed, brighter aspects of life then can be seen. In 1873, the first

[1] Facts about the 1870's taken from *Detroit in Its World Setting, A 250-year chronology, 1701-1951.* Detroit Public Library.

permanent, public school kindergarten in the United States was opened in St. Louis, Missouri. In 1874, the Michigan State School at Coldwater was started, the first of its kind in the world. The same year, the "Kalamazoo Case" established the legal right of school boards to use the primary school funds for high schools. Under the vigorous leadership of Frances Willard, the Women's Christian Temperance Union was organized in 1874. With their strong views on Temperance, the Methodists soon welcomed the efforts of the W.C.T.U. That same year, the assembly at Chatauqua, New York, was begun. Its purpose was to encourage Bible study and the training of Sunday School teachers. Annual Conference committees repeatedly stressed the need of more and better teachers for young Methodists. In 1878, the Chatauqua home study and reading courses were first developed. These were quickly copied here in Michigan at Bay View.

In the area of sanitary improvement, the first Michigan State Board of Health was established in 1873. The city of Detroit set up a Board of Public Works that same year. Construction of a large new waterworks for Detroit began in 1874 and went into use in December, 1877. The streets and many of the homes had gas lights too. Electric arc lights were first demonstrated in Detroit in 1879 and a few business firms began to use them in 1880. Osteopathy was first practiced by Dr. Andrew Still in Missouri, that same busy year of 1874. The first adhesive tape and medicated plasters were made then in New Jersey. Probably more disturbing to the Methodist preachers in Michigan was the fact that Mary Baker Eddy founded the Christian Science Church and published the first edition of *Science and Health* in 1875.

Charles Darwin published *The Descent of Man* in 1871. The theories of evolution produced the most bitter arguments in the 1880's. Open disagreement between religious liberals and the orthodox did not come until after John Fiske published his *Outlines of Cosmic Philosophy* in 1874. Unusual Christian sects were anathema to many Methodist preachers in this period. The establishment of a Universalist Church in Detroit, in May 1879, was not exactly welcomed by those of orthodox views religiously. Universalists were usually held to be Unitarian in their beliefs. William Booth established the Salvation Army in England in 1878 and its American branch in 1880. Again its ways were too unconventional for orthodox Church people. Regarded with great suspicion by practically all Methodist preachers in this time was the Roman Catholic Church. This may have been due in part to the ever-growing flood of immigrants to the United States from the south European and Catholic nations. But it was also the result of the doctrine of papal infallibility enunciated by the general church council called at the Vatican by Pope Pius IX in 1869 and 1870.

How much did all these happenings actually concern or change Michigan Methodists? Much of the State of Michigan was sparsely settled, especially the northern part. Farming and lumbering were still the usual methods of earning a livelihood. The Civil War was so near in memory that Republican political ideas were accepted without question. In religion, the Industrial Revolution at first had very little effect outside of the one big city in the State. Methodist members and ministers continued to follow oldtime rural customs throughout the last three decades of the 19th century and even into the first decade of the 20th. Circuit riding, Class meetings, and Quarterly Conferences were still widely prevalent, no matter whether they took place in connection with a Methodist Protestant or a Methodist Episcopal Society. It took the invention of the automobile, the First World War, and the acceptance of the Social Gospel to alter profoundly the Methodism found in Michigan.

Methodist Church Life in the Latter Third of the 19th Century

Due to the efforts of the Church Extension Society and of occasional zealous and well-to-do individuals, quite a large number of small Methodist Episcopal and Protestant churches had been scattered over the State. For a generation after the Civil War, the religious and social life of Methodists centered in these frame or brick buildings to an extent hard to realize today. So many little towns had scarcely any places of public assembly except their churches. If a theater or opera house existed, the local Methodist minister distinctly disapproved of any of the members of his church attending performances there. Dancing and all card games were just as strongly condemned as the instruments of the Devil.

People ate well from their farms or gardens but were very short of ready cash. Many churches had heavy debts, particularly in the hard times of the 1870's. Annual pew rents were counted on to pay most of the pastor's salary. In rural areas, the auction of the various pews was done publicly at 1 P.M. on a mid-week day. Most churches were in need of more money but the ideas of tithing and stewardship had not yet been developed in Michigan. Lacking the professional and mechanical forms of entertainment so common today, Church people made their own good times and helped to support the denomination at the same time.

1) Woman's Part in Church Work

Methodism was still a male dominated Church but the women members were steadily increasing in importance during the years from 1865 to 1900. More and more, the male official boards turned to the women of the church, usually the Ladies Aid Society, for help in enlarging the church building, redecorating the parsonage, or any emergency in the financial affairs they were supposed to handle. But the ministers were not yet ready to admit women to those quadrennial Lay Electoral Conferences so recently established.

Still less were they able to conceive that a woman might be licensed by a Quarterly Conference to preach and some day become a travelling elder. In 1876, the Detroit Annual Conference, through its presiding bishop, E. R. Ames, refused a renewal of her local preacher's license to Mrs. Frances D. York. She had been allowed to preach two years by the Ann Arbor District Conference and one year by the Detroit District Conference. Then a question of the legality of so allowing her was raised and her Presiding Elder, E. H. Pilcher, ruled that there was no authority so to license her. Manasseh Hickey brought her appeal to the Annual Conference but to no avail.[2]

The origins of the Ladies Aid Society have never been clearly established.[3] Michigan had a few women's organizations in the 1850's but the impetus given by work for the soldiers in the Civil War was the most influential factor in Michigan. Women who had worked in a soldiers aid society or for the Sanitary Commission and Christian Commission had learned how to organize their activities and the strength to be found in united effort. The Ladies Aid Society was always a local concern. It never had any central direction nor organized statistics. One might think it never existed if only the Annual Conference Minutes in Michigan were consulted.

There is record in these same Annual Conference *Minutes* of an organization created by the General Conference of 1872. It bore the cumbersome name of "The Ladies' and Pastors' Christian Union." A national board urged the creation of such a society in each Annual Conference with auxiliaries for every church. Perhaps it was successful in other States but in Michigan it did not last so very long. Conference officers were printed in the Minutes in Michigan for a few years in the mid-seventies and then quietly dropped. The Secretary of the Detroit Annual Conference complained that she could not find out what any of the auxiliaries were doing and wished they would make more reports. The Annual Conference Ladies and Pastors Christian Union always had a minister president and another for vice-president while the ladies held the lesser offices. Presumably this new organization was dropped in favor of the already existing Ladies Aid Societies.

In a general way, the duties of the various Ladies Aid Societies in-

---

[2] Detroit Annual Conference *Minutes* for 1876, p. 15.

[3] Ronald A. Brunger, "The Ladies Aid Societies in Mich. Methodism", *Methodist History*, Jan. 1967, V, #2 , pp. 31-48. See also Mr. Brunger's two articles "Church Social Life before 1900" and "Methodism and the Horse and Buggy Days" in *Michigan Christian Advocate*, February 21 and May 9, 1957. LXXX, #8, pp. 8, 18; #19, p. 10.

cluded helping to raise the pastor's salary, pay the current expenses or any special ones growing out of needed repairs on the church building, and make itself useful in any way that the Official Board felt was needed.

Judging from local newspapers, diaries, letters, and the reminiscences of old ladies, most of the Michigan Ladies Aid Societies planned to have at least two meetings a month to raise money. But it was never put as bluntly as that. They held picnics, lectures, socials, or anniversary celebrations according to the time of the year. The so-called "social" could be as varied as human ingenuity could invent. A "warm sugar" social gathered to eat maple sugar and syrup. The names of a pumpkin pie social, a lemonade or ice cream social indicate their nature.

But "a box social" requires explanation today. Each woman put up lunch enough for two in a fancily wrapped box with her name inside. Then the men bid on the various packages and so determined their partners for that evening. Sometimes the decoration outside was better than the inside contents. Occasionally, an elaborately iced cake would be sold to the highest bidder. Once at New Boston, Wayne County, a fine cake all decorated with candy was sold to a man who proudly took it home only to discover when he cut it that it was nothing but corn bread. That caused a great deal of talk.

The wintertime "oyster suppers" also deserve mention. Their menu consisted of raw oysters, oyster soup, scalloped oysters in succession accompanied by crackers, celery, pickles, and catsup. The dessert was cake and coffee. Chicken pie suppers were very popular too. The standard price for all these meals was 10¢. Donation parties of food for the minister and his family occurred about twice a year and a hearty supper was usually brought in and eaten at the parsonage before the members went home.

At the monthly meetings of the ladies by themselves, the proceedings often opened with prayer and then the repetition of Bible verses by each in turn all around the room. Then the pastor or a returned missionary might speak. Sometimes a dialogue or a simple play with a moral would be given. But business also took much time. When the church needed new carpet or decided to refinish and upholster the pulpit furniture, the ladies did most of the work. If the men arranged for papering the church or building some horse sheds at the back of the property, the ladies got invited to help on the costs. This they usually did only if the paper was all hung correctly.

One other factor needs emphasis today. Members of the usual Methodist Church then enjoyed the fellowship that all these activities and hard work done together produced. Women were far more isolated in their homes then and their daily housekeeping was more hard and monotonous hence even so strenuous a task as an oyster supper or a strawberry and homemade ice cream festival made a break in their routines. People lingered after a church supper to talk with each other and looked foreward to the celebration together with their fellow Methodists of the year's recurrent anniversaries. It had a more intimate flavor because most of the activities took place in the homes of the members. Very few churches originally were bult with kitchens, dining rooms, and lecture halls. Some official boards objected to the serving of food or the holding of a non-religious program in the church building proper.[4]

2) A Calendar of Methodist Church Events

The yearly round began with the Watch Night services on New Year's Eve. In January and February, the minister would hold "protracted meetings," a form of winter revival services. Preaching was held every night in the week except Saturday. Sometimes a preacher carried the burden alone but more often he sought outside aid. A great many people attended for religious reasons no doubt but some were there to see who would go forward to the "mourner's bench" that night. Undoubtedly, a few of the winter converts would backslide the next summer and return to repeat their actions the next winter.

Summer brought the big community and church celebrations of the 4th of July. Perhaps Memorial Day had also been a church project but if so was mostly devoted to decorating the graves in the local cemetery. The centennial, on July 4, 1876, produced special efforts everywhere. Back in 1874, the Annual Conferences in Michigan arranged for a special Centennial sermon at their sessions in September, 1875, and then were urged to preach a like Centennial sermon in their own local churches. The Centennial Exposition of 1876 was the first, big, public exposition in this country. Held in Philadelphia, it attracted world attention to our inventions, especially the telephone, and to our advances in science and architecture. Surely many of the Michigan Methodists, members and ministers, must have attended it.[5]

The biggest occasion of the church year to the children was the Christmas program. The Ladies Aid, the Sunday School, and almost everyone else in the church had a part in this. A large tree was set up in the church and ornamented with strings of popcorn, apples, small

[4] The late Mrs. Hugh Kennedy (Mary Louise White), then of the Clark Home, wrote out her recollections of what the church at Lake City was like in her childhood. She was then 86 years of age. Much of what is written in this chapter about church life in the late 19th century is based on her remembrance of a church founded in large part by her parents.

[5] The Rev. E. E. Caster, the author's grandfather, made a trip to the Philadelphia Centennial Exposition where he bought gold bracelets for his two daughters and a glass plate which the author still has. Independence Hall is pictured in the middle and the alphabet makes the border. Mr. Caster very likely had the usual ministerial half fare ticket.

bags of hard candy, and gifts for the children. A few of the children spoke a piece or sang a short song and then the Sunday School Superintendent distributed the gifts. Many people did not have a tree in their homes and gave their gifts to their own children at the church celebration rather than in their houses individually.[6]

The ministers took their full share in the social as well as the religious activities of the churches to which they had been appointed. Faithfully attending the socials and suppers of the Ladies Aid Societies, they and their wives presided and then prayed at various programs from lectures to missionary concerts. Again accompanied by their wives, they gave much time to calling on the people of the town. Their visits were by no means confined to Methodists alone. Sometimes, they called at every house on one side of the street for several blocks. In his pocket diaries of this period, the Rev. E. E. Caster often noted that he and his wife had made from ten to eighteen calls in a single afternoon. Each one must have been very brief. Once Mr. Caster visited a tavern and conversed with the men there whom he referred to as the "inmates." The letters and records leave the impression that the average Methodist minister gave far more time then to uninvited calling than such a man would be likely to do today.

Many a preacher gained a reputation for a secular lecture which he gave repeatedly for the benefit of his and neighboring Methodist churches. The subject might be Lincoln, the Civil War, a current event, or any odd topic that caught the public interest. Mr. Caster had one he called "Dirt." Travel lectures were the most popular. Any preacher who had been abroad, particularly to the Holy Land, had more calls for lectures than he could conveniently handle. This was true well into the 20th century. When Elijah H. Pilcher was planning to travel abroad, he addressed the Detroit Annual Conference before he went as well as after he returned. He also wrote long letters to the church papers while he was in Europe and the Near East.

3) *Methodist Sermons*

The average minister preached more often and at far greater length than his counterpart would do today. A stationed man preached twice at least on Sundays and one with a circuit or perhaps an out appointment to cover might preach from three to five times in one day. Presumably some were the same sermon repeated. A funeral demanded a

---

[6] Based in part on Mrs. Kennedy's reminiscences. She retained the most vivid impression of the wonderful surprise when the Superintendent handed down from the tree her favorite doll dressed in a new frock of red velvet made from her mother's best bonnet. The author clearly remembers speaking a short piece at a Christmas church occasion and how frightened she was but she also clearly visualizes the striped bag of candy and the tiny monogram ring that she was given afterwards. An orange with the candy was also something special then.

regular sermon in those days. Most sermons consumed more time than they would now. An hour to an hour and a half was average but some stalwarts were capable of preaching for two hours or more. They must have been quite repetitious.

Some thirty sermon outlines preached in the 1870's at the Fenton, East Saginaw, and Detroit Jefferson Avenue Churches by the Rev. E. E. Caster illustrate the trends of that time. Tthey were all written by hand in black ink which was emphasized by the use of red ink in capital letters and under key words. In length they vary from eight to thirty-two pages of paper about five by eight inches in size. The sentences are complete but illustrative examples were usually indicated by a word or two. Incidentally, the longest one, thirty-two pages, was a strong attack upon dancing and its evils. The text was "And David danced before the Lord."

All of these sermons seem very characteristic of their time. Purely religious sermons were fundamentalist in approach, rather emotional or sentimental in examples, and strict for the Biblical law of the Old Testament. Death and the judgment thereafter were frequently dwelt on in quite a literal way.

The strongest general impression left by reading and re-reading these sermons is of how many things the Methodist Episcopal Church and one of its ministers was opposed to in those changing times. Great stress was laid on the evils of drink, card playing, dancing, and the use of tobacco. Other denominations were mostly an object of suspicion too. Mr. Caster preached sermons specifically *against* Universalism, Mormonism, and the "Close Communion" Baptists. Methodists generally felt that sprinkling was quite enough in baptism. But the Methodist Protestants were on very close and friendly terms with the "Free Will" Baptists.

Mr. Caster was the chaplain of the Saginaw lodge of the American Protestant Association. This was an anti-minority group of the kind too often found in the history of the United States. The most bitter phrases used by Mr. Caster in any of his sermons were reserved for the Catholics with their "mummeries" and their priests "dominated by a foreign power."

During the violent railroad strikes of the late 1870's, Mr. Caster displayed an individualistic and pioneer attitude toward such crises. Foreign agitators were blamed or the wickedness of evil men in attacking those who had gained wealth by their own efforts. This minister predicted that American millionaires could not be scared by the threats of an idle gang of lawless wretches. He thought extreme poverty was a man's own fault for not working harder, staying sober, and obeying the church's precepts. The "Social Gospel" had not yet been born here in Michigan.

On the first Sunday after the Annual Conference of 1877 under reappointment for his third year at the Jefferson Avenue Church in East Saginaw, the Rev. E. E. Caster called his sermon "A Sketch — My Anxiety." He made the following points:

How shall we Succeed:

1. The pulpit must and shall be earnest and orthodox.
2. *You* must strengthen and not discourage the pulpit.
3. Cultivate personal piety.
4. Be regular and dont run about. You will get more good at home.
5. Be on time at the services.
6. Be zealous.
7. Be sectarian, love your own home best.
8. Be social.
9. Know as little as possible of the faults of each other.
10. Welcome strangers at Church.
11. Bear a part of the financial burden of the Church.[7]

Church Trials Again

The *Minutes* of the various Methodist Annual Conferences in Michigan reveal more clearly than other records do the advances and troubles of the years from 1872 to 1880. Human failings, administrative problems, and worrisome debts in hard times are all evident. Conference investigation or even trial by a special committee of five among the Methodist Protestants or by a "select committee of fifteen" in the Methodist Episcopal Church was still the way of dealing with an erring minister. He was a bit more likely just to be quietly dropped or go unassigned by the Methodist Protestants. Public reproof and expulsion was more likely to be the method of the Methodist Episcopalians. Fine legal points in the Discipline received what today seems an undue amount of attention. The "pettifogging spirit and practice" which the Michigan Annual Conference had deplored in 1870 went on increasing throughout that decade.

In the eight years beginning with 1873 and continuing through 1880, the two Methodist Episcopal Annual Conferences in the State of Michigan had at least forty-eight cases involving local or travelling elders. The Michigan Annual Conference had thirty-one of these and the Detroit Conference seventeen. The year 1874 saw five in the Detroit Annual Conference and six in the Michigan. In 1880 only one occurred in the Detroit Annual Conference but the Michigan Annual Conference

[7] This Sketch was found in the Henry W. Hicks Collection of letters in the Detroit Annual Conference Historical Collection, Adrian College Library. Mr. Caster and Mr. Hicks were close friends who corresponded often all through their lives. It was to be expected that he would share his new sermon outline with his friend Hicks. The thirty sermon outlines mentioned are in the possession of the author.

had ten. It is hard to estimate how many the Methodist Protestants dealt with in these same years as their *Minutes* were even more inadequate than those kept by the larger Methodist Episcopal Conferences. But not a year went by without at least from one to five ministers being listed as "unstationed," "dropped from roll," "left in the hands of the President," "received letter of withdrawal," "left irregularly," and once "ordered his name be stricken and· his papers demanded." The years in which the Methodist Protestant Annual Conference dealt with more than one or two óf such cases were 1872, 1874 and 1879.

Charges were often stated with extreme vagueness in the *Minutes,* perhaps intentionally so. The most frequent phrase was "conduct unbecoming to a minister." This might mean petty spite or something very serious. In the Methodist Episcopal records may be found such things as "immoral conduct," maladministration of the finances, and even "violation of the Sabbath and dealing in wheat options." The Methodist Protestant statements of such items give an impression that either debts and bad financial management were involved or perhaps what would be called today "personality conflict" had developed. In 1873, the Methodist Protestant Conference for the east half of Michigan noted that two ministers, the special committee and the church trustees concerned had examined the accounts and the two "brethren, after conversing with each other on the matter of difference morally, agreed that all difference being removed by such conversation., they are mutually agreed that all differences are now and forever settled."

Some Methodist Episcopal cases were dismissed because proper warning had not been given in time or the evidence was too scanty. Then the man's character was usually passed at once. More cases were turned back to the man's own Presiding Elder for further investigation or preliminary trial before the District Conference. A really serious charge usually got a preliminary committee to choose a larger committee to conduct the trial, a President of the court, a minister for the defense and two more for the Church. Fully carried through, such a trial resulted in the expulsion of the man from the Methodist ministry and even from membership in the Church at large. One case of heresy and several of immoral conduct received such treatment. A lesser punishment was "admonishment" from the presiding bishop in open Conference session. Sometimes as soon as the charge and trial date had been announced, word would be brought to the session that the man concerned had withdrawn from the ministry and had returned his "parchments." It was usually presumed that such action was a tacit admission of guilt.

The Detroit Annual Conference was still vexed by John Levington. He made a motion in 1873 and again in 1874 for appointment of a committee of five "on Secret Societies." This subject was almost a phobia

with him. After that long trial in 1872, the Conference was compelled
to proceed in exactly the same way with him in 1873. The charge was
"Evil Speaking" and was related to the things that Levington had written in a paper called the *Methodist Free Press*, published in Illinois.
Who had lied about whom and who was a Mason or not were unsettled
questions that complicated the hearing. Finally it was agreed that the
charges related to "questions concerning which . . . . he is not fully responsible for his course." Levington was continued as a superannuate.

But in 1874, he was made effective again and then, a couple of days
later, was located "at his own request." He must have been licensed
as a local preacher by the Simpson Church Quarterly Conference in
Detroit. In 1879, the *Minutes* show that Levington, through the Presiding Elder of the Detroit District, appealed for a review of the Simpson Church action "whereby he was suspended from the functions of
the ministry." Again he received the full legal procedure, a committee
of review of fifteen members with two ministers as counsel for the
Church. Levington insisted on acting as his own counsel. "After patient and careful consideration," the committee unanimously refused
Levington's appeal. A small note of interest is that James S. Smart,
who had been a Civil War chaplain and was the Presiding Elder of the
Saginaw District in 1879, was chairman of the committee and Joseph F.
Berry was the assistant secretary who kept the record. Of course, he
was the man who later became a bishop.

No other Methodist organization in Michigan ever had quite so
irksome and long enduring a case as that of John Levington was to the
Detroit Annual Conference. The Methodist Episcopal Michigan Annual
Conference had at least one that ran on for four years. A. W. Torrey
was first brought to trial in 1872 on a charge of a financial nature. He
received a public reproof from Bishop E. R. Ames and was made supernumerary. In 1873, a committee of three investigated him again and on
recommendation of his Presiding Elder, H. C. Peck of Kalamazoo District, his character was passed but he was left without appointment.
But Mr. Peck must have changed his mind about Mr. Torrey. In 1874,
he brought charges against Torrey and a committee of inquiry ordered
a complete investigation. Ie ended in Torrey's expulsion from the
Methodist ministry. The decision seems a bit odd because the committee
that recommended the expulsion in 1875 stated that "a long time had
elapsed since the events covered by the evidence and there are many
palliating circumstances connected with the case." It also thought that
Torrey "had been doing much during the intervening time to redeem
his Christian character." The committee may have thus implied that
they wanted Torrey to leave the ministry but not the membership of
the Methodist Episcopal Church.

The Presiding Elders:
Their Work, Rewards, and Burdens

Of all the positions and ranks in the Methodist hierachy at that time, the Presiding Elder had the most difficult tasks and the position most exposed to criticism or even attack. Charges of maladministration were leveled against the Rev. Elijah Pilcher in 1874, although nothing seems to have come of it. In the Michigan Annual Conference, the Rev. D. D. Gillett tried repeatedly, in the years 1874, 1875, and 1876, to bring charges of maladministration against Presiding Elder H. C. Peck of Kalamazoo District. Yet Gillett was not then holding a charge in the District which Peck supervised. It seems to have been a disagreement over the legal interpretation of the *Discipline*. In each of the years cited, a select committee dismissed Gillett's charges, doing so twice on the grounds of lack of proper time and notice having been given.

The rewards of holding the Presiding Eldership must not be overlooked. Some of them were universally respected, held the position beyond the customary term of eight years and, upon leaving the office, received handsome testimonial gifts. In 1872, the ministers of Coldwater District presented Rev. Resin Sapp with "a package of money." Mr. Sapp had been eight years on the District work but Bishop Ames asked for an exception to be made and appointed him to the Grand Rapids District. There he died on May 5, 1873, having served thirty-four years as a Methodist minister. At the Conference session of 1874, Resin Sapp's widow was presented with a large framed picture of her husband surrounded by the pictures of the members of the class of 1868, who were admitted on trial upon Sapp's recommendation while he was Presiding Elder of Kalamazoo District.

The Presiding Elder of Ionia District, D. F. Barnes, was given a purse of $175 at the Conference session of 1873 by the ministers of his District giving $75 and a few friends adding $100. In 1874, the ministers of the Niles District gave Rev. and Mrs. C. C. Olds, their Presiding Elder and his wife, "a beautiful silver tea set." The times may in general have been hard but a change had certainly come over the Methodist Episcopal Church when such gifts were presented to its Presiding Elders. That oldtime circuit rider would have had no place to carry or keep a silver tea set and $175 was decidedly more money than the average pioneer circuit rider saw in a year.

Administrative reform was being much agitated in the mid-1870's by the Methodists. Among the ideas under discussion were election of the Presiding Elders by the ministers of the Annual Conferences instead of appointment by the presiding bishop of that Conference session. Laymen were eager to attain equality and power in the Annual Conferences. And in some States dividing the Conferences into smaller units in both area and numbers was urged. In Michigan, many of the ministers urged the creation of a third Annual Conference to be called the Northern one. Also they wanted to see the number of Districts drastically reduced partly to save money but also partly to reduce the power of the bishop and the Presiding Elder as would surely occur if the latter was elected.

These various reforms were discussed at length in both the Detroit and Michigan Annual Conference sessions of 1875. This was because General Conference was scheduled to meet in the spring of 1876 before the sessions of that year would be held in Michigan. It was also the time for more Lay Electoral Conferences in 1875 and their views reinforced those of the ministers.

The Michigan Annual Conference was less aroused by the reform of election of the Presiding Elders than the Detroit Conference was. It caused less preliminary argument and was dealt with immediately and decisively. The Rev. J. H. McCarty introduced a statement and a resolution that the Presiding Eldership should not be changed. This was at once adopted by a vote of 74 to 31. Among the reasons which he gave for his attitude were these:

> Such a change would be radical, striking at the essential features of our system; . . . we believe that popular elections are generally attended with more or less irritation, and in their results not always more satisfactory than prayerfully-made appointments.

Either a demand for greater democracy was felt in the Detroit Annual Conference or some of the ministers were unhappy with their Presiding Elders. On the first day of the session, September 1, 1875, the Rev. J. S. Smart introduced two resolutions with a long preamble. Clearly he very much wanted to have the bishop's power, to form the Districts and appoint the ministers, limited in some decisive way. Smart declared that the members of any Conference knew more about local situations than any visiting bishop could, an elected Presiding Elder would have more self-confidence, the ministers if they had chosen him would offer more enthusiatic support to his efforts, and previous use of the ballot to fill high positions in Methodism had been successful. It was simply not decent to have such an office ever fall into the hands of an unsympathetic minister. It must never be forgotten that "all the temporal interests of Methodist ministers, including home, salary, associations, reputation, and sometimes even health and life, are largely in the hands of the appointing power."

The Detroit Annual Conference twice debated Smart's resolutions at length but finally rejected them and accepted a substitute offered by William H. Shier and William X. Ninde (The latter was a future Bishop.) The accepted resolution said the Presiding Eldership was "indispensible to the most vigorous working of our church economy." But "if practicable" the next General Conference ought to find some way of making him "elective by the concurrent action of the ministry and laity."

The Detroit Lay Electoral Conference even debated a motion either to abolish completely the office of Presiding Elder or to require him also to serve a single church as pastor. A few laymen appear to have thought that the Presiding Elder did not have enough to do. Either that or else they had absorbed some different ideas from the procedures of the Methodist Protestants. All these new lay ideas were tabled by a large majority.

*   *   *

The two Methodist Protestant Annual Conference in Michigan ran their affairs in complete democracy it is true. Yet at the same time it was extremely inefficient and functioning only in small rural and village churches. Everything that was done began with a committee. If anyone, concerned in the work given it to do, objected to the make-up of the group then its membership was changed. In 1875, by "unintentional oversight," the Michigan M.P. Annual Conference did not appoint any committees on Adrian College, Missions, Ministerial education, or Publications. The Conference simply voted on its last day that they reaffirmed their actions of the last year on each one and again recommended them to the people as worthy of support.

Just as the M.P.s had no bishops, they also had no Presiding Elders. The President of the Conference was also pastor of a Church and was authorized to call on any minister in the area to help him once during the year. This seems to have meant preaching for the President while he was checking another Church and probably preaching there too. In 1872, an effort to divide the Conference into six small Districts, only five to seven circuits or missions in each, failed of adoption. Each District was to have had a Chairman already the pastor of a church in that subdivision. The scheme was adopted in 1873 with eight subdistricts as they were then called. Next year nine divisions were made and a year later the number was returned to eight. Sometimes the number of appointments in one subdistrict was as low as three. It was soon found that the mission and financial needs of the churches could be more effectually conducted through this subdistrict plan. But because the Stationing Committee reported the districts and subdivisions for Conference approval, changes were often made from year to year just as the boundaries of particular circuits were also changed.

Any chairman of a subdistrict visited each charge in his part of Michigan at least once a year, held a missionary meeting at each place, and inquired into the character of the Quarterly Conferences too. He reported conditions in his subdistrict at the next Conference. Also he was expected to act as the President of Conference would during his absence from that division. All this resembles the work of a Presiding Elder. But a chairman had no control over appointments unless elected to the Stationing or Pastoral Relations committees in Annual Conferences.

Reporting to the M.P. Michigan Annual Conference in 1877, the Publishing Interests Committee declared that their own books and papers were one of the few general interests that bound them together. These three ministers, one of them President of Adrian College, saw the dangers of their situation. The committee said in part:

> The need of these general interests is the more particularly pressing in the case of a denomination which, like the Methodist Protestant Church, has none of those great centralising forces afforded by the personal and official rank of individuals chosen for their distinguished administrative and organizing abilities, and to whom has been committed the general and authoritive supervision and management of the bodies they represent. These so-called General Interests are to us as a people, with our peculiar governmental polity, our only bonds of denominational union. In these we can sink those little prejudices and differences which are due to the peculiarities of local training and geographical position.

The report was ended with a strong plea for every pastor to feel it his duty to place in every home on his charge a Bible, a *Discipline*, a hymnal, and copies of the denominational papers, more particularly the *Methodist Recorder* and the *Morning Guide*.[8]

* * * * * *

Michigan Petitions to the General Conference of 1876

The only reform on which all the Methodist Episcopal lay and ministerial Conferences in Michigan agreed was lay representation in the Annual Conferences equal in every way with the ministers. The Michigan Conference laymen also wanted the power to ordain women as ministers.

Authority for their Annual Conferences to determine the number of districts and their boundaries was much desired by some of the Michigan Methodist ministers. If the details were left to the bishop and the Presiding Elders, the Annual Conference ought to be asked to approve their decisions.

Each Lay Electoral Conference in this State had an element that was outspoken about its desire to reduce drastically the number of Districts and Presiding Elders. The Michigan Laymen said their goal was "at least one-half the present number." Detroit Conference Laymen debated a resolution that said the Presiding Eldership must be modified in some way "that will cut off or largely diminish the expenses of the office." But they found themselves unable to agree on that or any other resolution except the one asking for equal lay representation in the Annual Conference.

[8] *Minutes* of the 36th session of the Michigan Annual Conference of the Methodist Protestant Church in 1877, pp. 14-15.

The General Conference of 1876 sent the change in the *Discipline,* to give each Annual Conference authority to determine the number of its own Districts, to each succeeding Conference session as it was held, in order to get the opinion of all the Methodist Episcopal ministers. It seems odd that the two Annual Conferences in Michigan each voted almost unanimously *against* the proposed change. This may have been because the reform was to restrict the Conferences to from two to eight Districts with never any more than sixty appointments in any one District. Or it may be that they were conservative and when such a change really was offered, the majority found that they preferred to leave the power of reform with the General Conference and bishops.

Michigan Changes the Districts

The Michigan Annual Conference had been organized in ten Districts since 1869 and the Detroit with eight ever since 1865. The latter debated in 1875 a request to the presiding bishop to reduce the number of its Districts to five. But the previous eight were kept. In 1876, debate on the same change was extensive and finally a resolution asking for six Districts was adopted. The Rev. E. H. Pilcher wanted the number raised to ten. That year the Presiding Bishop, E. R. Ames, complied with their wishes. The Ann Arbor and Romeo Districts were abolished and appointments in the first were divided between the Detroit District with twelve and the Adrian District with ten.

More juggling around was done in the Thumb area. Saginaw District received four appointments from the Port Huron District and four more from Flint. Then the Flint District took eleven of the former Romeo District charges and the Port Huron District got the remainder or twelve appointments.

Not until 1879 was another District added to the Detroit Annual Conference. Then the Alpena District was established with fourteen appointments. Of that number, eight had been transferred from Saginaw District and the rest were new places for Methodist pioneer ministers to develop. Among them were Gaylord, Burt Lake, Cheboygan, and Roscommon. In 1880, the one-year old Alpena District had twenty-one appointments including Grayling and West Branch.

The changes made in the Districts of the Detroit Annual Conferences seem to have been more acceptable than those in the Michigan Annual Conference. Perhaps the west half of the State had its idea of a third Annual Conference more firmly fixed or else the changes did not fit with the accustomed travel patterns of that area. In 1874, the Michigan Annual Conference appointed a committee of ten ministers, one from each District, to confer with a like group from the Detroit Annual Conference on the question of division of the Conferences then functioning in the State. It was soon found that the Detroit committee had been appointed "more as a matter of courtesy than with the desire of division." The Michigan Conference committee even visited the Bishop's room and polled all the Presiding Elders on the question. Of course, this was done with the consent of Bishop W. L. Harris. All the ministers consulted voted against any division of the Conferences. The joint committee concluded, by a vote of seven to five, that it was inexpedient to divide the Conferences or change their boundary lines at present.

The same thing as had happened in the Detroit Annual Conference in 1875 also occurred that same year in the Michigan Annual Conference. A resolution to reduce the number of Districts was debated but was laid on the table and the number of Districts remained ten for another year. On the second day of the Conference session of 1876, Bishop Haven was asked by a formal resolution to arrange the Conference in seven Districts. This led to "considerable discussion and the offering of various amendments which were lost." When a recorded vote was taken the result was 79 for the resolution and 77 against it. Reading the names on the record vote leaves the impression that the oldtimers and former Presiding Elders were opposed to the reduction of the number of Districts.

The ten Districts of 1875 were made eight in 1876. Albion and Coldwater Districts were abolished and a Jackson District was created with sixteen appointments from Albion and thirteen from Coldwater. The Kalamazoo District received four from Albion and seven from Coldwater District. Next the Pentwater District was also abolished and thirteen of its appointments were added to the Big Rapids District.

This arrangement evidently was not liked for in 1877, the Michigan Annual Conference was raised to nine Districts by the abolition of that new Jackson District and the restoration of the Albion and Coldwater Districts. With only two or three exceptions, the restored Districts received again the same appointments as they had contained in 1875.

The rest of the Districts in the Michigan Annual Conference had only minor shifts in 1877 and little new in appointments can be discovered about them. From 1877 through 1880, these Districts remained nine in number with an entire Conference increase of perhaps ten to twelve charges each year. The increase in the number of churches is difficult to determine accurately in that period because two or three small societies would be joined in one circuit one year and split with a minister to each place the next.

All that argument and struggle to decrease the number of Districts and hence also the number of Presiding Elders was probably due to the hard times prevalent over Michigan in the mid-1870's. It does not seem reasonable that so many ministers should suddenly have grown so hostile to their immediate superiors, the Presiding Elders, that they would want to abolish their positions if at all possible.

The Influence of Hard Times on Michigan Methodism

The worst years of the Panic of 1873 for Michigan were those from 1875 through 1878. A good many churches in both Methodist Episcopal Conferences were in a desperate financial plight just then. Those that had just built a church beyond their immediate means to pay for were in danger of having the building sold to satisfy the mortgage holder. The more desperate cases came up again and again year after year in the Annual Conference sessions.

The Methodist Protestant churches were not as seriously effected by the Panic of 1873 or else they did not lay their financial difficulties to that cause. Their Conference *Minutes* reveal that the ministers were trying to introduce a more systematic method of money collections, that in nearly half the charges they were unable to obtain the sums that had been pledged for their salaries, and that Adrian College was in trouble with heavy debts during all these latter decades of the 19th century. For several years the M.P. Conferences borrowed money each year from the Preachers Aid Society funds in order to print the *Minutes*. At the end of the year, the money was repaid together with the interest and then promptly reborrowed to print the Minutes again. Among the churches in specific financial trouble were Pontiac, Warren and Riley Center. But none of these charges held their debts were due to the hard times then prevalent. It seems today that the lack of central authority and the business incompetence of many of the ministers were the chief causes.

Perhaps the general locations of the Methodist Episcopal and Methodist Protestant churches had something to do with their financial hardships. While both branches of Methodism had plenty of small, struggling Societies, the M.P.'s were more generally very small and rural in location. The Methodist Episcopal Church when it was located in a large town or city was more likely to have just built a larger and more elaborate church just before the Panic of 1873 began. Some congregations, in their desire to complete a handsome structure immediately, had borrowed money much beyond their capacity to repay with interest in any sudden emergency. As the hard times spread over the country, neither the ministers nor the members of the congregations were able to cope with their own mortgages let alone the big one on the church building. Many ministers were better preachers than they were business men. Money generally was very scarce and when local banks failed or refused more loans then frantic appeals reached the Annual Conferences. This situation helped to increase the demand for more lay representation in the business dealings of Methodism.

The northern churches in the Lower Peninsula were usually quite small and only recently organized. The Panic of 1873 influenced the finances of such Societies in two ways. Many of them did not yet have a church building to lose. Rather slowly, at the rate of $50 to $100 a year, the salaries paid their ministers declined from about $1,100 to around $500. Next the collections for the organized charities of Methodism suffered visibly for several years between 1875 and 1880.

The gaps in the statistical reports, found in the annual *Minutes* are very evident. This may have been due to just plain carelessness on the part of the pastors but is more likely to have been the result of the prevailing hard times. Perhaps some ministers had been unable to collect anything and could not face such an admission in print. The Michigan Annual Conference Treasurer of the Church Extension Society, L. R. Atwater, added a note to his Conference reports in 1878 and 1879 in which he lamented that forty-five of the ministers had failed to take any collection at all for his organization. He thought it "somewhat singular" that the number was the same both years and he called the attention of the negligent forty-five to the parts of the *Discipline* relating to finances. He also reminded all the ministers, "All our preachers, before being ordained, pledge themselves to keep our rules."

In the years 1877, 1878, and 1879, the Detroit Annual Conference instructed their Treasurer to list at the end of all the general statistics half a dozen places which had made no reports. In 1879, a sentence was added which stated, "If these charges had reported, instead of the apparent decrease, a real increase of more than 200 members would be shown."

Each Annual Conference had half a dozen churches in deep trouble with debts so huge that the danger was their building might be sold at public auction to satisfy the mortgage holders. The latter were not even getting their interest paid in the late 1870's. The most chronic and long-continued cases were at East Saginaw and Olivet. The first-named had been in trouble financially ever since the Civil War. Repeated efforts to help had been made by previous Conferences, particularly in 1866 and 1872. As shown in Chapter X, pledges of thousands of dollars had been obtained some years earlier. The East Saginaw Church debt of $28,000 in 1872 had by great effort been reduced to $5,000 in 1879.

The Olivet Methodist Episcopal Church was in such a bad financial situation that its affairs were brought up in every Michigan Annual Conference session from 1875 through 1879. It took two full pages of fine print to explain its predicament in 1876. It was afflicted with a second mortgage on top of a first one with the interest unpaid on both. Neither had the Church paid their pastor over $300 in 1876. The temptation was to use certain modest assets to pay the minister. A special Conference committee strongly opposed using money raised to liquidate the debt to pay the pastor. The result inevitably would be failure in efforts to raise money for Olivet Church debts in the Conference at large. The total debt was about $4,000 in a church with a membership of eighty-four.

Violent acts of nature nearly ruined one Church in each Conference too. The Benton Harbor Church was already embarrassed financially in 1874. So it asked the Michigan Annual Conference to appoint a financial agent to travel at large and collect for them. In 1875, the Agent sadly reported to Conference that the church building had been entirely destroyed by fire as the result of lightning. A "committee of relief" was appointed consisting of the Agent and another minister.

In the Detroit Annual Conference, the Port Huron Church reported in 1878 its utter inability to cope with a debt of $12,000. So it asked for a special financial agent to collect at large, with some success for in 1879 its debt was said to be $7,000. Alas! "On July 11th at ¼ past 11 o'clock, A.M., a tornado from the north and west struck the church and in a moment it was in ruins." The Lay Electoral Conference of 1879 asked the Annual Conference to set a date when all the churches in the entire Detroit Annual Conference would take a special collection for the relief of the Port Huron Church. This was done.

One Church in the Detroit Annual Conference and several in the Michigan Annual Conference went through financial crises due almost entirely to the hard times. The Michigan Annual Conference had more problems of this sort and at a later time too.

The Michigan Annual Conference of 1873 took special subscriptions for the debts of the churches at Grand Haven and Lowell. In 1875, the Holland Church was authorized to canvass at large in the Conference. In 1878, a special agent was appointed to collect for the churches at Olivet, Grand Ledge, and Marshall. In 1879, the Conference voted to send "a first-class man" to Marshall and also to ask the Missionary Society for $400 toward his salary. Also the Church Extension Society was asked for $500 each for the churches at Olivet and Kendall while the trustees of the Muir Church were authorized to sell their property in order to liquidate their debts.

The Monroe Church, with a debt of $10,000 and a membership of 148, had actually been advertised for sale under the mortgage in 1876 when the Detroit Annual Conference set up a very special committee of eight to help if at all possible. It included three laymen being David Preston, William Phelps, and T. C. Owen. The five ministers on the committee were all experienced and prominent men, such as Seth Reed and Francis A. Blades. The inclusion of John M. Arnold is to be noted as he ran the Methodist Book Depository in Detroit.

This committee must have known where to look for help. Just three days later, it was reported to the Conference that "a layman had been found who would advance money to save the church from immediate danger." In 1879, the debt of this Church had been reduced to $5,000.

Various methods were used by the Conferences in Michigan to help a debt stricken church. Most often a collection was taken then and there in the session. A special agent, a committee of three ministers or the local pastor concerned might any or all be authorized to collect anywhere in the District where the church was located. In hardship cases, collection in the Conference at large was allowed. Application to the national Missionary Society or Church Extension Society for a donation or loan might be used too. Lastly and reluctantly, the Conference in real desperation would allow the Society to sell its parsonage or church to pay its debts.

Both Conferences tried continually to obtain more businesslike procedures and more accurate, statistical reports. They urged the ministers all to study the provisions in the *Discipline* before undertaking a building project. Old and also new ways of finance sometimes brought criticism. The committee on the State of the Church of the Michigan Annual Conference of 1880 frowned on donation parties when held for support of the pastor because "it weakened our organic financial economy" and hurt the exact execution of the *Discipline*. The same committee did not think much of some of the new ways of money-raising in the Church. It said, "Festivals, Church fairs, etc. with their doubtful moral surroundings of fishponds, grab-bags and postoffices . . . to increase the revenues of the Church funds" harmed the morals of the people, lowered "the standards of Divine truth and compromised the purity and spirituality of the Gospel."

It is an interesting coincidence of views that the Michigan Methodist Protestant Conference of 1876 had a committee on "Moral Subjects" which declared in part:

> We bear our unqualified testimony against the popular amusements of the day, such as the Grab-Bag, Snap-an-catch-'em, Kissing Bees, etc., etc. Your committee believe that one and all of the above methods to raise money for Church purposes and pastors' salaries are wrong, and we enter our solemn protest against them.

While they were about it, the same committee condemned in no uncertain terms "Balls, Theaters, Circuses, Horse Racing, playing Croquet, Checkers, etc." They ended with strong support of "the Christian Sabbath as kept by orthodox Christians" and said that Sabbath labor, travelling or visiting were all "contrary to the word of God, and unless repented of will call for retribution at the Judgment Day."

A United Effort Produces Freedom from Debt in Detroit

The Methodist Episcopal Churches in the City of Detroit learned in 1880 that mutual alliance brought increased strength and freedom from debt for all of them, large or small, strong or weak. The Sunday Schools of the city had been working together ever since 1854 when the

Detroit Methodist Sunday School Union was formed. The group had grown used to striving together to improve the instruction and the materials used in the classes. In the summers, joint picnics and excursions were popular.

Sometimes, a mission Sunday School that the Union started became another church in time. Fort Street and Simpson Churches had both begun in this way. In 1868, the Sunday School Union became the Sunday School and Missionary Union of the Methodist Episcopal Church of Detroit. This group helped the Simpson Society build their first church. Then in 1878, the Methodist Episcopal Church and Sunday School Alliance was organized to strengthen the religious efforts in the city. The burden of debt carried by the smaller urban churches was painfully evident. The new organization, by an immense effort for that time, raised enough money to clear all the debts from all the Detroit Methodist Episcopal Churches in 1880. This was a modern goal achieved in a distinctly modern way.

In the beginning of this movement, the thought had been to bring the various Methodist churches of Detroit into closer harmony with a view to taking a larger view of the entire situation and enlightening the localism of the smaller churches. The Official Boards of these six churches had never held a joint meeting until Presiding Elder Washburne and his committee of three ministers arranged one.

A few statistics about the Detroit churches as they were on May 2, 1879 may make the situation more understandable.[9] Here are:

Churches	*Members*	*Debts*	*Officers & Students of Sunday Schools*	
Central	779	$ 8,000	118	1,217
Simpson	337	$ 8,500	49	676
Jefferson Ave.	236	$ 3,700	36	340
Tabernacle	230	$12,000	25	247
Fort Street	122	$ 2,200	32	250
16th Street	100	$ 1,100	20	180

A lay member of Tabernacle Church, Reuben Robinson, seems to have been the one who first suggested that all the city Methodist Churches should pool their debts and ask Central to help the rest of

---

[9] J. M. Arnold, A Sketch of the History of Methodism in Detroit, *Mich. Pioneer Coll.*, III, 225-243. His statistics do not always agree with those in the Detroit Conference *Minutes* for these years. Even the ministers complained that their *Minutes* were carelessly done then. Arnold included both probationary and full members in his figures. Also his were taken at a time midway between the Conference sessions when their statistics were reported. Central was the Church formed by the union of First and Congress St. Simpson was the outgrowth of Walnut St. Mission Sunday School. Tabernacle was the descendant of Lafayette St. Church also known briefly as Trinity. It had such a large debt because it had just erected a large brick church building. Fort St. was started in 1874 and 16th St. in 1872.

them clear off all debts in three equal installments. The total debt was then about $35,500 and the hope was to raise $12,000 in each of three big drives. The date of completion was first set for July 1, 1881. The two German churches in Detroit withdrew from the Alliance when the financial campaign got under way.

The chief guarantee of success was the appointment of David Preston as Treasurer. He was the man who raised the endowment fund for Albion College. Another promise of success was the agreement by the Official Board of Central Church to assume 2/5 of the total debt although that Church's own debt was a little under 1/4 of the entire amount.

The earnest, Christian spirit of a handful of Methodists finally brought success to the campaign. Beginning on March 17, 1879, a small prayer meeting was held at noon every weekday for three months in the parlor of Central Church. The attendance varied from ten to twenty but the general spirit remained warm and zealous. By February, 1880, $12,000 or the first third was raised. Then the work dragged as the summer came on. Preston was probably the one who urged them to shorten the time and attempt to reach their goal by Thanksgiving Day.

Without advance warning of the reason, invitations were sent to all reasonably well-to-do Methodists in Detroit for a dinner at Central Church on November 16. The men provided a caterer as they were determined their wives should be guests and not the kitchen helpers. The unpledged, remaining debt was $2,600 but before the evening was over the 125 guests had agreed to pay $1,600 more. By personal effort, David Preston raised the rest by the day before Thanksgiving.

In a speech he gave at the Thanksgiving celebration, Preston told how it was done. The first contribution was $2 from a poor man and the second was from a prosperous member who said he would not sign a pledge but would give him $100. Both incidents took place while Preston was walking from Central Church to his own office. More than 3,000 people had contributed. The amounts varied all the way from hundreds of 50¢ each to one of $1,500 and four of $1,000.

When just $1,000 was left to raise, Preston invited seven leading business men to meet in his office and obtained $700 from them. He raised the rest by walking down the street speaking to Methodists he met and by a personal call on Joseph Hudson and C. R. Mabley in their store. They gave him $130. Preston returned to his office and wrote in his account book in red ink the last contributors and the amounts they gave, signed his name and the time — 4:15 P.M. November 24, 1880. Finally he wrote, "It is finished. I am released from the burden."

No wonder the Methodist churches of Detroit held an elaborate celebration of Thanksgiving Day, November 25, 1880. Central Church was decorated with ropes of evergreen with a motto of the same material, saying "Praise God from whom all blessings flow." Plants and flowers were placed all around the pulpit and a "floral banner" bearing the words "Union — Success." A souvenir program was provided for everyone in the audience. The services lasted for two hours in all.

All the ministers appointed to Detroit took part. Presiding Elder Washburne was chairman and led in responsive reading of the 98th and 100th Psalms. The Rev. George W. Lowe of Fort Street Church led in prayer, William Dawe of Tabernacle Church read the Governor's Thanksgiving proclamation, John M. Arnold gave a twenty minute historical address, a large choir sang, and five other ministers gave "brief addresses."

The high point was reached when David Preston stood up and called on the Boards of Trustees of the six churches to come forward. To each he presented their cancelled obligations of debt. The men there present ran in age from the obviously young in years and church responsibility to John Owen, fifty-eight years a Methodist in Detroit.

It was a pleasing coincidence to the audience that all the Congregational churches were holding a similar meeting at exactly the same time to celebrate clearing their buildings of $27,000 in debt. A congratulatory message was sent to the Congregationalists and a similar reply received before the services ended.

In the long run, the best effects of this great, combined drive were not financial at all. It led eventually to the Methodist Union in Detroit, produced a much better spirit between the different congregations, and future Methodist churches were planned for better location and distribution. At that Thanksgiving service, the Rev. John M. Arnold had said it was his opinion that the local Societies had been far too "self-absorbed." Inevitably in considering only local interests, they did not always place a church where it would best serve the larger interests of the Methodist Episcopal Church.

❊   ❊   ❊   ❊   ❊   ❊

Michigan Methodism was fortunate in making three other, lasting achievements in the 8th decade of the 19th century. Bay View, Crystal Springs, and *The Michigan Christian Advocate*, how familiar those names are to most Michigan Methodists today. All three of them were the product of the mid-1870's. And how they have changed since their modest beginnings. Each one had different sponsors. Bay View was to be a Methodist State Camp Meeting established and run by the joint efforts of the Detroit and Michigan Annual Conferences. Crystal

Springs was the work of the Niles District Conference and Ministerial Association. It was not exactly born in the mid-1870's because the southwestern part of the State had held camp meetings from the early days of settlement there. But acquisition of more land and the building of more permanent facilities came about 1875. *The Michigan Christian Advocate* was neither a State, Conference, or District creation. Only by forming a private business corporation of Methodist ministers and laymen in Detroit was a local religious paper started. Both the Michigan and the Detroit Annual Conferences were very cool toward it in its first years.

✻ ✻ ✻ ✻ ✻ ✻

Bay View

The founders of Bay View were Samuel O. Knapp, a Methodist layman, and his pastor, the Rev. Joseph H. McCarty, of the First Methodist Episcopal Church in Jackson. Knapp had an invalid wife and they were searching for a summer place that would relieve her lung condition. They spent the summer of 1874 in Petoskey, then an outpost of about 1200 people in Emmet County.

Deep primeval woods covered two hundred miles of that region and 65% of the inhabitants were Indians. Several small Indian missions labored in the area but not until October, 1873, was the first sermon preached to the white people by the minister appointed to Charlevoix. In 1874, a class of eleven members was organized in Petoskey. Housing was so scarce that meetings were held in a passenger coach of the Grand Rapids and Indiana Railway. Mr. Knapp thoroughly explored the whole region around Petoskey and is said to have discovered the site of Bay View with its natural terraces and fine outlook over Little Traverse Bay.

Presumably during the ensuing winter, Mr. Knapp persuaded his minister in Jackson to accept his plans for Bay View. Mr. McCarty addressed both the Detroit and Michigan Annual Conferences during the first two weeks in September, 1875. He explained that the G.R. and I. Railroad had made an offer of land for a State camp meeting ground. Therefore he asked for appointment of a joint committee drawn from both Conferences. Appointed by the Detroit Annual Conference were E. H. Pilcher, Seth Reed, Robert Bird, and David Preston. Those on the committee from the Michigan Annual Conference were J. H. McCarty, W. H. Brockway, T. H. Jacokes, A. A. Knappen, and L. M. Edmonds. With the single exception of David Preston, the joint committee was composed of experienced ministers of wide reputation. The choice of preachers of such calibre for the committee indicates that the Conferences viewed this new project with sufficient seriousness. Neither could any work of importance in Michigan Methodism then get under way without the services of that layman-banker, David Preston.[10]

On November 9, 1875, the joint committee met for the first time at Jackson First Church. S. O. Knapp was also present. E. H. Pilcher was made temporary President and Seth Reed temporary Secretary. The latter remained as Secretary for thirteen years and also suggested the name BAY VIEW for the camp ground. Pilcher transferred to work in the Canada Conference in 1877 and so William H. Brockway became the second President of the project.

At that first meeting in Jackson, the joint committee drew up articles of incorporation under the Michigan statutes and appointed a Board of Trustees of nine members serving staggered three year terms. It was started with a one year term for one third of the trustees, two years for the second third, and three years for the remaining third. Thus it became a continuous organization. Knapp and Preston were the only lay members and they were both placed in the group of trustees with full three year terms.

That same day the group also stated that, in addition to maintaining a camp meeting ground, they proposed to establish a place for "summer residences" in connection with which religious services might be held and Christian standards of conduct upheld. Michigan and its Methodists were changing when time and money were available to set up summer homes in Christian surroundings presumably for more comfort during the hot weather.

The second meeting was that of the trustees on January 20, 1876, at Grand Rapids. Committees had investigated several sites and the decision was made that day in favor of three hundred acres of land just north of Petoskey offered by the G.R. and I. Railway. It promised to run its tracks a mile from Petoskey to Bay View, to build a station there, and to aid in clearing the land. It also sent two men out that winter, in a cutter sleigh, to visit all the Indians round about and get their titles to the land.

In return to the G. R. and I., the Methodist Episcopal Church was to have a warranty deed in which it promised to spend $10,000 in five years on improving the grounds and to conduct a camp meeting there annually for at least fifteen years. Not until 1890 did the Church have a quitclaim deed to the property. The citizens of Petoskey helped by raising some of the needed funds for improvement.

"A walking session" of the trustees was held on the Bay View camp grounds on May 2, 1876. It must have been strenuous for the forest was

---

[10] The Conference *Minutes* for both Detroit and Michigan from 1875 on usually have brief references to Bay View each year. More enlightening are C. S. Wheeler, *Bay View, 1875-1950*. Seth Reed, *The Story of My Life*, passim. E. H. Pilcher, *Hist. Prot. Mich.*, pp. 437-445. Emma L. Baker, *Stories of Bay View*, pp. 11-55.

full of low growth known then as "shintangle." Specific planning and work must begin for the intention was to hold a camp meeting there that summer. A spot for the pulpit and a public worship area were selected, near where the auditorium is today, and then they began platting of the grounds into blocks and lots. Seth Reed did most of this very hard work. Streets were not named and numbered until 1895. The ground was covered with ashes and small tree stubs at the first camp meeting held the first week in August.

Lumber was both cheap and plentiful so that, by the time the camp meeting opened, a speaker's stand "after the Swiss cottage style" of architecture had been built in addition to the boarding hall and a "lodging barn." Presumably the latter was for the horses. The humans slept in tents. The first year, about twenty tents were erected for the camp meeting. It was estimated that between 500 and 600 people attended.

The reminiscences of old timers make it seem very primitive. One of them slept on shavings and many more on hemlock boughs. Co-operative living certainly went on for one woman remembered "We all borrowed from one another everything, from case knives to dish cloths." Another could never forget the sleeping tents in which eighteen people slept with a curtain in the middle to divide the men's quarters from those of the women. The "outerenders" got scarcely any blankets and not so very much of the hemlock mattresses either.

The camp meeting was much like any other in its program of two to four sermons every day, prayer services at dawn and dusk, and earnest efforts at conversion or attainment of "Christian Perfection." The

The first Camp Meeting at Bay View in 1876.

latter was a second, deeper, religious experience. The opening sermon was preached by E. H. Pilcher. Then, assisted by all the other ministers present, he dedicated the grounds to religious use. In the report that Pilcher made to the Detroit Annual Conference that year, he said that the camp meeting "was as well attended and as profitable as we had any reason to expect."

The first annual meeting of the Michigan Camp Ground Association to elect the trustees was held in the edge of the forest during the week of camp meeting. Members of the Association were the people who had leased a lot and intended to build a cottage. A life membership cost $10 and an annual lease ran from $2 to $10. Years later some of them remembered that they were so few that all were able to sit on the trunk and branches of a fallen hemlock tree. The first cottages were built in 1877 for Samuel O. Knapp, T. R. Damon, William H. Shier, Mark Chittenden, and D. Carpenter.

Perhaps as early as this first Association meeting, plans were laid for a mutually helpful relationship with the tiny Methodist churches of the region. When Robert Bird was appointed to the Petoskey Society at the Conference session a few weeks after the first camp meeting, he was also made the Custodian of Bay View Camp Grounds.

All the northern part of Lower Michigan needed outside help to build churches and establish Methodism strongly. Mr. Bird was supported by both the Annual Conferences in Michigan with modest sums, also by the national Missionary Society, and by the ladies of Central Church in Detroit. He managed to build a modest church in Petoskey in 1877. His Sunday School received books and papers from various other Methodist churches in Michigan. Occasionally the Bay View Camp Meeting took a special collection for the "northern work." But this was always sent to the Michigan Annual Conference Treasurer and carefully divided among several small and struggling churches in Grand Traverse District. Still later a day was set aside during the camp meeting for Methodists living in Grand Traverse District to gather in their own meetings and activities at Bay View.

The trustees expanded their efforts for 1877. Some ten thousand circulars, describing the attractive location and health advantages of Bay View, were sent out. Besides pure water, they boasted of "air free from all malaria, as it comes sweeping across a hundred miles of fresh water from the west and northwest."

Construction work began as soon as the weather allowed. In addition to the five cottages built in 1877, the Bay View House was built, being two stories in height and 25 by 75 feet on the ground. This boarding house or hotel was repeatedly enlarged until 1929 when it burned to the ground.

In addition to the second camp meeting, plans were laid for a general Sunday School Congress to be held the week previous to the other gathering. A large committee of ministers and laymen from all over the State was to have charge and all Sunday School workers were invited "irrespective of denominations."

Conditions were still too primitive for some people. Circulars gave warning to bring your own blankets, pillows, carpet, and bed tick. Lodgings, provided by the Association, were wooden bunks and straw. Years later Seth Reed told of a man who came with a friend and a tent outfit the second year. He trudged around in the woods for some time trying to find the trustee. When located he was busy chopping down the huge hemlocks on his own lot. The traveller and his friend were both sure the place was "a sell, just roping folks in here."

Even though conditions were primitive and the camp meeting routine that of others held in Michigan, some were deeply impressed by the surroundings. An "old-timer" wrote later:

> I shall never forget . . . the evening service at the first camp meeting. The scene was worthy of an artist. Torches lighted up the earnest faces of the crowd around the speakers' stand; beyond stood a circle of Indians like bronze statues against a background of gleaming white tents. The sighing of the wind through the giant trees of the impenetrable forest about us, the sound of the waves on the shore, the fervent responses, the weeping of penitents, made a thrilling accompaniment to the solemn words of the preacher.[11]

Crystal Springs

Crystal Springs was not the only District camp meeting in Michigan at that time. The Kalamazoo and Coldwater Districts held a combined camp meeting at Wasepi in an oak grove near a small lake for some years. The one in 1880 was long remembered for having drawn over two thousand people on Sunday to hear six preachers. It was felt an extra effort was needed just then because the famous atheist, Colonel Robert Ingersoll, was to lecture at Schoolcraft soon.[12]

Crystal Springs had a long history of meetings in various places on the Niles District. As early as 1860, the Ministerial Association of Niles District began to look for a permanent camp site. A site on the Dowagiac River with natural springs looked attractive to the ministers. It was located between Niles and Dowagiac about 5½ miles from the latter town. Some wooden buildings were erected but unfortunately it suffered a bad fire in 1868 which destroyed the buildings and the grove in which the meetings had been held.

Some rebuilding had been done by Presiding Elder Carmi C. Olds. A small chapel was erected in addition to a two story building with a

---

[11] Emma L. Baker, *Stories of Bay View*, p. 13. Name of old-timer not given.
[12] From the history of the Three Rivers Methodist Episcopal Church. Found in Michigan Conference hist. coll., Albion College Library.

The Crystal Springs Camp Ground near Dowagiac was the first District Camp meeting in Michigan. It was greatly improved and became a large and successful Camp meeting under the leadership of Rev. James W. Robinson, Presiding Elder of the Niles District, 1874-78.

dining hall on the first floor and sleeping rooms upstairs. A State Fish Hatchery was located at Crystal Springs from 1873 to 1878 and was responsible for some improvement in the grounds. In 1874, a "tent-holders meeting" decided that all the camp meeting ground must be fenced and the area within the circle of tents be provided with five thousand seats. A police force must be at the gates and around the fence. An admission fee of 25¢ for the week or 10¢ for a single visit was to be charged. Some sort of disorder or else so large a congregation that it got out of control must have occurred. For that meeting declared the changes listed must be made or "our groves will be destroyed and we will have a disorderly congregation."

The Rev. James W. Robinson was later regarded as "peculiarly successful" as the Presiding Elder of Niles District from 1874 to 1878. During his four years "on the District" three thousand people became members of the Methodist Episcopal churches there. He edited and published a *Niles District Record* which began as a quarterly and then was issued monthly in 1877 and 1878 until the end of his term at Conference time in September. He had much to do with many changes and improvements at Crystal Springs. He even turned the monthly *District Record* into a *Daily Record* during the ten days of the annual camp meeting in mid-August. After Robinson died in 1881, his Conference Memoir said, "Crystal Springs became the most numerously attended, orderly, and successful gathering of its kind in the State under his management."[13]

A District Board of Trustees was created for Crystal Springs. Many cottages were built and the fencing and seating done as had been planned. The new Trustees promptly bought twenty acres more of land and put in a water works involving a steam engine which delivered the water to several hydrants scattered around the grounds.

The place drew unbelievable crowds immediately. It was claimed that eight thousand attended in 1877. Supplementary field meetings were needed to accommodate all the crowd. Robinson had added a Temperance Day to the program and this drew the Temperance Societies, who attended in a body on that day. A Woman's Day, featuring mothers' meetings in the tents was also successful. Also Children's Day meetings were usually held. Every year, special excursion trains were run to Pokagon, some two and one-half miles from the camp.

Examination of the *Daily Record* for the years 1875 through 1880 leaves the impression that Crystal Springs Camp Meeting was run like an army. Bells rang at intervals all day, precise occupation was provided for every waking moment, and zeal was displayed in all aspects of the work. In 1880, the day's program was as follows:

> Rising bell 6 A.M. Tent worship 6.30 A.M. Breakfast 7 A.M. Warning Bell 15 minutes before each service. Calling bell at hour of service. ·Prayer or Bible reading 8 A.M. Preaching 10 A.M. Class meeting 1 P.M. Children's meeting 5 P.M. Mother's meeting in the tents. 5 P.M. Young People's meeting 6 P.M. Preaching 7.30 P.M. Evening bell 9.45 P.M. Closing bell 10 P.M. when the gates will be closed and hush come over the encampment.

How did either the ministers or the audiences endure all the preaching? Music was provided by a cornetist and organist. The sheriff of Cass County took charge of policing the gates. Six ministers divided the responsibility for the preaching services. In addition, committees on "grounds and supplies, corals (*sic*) and barns, ticket office and foot gates" functioned busily.

The problems centered around what might be called creeping worldliness. A general supply store, soda fountain and barber shop were allowed on the grounds. Carts with fresh fruit and vegetables for sale

[13] For memoir of J. W. Robinson see Michigan Annual Conference *Minutes* for 1881, pp. 67-68. A bound volume of most of his *Niles District Records* is in the Michigan Conference historical collection, Albion College Library. It is valuable not only for the current notices but also because he ran a series of pieces about the history of many churches in that region. It is surprising to find what an interesting little paper it was. Apparently it was not continued by the next Presiding Elder. See also Fanny Springsteen, *The First Hundred Years of Crystal Springs*. This is a typed article found in the Michigan Conference historical collection, Albion College Library.

toured the grounds mornings. None of this commercial activity was ever allowed on Sundays. Consequently some men tried to sell their wares just outside the gates. Finally the police stopped all outside commercial activity as the law forbade such transactions within two miles of a camp meeting.

Undoubtedly a religious atmosphere so sustained for a week or ten days would powerfully influence many people. Some of the sermons were printed in full in the *Daily Record* for the people to reflect upon afterwards. It was said of an 8 A.M. prayer meeting on August 12, 1880, "Divine unction was there." After one of the evening sermons during the week, a consecration meeting was held. "The ministers and the fathers and mothers in Israel came into the altar and the rest of the congregation fell on their knees . . . a full salvation meeting was evident. People were intent to seek for the sanctifying grace."

Complete abstinence was strongly advocated in the Temperance meetings. In the mothers' meetings, it was declared that the "farmer's cider barrel is the bane of the temperance cause and a wicked gate to a drunkard's life." The mothers were plainly told to make their mince pies without cider. On another day, the District W.F.M.S. met with a returned missionary, Miss Lucy Hoag, speaking on the needs of the work in China.

In 1875, a minister of the Southern Methodist Episcopal Church, Dr. Warren, preached to the camp meeting and also in the Niles Church. He was the President of Warren College in Kentucky. Being of a genial nature, he was very well received and Presiding Elder Robinson noted this in the Niles *District Record* with the comment, "The blood of atonement avails to quench the flames of war and make the north and south one in Jesus Christ."

Occasionally in the Niles *District Record* Presiding Elder Robinson made short comments that reveal conditions in the Methodist Episcopal Church then. Perhaps this was done when bits of space remained to be filled just before going to press. In 1875, he stated that many of the churches were burdened with large debts which he called "cancers engaged in destructive eating of the Church." A great many curative plasters had been tried but "only one will cure — Greenbacks."

In an editorial on Amusements, he discussed croquet, finally deciding that it was "not wrong or injurious if used properly but, if indulged, it can become seriously reprehensible and lead to neglect of one's duties including religion."

Perhaps his most amusing bit was on "The Minister we want." Published in September, 1875, it said:

1. We don't want last year's preacher.
2. We don't want a temperance or missionary fanatic.
3. We don't want the old or invalid.
4. We do want one who is studious and visits most of the time.

Just one glimpse of what it was like to be a minister in Michigan in hard times appeared in the *District Record*. Robinson estimated in 1877 that ministerial salaries that had been $800 to $1,000 were now down to $400 to $500. Depression afflicted the whole countryside. The number of first-class, desirable appointments had sharply decreased in the last few years at the same time that the number of "elderly ministers with dependent, worthy families had increased." Only about fifty of the charges that two hundred and fifty ministers were available to fill were at all desirable. Disappointments would not be the fault of the Bishop or of the Cabinet. He had heard Bishop Merrill say that he "dreaded to read the appointments." But Robinson felt that most of the men "accepted the situation in a Christian spirit."

Birth of the *Michigan Christian Advocate*

Only in the Adrian District under the Detroit Annual Conference was a paper similar to the Niles *District Record* published. And within six months of its birth, that had been expanded into a paper intended for the Methodists of the entire State. Three Methodist ministers, Orrin Whitmore, Isaac N. Elwood, and John M. Arnold were the men immediately responsible for its creation. The project had been discussed occasionally for years.

When ill health prevented him from preaching, the Rev. James V. Watson established at Adrian a small paper called the *Michigan Christian Advocate*. He supported himself and his family by publishing this paper in the years from 1850 to 1852. Then he persuaded the General Conference to establish an official paper, The *Northwestern Christian Advocate*, at Chicago in 1852. Watson became its first editor and his Michigan publication was given up. In the Detroit Annual Conference at Romeo in 1863, John Arnold had stirred up debate about having a local paper and then, a year or two later, brought up the same question at a Methodist State Convention in Jackson.[14]

From 1872 to 1875, the Presiding Elder of Adrian District was Orrin Whitmore.. Among the ministers of his District was Isaac N. Elwood stationed at Morenci from 1872 to 1874. Both men died in 1887. In 1930, Mrs. Elwood still remembered that "it was in the study of the Morenci parsonage where we were then living that plans were made by my husband and Rev. Orrin Whitmore . . . to start the publication of the Adrian *District Methodist*. Both men wrote articles and editorials

---

[14] No copies of that first *Michigan Christian Advocate* of 1850-52 have been found. From references to it which Watson made in the *Northwestern*, it was definitely anti-slavery in tone. See pamphlet by John E. Marvin, *The Advocate Story*. E. H. Pilcher, *Hist. Prot. Mich.*, p. 433. Autobiography of John M. Arnold, M. A. Boughton, editor. Found in Detroit Annual Conference hist. coll., Adrian College Library.

for it." Only one copy of this paper, the second issue in November, 1873, is known to have survived. It was a four page publication 13 by 18 inches in size. It cost 50¢ a year and was printed on the steam presses of the *Adrian Daily and Weekly Times and Expositor*.

The content of this one lone issue of the *District Methodist* is interesting. The leading and longest piece, on the front page, is an account of a recent meeting in New York City of ministers and laymen from "every shade of Protestant belief." This almost ecumenical gathering was agreed that the greatest enemies of Protestantism were Romanism and Unitarianism. The Michigan ministers then were evidently disturbed by the evolution theories and writings of Darwin, Huxley, and Spencer. Warning was given in the lead article on "Evangelical Alliance" that it was dangerous to attempt an answer to "scientific atheism." Another article on the first page was headed "Preach the Gospel to every Creature." This was one of the commands of Christ to his Disciples. But He had not told them to teach science, art, or literature. Ministers might refute "the monkey theories" in sermons until they were exhausted yet not convert a single soul.

The paper gave two full pages to a three-day District Conference held at Tecumseh in October, 1873. Popular amusements were of great concern to that meeting. The attitude displayed was much like that of the Annual Conferences. Strong disapproval was expressed of almost all the entertainments of that day. Especially condemned were the theater, dancing, horse racing, and cards. The editors also found room in their modest paper for a few notices of other Protestant churches. One of them stated that the Adrian Episcopal Church had raised $59 for southern sufferers from yellow fever.

As far as the surviving records show, only three issues of the Adrian *District Methodist* were ever published. Mrs. Elwood said many years later that it was printed until the *Michigan Christian Advocate* was started and then "merged into it." Unfortunately, she was not sure whether that action occurred in 1873 or 1874.[15]

John M. Arnold was the Sunday School Agent and also the manager of a Methodist Book Depository in Detroit. He had been promoting plans for a statewide Methodist paper for some time and making speeches on the subject whenever and wherever opportunity offered. He had

[15] Letter of Mrs. I. N. Elwood to Rev. N. N. Clark on Nov. 19, 1930, about the *Advocate* is in a scrapbook belonging to the Detroit Annual Conference hist. coll., Adrian College Library. The copies of the *Advocates* from 1876 to 1920 are in the Burton Collection, Detroit Public Library. The issues are not complete after 1877 and 1878 for the years through 1883. The original copy of the Adrian *District Methodist* is in the Detroit Annual Conference hist. coll., Adrian College Library. Its first page was reproduced as cover of *Michigan Christian Advocate*, April 16, 1964. Vol. XCI. John Marvin, "A Bit of History and a Mystery," in same issue, pp. 4-7.

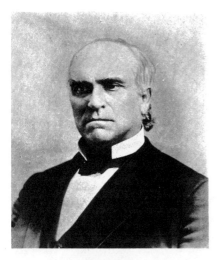

Orrin Whitmore (1823-87) served on frontier circuits from 1845; he became a prominent minister and served as presiding Elder of the Adrian District 1872-76. He was the founder of the publication of the Adrian District Methodist which was enlarged and made the Michigan Christian Advocate in January 1874. He directed Methodist relief in the thumb, following the forest fires of 1881.

John M. Arnold (1824-84) was a prominent minister and presiding Elder of the Owosso District, 1856-59. He had charge of the Methodist Book Depository established in Detroit in 1863; he was one of the founders of the Michigan Christian Advocate and was its editor at the time of his death.

advocated such a paper at a State Convention and later at a Preachers' Association meeting in May, 1873.

Some time in the ensuing summer, Arnold and Whitmore agreed to unite the Adrian and Detroit Districts in publishing a State Methodist paper. One of them might have known of Watson's earlier efforts in Adrian. They quickly agreed to call the new paper the *Michigan Christian Advocate*. In his Autobiography, Arnold said Whitmore already had "a Journal for his own District." Either the numbering of the sole surviving issue of the Adrian *District Methodist* is incorrect or Arnold had forgotten the exact date when he did get Whitmore's cooperation.

Some difficulty was experienced in getting enough money together

James H. Potts (1848-1942) was editor of the Michigan Christian Advocate from 1884 to 1916, following an earlier ministerial career in the Michigan Conference. A poet, and greatly beloved, he was a member of the Conference for over 72 years.

to begin. The scheme of a joint stack company with a capital of $10,000 divided into one hundred shares was tried. The Detroit Annual Conference met during the first week in September, 1873. But Arnold said the scheme did not do well at all at Conference. No reference to his plan was made in the Conference *Minutes* of that year. Arnold and Whitmore may have approached the ministers privately and individually.

Not until December, 1873, or possibly December, 1874, was the Methodist Publishing House Company organized and ready to do business. Arnold said the Company was formed in December, 1873. In his *History of Protestantism in Michigan,* E. H. Pilcher repeatedly stated that the Company was formed in 1874 and issued its first paper in January, 1875. Quite recently, discovery was made of a copy of the *Michigan Christian Advocate* for January, 1874, labeled Volume I, No. 4. The chances are that Whitmore and Elwood simply counted on from those three issues of the Adrian *District Methodist* in 1873. Then Pilcher, usually so accurate, evidently made a mistake. If this is true, then the *Michigan Christian Advocate* never had a first issue.[16]

The Articles of Association of the Methodist Publishing Company

[16] The first page of the first issue of the *Michigan Christian Advocate* (the so-called No. 4) was reproduced on page 4 of the *Michigan Christian Advocate* for April 16, 1964. See again also autobiography of Arnold, Marvin's pamphlet on the *Advocate,* and Pilcher's *Hist. Prot. Mich.*

show that twenty-eight men were stockholders, half ministers and half laymen. The largest number of shares held by any one man was thirty, taken by Erasmus D. Allen of Morenci. He is believed to have been a layman. John Arnold took eleven shares, the next largest number. Orrin Whitmore took five, Elijah Pilcher two and I. N. Elwood one share. Eleven men took one share costing them $100. John Owen, so active a layman then, held two shares. Arnold noted, in his autobiography, that $5,000 of the subscription intended to be $10,000 was paid in during the first year of the Company's existence.

The Articles of Association state that their intention was to run a job printing business in addition to publishing a religious newspaper. This double task was soon found too burdensome and the extra printing was dropped. The main office of the new paper was located in Detroit.

In the first meeting to organize the corporation, Pilcher was chosen President of the Company, Arnold Vice President, and George Robinson Secretary-Treasurer. Whitmore was continued as Editor and Lewis R. Fiske became Associate Editor. This arrangement lasted only a year or two because Pilcher transferred to work in Canada and Fiske became the Editor. But the latter was elected President of Albion College in 1877 and so John Arnold, after serving as Associate Editor and Business Manager, became the chief Editor. He was soon to receive valuable assistance from James H. Potts. He transferred from the Michigan Annual Conference to become the "Office Editor." Potts was the most influential for the longest time of any of the early workers on the *Advocate*. He served in its office from 1877 to 1917.

Those early numbers of the *Michigan Christian Advocate* resemble a newspaper rather than a modern magazine. The size of each page was about 18 by 24 inches. The four pages were very closely columned and no pictures broke the monotony of the fine print. The advertisements were often illustrated with drawings or diagrams. All the religious press of the Methodist Episcopal Church then accepted patent medicine ads that look fraudulent or vulgar to us today. Standards have improved in that respect.

The front page usually contained the religious articles on such topics as revivals, success, "Wanted — good men," and "Intermediate State." This last one tried to deal with the question of where the soul was between death and the last judgment. It managed to criticize evolution and the Catholic idea of purgatory in the course of a short article.

On the inside pages of the *Advocate* the local news was usually found. Revivals, protracted meetings, the overpayment of a pastor's quarterly claim, or the gift of some silver cutlery or a tea set to the minister and his wife, notices of a course of winter lectures for the benefit of some good cause, deaths or marriages among the ministers and their families were among the items most often reported from the small towns of both Annual Conferences and both peninsulas in the *Michigan Christian Advocate.*

Judging from the standing committee reports and the resolutions adopted, in the Annual Conference sessions between 1873 and 1880, the ministers were not at first too enthusiastic about the plan for a Methodist State religious paper. The Michigan Annual Conference was more lukewarm than the Detroit was. This may have been due to the fact that ministers of the Adrian and Detroit districts were founders of this local *Advocate.*

Yet even in the Detroit Annual Conference of 1874, opposition to the establishment of a local religious paper developed. Lewis R. Fiske offered three resolutions to the Detroit session on September 8, 1874. One approved publication of the *Michigan Christian Advocate,* another urged wide circulation all over the State, and the third recommended it be changed from a monthly to a weekly paper.

These three resolutions had not been through the periodicals committee but neither had the substitute offered at once by James Smart. A former Presiding Elder and appointed at Port Huron that year, Smart's resolution said, "We cannot, as a Conference, take any responsibility in the publication of the *Michigan Christian Advocate* and therefore respectfully decline to take any action in reference to it." After much debate, Smart's resolution was laid on the table and Fiske's adopted.

The Michigan Annual Conference apparently was not even very interested in the new paper. On September 12, 1874, Mr. Fiske presented to the session at Kalamazoo exactly the same resolutions as those just adopted at Romeo. He asked their endorsement "if consistent with their views of right and propriety." The matter was referred to a committee of three with Israel Cogshall as the chairman. The committee reported, on September 14, that it concurred in Fiske's resolutions and recommended that the paper be sold at a price not exceeding $1.25. Its report was "not adopted."

The Conferences at that time were concerned about improving the quality of the general Methodist religious press. In 1872, the Michigan Conference committee on periodicals had made a three page report urging larger, more expensive, and more "sanctified Papers." Above all, the ministers wanted to see a great "connectional" paper. This would circulate throughout the Church and discuss all issues, theological or political, in a lofty yet Methodist way. It was hoped the New York *Christian Advocate* might so develop.

Many ministers were also much disturbed by the so-called "premium swindle." Such was competition for subscriptions then that many papers or cheap magazines offered either "a beautiful chromo" or a brightly bound book with every year's subscription. In 1874, the Michigan Annual Conference committee on periodicals denounced premiums as "an unmitigated curse to the cause of true religion." What was needed was "good, honest, solid religious reading . . . at a price that will defy premium competition."

It may be that the incorporation and organization of the Methodist Publishing Company took place after the Conferences of 1874 at the same time that the publication shifted from a monthly to a weekly schedule of publication. This may be why the Detroit Annual Conference in 1875 accepted a resolution offered by W. W. Washburne from the floor after the periodicals committee report had been accepted. It originally made no mention of the *Michigan Christian Advocate*. Immediately after the report passed, Washburne brought up a resolution which said, "We are highly gratified with the success of the *Michigan Christian Advocate* and . . . we give it our hearty support and will present its claims to our people." This was immediately adopted with little discussion.

The Michigan Annual Conference in 1876 finally took notice of the new periodical in a report that first acknowledged the claims of the official periodicals and then said:

> We will, with pleasure, order the *Michigan Christian Advocate* for our people whenever desired, as we believe that, with its 5,000 subscribers, and the able manner in which it is edited, it is calculated to aid in building up our common Methodism.

At the Conference sessions of 1878, the Methodist Publishing Company presented $60 to the Superannuated Preachers Fund of the Detroit Annual Conference and $25 to the similar Fund in the Michigan Annual Conference. Thus this local *Advocate* began a policy for the use of its profits which the present editor of the paper, John E. Marvin, estimates has brought at least $93,000 to the ministerial pension funds of the two Annual Conferences. There is some feeling today that this money could have been more advantageously used to build more adequate quarters for the paper and to make the *Advocate* more independent. But who can tell how much good the pension funds have done the elderly ministers who could rarely save anything from their modest salaries toward their needs in retirement.[17]

Both Annual Conferences adopted resolutions on their local paper in 1878. The Detroit Annual Conference periodicals committee said in part:

> Our Michigan Advocate meets a felt want in two respects, — it gives local news and presents the needs of the Church in various portions of the State as no paper of a more general character could do, and its cheapness brings it within the reach of some who could not afford a

[17] Statement by Mr. Marvin found in pamphlet "The Advocate Story" pp. 5-6. Material from articles by Elmer Houser in 1933 in the same *Advocate* used in pamphlet. Detroit Annual Conference *Minutes* for 1878, pp. 16, 36. Michigan Annual Conference *Minutes* for 1878, pp. 11, 30.

more expensive paper . . . it should not displace the official paper in
the homes of those who are too penurious to pay the additional dollar
which the official paper costs. About 2,900 copies of this paper circu-
lates in Detroit Conference.

The similar committee in the Michigan Annual Conference said:

> We would gratefully acknowledge the courtesies which we, as a Con-
> ference and as individual pastors have received from the Michigan
> Christian Advocate . . . . We should however, deprecate allowing even
> this excellent paper to supercede in any measure the papers which are
> published under the direct control of the church.

The *Michigan Christian Advocate* made a strong beginning. In a
State with a total population of 1,184,059 in 1870 and 46,864 Methodist
Episcopalians in full membership in 1876, this new religious weekly
had achieved at least 5,000 subscribers within three years after it was
founded. In 1879, the Michigan Annual Conference periodicals committee referred to "our own loyal, useful and flourishing Michigan
Christian Advocate," discussed the evils of the secular press, and concluded, "Every family on our pastoral charges ought to receive one or
more denominational papers. With this conviction in our hearts, we
should nominate no rest for our feet until such a policy is in practical
operation."

    ❋   ❋   ❋   ❋   ❋   ❋

A few statistics show how Methodism developed in Michigan during
hard times. A full Methodist Episcopal membership of 41,696 in 1872
had grown to 53,477 in 1880. The Michigan Annual Conference grew
almost twice as much as the Detroit Annual Conference did, having
an increase of 7,330 to the Detroit's 4,451. Due to the inadequacy of
the statistics kept by the Methodist Protestants and also the incomplete
sets of their *Minutes* only a rough estimate can be offered. About 2,600
Methodist Protestants in the State of Michigan in 1873 had grown to
around 3,500 in 1880.

Both Methodist Episcopal Conferences together had 394½ churches
in 1872 and 572½ in 1880. Again the Michigan Annual Conference's
growth was greater. It had 105 more buildings to the Detroit's increase of 73. This really is amazing in such depression times as the
1870's. The building of parsonages still lagged behind the church construction. The total number of parsonages in 1872 was 241 which had
been built up to 291 in 1880. Of that total increase of 50, the Detroit
Annual Conference built 27 and the Michigan 23. The Michigan Conference of the Methodist Protestant Church had 24 Circuits and 20
Missions in 1873 but only 15 churches and 16 parsonages in both groups
of charges. Of course, most of the buildings were on the Circuits, only
one Mission at Pontiac having both a church and a parsonage. The

one at Capac had a church and Fremont a parsonage. By 1880, the M.P.'s had 45 Circuits and Missions with 32 churches and 24 parsonages. Nine of the total enjoyed the use of both church and parsonage on the same charge.

As to Sunday Schools, the M.P.'s had 48 in 1873 with 390 teachers and 1960 "Scholars." By 1880, they had 87 with 797 teachers and officers to deal with 3299 Scholars. In the Methodist Episcopal Sunday Schools of the State, 798 separate Sunday Schools in 1872 had become 869 in 1880, the increase being 61 in Detroit Conference and only ten in the Michigan Conference. A total of 8,249 officers and teachers in 1872 had become 9,613 in 1880. The increase was divided 838 in the Michigan Conference and 526 in the Detroit Conference. The total number of scholars in 1872 was 51,258 and by 1880 had become 66,596. However, the increase in each Conference was more nearly equal this time as the Detroit Conference had gained 7,838 scholars and the Michigan Conference 7,500.

The visible, statistical evidence indicates Methodism was a living, growing Church, particularly in its Sunday School work. Whether the Church was also growing in a deeper, religious sense is almost impossible to determine. Certainly the Methodist Episcopal Church was on the verge of great change but how was not yet fully clear.

PART V

THE UNITED STATES, MICHIGAN, AND METHODISM

1880 – 1900

In the last two decades of the 19th century, the material growth of the United States and Michigan was amazing. By the census, or any other measurable way of getting at the facts, constant increase was visible.

The population of the United States in 1880 was 50,155,783 but by 1900 it had grown to 75,994,575. The State of Michigan had a population of 1,636,937 in 1880 which had become 2,420,982 in 1900. Urban development around Detroit was like that occurring all over the north. Michigan's largest city more than doubled in population in those years from 1880 to 1900. A city of 116,340 in 1880 had become one of 285,704 in 1900. Detroit had risen to the 13th in size in the United States from the 17th in 1880. Also in 1900 its population was of mixed origin nationally. It had the highest percentage of people who could not speak any English – 11.98% – of any of the fifteen largest cities in the entire United States.

Statehood was almost completely established within the Continental United States too. Seven western States joined the Union. In 1889 the Dakotas, Montana, and Washington, in 1890 Idaho and Wyoming, and in 1896 Utah were admitted making a total of forty-five. Mostly by the Spanish-American War, the insular annexations were added in 1898 and 1899. Among these were Hawaii, Guam, Puerto Rico, the Philippine Islands, and American Samoa.

Republicanism was not quite so dominant as it had been in the first quarter century after its founding. Grover Cleveland, first Democratic President since before the Civil War, was first elected in 1884, renominated but not elected in 1888, and then reelected in 1892. Michigan elected a Democratic Governor in 1890. Edwin B. Winans was the first of that party to attain the chief executive's position in Michigan in forty years.

Political corruption was prevalent all over the United States then. But Michigan citizens were as shocked as the rest of the country when a disappointed office-seeker shot President Garfield in June, 1881. After weeks of suffering, he died in September. The entire United States mourned him. One result was passage of the first Federal Civil Service Act in 1883. Employees of the Treasury and Postoffice came under its provisions.

The passage of the Interstate Commerce Act in 1887 and the Sherman Antitrust Act in 1890 were indications of a changing attitude toward economic problems on the part of the Federal government. The tariff was also a concern that was constant in the last two decades of the 19th century. One real attempt to lower the tariff, made by Cleveland in 1888, was a failure. All the rest of the laws on this subject in the 1890's — McKinley, Wilson-Gorman, and Dingley — were exceedingly high and overprotective on many articles. Today it is thought that these tariffs aided the great fortunes then in the making and also increased the cost of living for ordinary citizens.

The 1880's were reasonably prosperous for most Americans except some of the farmers. But the 1890's were a different story. Another period of hard times centered around the year 1893 with lingering aftereffects much like the Panic of 1873. Imperialistic interest, which was growing, and then the Spanish-American War probably helped the return of prosperity around 1900.

The Industrial Revolution was developing rapidly throughout the middle west in the last part of the 19th century. Inventions were being made almost too quickly for the ordinary citizen to comprehend how they were changing the United States. Among the inventions of the 1880's were the electric fan, the electric iron, the box kodak, the fountain pen, incandescent gas lights, a process for producing aluminum cheaply, the first practical phonograph, and the adding machine. The first United States built automobiles appeared in small numbers in the 1890's. Ready-to-eat cereals began to be produced in 1893. The first of these products were grapenuts and shredded wheat. Wireless telegraphy was developed by Marconi in 1895. Rubber heels were patented by Humphrey O'Sullivan in 1889 and the first canned soup was also made that year.

Along with inventions for making life easier came almost continuous labor troubles. Samuel Gompers organized the American Federation of Labor in December, 1886. Strikes accompanied by violence were common in these decades. The Haymarket riots in 1886 in Chicago, the Homestead steel strike in Pennsylvania in 1892, and the Pullman strike on the railroads in 1893-1894 were the worst. A general goal was establishment of the ten-hour day for labor. Detroit underwent a serious strike by its street railway employees in 1891 for a ten-hour day and a raise in pay. A struggle to obtain municipal ownership of the street railways was also involved.

The changes and disturbances of that time produced a number of reform societies and third parties. Among the latter were the Greenbackers and Free Silverites with notions about the issuance of more cheap money. The Prohibition Party was also active and the Populists flourished briefly in the Nineties. A few Socialists and Single Taxers were also articulate about their ideas.

The beginnings of unified social aid may be seen in the organization of the American Red Cross in May, 1881, and in Detroit, an Association of Charities was formally organized in April, 1880.

Industrial development in Michigan in these decades was rapid. The manufactured products of Detroit alone in 1880 totalled more than $33,000,000. In general, the industries producing the most wealth for Michigan were extractive in nature: the enormous amounts of copper and iron mined in the Upper Peninsula, the lumber output of more than four billion board feet in 1888, and the salt extracted in the Thumb area. All this compensated in part for the widespread losses due to the great fires of 1881 which left a huge "Burnt Area." One of the largest manufacturing establishments in Michigan was the Peninsular Stove Company set up in Detroit in 1881. The first woven wire fences were produced in Adrian in 1883.

Improvements in transportation and communication also continued. In 1881, the Wabash Railroad completed its tracks to Detroit and the first through train from St. Louis arrived there. In 1884, the Michigan Central Railroad opened a new depot in Detroit and then, in 1893, use of a Union depot in Fort Street started. In 1881, railroad car ferry service was begun between the Upper and Lower Peninsulas. The Grand Trunk Railroad completed a tunnel between Port Huron and Sarnia, Ontario, in 1891. The next year the car ferries of the Ann Arbor Railroad began to run between Frankfort and Kewaunee, Wisconsin. In 1881, the Soo Canal and Locks were given to the United States government by the State of Michigan. The Federal government built an additional lock that same year and added another one in 1896. Michigan had certainly lost her isolation of pioneer days.[1]

Within Michigan, the coming of the electric street car and the bicycle helped local transportation. Horse-drawn street cars had long been used and did not entirely disappear from the streets of Detroit

[1] Dates are drawn from either the "Michigan Chronology" given by F. C. Bald, *Michigan in Four Centuries,* pp. 472-473, or from the 250-year chronology in *Detroit in Its World Setting,* pp. 155-193, by Detroit Public Library.

until 1896. But the Highland Park Railway had begun operating its electric cars on Woodward Avenue in 1886. The first electric interurban cars began to run in Michigan in the 1890's. A net work of lines connecting most of the towns of this State was laid in the last decade of the 19th century but their greatest use was in the first decade of the 20th century. The bicycle came into common use at that same time. The League of American Wheelmen was formed in 1880.

Larger organizations and extensions of lines and facilities meant improved communications for the United States and Michigan too. In 1881, the Western Union Telegraph was formed by the consolidation of the Western, American, Atlantic, and Pacific telegraph companies. In 1885, the American Telephone and Telegraph Company was organized. In 1893, long distance telephone service from Detroit to Chicago and New York City was attained. The city of Detroit had about four thousand telephones at that time.

An interest in organized sports and outdoor games was also developing in ways unknown to early pioneers. The bicycle and the streetcar were the sources of much entertainment. Group street car rides were popular in the 1890's. The first professional baseball was played in Detroit in 1881. The U.S. Lawn Tennis Association was founded that same year. Basketball was invented in 1892. And golf was first played in the United States in 1888. It was regarded as a rich man's game for many years. Roller-skating was also a new craze.

As reading matter for one's idle moments, cheap or yellow journalism developed in the 1890's, increasing through the rivalry of Pulitzer and Hearst just before the Spanish-American War. The *Ladies Home Journal* was founded in 1883. The poetry of James Whitcomb Riley was first published in the 1880's with ever-increasing popularity. Many a parlor table displayed an illustrated edition of his complete poems. Ben Hur was published in 1880, became an enormous best-seller and was dramatized in 1889. The Detroit Museum of Art was incorporated in 1885, bought a site at Jefferson and Hastings, began to build, and opened its first displays in September, 1888.

❊   ❊   ❊   ❊   ❊   ❊

Such profound economic and social changes inevitably influenced most religious denominations. Methodism was in a position to be quickly and widely affected by the industrial developments of that time. It has been said that, in the year 1880, Methodism was "the most evenly distributed church in the land." The circuit rider system received the credit for this achievement.

In the entire United States, all the branches of Methodism had about 3,305,000 members. The northern Methodist Episcopal Church had 1,742,922 members divided into 89 Annual Conferences. The southern branch had 832,175 members in 39 Annual Conferences. The Methodist

Protestants had 44 Annual Conferences with 130,000 members. Three groups of Negro Methodists had at least 600,000 members.[2]

Inevitably Methodism was growing in worldly wealth, in fine churches, in college buildings, in paid professional choirs, in organized national boards and commissions, and in demands for more education for its ministers and more democracy in its operations.

The oldtime institutions, geared to the achievement of individual conversions, were still in use but the zeal and fire once so evident were disappearing. The Class meetings were held on Sundays after the morning service, if held at all. Older members kept up the Classes but complained often that the spirit was not what it used to be. So also they said of camp meetings and revivals.

The professional evangelist was strong in the land for this was the heyday of the work of Dwight L. Moody. Professional advance preparation and aid in conducting revivals were widely in use. The summer camp meeting in tents in the woods for a week or two was changing into a middle class summer resort with permanent frame cottages, popular lectures on secular topics, handicraft classes, and religious services mostly held on Sundays. The business meeting was gradually taking the place of the prayer meeting. And the trustees of the church and parsonage properties were becoming more important than the Stewards and Class leaders. Ritual and formalism were creeping into the Sunday services in a way unknown in earlier Methodism.

The dislike of the recent ways and the uneasiness about the views held by the modern wing of the ministers led to the "Holiness Movement." This aimed to restore the older, heart religion. It was organized in 1867 in a camp meeting at Vineland, New Jersey, under the name "National Camp-Meeting Association for the Promotion of Holiness." This was intended to be undenominational but received most of its support from Methodists. It circulated various periodicals and organized State Holiness Camp Meetings. Much was made of attaining Christian perfection by receiving the second blessing. This movement was strongest in the 1890's in the rural areas and small villages of the west and south. Eventually many of the Holiness Associations separated into small pentecostal sects. The most important of some twenty-five of these was the Church of the Nazarene.[3]

The great need of a special organization to work with young people was widely felt in the Methodist Episcopal Church then. The Church Lyceum had flourished in the eastern United States in the 1870's. This was mostly absorbed by another young people's group called the Oxford League in 1884. At the same time, the Young People's Meth-

---

[2] All statistics taken from W. W. Sweet, *Meth. Am. Hist.*, pp. 332, 334.
[3] A good summary of the Holiness Movement is found in W. W. Sweet"s *Meth. Am. Hist.*, pp. 341-345.

odist Alliance was formed in Illinois, the Young People's Christian League in Boston, and the Methodist Young People's Union in Detroit.

All five of these societies sent delegates to a great meeting at Central Church in Cleveland in 1889. Out of this meeting, came the Epworth League, which spread rapidly across the northern United States and was officially approved by the General Conference in 1892. At the end of seven years, the Epworth League had 16,302 local societies. All were organized under four departments. Their names indicate their nature being Spiritual work, Mercy and Help, Literary, and Social work. Junior Epworth Leagues were also formed. The range of work of all these groups was really with young to middle-aged adults if the photographs of the local Epworth Leagues are to be trusted. Perhaps it was the mode of dress prevalent then but many of the members in the pictured groups look extremely mature.[4]

Modification of the itinerant circuit rider system continued to be demanded in the larger city churches. Change had last been made in 1864 when the two-year limit on an appointment was raised to three years. In 1888, it was lifted again to five years for the regular preacher in charge. Finally in 1900, all time limits were taken off by the General Conference.

Other significant changes were made that same year in the Methodist Episcopal organization. Agitation had been kept up for lay representation equal to that of the ministers in every way. As first established, a Lay Electoral Conference could only be held every four years in every Annual Conference for the sole purpose of selecting two lay delegates to the next General Conference. At least in Michigan, the lay delegates usually spoke their minds via some resolutions before they adjourned.

Not until 1900 did the laymen attain equal representation in the General Conference. This may have been delayed in part by a second demand, that for the inclusion of women among the lay General Conference delegates. Why such bitter opposition to such a mild reform should have existed so long is hard to understand today. It may have been part of the general male reluctance to grant to women equal political and social rights. The General Conference of 1872 had defined laymen as "all members of the Methodist Episcopal Church who are not members of an Annual Conference." In 1888, several women were among the elected delegates of the Lay Electoral Conferences of the Annual Conferences. But they were refused admission by the General Conference. Not until 1900 were women seated equally with the male lay delegates.[5]

---

[4] W. W. Sweet, *Meth. Am. Hist.*, pp. 348-350. Also based on the author's childhood recollections of a Junior League in Plymouth, Mich.

[5] R. M. Cameron, *Methodism and Society in Historical Perspective*, I, 267-271.

Two great changes in the attitudes and practices of the churches were already being talked in the United States in the 1890's but were not accepted in the Methodist Episcopal Church until the 20th century. These were the Social Gospel and the institutional church. Both were in part efforts to meet the religious needs of the rapidly growing cities. The Social Gospel preaches that the church must meet man's needs in this world as well as prepare his soul for the next. This would be done by a church which was open every day in every way that would aid all its members.

Chapter XII

A DISASTER, MUCH ROUTINE, AND A
FEW CHANGES

1880 – 1890

A few extraordinary events marked the history of Methodism in Michigan in the 1880's. The yearly routine of the 1870's still held sway in most of the State's Methodist churches. Toward the end of the decade, much more discussion of certain widely desired reforms took place. Those most often suggested were lay representation equal to that of the ministers in both General and Annual Conferences and full admission of women as travelling elders in the Annual Conferences. But all the debate had little in the way of real change to its credit. Really radical reforms did not come until the 20th century. The greatest thing accomplished in the Eighties was the drawing together in one denomination-wide group of the various young people's societies. This was the Epworth League, established in Michigan in 1889 the same year it was founded in Cleveland.

Much of what was written and said about the local religious outlook in the ninth decade of the nineteenth century resembles what was recorded in the 1870's People simply did not have the money to support the preachers and the great charitable endeavors of Methodism as they deserved to be. Perhaps this poverty was a bit more prevalent in the first half of that decade. Again and again, Methodist Episcopalians mentioned the "tight money market," the difficulties in any borrowing from any bank, and the lack of all financial resources on the part of Methodists engaged in clearing and settling what was then often called "our northern frontier."

References to the northern work, either M.E. or M.P., did not mean the Upper Peninsula primarily but rather the northern third of the

Lower Peninsula. Suggestions for the creation of a Northern Annual Conference were made almost every year. But somehow the money was so scarce and "aggressive" ministers so rare and the circuits so hard to travel and the results in more members so slight that the third Annual Conference in Michigan was never born. Perhaps also some ministers were reluctant to hazard all their future careers in an area where the opportunities for promotion to larger churches or substantial increases in salary were almost non-existent.[1]

The Methodist Protestant Annual Conferences in Michigan were operating on peculiarly small resources then. Their Conference *Minutes* were full of lists of circuits and missions that made no payments at all except to their pastors. The faculty at Adrian College were stated to be receiving "less than 40% of their salaries" in 1885. In connection with the Lansing Church, the Michigan M.P. Conference appealed to the West Michigan M.P. Conference for financial help because of "our utter inability to meet our obligations." When other churches, as in Pontiac, Saginaw, Dansville, and Bad Axe asked for monetary aid, the Michigan Methodist Protestant Conference committees used two phrases repeatedly in reply. Either it was recommended that a Church "secure the money in some way" or that the Conference "aid in some way." Sometimes very modest sums were had from Conference or national Church Extension Societies.

The Assassination of President Garfield

Shot by a disappointed office-seeker in mid-June, President Garfield lingered on all summer and died on September 19, 1881. Everything known then by physicians was done for him. Meeting early in September, the two M.E. Annual Conferences were very concerned about the wounded President. Meeting in August, as the M.P.s did, it was still thought the President would recover.

The Michigan Annual Conference, in session from August 31 to September 5, received all the latest bulletins about Garfield through the courtesy of the local Western Union telegraph manager. The President was said to be rapidly improving so the Conference sent him a telegram of "great sympathy and personal esteem." This was drafted and signed by Bishop Randolf Foster, Secretary H. M. Joy, and William H. Brockway.

The Detroit Annual Conference met from September 14th to 19th. On the 17th, it was learned that the President was worse and prospects of his recovery were discouraging. As its first act of the session, the Conference had already unanimously adopted a set of resolutions in-

---

[1] Comments based on two letters to the author from the late Rev. William C. S. Pellowe in 1963.

troduced by James S. Smart. These expressed an earnest sympathy and "profound and prayerful interest" in the President. Belief that God had saved his life thus far was stated and prayer was asked by everyone for "the President, his family, and the nation." Thanks was given to God that "the din of political strife has been hushed" and sympathy shown that demonstrated man's brotherhood under God.[2] Many of the first sermons of the new Conference year must have been devoted to President Garfield.

Michigan's Great Fire of 1881

The disaster of the 1880's in Michigan was the great forest fire of the first week in September, 1881, in the Thumb area. It did not cover so wide an area as the one a decade earlier had done but it caused greater loss of life. It is said that in 1881 some 282 people died, 15,000 were homeless, and 3,400 buildings were destroyed. The drought had been bad for two successive summers and, by the first of September, all the streams were dried up and even the swamps were hard baked clay.

[2] Detroit Annual Conference *Minutes* for 1881, pp. 6-7, 22. Michigan Annual Conference *Minutes* for 1881, pp. 12, 15, 29.

As early as 1757 Detroit had two sawmills operated by water power. It was not until the 1840's and 1850's that commercial logging and lumbering began on a large scale. Michigan white pine was the best in the world. After 1860 logging was a boom industry in the north. The peak was reached in 1888 when 4,292,000,000 board feet of lumber were saved, along with millions of shingles, staves, railroad ties, and squared timbers. As late as 1900 Michigan led the nation in the production of lumber.

Monday, September 5, 1881, was the peak day of the fire when a strong, southwest wind intensified the burning to a wall of fire that sometimes ran one hundred feet high. It was preceded by an intense darkness of smoke in which one could neither see nor breathe. In order of their greatest loss, the counties affected were Huron, Sanilac, Tuscola, Lapeer, and St. Clair. Among the small towns almost or entirely destroyed were Bad Axe, Minden, Huron City, Ubly, Deckerville, Carsonville, and Sand Beach. The latter is now called Harbor Beach. Bad Axe lost both a Methodist Episcopal and a Methodist Protestant church building. One can scarcely visualize the horrors of such a conflagration. It was claimed that the intense heat and smoke were felt and seen at least seven miles out in Lake Huron.[3]

John Bettes was admitted on trial to the Detroit Annual Conference in 1881. At the time of the fire, he was a supply preacher presumably with a local license for the church at Bad Axe and possibly also at Minden. He and his sister, Nancy, drove from Minden to Peck during the fire in a buggy with a long box. They had a wild ride and often had to jump their horse over fallen trees en route through smoke and flames. When they arrived at a hotel in Peck, a bundle discovered in the back of the buggy's long box was found to be a baby boy. His eight-year old brother, left with the baby while their parents fought the fire, had not been able to run fast enough to stop the buggy so he had thrown the baby into that long box for safety. Eventually after a week, the parents, the boy, and the baby were reunited in Peck.[4]

Meeting so soon after the fire, the Detroit Annual Conference was fully conscious of the desperate needs of the "Burnt District." Their deepest concern was for the Methodist ministers who would be appointed to that region. A special committee was immediately established to survey the situation and raise funds for relief work. This was not hard to do because anxiety was widespread for the "ministers who have suffered by fire." The sum of $373 was voluntarily sent for their relief. Southeast Indiana Conference gave $100, employees of the Cincinnati Book Concern $180, the Rev. Seth Reed $5, and "the son of a Methodist preacher" $5. That special committee recommended that $148, the largest sum, be given to John Bettes. The minister from Port Austin, John Maywood, received $100, John Andrews from Eyre had $75, and George Walker at Sand Beach $50. Bettes and Walker were returned to serve in the Burnt District the next year.[5]

The first Red Cross chapter in the United States had been formed by Clara Barton at Dansville, New York, just three weeks before the Michi-

---

[3] Gerard Schultz, *A History of Michigan's Thumb*, pp. 77-79. It has a chapter on "The Great Forest Fires of 1871 and 1881."

[4] This incident told me by the Rev. Ronald Brunger, who read it in an article on "The Sanilac Scene" by Bob Parks in the Port Huron *Times-Herald*.

[5] Detroit Annual Conference *Minutes* for 1881, pp. 41-42.

Religious News Service Photo

The Methodist Church at Caseville, near the tip of the Thumb, a Church that is popular with the tourists and often photographed.

gan fire. It was the first disaster that the Red Cross undertook to alleviate. A general relief committee was set up in Port Huron to dispense food and clothing. Such was the need that a general appeal by the Methodist Church to its own members for money and supplies was still needed. At least that special committee of the Detroit Annual Conference so decided but once collected it considered that distribution of aid could be handled most effectively by the three relief committees already in operation.

The Methodist Episcopal Church had a peculiar duty of its own in that tragic situation. General relief committees could house, clothe and feed people but could not possibly do anything for church congregations left homeless or ministers appointed to such desolate areas. That special ministerial relief committee of Detroit Annual Conference felt it would be cowardice not "to maintain the ordinances of religion in this devastated region." Therefore, an appeal must be made in all the Methodist church papers, a denominational fund raised under the direction of David Preston, and a committee of five named to manage the work. It must be under the direction of the Presiding Elder of Port Huron District aided by two ministers and two laymen of that region. It was specially noted that Bibles might be obtained for all destitute families by writing to the district superintendent of the American Bible Society in Kalamazoo.

The records of the Michigan Methodist Protestant Conference do not use the word fire anywhere in the Minutes of the 1880's but an annual concern was shown for the Bad Axe Church. In 1882, an appeal for help to "rebuild" the church at Bad Axe was made to the Conference session and the sum of $175 was raised then. A claim of $50 from the Church Extension Society was given to Bad Axe by one of the other ministers there. In 1883, the Rev. E. B. Sutton was left without an appointment and specially authorized "with suitable testimonials" to collect for building a church at Bad Axe. Presumably his efforts would be made both inside and outside Michigan. The results of his labors, if any, do not appear in the *Minutes*.

The Methodist Episcopal Church made a much greater and more sustained effort in the "Burnt District" than the M.P.s were able to do. A larger Church, more authority over its ministers, and a stronger connectional organization all helped. Even so, the effort had certain special difficulties. At the Detroit Annual Conference session of 1886, the special committee reported that eighteen churches and three parsonages had been built at a cost of about $20,000. Two more churches were under construction and would soon be finished. Three eligible building sites were paid for and would soon be used. The Rev. Orrin Whitmore had taken supernumerary rank in 1882 and given all his time and best efforts to working as the Agent for the Burnt District Relief Fund. The Conference decided to leave the tasks of closing the books of the

Fund and winding up all business involved to the Agent and the Presiding Elder of the Port Huron District.

How had so much been done in only a few years and with such modest funds? Zeal on the part of the ministers concerned, loans from the national Board of Church Extension, some help from the Missionary Society, and many items in the Methodist publications all contributed to the results. Each year detailed reports of the work were sent to the *Northwestern Christian Advocate* and the New York *Christian Advocate*. The Presiding Elders and the special Agent also signed notes and pledged their personal credit in cases of great necessity.

Unfortunately Agent Whitmore died on March 19, 1887. He had been appointed to the St. Ignace Church in September, 1886, and was trying to relieve its embarrassed financial situation. The Detroit Annual Conference session of 1887 appointed the Rev. Francis Berry to close Mr. Whitmore's accounts and the Burnt District Fund. This proved much easier to order than to do.

Mr. Berry reported to the Conference session in 1888 that two transactions still remained to be settled. First, Mr. Whitmore had placed a mortgage on the parsonage in Bad Axe as security for certain funds of the national Church Extension Board assigned to the use of another church. But the second church had been unable to use the money just at that time. Second, Agent Whitmore had advanced $200 to the Port Austin Church on the security of the personal note of his own Presiding Elder, Jacob Horton. The situations demanded ready cash which neither the churches nor the ministers involved could supply.

The Methodist answer to problems where solutions were not immediately visible was, as usual, appointment of a special committee. That time it was one on "the imperiled churches." To the Bad Axe and Port Austin situations caused by Whitmore's death were added the tasks of coping with the heavy debts of the Imlay City and Capac Churches. The lingering indebtedness of these small churches was burdensome to each of them and the Conference as well throughout the 1890's.[6] Drought, hard times, lumber camps that moved elsewhere, and people who had used all their ready cash to establish a land claim all helped to make finances very difficult for the small Methodist churches in the Thumb or northern parts of Michigan in general.

Problems of Administrative Division and Finance

In addition to the special problems due to the fire of 1881 all the branches of Methodism in Michigan were deeply concerned with their northern frontier work. The region was being rapidly settled but people

---

[6] References to the Burnt District occur throughout the Detroit Annual Conference *Minutes* of the 1880's: in 1883 pp. 11-12; in 1886 p. 60; in 1887 pp. 29-30; in 1888 pp. 24, 64; in 1889 p. 34.

Interior and exterior of the first Central Methodist Episcopal Church at Sault Ste. Marie. This Church stood on the present church site. It was built in 1874 and served for 20 years.

were widely scattered and very poor. Steamers and railroads had reached the borders of Lower Michigan but many small farms inland and away from those means of transportation were largely isolated and certainly untouched by the churches.

The Districts in the first four tiers of counties in the southern part of Lower Michigan changed very little in the 1880's. The substantial increases came further north. Albion District had 23 appointments in 1880 and 24 in 1890. Appointments in the Grand Rapids District were 31 in 1880 and the same in number in 1890. The Kalamazoo District had 27 appointments in 1880 and 34 in 1890.

In contrast, the Big Rapids District increased from 32 appointments in 1880 to 48 in 1890. And the Grand Traverse District rose from 28 appointments in 1880 to 41 in 1890. Little wonder that seven of the appointments on this last District were left "to be supplied" in 1890. The Presiding Elder there had a real problem on his hands.

The Michigan Annual Conference did not have a Burnt District to deal with but did have several churches that tottered on the brink of financial collapse. In the decade of the Eighties, special collections had to be taken at one or another Conference session for the churches at Benton Harbor, Kalkaska, Bellaire, White Cloud, and Chase. This latter church was in the Big Rapids District. In 1885, the committee on the State of the Church lamented that the total debt on the church properties of the Michigan Annual Conference had just about doubled in the last three years. Experience had taught the ministers that heavy church debts were no help to religious faith or conversions.

The Districts in the Michigan Annual Conference remained nine in number throughout the 1880's. The Detroit Annual Conference began the decade with seven Districts, divided the Upper Peninsula into two

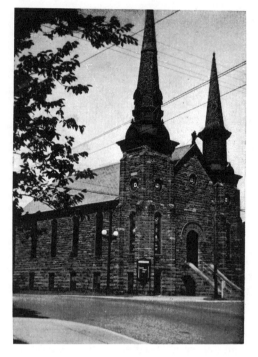

First Methodist Church, Marquette. The Indian missionary Pitezel found one wigwam here in the winter of 1846. The opening of the Jackson mine at Negaunee led to the establishment of the harbor at Marquette. Rev. William Benson organized the Society here in 1851. A wooden frame church was built in 1856. The present brownstone church was built in 1873 when the congregation numbered 125 members.

Districts during 1883 and 1884 and then returned to seven Districts from 1885 through 1890. The supervision of the entire Upper Peninsula by only one Presiding Elder was very strenuous not alone because of the weather but also because the 21 appointments of 1880 had increased to 46 by 1890. Eleven of those Upper Peninsula charges also had an out appointment. Hancock, Iron Mountain, and Ishpeming each had two churches by 1890.

The Alpena District was another unit of rapid change and expansion. Its name was changed in 1888 to the Bay City District. This was probably because Bay City and its two Methodist Episcopal churches was transferred from Saginaw District to Alpena District that year. Yet West Bay City had been part of the Alpena District in the earlier part of the same decade and the Presiding Elder maintained his headquarters there after 1881. Alpena District had 21 appointments in 1880 and 33 in 1890. Most of the new charges were small and struggling frontier groups, such as Au Gres, Greenbush, St. Helen, and Maple Ridge. Whoever was the Presiding Elder in that District followed a travel routine almost as strenuous as that of the early circuit riders. The railroad by no means reached all the places in which the Quarterly Conferences must be held at appointed times. A good horse was almost as important as it had been to James Gilruth in the 1830's. But the Presiding Elder of the later decade usually hitched his horse to a buggy or wagon and put his "grip" in the back instead of riding with well-stuffed saddlebags.

Any Methodist minister appointed to one of those new villages in the north had to have outside financial aid if he was to create a living church there. Throughout the Eighties, the Missionary Society sent from $5,000 to $8,000 to each Annual Conference in Michigan every year. This was carefully apportioned to the Districts and their poorer appointments in sums ranging from $25 to $250. Much the larger share went to Big Rapids and Grand Traverse Districts in the Michigan Annual Conference and to the Alpena-Bay City and Lake Superior Districts in the Detroit Annual Conference. Gifts and loans from the national Church Extension Society were also available. The Women's Home Missionary Society was organized in 1880 but not officially recognized by the Methodist Episcopal Church until the General Conference of 1884. That same year, the W.H.M.S. began work in Michigan in a modest way. In situations of financial crisis, the Annual Conference appointed a standing committee or a special financial agent to help a struggling church. Occasionally a collection was taken among the ministers in attendance at Conference to relieve some immediate, desperate need.

The Methodist Protestants in Michigan had the same problems of administration and finance that the Methodist Episcopalians did. But those problems were intensified for the M.P.'s by their smaller numbers,

Dr. Chandler Stephenson (1849-1921) a leader in the Michigan Conference of the Methodist Protestant Church, and father of Dr. Frank Stephenson. He wrote extensively for "Methodist Recorder," "Christian Herald," and "Homilectic Review"; was the author of many poems and two books.

lesser monetary resources, and organizational beliefs. Lacking bishops and presiding elders, an inadequate substitute was found in an elected President of Conference and sub-district chairmen. These officials all were responsible for a single church in addition to their supervisory duties. At times, the ministers refused to accept the sub-district divisions. Then argument would ensue in the annual conference sessions over whether the President should be located or travelling in his work. The feeling for a congregational form of administration was so strong, particularly in eastern Michigan that some ministers wished to work independently. One minister in the West Michigan Conference in 1888, Charles Clancy, even formed a Class of a dozen members who called themselves "Congregational Methodists." This was too much for the President of that Conference and so he read Clancy out of his charge at Fuller and put a notice of this action in the local paper and the *Methodist Recorder.*[7]

The M.P. Annual Conference known as West Michigan and North Indiana had fewer administrative troubles than the Michigan Annual Conference. It had three administrative Districts, named Lansing, Three Rivers, and Northern, throughout the 1880's. The number of charges in each division varied from eight to fourteen. Generally, Three Rivers District had more places than the Lansing one did.

The Chairman of the Northern District was sometimes known as the Superintendent of Northern Missions. Also he was pastor of a church in that District. His burdens must have been very heavy. Besides the hardships of travel there, he found a weakness and uncertainty in some small churches that must have been almost impossible to eradicate. Ministers might not even show up at their charges except at their own pleasure and convenience. At Leetsville in 1887, he "found all gone to the M.E. Church."

Finally, in 1889, a Conference Committee on Missions recommended that, if they were unable to send aggressive ministers and sufficient financial support, Methodist Protestantism should "cease our pretenses to what we do not perform and withdraw from the field." Specifically, any charge among the northern missions with less than forty members should be discontinued. As a result, the eight northern charges in 1889 become only four in 1890.

The Michigan Annual Conference of Methodist Protestants was unable to keep to the same ways of division and supervision in the Eighties. In 1880, it had eight sub-districts with a Chairman for each

---

[7] Charles Clancy was an irritating problem to the West Michigan Conference for several years. The basic trouble was that he had been given a letter of good standing in 1886. This commended him as a Christian minister to any other denomination. The Conference tried to get this letter back in 1887, and 1888 but Clancy refused and so did that new Congregational Methodist Class he had formed. W. Mich. An. Conf. *Minutes* for 1886, p. 15; for 1887, pp. 11, 17, 36-37; for 1888, p. 23.

who was also responsible for one particular church. The President of Conference was also to travel the District, as the Conference was often called by the M.P.'s. He was voted a salary of $700 which was never successfully raised above that sum during the entire decade. In 1881 and 1882, the sub-districts were reduced to five in number. Whenever districts were mentioned in the *Minutes* these five were maintained. Their names were Livingston, Clio, Port Huron, Lapeer, and Cass River. Nothing was said in 1881 about the President's travelling the Conference but in 1882 he was specifically required so to do. In 1883 he was not so required but the districts were increased to seven in number.

A first class disagreement about districts and the work of the President of Conference developed in 1884 and was not fully settled for three years. On August 28, 1884, the second day of the session, the Conference voted that the President should be required to travel the District during the coming year. On the fourth day, the decision to require travel of the President was reconsidered as was also his salary. "This motion elicited the most enthusiastic debate of the entire session, the laymen taking an active part." A formal vote was demanded but the effort to locate the President failed as a majority of eight ministers and eleven laymen voted for him to travel. Then a resolution was adopted to require every Quarterly Conference to tell their delegate to the next Annual Conference "whether they do or do not desire a travelling President." The salary was left as before. No sub-districts or chairmen were arranged for 1884-1885.

The Secretary carefully noted what happened at the session of 1885. On August 27th, the record reads:

> The roll was called to ascertain the desire of the circuits with regard to a travelling President, which resulted in twenty for travelling and sixteen against. A vote was taken to obtain the sense of the Conference on the same question. After an animated discussion, thirty-two voted for travelling and nineteen for locating the President. Voted that the President's salary be fixed at eight hundred dollars.

This last item, with its increase of $100 in salary may have been what triggered the rest of the events of that session. The next day the business of a travelling President was brought up again and laid on the table. Finally on the fifth day, the Conference reversed its previous decision, decided to locate its President and again have sub-districts with chairmen. Also it rescinded the vote to pay the President $800. No more mention of his salary was made in that year's *Minutes*. The sub-districts were made seven in number as had been done in 1883.

When the year 1886 came around, the Conference voted to pay their President $600 and require him to travel. Therefore, no chairmen nor sub-districts were established just as had occurred in 1884. But the Conference session of 1887 first voted to have a travelling President with a salary of $700. This was done on Wednesday but by Saturday afternoon the ministers must have been having second thoughts because they "voted that the Conference return to the old plan of Sub-Districts, and that Rev. Wm. Cope inform the Stationing Committee of this action of the Conference." Five districts were at once established being the same as had existed in 1881 and 1882. From 1888 through 1890, the sub-districts were seven in number. Adrian and Pontiac had been added to the five previous divisions. Whether the President also travelled in those years was not made clear in the *Minutes*, except that in 1890 Conference voted that he should travel at the same salary of $700. It would seem that even the independent-minded M.P.'s began to feel the need of help and advice from a locally based chairman in addition to that of a rarely seen Conference President.[8]

Problems in Selection of Conference Meeting Places

Expansion increased the problems connected with planning and holding the Methodist Episcopal Conferences in Michigan. The number of charges and the ministerial membership in each Annual Conference grew steadily. Judging from their registers of travelling elders and probationers, the Detroit Annual Conference expanded a little faster than the Michigan one did. Full membership in the Detroit Annual Conference grew from 236 in 1880 to 306 in 1890 and probationers from 18 to 48. In the same decade, the Michigan Annual Conference elders increased from 238 to 289 but probationers decreased from 26 to 15.

The costs of holding the annual sessions increased while the towns with enough space for both meetings and lodgings decreased. The Detroit Annual Conference appointed a special committee in 1888 on "Conference Attendance and Entertainment." It reported in part:

> Our increasing numbers make it more and more difficult to secure easy entertainment of the Conference. Already our numbers are above the ability of free hospitality of many places where a Conference session would be a great blessing, and make us dependent upon a comparatively few places, whose hospitality we regret to overtax.

This same committee also said plainly that the time had come when it was impossible to give free lodging and meals to all the ministers. It wished to see the ministers receiving salaries over $800 pay their own way. Suggestions for a plan of equalization of travelling expenses

---

[8] The record of all those shifts and changes can be found in the Methodist Protestant Annual Conference *Minutes* for Michigan according to the years mentioned in the author's account. It must be noted that the *Minutes* were most inadequate then with too many general statements that give no idea at all of what the subject matter of a resolution was. The spelling was most careless and very little proofreading could have been done. Most lists of names of ministers and delegates were not alphabetized either.

were included in the report but nothing beyond continuing the special committee was done then.

The Michigan Annual Conference encountered some of the same difficulties in the selection of locations for its sessions. Occasionally the choice of the next meeting place was left to the Presiding Elders. An invitation to come to Petoskey and Bay View was first extended in 1882 but not accepted until 1887. The choice fell on Muskegon in both 1880 and 1890. The Presiding Elders selected Lansing in 1884. There a very special meeting place was secured. Through the Michigan Secretary of State and the Board of Auditors, the Conference was invited to meet in the Representative Hall of the State Capitol. A special resolution of thanks and appreciation for the use of the place was adopted at the close of the session. It was said to have "ministered to our comfort and facilitated the transaction of the business of the church."[9]

The Michigan Annual Conference received an unusual offer for a session place in 1890. A. W. Wright of Alma wrote that he would assume the entire cost of entertaining the Conference if they would meet there. The Conference politely and regretfully declined on the ground that the next year was the quadrennial time for the attendance of lay delegates from about 300 charges in addition to the ministers. In such circumstances, it was felt that Alma was not large enough to accommodate them all.

Division of the two Methodist Episcopal Annual Conferences in Michigan was agitated again in the 1880's as it had been in the 1870's. Once more a joint committee, drawn from each Conference, debated the creation of three or four Conferences in the State. The General Conference of 1880 authorized Detroit Annual Conference to create a Lake Superior Conference in the Upper Peninsula. In 1887, the Detroit and Michigan Conferences united in a request to the General Conference of 1888 that they be given authority to divide the area into smaller Conferences "at any time during the next quadrennium on such lines as shall be determined by a majority of the members." But in 1889, another joint committee of the two Conferences decided that "the time for such division has not yet arrived."

Perhaps that joint committee so decided because of the poverty prevalent in the northern area of Michigan then. The largest and the most prosperous churches were in the first four tiers of counties in

[9] Michigan Annual Conference *Minutes* for 1884, p. 55. Detroit Annual Conference *Minutes* for 1884, pp. 27-28. Michigan Conference meeting places during the decade were Muskegon, Jackson, Coldwater, Albion, Lansing, Grand Rapids, Kalamazoo, Bay View, St. Joseph, and Greenville. Detroit sessions were held in Bay City, Port Huron, Detroit Central twice (1882 and 1888), Flint, East Saginaw, Pontiac, Adrian, Saginaw, and Alpena.

southern Michigan. As already suggested, opportunity for advancement by the ministers in the worldly sense and for mutual aid would certainly be reduced in any geographically equal division.

Changing Michigan Ministerial Personnel

Certain changes among the ministers composing the two Annual Conferences in Michigan indicate the beginning of modern Methodism here. In 1884, both the Detroit and Michigan Annual Conferences were very pleased when William Xavier Ninde was elected a Bishop and almost immediately assigned to hold both their annual sessions. He was "the first Michigan man ever elected to that high office" said the Michigan Annual Conference.

In 1870, Mr. Ninde had been transferred from the Cincinnati Annual Conference to Detroit where he was appointed to Central Church. After the permitted term of three years there, he taught at Garrett Biblical Institute, served again at Detroit Central Church and then was elected President of Garrett. For fourteen years, 1870-1884, he retained his membership in the Quarterly Conference of Detroit Central Church. So the Detroit Annual Conference had a special pride that "one of our members" had become a Bishop.

When Bishop Ninde pointed out the propriety of dropping his name from their register, the Detroit Annual Conference and a large audience adopted resolutions of regret. Nine of the older ministers formally presented him with these and assured Bishop Ninde that he would always have "a warm place in our hearts and a most cordial welcome *Home* whenever he shall . . . visit us." The Bishop lived until 1901, much of the time in Detroit but he never again presided over an annual session of the Detroit Annual Conference. In 1887, he did preside at the Michigan Annual Conference when it met at Bay View.

In 1880, the Michigan Methodist Protestant Annual Conference experienced similar feelings of pride when its members learned that Dr. G. B. McElroy of Adrian College had served as the elected President of the last M.P. General Conference. In a formal resolution that Conference stated its "appreciation of the high honor conferred upon our distinguished brother and through him upon this Conference." This was felt not to be enough evidently because in 1883 the ministers of the same Conference presented Mr. McElroy with a purse of $20. He was gotten before the Conference by asking him to come and help them out of a difficulty. Then one of the older ministers paid eloquent tribute to his wise counsel, noble devotion, and high loyalty to Adrian College. The Conference *Minutes* for 1883 state "the present was received in the same spirits in which it was given and the remarks made by the Doctor were listened to with rapted (*sic*) attention."

The work to which ministers were transferred and the places from which they came here also became more diversified and expanded in the 1880's. The lists of Methodist Episcopal appointments reveal ministers going as missionaries to Arizona, Dakota, and southern California. In 1889, the Detroit Annual Conference had four missionaries in North China, five in Bulgaria, and one a chaplain at the Eastern Michigan Asylum. In this same period, the Michigan Annual Conference sent ministers to Dakota, Nevada, Oregon, and Texas. Six missionaries departed for South India and one went to Liberia.

The Methodist foreign language Annual Conferences also expanded in Michigan in the last two decades of the 19th century. German speaking churches had been in operation in Michigan ever since 1846. Now in somewhat similar fashion to the manner in which the German work had been brought here, services were provided for people who were Norwegian or Danish. The impetus came from outside the State. The German speaking ministers came from Ohio or Indiana to the South. The Scandinavian speaking ministers came into Michigan Methodism from the West through Wisconsin and Illinois. Due to geography, the beginnings were made along the eastern edges of Lake Michigan.

The Northwest Norwegian Annual Conference was started in 1880 at Racine, Wisconsin. Among its appointments was that of the Rev. Henry Danielsen to Manistee and Frankfort under the supervision of the Presiding Elder of the Chicago District, the Rev. O. P. Petersen. In 1884, the new Conference was made the Norwegian *and Danish* Conference. It is said a Scandinavian language minister also labored at Escanaba. Probably the growth of such a foreign language church was slow and expansion even slower. By 1893, congregations, presumably with Quarterly Conferences, existed at Muskegon, Ludington, and Manistee.[10]

The transfers to Michigan from the eastern annual conferences of the United States continued in a small way just as they had done ever since the first pioneer times. But the influx from Canada rose noticeably in the 1880's. The tie with Canada had been very close in the early days and from two to five ministers had moved here from Canadian churches in every decade. Checking the register of 1890, it is found that the Detroit Annual Conference had received seventeen active ministers from the Canadian Conferences and eleven Methodist Protestant ministers during the previous decade. The Michigan M.E. Annual Conference in the similar period had received fourteen from Canada, three from Newfoundland, and seven Methodist Protestants.

In 1884 alone, six Canadian ministers entered the Detroit Annual

[10] Arlow W. Anderson, *The Salt of the Earth,* History of Norwegian Danish Methodism in America, pp. 84-85, 93, 152. This book was called to my attention by Rev. Ronald A. Brunger.

Conference and five the Michigan. Here was a trend that some of the native-born American Methodist ministers would soon resent.

The oldtime pioneer ministers died in proportionately greater numbers in the Eighties. The Detroit Annual Conference lost by death 44 of its members in this decade, the Michigan Annual Conference 40. The peak years took seven ministers away from the Michigan Annual Conference in 1883-84 and eight from the Detroit Annual Conference in 1886-87. The year 1887-88 shows only one death in the Michigan Annual Conference but that one was James T. Robe, who came into the ministry in 1830 in Indiana and, when southwest Michigan was part of the Indiana Annual Conference, preached all over that part of the Territory. He was the first to hold Methodist services in Kalamazoo and many other villages in that area.

A bad year for the Detroit Annual Conference was 1887 when it lost its leading layman, David Preston, in addition to Bishop William Logan Harris and eight ministers. Bishop Harris was next to the senior leader of the Church when he died and of interest to Michigan Methodists because he had begun his ministerial work in the Michigan Annual Conference session of 1837. David Preston was a very serious loss to the benevolent causes and financial boards of Methodism. A prosperous banker, he always gave liberally himself and had the power of inducing others to do likewise. Albion College owed much of its early endowment fund to his efforts. Among the ministers lost were Elijah Pilcher, Isaac Elwood, and Orrin Whitmore. Elwood was only 44 and Whitmore 63 at the time of their deaths. In the ordinary course of events, some years more of service might have been expected from them. Both had been connected with the creation of the *Michigan Christian Advocate.*

The passing of Elijah Holmes Pilcher deserves particular attention. He died at the age of 76 after the most remarkable career in Michigan Methodism. Preacher, Presiding Elder, Professor at Albion College, and author of the *History of Protestantism in Michigan,* Pilcher also studied law and medicine and was admitted to the State practice of these professions. In 1877, after the most urgent pleas for his help, Pilcher transferred to the Niagara Annual Conference in Canada to do what he could to build up the Methodist Church there. In 1882, he suffered a stroke which paralyzed his right side and he was thus forced to give up his work and live with his son, a Doctor, in Brooklyn, New York. He must have been a man of immense determination for he taught himself to write clearly with his *left* hand. In 1882, the Detroit Annual Conference restored Pilcher's name to its rank by seniority in the membership roll. He was well enough to come to Michigan in 1885 and attend the Conference session. His name stood first on the roll, he assisted with communion, and took a small part in the routine business. One of his sons, Leander W. Pilcher, was a missionary in China when his father died in April, 1887.[11]

＊   ＊   ＊   ＊   ＊   ＊

The process by which new men were admitted and trained to become Methodist ministers and full members of an annual conference was the same as it always had been. The first step was still a recommendation from the Quarterly Conference of the man's own local church. Then came four years of study and work as a minister done in accord with the rules in the *Discipline*. Specified books must be read and examinations thereon be given by older ministers each year at Conference time. Earlier, in the history of Methodism, a young man was assigned as a junior preacher on a double appointment with an older man, who became well acquainted with the new minister and acted as a kind of immediate supervisor.

As more stationed appointments were created, the only supervision was that of an overworked, Presiding Elder. M.E and M.P. Annual Conferences alike in Michigan complained repeatedly that the examinations were hasty, usually oral, done in competition with much Conference business, and not of the same degree of thoroughness or severity from year to year. Methodism was growing dissatisfied with its oldtime ministerial education.

The M. E. Michigan Annual Conference voted in 1880 that all future candidates must read all the required books and pass "a medium examination." If any had not done so then they must try again the next year. The Education committee's report that year said in part:

> The Conference ought not to ignore the imperative demand of the times for a high order of ministerial education. Our young men will soon make up, in their greater subsequent efficiency, the time spent in literary and special theological culture before assuming pastoral relations. . . . The modern Gospel minister must have a cultured mind as well as a zealous heart . . . ignorance is no longer tolerated in the pulpit. . . . One of our bishops says "the minister must study or go under. His great-grandfather's old musket has been shot clean out of the field."

In 1883, the M.E. Detroit Annual Conference declared that the current examinations were indefinite, hurried, disturbed by the business of the session and, in general, led many candidates to think it not necessary to pursue *all* of the Disciplinary course of study. So from thence forward, all candidates for admission on trial must come to the place of the session by 9 A.M. the day before Conference opened. If it was

---

[11] See account of Pilcher in Chapter IV. For his Conference memoir see the Detroit Annual Conference *Minutes* for 1887, pp. 27, 43, 56-58. Also see article by R. A. Brunger, Elijah H. Pilcher, Methodist Preacher Extraordinary, *Mich. Ch. Ad.* Feb. 20, 1964, XCI, #8, pp. 4-5, 18-19.

found that any man had not followed the *Discipline* in his studies, he must not be accepted under any circumstances.[12]

Almost every year after 1884, both M.E. Annual Conferences in Michigan listed men for re-examination in systematic theology, Ancient History, Christian Perfection, History of Methodism, or even now and then "the courses for which he has not prepared himself this year."

The consideration of ministerial education in Methodist Protestant Conferences in Michigan produced results and reports that read very much like those of the Methodist Episcopal Conferences. Both had more than their share of earnest, slow, hardworking men who just could not do all the required work in one year and hold a pastoral appointment too. The M.P. committees of examination tried very hard to give them the benefit of the doubt and rely on promises to review the material and study harder next year. Of course, they supported preparation for the ministry by attendance at Adrian College with study under the guidance of Dr. G. B. McElroy, Dean of its School of Theology.

Perhaps some of the older M.P. ministers needed to be convinced of the values found in systematic collegiate study. The Ministerial Education committee of 1885 said, "The standing of our church before the world . . . must depend largely on an intelligent and cultured ministry. We need more men thoroughly equipped. The water of life in the goblet of polished crystal is none the less the water of life."

Somewhat less elegantly yet more vigorously, the ministerial education committee of 1890, under the chairmanship of Dr. McElroy, said:

> Your Committee would recommend that the Michigan Annual Conference resolve . . . to give work to no man, and to continue no man in the work who will not *"study* to show himself approved" — who would rather talk than think; rather roam than read, and who persists in mistaking prosing for preaching.

The M.E. General Conference of 1884 had adopted resolutions emphasizing the importance of theological seminaries. It had also decided that a young minister might be left "without appointment to attend some of our schools." In Michigan, the school was usually Garrett but a few men went to Boston University. And in 1887, the Detroit Annual Conference committee on Education was pleased to note that DePauw University in Indiana now had a complete school of Theology in action.

Beginning in 1884, the two M.E. Conferences in Michigan each year increased the number of their members in attendance at one of the theological seminaries. Only seven from both Conferences were so occupied in 1884 but by 1889 their seminary students numbered

---

[12] For Michigan Annual Conference resolutions in 1880, see *Minutes,* pp. 23, 35. For Detroit Annual Conference resolutions in 1883, see their *Minutes,* p. 25.

twenty-four.[13] The M.P. Annual Conferences in Michigan seem not to have had more than two or three students in study at Adrian College in any one year. Lack of financial resources was probably the main reason their college theological students were so few in number.

A profound change was inevitable in Methodism as its clergy became more educated and better read in many fields. Whether the product of the theological seminary and its scholarly faculty was more deeply religious than the product of conversion in the camp meeting and training on the circuit under an experienced preacher was a matter of controversy for many years.

The frequent appearance of the phrase "to be supplied" in the lists of appointments in any Methodist Annual Conference *Minutes* in the 1880's shows that the supply of new ministers was not too abundant. The Detroit Annual Conference was so concerned about this shortage that, in 1885, it ordered the Education Committee to investigate "the cause of the alarming and continuous deficiency in Ministerial supply within the bounds of the Conference, and, if possible, to report an adequate remedy." In reply, the Committee sadly agreed that the churches were not producing their own supply of preachers. The causes were implied in the needed remedies. Among those suggested were more prayer, more cultivation of the spiritual life of the churches, regular efforts by minister and congregation to turn young men to the ministry and finally special pains must be taken to convince them that their theological education must be obtained in Methodist colleges. Last and most important of all, was "a steadfast resistance of the tidal wave of worldliness threatening to submerge society."

     ✻   ✻   ✻   ✻   ✻   ✻

The most important group in the personnel of the Methodist Episcopal Church in Michigan in the Eighties remains to be studied. The middle-aged travelling elders dominated the Annual Conference sessions, had passed all the preliminary training and study, and might be presumed to have many years of solid service still before them. Was the pessimism of that Education Committee's report in 1885 typical? Were they alert to the rapid changes taking place in the United States? What was their attitude toward their profession?

Generalization is uncertain because the differences were increasing among the ministers rather than the similarities. Education that was self-gained or from a theological seminary, wide variations in ministerial salaries, even greater differences in the church buildings and parsonages

---

[13] The ministerial students were usually listed together at the end of the appointments in each M.E. Conference's annual *Minutes*. For both M.E. Conferences in Michigan the seminary students were in 1884 — 7; in 1885 — 9; in 1886 — 11; in 1887 — 22; in 1888 — 18; in 1889 — 24; and in 1890 — 19.

were among the things that profoundly influenced the Michigan Methodist situation then.

A random study of the statistics in any Conference *Minutes* furnishes many examples of the differentiation. The Detroit Annual Conference *Minutes* for 1887 show that the minister at Central in Detroit received $4,000, the one at Tabernacle in the same city $1,600, the Birmingham minister got $900, Plymouth paid $800, and Royal Oak $515. But the Ypsilanti Church had a salary of $1,500 and Ann Arbor First Church $3,000. Again the *Minutes* show that Adrian paid $2,000 but Dexter only $500. In the Alpena District, out of a total of 28 appointments, only five of them paid $1,000 or over. These were Alpena, West Bay City, Cheboygan, East Tawas and Oscoda. Unfortunately the charges that paid the lowest salaries were frequently the places with no parsonages. So the minister paid rent out of his inadequate salary.

Examination of the *Minutes* of the Michigan Annual Conference for 1887 reveals a rather lower standard of salary in the west half of the State. The higest paying congregation was Division Street in Grand Rapids at $2,600 and next came Jackson First Church at $2,000. The First Church in Kalamazoo listed a salary of $1,800 but no other church than these three in the entire Michigan Annual Conference paid over $1,600. Also the farther north one went, the lower the salary pledge for the year and the greater the deficiency in payment. Statistics for the Grand Traverse District are revealing. Traverse City Church had a salary of $1,200 and all was paid too. Cadillac's $950 was all paid too. But Bellaire had pledged $445 and only paid $297. Kalkaska, which already had a burden of debt on its church building, pledged $528 and paid $450. This same District had 37 church buildings and only 25 parsonages in 1887.

The Committee on the State of the Church in the Michigan Annual Conference session of 1885 referred to the increase in "the spirit of worldliness and self-seeking in the matter of appointments; many charges clamouring loudly for the best man without regard to the wants of other places." It was felt that many church members were looking only for personality, youth, and dramatic preaching ability. On the other hand, some ministers were "giving to prominent charges the confidence that is due to God only."

Two incidents that happened at the Michigan Annual Conference session of 1883 were investigated by the Committee on the State of the Church in 1884. Each involved acceptance of older ministers by reluctant churches. These cases still disturbed the ministers in general in 1885.

The first case concerned the church located at Mason. Its congregation was determined to have a young pastor and believed that positive assurance of such an appointment had been given. Then Andrew Mason Fitch, an elder since 1842, a long experienced circuit rider, and unfortunately 68 on his last birthday, was sent there. The Official Board of the Mason Church refused to receive him, by some means found a preacher whom the congregation would accept, and paid Mr. Fitch $50 for his moving expenses. Mr. Fitch certainly was seriously embarrassed by it all and was eventually forced to accept retirement and died in 1887. The Mason congregation was pledged to pay a salary of $1050 in 1883. This was a reasonably good salary for the time and location of the church. It must be supposed that they were determined to get what they considered their money's worth.

Another similar incident about the same time took place in Charlotte. This church was pledged to pay $1150 in 1883. The minister appointed there, Thomas H. Jacokes, was refused because it was believed that he would not furnish them the wanted style of pulpit preaching. Mr. Jacokes was admitted to the Michigan Annual Conference in 1845. He was sixty-three in 1883 and had just completed his third term as a Presiding Elder. He lived until 1898.

In 1884, the Michigan Annual Conference Committee on the State of the Church expressed its opinion of the two incidents that had occurred in the previous year. As far as the Committee could see, those two official boards simply wanted the preachers they wanted. Nothing was said by either board against the ability, character, or experience of the men appointed to those churches. It was outright disloyalty, which would destroy the fundamental basis of Methodism if allowed to continue. Supposing the different charges were to be classified by income, buildings, size of membership, and degree of hardship then worldly rivalry and personal not religious qualifications would determine the appointments. This Committee concluded:

> All negotiations for ministerial supply, whether between pastors and presiding elders, or presiding elders and charges, are so clearly an invasion of Episcopal prerogative, and rights of parties, that our system cannot long survive its practice. Friendly and confidential conversation for the information of the appointing power is the utmost boundary of private or official rights in arranging supply for our work.

The position of the laymen in the Methodist Episcopal Church was very different then from what it is today. Only the Lay Electoral Conference had been established and it met only once in four years solely to elect two lay delegates to attend General Conference. Women had absolutely no legal standing in the Church at large then. Yet the Detroit Lay Electoral Conference of 1887 had two women delegates — Elizabeth Tracy of Detroit District Memorial Church and Celia Gibbs of Byron on Flint District. This same Lay Conference of 1887 chose Jennie B. Preston of Detroit as its first Reserve Delegate. She was the widow of David Preston, who had died about five months previously. It is doubtful if she attended the General Conference held in 1888.

The Michigan Conference Lay Electors also chose a woman as their first Reserve Delegate. She was Mary T. Lathrop of Jackson.

In their attitude toward women as ministers and delegates, the Methodist Protestants offer no contrast to the Methodist Episcopalians. With their democratic and congregational ideas of church government, it might be expected that they would welcome women equally with men as lay delegates but such was not the case. From 1885 through 1889, the Michigan M.P. Annual Conference had one or two women among the lay delegates each year but none at all were present in the period immediately before and after that time. Sister N. J. Remington was allowed to study for the ministry and the Michigan M.P. Conference appeared to favor the admission of women to their ministry then. But in 1881, when Sister Remington had by license filled a pulpit for three years and had been recommended, by the committee that examined the Senior Class for ordination, because she had completed the required course of study *then* the Conference changed its mind. First by a vote of 25 to 9 the earlier resolution favoring the ordination of women was reconsidered. Next by a vote of 32 to 12 the committee report on the Senior Class was "amended by leaving out the name of Sister N. J. Remington." Finally, the Conference voted "that Sister Remington be continued as a licentiate of this Conference." Male Methodist ministers then were delighted to have the women serve as collectors of funds for missions or to pay the church debts but they were not ready to welcome female preachers equally in the pulpit.

The travelling elders of all the Methodist Annual Conferences in Michigan were often simultaneously *pessimistic* and *optimistic* about the prospects for their denomination here. Many of the preachers felt that the *Discipline* was not being enforced as it was in the early days. The M.E. Michigan Annual Conference declared in its session of 1886 that the tendency was growing "to erase the sharply defined lines . . . between the world and the church; to make of the church a social rather than a soul-saving institution." Quite a few of the ministers thought that a successful revival was the result of the joint efforts of "the Lord, the Word, the people and the pastor" rather than the use of a professional and sensational evangelist.

The institutions of Methodism which seemed not to attract the church members as they used to do were the Class meeting and the prayer meeting. By inquiry, it had been found that from one-third to one-half of the members came and participated in the midweek prayer meeting. Some charges had no Classes and if they were organized had become most perfunctory. Good Class leaders were hardly to be found and when available were not generally doing their duty in calling on the members. The average Class was made up of the older members and met briefly after the regular Sunday church services. Testimony given at that time was apt to be stereotyped and meaningless.

Daily family worship was maintained in about half of the homes of church members. This alone produced great spiritual decline. Not nearly enough of the official church papers were taken either.

It was a disgrace that many ministers, just one week before Conference time, could give no exact idea of the total amount of money raised annually in their churches for religious purposes. This sad situation was not entirely the fault of the ministers as too many members left their financial duties until the last day of the Conference year. If any official board would adopt the policy of weekly payments on the disciplinary plan, its obligations would all be met and on time too. The old-fashioned donation party for the pastor weakened the whole budgeted economy and ought not to be used any more. All ministers ought to be more careful not to accumulate personal debts beyond their ability to pay in a reasonable period of time.[14]

Every year all the Methodist Annual Conferences in Michigan appointed committees on Temperance and on the Sanctity of the Sabbath. These committees, regardless of the year or the branch of the denomination, made annual reports that were long, minute, and very emphatic about the evils involved. Year in and year out the Annual Conferences advocated entire State abolition of the liquor trade. Both Conferences said occasionally that the prohibition views of the Methodist Episcopal Church must never involve it in politics or in active work for one party over the other. Any triumph gained in that way would be a temporary thing and not the permanent reform in full Prohibition that was desired.

While just as anti-liquor as the M.E. Church, the M.P.'s were more inclined to see the virtues of joining and working in the Prohibition Party. The Michigan Annual Conference of the Methodist Protestants gave a vigorous push to the anti-liquor cause when it created the position of Conference Temperance Missionary or Evangelist and appointed the Rev. E. B. Sutton to fill it. He labored mightily in the Cause from 1883 to 1887, judging from his annual reports. Here is what he said to the Conference session of 1886:

> Travelled 13,000 miles; visited 46 counties; spoke 430 times in public; collected in cash, $2,304; by notes, $6,999 . . . circulated $150 worth of literature; taken 200 subscribers to prohibition papers; payed, talked, prayed and voted for prohibition; been threatened of my life, egged, stoned, cursed, and by all these hopeful signs of the desperate condition of our enemy I think we are not far from the kingdom of prohibition.

[14] General comments here drawn from a summary report made in 1888 by a Committee on the State of the Church of the Michigan M.E. Annual Conference. That Committee sent out a questionaire to all their pastors and based their report on the replies received. See Mich. An. Conf. *Minutes* for 1888, pp. 64-67. Also a similar committee report in 1880 to same Conference in *Minutes* for 1880, pp. 32-33.

In the first part of the 1880's, sanctity of the Sabbath was advocated in a general way as giving both a rest for weary men and also a chance for religious improvement. Year by year, more restrictions were added by the Conference committees on Sunday observance. In 1884, the Detroit Annual Conference objected to "the flagrant desecration of this holy day in the annual review of our State militia by the Governor." In 1885, the same Conference protested the Sunday policy of many corporations compelling men to work then. It asked Methodists "to discountenance excursions by railroads and steamboats, taking mail matter out of the post office, visiting ice cream saloons, by which reproach is brought on the cause of Christ." In 1886, it said that the Sunday newspaper was "of such a character as renders it unsuitable for any Christian to read on the Lord's Day."

Camp meetings that ran their programs over Sunday were particularly disliked at that same time too. If Sunday services were held, the gates to the grounds must be closed, railroad excursions positively not allowed at all, and all trucking into the grounds stopped. In 1888 and again in 1889, the Detroit Annual Conference petitioned the U.S. Congress to forbid needless Sunday work in interstate commerce, in mail delivery, and in the military services in time of peace. The M.E. Michigan Annual Conference in 1885 considered that Christian ministers countenanced the desecration of the Sabbath whenever they started a journey by train on Sunday or wrote an article for the Sunday edition of a secular newspaper.

Naturally Methodist Conference standards of conduct on weekdays were very high too. Card playing, horse racing, dancing, theater attendance, and betting on anything were all vigorously condemned. A sacred concert given by a travelling opera troupe was not approved nor was the conduct of those "who stroll along the edge of a beer garden scene 'just to hear the beautiful music.'"

❈   ❈   ❈   ❈   ❈   ❈

All Methodist Annual Conferences were still dealing austerely with ministerial conduct not up to the standards set by the *Discipline*. The procedure always began with a committee hearing and then, if it was thought necessary, a formal Conference trial before a select number of older ministers would be held. Many erring men admitted their sins, withdrew from the Conference, and returned their parchments of ordination rather than face such an ordeal. The Methodist Protestant Conferences in Michigan had one or two men almost every year in the Eighties who were asked to appear before the Judicial Committee. Some of the complaints were recorded in such general terms that it is impossible today to determine what it was all about but the commonest trouble was failure to remain on the work to which the man had been appointed or else never even showing himself on his new charge. It may be that the somewhat more independent spirit of the M.P.'s and their looser form of organization encouraged that sort of thing.

The M.E. Annual Conferences in Michigan had cases at the beginning and end of the decade in each half of the State. The charges were variously stated as "conduct unbecoming to a minister," "longstanding and excessive debts," "withdrawal under charges," and once a case of "gross immorality."

In 1890, the M.E. Michigan Annual Conference had what to them was a troublesome affair involving one of their members but which has a faintly amusing air today. The Rev. John W. Arney kept several horses for "exercise, pleasure, and pecuniary profit." Occasionally he sent his best horses to professional trainers. Eventually he got involved in a horse race with his neighbors with entrance and gate fees. But Mr. Arney flatly and vigorously denied that he allowed any betting. Unfortunately the secular press got hold of what he was doing and played it up very sensationally. The minister's Presiding Elder could scarcely believe what he read in his newspaper but wrote at once to Mr. Arney to withdraw from such activities. However, the minister thought it had gone too far for him to quit at the last moment.

But at Annual Conference time, he apologized very humbly before a special committee, admitted his imprudence and wrongdoing, and deeply regretted any harm he might have done the Church. He then declared that "while he remains a Methodist minister he will never again engage in horse racing, and that he expects to remain a Methodist minister as long as he lives." His apology and promise before the Committee were sufficiently humble and sweeping that the Annual Conference, after some hesitation, "passed his character" and continued him in his second year as a travelling Deacon. As perhaps might have been expected, his lifetime promises lasted three years. In 1893, Mr. Arney withdrew from the ministry and also the membership of the Methodist Episcopal Church.[15]

Optimistic Aspects of Michigan Methodism in the Eighties

Plenty of optimism can be found in those same committee reports on the State of the Church as the pessimism just cited. In 1883, a Committee of the M. E. Michigan Annual Conference considered the Church at large and saw four needs of Methodism. These were a consecrated and educated ministry, a converted membership, cheaper literature, and an enlarged area of benevolence. It said in part:

> There never was a time when there were more and better churches built than during the present year, and more and better sermons preached. There never was a time when more prayers went up from family altars

[15] Found in M.E. Michigan Annual Conference *Minutes* for 1890, pp. 347-349.

than during the past year. And there never was a time when there were more Bibles in existence and more children that gathered together to study the same than at the present. And there never was a time christian churches were more united than they are today. Formerly they preached against each other, now they preach for each other. And there never was such a time when the church took such united advanced ground on moral reforms. On all moral questions it is taking front seats and it has come to stay. The world is advancing. The Church is taking the lead. The true light is shining and God is marching among the nations.

Among the moral problems upon which Methodism was taking a strong position of leadership were temperance, Sabbath observance, periodicals and books of sensational or dirty nature, and certain current questions. Total personal abstinence and Statewide prohibition were held to be the answer to the liquor problem. Every year cooperation with the W.C.T.U. was recommended. In 1890, both M.E. Annual Conferences in Michigan adopted resolutions urging the managers of the Chicago Columbian Exposition, scheduled for 1892-1893, not to allow the Fair to be open on Sundays. The fact that the secular press was so sensational and also cheaper than the religious press was noted repeatedly with ministerial distress.

Polygamy, Chinese immigration, and social purity were among the problems of a social nature upon which the Annual Conferences in Michigan took a public position. A special committee of the Detroit Annual Conference session of 1882 expressed its abhorrence of polygamy, regretted the Federal government had been so slow in adopting a law to suppress it, and hoped that the law recently adopted would be vigorously enforced until this evil was exterminated. In 1887, a resolution passed by the Detroit Annual Conference advocated a single standard of social conduct and urged the ministers to promote local chapters of the White Cross League, recently introduced from England. Its members pledged themselves to treat women with respect, avoid indecent language, and check the telling of "coarse jests." Again cooperation with the W.C.T.U. was urged and also with the Y.M.C.A.

Individual salvation had for so long been the sole occupation of the Church that these modest resolutions do seem to show that the ministers were becoming more aware of evil, social situations. They were also concerned about the sad plight of many minorities in the United States. Most consistent and long continued was the concern for the freedmen of the South. The work to provide schools for the Negroes was still pursued just as zealously as it had been right after the Civil War.

Now in the 1880's some concern was also felt for the Chinese laborers in the far west. The Michigan Annual Conference adopted a petition in 1886 to the State's national Senators and Congressmen about the ill-treatment of the Chinese laborers in the Pacific Coast States when they were supposedly protected by a treaty made in 1880. Such actions in the west led to retaliation in China, which had destroyed one Methodist mission at Chung King and forced all its workers to leave China. More laws to protect the Chinese were badly needed at once. A third group for whom some concern was expressed was the "Polacks" then coming to Detroit in large numbers. But little could be done for them as yet due to the heavy demands of the northern work.

Beginnings of the Women's Home Missionary Society

The desperate need for more money and more hands to do the work of Methodism in Michigan was answered in part by the Women's Home Missionary Society. The origins of this new group may be found in work done among the Negro women of the South. A group of wives of ministers had hoped that the General Conference of 1880 would give official approval to their work which was centered in New Orleans. Nothing was done and the original Missionary Society was very cold and legalistic toward this new women's group. Therefore, with the help of the Presiding Elder of the Cincinnati District, the Women's Home Missionary Society organized, drew up a constitution, and then elected a full slate of officers. It was a help in getting started that Mrs. Rutherford B. Hayes accepted the national presidency of the new society.

Not unitl the General Conference of 1884 did the W.H.M.S. receive official recognition. Their duty was to do for the "heathen women" of the United States what the W.F.M.S. was doing for such women abroad. In 1883, the M.E. Michigan Annual Conference declared:

> We recognize in the destitution of our frontier settlements, in the influx of foreign immigration, in the duties we owe to the aborigines, in the abominations of Mormonism, and in the ignorance of the Southern freedwomen, an ample field, and the exceeding necessity for this branch of benevolent enterprise.[16]

Work by local auxiliaries of the W.H.M.S. had already begun in the Michigan Annual Conference before official approval by the M.E. General Conference of 1884. As early as 1882, this work was favorably known to the local ministers for the annual session voted approval and cooperation. Sister E. C. Wright was asked to continue her work as the Conference Secretary until a slate of officers could be elected. Therefore in 1883, it could be reported that $146.50 had already been sent to the national Corresponding Secretary.

After official approval by the General Conference in 1884, the ministers of the Detroit and Michigan Annual M.E. Conferences turned eagerly to the W.H.M.S. for help, not for the "heathen women," rather

---

[16] Michigan Annual Conference *Minutes* for 1882, p. 41; for 1883, p. 43. For a summary account, see W. C. Barclay, *History of Methodist Missions*, III, 148-153.

for the almost destitute ministers and their families on the "northern work" in their own State. An advisory committee of laymen and ministers was appointed and the W.H.M.S. was asked to raise $2,500 within the bounds of the Detroit Annual Conference to be divided   exactly as the general missionary funds were. Three small auxiliaries were in existence when the request was made. By Conference time in 1885, the women had established 67 auxiliaries, had raised $2,250 in money, and had $1,200 in supplies. No wonder that the ministers pledged them a warm welcome to all their churches and the heartiest cooperation. It was urged that auxiliaries be organized, even in the poorest churches, to show their appreciation and to be prepared "in coming days to give as freely as they now receive."

By 1886, the Detroit M.E. Annual Conference numbered 92 auxiliaries with 1,700 members. That same year the W.H.M.S. organized a minister's circulating library made up mostly of the books of the Conference course of study. These were meant for the use of the men who were too poor to buy them. The Presiding Elders were to see to the distribution of the books. The Conference asked the W.H.M.S. to help extend religious instruction to lumber and mining camps through the auxiliaries on nearby circuits. One of the local members had made a personal call on the General Committee of the parent Missionary Society and thereby secured a raise of $2,800 annually in the appropriations for each Conference in the State of Michigan.

At the Detroit Annual Conference session of 1890 it was reported that the auxiliaries of the W.H.M.S. had raised $8,841 during the previous year. It is very noticeable that the Detroit District gave $5,308 of the total sum and the other divisions from 1/5 to 1/10 of it. The Society held an anniversary program on Friday afternoon of Conference week and had a full complement of officers who were women and advisors who were ministers.

The Michigan M.E. Annual Conference reported at its session of 1890 that the W.H.M.S. had collected $2,141 that year. Grand Rapids District gave the largest sum which was $435. It is probable that these statements of the total sums given included supplies such as shoes and clothing. It must be that it was in this period that the custom of packing a barrel for the missionary family began.

Certainly the ministers appreciated the help the women were giving judging in part from the resolutions of gratitude that they annually adopted. Their attitude toward women in Methodism also began to change. In 1883, the Detroit Annual Conference adopted a memorial to the impending General Conference asking for the licensing of women as exhorters and preachers. It would be particularly useful to have them so licensed in the foreign mission fields. In 1888, an effort was made to seat women in the General Conference. Each M.E. Annual Conference in Michigan elected women that year among the lay delegates. An advisory vote was taken in 1890 in the same Conference as to whether women should be eligible to become lay delegates to the General and Electoral Conferences. It was carefully specified that the vote was only to "ascertain the mind of the Church . . . not determine the final result." It must be remembered that the lay *men* were still trying to obtain equal representation in the General Conference with ministerial delegates and also direct membership in the Annual Conferences. None of the changes desired by lay men and lay women were made until the 20th century.

One action taken by the General Conference of 1888 was a help to both the Home and Foreign mission work. This was the creation of an order of deaconesses. The W.H.M.S. found their help particularly useful in the cities and soon plans for Deaconess Homes were made. In 1888 and again in 1890, the Detroit Annual Conference recommended the new order and asked for the creation of an advisory board for the deaconess work. In 1889, the Michigan M.E. Annual Conference praised the creation of the Deaconesses and declared this action was both "opportune and providential." It was thought that Grand Rapids would be peculiarly well suited for the establishment of a Deaconess Home.

The Care of Conference Claimants: Retired Preachers and Their Widows

A financial problem on which the Conferences in Michigan spent much time in the 1880's was the proper care of the aged Conference claimants. Annually the funds at hand were carefully divided on the basis of need and years of service to Methodism. The sad part was that the amount of money for this purpose was so pitifully small. Almost every year those to whom it fell to deal with the individual cases complained in their reports of how hard it was to care for those who deserved so much and received so little. The so-called Chartered Fund, sums long invested for the benefit of superannuated ministers, and the Book Concern each sent an annual check to every M.E. Conference. Usually this was presented by the bishop assigned to preside there that year. Then the Board of Stewards divided and delivered the money. Very few ministers got over $100 and the widows got about ⅓ or ⅔ of that sum.

Both M. E. Annual Conferences in Michigan concerted their efforts in the 1880's to increase their funds for the elderly ministers and their widows. It was agreed to say more to their congregations about the retired preachers and to try holding a Historical Day on the Sunday before Thanksgiving. A special sermon was to be preached, telling of the history of the local church, and efforts should be made to get the retired ministers and elderly lay members to attend. The claims of the superannuated should be explained and all collections taken on that day should go to their aid through the Conference Preachers Aid Society. Efforts to establish a permanent, endowed fund must be kept up and the suitability of bequests for that purpose made clear.

The results were an improvement but not by any means all the money that was needed. The Detroit Annual Conference in 1880 raised $1,281.82 and in 1890 collected $7,381.28. The Michigan M.E. Annual Conference Stewards had $1,692.22 in 1880 and $10,098.91 in 1890 to distribute. This seems a rather remarkable increase until it is realized that these amounts were never over half of what the Claimants were entitled to under the *Discipline* rules.

A number of special gifts and bequests encouraged the Conference in their efforts for the retired men. In 1884, the Detroit Annual Conference received $44.25 for the Conference Claimants from the Lansing National Holiness Camp Meeting Association as "part of the surplus of gate fees above expenses." The Rev. Henry W. Hicks got out a *Conference Daily* in the years from 1885 through 1887 making thereby $85 which he then gave to the Conference Claimants. In a few desperate cases, a Conference took a collection among its own members or the trustees of the corporate Conference would. The Rev. Luther Lee was very old and very poor when his wife died. A quiet collection among "friends" paid for her funeral and provided a burial lot in Glenwood Cemetery, Flint. A large plot with space for twenty-five burials was obtained and maintained for the use of those in need among Detroit Annual Conference ministers or their families.

The M.E. Annual Conferences in Michigan, in dealing with the funds for retired ministers, found it necessary to plunge much more deeply in to many business matters than had ever been done before. The Detroit Annual Conference had rather more of that kind of thing than the Michigan Annual Conference did in the 1880's.

In 1875, the Mary A. Palmer Fund was established by her son, Thomas W. Palmer, soon after her death. He felt that he was carrying out her last wishes when he gave $5,000 to start a permanent fund for the superannuated preachers. This first gift was restricted in that the interest was to be divided between Seth Reed, Elijah Pilcher, and Manasseh Hickey. These men had been her pastors and she specially wished that they and their widows should be helped. After all of them were gone, the interest would go into the general fund for the retired ministers.[17] In 1882, Mr. Palmer gave $5,000 more to the same fund without any restrictions upon its division. In its expression of gratitude to Mr. Palmer, the Detroit Annual Conference called it his "munificent gift."

[17] E. H. Pilcher, *Hist. Prot. Mich.*, pp. 145-147. Detroit Annual Conf. *Minutes* for 1882, p. 11; for 1888, pp. 19-20. Mary A. Palmer was the daughter of James Witherell, a prominent early citizen of Detroit. Pilcher died in 1887, Hickey in 1903, and Seth Reed in 1924.

The "Winters Fund" was also administered by the Detroit Annual Conference. This was the residue of her husband's estate which he wished Mrs. Winters to bequeath to the Detroit Annual Conference. Three ministers had explained to the couple the work of the Superannuated Preachers Aid Society. After some hesitation, the Conference trustees decided that they were entitled to use the interest for the elderly preachers. But investment of the money, mostly in land mortgages, was an anxiety to them for some years. Sometimes a farm mortgage had to be foreclosed and another one arranged.

Not until 1889 did the Michigan M.E. Annual Conference receive any substantial legacy. Melville R. Bissell was a lay member of the Board of Trustees of Division Street Church in Grand Rapids. Upon his death, it was learned that he had bequeathed to that Church for the Superannuated Preachers Fund the dividends upon eighty shares of the stock of the Bissell Carpet Sweeper Company. This gift seemed a bit uncertain to the executrix, Bissell's widow, and to the Board of the local Church. Therefore she offered to give $3,000 of the estate "to be kept at interest forever in exchange for the stock." The widow, the Board of Trustees, and the Probate Judge all felt that such an arrangement would help the aged ministers more than the stock dividends would. They agreed that "the stock is subject to fluctuations and contingencies affecting corporations." The members of the Conference were very pleased to accept this adjusted legacy.[18]

What would the old time circuit riders have thought of a Methodist Annual Conference dealing with dividends, interest, and mortgages! Incidentally, the Michigan M.E. Annual Conference session of 1885 presented three gold watches to three Presiding Elders, who were retiring from the District work, also a "silver bronze mantle clock" to the wife of one of them and a gavel to the Presiding Bishop, Henry W. Warren. In 1886, only one Presiding Elder got a gold watch. But in 1887, one Presiding Elder was given a purse of $50 and another one, also retiring, received "an elegant Bible."

1880-1890, The *Michigan Christian Advocate*

An additional source of funds for the superannuated ministers and what should have been an added source of optimism was the steady growth and success of the *Michigan Christian Advocate*. Its subscription lists increased every year and thereby the amount of money it was able to tender each Conference in Michigan for its retired ministers. A gift of $50 in gold to each M.E. Annual Conference in Michigan in 1881 was doubled in 1882 and tripled in 1883. By 1890, the MCA was able to split $2,500 between the two M.E. Annual Conferences. The total contributed in that decade to both Conferences by their own

[18] Michigan Annual Conference *Minutes* for 1889, pp. 162-163.

Advocate was $9,628.92. In 1882, this weekly paper had about 6,500 subscribers and in 1890 it had 15,736. It was hoped that it would soon have 20,000.

The Conference Periodical Committee reports in that same decade show a certain amount of unhappiness over the success of a *privately* owned, religious paper. A committee of the Detroit Annual Conference in 1886 reminded the ministers that the paper did not belong to "the officially recognized Advocate family of the Methodist Episcopal Church." Yet that same committee admitted that the *MCA* was the periodical "most generally patronized by our people . . . in solid worth the equal of any of its foster sisters, and in practical serviceableness to the church in our State, the superior of them all."

The Michigan M.E. Annual Conference Periodicals Committee in 1883 was a bit fearful that Methodists no longer gave enough attention to the *Northwestern Christian Advocate*. It was admitted that the *Michigan Christian Advocate* was newsy and "ably conducted" but every pastor ought to try to place one of our *official* papers in every home on his charge. Otherwise, the Methodist "connectional interest" might be endangered.

The continued success of the *Michigan Christian Advocate* and its annually increasing contributions to the retired preachers fund tended in time to change the tone of the ministerial comments about it to one of gratitude for its success. The information that it distributed over the State of Michigan must have greatly aided the growth of Bay View, Albion College, and the Epworth League.

John M. Arnold, of the Detroit Annual Conference, and James H. Potts, of the Michigan M.E. Annual Conference, were the editors who so greatly expanded the *Michigan Christian Advocate*. The first had entered the Detroit Annual Conference in 1849 and worked at a great many different places and jobs since then. Today he seems like the first of the modern business man-administrator-clergymen. Quite early he became interested in getting a branch of the Methodist Book Concern in Detroit and, after that was withdrawn, he ran a religious book store with a partner named Willyoung. The firm specialized in Sunday School library books for all the Protestant denominations. Later they carried the books that young ministers needed for their Conference courses of study. Arnold had a hand in most of the Detroit Annual Conference projects needing money. He was one of the founders of Bay View. Holding eleven shares of stock in the Methodist Publishing Company made him one of the organizers of the *Michigan Christian Advocate*. He was also Treasurer of the Detroit Corporate Conference as well as permanent secretary of the committee on Historical Day and the intended Centenary Fund.

Arnold died without a minute's warning in December, 1884. Little wonder that his loss was felt to be a catastrophe among the members of the Detroit Annual Conference. The writer of Arnold's Conference memoir in 1885 declared that at one time Dr. Arnold was too much influenced in his preaching by his business affairs and by a "plausible liberalism" but in his last years, while he was editor of the *MCA*, he had regained his devotion to spiritual Christianity. In his prayer at the Sunday morning service during the last Annual Conference session, Mr. Arnold had seemed like a man "who had power with God."[19]

The Michigan M.E. Annual Conference furnished James H. Potts, who served the *Michigan Christian Advocate* for forty years from 1877 to 1917. His was the longest term of service of any editor of that paper. He was an Associate Editor at first and listed in Conference assignments as Agent of the Preachers Savings Fund Society. When Lewis R. Fiske gave up the Chief Editor's position to become President of Albion College, Arnold assumed the head editorial position and Potts was brought in as office manager. He had been admitted to the Michigan M.E. Annual Conference in 1869 and, while serving various charges, had also written for the press. He had then begun to lose his hearing to the extent that it interfered with his work as a minister with a charge. But Mr. Potts still had many years of usefulness as the Office Editor in Detroit of the *Michigan Christian Advocate*. He always took a liberal position on reform questions in Methodism, repeatedly advocating·the admission of women to a position in the General Conference equal with that of laymen. Mr. Potts was not afraid to argue in the open session of the General Conference with the Rev. James M. Buckley, prominent editor of the New York *Christian Advocate*.

1880-1890, Bay View

Bay View developed especially in intellectual and social ways in the Eighties. The former Michigan State Camp Meeting was transformed in length, purposes and accomplishments. The original, dual aims of Bay View still dominated the work there during the first half of the decade. Dating from 1876 was the camp meeting and after it a general Sunday School meeting for teachers of all Protestant denominations. The religious atmosphere of the camp meetings can be seen in the testimony at the Michigan Annual Conference Love Feast on Sunday, September 15, 1889, of "Father S. C. Moon, over 90 years old." He said in part:

> A few years ago, at Bay View, I got a great uplift . . . it did seem to me I was up among the tops of those big trees, and I have lived up there ever since. Jesus, precious Jesus, permeates even to the outer rim of my

[19] J. E. Marvin, *The Advocate Story*, pp. 3, 5. E. H. Pilcher, *Hist. Prot. Mich.*, pp. 417, 419, 430-435. Memoir of Arnold in Detroit Conf. *Minutes* for 1885, pp. 54-58. For pictures of Arnold and Potts see pp. 317, 318 of this book.

being. I am now ready to depart. Surely the time of my departure is near at hand, but it is all bright ahead.[20]

In 1882, the Michigan M.E. Annual Conference received an invitation to hold their next meeting at Bay View and Petoskey. The invitation was declined on the ground that it was necessary to meet at Albion. This is presumed to have been because the lay Electoral Conference delegates would also be present in 1883. Hence the numbers at Conference would be so increased that not enough rooms would be available in the north. Then in 1886, the Conference decided to meet at Bay View the next year if the Presiding Elders could make "satisfactory arrangements with railroads and for entertainment."

Evidently this was done for the session in 1887 was held in the Chapel at Bay View. Bishop Ninde was delayed and wired the ministers to organize and begin the routine business. The Rev. J. M. Reid of New York City was chosen President and the regular rules were adopted, committees appointed, and examination of the characters of the elders started. Seth Reed, then Secretary of the Bay View Camp Meeting Association, was present and presumably welcomed the Conference. But when Reed presented the parchments of a minister, who wished to withdraw from the Conference, the ministers punctiliously voted that such a matter must be delayed until the Bishop was present.

If the wording of the *Minutes* is any indication, the Detroit Annual Conference was more enthusiastic about expanding the work at Bay View than the Michigan M.E. Conference was. In 1887, the Detroit Annual Conference voted its "hearty accord" with the efforts of the Bay View Superintendent to create a Bay View Sunday School Normal Course. The idea was to gain not just the cooperation of the Methodists in the Michigan Conference but also of the Baptists, Presbyterians, and Congregationalists. A short catechism, suggestions for Bible study, and practical hints for teachers were to be included in the new course of study. Then an effort would be made to hold a number of local teachers institutes to study the various plans. But the Michigan M.E. Annual Conference in 1889, and again in 1890, in the midst of long reports on the Sunday School and Tract Society, inserted one sentence of recommendation of "the Bible and Sunday School course prescribed by the Bay View Assembly."

Both M.E. Annual Conferences in Michigan realized fully for the first time in the mid-Eighties that they had in the Sunday Schools the future members of the Methodist Episcopal Church. The Detroit Annual Conference declared "the most promising field for revival work

[20] Michigan M.E. Annual Conference *Minutes* for 1889, p. 194.

is among the children." If all the Sunday School children could be received into the Church before reaching the age of twelve, they would be "saved from graduating into the streets, and finally into perdition."[21]

As the camp meeting and revival were changing so was Bay View. A young lawyer from Flint, John H. Hall, was largely responsible for the new developments. He had learned of the work of Bishop Vincent at Chatauqua, New York.

In the summer of 1886, Hall introduced a Michigan Chatauqua Assembly and started the CLSC. The initials stood for Chatauqua Literary and Scientific Circle. Locally these were reading clubs with a four-year plan of study. The headquarters were at Bay View. That same summer of 1886, a small summer school was in session and a program of lectures and music was conducted for four weeks. The Camp Ground Association was so pleased with the response that it incorporated the whole business as the Bay View Assembly in the fall of 1886.

The formal, summer classes were called both a summer school and a summer university. The idea of studying in the summer time was quite new in the United States then and it caught on at once with the school teachers of America. Study, a climate change, low costs, a pleasant vacation, and Christian surroundings were a very appealing combination. By 1888, four hundred teachers were in attendance at the summer school. Loud Hall, a permanent building for the school, was completed that same year. By 1890, education was being offered in a great variety of subjects. Among them were photography, English, cooking, music, geology, elocution, the Bible, business, and kindergarten training. In 1890, thirty-two instructors were required for the summer school.

The Assembly programs were changing too. In 1889, Frances E. Willard gave a temperance lecture. In 1890, Russell H. Conwell gave his famous "Acres of Diamonds" lecture. Both were to appear on the Bay View lecture platform many times. No longer were hymns the only music at Bay View for a great chorus sang the world's classical music.

Two modest legal changes took place in 1890. The name became Bay View Camp Ground Association of the Methodist Episcopal Church instead of Michigan. More important, the required occupation for fifteen years had taken place. Therefore the railroad gave a quit-claim deed to the Association and the property was at last fully in their own hands.[22]

---

[21] Detroit Annual Conference *Minutes* for 1887, pp. 77-78. Michigan Annual Conference *Minutes* for 1890, p. 359.

[22] Robert M. Garter, "Why Bay View Commenced," Mich. *Christian Advocate*, May 20, 1965, XCII, #20, pp. 3-4, 18-20. Jerome A. Fallon, "Bay View Revisited," *Michigan History*, March 1964, XLVIII, #1, pp. 18-34. The Detroit Annual Conference *Minutes* for 1886, p. 23. (approval of CLSC).

1880-1890, Albion College

The history of Albion College in the Eighties reveals the same combination of success in some fields and failure in others that characterized the Michigan Methodist Episcopal Church then in general. The Rev. Lewis Ransom Fiske was president of Albion College from 1877 to 1897. Judged from the year 1966, Fiske was the founder of the modern Albion College. Certainly he made many important academic changes in the twenty years he served as President. Yet, like other Presidents before him, Fiske was never able to establish the College on a sound financial basis. It must however be noted that the College was less deeply in debt in the 1880's and even had an occasional year when it had a few dollars left over after all the bills were paid. That was not true in the decade before or the one afterwards.

When he was appointed to the Presidency, Fiske was Editor of the *Michigan Christian Advocate* and also pastor of Tabernacle Church in Detroit. He said himself that he was reluctant to come to Albion partly because he would have to take a $1,000 cut in his salary but also on account of "the general conviction that the College would not and could not be made successful." Its attendance was small and its debts large. Efforts to create an endowment had not really succeeded. The Education Committee of the Michigan M.E. Annual Conference of 1880 observed that "Albion College has never yet had a bequest of a dollar."[23]

23. Robèrt Gildart, *Albion College, 1835-1960.* Chapter VI is on Fiske's Presidency. Statement by Fiske when he retired is given in full on pp. 153-158. Each year the M.E. Conferences in Michigan had reports on Education and reference was always made therein to the programs of Albion College.

Lewis Ransom Fiske (1825-1901) graduated from the University of Michigan in 1850. He served prominent pulpits in Michigan, and was president of Albion College for 20 years (1877-97). He was six times elected to the General Conference, and was an honored Methodist educator.

Worse yet, during the year 1880-1881, considerable agitation for the removal of Albion College to Detroit occurred. Not only the secular press but also the *Michigan* and *Northwestern Christian Advocates* favored such a step. No inducement of any value at all had ever been made from any town in Michigan. Moving the College to Detroit would mean that many Methodists in the western part of the State would send their children to nearer and non-religious colleges. Such drastic suggestions tended to disturb the faculty and students and certainly destroyed any local influence of the institution. A large city was in no way essential to a good college. Therefore, the special Conference committee, carefully chosen to deal with the question of the removal of Albion College to Detroit, recommended that all such agitation cease at once. And the Michigan M.E. Annual Conference of 1881 fully agreed with the committee opinion.

Several factors combined to produce the profound changes in programs, courses, and staff that President Fiske began in 1881. The student numbers were low. Only six graduated in 1879. Much open criticism had been made during the discussion of whether the College should be moved to Detroit. The College program had always been heavily classical with much emphasis on Latin and Greek. In the classroom, the ministerial viewpoint had dominated whatever the instruction might be. In 1882, the Michigan M.E. Annual Conference adopted a resolution of approval of the changes Fiske was making. It said, "The new departure is reversing the course of study in the classical and scientific courses, compelling the student to master the modern languages before entering upon the study of the ancient Greek and Latin." In History, the 19th century was to be studied first, the Latin Scientific program did not require Greek, and a Bachelor of Letters program was established with emphasis on English. The number and variety of courses were also greatly expanded. In 1880 the courses offered numbered 67 while in 1885 they had grown to 133. More electives were included too.

Another development in 1883 was the establishment of a weekly college newspaper, the *Pleiad*. Certain literary society papers had been published intermittently before then but the *Pleiad* was to enjoy continuous publication up to the present time.

An indication of somewhat lessened control by the ministers was a change in the College charter to allow representatives of the College alumni on the Board of Trustees. Until this time, the members of the Board of Trustees had been ministers appointed in equal numbers from the Detroit and Michigan Annual Conferences. Now the Board was to add six alumni chosen by the Alumni Society. This would make them equal with the ministers from one Conference. And eventually this would bring a more secular and business man's viewpoint to the College Board of Trustees.[24]

The year 1884 was the centennial of the Christmas Conference that chose Francis Asbury a Bishop and established the American Methodist Episcopal Church. Plans were laid in both the Conferences in Michigan, during their 1883 sessions, for a big anniversary program to take place as nearly as possible to December 28, the exact date of Asbury's consecration as Bishop. Much was to be made of Conference and national Methodist History. The twin goals of the fund drives, in connection with the Asbury centenary, were education and the Fund for the superannuated preachers. Meetings of the Albion College Board of Trustees with seven ministers and seven laymen from each Annual Conference in the State were held to plan a drive to collect an adequate endowment for Albion.

The theoretical organization of the Asbury Centenary Association took nine pages of fine print just to describe. District organizations, church auxiliaries, Sunday School junior groups, etc. were suggested. The goal was $500,000 and when this amount had been raised, it was suggested that Albion College should be renamed Asbury Centenary University. Of course, this was never done . Considering the economic conditions in Michigan then, how much of the State was still almost a frontier farming area, and the scope and detail of the plans, the project seems today to have been over-elaborated and over-large.

The ministers directly concerned must have realized that a project had been undertaken that would require many years for its completion. In 1885, the Centenary Association suggested to the M.E. Conferences in Michigan that the last Thursday in January should be observed as a day of prayer for colleges with particular attention given to Albion and its needs. As to the immediate Centenary celebration in December, 1884, many ministers felt that a significant religious service was of the first importance. Hence special revivals and District gatherings were held to honor the Asbury Centenary.

Throughout these years of special effort, James S. Smart had served as financial agent for Albion College. The financial side of the Centenary in Michigan received a setback when John M. Arnold died very suddenly in December, 1884. He was the Editor of the *Michigan Christian Advocate*, a member of the Centenary Association committee, and permanent secretary of the Detroit Annual Conference Historical Day in addition to the superannuated preachers fund raising. The committee told the next session of the Detroit Annual Conference that his death "seemed to check all our plans" as he was "the one on whom we had mainly relied." Besides a considerable "stringency in the money

---

[24] Detroit Annual Conference *Minutes* for 1882, p. 41. Gildart says in *Albion College*, p. 144, that only three alumni were to be elected.

market" had been felt in Michigan throughout 1884-1885. The need for more adequate publicity was felt for Albion College. So in 1889, a college lectureship to give the public more information on the value of a college education and the work of Albion was established. The Rev. Washington Gardner, then pastor of a large church in Cincinnati, was chosen as its first occupant.

Albion College at last had begun to grow in student population. The preparatory and college enrollment together in 1879-1880 was 243 while in 1889-1890 it was 496. This seems like a modest gain today but it had more than doubled in ten years.

The many changes introduced by President Fiske were apparently leading some Methodists to regard the College with greater favor. A sign of the changing times was the gift to Albion College in 1889 of $30,000 by Henry M. Loud for the endowment of a Chair of History. He was one of the trustees of the College, a lay member of the General Conference of 1884, and the donor of Loud Hall at the Bay View Assembly. His fortune was made in lumbering in Oscoda and AuSable.

1880-1900, Adrian College

Adrian College was the property of the Methodist Protestants alone in the Eighties. The former connection with the Wesleyans under the name Methodist only had been broken off in 1877 and that had left a residue of bitterness. The Michigan Annual Conference of the Methodist Protestants had tried to support the College and keep it a vigorous, growing institution. But the task was too much for a small and individualistic denomination, which lacked both the numbers and financial resources needed for the work.

The financial problems of Adrian College were very similar to those of Albion. Both Colleges suffered from inadequate endowments whose income did not equal the annual expenses of the institutions. Annual income from College Day collections in the churches was not what might have been expected either. The Methodist Protestant Annual Conferences each year repeated a promise to raise 10¢ per member for Adrian College. In 1881, the Michigan M.P. Conference received a report that the sum of $60.28 had been collected that year for Adrian College. The committee estimated that the amount was less than *one-fourth* of the dime per member assessed by the previous Conference. Returns were much the same in other years of the decade and in the West Michigan and North Indiana M.P. Conference. Heroic efforts on the part of President and faculty to keep expenses within income could not possibly succeed with such small collections. It caused rejoicing when the College got through a year without any addition to its total indebtedness as it did in 1882.

Local appreciation of Adrian College was stronger than that found elsewhere in Michigan. A bad fire destroyed the old North Hall in November 1880. It was almost immediately rebuilt "in a manner and style far better than before." The M.P. Conference committee on the College was pleased that "A subscription of over $3,000 by citizens of Adrian and vicinity" showed "better appreciation of the College by those nearest to it." Another sign of more approval was an increase in the number of local students attending the school.

Efforts were urged annually to increase the number of students in attendance at Adrian. Pastors were exhorted to preach or lecture every year at least once to their congregations about Adrian, its program, buildings, and needs. In the twenty years from 1880 to 1900, the best attendance at Adrian was that of the year 1881-1882 when "nearly 222" were reported to the Michigan M.P. Conference as "being the largest number ever in attendance during the time it has been in the possession of the M.P. Church." In 1900, the College had only 170 students.

Administrative difficulties capped all their other problems at Adrian College. In the twenty years between 1880 and 1900, *six* Presidents headed the College. All were no doubt good even devout Methodist Protestants but some were poor administrators or unhappy in such work, as the Rev. G. B. McElroy had been. Others were baffled by the various problems and above all by the debts and financial hardships of Adrian College.

An Acting President, Mark B. Taylor, served from 1880 to 1882. Then David Stephens was President from 1882 to 1888. He tried several new ideas such as a college paper with off campus circulation. But he left to become editor of the *Methodist Recorder.*

So many difficulties were encountered by Joseph McCulloch in the years from 1888 to 1893 that he tried to move the College to Ohio. The Adrian townspeople and the members of the First M.P. Church there united to stop his attempt. McCulloch may have had a good idea, at least in part, because Adrian's College's difficulties were due, it was thought then and since, to its location on the far edge of the strongest Methodist Protestant influence in terms of churches and numbers of members.

Dennison C. Thomas succeeded McCulloch as President but five years in the office were enough for him. Thomas in turn was followed by another Acting President, O. L. Palmer, who served for one year. Next the Rev. David B. Jones held a triple job as he was local pastor of First M.P. Church, a teaching professor and President of Adrian College from 1899 to 1902.[25] Continuity of policy must have been lacking in the Adrian of those years.

[25] F. W. Stephenson, Adrian College. Article in the Detroit Conference Archives, Adrian College Library.

The greatest influence for good in the late decades of the 19th century was exerted by Adrian College in the field of the professional education of Methodist Protestant ministers. The two Conferences in the State of Michigan followed the course of study laid out by the professors at Adrian for their probationary ministers. Young men were repeatedly urged to prepare for the ministry by college training rather than individual study. Dr. McElroy had great influence then upon the individual male students and upon the theology studied. This was not confined to two or three ministerial students from Michigan alone. The Committee on Ministerial Education of the Michigan M.P. Annual Conference of 1881 reported that there were "during the past year, thirty-seven young men in our two leading colleges preparing for the ministery (*sic*) — twenty-five at Adrian College and twelve at Western Maryland College." The "self-sacrificing labors of a few" kept the burdened College at work preparing a part of the Methodist Protestant membership for more adequate church leadership in the future.

New Organizations for work with M.E. Young Adults
1) The Wesleyan Guild

From the viewpoint of 1966, the most hopeful developments of the 1880's were the organizations for work with young adult Methodists. These were the Wesleyan Guild in Ann Arbor, a forerunner of the Wesley Foundation, and the Epworth League. The latter was formed in 1889 in Cleveland and spread rapidly over Michigan in 1890. These groups had a fresh viewpoint and were generally welcomed although some older members had doubts about them. The work of both groups was carried on among Methodist Episcopalians. The Methodist Protestants tended to favor and join the Christian Endeavor Societies.

Back in the 1850's, Michigan Methodists had been concerned to find more Methodist Episcopal Professors for the University of Michigan. Four houses for the Professors were part of the campus then and it was thought that one of them should always be occupied by a Methodist. The coming of the Rev. E. O. Haven to Ann Arbor relieved these Methodist anxieties for a time.

By 1882, the Ann Arbor Methodists were anxious to do more for the college students of their denomination than ever before contemplated. It was suggested by the Ann Arbor Quarterly Conference to the Detroit Annual Conference of that year that a building, to be named Haven Hall, should be erected for the lodging and boarding of young men and women students of the University. The Conference was interested, kept a committee going on the subject for several years but had so many calls for money that nothing much was done for Ann Arbor just then.

The Michigan M.E. Annual Conference was so engrossed in efforts to do something for Albion College that it paid little attention to the

University of Michigan at that time. In 1886, when its session was visited by the agent of the Student Christian Association in Ann Arbor, the ministers agreed that such work was needed and they hoped that Methodists would make a liberal response to his pleas.

The Detroit Annual Conference, in 1884 and again in 1886, expressed the same general approval of the S.C.A. But neither did it give any monetary assistance. In 1886, the report of the Committee on Education mentioned that the University of Michigan had 1,400 students, of whom 264 were members or adherents of the Methodist Episcopal Church. This was 78 more than the numbers of any other one denomination.

At last the members of the Ann Arbor First Church began to organize on their own initiative in order to do something for Methodist students. The first steps were taken in 1886 but it was quickly apparent that more money and a meeting place were badly needed. Other denominations were erecting buildings for student work there. Why could not the Methodists do likewise?

The name Wesleyan Guild was early chosen and steps were taken toward incorporation. The dual purpose was a Guild Hall and an endowed lecture series. At that time, New Testament Greek, Hebrew, comparative religions, and the history of Christianity were not taught in the University. Also young Methodists ought not to grow up in ignorance of the teachings of their own denomination. Thus far, the local Methodists, notably Junius E. Beal, had supported the project themselves but, in 1889, help was sought from the Conferences in Michigan. The Ann Arbor people would give the site if the ministers would raise the $45,000 needed for the building and the $15,000 necessary for the endowment of a future lecture course.

Under the incorporation, the affairs of the Wesleyan Guild were to be run by a board of trustees of nine members. Of the first board, five were professors in the University of Michigan. Among the five were Henry W. Rogers, Dean of the Law School, Joseph B. Steere, Professor of Zoology, and Alexander Winchell, Professor of Geology. An advisory council of fifteen was also provided. The Detroit and Michigan Annual Conferences were each asked to appoint two of their number each year to the advisory council. The minister currently appointed to Ann Arbor First Church should always be a member of the advisory board. Then the rest of the membership were to be elected by the trustees. Presumably the first trustees were chosen by the Ann Arbor church and after that were self-perpetuating. Bishops Vincent and Newman were members of the first advisory council. The Michigan M.E. Annual Conference appointed Levi Master and A. A. Knappen to that first advisory group and the Detroit Annual Conference sent William H. Shier and Charles T. Allen.

Some criticism was encountered in the early days of the Wesleyan Guild. People thought it was trying to compete with Albion College.

If parents wanted more Methodist education for their children, then they should have sent them to "our own institutions." But the possibilities inherent in contacts with students from all over the United States and even more with non-Christian foreign students were clearly seen by the founders of the Wesleyan Guild. At that time, the University had a number of Japanese students. Both Annual Conferences and also the Trustees thought that more promising young men might be drawn into the ministry through the Wesleyan Guild.

To meet the criticism and also report on the work done, the Wesleyan Guild got out a small brochure in 1890. Written by Professor Alexander Winchell, it included a number of letters of commendation for what was being done. Four Bishops and two editors, Arthur Edwards and James M. Buckley, having been to Ann Arbor gave the Wesleyan Guild their enthusiastic support. Enough money had been raised locally to support a course of six lectures each year for three years. Seven Bishops had been among the lecturers in the two years the course had existed. Of course, it was felt then that the Wesleyan Guild was inspired by John Wesley's famous Holy Club at Oxford. For a number of years, the Guild made use of the social rooms and auditorium of the First Methodist Episcopal Church at Ann Arbor.[26]

2) The National Methodist Board of Education

Attention should be called to the increased importance of the national Board of Education of the Methodist Episcopal Church. This had been created as one of the results of the Centennial Commemoration of 1866. The General Conference of 1888 had raised the Board of Education to equality with the other great national boards of the Methodist Episcopal Church. The Secretary of the Board of Education was made a General Conference officer. Its work was to be broadened, the Methodist colleges and schools drawn closer in a more systematic way, and the "connectional" bonds tightened. The chief function of the Board of Education at this time was the administration of the Student Loan Fund. This was created also in 1866 to become the result of the collections taken on Children's Day all through the Church. It made a great many student loans through the years and helped many a deserving Methodist student to stay in college. Albion College authorities, the Board of the Wesleyan Guild, and the officers of the new Epworth

---

[26] Michigan Annual Conference *Minutes* for 1889, pp. 220, 236. Detroit Annual Conference Minutes for 1888, p. 15; for 1889, pp. 71-73; for 1890, p. 73. Alexander Winchell, *The Wesleyan Guild at the University of Michigan*, 1890. A brochure printed by Courier Printing House, Ann Arbor, Mich. A copy of this booklet was obtained through the efforts of Rev. Charles Cooley, Wesley Foundation Director, Western Michigan University.

League would all in their own ways find that Student Loan Fund helpful.[27]

Origins of the Epworth League

For many years a gap existed between the work with the children in the Sunday Schools and the labors of class leaders and ministers with the adult Methodists. A considerable variety of societies for filling this gap already existed before 1889. Reading a large number of individual church histories leaves the impression that the majority of them claim to have had some kind of a young people's society before the Epworth League was ever thought of or organized. In general, these local young people's societies met at 7 P.M. Sunday nights in the church building and included almost everyone who was not still in the Infants Class in the Sunday School or, on the other hand, too old and feeble to come out to the church.

A veneer of non-religious purposes was sometimes given to the early local young people's societies. Literary Societies were very common then so perhaps the pastor suggested a young people's society with Christian literary exercises. One called simply The Young People's Society was formed at the minister's suggestion in Tecumseh in March, 1888. Again a temperance motive might be combined with the literary and religious themes. The I.O.G.T. — Independent Order of Good Templars — was quite strong in the Seventies as also were the Red Ribbon Societies. Both made a special appeal to young adults. The W.C.T.U. used the white ribbon as a symbol for total abstinence but the red ribbon is thought to have represented moderation and a Christian attitude in all social activities. A Red Ribbon Society was formed in the West Leroy Church, south of Battle Creek, in April, 1878.[28]

Of the organized societies, the most numerous in Michigan was the Young People's Methodist Alliance. It was stronger in the Michigan M.E. Annual Conference than in the Detroit Conference. The Y.P.M.A. was started at a camp meeting at Desplaines, Illinois, in August, 1883. The Rev. Morton D. Carrel, of Michigan Annual Conference, became its General Superintendent in 1888 but retained his Quarterly Conference connection in St. Joseph. He evidently was a vigorous worker because it was announced in December, 1888, that over one hundred local alliances had been organized and four Annual Conferences, including the Michigan one, had also joined.

The Y.P.M.A. took itself and its work very seriously. The pledge, taken upon one's knees when joining, promised to seek heart purity, pray and work for the salvation of souls, engage in regular Bible study

[27] Detroit Annual Conference Minutes for 1888, p. 63.
[28] R. A. Brunger, "Forerunners of the Methodist Youth Fellowship," in Michigan Christian Advocate for April 4, 1957, LXXXIV, #14, pp. 6-7.

and avoid worldly amusements such as cards, theater, dancing, opera, drink, and tobacco. Much attention was given to training schools in which the members were taught how to do Christian work. One was held at Crystal Springs in the summer of 1888. Y.P.M.A. members were inclined to look with suspicion on other youth groups and feel that their organization was the best. They disliked particularly the Christian Endeavor Society, which just then was making an effort at an inter-denominational growth.

At the Michigan M.E. Annual Conference of 1888, the Y.P.M.A. held a large and enthusiastic Friday evening meeting in the Benton Harbor Church. Mrs. Willing, sister of Bishop Fowler, and Harry Date, known as the "Little Evangelist," gave enthusiastically received addresses and appealed for a religion that lasts all year around. The same Conference's Committee on the State of the Church commended the Y.P.M.A. for its "royal work within the church in arousing our young people to Christian activity, and teaching them to become soul-winners." On Saturday of that week, the Conference set up a committee to consider whether a Conference Y.P.M.A. should be organized, heard from various ministers on the subject, and then adopted a favorable report along with a recommended slate of officers.[29]

In the Detroit Annual Conference, the youth movement was led by Detroit's Central Church under the name Detroit Conference Young People's Society. However it was never officially accepted. The Secretary of the D.C. Y.P.S. was the Rev. Frederick A. Smart, then pastor of the new Woodward Avenue Church in Detroit. His youth at Woodward Avenue planned a program for a social evening that disturbed some good, elderly Methodists. It involved some simple games so these people felt that such activity would lead inevitably to "worldliness and frivolity." The first society was organized late in 1887 but early in 1888 changed its name to the Methodist Young People's Union. It now began a rapid growth, which alarmed the leaders of the Y.P.M.A.

One other organization for young Methodists had some societies in Michigan before the Epworth League was born. This was the Oxford League, formed by Dr. John Vincent in 1884. The name was again a commemoration of Wesley's Holy Club. This group began with social, literary, and intellectual activities and then proceeded to religious questions. It was somewhat more highbrow and did not expand as fast as the young people's societies did. The Allegan Methodist Episcopal Church had an Oxford League, organized in 1887, with nine members. The general constitution of the Oxford League was said to be the basis for that of the Epworth League.

---

[29] Michigan Conference *Minutes* for 1888, pp. 40, 42, 60, 66, 81. Also paper on "Young People's Work in Michigan" by Rev. Russell Hopkins. Located in Detroit Conf. Hist. Coll., Adrian College Library.

Pastors and people were complaining about the overorganization of the young people's work. The Y.P.M.A. held a convention in Chicago in September, 1888. Overtures for a larger union were presented there by representatives of the Detroit Conference Young People's Society, the Oxford League, and the Young People's Christian League of New England. A layman from St. Joseph, Michigan, was corresponding secretary at the convention. The Y.P.M.A. was not so very cordial being fearful that their goals and values would be lost in another and larger organization.

The other young people's societies kept pressing the advantages of a larger union, particularly at Y.P.M.A. state conventions. The Young People's Alliance of the North Ohio Annual Conference established a special group to work for union. Then the Rev. B. F. Dimmick, pastor of the Cleveland Central Church, invited representatives of all the young people's societies to meet at his church. Out of a week of meetings by the representatives of the many societies was born the Epworth League on *May 15, 1889.* At the time the importance of this particular meeting was not generally recognized in the Methodist Episcopal Church at large.

Eight men from Michigan attended at Cleveland. Two were from the Michigan M.E. Annual Conference: Wilbur I. Cogshall, Presiding Elder of Niles District, and W. W. Cooper, layman from St. Joseph. The Detroit Annual Conference ministers who were there were W. Wallace Washburn of the Saginaw Washington Avenue Church, Frederick A. Smart of East Saginaw Hess Street Church, Charles H. Morgan of Adrian First Church, Claudius B. Spencer of Owosso Church, Samuel Plantz of Detroit Woodward Avenue Church, and James E. Jacklin of Flint Court Street Church. The Michigan Conference men represented the Y.P.M.A. and the others the Detroit Conference Young People's Union. Of the seven ministers in attendance from the State of Michigan, four had been admitted to full standing as an elder in the 1880's, two in the 1870's, and only one, Washburn, in 1869. Their ages were between 37 and 52 years.

Delegates numbering twenty-seven attended the Cleveland meeting and, at first, the outlook was not hopeful because the Oxford League men withdrew. But they returned that evening. The name was one cause of trouble. The Epworth League was finally accepted. It was said to have been taken from the Epworth Hymnal. Many compromises were made but more of the Oxford League pattern was retained. The pin in the shape of a maltese cross with the initials E.L. and the motto "Look up, Lift up" was drawn from that of the Oxford League. The society was to be organized on local, District, Annual Conference, and General Conference levels. A national Board of Control was established.

A weekly paper was taken over from the Detroit Conference Young People's Society. Originally called *Our Young People*, the name had been changed to *Our Youth*. The gathering at Cleveland renamed it the *Epworth Herald*. The Rev. Joseph F. Berry, associate editor of the *Michigan Christian Advocate* was made Editor of the *Epworth Herald* in 1890. The Rev. James E. Jacklin took his place with the *Michigan Christian Advocate*. How so much was accomplished in one week's time is almost beyond belief. Later Editor Berry declared that the task was done by "knee work" by intensely earnest men in a storm of optimism, indeed a "Pentecost."

Certain symbolisms were very helpful to the League's growth. The pin, the motto, and the wheel were most successful. The spokes of the wheel were the heart, head, hand, feet, pen, and pocket. That was the way it was repeated in the Junior Epworth Leagues for those under the age of fourteen. These words stood for the departments of work in the League. To the young adults, these were Spiritual or Christian work, Literary work, Mercy and Help, Correspondence, Finance, and Social or Entertainment. This last one still caused some criticism among older people. The constitution of the Epworth League provided a pledge "to abstain from all those forms of worldly amusement forbidden by the *Discipline*."[30]

The first Epworth League chapter in the State of Michigan was formed either at the Saginaw Hess Street Church or at the Decatur Church. Each claimed to be the first in Michigan. The pastor of the Saginaw Church was Frederick A. Smart, son of James S. Smart, and one of the six delegates from the Detroit Annual Conference to that meeting at Cleveland, Ohio. Upon his return from Cleveland, Mr. Smart organized both senior and junior chapters of the Epworth League in his Church. And in December, 1889, when his congregation dedicated a new church building *not* located on Hess Street, the name was changed at Mr. Smart's suggestion to Epworth Methodist Episcopal Church. The League of Epworth Church was said to be the second chapter in the entire Methodist Episcopal Church.

The minister at Decatur in 1889 was the Rev. Warren W. Lamport. Many years later, he wrote to the Rev. Robert E. Meader:

> On the first Sabbath evening following that convention our Young People's Methodist Alliance there transformed itself into a chapter of the Epworth League, and in so doing became the first Chapter in the

[30] Joseph F. Berry, *Four Wonderful Years*, A sketch of the origin, growth, and Working Plans of the Epworth League, *passim*. Also article on the Epworth League by Russell H. Hopkins.

State of Michigan. I have a letter from the General Secretary congratulating us on that fact.[31]

Mr. Lamport felt that the 50th anniversary of the Epworth League, in May 1939, ought to be celebrated. Also more recognition should be given to the first place of the Decatur Chapter. Probably, the Messrs. Smart and Lamport organized their respective chapters on the very same Sunday. Certainly the Epworth League at Decatur was the first in the Michigan Annual Conference and the one at Saginaw Hess Street Church the first in the Detroit Annual Conference.

Further organization went on rapidly in Michigan. Each Conference, meeting in September, 1889, paid some attention to the new society. The Detroit Annual Conference held a gathering of "Young People's Societies" as a result of which a Conference Epworth League was formed. Three of the men who had been at that meeting in Cleveland took part in the program. One of them, James E. Jacklin, was elected to the 8th General Conference District Board of Control of the League. A Detroit District meeting was held in Central Church on October 17, 1889. If any church had no organized League, it was asked to send its minister and two delegates to the October meeting.

In 1890, the Detroit Annual Conference was pleased to learn of "the wonderful growth" of the League. Joseph F. Berry was the reporter, he having just been elected editor of the *Epworth Herald*. He had been the associate editor of the *Michigan Christian Advocate* since 1886. A future Bishop was taking a step which would make him better known to the Church at large. A meeting of the Conference Epworth League was held in 1890 but Detroit Conference did not establish a standing committee on the organization.

The Michigan Annual Conference of 1889 at once created a standing committee on the Epworth League. Of its five members, M. D. Carrel had been very active in the Y.P.M.A. None of them had been at the Cleveland meeting. But the committee said they "most heartily transfer our loyalty to the Epworth League as the accepted society for the church." It warned that the central object of the League must always be "religious growth . . . not a literary circle or a social guild." As their District Board of Control member, John W. H. Carlisle was chosen. He was then pastor at St. Joseph. The Big Rapids District held the first District meeting in the Michigan Annual Conference at Luther on September 25 and 25, 1889.

The Rev. M. D. Carrel told the Michigan Annual Conference of 1890 about the League. He was just about to become "superintendent

---

[31] Letter of W. W. Lamport, to R. E. Meader, August 30, 1938. Found in Michigan Annual Conference Historical Society files, Albion College Library. For Saginaw Hess St. Church see *Michigan Christian Advocate*, October 22, 1964. XCI, #37, p. 19.

of the Epworth League Department of the Western Methodist Book Concern." So two men rose to larger areas of usefulness through the creation of the Epworth League.

A few statistics were presented to the Michigan Annual Conference of 1890 by its standing committee on the League. Organized Leagues with a membership of 5,724 in 136 charges already were at work. Junior Leagues numbered 24 with a membership of 1,121. But 149 charges were still unorganized. Eleven District conventions had been held and many of the camp meetings had given a day's program to the League. The Niles District had the most charges organized and Grand Traverse the least. By total membership, Lansing District led and Kalamazoo District had the fewest. Four Districts — Albion, Coldwater, Ionia, and Kalamazoo — had no Junior Leagues. Grand Traverse and Ionia Districts had held no general conventions.

Half the charges organized in one year was an inspiring result but every last one of the others must be reached. "The unorganized charges are precisely the ones most needing the League." The committee was glad of what had been accomplished but now "we press forward toward the better things and then still on to the best."

1880 — 1890

A Statistical Comparison

Statistical study of the various branches of Methodism in Michigan reveals a steady, material growth in all aspects of the Methodist Episcopal Church. But similar comparison of the Methodist Protestants in the Eighties shows a more erratic development. The M.P.'s grew in some aspects, such as total membership and church buildings, but declined in others, notably in their Sunday Schools. Their ministers were concerned about that last aspect themselves.

The Michigan Annual Conference of the Methodist Protestants reported 2,511 full members in 1880 and 2,740 in 1890. Probably around 1,200 should be added to those figures for the members of the West Michigan and North Indiana M.P. Annual Conference.[32] The Michigan M.P. Conference had 32 church buildings and 24 parsonages in 1880. These had increased to 51 churches and 27 parsonages in 1890. The parsonages were surely one to a charge or none at all but the distribu-

---

[32] Statistics of the Methodist Protestants have exactly the same failings as those of the Methodist Episcopalians: inaccurate arithmetic, charges that failed to make any reports, and poor proof-reading. In addition, the western M.P. Conference in the State of Michigan has special problems for the historian. It was called West Michigan and North Indiana in 1880 and this was changed to West Michigan alone in 1888. Statistics that were of Indiana are too difficult to separate from those of Michigan. The Conference *Minutes* in the historical collections in Adrian College Library are also incomplete for a few years around 1880. But it looks as if the West Michigan division declined in total membership about 200 in the Eighties.

tion of church buildings is harder to visualize. In 1880, the appointments were all labeled circuits or missions. The Flint Circuit had four churches and Shelby Circuit three. Six Circuits had two churches in 1880. Twenty-three charges had no church in 1880. Most of these were still missions. Sixteen had no churches in 1890 and the name circuit had been dropped although ten were still labeled missions.

The Sabbath School Committee of the Methodist Protestants in the Michigan Annual Conference was quite disturbed about that situation in 1890. Ministers England and Kinney commented, at the bottom of their statistical report, "We are sorry to notice that there is not the growth in our Sunday Schools that we should expect in our denomination, and therefore recommend that each pastor give more attention to this department of church work." The Michigan M.P. Annual Conference had 87 Sunday Schools in 1880 and 76 in 1890. Officers and teachers of Sunday Schools totalled 797 in 1880 and 746 in 1890. The "Scholars" numbered 3,299 in 1880 and 3,127 in 1890. What probably worried the ministers more was the printed fact that the Sunday School scholars had numbered 3,824 in 1889.

In the 20th century, it seems as if their financial situation would have needed the most attention of all the problems confronting the Methodist Protestants then. From the elected President of the Annual Conference on through the roll of the stationed ministers, at least ¼ to ½ of them did not receive their assessed salaries. Most of them were supposed to receive from $300 to $500 with the President to get either $700 or $800. Deficiencies of $100 or a little less were regularly reported. Probably donations of food were often helpful. The mission funds also were small. In 1880, the Michigan M.P. Conference reported an apportionment of $251.10 of which $185.17 was received for missions. In 1890, the apportionment was $359.58 and the sum received for home and foreign missions was $207.20.

Methodist Episcopal growth was vigorous overall but uneven in the Districts comparatively noted. The Michigan M.E. Annual Conference had 28,879 full members in 1880 and 37,968 in 1890. Its Sunday Schools numbered 449 in 1880 with 5,124 officers and teachers for 33,236 scholars. By 1890, it had 608 Sunday Schools with 7,003 officers and teachers for 48,327 scholars. The church buildings numbered 291 in 1880 and 446 in 1890. The parsonages lagged behind among the M.E.'s just as they did in the M.P. Conferences. Michigan M.E. Conference had 149 parsonages in 1880 and 206 in 1890. Giving for missions, outside of the women's efforts, amounted to $6,946 in 1880 and $13,951 in 1890.

The Detroit M.E. Annual Conference began this same decade with 24,598 full members and ended it with 36,032. Their Sunday Schools were 420 in number in 1880 and 515 in 1890. The 4,489 Sunday School officers and teachers of 1880 had become 6,579 in 1890. Their scholars numbered 33,360 in 1880 and 50,352 in 1890. Church buildings that numbered 281½ in 1880 had increased to 395 in 1890. Also 48 new parsonages had been added to the 142 of 1880. Giving for missions rose from $7,165 to $16,068 in this one decade.

Comparison of the charges within the various Districts one decade apart reveals a quite uneven growth. A few Districts, such as Adrian and Albion, remained nearly static. Increase was often the result of division of two churches previously on one circuit.

In contrast, the northern Districts were very busy starting societies and then charges where none had been before. Big Rapids District had 32 appointments in 1880 and 47 in 1890. In the Upper Peninsula, 21 appointments in 1880 had become 46 in 1890. These figures are only approximately correct because places changed their names or circuits were rearranged with villages moved from one District or Circuit to another at the convenience of the Presiding Elder and ministers.

Another tendency was the creation of a second and third church in a town where only one had been long established. The increasing population was easier to handle in two or three neighborhood churches. Battle Creek, Port Huron, Ludington, Kalamazoo, and Owosso all had added a second church to the original one by 1890. Grand Rapids had four Methodist Episcopal churches in 1880 and six in 1890. But Detroit had the most rapid urban growth in this decade of any Michigan town. Its six churches in 1880 had become thirteen in 1890. New ones were created while others were split, united, or renamed. Certainly an effort was being made to follow the expanding population.

The pattern of church creation in Detroit began with a mission Sunday School, usually meeting Sunday afternoons, with the teachers provided by an old, long-established Methodist Episcopal Church. When the Sunday School was well started then the parents would be invited to come in and a few adults from the other church would join in the establishment of a society, a congregation, and a Quarterly Conference with some small share in the time and efforts of a circuit preacher. If rapid growth ensued, the congregation would soon build a modest church and attempt to walk alone. It might be necessary to move the location or unite with another small or weak congregation.

The names used would change with the development too. It began usually with only a location name, such as Jefferson Avenue or 16th Street. The renaming might be for John Wesley, a prominent Bishop, or some wellknown lay member. The names of Bishops Asbury, Haven, and Ninde were all used for churches in Detroit between 1885 and 1887. Jefferson Avenue Church was moved four blocks, built again, and named Mary W. Palmer Memorial Church in 1884. Thomas Palmer, her son, gave the money for this church in the name of his mother, as he had also given a sum in her memory to the Conference Claimants Fund. A new church was named for John M. Arnold in 1890. David Preston

Church was a merger of Fort Street and Wesley formed soon after the death of that layman, in 1887. He had been connected with every good cause in Detroit. From 1883 through 1890, a new church or division of an old circuit was made each year. Only Central, Tabernacle, and Simpson remained the same on the Detroit Conference records throughout the 1880's. After 1883, Cass Avenue was also there and the same appointment.

Each of those last four churches was helpful to the mission churches then. Central, formed as it was by the union of the First and Congress Street churches, was the Mother Church of Detroit. Among the churches it helped start were Tabernacle, called Lafayette Street Mission then, the Cass Avenue Church, Jefferson Avenue, and Simpson Church.

The Tabernacle Church also helped in formation of Simpson Church. But Tabernacle, earlier briefly called Trinity, was not so conveniently located for many of its members as the city grew. Its debts were heavy and some members felt it ought to disband. In 1882, a meeting was held to discuss the future. One member, Mr. P. W. Nicholson, turned away the pessimistic tide and united Tabernacle Church in a great new effort when he said:

> We ought not to be discouraged. It is true that our life as a church has been a great struggle to make ends meet, but the work has not been in vain. Have we not sent forth workers all around us, and started missions which have since been organized into churches? Do not say or feel that Tabernacle Church is a failure. If we have done so much in the past, surely there is a work for us in the future. Let us struggle on for a little longer, and the Lord will bless us.[33]

[33] Alice Nash, Golden Jubilee *History of the Tabernacle M.E. Church*, p. 64.

Chapter XIII

DEPRESSION AND STAGNATION

1890 — 1900

The Committee on the State of the Church appointed by the Michigan Annual Conference of 1896 said to the ministers:

> To make a report on the "State of the Church" is almost as difficult as to make a report on the state of matrimony. Everyone knows about his own family and very little about his neighbors. Every Pastor knows about the financial and spiritual condition of his own Church, and very little about the real condition of others. We have a very inadequate idea of what the great Methodist Episcopal Church has done and is doing throughout the world.

Yet that committee felt sure that progress was being made in the construction of churches and parsonages, paying of chronic debts, and saving of souls. The great task of Methodism had been and still was "spreading scriptural holiness" through revivalism. Its chief danger was compromise with worldly amusements. If only Methodist doctrines and machinery were faithfully maintained and constantly used, then "intemperance, gambling, prostitution, Sabbath desecration, business dishonesty and political corruption" would decline.[1]

Annual Conference *Minutes* and statistics plus such sermons and letters as have survived give the impression of a Michigan Methodist Episcopal Church, in the last decade of the 19th century, that was striving with all its might to keep what it had gained in bygone years. Revivals, Classes and camp meetings had their wonted places in the yearly round of activity and church business was carried on much as it always

---

[1] Michigan Annual Conference Minutes for 1896, pp. 68-69. The five ministers on that committee were R. H. Bready, George A. Odlum, A. P. Moors, W. W. Lamport and G. W. Tuthill.

The Central Mine Church. This Church is 25 miles north of Calumet, marks the site of a former flourishing copper mining town inhabited largely by Cornish immigrants, (immigrants from County Cornwall, England). In 1890 the Sunday School reported a membership of 338. The mine ran out around 1900; a wholesale migration took place. Descendants of the former residents belong to a Homecoming Association. Once a year they return to hold a service and picnic on the grounds.

had been. Annually discussions occurred about administrative reforms but were not yet fully put into effect. Equal lay representation had repeatedly been discussed and approved in both the Detroit and Michigan Annual Conferences. It was not yet attained in the Church at large. Efforts to admit women to the ministry in Michigan had been made but, while theoretical approval of such steps was expressed, the result was usually a local license or status as a deaconess. The only social concerns actively promoted in Michigan, as for many previous decades, were temperance and Sunday observance.

American achievement of world power in the political and industrial areas occurred in the last decade of the 19th century. Hawaii was acquired and, by means of the Spanish-American War, the United States got Puerto Rico, Guam, and the Philippines. New immigration from central and southern Europe was flooding the United States in larger numbers each year. Urban development was more rapid than ever. Labor troubles were serious and constant involving such disturbances as the Pullman and Homestead strikes. Third party reform movements, such as Free Silver and Populism, reached their peaks in the Nineties too. Hard times troubled most of the United States in 1893 and the years just afterward. While that depression was sharp and severe, it did not last quite as long in Michigan as the Panic of 1873 had. So many large national changes inevitably also influenced American religious denominations.

Any historian, writing in 1966, is more conscious of the significance of the events of the 1890's than were the Methodists living in Michigan then. Possibly no contemporary can truly judge the events through which he lives. This was a Michigan still heavily *rural* except for Detroit. It was almost as strongly *Republican* and *conservative* in its political views. The Rev. Elisha E. Caster, then stationed at the Howell Methodist Episcopal Church, mentioned the election of 1900 in two letters to his longtime friend, the Rev. Henry W. Hicks, appointed that year to Pinckney and Unadilla. On the day before the presidential election, November 5, 1900, Mr. Caster wrote in part:

> Hurrah for McKinley and the Republican party! May Bryanism be so deeply buried as to never experience a resurrection in this or any other country. I am a thorough Prohibitionist but I can't see it to be my duty to tramp around the edges of nothing in the way of a party when there are great national interests that demand my ballot.

On November 14, 1900, Mr. Caster wrote again to Hicks about the election results as follows:

> Well didn't we give it to those Bryo-Dem-Pop-Silver-Anti-Bob and Rag-tail fellows a week ago? My I should think that Bryan . . . would apply to Aguinaldo for the Colonelcy of a regiment and learn how to run.[2]

Then too this was the Methodist Episcopal Church in Michigan not the Protestant Episcopalians nor the Congregationalists with whom we are concerned. Those other denominations were leaders in the development of the Social Gospel in the United States. Henry F. May pointed out, in his book *Protestant Churches and Industrial America,* that Methodism was founded among artisans and small storekeepers. In the early United States, members were mostly pioneer farmers. Only since the Civil War, were wealthy businessmen rising to a prominent place in the Church. Wesley preached and all those early groups practiced frugality, hard work, slow saving, and modest charity to deserving individuals. Methodist theology and practice were deeply concerned with sin and the conversion of the individual soul. Revivals causing deep human repentance were considered the answer to all social evils.[3]

The Annual Conference statistics of 1898 revealed a decline in both probationary and full members of 1756 in Michigan M.E. Conference. The decrease in the Detroit M.E. Conference was 652 that year. In 1899, the membership decrease in the same Conference was 728. But

---

[2] Caster-Hicks letters are in the Hicks Collection, Detroit Conf. Hist. Soc. Coll., Adrian Public Library.

[3] H. F. May, *op cit.,* pp. 188-190 in his chapter on The Social Gospel and the Churches.

the Michigan M.E. Annual Conference only numbered a decline of 380 all among the probationers.

When its statistical secretary reported a membership decline for the second year, the Detroit Annual Conference voted to hold "the third Friday of October . . . as a day of fasting and prayer in view of our humiliation." Whether any discussion of the basic causes of this situation occurred either was not recorded or else simply did not take place.[4]

How different was the expressed attitude of the Michigan M.E. Annual Conference. Its committee on the State of the Church noted in 1898 how painful was the reported decline in membership. It held that "the slums of our cities are better served with the gospel than is the country." Strong regret was felt over the disappearance of the country circuit, the local Sunday school, and the travelling preacher. Only prayer, altar services, powerful preaching, and more pastoral visitation would bring again "that oldtime increase." Why should the most talented ministers be sent to the cities to fight a hopeless and competitive battle with other denominations. In its conclusion, the committee revealed how the ministers clung to the older attitudes of Methodists in Michigan. It said:

> To our minds no stupidity exceeds that of attempting to compete with a population four fifths of which are foreigners who speak or preach in a foreign language and who belong to an imported church. In such a state of things, there is no promise nor hope for us.[5]

Only very general concern for the urban working man was expressed and that rarely in the Michigan M.E. Annual Conference *Minutes*. In 1893, Presiding Elder Wilbur I. Cogshall, of Grand Rapids District, reported that the churches in the region around Muskegon were suffering a decline in financial support because "by reason of the stoppage of factories, many of our people . . . have been compelled to move away from the city."[6]

But in the northern and western parts of the Michigan M.E. Annual Conference, many presiding elders were apt to express annually their concern for the poor farmers who were trying to bring the cutover lumbering lands under cultivation either with fruit or general crops. Metho-

---

[4] Detroit Annual Conference *Minutes* for 1899, pp. 23, 78. Because the Michigan M.E. Annual Conference printed the reports of its presiding elders and the Detroit Annual Conference did not, it is easier to determine Methodist attitudes on current changes in the west half of the State than it is for the eastern half. The city of Detroit may have early modified the rural attitude of the Detroit Conference too.

[5] Michigan M.E. Annual Conference *Minutes* for 1898, pp. 298-299. Members of that committee were all holders of village appointments being at Ada, Leslie and Charlevoix. None were prominent in the Conference roster.

[6] The same Conference in *Minutes* for 1893, p. 214.

dist ministers then understood more easily the rural hardships of small farmers than the urban problems of city factory workers.

An attempt was made to present a very modern problem to the Detroit Annual Conference session of 1897 but seems to have had no serious discussion, at least in the open meeting. The Rev. Oscar W. Willits, stationed preacher at Alpena, presented a motion for a committee of five to study and express an opinion on "the public policy of federal injunctions against the use of the public highways and other usual rights of citizens." He requested and got as members of the special committee Arthur Edwards, longtime editor of the *Northwestern Christian Advocate,* President Lewis R. Fiske of Albion College, J. M. Thoburn Jr. of Detroit Central, Albert B. Storms of Cass Avenue in Detroit, and Matthew C. Hawks of Michigan Avenue in Saginaw. Appointed on the second day of the session, the committee was ready to report on the sixth day, was put off until afternoon so that their report might be printed and, in the evening, "indefinitely postponed because of insufficient time to discuss it." It may have been that some of the ministers considered it too politically controversial a topic for an official stand by the Conference. How much one would like to know the exact nature of that committee report.[7]

The Spanish-American War and its attendant imperialistic actions by the United States had scarcely any effect upon Michigan Methodists. The situation was entirely different from that during the Civil War when twenty-four regiments were raised for the Union army in Michigan and then the fighting continued for four years. That little war in 1898 had only two regiments in it from Michigan and lasted from April to August. Hence the entire incident occurred between the Anual Conference sessions of 1897 and 1898.

The Methodist Annual Conferences in Michigan produced only the briefest of resolutions about the war. In fact, the two Methodist Protestant Annual Conferences made no mention of the war nor of the newly acquired territories. Their missionary societies were interested in work in Japan and its extension to China if possible. Also some attention was given to doing ministerial work in German within the State of Michigan by outside assistance. Extension of M.P. churches into the Upper Peninsula concerned the ministers in Michigan far more than work in the islands of the Pacific Ocean.

On the last day of the session, the Detroit M.E. Annual Conference of 1898 hastily adopted five resolutions. One of them praised the presiding Bishop Andrews, another expressed gratitude to the ministers and local churches in Mount Clemens, site of the meeting, and the rest dealt with international happenings. Clearly God was favoring and helping the United States in the breaking of the cruel Spanish control over

---

[7] Detroit Annual Conference *Minutes* for 1897, pp. 13, 21, 24.

Cuba, Puerto Rico, and the Philippines. Those lands must never revert to Spanish rule again but be assured "civil and religious liberty, popular education, and a pure Gospel."

In the preamble to the five resolutions, gratitude was declared for President McKinley's "large measure of wisdom, conciliation, humanity and justice." But in the second resolution, after stating it was "noble for our sons to die for fellowmen," the absolute necessity of a formal investigation of the incompetence and "avoidable evils of our camps" was affirmed. It was only proper that President McKinley had ordered a thorough examination to determine who was responsible for the mismanagement. The last of the five resolutions approved more friendly relations with Great Britain and also welcomed the disarmament proposals of the Czar of Russia.[8]

In that same Conference session, the committee report on the W.H.M.S. stated that the ministers were pleased that now "the eyes of our sisters are cast toward Cuba, and Puerto Rico, the Philippine Islands and Hawaii" because "the bounds of their work is co-extensive with the ground over which floats the Stars and Stripes."

Establishment of Methodist Deaconesses in Michigan

A small and consecrated band of Methodist women worked, with genuine social concern for their fellow human beings, in Michigan in the 1890's. These were the Deaconesses who had the official approval of both the Detroit and Michigan M.E. Annual Conferences. The money and supplies they needed were raised by the Women's Home Missionary Society through their many local church groups. By 1900, a Deaconess Home was established in each M.E. Annual Conference in Michigan. The one in Detroit was larger in membership and had a building on Elizabeth Street several years before the Michigan Annual Conference was able to locate and build a Home in Grand Rapids. The latter just had the foundations of a headquarters laid in the year 1893. Hard times and the cautious attitude of the local Board of Managers about going into debt delayed completion of the Michigan Conference Deaconess Home for several years. By 1900, the Detroit Annual Conference had a dozen Deaconesses at work most of the time while the Michigan Annual Conference had three or four.[9]

Deaconesses were classified as nursing or visiting according to the nature of the work they did. About half of each Conference group were probationers for whom regular class work was provided. After a

[8] Detroit M.E. Annual Conference *Minutes* for 1898, p. 65.

[9] Comments on the Deaconesses based on an examination of the annual reports of the Conference Deaconess Boards, the same for the W.H.M.S., and occasional discussion in the business sessions of both the M.E. Annual Conferences in Michigan for the decade, 1890-1900.

year or two probationers were recommended by a nearby church Quarterly Conference for formal license as a Deaconess. In order to give an air of solemnity, the licenses were usually bestowed by the presiding Bishop on Conference Sunday just after he ordained the Deacons and Elders.

As usual in Methodist interests, organization and connectional aspects were emphasized. A Home Board of Management was appointed and always included a minority of prominent, resident, local women. Also a Conference Board of Deaconesses was established, set up so that it would be continuous in action. Membership was usually nine with three leaving the Board each year. Two or three women were among the members of the Conference Board of Deaconesses.

President Lewis R. Fiske of Albion College was most interested in the Deaconess work from the time of its origin in the Detroit Annual Conference. In 1891, when the Detroit Conference Board of Deaconesses was created, he became its first President. On Conference Sunday, September 20, Fiske conducted the service of licensing the first two Deaconesses, who were Miss Lucretia A. Gaddis and Miss Elizabeth Thornborough. He did this at the request of the presiding Bishop Newman. Miss Gaddis served as Superintendent of the Detroit Deaconess Home from 1891 to 1899.

In the Michigan Annual Conference, Mrs. Laura C. Aldrich deserved most of the credit for getting the Deaconess work started. She was the widow of the Rev. William J. Aldrich. He had been a prominent minister and had died rather suddenly in September, 1890, as he was preparing to leave Muskegon Church and become a Presiding Elder again. Mrs. Aldrich was chosen Superintendent and Matron of the Conference Deaconess Home in Grand Rapids before there was one. She devoted the year 1892 and part of 1893 to visiting many local churches in order to explain the deaconess work and solicit funds for construction of a Deaconess Home. Then for five months in 1893, Mrs. Aldrich attended the Lucy Webb Hayes Training School for Deaconesses in Washington, D. C. Finally on September 10, 1893, Mrs. Aldrich was "consecrated by Bishop Bowman to the office and work of a Deaconess in the Church."

It is interesting to note that the need of specific training was felt even by a widow of a Methodist preacher. Presumably she was middle-aged and possessed extensive experience in church work on her husband's different pastorates. She continued as the Superintendent of the Deaconess Home in Grand Rapids until 1908. When she retired the Board of Control of the Home took formal note of her "long and valuable service" and gave her the honorary title of Superintendent Emeritus. The Home itself was already known as Aldrich Memorial but presumably that was in honor of her husband.

The daily work of those early Michigan Deaconesses can easily be visualized from the detailed and careful reports made each year in the Annual Conferences. The nursing Deaconesses did day or night duty in hospitals and homes. The visiting Deaconesses were more directly concerned with religious work. They must have done a great deal of calling from door to door. An entry made annually was "Opportunities for Bible reading and prayer improved." In 1893, the Detroit Conference Deaconesses had made 3,670 of those. Prayer was offered with the sick, classes taught in Sunday Schools, tracts distributed, and meetings held to explain the Deaconess movement.

Much direct charity was given. Shoes to the needy, garments to the number of 2,520, bed quilts and comforters numbering 34, and also baskets of provisions were among the items listed in the report to the Detroit M.E. Annual Conference in 1893. A good deal of the food was contributed by local branches of the W.H.M.S. Some 300 quarts of fruit and fifty glasses of jelly were distributed. By 1895, mention was made in the yearly list and report of boots and rubbers, suits for boys, cloaks for girls, and meals furnished as needed.

As the decade went on, teaching in Sewing and Industrial Schools was mentioned. For several years, Mrs. Kellar was in charge of what was then called the Tillman Avenue Mission. This is a street running north from Michigan Avenue one block east of 23rd Street. Today it lies between the New York Central and Wabash or Grand Trunk Railroad lines. Then it was located as being in the "Polish District." This Mission may in reality have been practically a Settlement House. It was also more active in holding religious services at the Mission building than the Deaconess Home was. Mrs. Harriet Kellar was ranked as an Associate Deaconess and probably lived at the Tillman Avenue Mission. A kind of affiliation with Simpson Church was maintained. Its stationed minister saw that children were baptized, communion was given, and a probationary membership class organized at the Mission. So the work among the non-English speaking immigrants was not entirely neglected.

One of the problems of the early Deaconess work was meeting the demand for such trained women. In 1897, Miss Mary Hartwell became Superintendent of the Florence Crittenden Rescue Mission. In 1895, one Deaconess, Saddie Kissack, left for work in West China and another, Laura Wright, expected soon to sail for Muttra, India. In 1892-1893, Mary Henderson labored at Bliss Hospital in Saginaw. A few Deaconesses were held ready to help any pastor with special needs during revival services. In the Michigan M.E. Annual Conference, such calls were answered from Second Street and the Plainfield Avenue churches in 1897. And Deaconess Margaret Bell was sent to Jackson "to open work in the slum portions."

An un-cooperative attitude on the part of some of the women members of the local churches may have made the raising of money for the

Deaconess work a bit more difficult. The Women's *Foreign* Missionary Society was to some degree in competition with the Women's *Home* Missionary Society in the smaller churches. It was felt by the older society that the parent national Missionary Society spent a great deal of money in grants to struggling churches within the United States, therefore the home work was not so necessary as that with foreign heathen women. Some women held office for years in one Women's Missionary Society and absolutely refused even to give a small amount to the other.[10] This attitude plus the hard times of the 1890's kept the monetary aid to the Deaconesses in their first decade here in Michigan far below what could have been profitably used in the State.

As far as the records show, the Methodist Protestant Annual Conferences in Michigan had no Deaconess work in the 1890's but did have active branches of the Women's Home and Foreign Missionary Societies of their denomination working throughout the decade. In 1892, at the request of the women concerned and after an offer to pay for their share of the printing, the annual minutes of the W.F.M.S. Conference meeting began to be printed in the back of the Conference *Minutes* of the ministers. But the local groups were quite small and had the monetary problems common at that time.

Three problems, largely social in nature, were still of great importance to most Michigan Methodists. As in previous decades, the two M.E. Annual Conferences were constantly concerned with negro education, temperance, and proper Sunday observance. The last two also were annually discussed by the two M.P. Annual Conferences.

1) *Southern Negro and White Education*

Conference resolutions expressed concern for the southern Negro and the poor White in much the same language as those of any year since 1865. But the sums collected each year in individual churches were very modest. Rarely was the amount requested achieved. In 1890, both M.E. Annual Conferences in Michigan raised a combined total of $3,447. By 1900, the amount given for this cause had become $5,426. The offering was more evenly distributed over the Districts in the Michigan Annual Conference, none of them being able to raise over a few hundred dollars apiece. In the eastern half of the State, Detroit City District always gave about three times as much as any other one District. In the latter part of the decade, aid to freedmen given by Lake Superior District declined about one quarter. An average of forty

---

[10] Based in large part on the recollections of the author. She remembers clearly that, in her childhood, her Mother explained how a relative labored only in the Foreign Missionary Society and could not be interested in the needs near at hand "while we give our money and time to the Home Missionary Society where we can see how great the demand for help really is at any time."

appointments making no contributions to the freedmen existed through-
out the 1890's in both the Detroit and Michigan Annual Conferences.
This particular benevolence did not touch the hearts of Michigan
Methodists as the foreign missions did.

Many of the committee reports on freedmen's aid, made to the Annual Conferences in Michigan, were stereotyped and similar from year
to year. Constant refrains were the continuing need of the former slaves
for education and the growing debts of Methodist southern schools
which must somehow be paid.

The committee on Freedmen's Aid and Southern Education of the
Detroit Annual Conference session of 1891 made a long report with a
20th century tone. That year was the 25th anniversary of the Freedmen's Aid Society. In that period, the Society had spent nearly $3,000,000
to establish forty-one schools in sixteen States with 330 teachers and
9,275 pupils. Thirteen of the schools were of collegiate rank, one theological and the rest academic. Manual training departments were
being added at many of the colleges. But the committee was disturbed
by the fact that Conference collections for these schools were always
so small. This was true all over the United States. During the previous
Conference year, the national Society had asked for $235,000 and had
received by collections in the churches $106,651.

Reasons for this failure were to be found in race discrimination as
practiced in southern church supported schools. The official, declared
policy of northern Methodism was "no exclusion on account of race,
color, or previous condition." But it was also official and stated policy
that "Separation in schools as in conferences is to be the voluntary
choice of the people themselves."

Of those forty-one southern Methodist schools, three colleges and
sixteen academies were for whites only. The fact was not questioned
that southern poor whites needed education. Nor that southern whites
always said that the northerners did not understand the situation and
certainly supported northern segregated schools too.

As that 1891 Detroit Conference committee saw it, the remedy was
a vigorous stand for what was right but not necessarily expedient. Its
report said in part:

> The negro wants more than teachers or preachers. He wants the
> recognition of his manhood. Christianity is not the wisdom of God
> and the education of men, but the love of God and the brotherhood of
> men. We have no business in the South at all if it be not to declare
> the gospel of equality in Christ. . . . Who can read the history of the
> Methodist Episcopal Church in its relation to African slavery without
> a sense of humiliation and shame? We have had enough of that kind
> of compromising with what God hates.

More ministerial effort must be devoted to increasing congregational knowledge of the southern work. It was hoped that such efforts would enlarge the collections for negro education. The committee concluded:

> We instruct our delegates to the coming General Conference to do all in their power to secure such legislation as shall forever do away with the reproach that we have betrayed a solemn trust, and sacrificed our Negro membership to secure peace in a godless community and fraternal relations with a time-serving church.[11]

2) *Temperance or Prohibition*

Michigan Methodism in all its branches was just as uncompromisingly opposed to the use of liquor in the 1890's as it ever had been. However, judging from the Conference resolutions, new aspects of that old evil appeared on the national scene and within the State.

Both M.E. Conferences in Michigan repeatedly objected to the sale of liquor at Washington, D.C. within the Capitol and also to the offering of wines and liquors to guests at White House receptions. Exception was also taken to the "canteens" provided at army posts because liquor was thereby made more easily accessible and young soldiers were by order assigned to serve it.

The committee on Temperance of the Detroit M.E. Annual Conference session in 1891 declared:

> That we look upon the provision of wines and liquors for the banquet at the last national G.A.R. encampment in Detroit as a gross violation of propriety, an insult to the intelligence and virtue of the nation, and an undeserved stigma upon the fame of our brave citizen-soldiery, meriting unqualified censure.[12]

Within the State of Michigan, Methodist ministers were saying that the only possible goal was Statewide prohibition of liquor. Licenses and local option were not being used effectively. The first led to bribery and corruption while use of the second only drove the problem into a nearby area.

A new organization to fight the liquor evil was formed in Ohio in 1893. This was the Anti-Saloon League, organized in Michigan by 1896. In his *Story of my Life*, Seth Reed states that he was one of the original organizers of the Anti-Saloon League. The North Ohio Annual Conference furnished the Rev. John F. Brant, who became, by episcopal appointment, the first Michigan State Superintendent of the Anti-Saloon League. Actual organization took place at Grand Rapids but Mr. Brant

---

[11] Freedmen"s aid resolutions in the Detroit Annual Conference *Minutes* for 1891, pp. 79-81. The committee on Freedmen's aid consisted of Oscar W. Willits of the Kingston church, John P. Varner of Saginaw Epworth, and Orton F. Winton of Grass Lake.

[12] Detroit Annual Conference *Minutes* for 1891, p. 78.

had his office at Lansing. He soon had two field assistants drawn from the ministers of the Detroit Annual Conference. They were Gilbert C. Squire and Julius F. H. Harrison. The latter served by appointment as Conference Temperance Evangelist from 1897 to 1899 without a specific church charge. It may be remembered that the Michigan M.P. Annual Conference had used a similar arrangement in the 1880's. The Temperance committees of the Detroit M.E. Annual Conference were authorized to appoint annually delegates to Anti-Saloon League conventions. It was never an official organ of the Church but Anti-Saloon League principles were held to be in agreement with the *Discipline*.

The sale of liquor to students at the University of Michigan was also of concern to Michigan Methodist ministers. In 1891, the churches of Ann Arbor joined with the University Student Christian Association to petition the Legislature to forbid "all traffic in intoxicating liquors within five miles of the University of Michigan." The Detroit M.E. Annual Conference thoroughly approved of this idea but nothing came of it then.

Strengthening the temperance work often concerned the Annual Conference sessions in Michigan. Every minister was asked to preach an annual temperance sermon. A monthly temperance prayer meeting ought to be organized. Holiday celebrations might well be combined with temperance suggestions. It was felt that this was especially needed at the Fourth of July anniversaries. The patriotism of that national holiday was often contaminated with a good deal of disorder and drunkenness.

3) Sabbath Observance

Now and then the committees of the Annual Conferences on temperance and Sabbath observance combined their efforts. Saloons and beer gardens, wide open on the Sabbath, made the day anything but one of quiet rest and worship. The Detroit Annual Conference committee on Sanctity of the Sabbath declared in 1891 that it was every minister's duty to "emphasize the teaching of the Discipline . . . that we are to avoid the profaning of the day of the Lord either by doing ordinary work therein or by buying or selling."

Some of the responsibility for the deterioration of Sabbath observance was laid by the Detroit Annual Conference at the feet of immigrants who brought with them the Continental European idea of Sunday. The Michigan M.E. Annual Conference was concerned by the sudden growth of summer resorts with many Chicago inhabitants on the Lake Michigan shores. Its committee on the State of the Church declared in 1897:

> Nearly the whole western shore of this great state is becoming dotted
> with Health Resorts, where thousands from all parts of the country

spend a portion of the summer. Chicago furnishes no small portion of this migratory class and the most of them trample on our laws enacted by our legislature to secure quiet and rest on the Lord's day. . . . The influence of the popular resorts of western and northern Michigan on our American Sabbaths is one of the most serious evils we have to encounter.[13]

The Michigan branches of Methodism had not yet quite decided whether use of the bicycle was harmful or beneficial morally. In 1897, the Detroit Annual Conference committee on Sanctity of the Sabbath said in part:

The church of Christ must stand with ceaseless vigilance as the protector of her Lord's Day. With the increasing use of the bicycle, a fresh temptation is presented to our young people to turn the Sabbath in whole or in part into a holiday. We pledge ourselves as a Conference to use all our influence, by word and example, to check and destroy the growing custom of bicycle riding for pleasure on the Sabbath.

But the Rev. Henry E. Wolfe, then pastor of the Court Street Church in Flint, looked at the bicycle in a different way. He wrote in March, 1897, of how he disliked the lingering winter and wished the snow was all gone "so we can again use the bicycle. One-third more pastoral work can be done with that valuable assistant." Mr. Wolfe had even formed a bicycle club among the members of his Sunday School and Epworth League.

Hard Times and Natural Disasters Again

"The times are stringent and money is tight" were complaints often heard among the Michigan Methodist clergy in the years from 1893 to 1898. Just twenty years earlier, the Michigan Methodist Church had weathered a similar, financial crisis. Judged by the Conference *Minutes* and ministerial correspondence, the Panic of 1873 was longer lasting and more severe in its effects. On both occasions of crisis, the Church, its ministers and members were all in debt and unable to meet financial subscriptions on time. In the last decade of the 19th century, hard times were first mentioned in the Annual Conference *Minutes* here in 1893. By 1898, references can be found to returning prosperity.

A few churches were compelled to appeal for Conference help or permission to solicit pledges in other Districts. Among those in monetary straits in the Detroit Annual Conference were the churches at Ironwood and Ishpeming. In the Michigan M.E. Annual Conference, urgent appeals were received from the Methodists at Chase and Olivet.

---

[13] Michigan M.E. Annual Conference *Minutes* for 1897, p. 177. The committee also urged writing to the office in Chicago for plans which had been drawn by the Sunday League of America to combat such evils.

Albion College also suffered from an ever-increasing debt throughout the 1890's.

Ordinarily the Annual Conferences responded to such financial appeals by authorizing the minister to solicit at large, by taking a collection at some Conference session at which the public audience would be large or by use of missionary or church extension funds. The Conferences in Michigan found the hardships of stringent times increased by great, natural catastrophes. Fire, drought, early and late frosts ruined wheat and fruit crops and certainly increased the financial worries of church and ministers.

Forest fires still recurred each summer in Michigan although none of those in the 1890's were as extensive as the earlier ones. Not long before the time for Annual Conference in 1892, "a great fire at Bay City had completely destroyed the Fremont Avenue Church and parsonage." The Rev. Edward A. Bray, pastor of that church, even lost his parchments of ordination. Presiding Elder Elisha Caster declared to the Detroit Annual Conference session that, if the church was to rebuild, outside aid was "an absolute necessity." Conference at once authorized the Presiding Elder and the local pastor to visit churches in order to seek monetary help from ministers and members. This particular church was a continued problem to the Detroit Annual Conference. In 1893, a special donation of $2,500 was sought for it from the national Church Extension Society. In 1895, the same Conference again authorized the local minister and the Presiding Elder to seek for outside aid due to "the continued serious financial embarrassments of Fremont Avenue Church of Bay City."

The city of Saginaw also had a very bad fire in the spring of 1893. The Detroit Annual Conference Woman's Foreign Missionary Society President, Mrs. Arvilla Lake, lost her home and most of her worldly possessions in that Saginaw fire. She wrote to Mrs. Carrie C. Faxon, the Recording Secretary, on May 26, 1893:

> You can get some idea of the fire from newspaper accounts, but it must be seen to be realized. Women crying, children lost, horses frightened, men trying to save a few goods, and over all the roar and crackling of the flames. And Oh! the heat! Though our loss is irreparable, I cannot feel as some do; I have not shed a tear, and am ready to commence over again. . . . I believe my heart is not set on the things of this world. When I saw all in ashes I felt thankful that I had a "house not made with hands, eternal in the heavens."

Mrs. Lake died in some sort of train accident one week after she wrote that letter. Neither her memoir writer, Mrs. Faxon, nor any of the other women, who had been at the Conference Foreign Missionary meeting in Saginaw, could forget how Mrs. Lake, in her closing speech to that group, had said, "I am deeply impressed with the solemn thought I shall never see you all again." After a moment of deep quiet, all present had joined in singing "God be with you till we meet again."

Saginaw Epworth Church was in financial straits throughout this decade. It is not clear from the records whether that bad fire destroyed any of the church property or not. But Epworth Church had special attention from the Detroit Annual Conference session of 1892. The Panic of 1893 did this church no good either. And in 1894, the Detroit Annual Conference session again struggled with the problem of how to raise $900 still unrepaid to the Church Extension Society. Only when the Detroit Conference guaranteed the loan had it been made in the first place. Eventually in view of the hard times, it was decided to ask for a year's extension of the life of the grant. In 1893 and again in 1894, the Detroit Corporate Conference trustees voted to give all the interest from one of their funds to the Saginaw Epworth Church. The fund was the result of a bequest in a will. If the statistics can be trusted, a debt of $2,000 still burdened the Epworth Church in Saginaw in 1900.

The Michigan M.E. Annual Conference suffered rather more than the Detroit one from disasters due to the weather. At least they said more about such troubles in their Conference *Minutes*. In 1891, it was noted that "the territory bounded by the Grand Traverse and Big Rapids Districts . . . have been devastated by drouth, frost and fire, causing great destitution and suffering." In 1893, the church at Spring Lake was destroyed by fire. In 1895, the Rev. John Graham, Presiding Elder of Albion District, mentioned in his annual report that the farmers were suffering from "low prices, short wheat crop, and a long drouth." The same complaint was made in the Coldwater District where Presiding Elder A. M. Gould said their benevolences and ministerial salaries had been seriously affected. The Grand Traverse District had its fruit crop ruined by a heavy snow and a severe frost on May 13, 1895. Drouth, forest fires and grasshoppers had also afflicted them. A few of the ministers had been forced to take up "secular pursuits" to support their families. The Rev. Levi Master, Presiding Elder of Kalamazoo District, declared that 1895 was "the hardest year in Church finances we have ever known. In some parts of my district the crops have been an utter failure."

An undue amount of fatal disease seems to have been prevalent too if judged by the sanitary standards of the 20th century. Ministers suffered from "lung trouble" and la grippe and their small children died of scarlet fever and diptheria, at least to the extent of several cases each year. Mourning ministerial parents were usually reported as bowed in humble submission to the will of God.

The hard times that began in 1893 were not much alleviated before 1897. In each M.E. Annual Conference in the State of Michigan, half a dozen of the churches labored under such a burden of debt that it

was feared that their buildings might be sold in payment of the mort-
gages. Strenuous efforts of pastors backed by their respective Presiding
Elders together with small sums of money from the Church Extension
Society and the Missionary Society, saved most of them.

Olivet Church seems to have been the only exception and the only
building that was sold then. This Society had struggled with increasing
debts for at least twenty years. When the trustees of Olivet College
made an offer of $1,600 for the property, everyone consulted thought
that it was the Church's last chance. Even Bishop Ninde made a special
trip in order to inspect personally the ground and general situation.
So in 1895, the sale of Olivet Church took place thus enabling the trustees to pay a longstanding debt of $500 and much accumulated interest
to the Church Extension Society. The Olivet Society had 86 members
the year before the sale of the building and its Presiding Elder, the Rev.
John Graham, said "There we lived at a poor dying rate." Olivet did not
appear in the lists of appointments for the rest of the decade.

The *Minutes* of the Methodist Protestant Conferences in Michigan
make hardly any mention of the hard times associated with the year
1893. Perhaps it was because those M.P. Churches were largely in small,
country villages and were not so sharply affected by hard times as the
larger cities. But their records give the impression that most of their
church units had a small membership and scanty, financial resources
all the time.

Consideration of the annual reports of the various Presiding Elders
and of the subjects, under continuing debate from year to year in the
Annual Conference sessions, leaves the impression that a period of depression was not the only cause of the financial distresses of Michigan
Methodist churches then. A transition from the pioneer church with its
donation parties and general ignorance of businesslike ways was in
progress. Too many trustees and stewards did not attend promptly to
the duties of their positions. And too many ministers, especially in the
smaller, rural churches, were ignorant of modern record keeping and
business procedures. Typical of what many Presiding Elders said of
the situation was the comment of the Rev. John Graham of Albion District. He wrote to the Michigan Annual Conference in his report made
in 1894:

> The stewards neglect the finances the first two quarters of the year.
> The salary falls behind and rarely catches up. Some churches have
> methods, others have none, and even in the case of the former some
> are so badly worked that the same policy pursued in national affairs
> would wreck the government; and this very management is wrecking our
> smaller churches. Then to pay the preacher by having him move to
> another charge may be good diplomacy but bad practice and worse
> morality. . . . Let us hope for a better day . . . when the pastor shall

have something more tangible for the getting of his scanty stipend than the cheap sentiment and pity of the community for the preacher as he is going to Conference.

The most pronounced effect of the Panic of 1893 upon Michigan Methodism was a long, slow sagging into increased debt in the individual churches and also in the Annual Conference projects. Ministerial salaries were not fully paid nor the assessments for such objects as the salaries of the Bishops and Presiding Elders. The many benevolent causes also suffered in the years from 1894 through 1897. It seems a little odd that the total Methodist church membership in Michigan did not fall until the years 1898 and 1899. Then the worst of the panic was thought to be over and people had begun quite generally to believe that better times had returned.

Certain tasks of the Annual Conferences were perennial mostly because of the hard times and the lack of proper business methods in the management of the worldly affairs of Methodism. High on the list must stand the struggle to find and divide fairly the funds for the Conference claimants. Other acute financial problems included the effort to pay for an episcopal residence in Detroit, to endow a bed in the Brooklyn Methodist Hospital and to find some way to settle the very, heavy debts of Albion College.

1) *Efforts to support the retired ministers*

The claims of the elderly and feeble superannuated ministers lay heavy on the consciences of the two Annual Conferences in M.E. Michigan Methodism throughout this decade. Certain invested funds were bringing in about $1,000 in interest each year. These were the results of a small number of bequests. The *Michigan Christian Advocate* editor annually presented a sum either a bit over or under $2,000. Moneys were also still received from the Book Concern and the Chartered Fund. But the number of superannuates was steadily increasing and so were the ministerial widows. In 1898, the Detroit Annual Conference decided that, except for a small sum immediately after her husband's death, no widow should ever receive an allowance who had "never been with her husband in the itineracy."

The amounts of money given in pensions were necessarily very small. The usual range was from around $22 to $175 per annum. Theoretical claims were set up for a range of pensions by years of service. But these were about twice the sum that anyone actually received. This disturbed the active ministers very much. A special hardship case might there and then have a collection taken for him on the Conference floor. Efforts were also made to get the elders to contribute one-half of one per cent of their salaries for the superannuates. In 1894, about half of the ministers on the active list of the Detroit Annual Conference contributed such an amount for the retired men. The claims of their retired brothers always came ahead of any urgent charitable or construction projects of the Annual Conferences in Michigan.[14]

2) *Supporting a Bed in the Brooklyn Hospital*

In 1888, the Detroit and Michigan M.E. Annual Conferences had each agreed to support and endow a bed in the Methodist Episcopal Hospital at Brooklyn, New York. It was understood that a collection should be taken annually for this purpose on "Hospital Sunday" then the last Sunday in December. It was also agreed that the first $365 collected each year in each Annual Conference should support the bed until such time as the full endowment might be obtained.

What were the reasons for undertaking this charitable project? This was the first Methodist hospital to be established. The Agent of the Brooklyn Hospital, Dr. J. S. Breckenridge, had visited each Annual Conference and addressed the ministers there. The Rev. Elijah Pilcher died in Brooklyn in 1887. He might have been a tie with the hospital project for the Michigan M.E. Annual Conference, in its session of 1890, stated that "several sufferers from this state have already been cared for in this Institution." Perhaps once the pledge was made, the Conferences did not quite know how to escape therefrom.

The hard times of the 1890's were undoubtedly the main factor that prevented the two Annual Conferences from fulfilling their promises. In the Detroit Annual Conference in 1893, it was stated that the Presiding Elders had written to Brooklyn some months previously that nothing more could be done for that hospital because Annual Conference support for Bliss Hospital in Saginaw had been pledged. This action was disliked immediately and again in the Conference meeting in 1894. An effort was made to get a formal release from the pledge of endowment but the matter was put in the hands of a large committee which, as far as the records show, never made any report. The treasurer of the Detroit Annual Conference reported that he received $6 for Brooklyn Hospital in 1894 and the same amount in 1895. The Michigan M.E. Annual Conference had the same difficulties in attempting to provide for its Conference bed in the Brooklyn Hospital. In 1894, it was still hopefully appointing another committee to further the work of collection if at all possible. A Conference hospital bed in Brooklyn,

---

[14] Detroit Annual Conference *Minutes* for 1894 lists the ministers and the amounts they gave to the "percentage fund for superannuates," pp. 16, 42-43.

New York, may have seemed very far away and unimportant to many Methodists.[15]

3) *Buying an Episcopal Residence*

The desperate efforts made by both M.E. Annual Conferences in Michigan to provide an episcopal residence in Detroit were within the confines of their State but many lay members did not see any necessity of buying an $18,000 mansion for a Bishop, even for their beloved Bishop Ninde. If it had not been for the valiant efforts of the Rev. James Jacklin and the *Michigan Christian Advocate*, the Detroit Annual Conference would have been financially disgraced by its inability to repay three prominent Detroit laymen who had personally assumed the debt in question.

The laymen were active from the first in the matter. In 1892, the Detroit Annual Conference session was addressed by William L. Holmes, a layman of Detroit. He stated that a very desirable property in a fine part of the city of Detroit could be gotten for $18,000. To raise this sum, the Methodists of the city of Detroit would be responsible for $6,000, the rest of the Detroit Annual Conference an equal sum and the Michigan Annual Conference the remainder. A joint committee of twelve would manage the purchase and repair of the property. Each Annual Conference was asked to appoint three ministers and three laymen. The Detroit Annual Conference laymen included Horace Hitchcock, H. M. Loud, and Frank Beal. Seth Reed and William Dawe were the best known of the ministers on the committee. The Michigan Annual Conference left the entire matter to three Presiding Elders: J. I. Buell, Levi Master and George S. Hickey of the Ionia, Kalamazoo, and Lansing Districts respectively.

The joint committee made the most strenuous efforts it could to raise the money. Printed appeals were sent to every charge, collections of 16¢ per member were requested and letters of reminder were mailed. In the first year, the city of Detroit raised $2,200 and the rest of the Detroit Annual Conference $700. But the whole Michigan M.E. Annual Conference had only raised $450. Worse still, "two or three generous laymen of Detroit have put themselves under the burden of carrying some $5,500 at the banks to secure the ready money required for the purchase." Surely 5¢ per member could be collected until the goal of 16¢ from each member was reached.

---

[15] Such records as there are seem most inadequate on the Brooklyn Hospital beds project. Neither Secretary nor Treasurer were always accurate or complete in the records they kept. Detroit Annual Conference *Minutes* as follows: for 1888, p. 13; for 1893, p. 66; for 1894, p. 15. Also Michigan Annual Conference *Minutes* for 1894, p. 335.

But all these plans were made in *1893!* How dismayed those members of that joint committee would have been if they had known that the property would have to be sold and the still remaining debt would not be finally settled until 1906. Repeated and most strenuous efforts brought such small results. In 1895, Michigan M.E. Annual Conference raised $351 and Detroit Annual Conference $242 for the episcopal residence. By 1896, a few Detroit laymen were much burdened by their personal assumption for the Church of that note for $5,300 plus its unpaid interest. Once again, both Conferences urged the ministers to do their duty and make every effort to raise the portion of the loan assigned to them by the Presiding Elders.

All the annual reports to the Conference sessions about that episcopal residence business are exactly the same until the year 1903. That year the Rev. William Dawe sadly reported to the Detroit Annual Conference that the property had been sold. But a debt of almost $6,000 still burdened those laymen and indirectly the Church. It was decided to try to raise ⅔ of the debt in the Detroit Annual Conference and ask the Michigan Annual Conference to do whatever they could to get the other third.

At this point the Rev. James Jacklin came to the rescue. He had been Associate Editor of the *Michigan Christian Advocate* since 1890.

All his efforts for the next two years were devoted to clearing away that debt. In 1905, the Detroit Annual Conference showed their appreciation of "his persistent and valuable services in collecting the debt" by a rising vote of thanks. When the debt was reported all paid in 1905, similar gratitude was recorded to the *Michigan Christian Advocate* and Jacklin again. The Michigan M.E. Annual Conference was never able to raise as much money as Detroit did but its gratitude and relief was just as great when the debt was all paid. Was there any feeling that Bishops did not need such expensive homes?

Albion College Again

Like most of the other institutions of Michigan Methodism, Albion College was profoundly affected by the Panic of 1893. To the Board of Trustees and the President, the business statistics of the College were a disaster. The previous slow, slight, annual increase in the total debt accelerated considerably during the depression. In 1890, the total debt of the College was not over $10,000. Each year it proved to be impossible to meet the current expenses and by the end of 1900, the total debt had grown to $92,000.

A variety of causes were responsible for this financial burden. Widespread hard times rendered the task of the Agents and Board of Trustees doubly difficult. That eloquent preacher, the Rev. Washington Gardner, served for some years as the College Financial Agent and

Lecturer. But the results of his labors seem to have been meagre in a period when pledges meant nothing because no one had any ready cash. Temporarily the answer, thought the Trustees, was cutting back on the college expenses as far as possible. That meant substantial decreases in salary for most of the faculty and dismissal for a few of them.

Another factor was the unproductiveness of some of the College endowment funds. Much of it was tied up in real estate, which was subject to the claims of annuities and taxes beyond its own productiveness. Opportunities for investment in stocks and bonds were not then available as they would be today.[16]

A more significant reason for the growing debt was the increasing enrollment in the College and hence the expense beyond what had been esctimated might be needed. Albion was in process of becoming a real acadamic community with a respectable reputation as a liberal arts college. The entire number of preparatory and college students was 496 in 1890 and 475 in 1900. Such figures do not reveal the true situation. Slowly and steadily the number of *college* students was growing. They numbered 121 in 1890, had become 188 in 1892 and had attained the decade's peak of 251 in 1896. Then the depression finally hit Albion and the College enrolled 228 students in 1897. In December 1896, President Fiske reported to the Board of Trustees:

> The attendance of students has fallen off somewhat. A large number of last year's students had used up their means and were unable to earn much in the long vacation, so that they could not return . . . notwithstanding the hard times, the Freshman class numbers nearly ninety students, among the largest Freshman classes we have had. . . . The Departments where the largest fees are charged have suffered the most.[17]

From the viewpoint of the Faculty, the period was one of trouble in many ways. Teaching long hours to save the college money, soliciting at large in the Methodist churches of Michigan in efforts to help raise the interest on the debts, anxious about their own family necessities, the Albion College faculty of that time deserve a special tribute of our gratitude.

Their anxieties were increased by the sudden change in the presidential administration of the College in 1897-1898. After twenty years as President, the Rev. Lewis Ransom Fiske submitted his resignation to the Trustees in May 1897. Exactly when he did retire seems to be unknown but Fiske's successor, Dr. John P. Ashley, made a report to the Trustees in December, 1898. Possibly Fiske, who would have been

[16] Robert Gildart, *Albion College*, 1835-1960, pp. 146-152. Both Annual Conferences have many references in their *Minutes* to the College hardships every year of the Nineties. An education committee report and also the Board of Trustees report were often printed.

[17] Gildart, *Albion College*, pp. 151-152.

seventy-two on his next birthday, was forced to retire on account of his health or age.

Dr. John P. Ashley came to Albion College from the presidency of Genesee Wesleyan Seminary in Lima, New York. He held a Ph.D. from Boston University and had studied abroad. Perhaps he had been over-rated intellectually or did not possess the qualifications requisite for a Methodist College President. He stayed only three years and one month at Albion College. Then he left quite suddenly and the Detroit Annual Conference evidently removed him from the ministry but not from the membership of the Methodist Episcopal Church. Gossip was rampant about both Ashley and Fiske at the time but evidence of just what happened seems not to exist today. The full details of why Mr. Fiske retired or why Mr. Ashley left cannot be determined now from the written records.

Student life at Albion College in the Nineties cannot be understood by much emphasis on administrative problems and financial burdens. Albion was a small college but it had most of the educational essentials and social trimmings then common in higher education. Its graduates were lifelong friends and loyal alumni of the institution. Challenging faculty teaching, athletics, fraternities, and a college paper, the *Pleaid*, were all to be found then at Albion.[18]

During the years 1886-1888 and 1889-1892, Smith Burnham was a student at Albion College. He taught History in the Preparatory Department of the College part time for two years before he earned his degree in 1892 and then full time from 1892 to 1898. He received an honorary LLD from Albion in 1928 and was for years an alumni member of the College's Board of Trustees. His wife, Ella Lillian Caster, also graduated from Albion College in 1892. In later years, Mr. Burnham was fond of saying that "propinquity got in its deadly work" because Mrs. Burnham was seated next to him in the classes for three years.[19]

Mrs. Burnham was the daughter of the Rev. Elisha Ezra Caster, a member of the Detroit Annual Conference. Hence it was probably inevitable that she should attend Albion College and follow a Classical course of study which included Greek. Mr. Burnham hesitated between M.S.U. and Albion but, after careful comparison of their catalogues, chose Albion because its course of study "laid more stress on the humanities and less on the sciences." Albion College advertised

---

[18] Ann Hollinshead, *Eminent and Interesting Albionians,* I, *passim.* Comments on Albion student life also based on the author's recollections. Both her parents, three uncles and two aunts graduated from Albion College.

[19] Comments on the Burnhams drawn in part from remembered family reminiscence. See also *From the Pen of Smith Burnham* edited by the author in 1954 from recollections that Mr. Burnham wrote down during the years from 1942 to 1947. For Albion College see particularly Chapter VII on "My Education."

then that its courses of study aimed to be practical rather than abstract, to give a wide range of electives, to deal with the living present in addition to the dead past, and to offer opportunities for research with specialization.

Ella Caster entered Albion on a diploma of high school graduation but Smith Burnham had not been adequately prepared for college and so spent most of his first two years in the Preparatory Department. The change from that kind of background to the high school accreditation of today was just beginning. More and more of the freshmen class, in each year of the Nineties, were admitted on high school diplomas. This had a connection with the proportionately greater growth of the college than the preparatory division.

Mr. Burnham earned his own way through Albion College. Twice he dropped out and taught a country school for a winter term. The first time he also carried twelve hours of work at Albion College in absentia and passed examinations there in upon his return to the school. In the years from 1889 through 1892, he was steward of "Mary's Club." This was a cooperative boarding club on Porter Street across from the college chapel. Mary Heimbuch owned the house and did the cooking. Mr. Burnham said of his work there:

> My duties were to do the marketing, keep the books, and collect their board bills from the students, the last the most difficult of the three. My pay was my board and ten cents per week from each student in the club, about forty in number. During these years, the price of board at Mary's Club averaged $2.10 per week.

Some of the faculty at Albion College made a deeply favorable impression on Mr. Burnham while of others he was rather critical. As was often the custom then, President Fiske taught some classes. These were in logic, ethics, and philosophy. The teaching was formal and probably dull much of the time. In Mr. Burnham's opinion, the one *great* teacher at Albion then was Fred Manville Taylor in the area of the Social Sciences. Later he was the head of the Economics Department at the University of Michigan for many years. Mr. Burnham studied and later taught under Professor Taylor's supervision and it was due to his influence that the teaching and writing of History became Smith Burnham's life work. Mr. Burnham recorded many years later his opinions of his Albion teachers. He said in part:

> In calling Fred M. Taylor the only great teacher in the Albion College of my student days, I do not mean to imply that there were not other good teachers on the faculty then but only that, as good as some of them were, they fell far below him in the classroom.
>
> Delos Fall was a careful, painstaking teacher of chemistry who trained some of the leading chemists of America. Moreover, he per-

sonified the good citizen. He was a useful member of the city school board, . . . a member of the State Board of Health, and later State Superintendent of Public Instruction.

Mr. Burnham did not mention the two buildings that Albion built in that decade. The first gymnasium was completed in the fall of 1892 and the McMillan Chemical Laboratory was built in 1893. This was a substantial, four story brick building given by U.S. Senator James Mc-Millan. The Rev. Washington Gardner and Professor Delos Fall obtained the gift of the money for it. The first made the contact with Senator McMillan and Mr. Fall convinced him of the great need for more adequate laboratories for teaching Physics and Chemistry. Professor Fall taught at Albion College for forty-one years. More than any other person, he established Albion's later reputation for excellence in science teaching.

Professor Frederick Lutz taught foreign languages at Albion College for thirty-five years from 1885 to 1920, although he did not die until 1935. Of him Mr. Burnham wrote:

> Frederick Lutz, Professor of Modern Languages, was preeminently the gentleman, quiet, modest, refined, considerate, generous, and gracious. These qualities ripened in him with the passing years. Professor Lutz was not a good drill master in elementary German and French, but he was a scholar who opened to his advanced students the rich treasures in the literature of those languages . . . this thought impressed me when I first saw his private library. He was a diligent student in his own field.

The most widely known member of the faculty that Albion College ever had came there in the 1890's. He was the Rev. Frederic Samuel Goodrich, brought to hold a recently endowed chair of English Bible. At first he also taught Greek. He served Albion for forty-three years as a teacher and then after his retirement, as the chaplain. Goodrich's name first appeared in the college catalog for 1892, but his transfer to an Annual Conference in Michigan was not until 1895. Then he came from the North Ohio to the Detroit Annual Conference with his membership in the Central Detroit Quarterly Conference. Yet Albion College is located in the Michigan M.E. Annual Conference. It may have been done because President Fiske also had his membership in the Central Detroit Quarterly Conference.[20]

The formal and academic side of Albion College was by no means the only aspect that the alumni remembered with gratitude and inner pleasure. Mr. Burnham noted, "I did not let my studies interfere too much with my education." His extracurricular activities were many

[20] Detroit Annual Conference *Minutes* for 1895, pp. 19, 30, 40. Gildart, *Albion College*, pp. 160, 185-186.

and varied. All his life he felt that they did quite as much as the more formal work to prepare him for his lifetime of teaching and lecturing. Literary societies, fraternities, political clubs, athletics and a college paper were all part of the college scene in spite of the rather austere, social attitudes of any Methodist sponsored college then.

The occasional parties at Albion might have an elaborate grand march and refreshments but never provided for any dancing if the college authorities had anything to do with the occasion. Even as an old lady, the author's mother faintly regretted that she was never allowed to dance.

National fraternities were then fairly recently installed at Albion College. Mr. Burnham joined the local chapter of Sigma Chi. It was the outgrowth of a local society called the Impromptu Speaking Club or I.S.C. The fraternity still had weekly programs of extemporaneous talks upon topics assigned as one got up to speak. During Burnham's years in Albion, his fraternity built a lodge on the campus and he helped to dig the cellar under the place.

The literary societies had a dominant place then. Mr. Burnham wrote of them:

> Sixty years ago there were two flourishing literary societies in Albion College, the Erosophian, and the Eclectic and Atheniades, the latter commonly known as the "Tics." Each of these societies had a hall on the third floor of the North Building. I joined the Erosophian Society. The active part I took in its work gave me some acquaintance with parliamentary law, led me to try to organize my thinking, and developed in me some facility in public speaking. Incidentally, the society elections introduced me to the kinds of political activities that produce results.

The dominant political party in Michigan being Republican then, of course the college had its Republican Club. Mr. Burnham wrote of it:

> College students were much interested in politics. By heredity, at least, I was a strong Republican. I helped form the Albion College Republican Club and early in 1892 it sent me as one of its delegates to the first national convention of College Republican Clubs in Ann Arbor. It was most interesting to meet young men from colleges all over the land. At this meeting I saw William McKinley . . . he spoke before the convention on the tariff and at the evening dinner made a short patriotic address which pleased me very much. I recall that I thought McKinley was a strikingly handsome man.

The author has heard Mr. Burnham tell repeatedly of how the Albion College Republican Club bought all the yellow ribbon in town, pinned big bows of it to their coat lapels, and stood in two rows at the station as the campaign train of William Jennings Bryan went through the town in 1896. Free Silver got no sympathy from them.

The achievement of his Albion years that Mr. Burnham remembered all his life with great pride was serving as captain of the only Albion College football team that, in forty years, beat the University of Michigan team. Football was first played at Albion in 1884 and by 1891, a formal schedule of games was established. When Mr. Burnham was captain in the fall of 1891, the opponents included Hillsdale and Olivet Colleges, the Detroit Athletic Club, and the University of Michigan. Olivet was then regarded as the chief rival. That College had defeated Albion at a game played in the spring of 1891 at the Intercollegiate Field Day.

Revenge over Olivet was much on the minds of the team and so, as an extra bit of preparation, a game was scheduled with the University at Ann Arbor. To the surprise of everyone, including the Albion team, the final score was ten to four in favor of Albion. To their still greater astonishment, the midnight train to Albion, on which the team returned home, was met by hundreds of students and townspeople. The scene was enlivened by a brass band, fireworks and torches. A large hay wagon, drawn by some of the students, took the team to the campus where, by the light of a huge bonfire, Captain Burnham and the other players told all about how it happened. Incidentally, Albion College beat Olivet College by 24 to 6 that year too.

Clearly Albion College had a vital intellectual and social life of its own then that was not at first much hindered by the Panic of 1893. Mr. Burnham was happy in his first years of teaching there. He left because the salaries and positions were cut to the bone in desperate attempts to cope with the increasing debts. The teaching position he had held in the Preparatory Department was simply abolished. At once, Mr. Burnham obtained a teaching position in a Pennsylvania State Normal School where he received slightly over twice as much salary as he had ever had at Albion College. It took a new President, Samuel Dickie, working in the 20th century to cure Albion College's monetary ills.

Administration and Personnel
1890-1900

Hard times and human ambition together created problems for the Methodist Episcopal Church in Michigan. Many of these were administrative and connected with the personnel of the Annual Conferences in ways familiar in previous decades. The perennial question of a third Annual Conference in Michigan, the extent to which ministers might be transferred between the Conferences, the selection and education of ministerial candidates, the choice and length of term of Presiding

DISTRICTS.

DETROIT CONF.

№ 1. ADRIAN.
" 2. BAY CITY.
" 3. DETROIT.
" 4. FLINT.
" 5. LAKE SUPERIOR
(EASTERN HALF)
" 6. PORT HURON.
" 7. SAGINAW.

MICHIGAN CONF.

№ 1. ALBION.
" 2. BIG RAPIDS.
" 3. COLDWATER.
" 4. GRAND RAPIDS.
" 5. GRAND TRAVERSE
" 6. IONIA.
" 7. KALAMAZOO.
" 8. LANSING.
" 9. NILES.

Elders, and the proper use of professional evangelists were recurrent questions in almost every Conference session of the last decade in the 19th century.

There was agitation again for another Conference. Why the idea of forming a new and third Annual Conference covering the Upper Peninsula and the northern part of the Lower Peninsula, should have had such an appeal then is hard for us to understand today. A good many ministers felt that each Conference in Michigan was too large. It was difficult to find towns capable of entertaining the Annual Conferences. They assumed that northern Michigan, after the forests were cleared, would speedily develop as had southern Michigan. They did not realize that the population potential of northern Michigan would prove more limited.

In 1893, the Michigan Annual Conference appointed a committee of nine of its ministers to hold joint meetings with a similar committee of the Detroit Annual Conference "with the view to dividing our State into three Conferences." Some thought such a division might be achieved in 1895 because the Bishop presiding in Michigan that year, John M. Walden, was asked to arrange the two Conference sessions for the same date in mid-September, 1895. When that time came, economic conditions were "stringent" and the Detroit Annual Conference discharged the committee. It also voted "that there be no division. It does not seem advisable at this time, and there is no special demand for it."[21]

Perhaps the recent hard times and the consequent church debts together with unpaid ministerial salaries, at least not in full, in many smaller appointments led to a resolution about transfers presented to the Michigan Annual Conference session of 1897. It was signed by fourteen ministers, of whom five were or had been Presiding Elders, was immediately adopted by the Conference, and then "most respectfully" sent to the presiding Bishops in Michigan. The ministers asked that no man should be transferred into the Conference "unless an exchange can be so effected as to maintain an equality of appointments."[22]

As in previous years, the concern for the quality of the men entering the Conferences on trial was maintained. A majority in both Annual Conferences were anxious that the examinations should be searching, marked on a high standard, and carried out with due time and attention. In 1897, the Michigan Annual Conference ordered a fee of $1 to be paid in advance of the examinations. Some complaint was made of ministerial examiners who tested candidates on unpublished books often being those written by the older man himself. In that same year, the De-

---

[21] Detroit Annual Conference *Minutes* for 1893 p. 10; for 1894 p. 30; for 1895 p. 23.

[22] Michigan M.E. Annual Conference *Minutes* for 1897, p. 141.

troit Annual Conference ordered that no one should be given an examination for admission on trial unless he first had filed his "answers to the
disciplinary questions concerning debt and the use of tobacco."

The deepest concern was felt for the many fine, young, ministerial
candidates of high character and deep, religious faith but with most
inadequate education for the demands of the age. Many of them earnestly promised to attend a theological seminary immediately but did
not do so. Such schooling really ought to be obtained before even
seeking admission to any Annual Conference on trial. After this preliminary complaint, the Detroit Annual Conference session of 1898
modestly agreed that no man should ever be recommended for admission
on trial without "at least the equivalent of a High School education."
Today this seems a very minimum rule.

The scholastic standards for Annual Conference admission may have
been kept rather modest because too many of the older ministers were
the product of self-education while serving as a junior preacher on a
circuit. Was a personal, religious experience or graduation from a
theological seminary more important to a minister? During this very
time, the Rev. Elisha E. Caster stated his opinion on this question in
letters to his friend, the Rev. Henry W. Hicks. On January 1, 1896, Mr.
Caster wrote from Milford:

> That senseless unholy cry for "college graduates" will yet cause
> God to forsake the Methodist Church I fear. I would encourage the
> schools, but when God's called one are rejected because someone is at
> the door who has been to college and that is all he has to recommend
> him then it is time for an ecclesiastical funeral.

And again on April 5, 1897, Mr. Caster wrote in part:

> We as a Church are a-going to grieve God on that school question
> yet. There is a drift to make it the all in our Church. I appreciate the
> trained minister but God can make up preachers after the pattern in
> the Mount, a half dozen of whom would be worth a whole regiment of
> mere scholastics. I know some men who could not get in the Con-
> ference now yet as preachers can knock out most of our college sprouts.[23]

The Nineties were still the heyday of the winter revival and the
summer camp meeting but more reliance was placed on the professional
evangelists than in earlier years. The Conference *Minutes,* the sermons
and even private letters refer to the sensational ways of the "cheap"
evangelists. The committee on the State of the Church, in the Michigan
M.E. Annual Conference session of 1891, expressed contempt for the
vulgar songs and "irreverent antics" by which some traveling evangelists
drew a crowd. Experience had clearly shown that "the permanency of
results from revival labors depends on apostolic methods rather than the

[23] Two letters copied from the Henry W. Hicks Papers, Adrian College Library.

flippancy of eccentric vulgarity and euphonious blasphemy, too often exhibited in evangelistic work."

Repeatedly in their annual reports, committees and Presiding Elders pointed out that the real test was not the number of converts at one week of special meetings but rather how many of those same converts were received into the nearest Methodist Church as probationers and, still more of a test, how many of them finally became full members of that same church. Sometimes in the statistics, a gap of several hundred may be found between claimed converts and actual new members reported by the local ministers.

An examination of the work of a professional evangelist from the viewpoint of the local church pastor is also found in those letters from Mr. Caster to his friend, Henry Hicks. On January 30, 1890, Caster wrote from West Bay City about the services then taking place in the First Church there. He said in part:

> Date is here working with Morgan and is an earnest worker. He is no preacher in the sense of a sermonizer. Six or eight were forward last night. But dear me, so much — "Now stand up" — "Now raise your hand" — and a score of other things that are to me belittling to the Gospel. I can't work with real old Methodist heart. It seems to me that births in Zion are brought about by preaching the Word. I mean births that are births.[24]

After completing his term as a Presiding Elder, Mr. Caster was appointed to the charge at Milford. From there he wrote on January 1, 1894, of his plans to observe the Week of Prayer and then go into protracted meetings. It seemed to him like the good old days of his youth to plan such activities. When he wrote again on January 16, he hinted that the daily sermons all alone were tiring and "a few evenings from a brother would help much."

The Presbyterians were also holding similar meetings but several of the neighboring pastors were helping in the preaching. Even the Roman Catholics were having "a Paulist Father preaching in the Hall. Many go to hear him out of curiosity." Mr. Caster had given his own congregation "a short dose of Catholicism last Sunday and it sort of hedged up the way so that very few attend there."

The Methodist meetings were still going on in February when Mr. Caster again urged Mr. Hicks to come and help him. He reported, on February 5, that he had "a score of great big sinners on the ragged

---

[24] In 1890, Mr. Caster was the Presiding Elder of the Bay City District so that the West Bay City Church was not his own immediate responsibility although he did help out by preaching there a few times. Date was Harry Date, who was widely known as the "little evangelist." Morgan was the minister appointed that Conference year at the First Church, West Bay City. As previously cited, letters were found in the Henry W. Hicks Papers, Detroit Annual Conference historical collection, Adrian College Library.

edge but only a few converts yet." He thought the reasons for the slowness of the services were evident, as follows:

> The Church here has had evangelists until they have been led to feel that they can do nothing. They have not even been taught to pray. In all this Church of 400 members not more than a half dozen could take part in public prayer when we began our meetings. . . . They do better now but it is not like the olden times. I lay it all to the shallow methods of the itinerating evangelists. When I came here we rallied six and eight in class — now we have 40 and 50. God help me to put the knife clean down to the bone.[25]

Intermittently in the 1890's the Michigan Annual Conference had its own special Revival Band. These seem to have been local preachers under the supervision of an elder of the Michigan Annual Conference. The group had their own tents and tried particularly to help on the weaker charges. When they could raise enough money, revivals were maintained the year around. They even had a small paper called *Live Coals*. Lack of provision in the *Discipline* for adequate supervision of such evangelists, as those who were not appointed to any local church or District, was held to handicap such work and also prevent its adequate finance. Many ministers were of the opinion that "the work which lasts the longest, seems the most thorough, is most valuable to a community, preserves unity in the church and builds up the strongest Christian character, comes out of that revival led by the regular pastor.[26]

Criticism of the Presiding Eldership.
Suggested Reforms

The Presiding Elder was far and away the most criticized figure in the Methodist Episcopal Church then. After six years as the Presiding Elder of Kalamazoo District, the Rev. Levi Master declared that the office of Presiding Elder was "sometimes the least understood, and sometimes the most unpopular, and yet, one of the most important" positions in the entire Church. The family life, professional career, and general zeal of the ministers often depended upon the character of the Presiding Elder. Yet wide mistrust of this official was evident in the 1890's[27]

[25] Copied from a letter to Hicks in the Hicks papers, Adrian College Library.

[26] Many references to revivalists in successive Annual Conference *Minutes*. As in the Michigan Annual Conference *Minutes* for 1892, p. 55. Again in same Conference *Minutes* for 1895, pp. 472, 508.

[27] Report by the Rev. Levi Master for Kalamazoo District was printed in the Michigan M.E. Annual Conference *Minutes* for 1897, p. 202. The *Minutes* of the Michigan Annual Conference for the decade of the Nineties contain summaries of all the annual reports of their Presiding Elders. The Detroit Annual Conference did not then do so in their annual *Minutes*.

The Detroit Annual Conference voted in 1890 and again in 1891 to ask the Bishops and the committees on Missions not to use any of the missionary money "for the support of presiding elders." This resolution created much debate both years and finally was adopted with qualifying phrases: in 1890 "if practicable" and in 1891 "unless in the judgment of the Bishop and presiding elders it becomes necessary."

Undoubtedly the reduction in 1897 of the number of Districts in the Michigan Annual Conference from nine to seven was due primarily to the need for financial economy. But the position and its occupants were the subject of frequent criticism then. Some of the ministers thought that Presiding Elders did very little to earn their salaries. While the Rev. Elisha Caster was stationed at Milford in the mid-1890's, he wrote to the Rev. Henry Hicks of how his Presiding Elder had not arrived to hold the second Quarterly meeting until nearly night. Mr. Caster had preached alone on Sunday morning. The Presiding Elder "preached the best he could I suppose in the evening and this morning was with us in quarterly conference, took his 15 cash and departed . . . really he could not get a work that would cheerfully pay him $600 a year."

In 1897, the Michigan M.E. Annual Conference gave the most careful, preliminary consideration to reduction of the number of Districts. Presiding Bishop John H. Vincent laid the matter before the session on its first day of meeting. Then he asked that "the effective Elders present express their own opinions by secret ballot placed in his own hands." The Elders evidently favored the reduction because the Coldwater and the Ionia Districts were abolished and their appointments were distributed between the three Districts of Niles, Kalamazoo, and Grand Rapids. The Niles District received more of the Coldwater appointments and Grand Rapids District got more of the Ionia churches. In addition, the District organizations of women's missionary societies, camp meetings, and Epworth Leagues were "annihilated." But it was felt that thereby the District groups in the surviving parts were enhanced in numbers and influence. Notice was taken by several ministers that the Crystal Springs Camp Meeting, located in the Niles District, was the largest and best ever held. The District Sunday School conventions also had grown.[28]

Most of all in their dealings with Presiding Elders, the ministers of the two M.E. Annual Conferences in Michigan wished that the Bishops would alternate six years of work on a District with a term in a pastorate. Immediate reappointment in transfer to another District savored of favoritism and was apt to cause envy among such ministers as had never been Presiding Elders. More than once, formal Conference resolutions were adopted saying that any retiring Presiding El-

[28] Michigan M.E. Annual Conference *Minutes* for 1897, p. 138; in the same Conference for 1898, p. 323.

der ought to serve three years as a pastor before undertaking the burden of supervision again.

The Detroit Annual Conference adopted such a restrictive statement in its session of 1897. But the Michigan M.E. Annual Conference enunciated opposition to such immediate reappointments throughout the decade. In 1891, both the ministers and the Lay Electoral Conference cautioned that any Presiding Elder, six years in service on one District, needed contact with the needs of a congregation through the pastorate. Such a stand was reiterated in the Michigan Conference session of 1895, 1897, and 1898. The resolution offered in that last year was signed by 49 ministers. Among other things it declared that repeated reappointment to the Presiding Eldership "destroyed the charm of true comradeship." This resolution was tabled and another adopted which said that they had "perfect confidence in the integrity . . . and godly judgment" of the Presiding Bishop. But this substitute was refused until one sentence was added saying that all the previous Conference resolutions on this subject were wise and were hereby reaffirmed.[29]

Who or what they feared is not clear today. Analysis of the records of the two Annual Conferences does not reveal undue monopoly of the office of Presiding Elder. In the Detroit Annual Conference, Seth Reed, Elijah Pilcher, and James Smart served more than one term as Presiding Elders. In the Michigan M.E. Annual Conference, William J. Aldrich, Thomas Jacokes, and William Brockway had two or more appointments each to the same office. Only a few of their terms in the Presiding Eldership were consecutive. But by the middle of the decade of the Nineties, all these ministers, except for Seth Reed, had died. It may have been the fear of such a continuity of power that alarmed the ministers rather than the actual reappointments themselves.

The Work of a Presiding Elder as Shown in His Letters

How one Presiding Elder regarded his position and work can be seen in the letters of the Rev. Elisha E. Caster to his longtime friend, the Rev. Henry W. Hicks.[30] Mr. Caster was admitted to the Detroit Annual Conference on trial in 1857 and then to full membership in 1859. Among his appointments since then had been Corunna, Fenton, Flint Garland Street, Marquette, and East Saginaw.

[29] Michigan M.E. Annual Conference *Minutes* for 1891, p. 497; and also for 1895, p. 471; for 1897, p. 151; for 1898, p. 269. Detroit Annual Conference *Minutes* for 1897, p. 15.

[30] The Caster letters are all in the Henry W. Hicks Papers, Adrian College Library. Those from Caster to Hicks number 279 and run from 1859 to 1912, the latter being the year that Hicks died. Mr. Caster preached his funeral sermon. None are in the collection for the decade of the Eighties. Presiding Elder Caster's letters commence with January 14, 1890 and end with August 18, 1893. A few letters from Mr. Hicks are in the Michigan Historical Collections, Ann Arbor.

From 1887 to 1893, he served as the Presiding Elder of the District in the northeastern part of the Lower Peninsula. It was first named the Alpena District and then later was called the Bay City District. This region was very long and thinly settled as yet in its northern parts. Covering the District at all its Quarterly Conferences meant journeys from Bay City to East Tawas, Oscoda, and Alpena on the shore of Lake Huron and thence inland to such towns as West Branch, Roscommon, St. Helen, Gaylord, and Cheboygan. Unfortunately only the letters for the last half of his term as Presiding Elder were preserved. It is not known what happened to the earlier ones. Mr. Hicks seems not to have ever deliberately destroyed any letters or receipted bills.

In contrast to James Gilruth, who was appointed as Presiding Elder to the Detroit District from 1832 to 1836, Elisha Caster journeyed by train over more than half of his trips to the churches and supplemented that mode of travel with occasional steamer trips from Bay City to Alpena or Oscoda. Outlying appointments on a large circuit were reached by stagecoach, logging train or with a horse and buggy. Gilruth now and then if he had his family along went with horses and an open wagon but mostly he rode horseback unless he was forced to walk because the horse could not get through. In January 1890, Mr. Caster expected to go to Alpena by train on Saturday, hold the Quarterly Conference and preach there on Sunday morning, ride twenty miles in a buggy to Long Rapids, preach and then hold another Quarterly Conference there, ride back by buggy to Alpena, arriving there about 2 A.M. in order to catch an early morning train so that he might lecture at Mount Morris Tuesday evening.

A winter series of lectures, usually sponsored by the Epworth League, were very popular then in Michigan. Single admissions were from 10¢ to 25¢ but most churches tried to sell as many season tickets at $1 as could possibly be done. Experience had shown that a better attendance was secured by the promotion of season tickets. Mr. Caster once heard another minister lecture on "Epitaphs or Grave Jokes." But he was far more likely to do the lecturing himself. Repeatedly he said in his letters that he had more calls than he was able to handle. Usually the local church paid him $5 and his expenses. One of his lecture topics was "Romanism and the Public Schools."

Mr. Caster was especially in demand after he made a trip to Europe and the Holy Land in the summer of 1891. The Rev. Edward W. Ryan, also a member of the Detroit Annual Conference, went with him. They toured England, France, Italy and Egypt enroute to Palestine. Part of the time in the Holy Land, a group, composed of the two Methodist ministers, one Catholic priest, and two Congregational clergymen, journeyed together.

The high point of the entire trip to Mr. Caster was the week he spent travelling on horseback alone with only an Arab guide through the mountains of Israel. He spent most of one day in a boat on the Sea of Galilee. At the last moment, Mr. Ryan had refused to attempt the trip and had remained in Jerusalem. When Mr. Caster returned to Michigan, he brought bottles of water from the Jordan River and the Dead Sea. These he used in baptisms of special importance to him in his later life.[31]

His experiences in Palestine were the basis of both sermons and lectures. After he left the Presiding Elder's office, he used his Holy Land trip as the thread of connection for a series of one dozen Sunday evening sermons in Milford and later at Howell. He confided to Mr. Hicks that at first he was uneasy that such a project would not be religious enough. But he soon learned that it demanded constant use of the Bible stories.

Such trips to the Holy Land were rare then. As far as the record shows, no other ministers of the Detroit Annual Conference had gone there since Elijah Pilcher's journey some twenty years previously. Hence the popular demand for lectures on so unusual a trip certainly increased Mr. Caster's work. On February 12, 1892, he wrote to Mr. Hicks from Clio, where he was giving two lectures on successive evenings. How he had maintained that week's schedule is a mystery.

Mr. Caster wrote in part:

> Both you and I after having passed our 50th milestone on the highway of life are able to go further, preach oftener and longer and louder and better in the same length of time than any of the machine-made tender-plant theologues of the present day.
>
> Look at my record for the present week. Last Saturday I went to Prescott, Sunday morning I preached and administered the Sacrament, after dinner walked ten miles to Whittemore where I preached in the evening and again administered the Sacrament. Monday morning I held Quarterly Conference and went to East Tawas, lectured three hours in the evening, next day held Love Feast, Sacrament, Quarterly Conference and lectured at the church on the circuit. Next day I was at Tawas City, got a telegram to attend a funeral, took the train home, and at 7 a.m. next train to Bennington, preached the funeral at 11 a.m., went to the grave, jumped into a carriage in waiting and almost flew to Owosso, took the 2.25 train for East Saginaw where I caught the 6 o'clock train on the F. and P.M. for Clio where I lectured 2 hours and 40 minutes, after which took some refreshments and went to bed.

The numerous funerals Mr. Caster was called on to conduct, plus his lectures and all the details of the regular work of any Presiding Elder, kept him almost literally on the run for the three years which his letters to Mr. Hicks record. Now and then in his notes of constant activity, Mr. Caster would write, "A comfortable pastorate would be more enjoyable." On January 14, 1891, after telling Hicks that he had only two hours of sleep the previous night, Caster said, "I guess I will

[31] The author has Mr. Caster's diary of his trip to the Holy Land. The most careful notes of the appropriate Bible chapters and verses were made.

never see the time again that I shall not be in a hurry. . . . I wonder if it is right for a man to allow himself to be so hurried and driven."

While Mr. Caster was abroad, his wife and daughter maintained the correspondence with Mr. Hicks. Mrs. Caster said in part of her letter, "I certainly do not enjoy being a Presiding Elder's wife and it does not seem like home with him gone so much. Although I can do as I am a mind to more . . . have just got the hardware man to come and set our coal stove in the corner of the kitchen."

The most difficult and sometimes the most unpleasant part of the yearly round of work carried out by any Presiding Elder was the help he was expected to give the presiding Bishop in his "Cabinet" labors at the Annual Conference sessions. Final determination of the annual appointments involved keeping both the ministers and the congregations satisfied with the episcopal decisions. A disgruntled minister and a disappointed congregation could create much trouble for their Presiding Elder.

On September 28, 1890, Mr. Caster wrote to Hicks from West Bay City:

> It was a good Conference but I never had harder work in the Cabinet. Had to fight to keep Ryan at Madison Avenue [Bay City]. Some are already looking to General Conference delegates [the next one would be in 1892]. I begin the rounds again a week from today at Au Gres.

Writing in pencil a week later from Godar, he explained his previous remark:

> Our Conference as a whole was more than usually harmonious. Perhaps I failed to see its true inwardness by reason of my big fights in the Cabinet. I have never had so hot contests. Smart was bound to have Ryan, and 4 or 5 members of the Madison Avenue Church helped but I fought it to the end and won. The preachers begin to think that I am a good deal of a Smart fighter. He hasn't floored me once yet. He wanted his Fred to be Secretary of Conference but he got only a few votes. At that Fred would be better than Dawe is. Smart has his District all manned for his election to General Conference. I tell you — honors of men cost one a good deal of anxiety and scheming. . . . The secret of happiness is contentment with one's lot.[32]

---

[32] The minister named Smart was James Shirley Smart then in his 4th year on the Flint District as Caster was in his 4th year on the Bay City District. "His Fred" was Mr. Smart"s son, Frederick A. Smart, who after serving at Epworth Church in Saginaw was a financial agent for Albion College in 1891-92. Previously James Smart had been a Civil War chaplain and also a Presiding Elder. He was the 3rd delegate elected to General Conference on the 5th ballot by Detroit Annual Conference. But he never attended because he died suddenly of apoplexy in March, 1892, while en route home from a Quarterly Conference. Mr. Caster never was a delegate to General Conference although family tradition says that he wished to be.

The ministers sometimes bothered the Presiding Elder about the appointments they did not attain or were unhappy over the churches they had gotten. Again writing to Hicks on December 25, 1890, Caster noted that his elder daughter was home from Albion College and that the family had just finished their attack on a "Christmas bird of 15 lbs." Then he said:

> I have been four years on the District at the end of the present year. A certain minister was Considerably disgruntled because he could not go to a certain church but I knew better than he did that he was not wanted there. It is a pretty difficult thing for a presiding elder to just please everybody. Fenn was not pleased at all with the idea of going to West Branch but now he tells me he was never more pleased than he is now. . . . I tell you the greatest ministerial enjoyment is not always had in the professedly great appointments.

In April 1890, Caster wrote to Hicks about the minister at the First Church in West Bay City. As the man's Presiding Elder, Caster found him "hard-working but I get complaints of his sermons having sameness. I was in hopes that he would go through here for three years on the run. . . . Did you not suppose that great schooling would put a man beyond criticism? God be thanked for something that is inborn."

Appointment determination never became comfortable work for Mr. Caster. As late as August 15, 1891, he wrote to Hicks that he was still unsettled in his mind about remaining on the District. Many of his ministers had said they wanted him to stay. Clerical politics was evidently warming up for he knew of twelve ministers who were open candidates for election to General Conference. But he also knew "some who will not go by my vote." A few ministers had urged Mr. Caster to become a candidate himself. He estimated that he could count on twenty votes from his own District. As Annual Conference time drew near, "the pulling and hauling" increased every day. At least twenty men would change churches just on his District. He concluded, "I dread the tussle."

Any Presiding Elder, who served the full term of six years on a District, became a well-known, public character in the many, small Michigan towns he visited approximately every three months. As such he was often called on to participate in important community events not strictly Methodist nor even entirely religious in nature. In April 1890, Presiding Elder Caster was asked to give a public address in Bay City on the 14th in remembrance of the 25th anniversary of Lincoln's assassination and the fall of Fort Sumter. He reluctantly agreed to do so because he knew it would mean much extra work "to build entirely new." In April 1893, Mr. Caster made public addresses for the Y.M.C.A. in Alpena and for the Odd Fellows in Oscoda. He also gave the dedication prayer for a fine, large, new Masonic Temple in Bay City.

If a public occasion involved Catholics, Mr. Caster flatly refused to have anything to do with it. While he was waiting on the dock in Bay City for the steamer to Oscoda, Caster wrote again to Hicks. The date being July 5, 1890, he told of the local celebration on the Fourth:

> The very Father O'Reily of Detroit gave a tirade against England for oppressing Ireland. It was an outrage to hand over our national holiday to a lot of priests who have sworn allegiance to a foreign potentate. All the priests in the adjacent country were on the platform. Not a Protestant minister was there. Ryan and I were invited to go onto the platform but we replied that we did not keep that kind of company.

Building new churches or remodeling old ones also meant added responsibility for any Presiding Elder. From East Tawas on January 14, 1890, Caster wrote to Hicks of how he had spent the previous day at Whittemore. The entire day had been given to settling a dispute between the church people and a local builder over part of the work on a new sanctuary. The Presiding Elder was thankful that the man was not one of the local Methodists. The dispute was about acceptance of some work done under a contract. From his own early experience as a carpenter, Presiding Elder Caster could see at once that the contract had not been carried out and that the work would have to be all ripped out and done over. When offered $30 in full settlement of his bill, the builder "kicked lustily but finally wrote out a settlement, passed receipts, and all parties felt better. Of course, under the circumstances, I preached an extra good sermon in the evening." By his 6th year in office, the burdens of the position had increased for Mr. Caster. On April 28, 1893, he wrote to Hicks, "I am building six churches on the District. It would not be quite so pressing if this were not my last year on the District."

As early as April in his last year on a District, Presiding Elder Caster speculated in his letters to Hicks about where he might be sent on his next appointment. He had been approached about editing a newspaper in Bay City, about being appointed to two churches within his District, and also about going to two churches outside his own administrative territory. He was sure of only one thing, that he was thoroughly weary of the Presiding Eldership. He much preferred to be more at home with his family and in a single church where he could concentrate his efforts. He also was positive that it was unwise to stay in the District where he had just been the Presiding Elder, mainly because he had preached so often and so much at all the points therein. As to becoming a newspaper editor, he was doubtful because "I do not think that my commission to preach the Gospel has run out." Eventually Mr. Caster was appointed to the church at Milford on the Flint District.

But before leaving his District, Mr. Caster preached farewell sermons, attended farewell receptions, and received parting gifts. He wrote to Hicks from East Tawas on August 7, 1893:

> I had a great time here and at Tawas City yesterday. It is my last round and the people either because they wanted to give me a good send-off or because they wished to testify their delight that they should see my face no more packed the churches to repletion. I had a good time preaching at both places. I wish you could see the complimentary resolutions they presented me. I would not be human did I not appreciate them. At Alpena . . . they presented me a beautiful silver coffee service. It was a complete surprise to me but, even now, I approve of it. I do have a sense of sadness in the thought of last things, last days, last interviews, last words, etc.

Mr. Caster soon settled into a pastorate again. Writing a long letter to Mr. Hicks just before Christmas, 1893, he told first of the funerals for which he had preached lately, of his many calls to speak for the various Epworth Leagues, and of his expectation that both his daughters would be home from Albion for Christmas. He concluded, "I am now ready to work in my Study and I tell you it seems good too not to have to grasp my grip every Saturday and oftener and run for the train. I hope to make some good sermons God helping me."

Methodist Work with Young People
1890-1900

In a decade of depression and debt, the most vigorous parts of Michigan Methodism were the Epworth League and the Christian Endeavor. Their development in numbers, organization, and work for their denominations was amazing. Their varied activities aroused doubts in the minds of the older church members and ministers but are really indications of how rapidly Methodism was changing.

The Methodist Protestants in Michigan turned for the affiliation of their work with young people to the Y.P.S.C.E., as their statistical record called it. The Young People's Society of Christian Endeavor was started in 1881 by a New England Congregational minister named Francis E. Clark. It is probable that the rather Congregational attitudes and organization of the M.P.'s influenced them to turn to the Y.P.S.C.E. when a desire was felt for more adequate work with the younger church members . Several Protestant denominations turned to the Y.P.S.C.E. about that time.[33]

As with so many other matters, the C.E. records are skimpy and none too accurate. The M.P. Annual Conference Minutes in Michigan

---

[33] W. C. Barclay, *History of Methodist Missions*, III, 102, 104. A footnote indicates that the C.E. did not have the all-around view of the young Christian's life and work that the Epworth League took.

each have one page devoted to the C.E. reports but that scarcely shows the skeleton of the work. The first mention of the C.E. Societies in the Michigan M.P. Annual Conference can be found in the *Minutes* for 1892. Thirteen local C.E. societies were listed together with their respective membership — active, associate, and honorary — plus the name and home town of the local corresponding secretary. A total of 261 active members were reported. The Rev. W. H. Flint had drafted the report and he urged the "brethren" to look on the C.E. as a source of real strength and "boom" it on every circuit. The M.P. Michigan Annual Conference had 24 C.E. societies in 1893, 64 in 1896, 59 in 1897, and 49 in 1898. That last was one society for every charge but not necessarily in every church on a given circuit. In 1900, 31 societies were reported for the M.P. Michigan Annual Conference. The C.E. Society of the West Michigan M.P. Conference was approved in general by the Conference session of 1892 but not until 1894 was any report printed in its Minutes. Then 22 local societies were reported and that total had dropped to 17 in 1900. The number of Junior C.E. societies in both the M.P. Conferences in Michigan was never over four to seven in each one.

Somehow the few statistics leave an impression that the C.E. societies were not as vigorous as the Epworth Leagues were. The emphasis was more strictly religious and not social or literary. Careful records were kept of numbers of conversions, withdrawals, dropped, and deceased. Very modest sums of money were raised for the church and Sunday school, for benevolences, and for "all purposes." The total amounts of money raised in the M.P. Michigan Conference varied from slightly over $700 to only a bit over $200. The entire active C.E. membership in 1900 numbered 1,218 of whom 923 were in the Michigan Annual Conference.

The records for the first decade of the Epworth League in Michigan are most inadequate. No mention of it was made in the various statistics of the Annual Conferences. Occasionally a Presiding Elder gave a few figures in his annual report. The committee on Epworth League of the Michigan M.E. Conference session of 1893 stated that there were a total of 562 chapters in the entire State averaging over sixty per group. Of that total, 269 were in the Michigan Annual Conference and 266 in the Detroit Annual Conference. By the end of that decade neither committees nor Presiding Elders were giving any figures for the Epworth Leagues. It may be that one must assume that practically every charge had at least one chapter. One Indian Epworth League was reported as well started in the Michigan Annual Conference at Northport.

It must be remembered always that this organization was really composed of young to middle-aged adults and not of Youth as we might think of them today. An Epworth League Sunday meeting at 6 P.M. might include everyone except the babies and those too old or feeble to walk to the church. No one seems ever to have been told that it was time he dropped out of League activity. And the Junior Leagues, like the junior C.E. societies, were never as numerous as the older groups.

Elaborate organization grew with the increased number of Leagues. Each Annual Conference in Michigan had a conference president, vice-president, secretary, and treasurer of the Epworth League. The Detroit Annual Conference organized more elaborately than the Michigan Annual Conference ever did. The first had a Board of Control of the League made up of the corresponding secretaries of the District Leagues. It also thought two vice-presidents were needed while the Michigan Annual Conference got along with one. Usually a standing committee on the Epworth League was appointed annually in each Conference. Their reports were longer and more detailed at the start of the decade than at its end. It may have been felt that more guidance was needed when the Epworth League was so very new. Each District in each Conference had a similar organization supervised by its Presiding Elder. In a large District or one handicapped by few railroads or steamers, sub-District organization might also develop. This was the case in the Grand Traverse District of the M.E. Michigan Annual Conference. And finally each local chapter had its full quota of officers plus many committee chairmen dealing with such things as devotions, programs, refreshments, reading lists, and visitation.

Annual Conventions flourished during the first 25 years of the Epworth League from its founding in 1889 to the First World War. These might be citywide, subdistrict, District, State, and International. Those for the larger areas drew huge crowds, lasted for at least three days, and presented a most elaborate program. The logistics of a Michigan State Epworth League Convention must have been almost as precise as those drawn up for an army.

During the Nineties, State Epworth League conventions were held at Albion, Jackson, Saginaw, and Detroit. Each chapter was entitled to two official delegates in addition to its pastor. Official badges must be worn at all times. The official delegates got a special railroad rate of one way and one third instead of the round-trip full fare. Lodgings in Methodist homes and all meals, except dinners, were provided. In March 1895, when the State convention was held at Detroit's Central Church, the ladies of the Tabernacle Church provided dinners at a nearby store at a cost of 25¢ each. Badges also entitled one to a reserved seat on the main floor of the Church. A reception committee met all trains on the convention days. Everyone expecting to attend and have lodging provided was required to register at least two weeks in advance of the opening session.

These State conventions had a very full program for all three days. National leaders always attended and meetings were divided by the Epworth League departments of finance and correspondence, mercy and help, literary, social, spiritual, and junior work. At that 1895 convention in Central Church, Detroit, Bishop Cyrus Foss of Philadelphia gave one evening lecture and the Rev. S. A. Steel, Secretary of Southern Methodist Epworth League work, gave another. Among the topics in the divided meetings were such items as systematic visitation, use of the local press, the location, features and aim of a social evening, church debts, and use of the Bible in the literary and spiritual departments. This final topic was conducted by Dr. Frederic S. Goodrich of Albion College. He frequently was called to lecture on the Holy Land at District and State conventions.[34]

Many years later, Mrs. Hugh Kennedy wrote of her memories of Epworth League work in the Lake City Methodist Episcopal Church, later in Albion College, and in Statewide service. She said in part:

> How well I remember my first childhood venture in State work. Of course, I worked in Epworth League and managed Junior League and taught Sunday School classes and played the organ when I was really too young but it helped me perhaps more than it did the children. Then the Epworth League sent me to a State convention in Saginaw, my first trip away from Lake City and what a thrill! The meeting and the kindness of being entertained in a Christian home, etc. made a great impression on me.

Mrs. Kennedy entered Albion College in 1894 where she was very active in Y.W.C.A. work and also the Student Volunteer Movement. She often worked with Dr. Goodrich and the State President of the Y.W.C.A. Soon she was speaking frequently to local and District meetings of the Epworth League. She wrote of this work and also of its unexpected consequences for her:

> Dr. Goodrich planned to have the Epworth Leagues in the State buy a bunch of 15 books for $10 (paper covered) to acquaint them with the missionary work to date, i.e., Livingston, Stanley, Adoniram Judson, etc. I was the one to further the plan in Grand Traverse District, hence I spoke in Big Rapids, where Reverend Nicholson (later bishop) was pastor, and also in Boyne City, where the editor of the paper entertained me. It was my first visit to northern Michigan. . . . After my talk, telling of our early missionary work in various denominations, the plea was made to the Epworth League to raise $10 for the books to read and study. To my amazement, a gentleman in the audience right away offered to buy the books for the Epworth League. It intrigued my interest. It was W. H. White and a year and three months later, he became my husband. So you see how much *both* of *us* owed to our Church.[35]

---

[34] A large scrapbook, kept by Dr. Goodrich in the 1890's, is in the Michigan Historical Collections, Rackham Bldg., University of Michigan, Ann Arbor. It has dozens of programs of Epworth League meetings at which Dr. Goodrich lectured. Sometimes he wore the garb of the natives of the Holy Land.

[35] From reminiscences by Mrs. Hugh Kennedy (Mary Louise Reeder White) written at the urging of the author in 1963. Mrs. Kennedy died in 1965 at the Clark Home in Grand Rapids.

Buildings for Epworth League work began to appear early in the history of the organization in Michigan. Bay view by 1891 had built an Epworth League Home at a cost of $3,000. Short courses in the study of the Bible were regularly given there in the summers. In a form of reciprocity, many a minister and also the two Annual Conferences recommended that their Leagues should pursue study of the Bay View and Chatauqua reading courses. Another Epworth League Cottage was built by 1891 at the Eaton Rapids Camp Meeting Grounds. Crystal Springs added an Epworth League Rally Day to its camp meeting program. In the Detroit Annual Conference, an Epworth League Cottage was built at Lake Orion Camp Meeting Grounds.

Epworth Heights at Ludington

What was intended to be a second Bay View was started at Ludington in 1894. Its official name was the Epworth League Training Assembly but it was usually called Epworth Heights or the Epworth Assembly. The aim was to provide a summer school for all aspects of church work including a Bible study school, training for Sunday School teachers, work for young preachers still engaged in the Conference course of study, and lastly skilled guidance in all aspects of Epworth League work. It drew a little upon the old-time camp meeting ways but took far more from the methods of the Chatauqua movement. Ministers in the Big Rapids District of the Michigan Annual Conference started it. Presiding Elder Daniel Westlake Parsons, just completing his six-year term there, was the leader in collecting local donations to start the Epworth Assembly. Active in aiding him in this project were the Rev. Thomas Nicholson and the Rev. William M. Puffer. The first was then stationed at Big Rapids and the second at Manistee.

These three founding ministers were very fortunate in their donation collections. The city of Ludington gave $10,000 and eighty acres of land. A local Development Company gave $1,000 and 150 acres of land. The F. and P.M. Railroad gave $10,000. By mid-September in 1894, the grounds had been cleared and both a large frame auditorium and an hotel built.[36]

Steady growth in its first years characterized the Epworth Assembly. In 1896 it enjoyed better attendance than most other such gatherings in the entire country. By 1900, thirteen cottages had been built, several more were planned, and the contracts for their construction had been

[36] Michigan M.E. Annual Conference *Minutes* for 1894, pp. 374-375. See the annual report of Presiding Elder D. W. Parsons of Big Rapids District. It is strange that no notice was taken of Epworth Heights in the 1890's by the Michigan Annual Conference in its business sessions. Either the record was incomplete or the place was only the concern of the District. No mention was made of the new Assembly in any of the *Minutes* of the 1890's until 1900.

given. Olney Rest Cottage, intended for the use of returned women missionaries, was being built by the combined efforts of the Ladies Aid Societies of the Big Rapids District. The receipts from collections during the programs and the numbers of people who spent the summer at Epworth Heights were greater in 1900 than at any previous assembly there.[37]

Some concern was felt by Methodist ministers that the college students of the denomination in Michigan might be overlooked in pleasant preoccupation with the rapid growth of the Epworth League in chapters and total membership. The committee on the Epworth League, in the Michigan M.E. Annual Conference session of 1895, expressed pleasure that a separate chapter had been organized in Albion College. It was commended to the sympathy and support of the faculty. Only by fostering student religious life and keeping them constantly in touch with Methodism would the College ever achieve "added financial support and increasing patronage."

In the Detroit Annual Conference session of 1897, the Epworth League committee recommended that the secretaries of the chapters at Albion, Ypsilanti, and Ann Arbor should be notified "by the Home Secretaries of students entering these institutions." The same Conference in session in 1894 had heartily endorsed the efforts of the Wesleyan Guild in the Ann Arbor church to provide a full-time paid Epworth League Secretary "to promote the interests of Methodism and practical Christianity among the students of the University of Michigan."[38]

In spite of the widespread endeavor to increase the number of Epworth League chapters in Michigan, some ministers drew back from such work in certain communities. These were the towns where they found a vigorous Christian Endeavor Society already at work. From the Y.P.S.C.E. statistics of the M.P. Conferences in Michigan, such places were usually small villages and did not by any means cover all the State. Hence if a newly appointed M.E. minister found a Christian Endeavor society at work, and several subscriptions taken to a paper called *Our Young People*, in the town to which he had been called, he was likely to hesitate and decide not to try to introduce the Epworth League there. Indeed the M.E. Annual Conferences felt that it was best to leave the situation as it was in such circumstances.[39]

Furnishing adequate leadership for the Epworth League, in both local chapters and Statewide activities, was a growing problem for the youth organization. Such a multitude of offices, committees, and activities demanded more time than many lay Methodists had to give. High standards were set and devotion to duty was emphatically expected of

[37] Michigan M.E. Annual Conference *Minutes* for 1900, p. 79.
[38] Detroit Annual Conference *Minutes* for 1897, p. 62; the same for 1894, p. 27.
[39] *History of American Methodism*, II, 646. From a section by Gerald O. McCulloh on the theology and practices of Methodism, 1876-1919.

all officers. The work quite often lapsed into one more task for an already over-burdened minister. The Junior Leagues were frequently under the guidance of the local minister's wife. Exclusively professional, religious leadership for the Epworth League occasionally defeated the aims of that work. Dr. F. S. Goodrich once spoke at a Michigan State Epworth League Convention on the subject "Impropriety of One Leader for Devotional Meetings for any Considerable Period of Time." Among the other topics often used in speeches by Dr. Goodrich were "The Evolution and Revolution of the Epworth Wheel," "The Epworth Leaguer in Business," "Backlook, Uplook, Outlook," and "Proper and Improper Church Entertainments."[40]

Wherever the appointed minister kept a strong hand over his Epworth League, an argument or even a serious rift in the Church might develop over the social entertainment allowed the young people. All Methodist ministers were strongly opposed to dancing just as of yore. But some of the incidents do seem just a bit absurd today. In 1893, the Epworth League at Lyons had worked up a "literary contest" in which the winning side would be treated to a supper. The local minister said it was "a form of gambling" and stopped it immediately. A Halloween Hide and Seek party, in which the ladies hid and the men looked for them, was also disapproved by the minister. If found within a certain, short time, the ladies would pay for the supper and if not then the men would. One group of young women hid in the local icehouse and did not hear the bell rung for the end of the contest and the serving of supper. They nearly froze before they decided to return to the church.

The Portland Epworth League held a "7¢ autograph party" on the seventh anniversary of the founding of the Epworth League. In winter the Epworth Leaguers often went sleighing or bobsled riding. Another favorite custom was a surprise party for some member living in a country area. The members would assemble as quietly as possible on the designated person's front porch and then, at a signal, all yell together. It is to be hoped that the group took food with them.

Perhaps some of the trouble between minister and Epworth Leaguers arose from the fact that very few churches had separate social rooms or parlors then. Social gatherings either had to be held in homes in the parlors or else in the sanctuary room where the minister prayed and preached each Sunday.[41]

If any local chapter of the Epworth League was not raising money for some Methodist missionary, it was likely to be raising money and collecting materials to carpet the church, to paint the building too, or the commonest project in the 1890's appears to have been building

---

[40] Speech topics found in that scrapbook kept by Dr. Goodrich, now it is in the Michigan Historical Collections, Rackham Bldg., University of Michigan, Ann Arbor.

[41] Social incidents drawn from numerous individual church histories in the Michigan Annual Conference historical collection files at Albion College Library.

horse sheds back of the meeting house. Usually if one gave money or lumber and nails, he was entitled on Sundays to preempt one of the stalls for his own horse. It does seem as if concern for the horse's comfort arose only near the time when the automobile would come into wide use.

When Court Street Church in Flint acquired a new bell for their steeple in 1894, the Epworth League gave a "Bell Social" at which the privilege of ringing the bell was auctioned off with the highest to be allowed to do so at 10 P.M. The Epworth League also helped to pay for and introduce the individual communion cup in this same Church in 1895. The Detroit Annual Conference first used individual communion cups in 1896.

On some projects, the Epworth League and the Sunday School combined forces. Together these two organizations at Court Street in Flint raised enough money to buy a piano for the Church. But the key had to be kept at the parsonage because many of the older members had been very opposed to such a purchase. Also at Court Street, the Epworth League gave an annual reception for the new members of the congregation.

In May 1896, the Rev. Elisha Caster preached on the Epworth League to his congregation at Milford. His text, in Job 29:15, was "I was eyes to the blind, and feet was I to the lame." He began by reminding them that the Epworth League was born at Cleveland just seven years ago. Its growth in so short a time was little short of miraculous. His sermon was organized around the aims of the League, each of which he discussed in turn. Mr. Caster felt that every young Methodist could surely find "scope for his or her aptitudes in this four-cornered work.'"

To a minister the spiritual work naturally stood first in importance. It could be done only by personal, individual work. Mr. Caster said in part:

> Here is the secret of power. The sinner is to be converted, as a rule, through human agencies. Not at long range but by earnest personal acquaintance. . . . It was a class sentiment of assumed sanctity that refused the Publican a place in the shouting throng and drove him up a tree — no place on earth for the poor fellow. But see! A look and a word of personal recognition by the Man of Galilee, not only won his heart but made of him a convert, a Christian.

Methodist ministers commonly thought the social side of the Epworth League of the least importance. Contrary to this usual attitude, Mr. Caster believed in specific meetings for social entertainment only. Here he declared:

> It would be greatly to our advantage to come together, say once a quarter, to eat a bit of fruit, or a piece of cake, and drink a cup of coffee, *not to make money,* but to become better acquainted with each

other, welcome strangers, and so enlarge the circle of our influence.
. . . We can't afford not to cultivate the social element that is within us.
It is twin sister to spiritual power, and so is God's order . . . if we will not
use the gifts with which our Maker has honored us, we shall fail to
find jewels and prove ourselves worthy of our origin.

Literary work was the third field of League effort. Here one's
leisure time might be profitably employed. The minimum goal should
be one hour a day for a year devoted to serious reading. Among the
books Mr. Caster recommended were Rollins *Ancient History,* Plutarch's
Lives, Macaulay's *England,* Prescott's *Ferdinand and Isabella,* and
Goodrich's *United States.* Poets like Milton, Cowper, and Goldsmith
were for "snatch reading." Above all, every League member ought to
give much time to the Bible. Mr. Caster held that the literary work of
the League was too often "insipid and neglected."

Mercy and Help constituted the fourth aspect of the League's activities. The words were of divine origin. We were not put in this
world for self alone but to be good and do good. Those who can achieve
that double goal "are worthy of double honor." No service was menial
that gave mercy and help in any way. He urged his hearers to walk
a bit farther to bring a blind or elderly person to church. And visits
to lonely, struggling human beings were always needed. Mr. Caster concluded, "This poor world needs sympathy and help. Money? Yes.
But suppose we have none, but have what is better – a heart, courage,
and brawny arms – we can help across a hard place some one who has
neither. We can be 'eyes to the blind and feet to the lame.' "[42]

A Statistical Comparison
1890-1900

The usual statistical decade comparisons show that growth was not
as all inclusive nor as great as the year 1890 had revealed in contrast
to 1880. Growth was visible but in the M.E. branch it tended to be
from one-half to two-thirds of what it had previously been in Michigan.
In contrast the M.P.'s were doing somewhat better than in the previous
decade. This was particularly noticeable in their Sunday Schools,
where ministerial concern had been great. Hence more attention had
been recommended in both Annual Conferences.

Both the Michigan and Western Michigan Methodist Protestant
Annual Conferences increased in numbers of members, churches, and
parsonages during the Nineties. The Michigan M.P. group had 2,740
members in 1890 and 3,567 in 1900. The West Michigan side had 1,128

[42] This sermon on the Epworth League is in the possession of the author together with about twenty other sermons by the Rev. E. E. Caster. Like the rest of
them, the text and key words are emphasized by red ink touches to letters and
underscorings.

members in 1890 and 1,325 in 1900. This particular Conference always seemed to be smaller and less vigorous in various ways than the M.P Michigan Conference was. Fifty-one churches in 1890 for the Michigan Annual Conference had grown to eighty-nine in 1900. The West Michigan churches in 1890 numbered twenty-three and one-half and by 1900 were thirty. Parsonages reported as twelve in 1890 had only become fourteen in 1900 in the West Michigan Conference. But the Michigan Conference had twenty-seven parsonages in 1890 and had built to the total of forty in 1900.

When it came to Sunday Schools, the Michigan M.P. Annual Conference was doing much better than the West Michigan was. A qualification of all figures must be noted in that the statistics and the paper used plus the print thereon were all so poorly done that doubt of their accuracy must be maintained. Totals at the bottom of columns of figures are so blurred that new addition must be carried out to have any summary figures.

The Michigan M.P.'s had 76 Sunday Schools in 1890 and 106 in 1900. The West Michigan Conference had 54 Sunday Schools in 1890 and 44 in 1900. Officers and teachers together numbered 746 in the Michigan Conference in 1890 and 1,050 in 1900 But the same group in the West Michigan Conference numbered 447 in 1890 and 421 in 1900. As to "scholars" as the children were still called then, the Michigan Conference had 3,127 in 1890 and 5,093 in 1900. The West Michigan part had 2,084 in 1890 and 1,887 in 1900. Unless due to careless reporting and printing of the statistics, no explanation of the more noticeable decline in the West Michigan situation seems to be discernible. Hard times do not appear to have much connection with a falling off in Sunday School attendance.

On the Methodist Episcopal side of the denomination, the Detroit Annual Conference had 49,195 full members in 1900 as compared with 36,032 in 1890. Its Sunday Schools numbered 590 in 1900 with 7,520 teachers and officers for 59,445 scholars. In comparison, Sunday Schools numbered 515 in 1890 with 6,579 teachers and officers for 50,352 scholars then. The church buildings numbered 507 in 1900 as compared with 395 in 1890. The 234 parsonages of 1900 had grown from 190 in 1890. Outside of the collections of the women's societies, mission giving was $19,774 in 1900 and had been $16,068 in 1890.

In this same decade, the Michigan M.E. Annual Conference had 49,589 full members in 1900 as compared with 37,968 in 1890. Their Sunday Schools in 1900 numbered 663 with 8,145 teachers and officers working with 55,117 scholars. Previously in 1890, the west side of the State had 608 Sunday Schools with 7,003 teachers and officers for 48,327 scholars. Michigan M.E. Conference buildings numbered 559 in 1900 up from 446 churches in 1890. Parsonages became 255 in 1900 from 206 in 1890. Mission giving, not counting the women's funds, was $19,891 in 1900 which was quite an increase from $13,951 in 1890 especially in the decade of the Panic of 1893.

A superficial examination of all the statistics just given leaves the impression that all was well with Methodism because the figures for 1900 are generally larger than those for 1890. A more careful comparison with preceding decades reveals that adult membership just about held to the rate of growth previously shown. But the Sunday Schools were only increasing at about *half* the rate of the 1880's particularly in the numbers of teachers and scholars. Churches and parsonages continued to be built at an encouraging rate but the general giving for missions showed a rather small increase indeed, particularly if compared with the sacrificial triple increases of the Civil War days. How much the Panic of 1893 had to do with the statistics of growth is difficult to determine. Perhaps the missions, especially in the Detroit Annual Conference, were affected in their money raising but hardly the Sunday Schools.

The letters that have survived and the committee reports in the Annual Conference sessions reveal a kind of general malaise that pervaded the Methodist Episcopal Church at that time. The older members particularly were very unhappy with the changing ways of their Church. Why was less attention paid to the country areas? Why was the Class meeting almost extinct? Why was there none of the old-time enthusiasm of an emotional nature in the winter revivals and the summer camp meetings? Ought not the old rule of changing ministers every *two* years to be revived? Why should laymen and even women have so prominent a part in a Church which had been run by the Bishops and Travelling Elders quite satisfactorily in the past? Such questions were often repeated with no very adequate answers.

Were many of the ministers opposed to any reforms and perhaps hesitating and dragging their feet on recommended changes? The two M.E. Annual Conferences in Michigan voted twice in the Nineties to admit laymen *equally* with ministers in Annual and General Conferences. True a substantial majority favored the change but each time a strong minority, of from twenty-five to fifty ministers, vigorously fought such long advocated reforms.

        ❖   ❖   ❖   ❖   ❖   ❖

To the historian viewing the entire nineteenth century from the vantage point of the decade of the 1960's, it seems obvious that the pioneer and somewhat Victorian Methodism long prevalent in a rural America was declining and disappearing as a modern, industrial, urban America was being born. Methodism would be forced to accept drastic changes if it was to survive and grow in the twentieth century. But in 1900 very few people understood what was then happening. They clung to the religious ways of the rural or village America that they had always known.

The Episcopal Address to the General Conference of 1900 was a message to the Methodist Episcopal Church at large but it raised certain questions troubling both the Detroit and Michigan Annual Conferences then. It said in part:

> That many changes have occurred in the outward forms of Methodism is obvious. Which do they indicate, *growth* or decay?
>
> 1) The Class Meeting is considerably disused: have fellowship and spiritual helpfulness among believers abated, or do they find . . . *other expressions and other instruments?*
>
> 2) The rigid and minute Church discipline of former years is relaxed: Is this a sign of pastoral unfaithfulness or of *growing respect for individual liberty* and of *a better conception of the Church?*
>
> 3) The plainness of the early Methodist congregations has disappeared. Is this simply vanity and worldliness or is it . . . *the natural and justifiable development of the esthetic faculty* under more prosperous external conditions?
>
> 4) The strenuous contention for doctrine and usage of Methodism . . . is now rarely heard. Is this indifferentism or is it *a better discernment of that which is vital to the Church faith* and in part the result of *an acceptance by others of the once disputed opinions?*[43]

Only the oncoming twentieth century would reveal which of the alternatives posed by those Bishops in 1900 was correct. But this 20th century Methodist historian thinks that those Bishops in 1900 could only lead their Church by taking the more optimistic parts of their fourfold statement for the truth and doing all they could to promote their further development.

The author hopes to show in the second volume of this History of Methodism in Michigan what the automobile, two World Wars, the great Depression of 1929, and the unification of three branches of Methodism in 1939 did to the Church in this State. All of them had as profound influence upon the Methodist Annual Conferences in Michigan as the railroad, the Civil War and recurrent hard times did in the nineteenth century. The Methodists would unite to meet the new challenges as they had the old demands in the years now part of their history.

[43] Quoted by John N. Norwood in *Church Membership in the Methodist Tradition,* p. 9. The arrangement of the quotation in separate parts with portions in italics is not that of the Bishops or Mr. Norwood. It was so written by the author of this history of Michigan Methodism in order to show more clearly the hopeful aspects of the questions raised in that Episcopal Address.

A BIBLIOGRAPHICAL NOTE

A full bibliography of all books, magazine articles and other items used in the preparation of this history of Michigan Methodism will be given at the end of volume II. Here only an acknowledgement is made of the libraries, books, and people most helpful to the author.

The materials for the study of Methodism in Michigan are divided and widely scattered over the middle west. A central location with adequate housing and a trained librarian-archivist to collect and catalog all the various source materials is greatly needed.

The Michigan Annual Conference at present keeps its historical collections in the Albion College library. The Detroit Annual Conference does likewise in the Adrian College library. Any Annual Conference historical collection is only as good as an interested and zealous minister curator can make it. Such work demands sustained attention over a period of some years. The Michigan Annual Conference has been unfortunate in its lack of a long period of effort on the part of one man to build up its materials. The late Rev. Spencer Owens began an improved reorganization of the Michigan Annual Conference materials and Rev. Richard Wearne has devoted a great deal of time and effort to the expansion of the collection. But the Detroit Annual Conference has over twice as many individual church histories as the Michigan Conference does. This is due to the devoted labors of the late Rev. William C. S. Pellowe in his eight years as curator of the Detroit Annual Conference Historical Society. Perhaps the most useful material in either Conference collection is the complete collection of the *Minutes* of the yearly Conference sessions. Early M.E. and M.P. Conference *Minutes* have been copied for the collection at Adrian College.

Detroit and Ann Arbor must also be visited in the search for the sources concerning Michigan Methodism. The Burton Collection of the city of Detroit's Public Libray contains many useful items. Of course it has much more material on the Methodist churches in the city of Detroit than for the rest of Michigan. Its very detailed card catalogs give an author easy access to the many small notices about Methodist churches

435

and ministers which appeared in the Detroit newspapers. Some years ago, a previous editor of the *Michigan Christian Advocate* placed the copies of that periodical for the years before 1920 in the Burton Collection. The bound volumes are not entirely complete in every number for the years before 1881. The file of the years since 1920 is to be found at the *Michigan Christian Advocate* office in Adrian. A bound set of the paper for the years since 1890 is also located at the Albion College library.

The Michigan Historical Collections of the University of Michigan are located in the Rackham Building in Ann Arbor. Its card catalogs are just as helpful as those of the Burton Collection. The material is somewhat more miscellaneous and scattered over Michigan in its subject matter than that in Detroit. Because the Rev. Guy Beckley was a Methodist minister in addition to being the editor of an early abolitionist paper, *the Signal of Liberty*, its files are most helpful for the early days of the Michigan Annual Conference and the Michigan Methodist attitudes toward slavery. A few papers of the Rev. Seth Reed are also in the Michigan Historical Collections. Because the Rev. Frederic S. Goodrich was a friend of the director of the Michigan Historical Collections, it has a number of items, including a large scrapbook, related to Goodrich's early work in Michigan.

Outside of Michigan, the most helpful material was found at the Garrett Theological Seminary library in Evanston, Illinois. It has what the author believes to be the only complete file of the *North-Western Christian Advocate* in the United States. It had several thousand subscribers in Michigan and also a minister-editor from this State in its early days. As it was started in 1852 and the *Michigan Christian Advocate* did not appear until 1874, the items concerning Michigan in the Civil War days made possible the writing of a far more full account of that critical time. The author is grateful to the Western Michigan College library staff for arranging with Garrett library an interlibrary loan of the volumes of the *Northwestern Christian Advocate* for the years 1861 through 1865.

Books concerned with Michigan, Detroit and Methodism in general were very useful for background. Two about the State were frequently consulted: *Michigan in Four Centuries* by F. Clever Bald, published in 1954 by Harper and Brothers, and *Michigan: A History of the Wolverine State* by Willis F. Dunbar, published in 1956 by William B. Eerdmans Co. Dr. Dunbar's *The Michigan Record in Higher Education*, published in 1963 by Wayne State University Press, was also helpful.

Three books about the city of Detroit were often useful. Silas Farmer's *History of Detroit and Michigan*, although it appeared in 1884, had both pictures and much detail about the earlier Detroit Methodist churches. George Catlin's *The Story of Detroit*, published in 1921, contained a few

Methodist incidents not found elsewhere. The basic chronological pattern of this book was in part determined by the very useful material in *Detroit in its world setting, A 250-year chronology,* 1701-1951. This little book was prepared by the Detroit Public Library in 1953, with Rae E. Rips as editor, for the celebration of the 250th anniversary of the founding of the city of Detroit.

The background of general Methodism, against which any State or Conference history ought to be written, was afforded by four books. Far and away the most useful was William Warren Sweet's *Methodism in American History* in the revision of 1953 published by the Abingdon Press. Also helpful was *The Story of Methodism* by Halford Luccock and Paul Hutchinson published in 1926 by the Abingdon Press. The recent three volume *History of American Methodism,* by the Abingdon Press in 1964, was loaned me by Mr. W. Fred Allen of Kalamazoo. While it is useful in matters of organization and general information about the Church, it is marred for a Michigan Methodist by incorrect statements about the year of founding and the first minister to preach here. The Rev. Daniel Freeman preached here in 1804 not someone named Morgan in 1803.[1] The various *Disciplines* of Methodism were often useful on such things as creed, offices and their duties, or the ritual. The *Discipline* for 1960 was the one most frequently consulted.

Two books on special aspects of Methodism were particularly useful. Wade Crawford Barclay has written a six volume *History of Methodist Missions* recently for the Board of Missions and Church Extension of the Methodist Church. The first three volumes were used many times for this book. Early American Methodism from 1769 to 1844 is the theme of the first two volumes. The third, called Widening Horizons, is on the years from 1845 to 1895. Not the least valuable part of Barclay's work is the introduction to the first volume on "The Wesleyan Heritage." Barclay's books were most helpful on the early part of Methodism in Michigan while the first volume of Richard M. Cameron's *Methodism and Society* was more helpful on the latter part of the 19th century. His two volumes were edited by the Board of Social and Economic Relations of the Methodist Church and published in 1961 by the Abingdon Press. Mr. Cameron's first volume is entitled "Methodism and Society in Historical Perspective" and deals with the social aspects of Methodism up the the year 1908.

More directly concerned with Michigan Methodism are two older books by Methodist ministers. The Rev. John H. Pitezel wrote very clearly of the hardships and annoyances of the early missionary's life in the Upper Peninsula in his *Lights and Shades of Missionary Life,* which was first published in Cincinnati in 1859. The author is grateful to Miss

---

[1] *History of American Methodism,* I, 404.

Kay Bush for arranging a loan of the copy of Pitezel's book owned by her father, Mr. Harry Bush of PawPaw. Without the labors of the Rev. Elijah Pilcher, scarcely anything would be known of the early days of Methodism in Michigan. He knew all but one of the first seven members of the first society organized in Michigan. He was indefatigable in collecting the reminiscences of early Methodists and then writing about the development of the Church here. His book, bearing the title *"Protestantism in Michigan*: Being a Special History of the Methodist Episcopal Church and incidentally of other denominations," was published in Detroit in 1878 by R.D.S. Tyler and Company. But it is clear that most of the book was written before the Civil War for Pilcher repeatedly tried to get the Detroit Annual Conference to print it. No mention at all is made of the Civil War and the last chapter with mention of Bay View and the *Michigan Christian Advocate* was so sketchy that it must have been added in haste just before publication. It is not always clear when Pilcher tells an anecdote whether he is relating his own experiences or not. And one could wish that his manner of organization was clearer, that items about the same preacher were all grouped in the same chapter, and that he had occasionally resisted the temptation to insert some piece of writing by another Methodist minister because he thought it was "interesting and profitable to read." Yet over all, any author seeking to write about Methodism in Michigan must be thankful that Pilcher was so zealous in pursuit of the truth about the Church in this State.

The people who were helpful in the work of studying and writing about Methodism in Michigan were of two kinds: those who in some way aided in provision of the source materials so badly needed and the group of ministers who read and criticized the manuscript as it was being written.

Bishop Thomas Pryor must be mentioned here because he was the first to recommend that the author be the one to write the history of Methodism in Michigan. He also gave the author his extensive collection of the *Minutes* of the Detroit Annual Conference, dating from 1853. These have been extremely useful in writing about Michigan Methodism.

The late Mrs. Hugh Kennedy (Mary Louise White) wrote many letters to the author and finally at some length her remembrances of the early days of her life in the church at Lake City and later at Albion College.

While William Warren Sweet printed in his *Religion on the Frontier*, one year of the diaries kept by the Rev. James Gilruth, the rest of his record during the years from 1832 to 1836 while he was a Presiding Elder on the Detroit District had never been printed. The author is most grateful to the descendants of James Gilruth for having the pertinent portions of the journal photostated for use in this history of Methodism in Michigan.

The response to the author's appeals for material, printed in the *Michigan Christian Advocate*, were mostly individual church histories. These will all be listed in the complete bibliography at the end of volume II. But the most curious item sent in must be mentioned here. Mrs. C. L. Wingeier of Fenwick contributed half a dozen copies of the *Northwestern Christian Advocate* dating from the years 1868, 1874 and 1878. They had been applied under frame siding on their house presumably for insulation. In spite of regular nail holes, they are largely readable.

The author especially appreciates the gift from her uncle, the late Dr. E. Wilbur Caster of Detroit, of the remaining sermons and diaries belonging to his father and the author's grandfather, the late Rev. Elisha E. Caster of the Detroit Annual Conference. An added reason for gratitude is that the sermons were all written in ink on a good quality of sermon paper. Most of all, the author is glad that she has a good memory that retains a distinct image of her grandfather although he died in 1914. One of the rewards of writing this book has been a deeper appreciation of her ancestor, Elisha Ezra Caster, through the reading and study of his letters to the Rev. Henry W. Hicks, now in the Detroit Conference historical collection in Adrian College Library.

This history of Methodism in Michigan is a joint project of the Detroit and Michigan Annual Conferences handled by an Area Historical Society created for this particular work. The Rev. Scott MacDonald has been the President of this Area Society during the time of its labors. His encouragement and advice is gratefully acknowledged. As President, Mr. MacDonald appointed an Editorial Committee consisting of the Rev. John Marvin, editor of the *Michigan Christian Advocate*, the Rev. Verner Kilgren of the Muskegon Heights Church, and the Rev. Ronald Brunger of the Fowlerville Church. The curators of the respective Conference Historical Societies had some connection with the work too. In the beginning, the late Rev. Spencer B. Owens, as curator, had something to do with the starting of the book. He was the first to interview the author about undertaking the book. After his death, the Rev. Richard Wearne became the curator and he also read most of the manuscript as written. His clear discussion of problems encountered in the writing has often been of great help to the author.

As curator of the Detroit Annual Conference, the late Rev. William C. S. Pellowe also served as chairman of the Research Committee and aided the author in finding her way through the masses of source material available. He also read and criticized the manuscript through chapter 11. Since Dr. Pellowe's death the position of curator of the Detroit Annual Conference has been taken by Dr. Frank Stephenson of Adrian. He has also been very helpful to the author, particularly in the provision of advice and materials about the Methodist Protestants. Messrs. Marvin, Kilgren and Brunger have patiently read all the manuscript, criticized the author's English where it needed it, and indicated small mistakes in historical facts. Any remaining errors are those of the author and not of the committee.

The criticisms of the committee collectively were conveyed to the author by the Rev. Ronald Brunger now of Fowlerville Methodist Church. As long as he lived, Dr. William C. S. Pellowe of Adrian also wrote often to the author about the book. His wise and experienced comments about Methodism often illuminated difficult topics for the author. Special acknowledgment must be made of the encouragement and helpful advice received from Mr. Brunger and Dr. Pellowe throughout the writing of this history of Michigan Methodism.

These Appendices were prepared by Rev. Ronald Brunger. The original spelling in the *Minutes* was retained throughout the lists.

APPENDIX A

SESSIONS OF THE METHODIST EPISCOPAL CONFERENCES OF MICHIGAN IN THE 19TH CENTURY

I. THE MICHIGAN CONFERENCE

Date	Place	Bishop	Secretary	Church Members
Sept. 7, 1836	Mansfield, Ohio	J. Soule	H. O. Sheldon	18,805 (4033)°
Sept. 6, 1837	Detroit, Mich.	R. R. Roberts	Edward Thompson	20,775 (4900)°
Sept. 5, 1838	Tiffin, Ohio	Beverly Waugh	Edward Thompson	25,149 (8476)°
Sept. 4, 1839	Ann Arbor, Mich.	J. Soule	Edward Thompson	25,032 (8204)°
Aug. 19, 1840	Marshall, Mich.	E. Hedding	H. Colclazer	11,523
Sept. 15, 1841	White Pigeon	R. R. Roberts	H. Colclazer	12,017
Aug. 17, 1842	Adrian, Mich.	T. A. Morris	H. Colclazer	13,928
Aug. 16, 1843	Ann Arbor, Mich.	J. Soule	J. S. Harrison	16,364
Oct. 2, 1844	Coldwater, Mich.	L. L. Hamline	H. Colclazer	16,537
Sept. 10, 1845	Detroit, Mich.	E. S. Janes	H. Colclazer	16,264
Sept. 23, 1846	Marshall, Mich.	E. S. Janes	H. Colclazer	16,514
Sept. 15, 1847	Ypsilanti, Mich.	T. A. Morris	E. H. Pilcher	16,737
Sept. 6, 1848	Kalamazoo, Mich.	E. S. Janes	E. H. Pilcher	16,844
Sept. 5, 1849	Adrian, Mich.	L. L. Hamline	E. H. Pilcher	14,787
Sept. 4, 1850	Albion, Mich.	T. A. Morris	E. H. Pilcher	15,562
Sept. 3, 1851	Monroe, Mich.	T. A. Morris	E. H. Pilcher	15,642
Sept. 15, 1852	Niles, Mich.	Levi Scott	E. H. Pilcher	15,767
Sept. 14, 1853	Detroit, Mich.	Beverly Waugh	E. H. Pilcher	15,552
Sept. 13, 1854	Ann Arbor Mich.	O. C. Baker	T. C. Gardner	16,959
Sept. 5, 1855	Flint, Mich.	E. R. Ames	T. C. Gardner	18,497
Oct. 1, 1856	Coldwater, Mich.	T. A. Morris	R. C. Crawford	
Sept. 26, 1857	Lansing, Mich.	Beverly Waugh	R. C. Crawford	
Sept. 15, 1858	Kalamazoo, Mich.	E. R. Ames	R. C. Crawford	
Sept. 14, 1859	Marshall, Mich.	E. S. Janes	R. C. Crawford	13,600
Sept. 27, 1860	Ionia, Mich.	M. Simpson	T. H. Sinex	13,828
Oct. 2, 1861	Battle Creek, Mich.	E. R. Ames	T. H. Sinex	
Oct. 2, 1862	Grand Rapids, Mich.	L. Scott	T. H. Sinex	13,520
Sept. 22, 1863	Jackson, Mich.	M. Simpson	T. H. Sinex	13,893
Sept. 28, 1864	Niles, Mich.	O. C. Baker	J. W. Robinson	13,349
Sept. 13, 1865	Albion, Mich.	E. R. Ames	L. R. Fiske	12,748
Sept. 6, 1866	Hillsdale, Mich.	M. Simpson	A. A. Dunton	15,260
Sept. 11, 1867	Lansing, Mich.	D. W. Clark	M. B. Camburn	17,620
Sept. 3, 1868	Three Rivers, Mich.	E. R. Ames	M. B. Camburn	17,836
Sept. 15, 1869	Grand Rapids, Mich.	L. Scott	M. B. Camburn	20,484
Aug. 31, 1870	Coldwater, Mich.	D. W. Clark	M. B. Camburn	21,627
Sept. 13, 1871	St. Joseph, Mich.	E. S. Janes	M. B. Camburn	22,376
Sept. 18, 1872	Jackson, Mich.	E. R. Ames	J. I. Buell	21,549
Sept. 10, 1873	Ionia, Mich.	I. W. Wiley	J. I. Buell	22,463
Sept. 9, 1874	Kalamazoo, Mich.	M. Simpson	G. B. Jocelyn	23,290
Sept. 8, 1875	Battle Creek, Mich.	L. Scott	G. B. Jocelyn	23,987
Sept. 13, 1876	Niles, Mich.	G. Haven	G. B. Jocelyn	25,766
Sept. 5, 1877	Grand Rapids, Mich.	S. M. Merrill	A. R. Boggs	26,300
Sept. 4, 1878	Three Rivers, Mich.	J. T. Peck	A. R. Boggs	26,950
Sept. 10, 1879	Ionia, Mich.	R. S. Foster	H. M. Joy	28,849

° The bracketed figure is the total membership reported within Michigan! The first figure for the years 1836-1839 includes the membership in northern Ohio, then included in the Michigan Conference.

Sept. 15, 1880	Muskegon, Mich.	T. Bowman	H. M. Joy	28,879
Aug. 31, 1881	Jackson, Mich.	R. S. Foster	H. M. Joy	29,171
Sept. 6, 1882	Coldwater, Mich.	E. G. Andrews	W. I. Cogshall	29,366
Sept. 5, 1883	Albion, Mich.	W. L. Harris	W. I. Cogshall	28,780
Sept. 19, 1884	Lansing, Mich.	W. X. Ninde	W. I. Cogshall	29,952
Sept. 21, 1885	Grand Rapids, Mich.	H. W. Warren	W. I. Cogshall	30,799
Sept. 15, 1886	Kalamazoo, Mich.	J. F. Hurst	W. I. Cogshall	32,424
Sept. 6, 1887	Bay View, Mich.	W. X. Ninde	I. R. A. Wightman	33,692
Sept. 4, 1888	St. Joseph, Mich.	S. M. Merrill	James W. Reid	35,512
Sept. 11, 1889	Greenville, Mich.	Cyrus D. Foss	James W. Reid	37,555
Sept. 10, 1890	Muskegon, Mich.	E. G. Andrews	W. I. Cogshall	37,968
Sept. 9, 1891	Grand Rapids, Mich.	J. P. Newman	W. I. Cogshall	39,511
Sept. 14, 1892	Hillsdale, Mich.	C. H. Fowler	P. J. Maveety	40,196
Sept. 6, 1893	Grand Rapids, Mich.	T. Bowman	P. J. Maveety	41,190
Sept. 12, 1894	Jackson, Mich.	W. F. Mallalieu	P. J. Maveety	44,336
Sept. 18, 1895	Albion, Mich.	John F. Hurst	P. J. Maveety	45,786
Sept. 16, 1896	Lansing, Mich.	John M. Walden	P. J. Maveety	47,594
Sept. 15, 1897	Kalamazoo, Mich.	John H. Vincent	P. J. Maveety	49,061
Sept. 14, 1898	Lansing, Mich.	S. M. Merrill	M. M. Callen	48,655
Sept. 13, 1899	Ionia, Mich.	C. H. Fowler	M. M. Callen	48,846
Sept. 12, 1900	Battle Creek, Mich.	D. A. Goodsell	M. M. Callen	49,589

APPENDIX A

SESSIONS OF THE METHODIST EPISCOPAL CONFERENCES IN MICHIGAN IN THE 19TH CENTURY

II. DETROIT CONFERENCE

Date	Place	Bishop	Secretary	Church Members
Sept. 17, 1856	Adrian	Thomas A Morris	Seth Reed	9,376
Sept. 2, 1857	Port Huron	Beverly Waugh	Seth Reed	10,680
Sept. 8, 1858	Ypsilanti	Osmon C. Baker	Seth Reed	13,067
Sept. 28, 1859	Pontiac	Edmund S. Janes	Seth Reed	14,303
Sept. 26, 1860	Dexter	Thomas A. Morris	S. Clements	14,552
Sept. 25, 1861	Detroit	Edward R. Ames	S. Clements	14,626
Sept. 24, 1862	Ann Arbor	Levi Scott	S. Clements	14,187
Sept. 16, 1863	Romeo	Matthew Simpson	S. Clements	14,564
Sept. 14, 1864	Adrian	Osmon C. Baker	W. H. Perrine	14,518
Sept. 13, 1865	Flint	Davis W. Clark	W. H. Perrine	14,535
Sept. 5, 1866	Hudson	Edward R. Ames	E. H. Pilcher	15,358
Sept. 4, 1867	Saginaw	Edmund S. Janes	E. H. Pilcher	16,856
Aug. 26, 1868	Ann Arbor	Edward R. Ames	C. C. Yemans	17,910
Sept. 1, 1869	Detroit	Levi Scott	A. Edwards	18,174
Aug. 24, 1870	Fenton	Davis W. Clark	A. Edwards	19,501
Sept. 13, 1871	Monroe	Matthew Simpson	A. Edwards	20,353
Sept. 4, 1872	East Saginaw	Edward R. Ames	A. Edwards	20,147
Sept. 3, 1873	Ypsilanti	Isaac W. Wiley	A. Edwards	19,824
Sept. 2, 1874	Romeo	Matthew Simpson	A. Edwards	20,931
Sept. 1, 1875	Flint	William Harris	A. Edwards	21,204
Aug. 30, 1876	Detroit	Edward R. Ames	A. Edwards	21,098
Sept. 5, 1877	Adrian	Randolph S. Foster	A. Edwards	25,037
Sept. 11, 1878	Ann Arbor	Stephen M. Merrill	A. Edwards	25,575
Sept. 10, 1879	Ann Arbor	Thomas Bowman	A. Edwards	25,436
Sept. 5, 1880	Bay City	Edward G. Andrews	A. Edwards	24,598
Sept. 14, 1881	Port Huron	Isaac W. Wiley	J. McEldowney	24,631
Sept. 13, 1882	Detroit	Jesse T. Peck	J. McEldowney	25,472
Sept. 12, 1883	Flint	William L. Harris	J. McEldowney	26,217
Sept. 17, 1884	East Saginaw	William X. Ninde	J. McEldowney	27,093
Sept. 10, 1885	Pontiac	Henry W. Warren	J. McEldowney	28,030
Sept. 9, 1886	Adrian	John F. Hurst	J. C. Wortley	29,333
Sept. 14, 1887	Saginaw	Williard F. Mallaliew	J. F. Berry	31,006
Sept. 12, 1888	Detroit	Stephen M. Merrill	J. F. Berry	32,834
Sept. 4, 1889	Bay City	Cyrus D. Foss	J. F. Berry	34,605
Sept. 18, 1890	Alpena	Edward G. Andrews	Wm. Dawe	36,032
Sept. 16, 1891	Detroit, Simpson	John P. Newman	Wm. Dawe	37,031
Sept. 21, 1892	Owosso	Charles H. Fowler	Wm. Dawe	39,037
Sept. 20, 1893	Detroit, Cass Ave.	Thomas Bowman	Wm. Dawe	40,660
Sept. 5, 1894	Sault Ste. Marie	John M. Walden	J. E. Jacklin	43,827
Sept. 11, 1895	Ann Arbor	John F. Hurst	J. E. Jacklin	45,715
Sept. 9, 1896	Flint, Garland St.	Charles H. Fowler	J. E. Jacklin	47,059
Sept. 15, 1897	Port Huron, First	Eart Cranston	A. W. Stalker	48,362
Sept. 21, 1898	Mt. Clemens	Edward G. Andrews	A. W. Stalker	48,268
Sept. 6, 1899	Detroit, Simpson	Daniel A. Goodsell	A. W. Stalker	47,548
Sept. 12, 1900	Pontiac	Isaac W. Joyce	Herman Scripps	49,195

443

APPENDIX B

SESSIONS OF THE METHODIST PROTESTANT CONFERENCES
OF MICHIGAN IN THE 19TH CENTURY

I. THE MICHIGAN CONFERENCE

Year	President	Secretary	Members	Ministers	Where Held
1842 – James Gay			7		Franciscoville, Washtenaw Co.
1843 – J. T. Pratt			18		Concord, Jackson Co.
1844 – Robert Bamford			22		Prairie Rd., Kalamazoo Co.
1845 – Robert Bamford			22		Sylvan, Washtenaw C.
1846 – W. B. Mack			23		Flourfield
1847 – W. B. Mack			23		Leoni, Jackson Co.
1848 – W. B. Mack			18		Adrian, Lenawee Co.
1849 – R. C. Lanning			16		Prairie Rd., Kalamazoo Co.
1850 – J. L. Turner			15		Jacison Co.
1851 – W. B. Mack			21		Jakson Co., Marbles home
1852 – W. B. Mack			21		Milton Niles Circuit, Cap Co.
No Records					
1867 – W. D. Tompkinson – (T. H. Beamish)			(1743)	39	
1868 – W. D. Tompkinson – (T. H. Beamish)			1743		
1869 – W. D. Tompkinson – (T. H. Beamish)			1743	39	Pomtiac
1870 – W. D. Tompkinson – J. D. Shults			2089	49	Richfield (Brown Church)
1871 – W. D. Tompkinson – C. B. Clark			2188	33	Plainfeld, Livingston Co.
1872 – Jared Warner – C. B. Clark			2162	49	Franklin, Oakland Co.
1873 – Jared Warner – J. D. Shults			2272	43	Clio, Genesee Co.
1874 – Cyrus S. Greene – J. D. Shults			2211	45	Burton, Genesee Co.
1875 – Cyrus S. Greene – C. B. Clark			1976	50	Davisburgh, Oakland Co.
1876 – J. F. Kellog – C. B. Clark			2058	44	Berlin Twns., St. Clair Co.
1877 – J. F. Kellog – W. Bradley			2018	40	Brockway Center, St. Clair Co.
1878 – J. F. Kellog – W. Bradley			2296	44	Dryden, Lapeer Co.
1879 – A. C. Fuller – W. Bradley			2582	60	Lapeer, Lapeer Co.
1880 – A. C. Fuller – W. Bradley			2511	59	Clio, Genesee Co.
1881 – W. Cope – W. Bradley			2483	63	Columbiaville, Lapeer Co.
1882 – W. Cope – W. Bradley			2337	50	Dansville, Inghan Co.
1883 – R. N. Mulholland – S. A. Long			2098	41	Franklin, Oakland Co.
1884 – R. N. Mulholland – S. A. Long			2114	39	Brockway Center, St. Clair Co.
1885 – Samuel Riley – C. W. Stephenson (P.T.)			2202	35	Fairgrove, Tuscola Co.
1886 – Samuel Riley – Ira Le Baron			2395	39	E. Saginaw
1887 – Samuel Riley – Ira Le Baron			2676	42	Clio, Michigan
1888 – F. Traver – Ira Le Baron			2627	57	Columbiaville, Mich.
1889 – F. Traver – C. W. Stephenson			2766	53	Leonard, Oakland Co.
1890 – F. Traver – C. W. Stephenson			2740	52	Franklin, Oakland Co.
1891 – A. C. Fuller – C. W. Stephenson			2919	54	E.S. Saginaw
1892 – F. Traver – R. Rutledge			3157	71	Adrian
1893 – J. E. Hubbell – M. R. Saigeon			3198	59	Yale (Form. Brockway Center)
1894 – J. E. Hubbell – M. R. Saigeon			2894	69	Capac
1895 – M. R. Saigeon – J. J. Beatty			3651	70	Fostoria
1896 – M. R. Saigeon – J. J. Beatty			3727	66	Clio
1897 – F. Traver – J. J. Beatty			3605	76	Lum
1898 – F. Traver – J. J. Beatty			3559	74	Mayville
1899 – F. Traver – J. J. Beatty			3430	77	Lapeer
1900 – J. W. Gray – J. J. Beatty			3567	77	E.S. Saginaw

444

II. WEST MICHIGAN CONFERENCE — Methodist Protestant Church

Year	President	Secretary	Members	Ministers	Where Held
25th 1883	C. P. Goodrich	B. Post	1306	46	Lagrange Ct., Ind.
26th 1884	L. D. Abbott	C. P. Goodrich	1268	45	Concord, Mich.
27th 1885	L. D. Abbott	C. P. Goodrich	1239	46	Barryville, Mich.
28th 1886	S. Reeves	C. P. Goodrich	1278	41	Hickory Corners, Mich.
29th 1887	Wm. D. Thompkinson	C. P. Goodrich	1296	42	Ainger, Mich.
30th 1888	Wm. D. Thompkinson	C. P. Goodrich	1291	35	Corey, Cass Co., Mich.
31st 1889	J. R. Stevenson	C. P. Goodrich	1113	37	Lagrance Ct., Ind.
32nd 1890	L. Dodds	C. P. Goodrich	1128	35	Diamodal, Mich.
33d 1891	L. Dodds	C. P. Goodrich	1144	38	Three Rivers, Mich.
34th 1892	L. Dodds	C. P. Goodrich	1241	35	Charlotte Ct., Mich.
35th 1893	L. Dodds	C. L. Ellis	1308	46	Bradley, Mich.
36th 1894	L. Dodds	C. L. Ellis	1431	47	Wakely, Cass Co. Mich.
37th 1895	S. M. Johnson	C. L. Ellis	1718	44	Ainger, Mich.
28th 1896	A. Smith	C. L. Ellis	1696	46	Lansing, Mich.
39th 1897	A. Smith	C. L. Ellis	1532	40	Flowerfield Ct., Mich.
40th 1898	A. Smith	C. L. Ellis	1416	44	Three Rivers, Mich.
41st 1899	C. L. Ellis	J. A. Moray	1287	39	Eaton Rapids, Mich.
42nd 1900	C. L. Ellis	J. A. Moray	1325	41	Lansing, Mich.
43d 1901	C. L. Ellis	J. A. Moray	1181	37	Langrange Ct., Ind.
44th 1902	C. L. Ellis	H. S. Sharuager	1225	32	Midland Pk., Gull Lk.
45th 1903	C. L. Ellis	H. S. Sharuager	1228	33	Midland Pk., Gull Lk.
46th 1904	J. A. Moray	H. S. Sharuager	1233	31	Barryville, Mich.
47th 1905	J. A. Moray	H. S. Sharuager			Flint, Mich.

In 1905 W. Mich. merged with the Michigan Conference

APPENDIX C

DISTRICTS OF THE METHODIST EPISCOPAL CHURCH
IN MICHIGAN DURING THE 19TH CENTURY

Districts arranged in chronological order of formation

Detroit District   1825-1900
  (Ohio Conference 1825-1836; Michigan Conference 1836-1856;
  Detroit Conference 1856 on)
Ann Arbor District   1835-1876; 1897-1900
  (Ohio Conference 1825-1836; Michigan Conference 1836-1856;
  Detroit Conference 1856 on)
Michigan District   1839-1840
  (in southwestern Michigan, Indian Conference)
Flint River District (Michigan Conference)   1837-1839
Marshall District (Michigan Conference)   1838-1865
Kalamazoo District (Michigan Conference)   1840-1900
Monroe District (Michigan Conference)   1840-1853
Mission District (Michigan Conference)   1840-1842
Indiana Mission District (Upper Peninsula, Michigan Conference)
       1842-1852
Shiawassee District (Michigan Conference)   1843-1844
Grand River District (Michigan Conference)   1844-1850; 1851-1853
Flint District   1850-1900
  (Michigan Conference 1850-1856; Detroit Conference 1856 on)
Coldwater District (Michigan Conference)   1852-1876, 1877-1897
Lake Superior Mission District (Michigan Conference)   1852-1853
Adrian District   1853-1897
  (Michigan Conference 1853-1856; Detroit Conference 1856 on)
Grand Rapids District (Michigan Conference)   1850-1851; 1853-1900
Lake Superior District   1853-1884; 1888-1900
  (Michigan Conference 1853-1856; Indian Mission District 1855-1856;
  Detroit Conference 1856 on)
Romeo District   1854-1876
  (Michigan Conference 1854-1856; Detroit Conference 1856 on)
Indian Mission District (Lower Peninsula, Michigan Conference)
       1855-1857
Lansing District (Michigan Conference)   1856-1900

Owosso District (Detroit Conference) 1856-1872
Port Huron District (Detroit Conference) 1857-1900
Grand Traverse District (Michigan Conference) 1858-1865; 1866-1900
Superior City District (in northern Wisconsin, Detroit Conference)
1860-1862
Niles District (Michigan Conference) 1862-1900
Manistee District (Michigan Conference) 1865-1866
Albion District (Michigan Conference) 1865-1876; 1877-1900
Ionia District (Michigan Conference) 1865-1897
Pentwater District (Michigan Conference) 1866-1876
Big Rapids District (Michigan Conference) 1869-1900
Saginaw District (Detroit Conference) 1872-1900
Jackson District (Michigan Conference) 1876-1877
Alpena District (Detroit Conference) 1879-1888
Sault Ste. Marie District (Detroit Conference) 1883-1884
Marquette District (Detroit Conference) 1884-1888
Bay City District (Detroit Conference) 1888-1900

APPENDIX D

I. THE APPOINTMENTS AT THE FIRST SESSION OF THE MICHIGAN ANNUAL CONFERENCE AT MANSFIELD, OHIO IN 1836

Detroit District, WILLIAM HERR, *Presiding Elder.*

Detroit, Edward Thompson.
Ypsilanti and Huron miss., William H. Brockway, Charles Babcock.
Plymouth, Wm. Sprague, David Burns.
Farmington, Luther D. Whitney, Mark Delany.
Romeo, Arthur B. Elliott, Larman Chatfield.
Mount Clemens, Hiram Gearing.
St. Clair, Robert Triggs.
Lapeer Miss., Philip Wareham.
Saganau miss., Oscar F. North.
Livingston miss., Washington Jackson.

Ann Arbor District, HEHRY COLCLAZER, *Presiding Elder*

Ann Arbor, Peter Sharp
Monroe, James F. Davidson.
Saline, Richard Lawrence, Allen Staples.
Tecumseh, William M. Sullivan, John H. Pitezell.
Coldwater, Peter Sabin, Lewis Smith.
Calhoun, Elijah Crane.
Spring Arbour, John Kinnear, Michael G. Perkizer.
Been Creek miss., Lorenzo Davis.
Grand River miss., Frederick A. Seaborn.

Maumee District, JOHN JANES, *Presiding Elder.*

Maumee and Perrysburg, Orin Mitchell.
Toledo, Ira Chase.
Waterville miss., Alanson Flemming, Wesley Shortess.
Defiance, M'Kendree Thrapp, Austin Coleman.
Culida, Andrew Hollopeter.
Lima, James A. Kellam, James H. Frees.
St. Mary's miss., Isaac Bennett, Joseph Santly.

Norwalk District, JOHN H. POWER, *Presiding Elder.*

Portland, John Quigley.
Elyria, Samuel M. Allen, Jonathan Hudson.
Wellington, John T. Kellam, Peter Howenstine.

Vermilion, John Morey.
Paris, Hiram M. Shaffer, John Mitchell.
Wyandott Miss., Samuel P. Shaw.
Frederick, Daniel M. Conant, Zephaniah Bell.
Mount Vernon, James M'Mahan.
Martinsburg, James Wheeler, James S. Saxby.
Norwalk Seminary, Jonathan E. Chaplin, Principal; John M. Goshorn, Agent.

Tiffin District, LEONARD B. GURLEY, *Presiding Elder.*

Tiffin, Thomas Thompson, Robart G. Dubois.
Sandusky, Leonard Hill, Wesley J. Wells.
Kenton miss., James Shaw.
Finley, Henry Whiteman, George W. Breckenridge.
Risdon miss., Wesley Brock, John O. Conoway.
Bucyrus, James Wilson, Ed. M'Clure.
Mount Gilead, Elam Day, David Hinman.

Wooster District, ADAM POE, *Presiding Elder.*

Brunswick, William Runnels, Andrew M. Fitch.
Medina, James Brewster, Oliver Burgess.
Richfield, George Smith.
Dalton, George Elliott, Miles Sanford.
Wooster, Elmore Yocum, Thomas Dunn.
Millersburg, Samuel Lynch, Sanford O. Parker.
Port Washington Miss., Wesley Clark.
Danville, David Grey.
Mansfield, Alvan Billings, Edmund Cone.
Ashland, Shadrack Ruark, Charles Reed.

Note: We have taken the liberty in this tabulation of changing the original order of the Districts, to give the Michigan Districts first, and then the nearer Districts in Ohio. The order of the Districts in the Conference Journal of 1836 ran thus: Wooster, Norwalk, Detroit, Ann Arbor, Maumee, Tiffin.

APPENDIX D

II. THE APPOINTMENTS AT THE FIRST SESSION OF THE DETROIT ANNUAL CONFERENCE AT ADRIAN IN 1856

Detroit District — WELLINGTON H. COLLINS, *Presiding Elder.*

Woodward Avenue—F. A. Blades
Congress Street—A . J. Eldred
Lafayette Street—James F. Davidson
City Mission—Manasseh Hickey
French Mission—To be sup.
Mt. Clemens and Lee Chapel
—John A. Baughman
Trenton—Andrew J. Bigelow
Flat Rock—J. J. Smith

Wayne—Jason W. Kellogg
Farmington—C. Mosher
Commerce—B. L. Deshetler
Pontiac—D. C. Jacokes
Birminghanm—John Glass, James Webster
Utica—Samuel Bessey
Plymouth—William Weaver
Northville—Richard McConnell

Ann Arbor District — GEORGE SMITH, *Presiding Elder.*

Ann Arbor City—Seth Reed
Ann Arbor City 2nd Charge to be
sup.
Ypsilanti—James S. Smart
Oakville—Alexander Gee
Henrietta—Joseph H. Holt
Augusta—E. Klumph
South Lyons—J. McAllister

Milford—Eli Westlake
Brighton—L. C. York
Pinckney—Wm. Benson
Dexter—Wm. Taylor
Chelsea—E. H. Brockway
Saline—R. Bird
Grass Lake—L. D. Burch

Adrian District — ELIJAH H. PILCHER, *Presiding Elder.*

Adrian—Toledo Street—W. H. Perrine
Church Street—to be sup.
Tecumseh—Wm. Fox
Ridgway—C. M. Anderson
Clinton—Wm P. Judd, D. B. Tracy,
supernumerary
Manchester—E. Steele
Napoleon—to be sup.
Franklin—S. P. Warner
Rome—J. Dobbins, one to be sup.

Hudson—F. W. Warren
Morenci—Wm. Donelly, J. J. Hogaboam
Palmyra—E. R. Hascall
Bedford—J. B. Greenlaw, Wm. Burnett
Monroe—Wm. E. Bigelow
Dundee—Solomon S. Littlefield

T. C. Gardner, agent of the Am. Bible Society, member of Toledo St. q.C.
James V. Watson, Editor of the North-Western Christian Advocate, & member of
Toledo St.

Flint District — SAMUEL CLEMENTS, *Presiding Elder.*

Flint—Geo. Taylor
South Flint—J. O. Bancroft

Hadley—T. Seeley, Isaac Crawford
Lapeer—A. Allen

Flushing—Wm. Mothersell
Grand Blanc—Rufus C. Crane
Genesee—One to be sup.,
    I. L. Holenbeck
Clarkston—Ira W. Donelson
Groveland—Thomas Wakelin

North Branch—Wm. Tuttle
Marathon—H. Carlton
Tuscola—L. Mitchell
East Saginaw—G. N. Belknap
Saginaw—J. Levington
Lower Saginaw—T. J. Joslin

Romeo District — JONATHAN BLANCHARD, *Presiding Elder.*

Romeo—E. W. Borden
Almont—B. F. Pritchard
Dryden—to be sup.
Armada—John Gray
Mill Creek—to be sup.
Memphis—J. B. Varnum
Columbus—J. G. Whitcomb
Clyde—O. Sanborn
Lake Port—H. O. Parker
Lexington—James S. Sutton

Port Sanilac—Ira H. Camburn
Port Austin—A. J. Black
Port Huron—John Russell
St. Clair—A. R. Bartlett
Newport—S. C. Stringham
Chesterfield—S. P. Lee
Washington—Wm. G. Stonex
Oakland—to be sup.
Oxford—to be sup.

Owosso District — JOHN M. ARNOLD, *Presiding Elder*

Corunna—O. Whitmore
Byron—Wm. Birdsall
Fentonville—to be sup.
Gaines—to be sup.
Hartland—J. H. Caster, Samuel
    Wilkinson
Howell—S. Calkins
Williamsville—B. H. Hedger, R.
    Johnson

Ingham—Albert McEwen
Fowlerville—to be sup.
Oak Grove—L. H. Dean
Antrim—E. B. Prindle
Bennington—Wm. Sly
Williamston—C. W. Seaman
Chesening—S. B. Murch

Lewis R. Fisk, Professor of Chemistry in the State Agricultural College, and member of the Williamston Quarterly Conference

Lake Superior District — A. C. SHAW, *Presiding Elder.*

Sault Ste. Marie—L. D. Price
Kewawenon—to be sup.
Ontonagon—F. W. May
Minnesota Mines—J. H. Burnham

Eagle River & Harbor—H. N. Brown
Portage Lake—David A. Curtis
Marquette—O. D. W. White

A. D. Wilbur trans. to Genesee; Thomas Carter to N.Y.; E. O. Haven to N. England; A. M. Fitch, A. L. Crittenden, B. F. Doughty to Michigan Conf.; C. B. Cocagne to Black River.

Index

The names of living people are not listed in this Index. All places are in Michigan unless the name of another State is cited. All male names without more data are those of Methodist Episcopal ministers. The abbreviations used are as follows: Bp. for Bishop, P.E. for Presiding Elder (called District Superintendent today), L for laymen, M.E. for Methodist Episcopal, M.P. for Methodist Protestant, W.M. for Wesleyan Methodist, Dt. for District, and A.C. for Annual Conference.